THE CLARKE PAPERS

THE CLARKE PAPERS

SELECTIONS FROM THE PAPERS OF WILLIAM CLARKE

Secretary to the Council of the Army, 1647–1649, *and to General Monck and the Commanders of the Army in Scotland,* 1651–1660

EDITED BY C. H. FIRTH

With a New Preface by Austin Woolrych

LONDON
OFFICES OF THE ROYAL HISTORICAL SOCIETY
UNIVERSITY COLLEGE LONDON, GOWER STREET
LONDON WC1E 6BT
1992

First published in two volumes 1891 and 1894
as Camden Society, New Series, Volumes XLIX and LIV

Reissued in one volume 1992

Distributed for the Royal Historical Society
by Boydell & Brewer Ltd
PO Box 9 Woodbridge Suffolk IP12 3DF UK
and Boydell & Brewer Inc.
PO Box 41026 Rochester NY 14604 USA

ISBN 0 86193 133 5

British Library Cataloguing-in-Publication Data
The Clarke papers: Selections from the papers of
William Clarke, Secretary to the Council of the
Army, 1647–1649, and to General Monck and the
Commanders of the Army in Scotland, 1651–1660.
I. Firth, C.H.
942.06
ISBN 0–86193–133–5

This publication is printed on acid-free paper

Printed in Great Britain by
St Edmundsbury Press Ltd, Bury St Edmunds, Suffolk

CONTENTS

PREFACE TO THE 1992 EDITION

'Mr. Firth's discovery of the *Clarke Papers* throws every other accession of material into the shade', wrote Samuel Rawson Gardiner in the preface to the final volume of his *History of the Great Civil War*, just a century ago. In that same year 1891 the Camden Society published the first of the two volumes now reprinted, superbly edited by Firth and introduced by a magisterial preface from his pen. Gardiner wrote his account of the New Model Army's sensational entry into politics with the help of Firth's proof sheets of volume I and of his transcripts for volume II. It was fitting that the great historian was enabled, just in time, to embody in his masterwork the first account of the Putney debates (among other stirring matters) ever to reach the broad reading public, just when his younger friend was in the process of presenting the pick of the Clarke papers to the world of scholarship in a model edition. Both men, of course, recognized instantly the richness and significance of the material before them; indeed one may well wonder whether there has ever in modern times been a more exciting archival discovery in any field of British history. Its fascination has spread far beyond the ranks of professional historians; surely no other seventeenth-century source is more widely read by history-lovers at large than the debates of the General Council of the Army. The glory of the collection lies in William Clarke's verbatim record of the impromptu speeches uttered in the heat of debate by both officers and common soldiers, not only at Putney, but earlier at Saffron Walden and Reading, and later (without the soldiers) at Whitehall. But the fame of these debates should not eclipse the other riches in these volumes: the vivid newsletters, the urgent missives to and from the agitators, the reports of confidential proceeding in General Fairfax's Council of War – all the raw evidence in fact of a fighting force that in its own words was 'no mere mercenary army' finding its political voice.

Although Gardiner credited Firth with discovering the Clarke papers, Firth himself acknowledges at the start of his preface that his attention was first drawn to them by H. A. Pottinger, the Librarian of Worcester College, to which they belonged. They had been briefly described in Coxe's *Catalogue of Manuscripts in the possession of Oxford Halls and Colleges* (1852), but Coxe missed the volumes containing the debates – Pottinger first discovered those – and no use was made of them until Pottinger put Firth on to the scent.[1] It is an intriguing thought that they would probably have been known earlier if William Clarke's son George had not been alienated in his later years by the internecine quarrels in All Souls, the College of which he had been a fellow since his earliest manhood, and for long a major benefactor. Had that not happened, William's whole collection would have gone to the college's Codrington Library, in whose design George as an amateur architect had taken an intense interest. Gardiner was a research fellow of All Souls from 1884 and would surely have found them for himself, even if no earlier scholar had turned them up in so prestigious a repository. But George Clarke was also a great benefactor of Worcester College, and to it he left the great bulk of his father's books and papers. The smaller body of his manuscripts which found its way into the possession of the Pophams of Littlecote Hall, and was calendared by the Royal Commission on Historical Manuscripts, has almost all been reunited since Firth's time with the main collection in Worcester College Library.[2]

Little more need be said here by way of introduction to the documents presented in these volumes, because Firth's own prefaces perform the task fully and accurately. A word of tribute is due, however, to his skill as an editor, especially in the case of the famous debates of 1647, whose texts present many problems. Clarke, it seems clear, had only newly learnt his primitive shorthand when he took them down, and when he deciphered his notes fifteen years or so later his memory could not always make good the deficiencies of his stenographic technique. His transcripts are bedevilled with gaps, confusions and apparent transpositions of sen-

1 Below, I, vii.

2 Below, II, vii–x; Historical Manuscripts Commission, *Leyborne-Popham Mss* (1899); G. E. Aylmer, Introduction to *Sir William Clarke Manuscripts 1640–1664* (Harvester Microform, 1979), p. 18.

tences or phrases. Firth laboured hard to produce an intelligible text with the minimum of alteration, and where he did emend or transpose he noted the fact meticulously. It is hard to imagine the work better done. His versions of the debates are somewhat harder going for the reader than the freer and modernized ones by A. S. P. Woodhouse in his justly popular *Puritanism and Liberty*,[3] but they are considerably closer to Clarke's own text. Just occasionally, in my own work on the debates, I found a passage where the manuscript would yield an alternative and more persuasive reading, but such cases were indeed rare.

In recent times G. E. Aylmer has given us fuller accounts of the careers of William and George Clarke than Firth and the *Dictionary of National Biography* furnished long ago.[4] They need not be retold here, but what contrasts they present! William was still in his early twenties when he was made secretary to the General Council of the Army and took down its debates, still in his thirties when Charles II knighted him and appointed him Secretary-at-War, and only about forty-three when he fell mortally wounded on the deck of Monck's flagship in the naval battle with the Dutch off Harwich. What were his thoughts, one wonders, when, already a minister of Charles II, he transcribed those speeches by soldiers and young officers which argued that the reason why the Lord had withdrawn his presence from their army was that it was 'going about to sett uppe the power of kinges, . . . which God will destroy'?[5] And were such passages ever read by his bachelor Tory son, whose long years in Oxford were punctuated by briefer employments as Secretary-at-War, Admiralty Secretary, and Lord Commissioner of the Admiralty?

In other respects Firth's prefaces need little amplification or correction, though much work has subsequently been done on the army

3 First published in 1938; 3rd edition, ed. Ivan Roots, 1986. Woodhouse's book remains valuable not only for his text of the debates but for a distinguished introduction and an excellent selection of supporting documents.

4 G. E. Aylmer, *op.cit.*, pp. 9–18; G. E. Aylmer, *The State's Servants* (1973), pp. 261–2, 278. On George Clarke see also H. M. C., *Leyborne-Popham Mss*, Introduction and pp. 259–89, and other sources cited by Aylmer in his introduction to *Sir William Clarke Mss*, p. 25 n. 13; also since this went to press Lesley Le Claire, 'Civil War to Arcadian dream: the libraries of William and George Clarke', *Oxford Magazine*, no. 74 (1991), 6–9.

5 Below, I, 377.

and its involvement in politics. His own last work, written in collaboration with Godfrey Davies, *The Regimental History of Cromwell's Army* (2 volumes, Oxford, 1940), is currently being reprinted. David Underdown's *Pride's Purge: Politics in the Puritan Revolution* (Oxford, 1971) is a masterly treatment of the whole political background to the documents in both the present volumes, and particularly strong on the interaction between parliamentary and army politics. Mark A. Kishlansky, in *The Rise of the New Model Army* (Cambridge, 1979) and in several related articles,[6] has thrown considerable new light on the genesis of the New Model Army and the development of its political role, though some of his contentions are questionable. By the time that this edition is in print, or very soon after, a full and balanced history of the army from its creation to 1653 will be available in Ian Gentles, *The New Model Army*. The political activity of the army between the first and second Civil Wars, and particularly its political debates from Saffron Walden to Putney and Windsor, are discussed in detail by the present writer in *Soldiers and Statesmen* (Oxford, 1987), which reassesses the relations between the army and the Levellers. On specific points it questions whether the 'new agents' of the autumn of 1647 were ever truly elected by their regiments, argues (*pace* Firth) that the agitators never returned to the General Council after 9 November 1647, and clears up the common misapprehension that the most famous debate of all, in which Ireton locked horns with the Levellers on the issue of manhood suffrage, took place either in Putney Church or in a session of the General Council of the Army. On the Levellers in general there has been a large literature since Firth's day. Perhaps the most recommendable titles are Joseph Frank, *The Levellers* (Cambridge, Mass., 1955, reprinted N.Y., 1969); Don. M. Wolfe (ed.), *Leveller Manifestoes of the Puritan Revolution* (N.Y., 1944, reprinted 1967); Pauline Gregg, *Freeborn John: A Biography of*

6 Mark A. Kishlansky: 'The Case of Army Truly Stated: the creation of the New Model Army', *Past and Present* 81 (1978), 51–75; 'The Army and the Levellers: the road to Putney', *Historical Journal* 22 (1979), 795–824; 'Consensus politics and the structure of debate at Putney', *Journal of British Studies 20* (1981), 50–69; 'Ideology and politics in the parliamentary armies, 1645–9' in John Morrill (ed.), *Reactions to the English Civil War 1642–1649* (1982), pp. 163–83; 'What happened at Ware?', *Historical Journal* 25 (1982), 827–39.

John Lilburne (1961); and on radicals more generally, Christopher Hill, *The World Turned Upside Down* (1972). There was much stir for a time over C. B. Macpherson's contention in *The Political Theory of Possessive Individualism* (Oxford, 1962) that the Levellers never advocated manhood suffrage or anything approaching it, but his critics – notably Sir Keith Thomas[7] – have argued persuasively that those adult males whom their spokesmen (though probably not all Levellers) would have excluded from the franchise constituted quite small categories, and not the majority as Macpherson imagined.

A very diffent influence on army politics is delineated by J. S. A. Adamson in an article which presages a major reappraisal of the role of the parliamentarian peers in the politics of the 1640s.[8] Adamson establishes that there was close liaison in 1647–8 between the army commanders and a group of Independent peers and M.P.s centring upon Viscount Saye and Sele and the Earl of Northumberland, though his attempt to reduce Ireton's role inthe drafting of the Heads of the Proposals to 'a secretarial capacity' may be thought to go too far. With regard to the Whitehall debates which fill much of Volume II, Barbara Taft has convincingly challenged the common view that the General Council of Officers was merely holding the Levellers in play while the king's trial and the erection of a conservative Commonwealth went ahead, and argued that the officers' amended version of the second Agreement of the People represented a serious attempt to devise a constitutional settlement that would unite the

[7] Keith Thomas, 'The Levellers and the franchise', in G. E. Aylmer (ed.), *The Interregnum: The Quest for Settlement 1646–1660* (1972), pp. 57–78.

[8] J. S. A. Adamson, 'The English nobility and the projected settlement of 1647', *Historical Journal* 30 (1987), 567–602. The scope of Adamson's work-in-progress can partly be gauged from his unpublished Cambridge Ph.D. thesis, 'The peerage in politics, 1645–9' (1986), and from his chapter on 'Parliamentary management, men-of-business and the House of Lords, 1640–49', in Clyve Jones (ed.), *A Pillar of the Constitution: The House of Lords in British Politics 1640–1784* (1989); see also his 'The baronial context of the English civil War' in *Transactions of the Royal Historical Society*, 5th series 40 (1990), 93–120. These and other pieces by Adamson are attacked by Mark A. Kishlansky in 'Saye What?' *Historical Journal* 33 (1990), 917–37. Adamson has replied in 'Politics and the nobility in civil-war England', *Historical Journal* 34 (1991), 231–55.

army and its friends in the country.[9] She has also published, from volume XVI of the Clarke manuscripts, the voting lists in the Council of Officers on four crucial days during the debates.[10]

Clarke left forty-seven volumes of manuscripts, besides sundry unbound documents and many books and pamphlets. Not all historians may be aware of the extent to which Clarke's collection of pamphlets, which includes quite a number of items that his contemporary George Thomason missed, complements and illumines the subject-matter of his more famous manuscripts. Firth of course published only a selection from the manuscript material, but it was a generous one by the standards of a century ago, and he chose well. In the past dozen years or so there have been two major advances in the accessibility of the rest of the Clarke manuscripts. One has been the publication by Harvester Microform of the entire collection on seventeen reels of mocrofilm, under the editorial direction of G. E. Aylmer. The other had been the cracking of Clarke's shorthand by Eric Sams, and the subsequent decipherment and transcription (still in progress) by Frances McDonald of all the documents that Clarke left undecoded.

Dr. Aylmer's introduction to the microfilm edition[11] provided such a good summary account of the contents of the whole archive and such a judicious appraisal of its value that only a brief indication need be given here of the sort of material that Firth left unpublished. A great deal of it is of interest primarily to students of army administration and army finances. But Clarke was in Scotland all through the 1650s, and since the line between military and civil administration in that country was often blurred, his papers are a rich source for the political history of Scotland in that decade. Firth published many of them in his two volumes for the Scottish History Society, *Scotland and the Commonwealth* (1895) and *Scotland and the Protectorate* (1899), and Frances Dow used both these and the unpublished manuscripts extensively in her *Cromwellian Scotland 1651–1660* (Edinburgh, 1979). There are also documents of consid-

9 Barbara Taft, 'The Council of Officers' *Agreement of the People*, 1648/9', *Historical Journal* 28 (1985), 169–85.

10 Barbara Taft, 'Voting lists of the Council of Officer, December 1648', *Bulletin of the Institute of Historical Research* 52 (1979), 138–54.

11 Cited in n. 2.

erable interest for English history, including a record in Clarke's hand of the trial of Archbishop Laud which adds appreciably to the printed versions, and a very full fair copy of the proceedings of the second High Court of Justice which tried the Duke of Hamilton, the Earl of Holland, the Earl of Norwich, Sir Arthur Capel and Sir John Owen early in 1649. Firth ommitted little of importance that bears on the army's political activity in 1647–9, but one exception is a series of lists of grievances drawn up by individual regiments under the initiative of their agitators in May 1647. Several historians have found valuable evidence in these concerning the early politicization of the New Model soldiery.[12] Cryptology is only one of the skills of Eric Sams, the scholar who has given us the key to Clarke's shorthand. Civil servant extraordinary, he is known to musicians for his authoritative works on the Lieder of Schumann, Brahms and Hugo Wolf, to Shakespearians as a proponent of the bard's authorship of *Edmund Ironside*, and to veterans of the war-time military establishment at Bletchley Park as a then youthful but already highly gifted cipher-breaker. He has contributed a most interesting short essay on Clarke's and other early shorthand systems to the microfilm edition of the manuscripts.[13] Following his breakthrough, Frances McDonald of New College, Oxford, has fully mastered Clarke's stenography and is now well advanced on a transcript of all the documents that Clarke left undeciphered. It currently runs to about 230,000 words, and will in due course be published.[14] Unfortunately she is not in a position to compare Clarke's original record of the great army debates with his own transcript of c.1662, since it was apparently his practice to destroy his shorthand notes as he deciphered them. But there is much valuable material to come from the shorthand volumes, most of it relating to the years 1651–1660.

Clarke did well to bequeath his papers to Worcester College, for they have been fortunate in their custodians. The perspicacity of H. A. Pottinger, who communicated his discovery of their value to their

12 J. S. Morrill, 'The army revolt of 1647', in A. C. Duke and C. A. Tamse (eds.), *Britain and the Netherlands* (*War and Society*), vol. VI, The Hague 1977, pp. 54–78, esp. p. 78; Kishlansky, *Rise of the New Model Army*, pp. 209–16; Woolrych, *Soldiers and Statesmen*, pp. 73–85.

13 *Sir William Clarke MSS*, pp. 29–34.

14 Information kindly supplied by Mrs. McDonald.

ideal editor, has already been mentioned. In more recent years the College has spent handsomely on its library and given its treasures a full worthy setting, where scholars may work on them in comfort and seclusion. Many historians have recorded their gratitude to Richard Sayce, who was Fellow Librarian until his untimely death in 1977. But no one has delved in Clarke's collection in the past twenty years and more without experiencing the quite exceptional helpfulness of Lesley Le Claire (formerly Lesley Montgomery), who was Assistant Librarian in Sayce's time and is now Librarian. Her unique knowledge of the Clarke papers is only matched by her readiness to share it with their readers and to communicate her own enthusiasm to them. Needless to say, her help has been sought and given for this preface. Her personal kindness is a happy memory for a whole generation of seventeenth-century historians, who may feel as this one does that it is really she who should be introducing this welcome reprint of a great jewel in the crown of the old Camden Society.

Caton, Lancaster — AUSTIN WOOLRYCH

PREFACE.

THE collection from which the papers printed in this volume are selected was bequeathed to Worcester College, Oxford, in 1736. Their donor, Dr. George Clarke, a great benefactor of that college and of the University, was Judge Advocate-General from 1684 to 1705, and Secretary at War from 1692 to 1704. His father, Sir William Clarke, was the original owner of these papers. Lives of both father and son are given in the *Dictionary of National Biography* (vol. x. pp. 424, 448). An account of the papers themselves is contained in Mr. Coxe's *Catalogue of Manuscripts in the possession of Oxford Halls and Colleges*, 1852, vol. ii. It is strange that no historian has hitherto thought fit to make use of them. My own attention was first called to the collection by the librarian of Worcester College, H. A. Pottinger, Esq., to whom and to the authorities of the college the thanks of the Camden Society are due for their kindness in facilitating the use of these papers, and the permission to publish them. Since the papers were inspected by Mr. Coxe, Mr. Pottinger has discovered some additional volumes, including the most valuable of all, that containing the debates of the Council of the Army in 1647.

William Clarke, who was probably born about 1623, was admitted a student of the Inner Temple in 1645. When the New Model was organised, John Rushworth was appointed Secretary to the General and Council of War, with William Clarke and another assistant as subordinates. Clarke acted as secretary to the commissioners who negotiated the surrender of Oxford in June, 1646, and to those who tried to arrange terms between the Parliament and the Army in July, 1647 (Sprigge, *Anglia Rediviva*, ed. 1854, p. 258; Rushworth, vi. 606). He seems to have taken part in the invasion of Scotland in July, 1650,[a] and from the autumn of 1651 to the Restoration was Secretary to the Army of Occupation in Scotland. From 1654 that army was under the command of Monck, and Clarke laid the foundation of his subsequent fortunes by gaining the confidence of his commander. Edward Phillips, in the narrative of the Restoration which he added to Baker's Chronicle, describes the attempts of Monck's opponents to win over Clarke.

> "He also writ to Mr. Clarke, the General's Secretary, who was an active useful Instrument in his affairs, to seduce him from his Service; the truth is, the greatest part of Clarke's Estate was in England, and he was a man of so civil and ingenuous a Conversation that he might have been the better excused in a Neutrality to both Parties, and his Interest did direct him to it. But he was resolved to hazard all his Fortunes in the General's Bottom, and would not by threats or cunning, which were both used by Lilburn to him, be prevailed with to quit his Party. For which his fidelity and constancy, at this time, he was ever after so much esteemed by the General, that he trusted him with his most secret transactions."—Ed. 1670, p. 688.

Not long after the Restoration Clarke was knighted and, on 28th January, 1661, appointed Secretary at War (*Cal. State Papers, Dom.*, 1660-1, p. 490). Sir William Coventry described him to Pepys as one of the "sorry instruments" by whom Monck was lucky enough to effect great things (Pepys' Diary, 12th July, 1666). Clarke accompanied Monck to sea in 1666, and was mortally wounded in the battle with the Dutch off Harwich, 2nd June, 1666. He was buried in the chancel of Harwich Church, where an elaborate tablet to his memory was erected by his widow. Monck, in commending her and his child to the favour of the King, wrote

[a] Some of his letters from Scotland are amongst the *Tanner MSS.* in the Bodleian. Cary prints Clarke's accounts of the captures of Stirling and Dundee (*Memorials of the Civil War*, ii. 327, 367). In August, 1651, he asked for the post of Keeper of the Scotch Records (*ibid.* p. 332). Other letters of his are printed in the newspapers. See also *Old Parliamentary History*, xx. 28, 56.

of Clarke that in him he had lost "a faithful and indefatigable servant," and that he could not express "too much kindness to his memory" (*Cal. State Papers, Dom.*, 1665-6, p. 471). Clarke had married Dorothy, daughter and coheiress of Thomas Hyliard, of Hampshire, and Elizabeth Kimpton.[a] A letter from Sir Thomas Clarges to her on her husband's death is preserved in the British Museum.[b]

"MADAM,

"I am so afflicted for the losse of my deare friend Sir William Clerk that I have more need to receive consolation from others then to give it. But I cannot omitt writeing to your Ladyship to desire and beseech you since this fatall stroke cannot be recalled that your Ladyship will have so much respect to that sweete pledge of both your loves, as for his sake to moderate your grief, that your health be not impaired by it."

The widow took the advice, married again in the same year, and lived till 1695. Her second husband, Samuel Barrow, who had been chief physician to the Army in Scotland, became at the Restoration physician in ordinary to the King, and Advocate-General of the Army.

The special value of the Clarke Papers consists in the light which they throw upon the history of the Army during the period when its political importance was greatest. By their assistance we can follow more closely the history of the quarrel between the Parliament and the Army, and appreciate with more exactness than before the causes of the revolutions of 1647 and 1648. The news-letters reveal the state of feeling in London and in the Army as the

[a] By this marriage Clarke became in some way connected with Gilbert Mabbott, another of Rushworth's assistants, whose numerous letters in this correspondence testify to their familiarity. Mabbott's son was named Kympton Mabbott.

[b] *Egerton MS.*, 2618, f. 125. The letter is dated from on board the "Royall Charles," 8th June, 1666. This volume contains other papers belonging to the collections of Sir William Clarke, including the key to a numerical cypher, dated Sept. 1656 (f. 49). Clarke's diary relating to the events of his last service at sea, April 23—June 1, 1666, is also in the British Museum, *Additional MS.*, 14286.

quarrel progressed. The correspondence of the Agitators shows how the revolt in the Army began and by what means it was carried out. The debates of the Council of the Army illustrate in the most striking manner the political views of the soldiers, the dissensions which arose amongst them, and the character of the Army leaders. They elucidate more than one dark passage in Cromwell's political career, and justify the high estimation of Ireton's ability expressed by his contemporaries.

In February and March, 1647, Parliament passed a series of votes for the disbanding of the Army. They also determined that a body of 3,000 horse, 1,200 dragoons, and 8,400 foot, to be drawn from the army of Sir Thomas Fairfax, should be employed for the reconquest of Ireland. An army consisting of 5,400 horse and 1,000 dragoons, together with about 10,000 foot for garrison service, was to be maintained in England. The terms on which the disbanding was to take place were calculated to rouse legitimate discontent. The soldiers were to receive a very small portion of the pay due to them, and they were offered very insufficient securities for their large arrears of pay. They were promised an Act of Indemnity for acts done in pursuance of the orders of their commanders during the war, but that Act when passed was regarded by them as insufficient for their protection. Finally, it was evident that the disbanding would be followed by severe measures for the enforcement of Presbyterian orthodoxy and the punishment of sectaries. As the policy of Holles and the Presbyterian leaders developed itself, protests against it multiplied both from the Army itself and from the Independents outside the Army. But all petitions against that policy were suppressed, and the petitioners sometimes punished (pp. 2, 26, 92).

About March 21, 1647, a petition was circulated amongst the officers setting forth their objections to the proposed scheme for disbanding.

1. "First, whereas the necessity and exigence of the War, hath put us upon many actions, which the Law would not warrant, nor we have acted in a time of setled

peace; we humbly desire, that before our disbanding, a full and sufficient provision may be made by Ordinance of Parliament (to which the Royall assent may be desired) for our indempnity and security in all such cases.

2. "That Auditors or Commissioners may be speedily appointed and authorised to repaire to the headquarters of this Army, to audite and state our accompts, as well for all former services as for our services in this Army; and that before the disbanding of the Army, satisfaction may be given to the Petitioners for their arreares, that so the charge, trouble, and loss of time, which we must otherwise necessarily undergoe in attendance for the obtaining of them may be prevented. . . .

3. "That those who have voluntarily served the Parliament in the late Warrs may not hereafter be compelled by press or otherwise to serve as souldiers out of this Kingdome. Nor those who have served as horsemen may be compelled by press to serve on Foot, in any future case.

4. "That such in this Army as have lost their limbs, and the wives and children of such as have been slain in the service, and such officers or souldiers as have sustained losses, or have been prejudiced in their estates, by adhering to the Parliament; or in their persons by sickness or imprisonment under the Enemy, may have such allowances and satisfaction, as may be agreeable to Justice and equity.

5. "That till the Army be disbanded as aforesaid, some course may be taken for the supply thereof with moneys, whereby we may be enabled to discharge our quarters, that so we may not for necessary food be beholden to the Parliament's Enemies, burthensome to their friends, or oppressive to the Country, whose preservation we have always endeavoured, and in whose happiness we should still rejoice."

Moderate though these demands were, Fairfax was directed at once to put a stop to any further proceeding in that petition, and to send up Lieutenant-General Hammond, Colonel Robert Hammond, Colonel Lilburn, Colonel Pride, and Lieutenant-Colonel Grime, who were concerned in promoting it, to answer for their conduct at the bar of the House of Commons (pp. 1-4, *Book of Army Declarations*, 1647, pp. 1-5). On March 30, the House of Commons passed a declaration, condemning the petition as tending to put the Army into a distemper and mutiny, and declaring that those who continued to promote it should be proceeded against as enemies to the State and disturbers of the public peace.

On April 15, six parliamentary commissioners were sent to Saffron Walden to confer with Fairfax and his officers on the engagement of the body of soldiers destined for the service of Ireland. A full narrative of their proceedings is given on pp. 5-15. The result of their mission showed a general unwillingness in both officers and soldiers to engage upon the terms offered. The officers in general maintained a somewhat neutral attitude, declining emphatically to engage themselves, but promising to promote and not to hinder the engagement of their soldiers (p. 7). A few of the higher officers undertook to go in person, but in more than one regiment soldiers refused to follow the example of their commanders, and mutinied when they were drawn out to march (pp. 12-15).

Left to themselves by the indecision of their officers, the soldiers began to act without them. In a paper entitled *An apology of all the private soldiers in Sir Thomas Fairfax his army to their commission officers*, they stated their grievances and called on their officers to stand by them for the redress of these wrongs.

"The Lord put a spirit of courage into your hearts that you may stand fast in your integrity that you have manifested to us your soldiers; and we do declare to you that if any of you shall not, he shall be marked with a brand of infamy for ever, as a traytor to his country and an enemy to this Armie. . . . We have been quiet and peaceable in obeying all orders and commands, yet now we have just cause to tell you, if we be not relieved in these our grievances, wee shall be forced to that, which we pray God to divert, and keep your and our hearts upright." [a]

A somewhat similar letter was at the same time addressed to Fairfax, Cromwell, and Skippon, which Skippon, on April 30, delivered to the House of Commons (Rushworth, vi. 474). It was signed by the representatives of eight regiments of horse and presented by three troopers. At the command of the House the three troopers were called in and examined; their answers are printed in Appendix B. on pp. 430, 431. The letter itself is printed, from the copy addressed to Skippon, in Cary's *Memorials*

[a] *Book of Army Declarations*, pp. 9-11. Compare the comments on page 15 of these papers.

of the Civil War, i. 201, and in the *Lords Journals*, ix. 164; other versions, with slight verbal variations, are to be found in Prynne's *The Hypocrites Unmasking*, 1647, and in the *Book of Army Declarations*, p. 9.

The immediate result of this letter was an order sending Skippon, Cromwell, Ireton, and Fleetwood to Saffron Walden to acquaint the soldiers with the votes of the House respecting their pay and indemnity, and to examine into the origin of the letter from the eight regiments (see pp. 20, 21, 33). A narrative of the proceedings of the commissioners is printed on pp. 27-31, and reports of the debates which took place between them and the officers on May 15, 16, follow on pp. 33-44, 45-78. These reports were probably taken down by William Clarke at the time in shorthand, though apparently his notes were not transcribed at length till 1662 (p. 31). It is obvious that the author was not at the time a very skilful note-taker. There are frequent blanks in the report and it is often very confused. It is also probable that the person who finally transcribed the notes added to the confusion by mistaking the order of some of the pages. Nevertheless, with all its errors, the report gives an extremely valuable and interesting picture of a curious scene. The meetings in the church at Saffron Walden on May 15, 16, were attended by about 200 officers and a certain number of private soldiers, probably representatives sent by different regiments. Skippon presided, and one after another the chief officers gave an account of the temper of their respective regiments and their reception of the votes of Parliament. Each regiment made a return of its grievances, and (by consent of the great majority of the officers) Lambert and others were appointed to collect from these regimental returns a summary of the common grievances of the whole army, to be presented to the commissioners and transmitted to Parliament (pp. 36, 42, 97). Over these returns a number of disputes took place. More than once varying returns were presented by different officers for the same regiment. Lieutenant-Colonel Jackson and Captain White quarrelled violently over the account presented from Fairfax's own foot regiment (pp. 53, 57). There were disputes also as to the regiments of Colonel Graves and Sir Hardress Waller (pp. 56, 59-62). Colonel Sheffield, as the spokesman of the minority willing to accept the terms offered by Parliament, objected to the presence of private soldiers, and fell foul of Colonel Hammond and Colonel Whalley (pp. 40, 65, 77, 85). Skippon had the greatest difficulty in maintaining order. More than once he urged the officers "to hear one another with sobriety," to "forbear acclamations," to "speak with moderation or else be silent." "God knows it is a very great pressure to my spirit to hear and observe such clashings and jarrings amongst you, I am sure there can no good come of it" (pp. 48, 49, 58, 77).

It was finally proposed that two of the commissioners should go up to London to represent the desires of the Army to Parliament, and remove any misrepresentations which might be made of the action of the officers (p. 76). In accordance with this desire, and in obedience to a similar order from Parliament, Cromwell and Fleetwood were sent up to London with an elaborate report signed by all four commissioners (pp. 94-99). Cromwell presented this report to the House of Commons on May 21, expressing his belief that the soldiers would disband when ordered, but would certainly not engage to go to Ireland (p. 99). The House replied by some minor concessions to the demands of the soldiers, but made no further addition to the eight weeks' pay before promised. On May 25 a series of votes were passed fixing the dates and places at which the different regiments were to be disbanded. Cromwell and Fleetwood remained in London for the rest of the month. Fairfax, whose stay in London had caused injurious comment, was ordered down to the Army (pp. 11, 85, 93, 101). He arrived at Saffron Walden on May 20, and removed his head-quarters to Bury on May 25. Immediately on his arrival he issued a letter to the commanders of the several regiments, informing them that they were to give notice to their soldiers, that the grievances of the Army had been presented to the House of Commons, and were taken into consideration by them. "I do therefore require the souldiers to forbear any further actings by them selves without their officers in any irregular ways, and all officers are strictly to see to it in their several charges, that there be no more such meetings or consultations of souldiers at Bury or elsewhere" (Rushworth, vi. 495). It was too late, however, for such an order to produce obedience. Already the soldiers had formed an organised council of representatives and agreed on their plan of action.

In their report the four commissioners had stated that in their opinion "the officers thus joyning with the soldiers againe in a regular way to make knowne and give vent to their greivances, hath contributed much to allay precedent distempers, to bring off the souldiers from their late wayes of correspondencie and actings among themselves, and to reduce them again to a right order and regard to their officers in what they do" (p. 99). This view was too sanguine. Concerted action amongst the soldiers seems to have begun towards the end of April, 1647, when representatives of eight regiments of horse drew up the letter to Fairfax, Cromwell, and Skippon. In their examination the three troopers said that the letter "was drawn up first at a rendezvous of several of those regiments, and afterwards they had several meetings about it by agents from each regiment in several places" (Rushworth, vi. 474, *cf.* pp. 21, 33). One consequence of the mission of the four officers to Saffron Walden in May was the introduction of a similar organisation amongst the foot regiments. One or two soldiers were chosen from each troop or company to draw up and present their statements of grievances (pp. 66, 96). "The committee of troopers met at St. Edmundsbury, and the foot, who chose two out of every company, sent them to confer with the troopers, and every foot soldier gave fourpence a piece towards defraying of the charges of that meeting" (Rushworth, vi. 485). Throughout the Agitators of the horse regiments continued to take the lead, sending letters to other regiments, and writing to the Army of the northern association to persuade it to stand by the new model (pp. 88, 89). The Agitators were in constant communication with London and received news of all the votes of Parliament directly they were passed. A remarkable paper entitled *Advertisements for the managing of the Councells of the Army* (p. 22), possibly from the pen of Sexby, sketches out the line of conduct which they adopted. The news of the votes of May 18 for the disbanding of the Army precipitated open mutiny. "Believe it, my deare fellowes, wee must now be very active to send to all our several regiments of Horse and Foote and let them knowe that nothing but destruction is threatened. Loving friends, be active, for all lies at stake" (pp. 85, 86). In reply to this exhortation from one of their correspondents in London the Agitators at Bury issued a circular letter urging their regiments to resist disbanding. "Resolve neither to take monie nor march one from another, but lett all your actions be joyn'd. And if any orders should come to your particular regiments to march from the rest of the Army, march not while you have consulted with the rest of the Army" (p. 87). The General was to be petitioned in the name of the soldiers "to have him, in honour, justice, and honestie, to stand by you." Skippon "and all other officers that are not right" were to be told to leave the Army (p. 100). A printing press was to be got into the Army in order to set forth the wrongs of the soldiers and to disabuse the people of their prejudices against them (pp. 22, 86). The counties were to be stirred up to petition for their rights, and to appeal to the Army to assert them (p. 101). The magazine and artillery train at Oxford, which the Parliament intended to remove to London, were to be seized by a party of 1,000 horse (pp. 105, 114). When the commissioners of the Parliament came to pay off the General's regiment of foot, which was to be the first disbanded, they and the £7,000 they brought with them were to be seized on the way (pp. 106, 107).

The question whether this plan of action was inspired by the officers, or to what extent the officers were cognisant of it, is of some interest. The three troopers who brought the letter of the eight regiments of horse, "being demanded whether any of their officers were engaged in it . . . answered that they thought very few of them knew or took notice of it" (Rushworth, vi., 474). A number of officers were active in framing petitions to Parliament against the proposed terms of disbandment, and some sought to procure the support of the soldiers to these petitions (pp. 2, 25, 45). Now and then one would exhort his soldiers to "stand for their liberties" and refuse to engage for Ireland, but most of them, whilst refusing to engage themselves, made no attempt to prevent their men from enlisting (pp. 7, 56). With the exception of two or three subalterns (such as, perhaps, Lieutenant Chillenden,[a] and certainly Cornet Joyce) none of the officers seem to have been implicated in the bolder schemes for active resistance to disbanding set on foot by Sexby and the Agitators. Sexby was perfectly able to conceive such a scheme unaided, and there were many other men of ability amongst the Agitators. Colonel Wogan attributes great importance to the action of Captain John Reynolds, but confuses the events of May with those of June, and draws liberally on his imagination to supply the defects of his memory (pp .421-429).

The question of the part played by Cromwell and Ireton with respect to this movement in the Army is of more importance. The theory of Cromwell's opponents is that he first, by his false protestations that the Army should disband whensoever they should be commanded, induced the Parliament to pass the disbanding votes, and then, by means of the Agitators, induced the Army to refuse to disband. This is the theory set forth by Colonel Wogan (pp. 425-427). It is also the theory of Clement Walker, who says, speaking of the disbanding ordinance—

"To the passing of this Ordinance, Cromwell's protestations in the House with his hand upon his breast, 'In the presence of almighty God, before whom he stood, that he knew the Army would disband and lay down their arms at their doore, whensoever they should command them,' conduced much: this was maliciously done of Cromwel to set the Army at a greater distance with the Presbyterian party and to bring

[a] Pages 85, 100, 105. References in the letters on pp. 83, 86 seem to show that some officers helped the Agitators with money.

them and the Independent party nearer together. . . . And at the same time when he made these protests in the House he had his Agitators (Spirits of his own and his son Ireton's conjuring up in the Army though since conjured down by them without requital) to animate them against the major part of the House . . . to ingage them against disbanding and going for Ireland . . . and to insist upon many other high demands, some private as souldiers, some publique as statesmen." (*History of Independency*, ed. 1648, pt. i. p. 31.)

A similar theory is embodied in Butler's well-known verses—

"So Cromwell, with deep oaths and vows,
Swore all the Commons out o' th' house,
Vowed that the redcoats would disband
Ay marry would they, at their command;
And trolled them on, and swore and swore
Till th' Army turned them out of door." [a]

The first votes for disbanding were passed on February 18, 19, 23, 25, 26, and during the first week of March, 1647 (*Commons Journals*). A news letter of February 18, 1647, observes, "Cromwell is dangerously ill with an imposthume in his head, whereby his party is now the weaker in the House," so that he was probably not in the House when the original decision to disband was taken (*Clarendon MS.*, 2,439). His dissatisfaction with the policy of the Presbyterians was notorious, and he openly showed that he would have no hand in forwarding it. "Young Vane and Cromwell," says a news letter, "often forbear coming to the House," and Holles complains that Cromwell and his friends purposely absented themselves from the Committee of both Kingdoms (*Clarendon MS.*, 2,504; Holles *Memoirs*, § 79). He even thought of leaving England and taking service in Germany under the Elector Palatine (Gardener, *Great Civil War*, iii. 36). Twice indeed, once apparently in March, and again on May 21, he did profess his belief that the Army would disband when Parliament ordered them; but to suppose that this was done merely to encourage the policy of which he was the declared opponent requires clear and conclusive evidence. (Lilburn, *Jonah's Cry*, p. 4; *Clarendon MS.*, 2,520). All the evidence points another way.

[a] *Hudibras*, pt. ii. canto ii.

These papers show the real origin of the movement which resulted in the election of the Agitators, and explain what Cromwell's attitude really was. He sympathised with the grievances of the soldiers, but urged them to accept the terms offered rather than cause a new war. He pressed the officers "to have a very great care to make the best use" they could of the votes of Parliament, and to employ their own influence with their men "to worke in them a good opinion of that authority that is over both us and them." He bade them remember that, "if that authority falls to nothing, nothing can follow but confusion" (p. 72). Ireton seems to have been equally desirous to mediate between the Army and the Parliament (p. 102). On this point the evidence afforded by these papers is confirmed by the testimony of their supposed accomplices, the Levellers and the Agitators.

"O Cromwell" wrote Lilburn on March 25, 1647, "I am informed this day by an officer out of the Army and by another knowing man yesterday, that came a purpose to me out of the Army, that you and your agents are like to dash in pieces the hopes of our outward preservation, their petition to the House, and will not suffer them to petition till they have laid down their arms, because, forsooth, you have engaged to the House they shall lay down their armes whenever they shall command them." (*Jonah's Cry out of the Whale's Belly*, 1647, p. 4).

In the autumn of 1647, when the Agitators fell out with Cromwell and Ireton, their backwardness at the commencement of the breach was made an argument against them.

"We hope it will be no discouragement unto you," wrote the Agitators to the soldiers, "though your Officers, yea, the greatest Officers, should apostatise from you; Its well known that the great Officers which now oppose, did as much oppose secretly when wee refused to disband according to the Parliament's Order; and at last they confessed the Providence of God was the more wonderfull, because those resolutions to stand for Fredom and justice began among the Souldiers only." ("*A copy of a Letter sent by the Agents of Several Regiments*," 1647.)

Still more definite are the statements of John Wildman in the pamphlet against Cromwell and Ireton which he entitles *Putney Projects*.

"I shall not prejudge the singleness of Cromwell's or Ireton's hearts as to public good, in their first associating with the Army at Newmarket, but it's worth the knowing that they both in private opposed those gallant endeavours of the Army for their country's freedom. Yea, their arguments against them were only prophesies of sad events; confusion and ruin, said they, will be the portion of the actors in that design, they will never be able to accomplish their desires against such potent enemies. They were as clearly convinced, as if it had been written with a beam of the Sun, that an apostate party in Parliament (viz. Hollis his faction) did subject our laws and liberties to their inordinate wills and lusts, and exercised such tyranny, injustice, arbitrariness, and oppression, as the worst of arbitrary courts could never parallel. But to oppose a party of tyrants so powerful; *hic labor hoc opus est*, there was a lion and a bear in the way. And lest mere suspicion of their compliance with the Army in any attempt to affront those insulting tyrants should be turned to their prejudice, they were willing, at least by their creatures, to suppress the soldiers first most innocent and modest petition. C. Rich sent several orders to some of his officers to prevent subscription of that petition. And the constant importunity and solicitation of many friends could not prevail with Cromwell to appear, until the danger of imprisonment forced him to fly to the Army (the day after their first rendezvous) for shelter. And then both he and Ireton joining with the Army, and assuming offices to themselves (acting without commissions and being outed by the self-denying Ordinance of Parliament, and the General having no power to make general officers) they were engaged in respect to their own safety to crush and overturn Hollis his domineering, tyrannical faction. And to that end their invasion of the people's freedom, their injustice and oppression, was painted in the most lively colours to the people's eyes, and petitions to the General against those obstructors of justice in parliament, drawn by Cromwell himself, were sent to some counties to subscribe, and then the most mellifluous enamouring promises were passed to petitioners of clearing and securing their rights and liberties, then the General engaged himself to them that what he wanted in expression of his devotion to their service should be supplied in action: and hereby their names were ingraven in the peoples hearts for gallant patriots, and the most noble heroes of our age."

But though the officers might at first hold back the time came when they were forced to decide. When they undertook to collect, to summarise, and to represent to Parliament the grievances of the soldiers, they practically made their cause their own. Parliament strove to separate the privates from their officers, but in vain (pp. 84, 87). The Agitators summoned the soldiers to stick by their officers as their officers had stuck by them. "Stand with your officers, and one with another you need not fear. If you divide you destroy all" (p. 87).

When the Council of War met at St. Edmundsbury on May 29,

the Agitators of ten regiments of horse and six regiments of foot presented a petition to the General, begging him "to appoint a rendezvous speedily for the Army, and also to use your utmost endeavour it be not disbanded before our sad and pressing grievances be heard and fully redressed" (*Book of Army Declarations*, p. 16). By 84 votes to 7, the Council resolved that a general rendezvous should take place, and by 82 to 4 passed the remonstrance against disbanding which a small committee had drawn up (pp. 108-111). See *The Opinion and Humble Advise of the Councell of Warre convened at Bury St. Edmunds*, 29 *May*, 1647. *In relation to the Votes of Parliament communicated to us by your Excellency, and the desires of our advice thereon.* (*Book of Army Declarations, p.* 12.)

"The officers," writes an observer, "now owne the Souldiers and all that's done, and doe beginne to bestirre themselves. . . . Itt is incredible the Unitie of Officers and Souldiers" (p. 113).

The friends of Sir Thomas Fairfax urged him to leave the Army in case it decided to oppose the Parliament's commands (pp. 104, 122). He chose to adhere to the votes of the Council of War, and wrote to the Committee at Derby House to announce that he could not undertake to draw out the regiments under his command to be disbanded at the time appointed (p. 116). At the same time he sent the Parliament the resolutions of the Council of War, and entreated them that there might be "ways of love and composure thought upon." "I shall do my endeavours," he added, "though I am forced to yield something out of order, to keep the Army from disorder or worse inconveniences" (May 30; *Book of Army Declarations*, p. 12 ; Rushworth, vi. 497-499).

Whatever Fairfax might desire, the Army was fast passing beyond control. His own regiment of foot, which was to have been disbanded on June 1, was, as the Agitators had designed, the first to break out into open revolt (pp. 100, 106, 113).

The commissioners came to Chelmsford on the evening of Monday, May 31, escorted by three troops of horse to guard the money. When they arrived they found that about two hours before they came the regiment had marched away towards Raine, on the way to the general rendezvous at Newmarket. Major Gooday, one of those officers of the regiment who remained faithful to the Parliament, had met his company on the march, and "demanding of them by what order they removed their quarters, they answered the horse caused them to remove; further expressing that they received orders from the Agitators" (Cary, *Memorials of the Civil War*, i. 220). Lieutenant-Colonel Jackson and Major Gooday reported that they had used their utmost endeavours to dispose the soldiers for the service of Ireland, and complained that some of their officers had refused to read the votes and declarations of Parliament to their companies (*Tanner MSS.*, lviii. p. 127). Next day Jackson and Gooday were sent after their men to endeavour to induce them to return.

The commissioners give the following account of the result:

"This day we sent Lievtenant-Colonel Jackson, Major Goodday, and Captain Heifeild to Raine, where we were informed that the souldiers of the Generall's foote Regiment had appointed a Rendezvous. There mett about a thousand. At the approach of the officers we sent thither, the souldyers cryed out, There comes our Enimies. When they were acquainted with the votes, declaracions, and ordinances of Parlement, they asked the officers, what doe you bringing your two-penny pamphletts to us? And afterwards they seized upon the wagons with what ammunicion was in them and the chirurgeons chests, and have carryed them away towards Halstead and Heueningham, where they quarter this night. To morrow they are to be at Sudberry and Lavenham; which is the quarter that is appointed them, by Gravenor, the quarter master Generall. By the way some of the souldiers have comitted very great outrages. At Braintry they broke open a man's house, and tooke away fiftie pounds. Upon complaint to the Lievtenant, they were apprehended, but those into whose custodie they were put gave them their libertie againe. Some part of the money was restored, but they conveyd away at least foure and twentie pounds. There is one Captain White who is the most active man in this buisines, and issues out orders as if he were the Lievtenant Colonel. There went away with this Regiment, as we are enformed, two Captains, and a Captain Lievtenant. Many of the souldyers haveing beene dealt withall, profess that money is the onely thing that they insist upon And that 4 moneths pay would have given satisfaccion; but for the present, are carryed away togeather, as in a torrent. Some officers of thes Regiments, as we feare, have fully recruited their companyes, under pretence, for the service of Ireland, but being listed, doe indispose them all they can as by experience is evident. We now conceive our being here is altogeather unprofitable in order to the service we are comaunded downe upon. And therefore offer it to your Lordships, &c. consideracion, whether it may not be convenient to require our returns.[a]

Of the objects of the Agitators three had now been gained. Fairfax and the officers had cast in their lot with the soldiers, a general rendezvous of the Army had been ordered to take place on June 5, and the disbanding of Fairfax's regiment had been prevented. It remained to secure the artillery train which had been left at Oxford on the surrender of that place in 1646. On May 31 the Derby House Committee had ordered the removal of the train and the magazine from Oxford to London (pp. 114, 117). Oxford was garrisoned by Colonel Richard Ingoldsby's regiment, which, though not represented amongst the Agitators who had signed the petition of May 29, was politically one of the most radical in the Army. The regiment was to have been disbanded at Woodstock on June 14, and money was sent down to pay them off. When too late the money was ordered back, but the soldiers mutinied and stopped the wagons which carried it. They were encouraged by the near neighbourhood of Colonel Rainborow's regiment, which, though ordered into Hampshire, and designed for the reduction of Jersey, had left its quarters, expelled its officers, and turned back to assist in the seizure of the magazine. Rainborow found his regiment on May 30 quartered about Abingdon, having thrown off any semblance of obedience.

"When I came," he writes, "I found most of my officers come up to the general quarters of the regiment, who all the time till then had not dared so much as to appear amongst them; but they had not been long in their quarters, ere the Major-serjeant was almost killed by his own soldiers; and his ensign, if he had not exceedingly well defended himself against another company, he had been cut all to pieces; but in defending himself he hath wounded divers of them, two whereof, I am confident, cannot possibly scape with life." (Cary, *Memorials of the Civil War*, i. 221.)

---

[a] *Tanner MSS.*, lviii. f. 129. The Earl of Warwick, Sir Gilbert Gerard, and Sir Harbottle Grimston to the Derby House Committee, June 1, 1647.

To assist in the seizure of the magazine a body of 500 or possibly 1,000 troopers from different cavalry regiments, under the command of Cornet Joyce of Fairfax's regiment of horse, had been collected by the Agitators and despatched to Oxford (p. 106). After making all safe at Oxford, Joyce with some 500 men started north to Holdenby, in Northamptonshire, where the King was in keeping. The King's guards consisted of portions of the regiments of Colonel Graves and Sir Robert Pye, and a few dragoons, all under the command of Colonel Graves. Whilst their commanders supported the Parliament, the soldiers themselves were completely in sympathy with the rest of the Army (pp. 44, 59-62, 113). The Parliamentary leaders were well aware of the disaffection of the King's guard, and there had been rumours a month earlier that some of the foot regiments would "go for Holdenby" and fetch the King. Of the importance of retaining the custody of the King Holles and his friends were well aware, but they seem to have been anxious to come to an agreement with Charles first, and whilst they deliberated and negotiated the soldiers acted. They were discussing the removal of the King, and negotiating for the aid of a Scotch army, when the news came that Joyce, on the morning of June 3, had seized Holdenby and secured the King.

A despatch from Bellièvre to Mazarin, $\frac{3}{13}$ June, 1647, gives the following account of the situation:

"Suyvant l'ancien usage d'Angleterre depuis dix jours nous deliberons sans rien conclure, cherchans les moyens d'empescher que le Roy de la Grande Bretagne tombe entre les mains de l'armée, puisqu'il n'a point d'asseurance qu' elle veuille faire aucune chose à son advantage. D'une douzaine de propositions dont la moins bonne eust mieux valu que de ne rien faire il n'a pas esté possible de obliger ceux du Parlement qui estoient dans ce dessein à en executer aucune, et cependant nous aprenons par un homme qui vient d'arriver de la part des Commissionaires qui sont a Humby, à la verité sans avoir de leurs lettres, que la maison est investie par un party destaché de l'armée qui demande le dit Roy, et quoyque celui qui le garde tesmoigne ne le vouloir pas remettre entre leurs mains, sans en avoir l'ordre du Parlement, il est à croire qu'il l'aura rendu, s'il est vrai qu'il soit pressé, n'estant pas en estat de resister aux forces qui environnent cette maison qui n'a pas ny fossez ny murailles qui la ferment."

On the plans of the Presbyterian leaders, Dr. Denton, a London physician, often very well informed on political movements, writes thus to Sir Ralph Verney, June 14, 1647:

"I have gathered many scraps and looked as far into the clouds as I can, and the result I make to myself is this (but I have only several collections for my grounds and those not very authentic) that the Scots and a Presbyterian party there of some members, not without the counsel of the Queen or some French party, had a design of carrying the King into Scotland, and to set him in the head of an army there, and to bring him up to London, and so to quell the Independent party; but, if I rightly guess, a false Presbyterian father betrayed them to his Independent son; and so the army to prevent them seized the King. Dunfermline is gone into France, sent it is thought to get the Prince into Scotland, and so to play the game the better by that means." [a]

In the fourth article of the charge of the Army against the Eleven Members it was asserted that Holles and others had invited the Scots to march into England, and had sent to the Queen in France, "advising her speedily to send the Prince into Scotland to march into this kingdom at the head of an Army."

The knowledge of these designs, and the desire to prevent their execution, decided Cromwell to cast in his lot with the Army. The possibility of the introduction of a foreign force to maintain the Presbyterian leaders in power, and restore the King to his throne without adequate security for religious or political liberties, demanded immediate action. Abandoning his vain attempt at mediation, he joined Fairfax and the Army in their opposition to the Parliament.

A letter written by a soldier in London, June 1, says:

"The greatest and newest newes is, our general hath declared his resolution to owne the Armie in this their just action, and hath sent for Lieut.-Gen. Cromwell downe to him. I heare he is going out of towne this day. The certainty of this I cannot averre but 'tis not very unlikely. I think before I can take another oppor-

---

[a] *Verney MSS.* This passage and the extract from Bellièvre were kindly communicated to me by Mr. Gardiner.

tunity I shall have matter of great moment to write to you. The Lord smile upon the Saints, and that will prove sufficient to astonish their enemies. The King's person is secured by o[r] armie or by some for it; this is not altogether unprobable tho' I doe a little question whether it be yet done. Very great are the expectations of this daye's business." [a]

Cromwell seems to have left London on June 3, and to have joined Fairfax at Kenford, near Bury, on Friday, June 4, or more probably, on Saturday, June 5. On the 4th, Fairfax had received news of the seizure of the King by Joyce, and on Saturday morning he was informed that the King had been carried from Holdenby and was on his way to Newmarket.

The question to what extent Cromwell was responsible for the seizure of the King has been often discussed. John Harris, in a tract published in December, 1647, entitled *The Grand Designe*, definitely asserts that he was directly responsible:

"It was by some persons at L.-Gen. Crumwel's, he himself being present, upon Monday at night before Whitsunday 1647 [May 31] resolved, that for as much as it was probable that the said Hollis and his party had a determination privately to remove the King to some place of strength or else to set him in the head of another army; that therefore Cornet George Joyce should with as much speed and secrecy as might be repair to Oxford, to give instructions for the securing the garrison, magazine and trains therein, from the said party then endeavouring to get the same, and then forthwith to gather such a party of Horse as he could conveniently get to his assistance, and either secure the person of the King from being removed by any other, or, if occasion were, to remove him to some place of better security, for the prevention of the designe of the aforesaid pretended traiterous party: which was accordingly done, both with the knowledge and approbation of L.-G. Crumwell, although he afterward (like a subtle Fox) would not be pleased to take notice of it."

Lilburn, in his *Impeachment of High Treason against Cromwell and Ireton*, 1649, adds these additional details, that the order was delivered to Joyce "in Cromwell's own garden in Drury Lane,

[a] *Tanner MSS.*, lviii. f. 123, signed W. R. This letter was read in the House of Commons June 3, and may have had something to do with Cromwell's leaving London. He seems to have left in the company of Hugh Peter.

Col. Charles Fleetwood being by." This he practically asserts on the authority of Joyce himself.

Major Huntington, in his Reasons for laying down his commission, says:

"Advice was given by Lieut.-Gen. Cromwell and Commissary General Ireton to remove the King's person from Holdenby, or to secure him there by other guards than those appointed by the Commissioners of Parliament: which design was thought most fit to be carried on by the private soldiery of the Army, and promoted by the agitators of each regiment; whose first business was to secure the garrison at Oxford, with the guns and ammunition there; and from thence to march to Holdenby in prosecution of the former advice; which was accordingly acted by Cornet Joyce."

Huntington also says that Joyce, "being told that the General was displeased with him for bringing the King from Holdenby, answered, that Lieutenant-General Cromwell had given him orders at London, to do what he had done, both there and at Oxford."

In a tract written in 1659, Joyce describes a quarrel between himself and Cromwell in 1648, in the course of which Cromwell

"called him a rascal many times, and with great threats said that he would make him write a vindication of him against a book entitled, *The Grand Design Discovered.* Wherein were many things declared concerning Cromwell's carriage towards Joyce, before he went to Holmby for the King; which afterwards he called God to witness he knew nothing of." (*A Narrative of the Causes of the late Lord General Cromwell's Anger against Lieut-Col. George Joyce.*)

Joyce's narrative is full of wild inaccuracies, but it is evident that Cromwell did not admit the truth of the definite statement published by Harris. How much did he admit? On this point Huntington's statement is definite and probably correct. He states that when Fairfax demanded who gave orders for the removal of the King, Ireton replied

"that he gave orders only for securing the King there, and not for taking him away from thence. Lieutenant-General Cromwell, coming then from London, said, That if this had not been done, the King would have been fetched away by order of

Parliament; or else Colonel Graves, by the advice of the Commissioners, would have carried him to London, throwing themselves upon the favour of the Parliament for that service."

Since Cromwell approved Joyce's preventing the removal of the King from Holdenby, his objection must have been to the second part of the story published by Harris.

Harris asserted that Cromwell gave orders not merely "to secure the person of the King there from being removed by any other," but also, "if occasion were, to remove him to some place of better security."

Cromwell constantly denied that he had sanctioned the removal of the King from Holdenby.

The account of the interview of the officers with the King on June 7 (p. 125) states plainly that all the officers, amongst whom were Cromwell and Ireton, told the King that he had been removed from Holdenby "without their privity, knowledge, or consent" (*cf. Memoirs of Sir P. Warwick*, p. 299).

Fairfax writes in the same strain to Lenthall on June 7: "I can clearly profess (as in the presence of God) for myself, and dare be confident of the same for all the officers about me, and the body of the Army, that the remove of his Majesty from Holdenby was without any design, knowledge, or privity thereof on our part" (*Old Parliamentary History*, xv. 410). As Fairfax had two days before heard the statements of Cromwell and Ireton which Huntington reports, it is clear that he drew a sharp distinction between the King's removal from Holdenby and what the commissioners term "the changing of the King's guards." Ireton's answer defines Cromwell's position. Cromwell, like Ireton, had authorised "securing the King there, not taking him thence." If that be so, Joyce was not telling the truth when he said that Cromwell authorised both the seizure and the removal of the King, and Harris was misinformed when he repeated Joyce's statement. The earlier statements of Joyce are of considerable importance. The narrative printed by Rushworth, and attributed by Masson on good internal evidence to Joyce himself, affords conclusive proof that the removal of the King from Holdenby was an afterthought, and not part of Joyce's original plan. Joyce states that he seized Holdenby early on the morning of Thursday, June 3, occupied the house, set his guards, and dismissed the troopers to their quarters.

"All this being done it grew towards noon . . . . All was quiet in the said present security of his Majesty till tidings came that Graves was gone quite away . . . . None could tell what was become of him, and some of his damning blades did say and swear they would fetch a party, which party could not be from the Army, but must be from some other place. And therefore to prevent disturbance and blood and for the peace sake of the Kingdom, all declared unanimously, that they thought it most convenient to secure the King in another place from such persons as could cunningly or desperately take him away contrary to order." (*Rushworth*, vi. 514.)

About ten o'clock the same night the soldiers sent Cornet Joyce to the King, and Joyce saw the King in bed and announced his intended removal to him. Early next morning, Friday the fourth of June, they set out for Newmarket.[a]

Two other pieces of evidence confirm the view that the removal of the King was not at first intended. The Declaration delivered by Joyce to the commissioners in charge of the King speaks only of preventing a design to take away the King. Moreover Joyce was uncertain whither to take the King, and suggested first Oxford, then Cambridge. Newmarket was proposed by the King himself. If the removal of the King had been pre-determined his destination would also have been pre-arranged (*Old Parliamentary History*, xv. 394; Rushworth, vi. 516). So the story originally told by Joyce is both consistent and probable. If it be true that the removal of the King was not part of Joyce's original design, is it

[a] The statement that the removal of the King was first determined on in the interview on the evening of June 3 is confirmed by the letters of Lord Montagu of June 3 and 4, and his narrative of June 8. (*Old Parliamentary History*, xv. 393, 396.)

probable that it was part of his original instructions? Joyce's later statement that he removed the King from Holdenby in pursuance of instructions received from Cromwell is inconsistent with his earlier statement that the removal was forced upon him by the demands of his soldiers.

As soon as Joyce had seized Holdenby and secured the King he wrote a letter announcing his success. Holles gives the following account of it in his Memoirs:

> "Joyce, after seizing and carrying away the King, immediately sends up a letter to certify what he had done, with directions that it should be delivered to Cromwell, and, if he is absent, to Sir Arthur Haslerig or to Colonel Fleetwood; which letter was given to Colonel Fleetwood, as one Lieutenant Markham informed the House, saying that the messenger that brought it told him so; nor did Sir Arthur Haslerig make a clear answer, when he was asked concerning it in the House: Colonel Fleetwood being at that time gone to the Army so that he could not be examined." (*Memoirs*, § 96.)

The story as told by Holles was written several months later, and the note entered by Lawrence Whitacre in his diary on June 8 is probably more accurate.

> "The House was informed by Mr. Holles of a letter was come to his hands written from Holmby by Cornet Joyce with directions that it should be delivered to Lieut.-Gen. Cromwell, or in his absence to Sir Arthur Haslerig or Col. Fleetwood; whereby Mr. Holles would have inferred that those three gentlemen held correspondence with that Cornet, and so had intelligence of that party's carrying away the King and the Commissioners from Holmby; but Sir Arthur Haslerig denied any knowledge he had thereof, and the names of none of those gentlemen did appear upon the superscription of that letter, so that there was no further proceeding upon it at that time."

The letter printed on p. 118 is probably the letter thus referred to by Holles and Whitacre. There is no superscription, but it was evidently written to some superior officer who was largely responsible for what Joyce had done. He practically says, 'I have carried out your instructions, send me fresh instructions at once.' Its contents substantially correspond to the orders which may be supposed to have been given by Cromwell to Joyce. 'I have secured the King. I have not arrested Colonel Graves because he has escaped. I shall attend to the directions of the parliamentary commissioners within certain limits, but on other points obey no orders but those of the General.' Nothing is said of the removal of the King from Holdenby to Newmarket, or to any other place. If the conclusion that the letter was addressed to Cromwell be accepted, it confirms the view of his relations to Joyce which has been stated in the last few pages.

Fairfax, in his *Short Memorials*, states that he "called for a Council of War to proceed against Joyce, but the officers, whether for fear of the distempered soldiers, or rather (as I suspected) a secret allowance of what was done, made all my endeavours in this ineffectual" (Maseres, *Select Tracts*, i. 448). Some inquiry there probably was into the conduct of Joyce, and it is probable that it was in connection with that inquiry that Clarke obtained copies of the two letters from Joyce here printed (pp. 118-120). The officers in general certainly held that Joyce had done good service to the Army, and he was not only pardoned but promised promotion.

On September 4, 1647, the "Committee of General Officers" passed a resolution "that Commissary-Generall Ireton and Colonel Rainborow bee desired to move the Generall that Cornett Joyce may have the troope of Captain Layton, latelie deceased, in Colonel Fleetwood's regiment, the Generall having engaged to give him the first that falls." (*Clarke MSS.*, vol. lxvi.)

On the treatment of the King whilst he was in the custody of the Army there are several papers in this volume. After Whalley had delivered him from the hands of Joyce he refused to go back to Holdenby, and insisted on continuing his journey to Newmarket (pp. 122, 123). A news letter from the latter place describes his first interview with Fairfax and the officers (p. 124). Fairfax ordered special precautions to be taken by Whalley for the security of the King's person, fearing a rising in Norfolk (p. 130). The King requested Fairfax to allow the Duke of Richmond and two favourite chaplains to attend him ; but Fairfax was unwilling directly to sanction their admission, as it was contrary to the orders of Parliament (p. 137). He was also afraid of some " intention to surprise the King to London," and warned Whalley to be on his guard against it (p. 139). " Be careful of the King's secureing," wrote Cromwell and Hewson to Colonel Whalley; but at the same time they urged him to be " exact only in faithfulness to his trust," and in other things to consult the King's wishes as far as possible (p. 140). Hoping for a speedy accommodation with the Royalist party, they freely allowed the Royalists to come to see the King. " When the Army was in their greatest glory, and the enemy under their foot, yet we were ever humane and Christian to them, and now, being so near a reconciliation, we should not shew any aversion or indisposition " (p. 216).

The mutiny in the New Model, crowned by Joyce's seizure of the King, was followed by similar acts of insubordination amongst the military forces in the rest of the kingdom.

Skippon's regiment at Newcastle sympathised with the regiments stationed in the south (p. 125). The Army of the Northern Association, a separate organisation under the command of General Poyntz, resolved, in spite of the efforts of its commander, to associate itself with the demands of Fairfax's forces. In May the Agitators of the eight regiments of horse had sent a declaration to the Northern Army, explaining the cause of their proceedings, and had also despatched three of their number to arrange joint action (pp. 90, 92, 121).[a] Vainly Poyntz issued orders prohibiting meetings amongst the soldiers, and requiring the arrest of these incendiaries (p. 142). On July 8 he was arrested in his own quarters, and carried prisoner to Pontefract (p. 163). The three Agitators wrote

[a] A similar manifesto from the Agitators to the soldiers in Wales was issued later (p. 159). In several counties a large party seems to have sided with the Army against the Parliament (pp. 130, 138, 222).

to Fairfax giving an account of what they had done, and forwarding a series of charges against Poyntz, signed by representatives of every regiment in the Northern Army (pp. 163-170).

One result of the division in the Army was naturally a change in the officers of many regiments. Fairfax was on July 19 appointed commander-in-chief of all the land forces in the pay of the Parliament (*Lords' Journals*, vii. 339); but even before that date he had commenced appointing new officers in the regiments immediately under his control to take the place of those who had seceded. Barkstead became colonel of Fortescue's regiment, Pride of Harley's, Overton of Herbert's, Harrison of Sheffield's, Horton of Butler's, Thomlinson of Pye's; Scroope succeeded Greaves, and Twisleton, Rossiter. Many officers of lower rank either left the Army, or were even in some cases expelled by their soldiers (see pp. 139, 428).[a]

To restore or to maintain any semblance of order amongst soldiers who had thus shaken off the bonds of discipline was a task of very great difficulty. Equally difficult was the task of uniting these

[a] It would not be difficult to estimate the number and fix the names of the officers who separated themselves from the Army at this period. The list given in Sprigge supplies a list of the officers of the New Model in 1646. The engagement of various officers on March 22, 1647, supplemented by the report of the parliamentary commissioners on April 27, gives the names of those who expressed themselves satisfied with the concessions of Parliament, and undertook to serve in Ireland. (*Lords' Journals*, vii. 114, 152, 220, 345; *Rushworth*, vi. 465). In Fortescue's, Lilburn's, Herbert's, and some other regiments, a considerable number of soldiers engaged for Ireland. On the rupture with Parliament in the beginning of June several officers succeeded in bringing off part of their soldiers; for instance Colonel Greaves (*Lords' Journals*, vii. 243, 267), Sir Robert Pye (*Lords' Journals*, vii. 243), Lieut.-Colonel Jackson (*Lords' Journals*, vii. 243), Captain Farmer (*Lords' Journals*, vii. 258). Part of Fairfax's lifeguard left him (*Lords' Journals*, vii. 264, 282). On the other side the names of those who adhered to Fairfax may be gathered from the signatures to the Petition presented April 27 (*Rushworth*, vi. 471), and from the lists of attendances at various councils of war given in the book of Army declarations published in 1647.

armed politicians for common political action. In the rendezvous at Newmarket on June 4 and 5, a common statement of the grievances of the Army was agreed to and subscribed by the officers and soldiers. On the second of these dates "a Solemn Engagement of the Army" was read, assented to, and subscribed, which forms a sort of military version of the "Solemn League and Covenant." It began by a recital of the causes which led them first to elect Agitators to represent their grievances, and now to refuse to disband. It concluded by an assertion of their willingness to disband when their just demands were satisfied; and a refusal to disband, divide, or suffer themselves to be disbanded or divided, until their demands were satisfied and security given against future wrongs. What satisfaction and security should be regarded as sufficient was to be decided by a council,

"to consist of those general officers of the Army (who have concurred with the Army in the premises) with two commission officers, and two souldiers to be chosen for each Regiment, who have concurred and shall concur with us in the premises, and in this agreement; and by the major part of such of them, who shall meet in Council for that purpose, when they shall be thereunto called by the General.[a]" (Rushworth, vi. 505–512.)

The idea of reinforcing the slackened bond of discipline by this Act of Association for common political ends may have occurred to many: its actual form was pretty certainly due to Ireton. To Ireton also was due the Declaration of the Army of June 14, in which they went beyond the statement of their grievances as soldiers, and proceeded to propound their desires "for the settling and securing of our own and the kingdom's common Right, Freedom, Peace, and Safety." (Rushworth, vi. 564-570.)

That Declaration contains in it the demands afterwards embodied in the "Heads of the Proposals of the Army," which are developed in the latter into a number of definite articles offered for the consideration of Parliament and people.

Here, as in the letter of the officers from Royston, the soldiers demand a voice in the settlement of the kingdom on the ground

"that we are not a meer mercenary Army hired to serve any Arbitrary power of a State, but called forth and conjured by the severall Declarations of Parliament to the defence of our owne and the people's just Rights and Liberties; and so we took up Armes in judgement and conscience to those ends, and have so continued in them, and are resolved according to your first just desires in your Declarations, and such principles as we have received from your frequent informations, and our own common sense concerning those our fundamental rights and liberties, to assert and vindicate the just power and rights of this Kingdome in Parliament for those common ends premised against all arbitrary power, violence, and oppression, and against all particular parties or interests whatsoever."

It contains also a memorable vindication of the right of the Army to resist the authority of Parliament in defence of their just rights and liberties, which is frequently appealed to in the debates of the following October (pp. 260, 268).

Ireton bases the right of resistance on the "Law of Nature and of Nations," citing the example of the Scots, the Dutch, and the Portuguese.

"Such also," he continues, "were the proceedings of our ancestors of famous memory to the purchasing of such Rights and Liberties, as they have enjoyed through the price of their bloud, and we (both by that and the later bloud of our deare friends and fellow soldiers) with the hazard of our own, do now lay claim unto."

Whilst thus asserting the theoretical right of the Army to resist under certain conditions the authority of Parliament, Ireton is careful at the same time to fix a limit to the practical exercise of this right.

The first aim of the Army is declared to be to have Parliaments "rightly constituted, that is, freely, equally, and successively chosen." Parliament is to be purged of delinquents, corruptions, and members unduly elected. The duration of this and of future Parliaments is to be legally fixed; new Parliaments are to be summoned at definite intervals, and to continue sitting for a definite time. When these reforms are effected, the Army will willingly submit to the authority of Parliament.

> "Thus a firm foundation being laid in the authority and constitution of Parliaments for the hopes, at least, of common and equall right and freedom to ourselves and to all the freeborn people of this land; we shall for our parts freely and cheerfully commit our stock or share of interest in this kingdome into this common bottome of Parliaments, and though it may (for our particulars) go ill with us in one Voyage, yet we shall thus hope (if right be with us) to fare better in another."[a]

Just as the Army promises to submit to the authority of Parliament, provided certain reforms in its constitution are granted, so it also professes that it seeks neither "to overthrow Presbytery or hinder the settlement thereof," provided that some toleration for "tender consciences" be guaranteed. They demand

> "that such who, upon conscientious grounds, may differ from the established formes may not for that be debarred from the common Rights, Liberties, or Benefits belonging equally to all as men and members of the Commonwealth, while they live soberly, honestly, and inoffensively towards others, and peacefully and truthfully towards the State."

This promise to accept the establishment of Presbyterianism, if freedom of conscience were provided for, is more than once repeated. It is stated with equal clearness in the letter of Fairfax and his officers to the City of London (June 10), which Carlyle on good grounds supposes to have been written by Cromwell.

Again on September 9, in a discussion in the Council of War at Putney, Cromwell

> "expressed himself to this effect. That whereas it hath been suggested to this Kingdom that hee hath a desire to cast down the Foundation of Presbytery, and to

---

[a] Rushworth's text of this Declaration, vol. vi. pp 564-570, differs in some phrases from that printed in the *Book of Army Declarations*, 1647, pp. 36-46, and the version in the *Old Parliamentary History*, said to be reprinted from the original Declarations printed at Cambridge, gives two very important paragraphs not contained in either of the others (xv. 466).

advance and set up Independency, hee declares, that hee desires nothing more then to see this poore tottered nation established in Truth and Peace, and this languishing Commonwealth restored to their just rights and liberties." (Two Declarations from his Excellency Sir Thomas Fairfax, etc., 1647.)

There was, however, one point in which the Army would be satisfied with nothing short of complete surrender. They demanded that "those persons who in the late unjust and high proceedings against the Army appeared to have the will, the confidence, credit and power, to abuse the Parliament and Army and endanger the Kingdome," should "not continue in the same power," but "be made incapable thereof for the future." This was emphasised by the impeachment of Holles and ten other Presbyterian leaders. Permanent exclusion from political power was a thing to which Holles and his friends would not submit without a struggle. They would have appealed to arms as soon as the news came that the Army had refused to disband, if only the City had been ready to back them (p. 117). A news letter amongst Clarendon's papers, says:

"on the 3rd [of June] the Mayor of London called a Common Council to consider of the present affaires of the Citty, wherein it was resolved by one unanimous consent that they would have noe more war. Concerning how the Parliament took this I have noe more, but that at the first there were some that were pleased to show their mettle in very high expressions, but at last without taking any resolution they rose in very great distraction, being now informed of the resolution of the City whereon they built their chiefest hope." (*Clarendon MS.*, 2527.)

Incitements to the citizens to fight were not wanting, but produced no effect.

Another news letter, of June 7, adds: "Yesterday Col. Massey as he passed through the streets in his coach, exhorting the cittizens to defend themselves against the madd men in the Army, who if they should prevaile would demand the heads of the best citizens, and of the chief men of the Parliament as well as his head" (*ibid.* 2528).

On the news that the Army was marching on London, and was come as far as St. Albans, a more warlike spirit prevailed, and the trained bands were called out (June 11-12); but the next day a conciliatory answer was sent to the letter of the officers of the Army, and the idea of resistance abandoned (pp. 132-135). More than once there were riots caused by the disbanded soldiers and officers of the old armies of Essex and Waller, who clamoured for their pay at the doors of the House of Commons, and threatened the lives of unpopular members (pp. 136, 141). The Presbyterian clergy openly denounced Fairfax and his soldiers in their sermons (p. 150). Whilst the commissioners of the Army and the commissioners of the Parliament were negotiating, news that soldiers were being enlisted in London reached head-quarters (p. 152).

In May, 1647, an ordinance appointing a new committee for the control of the London militia had been passed, by which a number of aldermen and officers belonging to the Independent party, who had done good service during the war, were put out of the committee and their places filled up by Presbyterians (*Rushworth*, vi. 472, 478). The Presbyterian commissioners now proceeded to purge the London trained bands by expelling officers who were accused of being Independents or suspected of supporting the Army, and the officers thus expelled applied to the Army for redress (pp. 152-156).

On July 16 the Agitators laid before the General Council of the Army (or "the General Council of War" as it is here termed) a paper in which they demanded an immediate march on London, in order to obtain the restoration of the militia to the hands of the old commissioners, the release of all prisoners illegally committed, a declaration against the entrance of any foreign forces into England, and the placing of all military forces in the country under the command of Fairfax (pp. 170-175). A great debate took place in the Council of the Army on the question of marching up to London. Over 100 officers and Agitators were present, and the discussion lasted till twelve at night (p. 214). Cromwell and Ireton vehemently opposed a march on London, and succeeded in persuading the Council to be content to send a summary of their demands to Parliament, and require an answer within four days. Cromwell was especially anxious to arrive at a settlement of the differences between the Army and Parliament by means of the treaty which was still being negotiated.

"It will be for our honour and honesty to do what we can to accomplish this work by way of a treaty. . . . . Whatsoever we get by a treaty will be firm and durable, it will be conveyed over to posterity. We shall avoid the great objection that lies against us that we have got things of the Parliament by force, and we know what it is to have that stain lie upon us" (p. 185).

At the same time he held that certain preliminary demands necessary for the present security of the Army during the treaty, and certain grievances whose redress admitted of no delay, might be properly obtained by an ultimatum requiring an answer within a certain specified time (p. 191). Force was not to be used except in the last resort, "except we cannot get what is for the good of the kingdom without force" (p. 202). At the same time he urged that the friends of the Army in the House of Commons were steadily gaining ground; that any appeal to force would alienate the middle party in the House who were neither Presbyterian nor Independent, and stop the mouths of their friends; he reminded his hearers of their old hopes of obtaining their ends through Parliament, and begged them not to abandon those hopes.

"It hath been in most of our thoughts that this Parliament might be a reformed and purged Parliament, that we might see there men looking at public and common interests only. . . . . . This is the principle we did march upon when we were at Uxbridge and when we were at St. Alban's, and surely the thing was wise and honourable and just. . . . . . If we wish to see a purged Parliament let me persuade every man that he would be a little apt to hope the best" (p. 192).

Ireton opposed the march on London for reasons very similar to those put forward by Cromwell. He expected less from the treaty, deemed the question of the London militia of less importance, and urged that there was no sufficient ground for the proposed movement (pp. 194-199). Above all, however, he was anxious that before any new quarrel with the Parliament took place the Army should vindicate the integrity of its intentions by declaring publicly to the kingdom what its political objects were, and how it meant to secure the liberties of the people (p. 179). He had been charged by the General and the rest of the commissioners of the Army appointed to treat with Parliament to draw up a series of proposals for the settlement of the kingdom. With a single assistant, apparently Lambert, he had sketched out the first draft of the document afterwards known as the "Heads of the Proposals of the Army." In it he hoped "to set down something that may be a rule to lay a foundation for the common rights and liberties of the people and for an established peace in the nation" (*cf.* pp. 343-349).

The scheme thus drawn up was to be tendered to the parliamentary commissioners, and to be transmitted by them to Parliament as the basis of a settlement. It would serve also as a manifesto from the Army to the nation, and for that reason Ireton was eager to get it adopted and published before a new breach took place between the Parliament and the Army. On July 17, the day after the debate on the question of marching to London, the draft of the proposals was submitted to the Council. Unfortunately Clarke's report of the discussion ends abruptly, but a few references to the debates are to be found in his reports of the October meetings of Council (pp. 181, 189, 197, 211). The result was that the draft propositions were referred to a committee of twelve officers and twelve Agitators (p. 216).

Parliament yielded to the peremptory demands of the Army, and passed an ordinance replacing the London militia in the hands of the old commissioners (Rushworth, vi. 626, 629, 632-5). At once counter-petitions were set on foot in the City; tumults began, and on July 26 the two Houses were forced by mob-violence to recall their votes. The riots of July 26, the flight of Lenthall to the Army, and the entry of the Army into London are the subject of letters printed on pp. 217-223. Before the Army entered London the "Propositions" had been finally revised, and they were published on August 2 with a declaration to the Parliament and the nation. In the fortnight which had elapsed since the draft was laid before the Council the propositions had undergone some modification in the hope that they would obtain the King's concurrence. Sir John Berkeley describes Ireton as permitting him to examine the draft of the proposals and to make certain alterations in them. "He permitted me to alter two of the articles and that in most material points; and I would have done a third, which was the excluding seven persons from pardon and the not admitting of our party to sit in the next parliament" (*Memoirs of Sir J. Berkeley*, Maseres, p. 363).

When the proposals were privately submitted to the King he objected to the two points mentioned by Berkeley, and still more to the fact that though there was nothing against the Church government established, yet there was nothing done to assert it. The latter reason had great weight with the King in his final rejection of the Army terms (*ibid.*, pp. 367, 368). Major Huntington confirms the account of the private submission of the "Proposals" to the King, which probably took place about July 21 (*Reasons for laying down his Commission*, Maseres, p. 401). He states that Ireton, Rainborow, Hammond, and Rich "attended the King at Woburn, for three hours together, debating the whole business with the King upon the Proposals; upon which debate many of the most material things which the King disliked were afterwards struck out, and many other things were much abated by promises." The precise nature of these changes is thus stated by Wildman in his *Putney Projects*," 1647, p. 14.

"When the Proposalls were first composed, there was a small restriction of the King's negative voice: it was agreed to be proposed, that whatsoever bill should be propounded by two immediate succeeding Parliaments, should stand in full force and effect as any other law, though the King should refuse to consent. . . . . This was expunged."

(2.) "In that rough draft it was proposed, that all who have been in hostility against the Parliament, be incapable of bearing office of power, or publique trust for ten years, without consent of Parliament. But in further favour of the King's interest, these ten years of excluding delinquents from power or trust, were changed to five years."

(3.) "It was further added, after this intercourse with the King, that the Councell of State should have power to admit such Delinquents to any office of power or trust before those five yeares were expired . . . ."

(4.) "In the composure of the proposalls it was desired that an Act for the extirpation of Bishops might be passed by the King. . . . . This Proposall was so moderated that the office and function of Bishops might be continued; and it is now only proposed that the coercive power and jurisdiction of Bishops extending to any Civill penalties upon any be abolished."

(5.) "After this Treaty with the King, the proposall for passing an Act to confirm the sale of Bishops lands was wholly obliterated; and though the Army afterward desired the Parliament to proceed in the sale and alienation of those Lands, yet that was none of their proposalls in order to a peace with the King, but according to their proposalls for a setled peace, the King was first to be established in his throne with his usurped power of a negative voyce to all lawes or determinations of Parliament, and then they knew that the King might be at his choyce, whether he would permit an alienation of these lands."

One of this committee of four who discussed the "Propositions" with the King, viz. Colonel Rainborow, gave John Lilburn "a full account of that business," and of Ireton's "base juggling and underhand dealings" (Lilburn's *Impeachment of High Treason against Oliver Cromwell and Henry Ireton*, 1649, p. 55). It was doubtless Lilburn who supplied Wildman with the information he embodies in his tract.

A detailed criticism of these Heads of Proposals is given by Mr. Gardiner in the preface to his *Constitutional Documents of the Puritan Revolution* (pp. xlviii.-l.). "It contained," he concludes, "too much that was new, too much in advance of the general intelligence of the times to obtain that popular support without which the best constitutions are but castles in the air; and even if this could have been got over, there was the fatal objection that it proceeded from an army." Even after the occupation of London had taken place, Parliament, instead of taking up the Heads of the Proposals as the basis of a settlement of the kingdom, "sent to the King a revised edition of the propositions of Newcastle, differing mainly in this, that it proposed a limited toleration for dissentient Puritans, whilst forbidding all use of the book of Common Prayer." In his reply to their propositions, the King, on September 14, expressed a preference for the Proposals of the Army, as more conducive "to the satisfaction of all interests and a fitter foundation for a lasting peace (*Rushworth* vii. 810). Major Huntington's letter (p. 225) shows that the King expected the leaders of the Army to stand by him in procuring an offer of better terms from the parliament. The question of a new treaty was discussed in the House of Commons on September 22 and 23, 1647. Marten and his party were eager for the passing of a vote to make no further addresses to the King. Cromwell and Ireton on the other hand opposed Marten's motion, and the House finally resolved on September 23 that they would once again make application to the King.

This decision led to much discontent amongst the Levelling party in the Army as also outside of it, and "the credit and reputation" of both Cromwell and Ireton was much blasted thereby (p. 228). They were accused of falsely representing it to be the desire and sense of the Army that this new application should be made to the King. The charge is thus stated by Wildman in his *Putney Projects* (p. 43):

"When the answer of the King's was voted by the Parliament to be a denial of the Propositions, a question was stated whether any more addresses should be made to the King, and the determination was very dubious: but then a Cabinet Councell of the Grandees was called, Sir John Eveling, Mr. William Perpoint, and Mr. Fines, Sir Henry Vane, and Cromwell, and Ireton, *cum paucis aliis*: and O how was the quintessence of their braines extracted, in plausible arguments for a new addresse to the King! how were the imaginary mischiefs, and dangerous consequences of a refusall presented in most lively emblems! and I conclude from the event, that in such a Cabinet Councell the question was first concluded in the affirmative, and then the debate of the question was managed in the House with much seeming solemnity; but when the potency of reason, and justice, against any further addresses, began to tryumph over their feminine reasons, a Member (no question one of the same confederacy) produced a reason like Goliah's sword, with this inscription, there's none like this, its (saith he) the sense of the Army that a further addresse be made to the King: this led every reason captive, and so the debate ended. . . . . . Com. Gen. Ireton without a proxie sometime averred as much in effect in the House, 'You must (saith he) looke for opposition, whenever you shall cease your addresses to the King, and then your case would be sad, if you should have no strength adhere unto you, and if you now cease, I cannot promise you the Armies assistance.' "

When this charge was made against Cromwell by Sexby in the debate in the Council of the Army on October 28, he replied that what he had spoken in Parliament he had spoken as his own sense, and not in the name of the Army.[a] Ireton's answer was, that he did believe it to be the sense of the Army that a second address should be made to the King (pp. 228-232).

Whilst the public utterances of Ireton and Cromwell were thus misinterpreted by the Levellers, their private conferences with the King and their apparent intimacy with his agents Berkeley and Ashburnham gave rise to still greater suspicions. After the King came to Hampton Court,

"Mr. Ashburnham had daily some message or another from the King, to Cromwell and Ireton, who had enough to do both in the Parliament and Council of the Army, the one abounding with Presbyterians, the other with Levellers, and both really jealous that Cromwell and Ireton had made a private compact and bargain with the King; Lilburn printing books weekly to that effect, and Sir Lewis Dives afterwards acknowledged to me, that being his fellow prisoner he had daily endeavoured to possess him with that opinion; of which, although he were not persuaded himself, yet he judged it for the King's service to divide Cromwell and the Army. On the other hand the Presbyterians were no less confident of their surmises, and amongst them, Cromwell told me that my Lady Carlisle affirmed, that I had said to her Ladyship, that he was to be Earl of Essex and Captain of the King's guards. . . . . . These and the like discourses made great impression on the Army; to which Mr. Ashburnham's secret and long conferences contributed not a

[a] Other accounts of Cromwell's speech are given in the note on p. 230. Mr. Gardiner points out that the speech which Cromwell defends must have been made on September 22nd, as he arrived too late for the debate of the 23rd.

little; insomuch that the Adjutators, who were wont to complain that Cromwell went too slow towards the King, began now to suspect that he had gone too fast and left them behind him." (*Memoirs of Sir John Berkeley*, Maseres' Select Tracts, i. 368-372).

A pamphlet complains that the officers make an "idoll of the King."

"Why are they so familiar with Ashburnhame and others, his chief agents? Why permit they so many of his deceitful clergy to continue about him? Why doe themselves kneele, and kisse, and fawne upon him? Why have they received favours from him, and sent their wives or daughters to visit him, or to kiss his hand, or to be kissed of him? Oh shame of men! Oh sin against God! What, to doe thus to a man of blood, over head and eares in the blood of your dearest friends and fellow commoners?" (*A Call to all the Souldiers of the Army by the Free People of England*, 1647, p. 5.)

Another charge was that the engagement of June 5, referring the political government of the Army to the elected General Council of the Army, had not been kept, and that its authority had been gradually superseded by the Council of War, and by other committees of officers.

Lilburn wrote to Cromwell on July 1:

"You have robbed, by your unjust subtlety and shifting tricks, the honest and gallant Agitators of all their power and authority, and solely placed it in a thing called a counsell of war, or rather a Cabinet junto of seven or eight proud self-ended fellows, that so you may without control make up your own ends." (*Jonah's Cry*, p. 9).

Sir John Berkeley observes:

"Out of my discourses and inquiries, I collected these observations: First, that the Army was governed partly by a Council of War, and partly by a Council of the Army, or Agitators, wherein the General had but a single voice; that Fairfax, the General, had little power in either; that Cromwell, and his son Ireton, with their Friends and Partisans, governed the Council of War absolutely, but not that of the Army, which was the most powerful, though they had a strong party there also; but the major part of the Adjutators carried it. Amongst these Adjutators there were many ill-wishers of Cromwell, looking on him as one who would always make his advantages out of the Army." (*Memoirs of Sir John Berkley*, Maseres' Tracts, i. 364.)

Later the complaint of the Levellers became:

"that the General Councils (which according to their engagements ought to have consisted only of two select commission officers, and two private souldiers, chosen by every regiment, with such generall officers as assented to the engagement, and no other) were nevertheless overgrown with Collonels, Lieut.-Collonels, Majors and others not chosen, and many of them dissenters from the said engagement." (*England's New Chains Discovered*, pt. 2, p. 3, 1649. See also *The Hunting of the Foxes from Newmarket and Triploe Heath to Whitehall*, Somers' Tracts, vi. 45.)

The blame of these concessions to the King and the burden of the other charges was laid upon Ireton and Cromwell both, but most on Ireton. Wildman appeals to "my once much honoured Cromwell," as if hoping that his pen "could possibly awaken Cromwell's conscience from the dead" (*Putney Projects*, p. 37). Sometimes it is suggested that Ireton was the tempter.

"Before it be too late deal plainly with Ireton, by whose cowardly or ambitious policy Cromwell is betrayed into these mischievous practices . . . . And if Cromwell instantly repent not, and alter his course, let him know also, that ye loved and honoured just, honest, sincere and valiant Cromwell, that loved his country, and the liberties of the people above his life, yea, and hated the King as a man of blood, but that Cromwell ceasing to be such, he ceaseth to be the object of your love."

Sometimes it was suggested that they were accomplices, and that their occasional differences were but the clearer proof of their secret alliance.

"One of the surest tokens of confederates in evill, is not only when one of his fellowes is vehement, fiery or hot in any of their pursuits, to be patient, cold or moderate to pacify his partner, and like deceitfull Lawyers before their clients to quallify matters; but sometimes seeme to discord or fall out and quarrell in Councels, reasonings and debates; and yet nevertheless in the end to agree in evill; which they doe purposely, to hold upright men in a charitable (though doubtfull) opinion, that if such and such a man be not godly and upright they know not whom in the world to trust." (*A Call to all the Souldiers of the Armie by the Free People of England*, etc., 1647, pp. 4, 6.)

The dissatisfaction and suspicion roused by all these different causes found expression in renewed disturbance in the Army and amongst the Levelling party in general. Meetings took place amongst the soldiers, and several regiments elected new representatives under the pretext that the officers had broken their engagements (pp. 349, 367). A declaration published in November, 1647, by Colonel Whalley's troop, attacks the Agitators elected in June, saying:

> "That upon several informations that those formerly employed by us did more consult their own advancement than the public settlement, we were induced, about the 19th of October last, to make choice of two new Agitators for a regiment."

The authority given these new Agitators

> "was only to act according to our first engaged principles with the consent and advice of the General, the Council of War, and the Agitators first elected, to clear those things that seemed dubious to us, to prevent misinformations," etc. (Reprinted by Maseres, Select Tracts, i. lxv.)

These new representatives usually styled themselves "Agents," but are often described as "Agitators," both by themselves and others (pp. 259, 264, 279). It is convenient to use the term "Agents" in order to distinguish the new Agitators from the old. Five regiments of horse took the lead in this movement, those of Cromwell, Ireton, Fleetwood, Whalley, and Rich; and their representatives signed the "Case of the Army," which is dated October 9, 1647. By the beginning of November four other regiments of horse and seven of foot had also elected Agents, and associated themselves with the demands of the original five (Rushworth, vii. 859).

A certain number of persons, claiming to represent the Levellers of London and other districts, made common cause with the protesting soldiers (pp. 235, 251; *cf.* Rushworth, vii. 876-8). The most prominent of these was John Wildman, a follower of Lilburn's, who was adopted by the Agents as their mouthpiece, and was probably the author of the "Case of the Army," and some other tracts published in their name (pp. 269, 352, 356).

The new Agents commenced operations by the presentation of a manifesto, entitled "The Case of the Army stated," which was presented to the General on October 18. It is well summarised by Godwin, *History of the Commonwealth*, ii. 445; and was accompanied by a letter which is printed *in extenso* by Rushworth (vii. 485; see also these debates, pp. 227, 229, 241, 293, 304, 346, 354, 356, 360, 373). The General Council of the Army, at its meeting on October 22, appointed a committee to sit the next day for the consideration of the papers thus presented. On the 28th the Agents presented a further paper, clearing themselves from the charge of seeking to divide the Army. The summary of their political demands, entitled "The Agreement of the People," though not published till a few days later, seems to have been presented at the same time (p. 236; Rushworth, vii. 849, 850, 859; Godwin, ii. 449).

The debates to which the presentation of these papers gave rise extended from October 28 to November 11 (pp. 226-418). The reports now printed were probably taken down in shorthand by William Clarke himself.

At the General Council which met at Putney on October 28 the presenters of the "Case of the Army" were represented by two soldiers and two outsiders, and also by three of the original Agitators (p. 226). One of the latter, Sexby, opened the proceedings by a statement of the causes of the present discontents in the Army. Their leaders, he complained, had laboured too much to satisfy the King and to support the Parliament, instead of simply seeking to carry out the engagements of the Army and taking a direct course to settle the kingdom. He concluded by a personal attack upon Cromwell and Ireton for advocating a further application to the King in the parliamentary debates of September 22 and 23 (pp. 227–232).

The discussion then turned on the "Agreement of the People," and Cromwell, after some remarks on the importance of the constitutional changes demanded in it, replied, "Before we take this paper into consideration, it is fit for us to consider how far we are obliged, and how far we are free." The engagements of the Army as set forth in their public declarations must first be considered. When that was done they would know how far they were free to adopt the proposals of the Agents (pp. 236–240).

Ireton took the same line, whilst Wildman and Colonel Rainborow argued that the consideration of the justice of the demands now put forward should precede the consideration of earlier engagements (240-247). Cromwell proposed the appointment of a committee to consider the engagements in question, and Colonel Goffe suggested a prayer meeting (pp. 250-255). Both these propositions were finally accepted, but not till a long and excited discussion had taken place between Ireton and Wildman on the nature of obligations in general, and the question when they were binding and when they might be broken (pp. 257-279).

On the morning of October 29 the prayer meeting took place at the Quartermaster-General's quarters at Mr. Chamberlain's house (pp. 257, 259, 280-285). It was followed by a fresh discussion in the Council on the question of the engagements of the Army, in the course of which both Cromwell and Ireton emphatically disavowed any private and personal engagements whatever (pp. 293, 294). In an eloquent speech the latter declared that he desired the consideration of engagements not so much for the sake of the engagements themselves as for the sake of the reputation and good name of the Army.

"I would not have this Army . . . . to incur the scandal of neglecting engagements, and laying aside all consideration of engagements, and juggling, and deceiving, and deluding the world, making them believe things in times of extremity which they never meant" (p. 297).

The "Agreement of the People" was next read, and a general debate took place over the first article, which claimed manhood suffrage (p. 299). On this point the discussion was long and passionate (pp. 299-345). Ireton, while professing his willingness to support a reasonable extension of the franchise, opposed manhood suffrage as dangerous in itself, and still more dangerous from the principles upon which it was claimed (pp. 322, 333, 340). Cromwell and Colonel Rich supported Ireton (pp. 309, 315, 332). The former again proposed the appointment of a committee to agree upon a reasonable compromise (p. 328). The proposal was backed by Lieutenant Chillenden, Captain Rolfe, and others, and was finally accepted (pp. 337, 338). A fresh debate then arose on the question of the statements made in the "Case of the Army," and Ireton passionately vindicated the officers from the charge of dividing the Army, and retorted the charge on the new Agents (pp. 346-348). He went on to compare the "Heads of the Proposals of the Army" with the "Agreement," in order to show that the main demands of the latter were substantially contained in the "Proposals" (p. 349). Wildman in answer criticised the "Proposals" in detail, in order to show that by the authority they reserved to the King and the House of Lords "the foundation of slavery was rivetted more strongly than before" (p. 353). Ireton defended the proposals, and charged Wildman with being the author of the "Case of the Army" (pp. 356-361).

On October 30 the Committee of Officers and Agitators appointed to prepare "somewhat to be insisted upon and adhered unto for settling the kingdom," held a meeting, and agreed to a number of articles relative to the constitution of future Parliaments (pp. 363-367). With the exception of the article on the suffrage, these propositions were substantially the same as those contained in the "Heads of the Proposals."

The result of the deliberations of the Committee was a clause desiring the extension of the franchise "to all freeborn Englishmen or persons made free denizens of England, who have served the Parliament in the late war for the liberties of the kingdom .... or voluntarily assisted the Parliament in the said war with money, arms, etc." (p. 367). Though this guaranteed the rights of the soldiers, it did not go as far as the Agitators desired, and they seem finally to have obtained a vote in favour of manhood suffrage of the General Council.

In a letter from the Agents to the regiments which they represented, dated November 11, they say that the first article of the agreement having been long debated "it was concluded by vote in the Affirmative; viz. that all souldiers and others, if they be not servants or beggars, ought to have voices in electing those that shall represent them in Parliament, although they have not fortie shillings a year by freehold land. And there were but three voyces against this your native freedome." Cromwell and Ireton continued to oppose this further extension, the former saying that it "did tend very much to anarchy" (p. 411; *cf.* p. 309).

In the later constitutions and the suggested constitutions of the period the question of the suffrage was variously treated. The "Agreement of the People," presented to Parliament January 15, 1649, embodies the view finally adopted by the governing party in the Army. It proposed:

"That the electors in every division shall be natives or denizens of England, not persons receiving alms, but such as are assessed ordinarily towards the relief of the poor; not servants to and receiving wages from any particular person. And in all elections except for the Universities they shall be men of 21 years of age or upwards, and housekeepers dwelling within the division for which the election is."

The restrictions are those suggested in these debates of October, 1647 (pp. 313, 335, 341, 342).

Ireton, who in the "Heads of the Proposals of the Army" had first suggested the redistribution of seats according to the rates borne by the respective counties in the burdens of the kingdom, was probably also the author of this proposal for basing the franchise on the payment of rates for the relief of the poor. It does not appear in the scheme of the Levellers or in the Instrument of Government. The views of the former are contained in the "Agreement of the Free People of England," put forth by Lilburn and his friends, May 1, 1649. It gives the franchise "according to natural right" to "all men of the age of 21 years and upwards not being servants or receiving alms." The Instrument of Government, on the other hand, reproducing the scheme which the Long Parliament was engaged in passing when Cromwell expelled it, restricted the franchise in the counties to persons possessing real or personal estate to the value of £200, and left the right of voting in the boroughs unaltered.

The debates of the Council on November 1 turned mainly on the subject of the King and the House of Lords. Wildman argued that by the fundamental constitution of the kingdom neither King nor Lords had any right to a negative voice in legislation, and that they ought to be expressly deprived of the right which they had usurped (pp. 367, 385-387). Ireton had no great difficulty in refuting the proof of these statements which Wildman attempted to derive from the coronation oath (pp. 386, 387, 399), but his own opinion and the general sense of the Army were both strongly in favour of limiting the power of the Lords. The Committee appointed by the Council of Officers had originally decided that the Lords should possess a suspensive veto only (p. 396). For this a more elaborate scheme suggested by Ireton was finally substituted, stipulating that laws passed by the House of Commons should be binding for the people even without the consent of the Lords (pp. 394, 397, 407). But the Lords would not be so bound "for their own persons and estates as the Commons are" unless they expressly consented to it (pp. 391, 394, 397, 405). Lords who happened to be officers of state were to be liable to the judgment of the Commons; those who were not were to be tried and judged only by their peers (p. 409). The suggestion that Lords and Commons should sit together as one House appears to have been considered and rejected (p. 395). The Act of March 19, 1649, which abolished the Upper House as useless and dangerous, declared that such Lords, as had "demeaned themselves with honour, courage, and fidelity to the Commonwealth," should be capable of sitting in Parliament, "if they shall be thereunto elected." Ireton seems to have proposed a similar provision at this time, but the precise text of his propcsal is missing (p. 395).

The articles brought forward by the Committee treated the King's negative voice in the same fashion as the legislative power of the

Lords. The first draft of the "Heads of the Proposals" had given the King a suspensive veto. In their final form, however, nothing at all was said about the King's negative voice; it was simply passed over in silence (*cf.* p. 357). In place of that, the Army demanded the King's assent to certain stipulated concessions which were held essential to the peace and safety of the kingdom, and proposed that when these things were provided for he should be restored to his throne without diminution to his personal rights, and without further limitation to the exercise of his regal power (Art. xiv., *cf.* pp. 358-9) Wildman and his party insisted that this involved the restoration of the King with an unlimited negative voice, and that he could not safely be allowed any share whatever in legislation (pp. 362, 385). In reply Ireton pointed out that matters essential to safety were already provided for; that the King by confirming the ordinances made by Parliament would practically admit the right of the Parliament to make laws without his consent where the safety of the nation was concerned; and that the article proposed by the committee gave the House of Commons power to enact laws binding on all commoners.

"Itt takes away the negative voice of the Lords and of the Kinge too, as to what concernes the people; for itt says that the Commons of England shall bee bound by what judgement and above what orders, ordinances, or lawes shall bee made for that purpose by them; and all that followes for the Kinge or Lords is this, that the Lords or Kinge are not bound by that law they pass for their own persons or estates as the Commoners are, unlesse they consent to it" (pp. 389-391, 407).

The debates of November 3 are very briefly reported, and the reports of those which took place on the four following days are missing altogether. An attempt is made to supply some account of them in Appendix E. On November 5 the extreme party succeeded in obtaining a vote for a general rendezvous of the Army, and procured from the Council a letter to Parliament intimating that the Army was opposed to any further applications to the King. On November 8, however, Cromwell, who had long been sensible of the dangers of division and anarchy caused by these disputes in the Council, carried a vote recommending the General to order the representative Officers and Agitators to return to their regiments until the intended rendezvous had taken place (p. 412). On the following day the Council was adjourned for a fortnight; but before it separated a declaration was drawn up, explaining that the letter of November 5 was not intended to mean that the Council opposed Parliament's sending any further propositions to the King, "our intentions being only to assert the freedom of Parliament" (p. 416). It was also decided that instead of the one general rendezvous of the Army, which had been previously settled, there should be three separate reviews, to take place at different places on successive days.

The first rendezvous took place on November 15 near Ware. The Levellers attempted to convert it into the general rendezvous which they so much desired. The regiments of Harrison and Robert Lilburn broke loose from the control of their officers, and came to the field of the review intending to make it an armed demonstration in favour of the "Agreement of the People." Cromwell's action was again decisive, and the incipient mutiny was quelled by the execution of a single mutineer.[a] A remonstrance drawn up in the name of the General was read at the head of every regiment. Like the engagement of June 5, which it supplements and completes, it was evidently the composition of Ireton (v. p. 348). Fairfax declares that he and the other commanders have done their best to carry out the ends of the Newmarket engagement, and complains of the discontents and divisions which the Agents have caused in the Army. He announces that without redress of these abuses and disorders he will not continue in command, but professes his willingness "to adhere to, and to

[a] The best account of the rendezvous is given in a letter of William Clarke's, contained in a pamphlet entitled *A Full Relation of the Proceedings at the Rendezvous at Corkbush Field in Hartford Parish on Monday last*, 1647. It is reprinted by Maseres, Select Tracts, i. lv.

conduct, and live and die with the Army in the lawful prosecution" of certain specified aims. Those aims are the obtaining of six demands which concern the Army as soldiers, and the attainment of the following political objects for the kingdom at large.

"A period to be set for this present Parliament, to end so soon as may be with safety; and provision thereunto to be made for future Parliaments, for the certainty of their meeting, sitting, and ending, and for the freedom and equality of elections thereto; to render the House of Commons, as near as may be, an equal representative of the people that are to elect. And, according to the Representation of the Army of June 14, to leave other things to, and acquiesce in, the determinations of the Parliament; but to remind the Parliament of, and mediate with them for, redress of the common grievances of the people, and all other things that the Army have declared their desire for."

He concluded by exacting from the officers and soldiers of every regiment the subscription of a definite promise to be bound by the decision of the General Council of the Army as to the prosecution of the objects thus enumerated. On the other hand, "for the matter of ordering conduct and government of the Army," they were to be "observant and subject to the General, the Council of War, and their officers." (*Old Parliamentary History*, xvi. 340-345.)

By this new compact between Fairfax and his soldiers the political aims of the Army were clearly defined and its action was restricted to certain definite objects. The acceptance of the engagement was followed by the restoration of good relations between officers and men and by the revival of discipline. Some few of the discontented party continued to plot mutiny, but they were either reduced to submission or promptly expelled from the Army. A few weeks later the "General Council of the Army" itself ceased to exist, and the system of representation, established by the engagement of June 4, was never revived. A constitutional experiment so remarkable is worth tracing to its close.

The vote of November 8 had simply dismissed the Agitators and the representative officers to their several regiments, "there to reside until the said rendezvous be over, and until his Excellency shall see fit to call them together again according to the Engagement" (p. 412). The Council met again, on November 25, in the town hall at Windsor, and continued to meet throughout December and during the first week of January, 1648. There is little doubt that the Agitators continued to take part in its debates, privates as well as officers. Parliamentary Commissioners came to Windsor to arrange with the Council of the Army the question of pay and the disbanding of supernumeraries. A letter from Windsor, dated December 31, says:

> "The Parliament's Commissioners have been at the headquarters with us now this three days, and had divers meetings with our councils, and joined with us in prayer, and other things tending to the good of the kingdom and the army, and have had full satisfaction in all things upon the votes of the Houses, to their hearts desire and content. And the officers came to them and assured them the spirit of the army was, that since God hath put an opportunity into their hands of purpose to settle the kingdom, if God should honour the army to be further helping to them, the army would live and die with them and for them willingly. Whereby they were much joyed, and received their expressions with abundance of thanks. . . . . The Agreement was sweet and comfortable, the whole matter of the kingdom being left with the Parliament." (Rushworth, vii. 928, 935, 951.)

The most important subject treated with the Parliamentary Commissioners was the reorganisation of the Army and the disbanding and payment of those soldiers who were not to be included in the new establishment. With the concurrence of Fairfax and the Council, this was effected by a series of Parliamentary resolutions, in accordance with which a standing army of about 23,000 men was to be kept up (Rushworth, vii. 935, 992, 995). Supernumeraries, soldiers enlisted since the Newmarket engagement, and superfluous local levies were disbanded in large numbers (*ibid.*, 921, 929, 946, 953, 997, 1007, 1011, 1042). A number of rules were established for the billeting and quartering of the soldiers to be still maintained (*ibid.*, 956). Above all, a considerable reduction in the pay of the Army was agreed upon, though it was stipulated by the soldiers that the said reduction should hold good for time of peace merely, and that in case of a new war their pay and allowances should be again increased (*ibid.*, pp. 995, 996; see also an imperfect letter of Fairfax's amongst Clarke's MSS.,) One of the last acts of the Council was to vote an addition to the number of Army chaplains.

"The Councell of the Army having information of the willingnesse and readinesse of divers Godlye men of the ministrye to bestowe theyr paynes to preach the ghospell of Christ in the Armye, it was resolved by the Counsell that some of them whose hearts God should most incline to that worke, should be desired to come to the Army for that purpose and be assured from the Counsell of all encouragement thereto and good acceptance of theyr paynes therein." (Clarke MS. Jan. 9, 1647.)

In pursuance of this vote John Canne became chaplain of Robert Lilburn's regiment, and a number of other divines became attached to the Army.

Whilst the headquarters were at Windsor the Council of War frequently met to condemn persons implicated in the recent disturbances. Captain-Lieutenant Bray, Major Cobbet, and several privates were tried and condemned, but the proceedings closed with a general reconciliation and remission of punishments (Rushworth vii., 922, 937, 940, 942, 943). The meeting of December 21 is thus described in a letter which Rushworth reprints from the *Perfect Diurnal*.

"The General Council of the Army met in the Castle at Windsor; the greatest part of that day was spent in several declarations made by divers officers concerning the present juncture of affairs; many exhortations to unity and affinity, and motions made for passing by offences that had, through weakness, come from brethren.

"Major White laid hold of this opportunity, made an acknowledgement that he had spoken some words rashly at Putney, for which he was censured by that Council; desired that he might be looked upon as one that desired the good of the Army; and, that being restored into favour he should readily submit to the discipline of the Army. This was unanimously approved of, and the major accordingly readmitted into the General Council.

"Wednesday, December 22, was, according to appointment, kept as a solemn fast by the general and officers; the duties of the day were performed by divers of the officers, amongst whom there was a sweet harmony: the Lieutenant-General, Commissary General Ireton, Col. Tichburne, Col. Hewson, Mr. Peters, and other officers prayed very fervently and pathetically; this continued from nine in the morning till seven at night. In the evening a motion was made that whereas Col. Rainsborough had acted some things which gave offence, that in regard of his present acknowledgment, his former service might not be forgotten; but that the Council would move the General to write to the House, that he might be made Vice-admiral; which was assented to by all, and a letter written to Mr. Speaker accordingly.

"Thursday, December 23, the General Council of the Army again met. . . . . This day also the Council of War sat about the trial of Captain-Lieutentant Bray, Mr. Crosman, Mr. Allen, and others; but upon their acknowledgment of their rash and irregular proceedings, and promise to submit to the discipline of the Army for the time to come, they were dismissed and sent to their several regiments."[a]

The last meeting of the Council took place on January 8, 1648. "This Saturday the General Council of the Army met at the Castle at Windsor, where the appearance was great, and they were very unanimous in debate." Without a single opposing voice they agreed upon the Declaration presented to Parliament on January 11, announcing their satisfaction with the recent vote for no further addresses to the King, and promising to support the Parliament in settling the kingdom without him (Rushworth, vii. 959, 961).

"To-morrow," continues the letter, "all the council that met this day are to dine with the General in Windsor Castle, to congratulate the unity of the Army and to take their leaves each of other before they be dispersed into the several garrisons and great towns, which the Army will punctually perform against the 15th of January."

---

[a] Insubordination, however, was not yet entirely at an end. On February 23 some of the Lifeguard of Fairfax presented a petition to their General, protesting against the terms on which they were to be disbanded, and backed it by a mutinous demonstration, for which several were tried by a court-martial (Rushworth, vii. 1006, 1009, 1010). A certain William Clarke was condemned to death, but pardoned. Harrison's regiment mutinied when ordered into the west, for which Henry Gethings, an Agitator, and two soldiers were sentenced to death, but also pardoned. Another leading Leveller Corporal Thompson, who had escaped from custody, was arrested by Cromwell himself at the door of the House of Commons, and tried about the same time. (*The Kingdom's Weekly Post*, March 2-9, 164$\frac{7}{8}$; *A Vindication of Lieut.-Gen. Cromwell, etc., against a libell signed by one Tompson*, by A. C., March 7, 164$\frac{7}{8}$.)

So ended the assembly instituted in pursuance of the Engagement of June 5—the most thoroughly representative of all the different councils which successively spoke in the name of the Army. Subsequent councils contained no representatives of the common soldiers. The assembly which met at St Albans on November 7, 1648, though often spoken of as the General Council of the Army, was in reality composed solely of officers, and styled itself "the General Council of Officers of the Army" (Rushworth, vii. 1320, 1330, 1366. *Old Parliamentary History*, xviii. 160, 266, 458, 516).

In May, 1649, Colonel Scroope's regiment and portions of several others mutinied, demanding the re-establishment of the General Council of the Army according to the Engagement of June 5, 1647, which they accused their officers of having broken. The rising was suppressed by Cromwell at Burford, and one of the leaders, Cornet Henry Denne, published a pamphlet entitled the "Levellers Designe Discovered," in which he explained the aims of the mutineers, and retracted the opinions which he had held in common with them. On the question of the General Council and the reasons which led to its dissolution he speaks as follows:

"I shall declare what satisfaction I have received that so I may give the same satisfaction unto others. . . . . Such a councell indeed the ingagement required. And such a councell was constituted in the Army, acting, and transacting of matters pertaining to the discipline of the Army. And so long was this councell continued, untill the inconvenience thereof was so far manifest; that most of the Regiments of horse and foot did petition his Excellency to send back the severall agitators to their respective regiments untill he should be pleased to resummon them; professing a willingnesse in themselves to submit unto his Excellency with his Councell of War, according to the pristine discipline of the Army. His Excellency having received these petitions did not immediately send back the Agitators (as requested). But having first summoned a councell, and communicated the petitions unto them; it was by them concluded that according to the petitions of the severall regiments the Councell of Agitators should be dissolved, untill his Excellency should see cause to resummon them. Now this being so: his Excellency cannot be charged with violation of that ingagement, neither doth there remain any obligation on his

Excellency to have continued or revived any such councell." (*The Levellers Designe Discovered*, p. 4, 1649.)

Unfortunately the debates of the Council during the final meetings at Windsor are not recorded by Clarke, or at least have not survived. In some of these gatherings business of great importance was treated, but most of them seem to have been devoted to military rather than political affairs. The peculiar value of the reports of the debates on the Agreement of the people lies in the fact that in them the fundamental principles of politics were discussed. In the course of the argument the political theories of the two parties in the army, and the characters of their leaders, are clearly defined and exhibited. Both these points deserve and require a more detailed consideration.

The views of the extreme party amongst the sectaries are set forth in the pamphlets of Lilburn, Overton, and others, and are well summarised by Thomas Edwards in his *Gangraena*. In the third part of that work, published in 1646, he enumerates the erroneous opinions held by the "sectaries" in political as well as in religious matters. He complains that just as they neglected authority in religion so they rejected it in politics.

"As they do in matters of religion and conscience fly from the scriptures, and from supernaturall truths revealed there, that a man may not be questioned for going against them, but only for errors against the light of nature and right reason; so they do also in civill government and things of this world, they go from the lawes and constitutions of kingdoms, and will be governed by rules according to nature and right reason; and though the lawes and customes of a kingdome be never so plain and cleer against their wayes, yet they will not submit, but cry out for naturall rights derived from Adam and right reason" (*Gangraena*, pt. iii. p. 20).

Accordingly in these debates we hear much of the laws of nature and of natural rights. It was held that every man born in England, every "free born Englishman," possessed certain rights which were termed his "birthright." The phrase "birthright" was not altogether new in English political discussions, but had usually been employed in a more limited signification. "Subjects," said Sir Robert Berkeley during Hampden's trial, "have a birthright in the laws of this kingdom." The word is used in a similar fashion in the Act of Settlement. Ireton employs it with the same meaning in one of his speeches.

"If you call that your birthright, which is the most fundamental part of your constitution, then let him perish that goes about to hinder you of the least part of your birthright" (p. 325).

The Levellers sometimes used the term to denote certain inherited constitutional rights. They believed that the English commons had possessed these rights under the Saxons, and were unjustly deprived of them by the Norman Conquest (*cf.* pp. 318, 368). "To purchase our inheritances that have been lost," "to recover our birthrights and privileges as Englishmen," were alleged by them to be the cause for which they had taken up arms (pp. 235, 322).

The negative voice of the King, and the power of the House of Lords, they asserted to be a part of the bondage imposed on England by the Norman Conquest (pp. 401, 402). According to some of their pamphleteers the law and the constitution alike were part of the Norman yoke.

"The greatest mischief of all and the oppressing bondage of England ever since the Norman yoke," says Lilburn, "is a law called the common law. The laws of this nation," he adds, "are unworthy a free people, and deserve from first to last to be considered, and seriously debated, and reduced to an agreement with common equity and right reason, which ought to be the form and life of every government. Magna Charta itself being but a beggarly thing, containing many marks of intolerable bondage, and the laws that have been made since by Parliaments have in very many particulars made our government much more oppressive and intolerable" (Lilburn, *Just Man's Justification*, pp. 11-15; Edwards, *Gangraena*, iii. 194).

Park, in his edition of the *Harleian Miscellany*, reprints three pamphlets by John Hare, setting forth this theory of the consequences of the Norman Conquest, viz. (1.) *St. Edward's Ghost, or Anti-Normanism; being a patheticall Complaint and Motion, in the behalf of our English Nation against her grand yet neglected*

Grievance, Normanism, 1647 (vol. viii. p. 94); (2). *Plain English to our wilful bearers with Normanism*, 1647 (vol. ix. p. 90); (3). *England's proper and only Way to an Establishment in Honour, Freedom, Peace, and Happiness; or the Norman Yoke once more uncased; and the Necessity, Justice, and present Seasonableness of breaking it in pieces demonstrated*, 1648 (vol. vi. p. 36).

The theory which the Levellers thus put forward found eager acceptance in the Army. In attempting to find an historical basis for the rights which they claimed the soldiers were but following the example of the lawyers. When they represented the liberties they demanded as an inheritance from the past, fictitious though the pedigree might be, they adopted the conventional method of English political controversy. But in fact they rested their claims far more on abstract justice and pure reason, and demanded their rights, not merely as the lawful inheritance of Englishmen, but as the natural rights of all men. Their argument is well summed up by Edwards.

"That, seeing all men are by nature the Sons of Adam, and from him have legitimately derived a naturall propriety, right, and freedom, Therefore England and all other Nations, and all particular persons in every Nation, notwithstanding the difference of Lawes and Governments, rancks and degrees, ought to be alike free and estated in their naturall Liberties, and to enjoy the just Rights and Prerogative of mankind, whereunto they are Heirs apparent; and thus the Commoners by right are equall with the Lords. For by naturall birth all men are equally and alike born to like propriety, liberty, and freedom; and as we are delivered of God by the hand of nature into this world, every one with a naturall innate freedom, and propriety, even so are we to live, every one equally and alike to enjoy his birth-right and priviledge." (*Gangraena*, pt. iii., p. 16.)

First and most important of these rights was the right to a voice in the election of Members of Parliament. The only legitimate foundation of a government was the consent of the governed.

"I thinke its cleare," says Rainborow, "that every man that is to live under a governement ought first by his own consent to putt himself under that governement; and I doe thinke that the poorest man in England is not at all bound in a strict sense to that government that he hath not had a voice to putt himself under" (p. 301).

"Every man born in England cannot, ought nott; neither by the law of God nor the law of nature, to bee exempted from the choice of those who are to make lawes, for him to live under, and for him, for ought I know to die under" (p. 305).

Wildman lays down the same principle.

"That's the undeniable maxim of government; that all governement is in the free consent of the govern'd. If so then upon that account there is noe person that is under a just governement or hath justly his own unlesse hee by his owne free consent be putt under that governement" (p. 318).

We judge that all inhabitants that have not lost their birthright should have an equal voice in elections" (p. 300).

As Ireton points out, the argument for universal suffrage was based on an absolute natural right, paramount to existing laws or constitution (pp. 301, 307, 325, 327). The law of nature was invoked against the law of the land.

These natural rights were held to be inherent, indefeasible rights, which no positive law or constitution could take away. As the crown lawyers had asserted that some powers were so inseparable from the King's person, that Acts of Parliament to deprive him of them were void, so now the spokesmen of the soldiers denied that any law or custom could deprive the people of their rights. Edwards thus states their contention:

"That whatever the Fundamentall Constitutions of Kingdomes and Commonwealths have been by forefathers, whatever agreements, compacts have been of subjection and obedience of such a people for themselves and posterities to one, as under kingly government, or to more, yet the men of the present age, following many hundred years after, ought to be absolutely free from what their forefathers yeelded unto, and freed from all kinds of exorbitancies, molestations, without exception or limitation, either in respect of persons, officers, degrees, or things, and estated in their naturall and just Liberties agreeable to right reason." (*Gangraena*, pt. iii.)

Throughout the debates these principles are assumed by the supporters of the Agreement. "If there is a constitution that the people are not free, that should be annulled," says Mr. Pettus (p. 336). If the engagements of the Army had given away anything that was the people's right, they were unjust and therefore void (p. 251). If a thing were just and the people's due, no engagement to the contrary was binding (pp. 261, 301). In accordance with these principles the spokesmen of the soldiers demanded the abolition of the law which restricted the franchise to forty-shilling freeholders. "I think," said Rainborow, "that the law of the land in that thing is the most tyrannical law under heaven" (p. 311). They demanded on the same grounds the abolition of the power of the King and the House of Lords, and especially the taking away of their share in legislation.

"To give the Kinge a legislative power," argued Wildman, "is contrary to his own oath at his coronation, and itt is the like to give a power to the Kinge by his negative voice to deny all lawes. And for the Lords, seeing the foundation of all justice is the election of the people it is unjust they should have that power" (p. 386).

"Both the power of the Kinge and Lords," argued another, "was ever a branch of tyranny, and if ever a people shall free themselves from tyranny certainly itt is after seven yeares' warre and fighting for their liberty" (p. 352).

"Itt will never satisfie the godly people in the Kingedome unlesse that all government be in the Commons and that freely" (p. 398).

Already on May 20, 1647, a petition had been addressed to the House of Commons as "the supreme authority of this nation," and had been ordered by them to be burnt as a high breach of privilege.

To what extent the articles drawn up by the committee of the General Council limited the powers of the King and Lords, and how far the demand for universal suffrage was successful has already been shown (pp. l.-liii.). There were, however, other rights which were to be secured by a different process.

In the articles drawn up by the Committee of the Council of the Army the represented announce that they reserve to themselves certain fundamental rights which their representatives are not empowered to abrogate or give away (pp. 407, 409). No man is to be impressed; no man compelled to any form of religion; no man disquieted for acts done during the war. The idea of inserting these reservations and the substance of the reservations themselves are both taken from the first Agreement of the People, presented to the Council of the Army in Oct. 1647. The four reserves contained in that document ran thus:

"1. That matters of Religion, and the wayes of God's Worship, are not at all intrusted by us to any humane power, because therein we cannot remit or exceed a tittle of what our consciences dictate to be the mind of God, without wilfull sin: nevertheless the publike way of instructing the nation (so it be not compulsive) is referred to their discretion.

"2. That the matter of impresting and constraining any of us to serve in the wars is against our freedome; and therefore we do not allow it in our Representatives; the rather because, money (the sinews of war) being alwayes at their disposall, they can never want numbers of men apt enough to engage in any just cause.

"3. That after the dissolution of the present Parliament no person be at any time questioned for anything said or done, in reference to the late publike differences, otherwise then in execution of the judgements of the present Representatives or House of Commons.

"4. That in all Lawes made or to be made, every person may be bound alike, and that no Tenure, Estate, Charter, Degree, Birth, or Place, do confer any exemption from the ordinary course of legall proceedings whereunto others are subjected."

These reservations were practically a "Declaration of the Rights of Man" expressed by means of negatives and restrictions. Similar reservations, six in number, besides an elaborate article concerning the limits of religious freedom, are embodied in the second Agreement of the People, presented to Parliament from the Army in January 1649 (Gardiner, *Constitutional Documents*, p. 279).

In the desire to limit the powers of the government, and guarantee the rights of the individual, the Levellers went still further, and the third Agreement of the People, published by Lilburn and his friends in May, 1649, contains no less than eighteen provisions restricting the power of future Parliaments. To limit the power of Parliament was in fact the chief aim of these and similar stipulations.

The events of the spring of 1647 had sowed in the minds of the soldiers a deeply-rooted distrust of parliamentary assemblies, and a well grounded objection to their omnipotence. The exercise of an unlimited or arbitrary power by such as have been trusted with supreme and subordinate authority, and the prevalence of corrupt interests powerfully inclining most men once entrusted with authority to pervert the same for their own domination, are the chief reasons given for Lilburn's Agreement and for the reservations contained in it. Though these reservations disappear in the Instrument of Government, the imposition of a written constitution, the provisions it contains for the securing of religious liberty, the clause nullifying bills contrary to the tenor of the "Instrument," the absence of any provision for its amendment, and the opposition to all proposals for its alteration, are manifestations of the same feeling. Cromwell never more truly represented the views of the Army than when he forbade his first Parliament to alter the Instrument, and the distinction which he drew between fundamentals which must be accepted, and circumstantials which might be altered, is but an echo of the tenth article of the Agreement of January, 1649.

In any discussion of the political principles set forth in these debates one other point requires special notice. Speakers on both sides refer to society and government as resting on a contract. "The King," says Cromwell, "is King by contract;" referring no doubt to the fundamental contract between King and people which James II. was voted to have broken (p. 366).

"We are under a contract," says Ireton, and he proceeds to argue that on this contract or covenant between man and man private property both in land and goods is founded (p. 263).

Mr. Pettus goes further and states the origin and purpose of the contract.

> "Every man is naturally free .... when men were in so great numbers that every man could not give his voice .... men agreed to come unto some form of governement that they who were chosen might preserve propertie" (p. 312).

As these debates explain the political views of the soldiers, so they elucidate the character and position of their leaders. Fairfax himself was absent from the most important debates on account of illness (p. 226). When he was present he contented himself with presiding in silence, and left Ireton and Cromwell to expound his views. "He was of few words in discourse or council," observes Whitelock, and according to Sprigge he suffered at times from an impediment in his speech (*Anglia Rediviva*, ed. 1854, p. 325).

Ireton is a statesman to whose influence and ability historians have hardly done justice. To his military talents, he added great business capacity and indefatigable industry. Ludlow attributes his death to his "immoderate labours," and another of his associates in Ireland describes him as "seldom thinking it time to eat till he had done the work of the day at nine or ten at night, and then will sit up as long as any man hath business with him" (Cooke, *Monarchy no creature of God's making*, 1652). Bred a lawyer, he possessed a larger stock of political and constitutional knowledge than his fellow officers. Clarendon terms him "a scholar conversant in the law, and in all that learning which had expressed the greatest animosity and malice against regal government" (*Rebellion*, xiii., 175). He had also what Whitelock styles "a working and laborious brain and fancy" (*Memorials*, ii., 163). He was fertile in formulas, ingenious in devising constitutional expedients, and skilled in putting the political ideas of himself or others into legal shape. As no one amongst the superior officers possessed these varied qualifications to the same extent he naturally became the penman of the Army. Imperfect though the records of these debates are, they show that Ireton was also an excellent and sometimes an eloquent speaker. Above all he was a ready debater, expressing himself clearly and forcibly, swift to seize an argumentative advantage, to press home the the consequences of a principle, or to point out the importance of a precedent. Confident, however, of the soundness of his own logic, he did not always fairly appreciate the strong points of an opponent's case. His defect was that he was too positive and dogmatic, and sometimes his brother officers lost their tempers and declined to be dictated to. Less sympathetic than Cromwell, he roused more opposition, and was eager to convince when Cromwell was anxious only to unite. Over Cromwell Ireton exercised great influence—the influence which a man of definite views exercises over a friend whose mind is not yet made up about everything.

Ireton's own political position has been much misunderstood. Clarendon represents him as "so radically averse from monarchy and so fixed to a republican government, that if he had lived he would either by his counsel and credit have prevented" Cromwell's assumption of the protectorate, or "publicly opposed and declared against it" (*Rebellion*, xiii., 175). "Ireton," says Burnet, "had the principles and the temper of a Cassius in him. He stuck at nothing that might have turned England to a commonwealth" (*Own Time*, 1833, ed. i., 85).

As a matter of fact, so long as monarchy could be maintained, Ireton sought to maintain it. Throughout 1647 and 1648, he was the leader and spokesman of the moderate party in the Council of the Army. The constitution was always in his mouth; he was anxious to change as little of it as necessary and to preserve as much of it as possible. His declarations on this point are clear and frequent.

> "I doe not seeke, nor would not seeke, nor will joyne with them that doe seeke the destruction of Parliament or Kinge. Neither will I consent with those, or concurre with them who will not attempt all the wayes that are possible to preserve both, and to make good use, and the best use that can be of both for the kingedome (p. 233). Where I see thinges would not do reall mischief I would hold to positive constitution. . . . . soe long as I can with safetie continue a constitution I will doe it (p. 350). Rather then I will make a disturbance to a good constitution of a kingedome wherein I may live in godlinesse, and peace, and quietnesse, I will parte with a great deale of my birthright" (p. 324).

Hence the vigour with which he opposed manhood suffrage.

> "To me, if there were nothing but this, that there is a constitution, and that constitution which if you take away you leave nothing of constitution, and consequently nothing of right or property [it would be enough] I would not goe to alter

that, though a man could propound that which might in some respects bee better, unlesse it could be demonstrated to me that this were unlawful or that this were destructive" (p. 340).

Manhood suffrage, he maintained, would destroy property. Men might be elected who had no stake in the country, and they might vote down all property (pp. 303, 314). It would endanger liberty itself.

"If there be anything at all that is a foundation of liberty itt is this, that those who shall chuse the lawmakers shall be men freed from dependance upon others. . . . I think if wee from imagination and conceits will go about to hazard the peace of the kingdom to alter the constitution in such a point, wee shall see that libertie that we soe much talke of and contend for shall bee nothing by this our contending for it, by putting it into the hands of those that will give it away when they have itt" (p. 341).

Ireton's objections to the principles on which the demand was based were still stronger than his objection to the demand itself. He denied altogether that any man had by birthright any claim to a voice in the government of his country. He denied with equal bluntness the theory that no man was bound to obedience to any government, unless he had by his own free consent put himself under that government (pp. 302, 319). Arguments about abstract justice he abhorred and dreaded:

"When I do hear men speake of laying aside all engagements to [consider only] that wild or vast notion of what in every man's conception is just or unjust, I am afraid and do tremble att the boundlesse and endlesse consequences of itt" (p. 264).

Equally keen was his perception of the danger of appeals to natural rights and the law of nature.

"I wish wee may all consider of what right you challenge that all the people should have right to Elections. Is itt by the right of nature? If you will hold forth that as your ground, then I thinke you must deny all property too. . . . By that same right of nature, whatever it bee that you pretend, by which you can say one man hath an equall right with another to the chusing of him that shall governe him, by the same right of nature hee hath an equall right in any goods he sees, meate, drinke, clothes, to take and use them for his sustenance. . . . . If upon these grounds you doe paramount to all constitutions hold uppe this law of nature, I would faine have any man shew me where you will end" (p. 307; *cf.* pp. 303, 310, 314, 336).

In the heat of his opposition to these theories of abstract right which he heard put forward, Ireton denied all political rights to persons not freeholders possessing a permanent interest in the country (pp. 302, 307, 314). He answered the Levellers of 1647 very much as Lord Braxfield answered the Reformers of 1794.

"'A government in every country,' said Braxfield, 'should be just like a corporation, and in this country it is made up of the landed interest, which alone has a right to be represented. As for the rabble, who have nothing but personal property, what hold has the nation of them? They may pack up their property on their backs and leave the country in the twinkling of an eye, but landed property cannot be removed.'" (*State Trials*, xxiii. 231.)

In practice, however, Ireton was not prepared to push his opposition to the extremes to which his logic might have carried him. Throughout he announced his willingness to support a reasonable extension of the franchise, providing it was limited "to the fix't and settled people of this nation," to "men who are like to be freemen and not given up to the wills of others" (pp. 313, 344). At the same time no one was more eager for parliamentary reform of other kinds:

"I will not arrogate that I was the first man that putt the Army upon the thought either of successive Parliaments or more equall Parliaments; yet there are some heere that know who they were putt us upon that foundation of libertie of putting a period to this Parliament, that wee might have successive Parliaments, and that there might bee a more equall distribution of elections" (p. 333).

According to Wildman and Sexby the soldiers had engaged for their own freedom and for the recovery of their lost liberties (pp. 318, 322). They demanded securities for their personal rights, and a voice in the making of the laws they had to live under (pp. 318, 354). Securities for the rights of parliaments would not satisfy them, for they feared the parliament's privileges as much as the King's prerogative.

In Ireton's view the war had been originally undertaken "for the liberty of Parliaments," that the law of the Kingdom might be determined by its representatives in Parliament, and "that the will of one man should not be a law" (pp. 327, 333). Circumstances had led him to demand now not only securities for the liberty of parliament, but guarantees as to its composition. "The rectification of the supreme authority of the Kingdom," "the reduction of the supreme authority to that constitution which is due to the people of this Kingdom," he declared to be the necessary condition of the Army's submission to parliament, and a condition which it was justified in using force to obtain (pp. 267, 268). Further than this Ireton was not prepared to go. The devices by which he sought to reconcile the real sovereignty of the House of Commons with the concession of a nominal share in legislation to the House of Lords, and a strictly limited veto to the Crown, are significant illustrations of his statesmanship. He thought to effect a political revolution by a change in the machinery of the constitution without any alteration in its outward form, and without a corresponding change in the spirit of the nation.

Equally conservative in temper, Cromwell set less value on constitutional forms and had less faith in political machinery. He was not, as he expresses it, "wedded and glued to forms of government" (p. 277). His criticisms of the "Agreement of the People" deal not so much with the justice or even the expediency of the particular things proposed as with the general danger of change:

> "This paper doth contain in it very great alterations of the very government of this kingdom, alterations from that government it hath been under, I believe I may almost say since it was a nation, and what the consequences of such an alteration as this would be, if there were nothing else to be considered but the very weight and nature of the things contained in this paper, wise men and godly men ought to consider" (p. 237).

Other parties might be formed and put forth other schemes for new constitutions equally plausible and seek to impose them on the country:

> "And if so what do you think the consequence of that would be? Would it not be confusion? Would it not be utter confusion? Would it not make England like Switzerland, one county against another as one canton of the Swiss is against another? And if so what would that produce but an absolute desolation—an absolute desolation to the nation" (p. 237).

He proceeds to lay down the principle that, in proposing a change of such importance, the first thing to consider is "whether, according to reason and judgement, the spirits and temper of the people of this nation are prepared to receive and to go along with it" (p. 237). "In the government of nations that which is to be looked after is the affections of the people, and that I find which satisfies my conscience in the present thing" (p. 369). Compared with the question of its acceptance by the people, the question of the particular form of the government was unimportant. This he illustrates by the case of the Jews, governed successively by patriarchs, judges and kings. Under all these governments they were happy and contented. Moreover, there were other things more important than the form of the government. Even if you change the government to the best possible form of government "it is but a moral thing." "It is but as Paul says, 'dross and dung' in comparison of Christ." Why should they contest so much for merely temporal things? If every man in the kingdom were so bent on realising his ideal of government that he was willing to fight to establish it, the state would come to desolation (p. 370). His conclusion was that the question what government were fittest for the kingdom should be left to Parliament to determine. The Army should content itself with insisting that parliaments should be fairly elected, regularly summoned, and dissolved at regular intervals (*ibid*). Though willing to use force against the Parliament when he regarded it as necessary, he was anxious to limit the use of force to cases in which its employment was absolutely indispensable. "I do not know that force is to be used except we cannot get what is for the good of the kingdom without force" (p. 202, *cf.* p. 185). The good of the people he declares to be the principle by which his actions are guided.

"That's in all our hearts to profess above anything that's worldly the public good of the people, and if that be in our hearts truly and nakedly I am confident it is a principle that will stand" (p. 259). "If that be not the supreme aim of us under God our principles fall" (p. 277).

This does not mean that the wishes of the people are to be implicitly followed. "That's the question, what's for their good, not what pleases them" (p. 209). In these words there is already a foreshadowing of the Protectorate.

Many other illustrations of Cromwell's character are to be found in these speeches. The good sense with which he checks the exaggerated religious enthusiasm of some of his friends is specially notable. Accused of want of faith when he mentions the difficulties in the way of establishing the new constitution proposed by the Agitators, he replies:

"I know a man may answer all difficulties with faith, and faith will answer all difficulties really where it is, but we are very apt all of us to call that faith which perhaps may be but carnal imagination" (p. 238).

His dignified vindication of himself from the charge of being affrighted by difficulties is admirable (pp. 247, 289). Equally good is his criticism of the claims of those who assert themselves to have received special revelations or "particular dictates from God" (pp. 375, 379).

Other characteristic passages are his description of his own eager and sanguine temperament (p. 191), and his blunt answer to the charge of seeking his own ends (p. 179).

The speeches of Goffe and Rainborow are valuable to all who care to understand the temper of the Puritan soldier. Goffe was one of the mystical enthusiasts whom every revolution produces As he was an Englishman of the 17th century his enthusiasm took a religious rather than a political turn. He rejoiced to belong to that "company of saints" who were "chosen, and called, and faithful," whose desire was to "follow Christ wheresoever he goes" (p. 283). Cromwell in difficulties generally moved for a Committee; Goffe invariably proposed a prayer-meeting. Always "seeking the Lord," he fancied that he heard the voice of God answering his prayers, inspiring his resolves, and dictating his actions (pp. 253, 283, 374). In the revolutions which he witnessed he saw God "throwing down the glory of all flesh," the kingdom of Antichrist falling, the "latter days" beginning, and the personal reign of Christ at hand (p. 282). Three-quarters a Fifth Monarchy man, he differed from most of that sect in one very important particular. They were eager to realise their visions by force and at once, and believed that the day of their triumph had come. Their feeling is well expressed in the hymn of one of their preachers:

> "The Lord begins to honour us,
> The Saints are marching on;
> The sword is sharp, the arrows swift,
> To destroy Babylon."

Goffe on the other hand possessed a certain patience; a willingness, as he said, to wait upon the Lord till his own season. "It may be there is a better opportunity that the Lord will give us" (p. 284).

Rainborow was much more like a modern radical. His enthusiasm was more secular and more national. He, too, talks of "God's people," but it is merely as an occasional synonym for "the honest men of England" (pp. 246, 273). He had fought for no vision of a heavenly kingdom, but for his own freedom and "for the liberties of the people of England" (pp. 272, 273). By the people of England he meant neither an oligarchy of country gentlemen, nor a limited number of freeholders, but "every man born in England," "the poor man," "the meanest man in the kingdom" (pp. 304, 305, 309). If rich men alone were to have votes,

> "One part would make hewers of wood and drawers of water of the other five, and so the greatest part of the nation be enslaved" (p. 320). If there were to be no extension of the franchise "what shall become of those many men that have laid themselves out for the Parliament of England in this present war, that have ruined themselves by fighting, by hazarding all they had? They are Englishmen. They have now nothing to say for themselves" (p. 320).

Political difficulties might beset the attempt of the Army to secure the liberties of the nation, but they must be faced and vanquished as at Marston or Naseby.

> "Let difficulties be round about you, have you death before you, the sea on each side of you and behind you, are you convinced the thing is just, I think you are bound in conscience to carry it on; and I think at the last day it can never be answered to God that you did not do it. For I think it is a poor service to God and the Kingdom to take their pay and to decline their work" (p. 246).

How long Cromwell and Ireton would be able to hold back men like Goffe and Rainborow, and how far they would be able to control them, depended mainly on the turn which events took. More than once during these debates, voices had been heard demanding the punishment of the King. "Is it just or reasonable," asked Wildman, "to punish with death those that according to his command do make war . . . and then to say that there is a way left for mercy for him . . . who was the great contriver of all" (p. 384). At present, however, only one of the higher officers seems to have backed this demand. On November 11, Colonel Harrison "made a narration concerning some thinges that lay upon his spirit," denounced the King as a man of blood, and demanded his prosecution. Cromwell and Ireton answered him, the one putting several cases in which murder was not to be punished, the other urging that the Army ought not to take unlawful ways even to bring a delinquent to justice. Cromwell and Fairfax added that the question of the King's future treatment ought to be left to the determination of Parliament (pp. 417, 418). But whether in the end the Army would be content to leave the question to parliament did not depend entirely upon the wishes of its leaders.

It remains to add a few words on the editing of the papers printed in this volume. William Clarke appears to have taken copies of letters received at the head quarters of the Army, and to have kept draughts or copies of most of those sent out. These were transcribed into books at a later period. In the case of those now printed, this transcription took place in 1662. In some instances these original copies and draughts have survived, but they were generally destroyed when the second copy was made. In the same way the rough notes of the debates taken in shorthand in 1647 were not written out till 1662. The result of this system is seen in the large number of clerical errors which the letters contain. Where both copies have survived a comparison of the text of the two sometimes supplied a correction. At other times, in order to complete the sense, it was necessary to supply the words which are printed between square brackets. Some verbal slips were also corrected, and the punctuation frequently amended.

In the debates, errors of all kinds were still more frequent, though fortunately the most important speeches are also the best reported. In some cases the meaning of the speakers was obscured by inversions in the order of words, clauses, and even sentences. Sentences were often mixed together, and the tail of one sometimes inserted in the middle of the next. Where possible these mistakes of the reporter, or the transcriber of his notes, have been corrected, and the alterations made pointed out in the foot notes. Other obscure passages have been elucidated by supplying words between square brackets, or suggesting paraphrases below. The text has been also amended by omitting useless repetitions, and inserting stops. A certain amount of emendation of this kind was absolutely necessary in order to make the debates intelligible, but as few changes as possible have been made.

The Index will be contained in the second volume.

THE CLARKE PAPERS.

[*Letters from a correspondent in London to a friend in the Army.*]

London, 28th March, 1647.

I pray tell the Comptroller,[a] that it is the opinion of freinds heere that the Generall doe send to the severall Regiments the order of the House of Commons[b] to hinder the promoting of the Petition, and also the Copie of the Petition, but in noe kind to expresse any thing in that order which may anger the Souldiers,[c] and only to desire the officers to observe the order of the House of Commons and to be carefull in the same.

It is likewise the opinion of freinds heere that all our freinds doe not say any thing to hinder the Souldiers to goe with the 17 undertakers, for they doe but watch to gett advantage of any in our Army that shall give out speaches to hinder the Souldiers for going. But yet they doe all thinke this, that it may be told them, that most of those 17 undertakers doe not meane to goe to Ireland but only to drawe their men upp to the sea side and never

[a] Captain Richard Deane, Comptroller of the Ordnance. Peacock, *Army Lists*, ed. 2, p. 101.

[b] March 27. *Commons' Journals*, v., 127.

[c] The petition is given in the *Old Parliamentary History*, xv., 342, and in *The Journals of the House of Lords*, ix., 114. According to Waller the petition was drawn up about March 22, and then presented to the Convention of officers. *Vindication*, p. 51. The same day an engagement was drawn up and signed by 29 officers undertaking to serve in Ireland. They are probably the 'undertakers' referred to.

meane to goe, as Colonell Fortescue, Colonell Harvey, Colonell Sheffeild, Sir Robert Pye, Lievtennant Colonell Jackson.

All our freinds heere doe thinke these 17 undertakers will prove very knaves in their designes and therefore that wee doe lett them goe on quiettly. Thursday is the day to name the Generall that shall goe for Ireland. Bee carefull to whome you speake, for Fincher[a] is there but for a Spie.

London, 30 March, 1647.

I have write to the Generall, that the Lords have voted to send for him to the Parliament[b] (I thinke the Lords are all madd). Lett every man fitt himselfe with patience, for hee shall have a tryall to the purpose. Tell Mr. Saltmarsh[c] now is the tyme of tryall; since these warrs began there was never such a tryall of Men.

London, 30 March, 1647.

Yesterday the House satt very late in the night about the Army. They have voted all those that had any hand in the Petition to be proceeded against as Enemies to the State, and have sent for Commissary Generall Ireton, Colonell Hammond, Lieutennant Collonell Hammond, Collonell Lilborne, and Lieutennant Colonel Pride to appeare before the House.[d] They have likewise sent for Major Generall Skippon privately to come with all speed to the

[a] Quarter-Master-General of the Horse; v. Waller's *Vindication*, p. 51, and Sprigge, *Anglia Rediviva*, ed. 1854, pp. 60, 218.

[b] *Lords' Journals*, ix., iii.

[c] John Saltmarsh, a leading Independent preacher; see Fuller's *Worthies*, ed. 1811, ii., 519; Hanbury, *Historical Memorials*, iii., 74, 167; Rushworth, vii., 944.

[d] The letters which led to this vote are printed in the *Lords' Journals*, ix., 115; the declaration against the petitioners was drawn up by Holles: see Ludlow's *Memoirs*, ed. 1751, p. 74, and Waller's *Vindication*, p. 62. This Declaration, passed March 29, was erased by vote of June 3, 1647. *Commons' Journals*, v., 129, 197. It is printed in the *Old Parliamentary History*, xv., 344.

Army.[a] They have likewise ordered that those foote that are to bee transported shall have one moneths pay of their Arreares and a fortnights advance when they are on shippboard, and the Horse to have a moneths pay when they are over, and this to be performed, but when, they must not question.[b] There is likewise orders to be given imediately for the seperatting of the Forces intended for Ireland from those that are intended to be disbanded some miles distance, for feare those that intend not for that service should pollute the other, and all this bussinesse ariseth from an information that one of the Army gave to Colonell Harley which the House will not divulge.

London, 30 March, 1647.

Much adoe there was on Satturday last at the House about your Army. The Cittizens grumble vilely and will be satisfied with nothing but that you be presently disbanded, and they say nor will they trust you to goe for Ireland with your own Commanders unlesse first the Army be purg'd of Sectaries as they call them. A great stirr is made about the Petition[c] (term'd Independant) to which hands were getting in London, and some were committed about it, but Major [d] is againe discharged upon Baile, nor will the Petition I understand be thus stifled; but (tis said) the Petitioners or a great company of them will attend the House dayly to have their Petition restored, and that they may be allowed the libertie as others to make knowne their grievances, or

[a] Skippon was summoned from Newcastle on March 29, and voted by the Commons to command the forces destined for Ireland, with the title of Field-Marshal (April 2). This vote was agreed to by the Lords on April 6. *Commons' Journals*, v., 133; *Lords' Journals*, ix., 122. He accepted the command with considerable reluctance, and resigned it on July 21, 1647. *Lords' Journals*, ix., 138, 158, 348; *Commons' Journals*, 129, 156, 176.

[b] 27 March, 1647, when Clotworthy delivered the report of the Commissioners sent to the Army. *Commons' Journals*, v., 127.

[c] This petition is printed in the *Lords' Journals*, ix. 82; see also Godwin, *Commonwealth*, ii. 277.

[d] Major Tulidah: see Lilburne's *Rash Oaths unwarrantable*, 1647, p. 35.

otherwise they will appeale to the Kingdome in Generall. The Petition of your Army is likewise much talked of, some for it, and others against it. Some have been suspended in London for preaching being not ordained, yet they preach notwithstanding, as Mr. Knowles,[a] &c. One thing more much talked of in London, both new and strange newes, Mr. William Sedgwick, brother to Obediah, is lately come to London from the Isle of Ely, and prophesies that the World will be at an end within foureteene dayes, Christ then comeing to Judgment, and that Christ appeared to him in his studdy the last weeke at Ely and told him soe much. Severall Ministers went to discourse with him the Last Lords day but he refused to enter into argumentation with any of them further then this, that it was reveal'd unto him the World would be at an end within few dayes: thus much is talked of in London generally, but withall they say hee is distempered in minde, and say others, for soe much as he discourses he talkes very sencibly.

Since the writing of the former I understand that the Commons satt all the day yesterday and untill tenn at night in further debate of your Army; and it was strongly aimed at, to say noe further, to have the whole Army presently disbanded, and upon the result of it was voted that your Army both the Horse and foot should be disbanded, excepting only three Regiments of Horse,[b] vizt. Collonell-Gen. Pointz, Collonell Bethells, and Collonell Copley's. You may see by this how the tyde turnes, and how soone all the soe lately much admired services of your Army are forgotten. Nay the Cittizens or many of them have raised a new aspersion against you, that you are all at this present in armes and stands upon your guard at the Head Quarters at Walden, and this is the great talke at this present and soe confidently reported. I did not my selfe

[a] Hanserd Knollys.

[b] *Commons' Journals*, v., 128; Godwin's *Commonwealth*, ii., 285. The vote was that these three regiments should be part of the 5,400 horse to be still maintained.

knowe what to thinke of it, as conceiving in truth you had just cause soe to doe; but I went to the Secretary[a] and hee assured mee the contrary, and I have not been backward to tell some of the cheife Ringleaders their errors in reporting it.

A Narrative of the Proceedings at Saffron-Walden since the Commissioners of Parliament came thither concerning the sending of Part of this Army into Ireland.

Fryday the 9th of Aprill 1647. The Committee at Derby house wrote unto the Generall, that the Houses had designed part of the Army for Ireland and that they had referr'd it to a Committee, to conferre with his Excellencie and the Officers how they might be sent over, and to drawe out such as shall ingage for Ireland from the rest of the Army into a body, desireing the Generall to give them the best assistance hee can for the effectuall transaction of that service. This Letter came to the Generall's hands Aprill 13.

And the same day came another Letter to the Generall's hands from the Committee at Derby house dated Aprill 12th, expresseing that they had appointed a Committee to come to conferre with the Generall and Officers to drawe out such of his Forces as were willing to engage in the service of Ireland according to the Votes of both Houses, desireing him to have his Officers ready at the head Quarters at that time that the buissinesse may be effected with speed.

The same day the Generall yssued forth his Orders to the severall Regiments in the Army, that all the feild Officers in every Regiment and the Captaines and Lieutennants of every Troope of Horse

[a] The Secretary was John Rushworth, Secretary to the General. This letter I take to be written by Gilbert Mabbott, once Rushworth's servant, one of the persons who regularly supplied news-letters to the army, and a familiar acquaintance of William Clarke's. He was most likely the writer of the three previous letters also.

and Company of Foote should be in person at the head Quarters that were imployed about in relation to the service of Ireland.

Thursday Aprill 15th. The Commissioners[a] came downe to the Generall's Quarters, and after they had dined with him spake with him in private and in his chamber communicated unto him the Votes of both Houses and their Instructions, and withall declared that they were informed there was some speaches cast abroad in the Army to disaffect the People from the service of Ireland to the much retarding of that bussinesse, which they thought fitt to acquaint the Generall withall to the end it might be prevented. And for the better prevention thereof offered to the Generall the draught of a Declaration which they brought with them ready written to be published in the Army.[b] The Generall told them that if soe bee they could make it appeare there were any such in this Army that did goe about to hinder others that were willing to goe in this service he desired they might be made knowne, and hee would proceed against them and see them punnished; and for publishing a Declaration to his Army, as if in his opinion they were guiltie of giveing such obstructions, hee thought it might not be convenient unlesse hee had proofe of it, however he would when all the Officers did attend the Commissioners declare his intention in furtherance of that service, and give them it in charge to promote it though they should not be disposed to goe themselves; and besides there were expressions in the said Declaration to this purpose, that some persons did endeavour a retardment of that service by secrett objections and discouragments, and doth thereby require the Officers and Souldiers of the Army to discover such person as shall offend in the premises that he may be imprizoned and further punnished &c. For the Generall soe farr forth to adiudge his Army guilty before any proofe made that there were any that

[a] The report of the Commissioners is printed in the *Lords' Journals*, ix., 152. Sir William Waller gives a detailed account of their mission in his *Vindication*, pp. 77-93. See also Rushworth, vi., 457, 460, 463.

[b] Waller, p. 80.

did retard the service hee thought was very hard to have it put upon them, especially considering he offered the Commissioners soe freely to punnish any of the Army they could informe against.

Whilst the Generall and Commissioners were thus conferring together, the Officers were adviseing among themselves in the Church by way of preparation what to answere to the Commissioners at the meeting, and accordingly chose a certaine number of Officers to speake for all the rest, who afterwards coming downe to the Generall's Quarters (being nere 200 Officers) by command from him at the Commissioners desire, the Commissioners came downe to them and acquainted them with the Votes of both Houses and the substance of what they had in Commission to say in pursuance thereof.[a] Whereupon the Officers desired to knowe what satisfaction they could give to these particulars following which formerly were propounded at their first meeting vizt.

1. To represent their desires to knowe what was done in refferrence to the last Propositions sent unto the Parliament by way of Quærie.

2. To represent, that all those who in their owne person did not ingage for Ireland would be ready to promote the service.

3. That if the same conduct they have had, under which God hath soe exceedingly blest this Army and Kingdome, might be continued also as to the service of Ireland, it would conduce much to their encouragment and personall engagement.

It is to be observed that as these Officers were speaking for the rest propounding to receive satisfaction in the conduct &c. it being said by some of the Commissioners they spake only their owne sence, the Officers cryed out, All, All,—Declareing thereby their unanimity in those desires. Neverthelesse by the mouthes of those that were intrusted by the Officers to speake in their names, they freely offered their service in promoting that service severall times though they did not engage themselves in their persons. Whereupon the Commissioners declareing that it was not needfull for any

[a] Waller, p. 82.

that did not intend the service in their owne persons to attend any longer, most of the Officers departed to their severall charges, and the Towne (before very full) was of a suddaine emptied.

It may not be omitted to observe what the Generall said at that meeting in the presence of the Commissioners and all the Officers, both at the first meeting and afterwards, Expressing how necessary the worke was, and that who ever did not intend it in their owne persons should lay their hands to it, and use many other arguments to incourage that worke. And it is also observed what Representation was made thereof from the Commissioners here to the committee at Derby House, as by the Letter from the committee at Derby House of the 17th of Aprill appeares: vizt. That the Generall did publish amongst the Officers his oppinion of the honour and importance of that service and also of his dislike of any practice that might disrepute the same, and did also command that however any of their owne Resolutions might stand disposed, they should neverthelesse not prejudice but rather promote in referrence to others; which care of the Generall to remove all impedements in a worke wherein this Kingdome is soe neerely concerned the Committee were very sencible of, and did returne him thanks, and further desire him to proceed to declare the same as hee shall see occasion (which indeed hee did to every Officer that came to him afterwards that was not present at that meeting). And further the Letter saith, If you please to publish the same, it may be the better knowne to the Officers and Souldiers, and wee conceive it may the better produce the effect intended in it.

Upon this intimation from the Committee at Derby House, of publishing something in writeing, though they left him at libertie whether he would publish any thing or not, the Generall was pleased to drawe a letter to be written to the Colonell or Cheife Officers resideing with each Regiment in the Army, to publish to their Officers and Souldiers how much his desire was to promote that service, and that if they were not disposed themselves yett they should make the votes knowne, and his desires for the incouragement of itt, and imediatelie issued out to Sir Hardresse Waller's and other Regiments copies of that Letter, and the Votes of both Houses inclosed, to bee published by reading the same att the Head of every Regiment as by the Letter heerafter mencioned appeareth.[a] And withall, after such time as some copies were delivered out, sent a copy of the letter to the Commissioners that they might bee pleased to take notice of itt, and to give itt to such officers as had subscribed to goe for Ireland to make use of for the furtherance of that service if they thought fitt.

The next morning after these Letters were issued out Mr. Jessop, Secretary to the Earle of Warrwick and the Commissioners, wrote a Letter to Mr. Rushworth letting him knowe that he had it in command from the Earle of Warwick and the rest of the Commissioners, to desire him to move his Excellencie to forbeare issuing forth any more of these Letters to the Collonells whereof the copie was delivered last night, untill they had represented to his Excellencie their sence thereupon, as by the Letter appeares. Hereupon the Generall was made acquainted therewith, and a stopp made of yssuing out any more of those Letters, till towards evening there came a Letter from the Commissioners here present letting the Generall knowe that they were not satisfied with the coppie of that Letter he had sent them; they conceiv'd that an intimation from them, that such discouragments were scattered in the Army, was a sufficient ground for his Excellencie to take notice that there were obstructions of that nature, and to incert the same in his Letter to the Regiments, and to expresse a strict and peremptory injunction, they conceiving the word desire [not] to be sufficiently vigorous to effect their desires thereupon to his Officers &c., as by the Letter of the 19th of Aprill appeares; and in pursuance of this advice and intimation they sent a draught of a letter to the Generall, in such expressions as they thought it was fitt for the Generall to publish, wherein they would have the Generall to declare unto the Army,

[a] The letter is printed in Rushworth, vi., 461; for the comments of the Commissioners, see Waller, p. 85.

that hee was informed of some discouraging arguments had been cast among the Souldiers, which if really soe hee cannot but interpret it a fruit of disaffection to the welfare of this Kingdome and Ireland. At this passage the Generall was not satisfied,[a] haveing not received any information of Weight in the least kinde of any persons in the Army discouraging the service, or any thing that would beare that construction. Whereupon Mr. Jessop, who came with the Letter, told the Generall hee had in command to acquaint him for his satisfaction, that Captaine Audley had said in the presence of the Generall, that those that were now soe forward for the service of Ireland were not worthy to come neere to his horse tayle.

Upon this Letter the Generall did contrive an answeare in writing to this purpose,[a] that hee was ready to comply with them in what may conduce to the furthering of the service of Ireland and effect their desires, and that though the word 'require' was not expressed in it, it being his constant course to use the word 'desire' to his Officers, hee doubted not but it would find a ready obedience; and acquainted them further, that he had sent for Captaine Audley, whome they had informed against for speaking words in his presence to the prejudice of the Ireish service, to give their Lordshipps satisfaction in what hee said; and withall desired their Lordshipps to informe him of any person in the Army that did any thing to the obstruction of the Ireish service, and hee would proceed against him and see him punnished. To this answere of the Generall's there was never any reply made, but (as wee are informed) a post sent to the Committee at Derby House.

Lords Day: Aprill 18th. There came 16 private souldiers of Collonell Lilburne's Regiment, (all of his own company), and acquainted the Generall that their Lieutennant Colonell[b] had commanded them to march the next morning earely towards Cheshire, that the speach was they were to goe for Ireland, and that their

[a] Waller, pp. 85, 86.

[b] Nicholas Kempson.

Colonell's Captaine Lieutenant[a] told his Company that they should not have any pay till they had advanc'd their Quarters further from the Army, never acquainting them they were to goe for Ireland. Whereupon the Generall went to the Commissioners, and acquainted them with the occasion of the coming of the Souldiers, and that he desired there might be all faire dealing used by such Officers as did intend for the service of Ireland, which they desired to further; and he did conceive it would much contribute to the furtherance of that worke, that the Officers did drawe their Regiments to a Randezvouz and declare publiquely to the Souldiers the votes of both Houses for their encouragment to goe; and that such as would goe might be drawne a part, and according to the order given by the Commissioners immediatly to march to those Quarters they had appointed them. Whereupon the Commissioners said that they thought the course was very faire, and that just as his Excellencie came in they had given that order, but the Souldiers came to complaine an houre before, declareing their ignorance of any such intention, which indeed occasioned that Order.

Munday: Aprill 19th, the Generall received a letter (early in the morning) from the Committee at Darby House to stay his jorney to London,[b] whether hee had purposed that day to have gone to fall into a course of phisick for the recovery of his health, being brought very lowe by neglecting it; in which Letter the Committee doe expresse that the bussinesse of sending forces for Ireland did goe on very vigerously, and that it hath been very much promoted by the Generall's care and countenance, and doubted not but in a very few dayes to compleat the number designed, especially if the Generall continue there.

Upon this, the rather (though the Generall before it came had determined not to goe because hee did conceive the Commissioners here would take it as an obstruction to the service) but because it is mentioned in this Letter with such confidence that the worke

[a] Robert Fish. See *Lords' Journals*, ix., 154.

[b] See Waller, pp. 90, 91.

goes on prosperously, that the number designed will be compleated in few dayes. It is conceived the occasion of their mistake might arise by the subscription of the Life Guard and most of the Officers of Colonell Lilburne's Regiment.

That those Officers in whom they did first of all relie for the great encouragement in this service doe now withdrawe themselves from their former personall engagement in it, as namely; Colonell Harley, Colonell Fortescue, Colonell Butler, Lieutennant Colonell Jackson, Major Fincher, Major Alford, Major Duckett, Major Gooday, Captaine Robotham,[a] and divers others who subscribed to that paper delivered to the House of Commons, for which thankes was returned unto them, and upon confidence of these men's engagements and interests in the Army the House might reasonably conceive the number designed might have been procured.

It is to be observed That of all the Horse Officers in the Army from Captaines upwards not above six Captaines, Majors or Colonells have subscribed to goe in person: vizt. Colonell Sheffeild, the Lord Calfeild, Captaine Howard, (and Sir Robert Pye if hee yet goe) and two others, and not one Captaine in all Colonell Butler's Regiment nor in Colonell Sheffeild's doe ingage in person, of both which Regiments, by reason of their Colonell's engagement, the House had the greatest confidence; and besides Captaine Pennyfather and Captaine Burgis of Colonell Butler's Regiment had their names sett in the paper without their privity, which was presented to the House.[b]

For the Foote Officers that have subscribed the Commissioners knowe their names best because they have the list, but as wee are informed Colonell Herbert and Lieutennant Colonell Kempson are the two only Field Officers; the rest are Captaines and they

[a] A list of these officers is given in the *Lords' Journals*, ix., 114, viz. Edward Harley, Richard Fortescue, John Butler, Richard Fincher, John Alford, Charles Duckett, Sampson Gooday, Robert Robotham, and others, thirty in all.

[b] Thomas Pennyfather and Benjamin Burges. *Lords' Journals*, ix., 114.

but a few, and some inferiour Officers under them. For Colonell Herbert, before hee went to the Commissioners, hee declared[a] to Mr. Rushworth and others, that it was in vain for him to goe and delude the Commissioners by telling them his Regiment would goe, when he knewe their full purpose was against it, except one Officer that had some few men, that would goe with him; and besides hee declared, that upon the first intention to send that Regiment into Ireland, the Officers and Souldiers did unanimously declare they would not stirr unlesse they had their full arrears; which was true, for he wrote soe in a letter unto the Generall under his owne hand ready to be produc'd. But after his coming to the Commissioners they engaged him, and presently gave him an order to march away with his Regiment towards Chester. Only Captaine Shorte[b] who had formerly a longing desire after Ireland, subscribed to goe with him and a Lieutennant or two, and accordingly the Generall gave the said Colonell an Order to Randezvouz his Regiment upon Fryday the 23rd of Aprill at Hitching in Hertfordshire, where he hath power to draw away what men he could gett; Hee tooke his leive of the Generall and said hee must now serve his Lords and Masters.

For Lieutennant Colonell Kempson, hee and the rest of the Officers of Colonell Lilburne's Regiment[c] most greivously abused the Commissioners by telling them that hee had the consent of the whole Regiment to goe intire, which as conceived was a maine ground that the Commissioners did write to Derby House that the worke went on soe prosperously. For when some of his Officers came to drawe forth five of the Companies of Ireland, they were very much incenst against their Officers, holding jointly together not to goe, teareing the staffe and collours from Captaine Peckham,[d] who, as was supposed, had the greatest influence of any Officer in the Regiment, who hath been to make his complaint to the Com-

[a] See Rushworth, vi., 468.

[b] Nathaniel Shorte.

[c] Rushworth, vi., 460, 463, 467.

[d] Christopher Peckham.

missioners and would insinuate as if the Colonell (who is most innocent) had occasioned itt.

It is likewise remarkable the carriage of this Lieutennant Collonell[a] who Aprill the 20th when the Regiment was drawne to a Randezvous to see who would goe for Ireland, and whoe not; hee, whilst Colonell Lilburne was reading the Generall's Letter and Parliament votes to five companies, carried away fower companies with their collours without ever acquainting them with the Votes of the Parliament; and his misdemeanour was the greater in that he kept the Souldiers pay and would not give them a penny, and therefore the Souldiers seeing their Officers goe, the colours and the money goe, though they had noe minde to goe themselves, yet followed. But it hath produced this effect that Aprill 21st Captaine Weldon's[b] company (one of the fower) is returned back to the Regiment and say all the rest will followe; soe this man's carriage brings a disrepute upon their proceedings this way and by consequence a great disservice to the Parliament, and deserves blame. For those five companies where Colonell Lilburne was, after the Votes were read all those that would goe for Ireland were drawne out, who were in number threescore and one more. For Captaine Peckham's company they mutinnied, beat their Captaine, and would not come to the Randezvouz.

And whilst they were at the Randezvouz Lieutennant Generall Massey[c] came and told them for their incouragment, that Colonel Herbert[d] was already marching with his Regiment towards Cheshire, Captaine Orpin,[e] who was sent as one to beare witnesse of Colonell Lilburne's carriage, being of Colonell Herbert's Regiment, had much a doe to forbeare to tell the Lieutennant Generall hee was mistaken, and Mr. Woolsey who came with him upon that occasion knewe the contrary.

[a] Nicholas Kempson.
[b] George Weldon.
[c] On Massey's unpopularity see Waller, *Vindication*, p. 84.
[d] William Herbert.
[e] Edward Orpin.

The Officers of Colonell Fleetwood's Regiment are returned and bring this accompt, that the Regiment was drawne to a Randezvouz, Captaine Howard made knowne his desires, but the conditions was mightily slighted; though as to his owne person the Regiment was civill, hee could not gett, with all the interest he had in his owne troopes nor in the Regiment, more than a Quarter Master and five men: which soe much troubled him as he is gone to London in discontent, and speakes hardly of the Commissioners for putting him upon such a fruitlesse bussinesse.[a]

[*News-letter from London.*]

Queenstreete, 24 Aprill, 1647.

Yesterday was a great day in the House. Severall particulars were in debate, butt amongst the rest Mr. Hollis brought in an Apology which was pretended to bee from the Souldiers in the Army to their Commission Officers, the same that was brought to Colonel Whalley's Regiment; which though itt is soe weake and impertinent that few or none of the Army (especially if they have one dram of sence or reason) will owne, yett hee indeavoured to make itt the sence of the whole Army, and soe lanch't forth into high expressions against itt.[b] Some tooke him uppe nimbly and handsomely. Tuesday is assigned for the great day for the disbanding of the Army, when, how, and on what consideracion, nothing being done yesterday about itt, though some thinke six weekes pay enough, as much as Massies men had, and say, They deserv'd as much as this Army.[c] The Spiritts of the Godly heere

[a] Howard was a captain in Fleetwood's regiment, who offered to serve in Ireland, and was appointed by Parliament Colonel of a regiment of horse to be raised for that service. *Lords' Journals*, ix., 135, 137; Rushworth, vi., 459, 463. A list of officers who volunteered for Ireland, with their respective regiments, is given by Rushworth, vi., 460—464, and in the report of the Commissioners before referred to.

[b] *Commons' Journals*, v. 153-4; for the Apology itself see the *Book of Army Declarations*, p. 9.

[c] On the disbanding of Massey's brigade see Sprigge, *Anglia Rediviva*, ed. 1854, p. 314, and Hollis, *Memoirs*, ed. 1699, p. 81.

are very much carried out in expectation and hopes of great thinges from the Army, and are farre from our too cold and remisse posture. I feare wee shall sadden their hearts by being too fearfull of Man.

[*News-letters from Saffron-Walden.*]

Walden, 25 Apr. 1647.

Captain Rolphe with some others of Colonel Hamond's Regiment came this morning to Colonel Lambert and the rest of them which are appointed by the Generall for the affaires of the Army, with this account: that Captain Stratton hath drawne of their Regiment 36 men, Captain Ohara most of his Company, and another Lieutenant half his Captaine's Company; by this way of dealing with all their Souldiers, making of them drunke, and then gett them to sett their hands, which when they have done, they make them believe they have power to force them.[a] Which way cannott bee good, as I conceive, for when they come to understand that itt is left to their owne pleasure, and can noe way bee forced by the Officers, they will fall away from their Officers as Colonel Lilburne's doe, there being almost two of those Companies which were marched away so strangelie from the Randezvouze by the Officers returned, and may fall from them every day. All Colonel Fortescue's 6 Companies march away compleate and Adjutant Gray Colonell over them. None of Colonel Hewson's can be perswaded to goe for the service uppon those termes tendred. Horse they can gett none as I heare, the Parliament must thinke of some better termes for this Army, if they intend any should goe for that service. I suppose you have an account of Captain Dormer's[b] expressions to his Souldiers att the Generall's Quarters, how that the intention of

[a] On Hammond's regiment see Rushworth, vi., 466; the officers mentioned were Edmund Rolphe, William Stratton, and Charles O'Hara. On Stratton see also *Lords' Journals*, ix., 141.

[b] On the conduct of Captain (or Major) Francis Dormer see his own letter, *Lords' Journals*, ix., 153, where a full account of the disturbances in Colonel Robert Lilburne's regiment is given.

their drawing out was nott to promote the Irish service butt to goe against an independant Armie that was gathering together in the Kingedome, and many other wicked expressions, telling his Souldiers that hee would only desire them to tarry with him untill they saw what the Independents did, and then hee would give them passes to goe home, promising them their Arreares.[a]

Walden, 26 Apr. 1647.

On Thursday last Colonel Howard drew forth Colonel Fleetwood's Regiment and propounded the service of Ireland to them, butt nott one man offered himself. Colonel Fleetwood's owne Troope made a short Narration of what they intended, which was they were sorry they could nott give that answer the Colonell expected as to engage for Ireland, which they could nott till they were secured for acts done heere as Souldiers, their arreares satisfied, and to know their Cheif Conductor, and what way they should subsist there. Colonel Sheffeild's Regiment was drawne forth on Friday, and they gave the like answer; one of their answers is inclosed.

Wee, the Souldiers in Captain Evelyn's[b] Troope, desire,

First,

Before any man of us list our names for Ireland, wee desire satisfaccion for our arreares heere in England according to the Parliament's manifold Declarations and Remonstrances.

Wee desire a satisfactory answer to our Officers Request given in to their Commissioners when they first came downe to treate with the Army about going for Ireland; and before such time as these are answered, wee shall desire, neither to list, nor provide ourselves for that service. Though wee are perswaded that that Kingdome stands in neede of helpe, yett wee conceive that wee are nott soe to helpe them as wholly to deprive our selves of our just rights and liberties, and of receiving satisfaccion for former services.[c]

[a] James Gray, Adjutant-General of the Foot.

[b] Captain Arthur Evelyn.

[c] See Rushworth, vi. 465

[*List of the Strength of the Army in Officers and Men.*]

Horse.		
Generalls Regiment	70	519
Lt. Generall's	66	514
Com^ary Genll	68	496
Fleetwood's	70	584
Whalley's	65	517
Riche's	68	590
Pye's	65	529
Sheffeild's	64	504
Grave's	70	560
Butler's	64	467
Life Guard	11	100
	681	5380
Dragoones	115	0803
Foote.		
Generall's Reg^t	126	1220
Major Generall's	125	1284
Hamond's	126	894
Rainsborough's	124	1181
Pickering's	125	1073
Ingoldsbye's	126	945
Lambert's	126	1089
Welden's	124	1060
Harley's	125	1064
Waller	126	1074
Herbert	124	1177
Fortescue's (estimated)	125	0750
	1502	12811

Horse	0681 . .	5380
Foote	1502 . .	12811
Dragooners	115 . .	00803
Two Comp[s] firelockes and train .	22 . .	166
	2320	191160
		2320
		21480[a]

THE PROCEEDINGS OF THE ARMY UNDER THE COMMAND OF HIS EXCELLENCIE SIR THOMAS FAIRFAX, COMMENCING MAY 1ST, 1647.

[*A circular Letter to the Commanders of the different Regiments.*]

Major Saunders,[b]

The Generall was pleased during his absence, or untill the Major Generall[c] came, to give Colonell Hammond, Colonell Rich, Major Watson,[d] and us whose names are hereunder written, or any three of us, full power and authority to give orders upon all usuall occasions to the Army, as also for the calling of the severall Regiments of

[a] The regiments in Yorkshire and the North are not included, as this list refers merely to the New Model Army under the command of Fairfax.

[b] Major of Colonel Robert Hammond's regiment; probably the Thomas Saunders mentioned in the *Life of Colonel Hutchinson*, ii., 134.

[c] Skippon, arrived in London about April 27, took his seat in the Commons on April 29, and was sent down to the Army by order of April 30. Rushworth, vi., 463, 472, 474.

[d] Robert Hammond, Nathaniel Rich, and Leonard Watson.

Horse and Foote to a Randezvouz, to the end that such Officers and Souldiers as intend for the service of Ireland may be drawne out of the severall Regiments and Companies; and for their better encouragment according to our Instructions wee have here sent you inclosed the Generall's Letter[a] and Votes of both Houses, desireing that you will cause them to be read to the Officers and Souldiers in your Regiment at their Randezvouz; and if any of your Companies shall march intire for that service wee thinke fitt to certifie you, that it is the Generall's pleasure and order that they march with their Collours; but if only some few shall dispose themselves for the service, then that the Colours remaine still with the Company. If you please to encourage all who incline thereto, wee shall certifie your good service therein to the Generall who will very well resent it, and wee shall rest

Your etc.

Walden, May 3, 1647.

Letter sent to the Collonells or cheife officers of the respective Regiments.

Sir,

Wee desire you upon receipt hereof forthwith to repaire hither your selfe, with some Commission Officer of every Troope in your Regiment, to give unto us the best accompt you can concerning the present temper and disposition of the Regiment, in relation to some late discontents reported to have been amongst the Souldiers; and to receive from us an accompt of such things as wee are appointed by the honourable House of Commons to impart to the Army, concerning the care of that House for their Indempnity and Arrears; you are with the said Officers to be here with as much

[a] The letter of April 18. Rushworth, vi., 461.

speed as possibly you may, but at farthest faile not to be here on Thursday next.[a]

We remaine
Your assured freinds
P. SKIPPON.
OLIVER CROMWELL.
H. IRETON.

Walden, May 3d, 1647.

[*News-letter from Saffron Walden.*]

Walden, 3 May, 1647.[b]

Yesterday the Major Generall, Lieutennant Generall, and Commissary Generall came to Walden, and about halfe an houre after the afternoone sermon was ended there came Lievtennant Colonell Tubbs[c] to my Quarters, and informed mee that there was Intelligence given to him that morning that there was private orders sent by Collonell Middleton, Collonell of the Auxillaries to the severall

[a] Compare the letter of May 3, addressed by these three officers to the Speaker. Cary, *Memorials of the Civil Wars*, i. 205. On April 30, Skippon communicated to the Commons a letter addressed to himself, Fairfax, and Cromwell by the agents of eight regiments of Horse. Rushworth, vi., 474; Hollis, *Memoirs*, p. 89. The letter is printed in Cary's *Memorials of the Civil War*, i., 201, and in the *Lords' Journals*, ix., 164. Skippon, Cromwell, Ireton, and Fleetwood were ordered forthwith to go down to their charges in the army and employ their endeavours to quiet all disturbances in the Army, *Commons' Journals*, v., 158.

[b] In the MS., the date assigned to this letter is April 3. The references to Skippon and the mention of the meeting of the officers render this date impossible, and a second news-letter written the same day supplies the correct date.

[c] Should be Jubbes. John Jubbes entered the Army in April 1643, and after serving in Manchester's Army, became a member of the New Model. He was now Lieutenant-Colonel of Hewson's regiment. He left the army in April, 1648, for reasons stated at length in his *Apology touching his proceeding in a paper called Proposals for Peace and Freedom*, 1648.

Captaines that commanded under his command for the being in a posture ready to rise against the Army, which he was informed should be that night; whereupon he raised his Regiment for their better securitie, and drew them to a Randezvouz; but after hee had spoke with the Major Generall, Lievtennant Generall, and Commissary Generall and informed them of the bussinesse, they came together to the Major Generall's Quarters, and satt very late about it. In the meane time Captaine Reynolds [a] came in and informed them that the horse kept guards, feareing they should be surpriz'd; the Souldiers in the Towne were much nettled at the news of Collonell Hewson's Regiment,[b] and every man provided powder and bullett and kept guards with their swords drawne at the street corners, and durst not be knowne what was the reason they stood there; the other promised not to goe to bed that night, but this day all is very still and quiett. The examination of the Souldiers concerning this buissnesse was taken this day by Mr. Margetts,[c] who I knowe hath given you a full accompt. Orders are sent out for the Officers to meete here at Walden on Thursday next.

Walden, May 4° 1647.

Advertisements for the managing of the Councells of the Army.[d]

1. Appoint a Councell for the ordering the undertakings of the Army.

2. Keepe a partie of able penn men at Oxford and the Army,

[a] Captain John Reynolds, of Cromwell's own regiment of horse, knighted by Cromwell, June 11, 1655. See his life in Noble's *House of Cromwell*, ed. 1787, ii., 418.

[b] Rushworth, vi., 480.

[c] Thomas Margetts, a clerk of the Judge-Advocate of the New Model, Dr. John Mills. For a sketch of his life see Calendar of State Papers, Domestic, 1658-9, p. 378.

[d] No indication is given of the authorship of this paper. It was probably however the work of Edward Sexby, for it closely resembles his subsequent letters in the policy it advocates.

where their presses be imployed to satisfie and undeceive the people.

3. Hold correspondence with the Soldiers and well affected freinds in the severall Counties of the Kingdome, for prevention of uproars, interposition of parties, for disarming the disaffected, and secureing the persons of projecting partes, namely Presbiterians.

4. Doe all things upon publique grounds for the good of the People, and with expedition to avoid devisions and for the prevention of Blood-shed.

5. Bee vigilent to keepe yourselves from supplanting, secrett, open, or undermining Enemies, especially prevent the removall or surprizall of the King's person.

6. Present the generall Officers with the heads of your demaunds in writing, and subscribed, and soe agreed to by your appointed trustees in behalfe of yourselves and other Souldiers.

7. Desire redresse of all arbitrary and exorbitant proceedings throughout the Kingdome, and, according to the Covenant, call for publique justice and due punnishment to be inflicted upon all offenders whomesoever.

8. Crave [give?] some reasons for desireing Reformation in civill justice, and query how the pretended and respective ends of our taking up Armes hath been performed or comported with, according to the mutuall provocations and Declarations of Parliament put forth to engage us in bloud, and for ought wee yett find to entangle us in stronger chains, and to clapp upon our necks heavier yoakes or servitude.

9. Permitt not the Army to be long delayed, or tampered with too much. least Resolution languish and courage grow cold.

10. Persuade the Generall Officers not to depart from the Army untill these stormes be overblowne, the Subiects libertie confirmed, the Kingdome settled, delinquents detected and punished, the Souldiers and Sufferers satisfied and rewarded; in all which respects their conduct was never of more consequence, nor their interest in

the Army more usefull, the present Imployment being most important, tending to the consummation of all our cares, and the good concluding by the Establishment (in peace and truth) of the worke of the whole Warre.

11. That according to the premisses wee may bee speedily and respectively performed with, after which the Army may be reduced and [to ?] such a number of Horsemen as is not inconsistant with the Kingdomes safety; the rest, being justly dealt with in point of due and deserved pay, with honourable rewards for their severall services, may be disbanded, after an Act of Indempnity be made, and satisfaction be given as aforesaid not only to this Army, but to all the well-affected souldiers and subjects throughout this Kingdome.

Letter from[a]

I pray you tell Lievtenant Generall Cromwell that all our freinds doe hope the Army will be well united by this meeting (Horse and Foote), and for this time lett them demaund nothing but what is relating to them as Souldiers. It is much wondred that my Lord Pembrock[b] should soe rayle against the Army at a Common Councell the other day that 4,000 Cavaleers were in it (it is noe time to disband us) the King and all his party did wholly rely upon the Army; and spoke to the Citty as if it had been true the Army had sent to the King[c] Be carefull to whome you speake, but doe what you can to unite the Officers to the Army in demaunding things just and honourable relateing to them as Souldiers; if wee fall [on too] softly I perceive wee shall loose by it.

London, May 5th, 1647.

[a] No name is given, but simply an unintelligible cypher. It is probably by the author of the previous paper.

[b] Rushworth vi., 476. With reference to Pembroke's statement about the number of cavaliers in Fairfax's army see *Memoirs of Sir P. Warwick*, p. 253.

[c] See the Tanner MSS. in the Bodleian Library, vol. lviii., f. 46.

Upon debate yesterday of the Citty Militia,[a] the Lord Mayor and Aldermen Addams had like to have been seized of; hee had better never been named hee came of with such disgrace.

Relation from Walden.

Your desire in yours (which I communicated to Mr. Sparrow and other freinds) was granted before you came. I never found the Officers more unanimous. I was this afternoone with Captaine Goffe, Captain Grigson, Mr. Butler, Lieutenant Lloyd,[b] and other officers, and their resolutions at present are to drawe upp something in writing to expresse the Reasons why they cannot engage for Ireland; as, that they will see things settled here in relation to their priviledges and liberties before they engage abroad; that they will rather suffer with the godly party heere than goe away and leave them to the mercy of their Adversaries, &c. Collonell Sheffeild's Regiment continue their Red Collours, and say they are England's Collours, and that they will not goe for Ireland. Some of the Foote about Cambridgshire give out that they will goe for Holdenby and fetch the king, which gives much offence and scandall. The inclosed was printed at Cambridge, and sent to the High Constable's to gett subscribed and then presented.[c]

Walden, 5 May, 1647.

Letter from London.

Heere is little of moment since your departure worth the note-

[a] On this debate see *Commons' Journals*, v., 161; Rushworth, vi., 472, 478.

[b] William Goffe, and George Gregson, captains in Colonel Harley's regiment, and Lieutenant Griffith Lloyd. Rushworth, vi., 471.

[c] A petition for the disbanding of the army purporting to come from the inhabitants of the Eastern Association.

ing, but the continued clamours of the Citty against the Army, and which are now more high and generall then ever, occasioned by a late[a] speach of the Earle of Pembrock's at the Common Councill in London Monday last, telling the Cittizens that did they knowe soe much as hee, coming from the Fountaine's head of the Army, they would not scruple the lending of the 200,000li., to be ridd of the Army and to have them disbanded, for that all the hopes (hee told them) of the King and malignant party depended upon that Army, and that more he said they had sent to the King, delivered him a Petition and had received an answeare of it, and that all this put together hee conceived it were high time they were disbanded. This and more was spoken and which hath raised such a clamour in the City will not easily be taken off. This businesse truly I conceive concernes the Army in a high manner to consider of, both for vindication and reparation. The honest Petition of the well-affected Cittizens was on Tuesday last turned out of the House of Commons, with this answeare, that they approved not of the Petition nor manner of the representation.[b] Noe grievances are to be represented to the House, you may perceive, though in a way of Petition, but what they shall approve off. Alasse! poor England! when will be a remedy for thy malladies? or when will thy Egiptian Bondage end? Our good God sett us free in Jesus Christ, and make us denisons not of an earthly but of a heavenly habbition, for there is noe peace to be expected amongst the sonnes of men. The House of Commons on Wednesday called for the Ordinance for conferring the 2,000li. per annum on Lievtenant Generall Cromwell, which was read and committed; they likewise ordered the ordinance for the Generall's 5,000li. to be read on Tuesday next.[c]

London: May 6th, 1647.

[a] May 3.

[b] Rushworth, vi., 478; *Commons' Journals*, May 4, v., 162.

[c] *Commons' Journals*, v., 167.

[*A Letter from London.*]

Sir,

The rumour of the Armies holding intelligence with the King spreads a pace in the Kingdome, nay as farr as France, as lettres Thursday testifie, and it gives some cause to suspect that report was first framed there. It's talked of in the Citty further, [that] now your Army beginne to keepe strict guards and fortifie the head Quarters, nay say some further Major Generall Skippon will be deteyned untill the Army be satisfied in their demaunds; theis are London stories, and another I would be satisfied in, that a part of your Army should have been surprized by the Trayned Bands of Essex.

Sir,

On Thursday Sir John Sidley of Kent was three times called to the Barre in the House of Commons about Colonell Kenrick's Indictment mentioned in the Occurrances, for taking away of Horses &c. And upon full debate, though Mr. Hollis and Sir William Waller pleaded hard on his behalfe, hee was voted to be put out of Commission of Justice of Peace, out of the Militia, and made uncapable of bearing office in State and Comonwealth.[a]

[*Narrative of the Proceedings of Skippon and the Commissioners at Saffron Walden, May* 6, 7, 1647 [b]].

Yesterday[c] many of the Officers of the Army came to this Towne, but by reason that few of the officers of Horse came, the meeting

[a] Rushworth, vi., 479; *Commons' Journals*, v., 163-4, May 6, 1647. Sir John Sedley is the person meant.

[b] Rushworth, vi., 480.

[c] Friday, May 7. The Commissioners give an account of their first meeting in a letter to Lenthal, dated May 8. Cary, *Memorials*, i. 207.

was deferr'd till this day. The examination was yesterday taken of Lievtennant Wheeler a Lievtennant in Colonell Hammond's Regiment, to this effect: that being the other day at Royston the Postmaster there shewed him the Coppy of a Paper which was given him the day before by one Mr. Seely, who tooke post for the North there and gave himselfe out to be the Duke of Buckingham's Chaplaine; the paper was the same verbatim with that which goes abroad concerning the Army and his Majestie, which (it seemes) the Earle of Pembrooke declared to be true. The Postmaster further said that the Chaplaine told him that hee needed not to feare the truth of it, for that Sir William Armin had a Copie of it at Huntington, and yesterday Sir William sent a Copie of it to the Lievtennant Generall. The Officers, being acquainted with this designe and the Earle of Pembrook's relation are very sencible of the dishonour of the Army therein, and will desire repairation, as will appeare by the inclosed, which yesterday was resolved upon to have been offered to the Major Generall and the rest; but by reason it was apprehended the Officers could not give their sence without the Souldiers, it was not mentioned at all, therefore I was charged not to communicate it to any, and soe I have sent it in short hand for your owne use.

This day the Officers mett in the Church, not above 30 Officers of Horse and about 150 of Foote. The Feild Marshall Generall first made a Narration of the occasion of their comming downe to quiet the distempers of the army, that they should make it appeare that they were faithfull hearted for the publique good, that it would be conscience, justice, reason, and faithfullnesse in them that were Commanders to contribute their utmost endeavours for the alleying of all distempers. After the ending of this Speach the votes of the House were read, and Copies of them given to the severall Officers of each Regiment there present to be communicated to their Regiments Upon this, the Commissioners (for soe I may call them) withdrawing, the Major Generall returned and expressed himselfe concerninge the service of Ireland, how just and necessary the worke was, and how that service was altogether unthought of or unsought for by him ; I shall at present give you what he said in this particular at large, and leave the full accompt of the rest till the next: his words were,

Gentlemen,

I shall now desire you to heare mee a few words in relation to the bussinesse of Ireland ; I believe it is not unknowne or unapprehended by your selves how just, and honourable, how necessary that worke is. Altogether unthought of, unsought for, it hath pleased God to call mee to be imployed there if he please, a service truly that my exceeding unfittnesse for made mee exceeding unwilling to (to speake in relation to myselfe, for concerning the service you have heard what I have exprest). If I should have been excused, as I did most humbly and earnestly desire (I speake still in relation to my selfe), I would rather have been content to have laid downe all my other Imployments at the Parliament's foote, by their command, then to have undertaken this, for which I am soe unfitt. It is not a title, or preferment, or any selfe advantage that moves mee in this at all, but singly this, which I desire you to lay to heart, that it should not be said such a man was the delayer, was the obstructour, or the prejudicer of such a service singly. This consideration made mee in conscience to God to undertake that worke, with this expression, though it shall please God I perish in the undertaking of it, God's will be done. It was said on all hands, as I have many times heard, that if I would engage, a considerable parte of the Army, Officers, and Souldiers would engage ; if I did not engage they would not engage. Truly, as farr as still relates to myself, I have a great deale of reason to looke upon this as a testimony of love and respect from the Army. Now since that obstruction is taken away be pleased to take notice of it, and if my engagement may be any furtherance to the bussinesse I pray lett it appeare; and accordingly you may please to make knowne to your severall Regiments that, for those reasons I have partly mentioned, I was exceedingly desireious to decline it, upon that single consideration I was moved to entertaine it, that if my going may be any furtherance (God in mercy goe with us), I should improve it to the furtherance of that service. I thought good to communicate [this] to you; though it was not in our commission, yet it was not without advice and consent of those Gentlemen.

To this Colonell Hammond replied,[a] that at the meeting of the late Commissioners at Walden there was something offered by him in relation to himselfe and many officers of the Army, that they had that knowledge of the Major Generall's great honour, gallantry, and honestie, that they should as freely goe with him as any, except the Generall and Lieutennant Generall; not that his going would be an occasion of drawing the Army; and that if the Commissisoners or others had given him information otherwise, they have not done that which is right.

To this the Major Generall thus exprest himselfe: You will be pleased iudiciously, Christianly, seasonably, cordially, dilligently, and faithfully to take into consideration all those things I have propounded to you, and againe I beseech you, as men of integritie and honesty, improve your utmost interest for the service of the Parliament and of Ireland. Then Colonell Butler[b] desired to be satisfied concerning the considerable part of Arreares, whether the Parliament would doe any thing more then they had already voted vizt. 6 weekes pay, in regard the Souldiers would be desireous to knowe of them. The Commissioners replyed that they could not assure any further satisfaction, and that it did not lye in their powers to interperett the votes of the Parliament. Then some Officers desired to knowe the meaning of the House concerning distempers. To this the Commissioners answeared, that the cheife occasion of their coming downe was upon the letter of the 8 Regiments of

[a] See Rushworth, vi., 458. Colonel Robert Hammond.

[b] Colonel John Butler.

Horse; yet the House had been informed of some other proceedings which they conceiv'd illegal and out of discontents, and they were to receive the distempers of the severall Regiments, and for such as could give an accompt that their Regiments were free from distempers, they doubted not but it would be acceptable to the Parliament and to them. After this there was some debate whether the Officers then present should deliver in any thing of what they apprehended was occassions of discontents, and resolved that till they had consulted with their Souldiers it would be but halfe worke, and therefore nothing of their greivances should be then offered; hereupon the Officers were appointed to their severall charges to take the accompts, and to meete the Commissioners at Walden to-morrow sennight; and in the meane time, if they should be provided to give a full accompt the Commissioners declared that they should stay here, unlesse they had a command to the contrary, and receive the same from such as should be prepared before that time. The Officers are generally very unanimous, and I believe what will be proposed will be much according to the sence of the inclosed.

At the meeting Captaine Clarke of Sir Hardresse Wallers Regiment presented the inclosed Petition to Major Generall Skippon, desireing it might be publicly read, for the satisfaction of the Officers present and cleareinge of himselfe and the rest; but in regard it concerned themselves only it was not thought fitt to be communicated.

Walden 7 May, 1647.

[For the whole proceedings at this meeting, it is in shorthand, in the bundle upon Mr. Wragges Lettre, May 6th 1647.][a]

[a] This note was probably written in 1662, when the letter was copied into the book from which it is now printed. Thomas Wragge was one of the two clerks to Rushworth, the Secretary of the Army. I take this letter to have been written to Rushworth by either William Clarke or Wragge, but probably by the former. Rushworth, as his letters in the *Fairfax Correspondence* seem to show, was in London most of the month, with Sir Thomas Fairfax.

[*Petition enclosed in the preceding Narrative*].

To the right honourable Major Generall Skippon, Lieutenant Generall Cromwell with the rest of the honourable Commissioners of Parliament at Saffron Walden.

Wee whose names are subscribed, being Officers in Colonell Sir Hardresse Waller's Regiment,

Humbly present,

That whereas wee with diverse other Officers are exprest in print and otherwise as ingagers of the present service of Ireland upon the termes lately proposed, contrary to our intentions and resolutions, wee having formerly declared that wee were not neither as yet are resolved for that service upon those propositions, wee cannot but with griefe and sadnesse of heart sencibly apprehend it to be a strange designe of some who through false reports have endeavoured to vaile the eyes of those in publique authority to the grosse abuse of Parliament and Kingdome, who by false informers are much deceived and the releife of Ireland obstructed and retarded through such apparant delusions; which likewise may possibly render us unfaithfull and dishonourable, if it shall be conceived wee have engaged and yet declyne the present imployment, which indeed was not by us undertaken.

All which wee humbly pray may be considered.

John Clarke, Capt.
Ralph Wilson, Lt.
John Trailkins, Lt. (Filkins?)
Nath Chase, Lt.
Edward Allen, Ens.[a]

Copie of the Letter from the Officers to the 8 *Regiments.*

Sir,

When wee were in London there were three Letters delivered

[a] The names appended are corrected from Rushworth, vi., 466.

(the one to the Generall, the other two to us, all of the same effect) in the name of the 8 Regiments of Horse, whereof yours is one; which importing matter of dangerous consequence were imparted to the House of Commons, wee desire you to use your best endeavours to enquire where they had their rise, and to bring with you when you come on Saturday next[a] the best accompt thereof you can, and soe wee rest

Your very assured freinds

PHILLIPP SKIPPON.
OLIVER CROMWELL.

Walden, May 9.

The 8 Regiments are

The Generall's Regiment of Horse.
Lieutennant Generall's.
Commissary Generall's.
Colonell Fleetwood's.
Colonell Okey's.
Colonell Butler's
Colonell Sheffeild's.
Colonell Rich's.

AT THE CONVENTION OF OFFICERS AT THE CHURCH IN SAFFRON WALDEN SATTURDAY MAY 15: 1647.

Severall Speeches of Major Generall Skippon and other Officers at the 2d meeting in Walden.

Major Generall Skippon.

Gentlemen, Fellow Souldiers, and Christian Freinds.

Wee are heere according to appointment at our last meeting in

[a] 15 May. The letter referred to is that mentioned on p. 21, note a, the letter read in the House of Commons on April 30.

this place, to receive from you an accompt how you have improved your vtmost endeavours with your severall Regiments and Companies, to make them sencible of the care of the Parliament for them expressed in those votes that you have received from our hands concerning indempnity, arreares, and auditing of your accompts; and also to receive an accompt from you how you finde the temper of your severall Regiments, and this is the bussinesse for which wee are mett together at this time; and wee hope [you] have soe Christian like, soe judiciously, soe impartially, soe faithfully discharged your duties, as wee shall receive a very good accompt from you in relation to these things.

Lievtenant Generall Cromwell

Then said, that what the Major Generall exprest was the sence of them all.

Colonel Whalley.[a]

Sir,

I thinke it is the souldiers desire and request that you would give them three or fower howres respite to consider together, that soe they may present you with the whole bussinesse, because they are not prepared to give you a satisfactory answere.

Souldier.

They are not all the greivances of the Souldiers; they desire soe much time before they returne that they may answere other greivances.

[a] Colonel Edward Whalley, a life of whom is given in Noble's *House of Cromwell*, ii., 143.

Heere upon the 4 Officers advised together, and then the Major Generall spake as followes.

Major Generall Skippon.

In answere to that which Colonell Whalley desired in the name of the rest of the Officers or you heere present, if you be not at this present prepared to give us such an accompt as has been exprest in that I said before, you may have some howres respite; and let it be done with as much convenient speede as may bee, that wee may the sooner knowe it, and the sooner in discharge of our duties doe that that becomes us to doe. If the souldiers have anything to present, lett them doe it by their Officers, and wee shall take what is presented unto us into consideration, and in all faithfull heartednesse I hope towards God and man discharge our duties. One thing of my selfe; I shall be bould to desire, and to advise, and to admonish, as I have done formerly, that you will soe represent and soe adjutate thinges as may become your Christian profession, and as may become sober minded men, as may become servants to the publick.

Major Alford.[a]

Sir,

In obedience to those commands that wee had from you concerning that which you were pleased to give us in command in relation to the severall regiments, I thinke most of the officers have made a returne of what they have from the Regiments in writinge; as in particular to those two things you were pleased to speake of concerning indempnity and arreares, I have brought from my Colonell's Regiment an accompt in writeing. There are some other greivances also which lye upon the Regiment, which I have delivered to my Colonell and others I mett last night for that purpose.

[a] Major John Alford, of Colonel Rich's regiment, one of the subscribers of the engagement of March 22

Colonel Sheffeild,[a]

That hee did not knowe by what authoritie the Officers mett. In obedience to your command, I have brought in the returne from my Regiment which I find to bee their greivance which with others I I may bring in.

Lieutenant Colonell Jackson.[a]

My condition is the same.

(*The 4 Officers advised together.*)

Collonell Lambert.[b]

Give mee leave to speake something to what hath been already offerr'd.

Sir,

According to the directions which with the rest of the Commissioners were pleased to give the Officers of the Army att the last convention of them here, there hath been in several Regiments a perfect performance of what you then commanded; in the first place a faithfull publishing and makeing knowne those votes of the Parliament.

To the 2d part, which was to make a further search into the supposed distempers of the Army, they have made a dilligent inquiry thereinto, and have brought a returne thereof from the severall Regiments. They have likewise proceeded further into it, and have desired severall Gentlemen of this army, that they would be pleased to receive them, and come and collect out of them what are common, universall, generall to the whole Army, and as speedily as could be drawe them upp and represent them to yourselves. These were desired by the officers of the army and not sought by themselves; and I

[a] Thomas Sheffield, Colonel of a regiment of horse, and Thomas Jackson, Lieutenant-Colonel of Fairfax's foot regiment.

[b] John Lambert, succeeded in 1646 to the command of the regiment in the New Model which was originally Colonel Edward Mountague's.

thinke there is not a Regiment here that hath not made this their suite, and that whatsoever might relate to any one particular Regiment might be left out, and the generall greivances of the whole army represented. And this truly, as yet there hath not been time and opportunity to doe it, and it is their desire that you will be pleased to lett them have time till Monday morning for the perfecting of it.

Collonell Sheffeild.

Whereas Colonell Lambert saith, that every Regiment hath made a returne of their proceedings, for my part I knowe nothing of it; and I conceive I, beinge Colonell of a Regiment, may knowe of it, as well as a trooper or an inferiour officer.

Major Fincher.[a]

Wee were to take an accompt from our Regiment, and wee were to returne the answeare to you, as wee conceive, and not to any other.

Collonell Lambert.

This way that is propounded and hath been taken is by the unanimous consent of all, both officers and souldiers, and if you take any other way then this wee cannot helpe your differring from it.

Sir,

There is nothing desired but that these things[b] might bee represented to the Feild Marshall and the rest of the commissioners here; if you will doe otherwise you may take your course. It was agreed by those that were present of the officers.

[a] Richard Fincher, before referred to, p. 1, was Major of Sheffield's regiment.

[b] These particular petitions of the separate regiments may be found amongst the Clarke MSS., vol. xli., ff. 105-127.

Wee did suppose that the meeting of those Gentlemen to whome wee did deliver upp the greivances had been by order of the Commissioners.

Captain Rainborrowe.[a]

The command was generall to give a retorne, and not only to a particular.

I was at the Regiment when the Randezvouz was, and I was acquainted as well as the Colonell, though the Colonell be pleased to give the sence of the Regiment. They did give me their sence in writing, that there may bee noe mistake att all in the tender of their just greivances.

Colonell Sheffeild.

I doe not deny that; if you have delivered it, with all my heart, lett them make the best use of it they can: I only speake it as my sence.

Collonell Lambert.

I thinke it will be found when all is done that wee have not neglected our duties, but that wee have used all our interests to pacifie what was not faire in the army. When wee have done and presented what are the common grievances of the army to you, I make noe question but you will finde what wee say doth not proceede singly from us, but from the body of the army, and will appeare themselves what they are to yourselves and the world.

Major Generall Skippon.

Freinds,

In answeare to what Colonell Sheffeild hath said I shall now only say thus much; if Colonell Sheffeild or any other officer can give

[a] William Rainborowe, of Colonel Sheffield's regiment, not the more celebrated Colonel Thomas Rainborowe. See *Lords' Journals*, ix., 195.

in the state of their Regiment, and an accompt of their endeavours according to what hath been before desired, wee shall now presently receive it; if any other particular officer hath any thinge, upon just ground and in sober manner, to make knowne concerning that Regiment, wee shall be willing to receive it.

I thinke it not amisse to lett you knowe how precious time is with us, how much an accompt is expected from us; and therefore, though wee are loath to deny soe reasonable a request of giveing further time, a great part of you it seemes not being soe fully prepared to give us in an accompt of those things that wee have exprest, to morrowe by 5 of the clock in the afternoone, if God will, wee shall meet you here againe; because wee would willingly dispose and order our bussinesse soe as wee might loose as little time as wee could. And I thinke in relation to those things that wee are sent especially hither about to communicate to you the votes of the House of Commons and the sence of the Parliament, in that as it appeares since, and I shall tell you by and by, the resolution of the Parliament, soe farre as yet it appeares to us, and that you might fully knowe what wee can tell you to give you all the satisfaction that may be, I have received a letter even now which is from a very good hand, the Earle of Manchester that sitts in the chaire of the Comittee at Derby House, who is also Speaker of the House of Peeres, which doth assure mee that the Act of Indempnity is past large and full.[a]

(*The Letter read.*)

"Sir,

I have thought fitt to give you this accompt: that this day the House of Commons have passed an Act for Indempnitie large and full. They have like wise granted a fortnight's pay to those that

[a] On the question whether this ordinance was sufficient to secure the army from danger see the opinion drawn up by Judge Jenkins, May 24, 1647, and published as a pamphlet, entitled *The Armies Indemnity*. He decides that it was not sufficient.

shall be disbanded, and a fortnight's advance more to those that goe for Ireland."

This is from the Speaker of the House of Peeres pro tempore, the Earle of Manchester.[a]

And truly, Gentlemen, though I did not in that particular advise with those gentlemen about it, yet I did by their advice and consent make knowne somethinge concerning Ireland the last day, of which I heare nothing since; I hope it will be soe considered of as a service not to be forgotten, not to be neglected, not to be hindred; and that I shall referre, as I did all the rest, to your impartiall, judicious, and faithfull consideration.

Lievtenant Goodhand.[b]

If it please your Honours, I am to certifie to your Honours concerning the condition of the Life guard.

Major Generall Skippon.

I pray you lett us see our buissnesse, and see it before us, and then wee shall doe as honest men, and I hope you will behave your selves soe too, and I can expect noe other from you.

Trooper.

There's a returne from our Regiment, I humbly desire it may be read.

Collonell Sheffeild,

This is a meeting for officers, and if the troopers could come themselves, it had been needlesse for us to goe downe, and bring returnes of the sence of the Regiment.

[a] Rushworth, vi., 485, 489. *Commons' Journals*, v., 174, 181; *Lords' Journals*, ix., 192, 201. Manchester's letter must have been dated May 14.

[b] Andrew Goodhand of the Lifeguard.

Major-General Skippon,

It is more seasonable for us to receive all together, for I hope it is all our mindes not to hinder but further the bussinesse all wee can.

Lievtenant Goodhand.

Wee have call'd them together, and find them not in any distemper, and for indempnitie and arreares they returne thankes to the Parliament, and that they will lay downe their armes at the Parliaments command; soe much is presented for satisfaction.

There is a paper to satisfie more fully under Captaine Hall's hand.[a]

Captain Farmer.[b]

In answeare to those two for indempnity and arreares, there is the reply of my Colonell's Regiment.

Collonell Okey.

I heard my name mentioned for the Regiment; those papers which these gentlemen have delivered in are only for those troopers which are engaged for Ireland, and itt is not the accompt of the whole Regiment.

Captain Farmer.

Itt is the sence of those troopes that have engaged for Ireland.

Colonel Lambert.

If it please you, Sir, I shall offer thus much to you.

[a] Captain Henry Hall succeeded Charles Doyley as Captain of the Lifeguard. Sprigge, ed. 1854, p. 332; Rushworth, vi., 551.

[b] John Farmer, captain in the regiment of dragoons commanded by Colonel John Okey.

Major General Skippon.

Captain Farmer, everything shall be taken into consideration as farre as wee are able, and does concerne us to doe, in answeare to the trust reposed in us, when as wee see our bussinesse before us.

Collonell Lambert.

If it please you to heare a word or two concerning the bussinesse before you. It may be Colonel Sheffeild and some of those worthy gentlemen that are with him are unsatisfied with our proceedings, thinking wee only have carried on this bussinesse, and not acquainted them with what was done. I shall therefore desire to offer the reason of our soe doing.

One speciall reason was, because himselfe and many of them have already engaged for Ireland, and being soe they are not like to have those influences fall upon them as those in England; and in regard it did not soe especially concerne them, wee thought them not soe proper to them to be acquainted with itt.

Another was, because wee found the greatest grievance of the army is the rejecting the late petition and representation that was intended to be presented to the Parliament by the mediation of the Generall. That him selfe and many of the rest of the worthy gentlemen did declare as noe grievance at all, and soe did refuse to joyne in it; and therefore wee could not represent that as a grievance which they did never assent unto.

This I speake to take off hard thoughts concerning us; and whereas you were pleased to desire a particular accompt to be drawne out of those returnes that are brought in by way of returne from the severall Regiments, wee must needs say wee knowe of severall papers that are brought in by way of returne from the severall Regiments; yet notwithstanding there was this caution with it, that if any one particular Regiment did represent anything particularly, which they presented as their owne desire, and not as the desire of the whole army, it was desired that they might not be received, because it does not come as the desire of the whole army; and therefore, if wee should give them in, wee should be a little unfaithfull to that trust which was imposed in us, for wee must present some single things as the sence of the army; and therefore wee desire that you will give us as large a time as you can for the examining and compareing of the severall returnes together; and then wee shall represent them to you altogether, as the generall and universall greivance of the army, from as many as have made application to us; which wee thinke is the whole army, or very neere itt.

Colonell Sheffield.

I would very gladly knowe by what authority they have done this.

Colonel Lambert.

Sir,

If you desire to knowe by what authoritie wee have done this, if it shall be demaunded authoritatively I doubt not but there will be given a satisfactory answeare; and truly, Sir, all that I offer'd was to noe other end but to take off those reflections which you may lay upon us, when singly wee have done nothing but that which concernes the bussinesse in hand.

Major General Skippon.

To that end you have given in particular papers.

Colonel Hewson.[a]

Many regiments of the Army in bringing in their grievances have desired some gentlemen here that they will collect them into one perticular summe, and present them to you; the desire of those that are sent over was to avoid confusion; in regard they could not

[a] John Hewson had succeeded to the command of Colonel Pickering's regiment of foot on the latter's death in December, 1645. Sprigge, pp. 167, 329.

be represented by many without inconveniencies, it was thought fitt to appoint some gentlemen as a committee to put things into a forme for us, and it was done by the generall consent of the officers of the severall regiments.

Major General Skippon.

I doe not know at present, Gentlemen, what wee can say unto you more, but to desire and perswade you to deale as effectually as you can to make manifest yourselves Christian and faithfull men, to proceede soe as there may be noe just exception taken at the manner of your proceeding as well as of the matter. To morrowe at 5 of the clock in the afternoone, if God will, wee shall be here againe, and receive those things in relation to the particulars that wee have diverse times prest you about, and shall receive any papers from any other that they shall thinke fitt to deliver in to us, and I thinke that may give satisfaction to all. If this be your sence, pray you speake.

The other three officers and Members of Parliament declared their assent.

Lettre from the Troopers in Sir Robert Pies Regiment.

Gentlemen and Fellow Souldiers,

Wee cannot but ecchoe the rebounds of our constant desires to the first petition, and by reason of the declaration against that, the resolution of all the souldiers in our regiment is to joyne in the letter to his Excellencie, as freely in their subscriptions (and every other way) as they at first did to the petition. It is our unhappinesse that wee are soe farre distant in quarters from the 8 regiments (our troopes being also apart from the other), by reason whereof timely notice cannot be given us to aggitate according to our reall intentions, which are to adde our selves to them intirely as one man, Colonel Graves regiment (excepting some officers) being of the same resolution, and much discontented they had not true information of the candor of that first petition. The subscriptions of our regiment (both to the first petition and last letter to the Generall) are in readynesse to be delivered according to directions, though their's cannot be expected in respect of their officers obstructions. Thus, blessing God for exciting such instruments as you, wee waite all opportunities for the provocation of justice and judgment, that they may runn downe like a mighty current, which is the earnest desire of all.

Your assured faithfull friends and servants
T. I. O. B. &c.

May 13th 1647.

The bearer hereof wee have intrusted for what you shall thinke fittinge herein, hee is to stay at the head quarters.

Address. For our honoured freinds Captain Gladman, Captain Berry, Captain Lawrence, Mr. R. or any of them at the head quarters, these[a]

HEADS OF PROCEEDINGS IN WALDEN CHURCH. SUNDAY, 16 MAY, 1647.[b]

(The Votes of Parliament read.)

Major General Skippon.

. . . . . In those votes of the Army, and what sincere industrious and faithfull endeavours you have used to make them sencible thereof, and what distempers you finde in your severall Regiments, Troopes or Companies, that wee might knowe how you have in these particulars discharged your duties as conscientious Christians in the sight of God, and as men faithfull and obedient to the Parliament

[a] Captains John Gladman, James Berry, and Adam Lawrence, all three of Fairfax's regiment of horse. A life of Berry is given in the *Dictionary of National Biography*. Mr. R. I take to be John Rushworth. The letter mentioned is that of the eight regiments. The regiments of Pye and Graves were quartered at Holdenby.

[b] See on this meeting the letter of the Commissioners. Cary, i., 214. Rushworth, vi., 485, 487. Another version of this speech of Skippon's is printed by Rushworth, and dated 15 May.

of England. I am further to desire you, upon a motion made againe and againe at two former meetings, by my selfe in relation to the service of Ireland, that you will give us an accompt how you find your severall regiments disposed to that service. The justnesse, the honourablenesse, and the necessitie of which service cannot be unknowne to you. I desire to knowe and am persuaded it is the mind of these other Gentlemen that are sent downe, not under the name of Commissioners, but as Parliament men and Members of this Army to our severall charges in the Army, that you would in these particulars give us such satisfaction as I hope you can or shall make appeare to us, to the Parliament, and to all that shall have the heareing of our proceedings, that you have faithfully discharged your duty, as wee have desired, and shall endeavour to doe to the Parliament and for the service of the whole Kingdome. I pray that there may be an orderly proceeding amongst you in what you have to doe or say, if any man desire to speake lett him be heard without interruption. Lett all things be done discreetly, fairely, and orderly. I hope in the end of all wee shall finde that there is nothing aimed at on all hands, but that which tends to the reall service of the Parliament and publique good.

Lievtenant Generall Cromwell.

Although [*blank*]

Collonel Whalley.

The officers according to your commands have repaired to their severall regiments, and have served you with all faithfulnesse.

They have left [*blank*] but their actions sufficiently declares that to you, that they have done the Parliament reall and good service. They have conveen'd heere at the head quarters according to your command, mett together and declared their greivances in writing, which greivances either are the greivances of all or the greatest part of the Army.

Major General Skippon.

Of the great and faithfull services of this Army there cannot but be an ingenuous acknowledgment from our enemies.

Upon the endeavours of this Army—soe great successes to the great benefitt of the whole Kingdome—lett not any words I speake be misunderstood—That which I especially propounded, which you heare the rest of these worthy Gentlemen were pleased to approve as their sence, was that you would please as well to give us an accompt of your proceedings with your severall regiments in relation to make them sencible of the care of the Parliament for their indempnitie, for part of their arreares at present, and to have their accompts audited . . . . . and what distempers . . . . .

And truly Sir, except you please to give us that accompt, wee in that particular cannot but be unsatisfied, nor cannot tell what to say in it untill you expresse your selves concerning it; and therefore I pray that wee may receive such an accompt from you. In that wee doe . . . . .

Collonell.[a]

May it please your Honours I desire one word at the meeting. Before this all our names in our severall regiments were ready, if you please [to ask] the officers to give an accompt thereof. I have in writing under my owne and my Major's [hands] to testifie what returne it made to us, I believe according to trust, and I hope that will answeare your expectations; forI doe not really [merely?] speake to the matter of distemper that is supposed to be amongst us, but I likewise answeare to the Irish bussinesse.

Major General Skippon.

If you have any thing to offer . . . . .

Officer.[a]

Sir, As in relation to what concernes the Regiment . . . . .

[a] These two officers seem to be Lieutenant Colonel Jackson and Major Gooday of Fairfax's regiment, two of those who had engaged to serve in Ireland.

Commissary General Ireton.

Major, doe you deliver that?

Officer.

I doe deliver that as the sence of the Regiment, which was delivered to mee in the feild in writeing.

Com. Gen. Ireton.

That which was delivered I thinke I have seene, and it was not done . . . .

Maj. Gen. Skippon.

Gentlemen, I doe desire it againe and againe, and I thinke it is all our desires, that you will heare one another with sobrietie.

Captain White.[a]

Please your Honours to heare this concerning the Generall's Regiment of Foote: first, he speakes of carrying in the report as under his hand, for my[self] I doe not understand itt . . . to him and soe to our selves, if it had been soe then our meeting had been in vaine . . . .

Therefore to that end wee did conveene together, some of us agreeing with the rest of the officers, ... which Colonell Whalley hath delivered in, soe to that wee sett our hands, and it is the minde of the officers if not private souldiers.

Colonel Lambert.

Please you to lett us knowe, whether it is your desire that wee should give you a particular accompt of the overtures in the Regiments?

[a] Francis White of Fairfax's foot regiment, on whom see Rushworth, viii., 943, and his own pamphlet, viz. *The Copies of Several Letters presented to the Lord General Fairfax and Lieut-General Cromwell*, by Francis White, 1649.

If you extend to every particular, it may bee there may be something of weakenesse or ignorance.

I thinke Colonell Whalley hath already presented itt to you [the sense] if not [of all of] a great part of the Army.

Here the Officers generally cried All, All.

Maj. Gen. Skippon.

Gentlemen, if it please you, these acclamations might be forborne; for wee are desireous to heare every one speake, and according to our trust to deale impartially. Butt still, if it seeme good to you to lett us knowe whatt course you have taken in the particulars that I mentioned to you—your papers of those things which you call greivances—wee desire to knowe the distempers that you could observe to be in your severall regiments, or under your severall commands. Wee did also desire that you would (as I doubt not but you have done) contribute your utmost endeavours for the qualifying them. These papers we shall read, God willing; but, in order to our proceedings, I shall desire that you will give some such satisfaction that wee may knowe how to consider of things amongst our selves as befitts our imployments [that] wee may know what to say concerning them. You have communicated those votes to your severall regiments, you have endeavoured to lett them see the care of the Parliament for them in these particular votes. You have endeavoured to enquire out the distempers, you have putt to your helping hands what you could to pay [allay?] them. This will be a very proper way: I thinke with submission, I shall desire these Gentlemen to lett you know their sences.

Colonel Lambert.

I thinke wee shall all use our endeavours to the peaceable continuance of the Army for those things that I have mentioned before. I say there is something of weakenesse of which wee must desire the best construction of your selfe and the commissioners—if you decline that name—and the rest of the Members of the House. Wee dare clearely and fully satisfie you in the whole progresse, but I desire itt may not be soe publique as now it is.

Major Disbrow.[a]

If it please your Honours I shall make a relation of what I did, which is according to the acting of most officers heere.

According to your commands I repaired to the Regiment upon Monday last. I went from one division to another. I told them what you were pleased to represent unto us, and that was an apprehension of some . . . . . To that end I was commanded now to come to them to represent the Parliament's votes to them, which I read to each division, first to one, and then the other.

They told mee there was noe unquiettnesse amongst them . . . . . But withall told mee that there were diverse things which lay upon them as Greivances . . . . . which were their Greivances, I should represent them to you, and I must returne an accompt of what accompt I had from them; upon which they did . . . . . which for my part I did disallowe of, I told them soe to their faces . . . . . Allowe of the things I argued the case . . . . . and in the conclusion . . . . . prejudiciall and evill, and at last they did come to present mee with their Greivances. I did then beleive, and doe still, that they are very sober things, and therefore it is not only that which I have presented and which is said to be the sence of the Army, but itt is that which lies both upon souldiers and officers that wee have now represented to you . . . . . not mutinously intended and what is fitt to be answered and satisfied; and soe farre as I understand of the condition of the army, and those officers that I have spoke withall, they desire to be answered in some

[a] John Disbrowe (or Desborough), Major of Fairfax's regiment of horse.

particular things, and those particular things are there represented to you.

Collonel Hammond.[a]

I found my Regiment very quiett, only some Greivances and troubles were talkt of.

Collonel Whalley.

As Major Disbrough hath done for the Generall's Regiment soe I have the like accompt to give of mine. I find that both my officers and souldiers are not transported or carryed away by passion. Reason sways them; and truly reason is so prevalent with them, in these humble desires that they make in the way of greivances to Parliament, as I am confident they will deny themselves in every thing, if there may be as reasonable a reason given why they may not goe on.

Colonel Hewson.

Your Honour was pleased to communicate to us for to propound to our souldiers the bussinesse of Ireland, and to read unto them these votes, according as you were pleased now to expresse them. Wee have done it with faithfulnesse. We returned to our regiments. For my part I can give to your Honour this accompt: I read to them the votes [to] lett them knowe what care the Parliament had taken for them, their intention for indempnity and [for] a considerable summe for their arreares. I lett them knowe that your Honour was to goe for Ireland and to accept of that imployment. Truly I found them in noe distemper, but very quiett; only I find that there was some greivances lay upon them, something did trouble them. I mov'd about the Irish affaire; they seem'd to be utterly unwilling for to stirre in that untill such time as they had some satisfaction.

[a] Colonel Robert Hammond.

Major Cowell,[a]

Seing you expect an accompt from every regiment in particular I am able to give it for the Generall's Regiment of foote; I drew them upp on . . . . . last in two bodies, and for the returne of itt, itt is in those papers. This method they tooke: they desired some time to present their greivances unto us and by us unto your Honours; and being drawne into particular companies wee went from company to company. They had taken their resolutions. Wee demaunded of them if wee should rest confident that what those of every company should bring should be the sence of every particular company. They were brought to us at a rendezvous of the officers of every regiment, and upon our view there is our consent with itt. Wee made knowne unto them the grounds why they should goe, and of your present company and command over them, to try if that would drawe them. I am sorry wee can make noe other report, wee received nothing but a negative voice.

Lievtenant Collonel Read.[b]

According to your command I repaired to the Regiment and according to what Major Cowell hath declared . . . . . every particular company gathered together [brought] in the sence of itt.

Major.[c]

Concerning Collonell Fleetwood's I can give your Honour some accompt of that. According to your Honour's command I drew Collonell Fleetwood's Regiment to a Randezvous, and I read the votes which your Honour sent to be communicated to every troope . . . . . only this, they did say they had something to

[a] William Cowell of Colonel Harley's regiment, died a colonel in 1648. See Carlyle's *Cromwell*, letter lxix.

[b] Lieutenant-Colonel Thomas Reade of Colonel Herbert's regiment. Rushworth, vi., 466, 471.

[c] Major Thomas Harrison, the regicide.

deliver to mee, which they gave mee, and the greivances wee did returne in yesterday, your Honour received them.

Major Cowell.

Truly this I can say noe more, I found noe distemper nor any shaddowe of distemper amongst them.

Captain White.

An't please your your Honours, I gave in the paper of the particular greivances to my Lievtennant Collonell, wherein they gave in their desires; my Lievtennant Collonell left out some and sett downe others.

Lievtennant Collonel Jackson.

An't please your Honours, I thinke Captaine White doth forgett himselfe; I was willing to present their greivances; I did desire to knowe their greivances; I should be willing to receive them, or otherwise to heare them.

Captain White.

I shall speake only to the manner of proceeding; my Lievtennant Collonell hath soe endeavoured to obstruct that hee sent for mee, and questioned mee as high as my life, and committed mee to the Marshall, and afterwards brought mee to a heareing before the Major Generall; I pressed him either to enlarge mee or else to committ me, upon which the Major Generall did release mee; and soe lying under that same calumny I did seeke to vindicate my selfe from any man's person, to desire that the Major Generall would vouchsafe to be President of a Councill of Warre that the difference betweene my Lievtennant Collonell and I may be determined.

Commissary Ireton.

For the differences that are amongst them in relation to the buissenesse that you are now about, since they have severally spoken, it were necessary to take into consideration in regard of the difference of itt, and appoint them to attend you for itt.

Captain Leigh.[a]

I have only a word in relation to that Regiment. I was present in the field when the difference hapned, and did see what Captaine White did, and the truth is my sence is the same . . . . . willinge to concurre together in that way ; but when Captain White did declare his greivances they were not accepted of, neither did hee approve of those greivances, but did offer it to joyne with the rest.

Captain Audley.[b]

I shall speake something in referrence to that which Commissary Ireton pleased to order betweene officer and officer ; I only perceive there is some differences in your accompt ; your Lievtennant Collonell gives one, and you another, and for that the Major Generall[c] will take care of these privately without interruption.

Captain White.

Captain Audley, If it shall please my Lievtennant Colonell to present the greivances which his owne company hath there will be compleatly 8 companies, and he may take memorandum[d] then of this.

Major Sedascue.

May it please your Honour,

I have caused those votes and propositions that were sent to be read at the head of every troope in the regiment. Those

[a] William Leigh of Fairfax's regiment of foot.

[b] Lewis Audley of the same regiment. See on Audley, Burton's *Diary*, iii., 15, 37-45, 86.

[c] Major of Ireton's regiment of horse.

[d] MS. M[dum].

Parliament propositions being read I received from the severall troopes a paper, wherein they have exprest their severall Greivances they have sent hither. I have according to the consent of all the officers delivered them to Colonell Whalley, and the rest of the men who are to present it to your Honour.

Major Huntington.[a]

According to your commands I sent out, but they could not soe soone come to them as to others, they being soe farre distant. I read the orders which the Parliament were pleased to give for the arreares, and for the auditing of accompts, and for indempnitie, and after that I desired they would make knowne their greivances, that I might present them to your Honours; and upon this they chose 4 out of each troope to drawe upp their greivances, which wee have presented unto the gentlemen there, and are now putt with the rest. As for the bussinesse of Ireland, they desired their just desires might bee answered, before they resolved of that, and that the greivances which they had might be represented to them.

Lievtennant Collonel Smith.[b]

May it please your Honours,

In obedience to your commands I repaired unto Sir Hardresse Waller's Regiment, and randezvouz'd them as on Monday, and I read at the head of the regiment those votes which I received from your Honour. For distempers, I find not much, but some amongst them, and that was that there were some officers that had engaged for Ireland, and had declared that those that were not willing to goe now freely for Ireland should be forc'd to comply; which they find to be a great greivance and trouble, and they declared as the sence of the House to that purpose; other greivances I find none.

[a] Robert Huntington, Major of Cromwell's regiment of horse. On 8 April, 1647, the House of Commons voted that he should command Cromwell's regiment. *Commons' Journals*, v., 137.

[b] The Lieutenant-General of this regiment was Edward Salmon. *Rushworth*, vi., 466.

There was indeed some difference amongst some officers falling to some words, that had not I been present, might have been very inconvenient, and made very great mutinie in the regiment. Many greivances they did declare to mee which they had, which greivances they told mee they would draw upp, and they were delivered in with the substance of what is presented to your Honours.

Captaine Thomas.[a]

You were against the going for Ireland, that was the cause.

There was noe words of admonition, but that you your selfe did read the votes, more then these you would drawe upp the greivances, and drew upp an officer of each company to signe them for you. The Major comes after, and then cryes, 'Stand for your liberties and priviledges now and ever.'

Officer.[b]

An't please your Honour I am the man.

The word that was said was this; a corporall in Sir Hardresse Waller's regiment, a private souldier, comeing to knowe my advice, I said, 'I hope the souldiers may have their libertie.' The Lievtennant Colonell, heareing I did desire to knowe, lett him declare to the Lievtennant Colonell, whereupon th . . . . . in a mutinous manner struck mee for defending my owne innocency. This is that which I say to that which Captaine Thomas seemes to demaund.

Officer.

An't please your Honour my Lievtennant Collonell drewe the regiment to a randezvous. Captaine Thomas said as that wee were seditious, and that some had poysoned our souldiers, that wee were enemies to the peace of the Kingdome, which the souldiers desire to be vindicated in; and that though we were not willing to goe for Ireland, yett [wee should be forced to comply]. He used those words against us, which wee conceive tends much to the dishonour of the Army.

[a] Captain Daniel Thomas of Sir H. Waller's regiment.

[b] Major Thomas Smith.

Commissary Ireton.

If you please to hint to them that they may take the examination of what miscarriages have been.

Lievtennant Collonel Jackson.

May it please your Honours, I have one motion to make. If you please to give mee leave you shall have the bussinesse truly laid before you, which, as I suppose, itt is not yett.

Captain White.

For that paper which my Lievtennant Colonell speakes of that hee produced and hee desired us to signe, wee refused and drew upp one, which was signed in the same manner as it is exprest, with those hands of 7 companies of the regiment.

Captain Husbands.[a]

For that bussinesse that was even now spoken of, it does reflect not only on those officers, but upon the whole Army. Itt is of such an high nature that I thinke fitt hee may be secured in the meane time.

Collonel Sheffeild.

I doe not thinke but that any man hath a libertie to speake; 'tis true there are more officers of the one side then of the other.

Major General Skippon.

Freinds, I thinke itt is our desires that love and peace should be maintain'd amongst us, whether wee bee of the one way or other. I am sure it is our duty towards God in conscience, and towards one another as Christians; and truly I must needs ingeniously say, I am very sorrey to observe that there should be such a disagreement betweene you; the thing itselfe I hope cannot justly produce any

[a] Azariah Husbands, of Rich's regiment. "Hee," refers to Capt. Thomas.

such thing; and therefore it must be my advice to you that you would leave personall things, and apply your selfe to those things that wee are mett about; not but that there may be a convenient time and course taken to order these things.

That shall be my advice to you; and truly, as I said before, God knowes it is a very great pressure to my spiritt to heare and observe such clashings and jarrings amongst you; I am sure there can noe good come out of it, it is very likely noe good can come out of it.

And therefore I shall desire that you will leave these particular disagreements till another time.

Collonel Whalley.

An't please your Honours, itt was thought as a great burthen upon many heere present, those words which were spoken, yet wee did resolve not[a] to speake of itt, because wee would not trouble your Honours, though they are words not to speake of.

Collonel Okey.

According to your Honours commands I did declare to my Major that was here, and one Captaine Mercer that is with mee in Shropshire,[b] the votes that came downe with your Honour. By reason of the distance of place, which is 6 score miles where five troopes quarter, hee could not possibly returne the answere by this time; but 5 troopes that are quartered about Holdenby they were brought in yesterday by the Major.

Officer.

I could not be soe particular for my own part.

I knowe not who they were sent to; I heard they were sent.

[a] MS. "did not resolve."

[b] Major Nicholas Moore and Captain Charles Mercer of Okey's regiment of dragoons.

They were never communicated to the regiment, but soe farre as I perceive the condition is not any way distemperous but very quiett. Heere is my owne; I have delivered the sence of itt to the officers.

Commissary Ireton.

For Colonell Okey's regiment, if the votes be not communicated it is fitt some course should be taken for itt.

Major General Skippon.

Truly that is very well remembred of Commissary Ireton heere, I knowe not whether you tooke notice of itt.

Hitherto I knowe you have not had time to speake with your regiment about it more particularly, and to prevent distempers, but the bussinesse is of such concernment as wee cannot tell how to avoid itt, but pray that you will take especiall notice of itt; for I had it from a very good hand, that the House of Commons have passed an Act of Indempnity large and full, [two] moneths arreares to those that goe for Ireland; soe that you shall doe well to make all the advantages that you can to give satisfaction unto your severall officers and souldiers, and to discharge your duty in all faithfull obedience to the Parliament, and not to question the justice and honour of the Parliament in further proceeding to give you satisfaction I hope.

Major Scroope.[a]

May it please your Hononrs, I doe conceive and doe partly knowe that these votes have not been communicated to Collonell Graves' regiment, and therefore I doe not see how any just accompt had been given in the bussinesse; and if your Honours would please to

[a] Adrian Scroope, the regicide, Major of the regiment of horse of Colonel Richard Grevis, or Graves, which was at this time guarding the King at Holmby. Scroope afterwards succeeded to the command of that regiment.

direct what way wee may take to deliver in our accompt before the day appointed . . . . .

Captain Holcraft.[a]

Sir, I had the [votes] delivered to mee. I did carry them first to my Collonell, and by his command went to the regiment; but the regiment was not called to a randezvous by his command, but they are according to your approbation; likewise it being made an objection before wee went away whether that course might be taken, itt was communicated to severall troopes. To Captaine Flemming's troopes the votes were not sent. I am sure they were communicated to all but Captaine Flemming's[b] troope, and Captaine Barton's Quarter.Master received them.

Quarter Master.

I never received them.

Officer.

The Troope never heard of them.

I can assure you the troopes were not called together; that was left to the discretion of the officers.

[Captain Holcraft?]

They were in the same posture they ever have been, to those troopes they were communicated according to their sence.

Quarter Master.

It was only the sence of the officers.

Major General Skippon.

I shall speake only to this present bussinesse of Colonell Graves'

[a] Charles Holcroft of the same regiment, one of those officers who had signed the engagement of March 22, promising to serve in Ireland.

[b] Captain Fleming, of Graves's regiment, was adjutant-general of horse in the New Model, colonel in 1648, and killed in the war in Wales. Phillips, *Civil War in Wales*, i., 401.

Regiment. I thinke by what hath been said that the votes have been communicated to fower of the six troopes, and not to the rest.

But sure, Captaine Holcraft, I did desire you yesterday that some might goe to the other two troopes.

Captain Holcraft.

Sir, According to your command I communicated the votes to the troopes; if you please to peruse the papers, and then I am confident you will finde that to be the sence of that regiment to be delivered in fully.

Major-General Skippon.

Those that are brought in wee shall read.

Major Scroope.

That was all that I have to say because the Regiment was not called together.

Commissary Ireton.

You may remember that the coppie of the votes to the Regiment were delivered to Captaine Holcraft ; Captaine Holcraft and three more officers have made a returne, and I doe not remember what they did make . . . . . if it had not been done through want of time or otherwise . . . . . But, Sir, now I perceive by what Captaine Holcraft sayes that it was communicated to the troopes, all but Captain Flemming's, I desire that Captaine Holcraft may declare possitively, cleerely, and expressly: whether hee knows that they were all drawne together.

Captain Holcraft.

I knowe that my Collonell's Troope was drawne together, and that upon my conscience and honour I have given that which was their sence.

For my Major's Troope I understand that their troope was called together; for Captaine Flemming's Troope, his Lievtennant was in towne, and hee did not tell mee that his Troope was not called together till hee had signed what was delivered in there, for at my Major's desire wee were to drawe upp the sence of the Regiment; for my Lord Caulfeild's Troope it was drawne upp and the greivances given in according to the sence you have there; for Captaine Barton's Troope itt was drawne upp with the rest.

Captain Barton.[a]

I can affirme this not to be true, for all the Regiment was not call'd together, of severall troopes there were not halfe his troopes gathered together.

Collonel Rich.[b]

For the bussinesse of my Regiment you have had severall hints; the truth of itt is I was not there my selfe, and itt was for noe other end but because I was not well, and I had a particular dispensation from the Generall to be absent. My Major and all the Captaines of my Regiment are here in towne; they have both particularly by themselves, the Major joyntly from the whole Regiment, given mee a little accompt of those things of which you desired an accompt; and truly as to those votes that you laid your commands upon them to read to the Regiment in referrence to Arreares and Indempnitie, I find that of this Ordinance of Indempnitie they give us some hopes that wee shall be indempnified fully.

Truly as to arreares, that same considerable proportion which the votes does mention they tell mee that they doe not very well understand, unlesse it be that six weekes pay which the House of Commons have voted at their disbanding; and they would be very glad if the House would soe favour them as once againe to

[a] Captain ——— Barton.

[b] Colonel Nathaniel Rich; his major was John Alford.

take that into consideration. In refferrence to distempers I am sorrey to see my Major and some of my officers differ in their accompt. My Major did indeede give me an accompt under his owne hand and the hand of some of my Captaines, as that which was the sence of the whole regiment, and that which hee hath signed; and truly I doe finde in that, as I have in that from another regiment, some things not fitt, and impertinent and extravagant, and that was the reason and the only reason that that course which you see was taken, that wee extract out of all that was brought in that that wee thought might be most pertinent upon this occasion, and to leave out those things that were impertinent or otherwise. But lastly, as to that which you speake in referrence to the Ireish service; truly I am verry sorrey to see soe little accompt given generally. For the particular accompt of my regiment, for I speake [to] noe more; wee who are horsemen are not very willing to crosse the seas, but wee must also desire that wee might further be made happie in haveing such a Commander as we could approve. Wee are told of an officer of the Cavaleeres that should beare immediate command over us; as to that person to serve under him either in or out of the Kingdome I knowe nothing that I can speake or thinke to detract from him; hee is a person of honour, butt hee is a stranger to mee and to my regiment, and as on the one side wee should be very glad to have one with us that wee have had experience of, soe on the other side itt is their oppinion to be wedded to noe man to goe under his command out of the Kingdome, before they receive some satisfaction in some competent measure.

Souldier.

May it please your Honour to be acquainted with the temper of your Regiment, and to see in what condition wee are; itt is not only the desire of the Regiment to knowe their commands, but in matter of Greivances which now lie upon them [they desire they] may accordingly have redresse from those in power, and remedies applied according to the diseases; and then wee desire that the justice of our proceedings may noe longer be censured, and condemned, butt judges [a] in the proper spheare of them, that soe wee may bee noe longer misapprehended, which I represent to your Honour and to this honorable company.

Collonel Rich.

I perceive this is an honest souldier of the regiment who has been a witnesse of all things that have passed; from this bussinesse in hand that doe respect the souldiers as well as the officers, if I have falne short in any thing, if you please to permitt him to give mee some private notice.

Souldier.

I cannot say that I knowe every particular, but it is the generall desire of the Regiment that they may be represented before you.

Collonel Rich.

I have done faithfully my endeavour for your satisfaction.

Collonel Sheffeild.

Sir. there is one thing that an officer in Collonel Hammond's Regiment said just now: that they were ready to accept of the termes with a great deale of chearefullnesse, that I did tell them that you did engage into Ireland, and Major Generall Skippon to command them, and I am sure itt is as great a comfort as any they have.

Collonel Hamond.

To what that Gentleman said, I find my Officers and Souldiers very willing; and though they doe confide in you, yet unlesse they have satisfaction as to indempnity and arreares, I must needes

[a] judged ?

say — when wee are satisfied in them as wee are in the point of conduct under the Major Generall, provided that the conduct be soe settled upon the conditions before mentioned — to engage themselves and the army that is to serve with them upon that service. Truly, Sir, if they may be soe satisfied upon those termes, that they will then chearefully, faithfully and honestly, not out of any ends of their owne, but out of a cleere and candid sence, freely and chearefully venture their lives for the service of the Kingdome as they have hitherto done; and this I speake to you not from my selfe alone, but from very many that have desired mee to speake.

Collonel Sheffeild.

I shall desire your favour in this: I beleive Collonel Hammond hath made a mistake, I am confident my men would as willingly have their owne officers, and I am confident that they desire nothing more then to serve the Parliament in what the Parliament shall command them in; and, for the ends, if Collonel Hammond does meane mee, I thinke I have as little cause otherwise as any other.

Collonel Hammond.

I did not intend itt of Collonell Sheffeild or any other in [relation to] that service, I only speake in relation to the Act of Indempnity which I am not ashamed to owne. But there is some exceptions for Captaines to be Lievtennant Collonells, Lievtennants to be made Captaines and Sarjeants to be made Lievtennants and Ensignes; this they have done in my Regiment.

Captain Rainborowe.

May it please your Honour, not haveing heard any thing fully spoken as to my Colonell's Regiment, though superiour officers are heere, I hope I shall not be mistaken in that which I am now to speake.

And that is to tender the accompt of what I have proceeded in my troope in Collonell Sheffeild's regiment. I had my troope at a randezvouz by themselves, thinking it the best way whereby I might impart and encourage them to the satisfaction desired of the Parliament, which I did in as faithfull a manner as I thought I was called unto. I advised them not to doe any thing too rashly but consider of itt. In conclusion they did tell mee, that if such and such things, which they did apprehend was very just and necessary as to their good and satisfaction, and according to the engagements of the Parliament, should be made [good] unto them, they should shewe the same affection.

And as to the bussinesse of Ireland they did include itt in these expressions. And as to the regiment, the Colonell and Major, the Captaines and my selfe was present when the letter was read and the votes of both Houses read unto them. I heard noe questions at all made, but that which they said their answeare was, this, jointly, one and all, that they could not be satisfied till they had an answeare to their petition.

And as to that of Ireland, I did not heare it moved in publique by any Officer at the Randezvouz. And as for the full of the Souldiers meaning and answeares to the votes, they have appointed severall of the regiment to bring upp their resolucions; they did not seeme to vent any distempers, for I saw not any thing done but that that did become them as souldiers, but these men are come upp and have signed these greivances which are signed. The whole Regiment signed them, they choose two out of a troope to bring them; and to speake seriously many of them did not knowe what they did, for many of them cryed out 'Indempnity,' 'Indempnity,' and afterwards ask't mee what it was.

Lieutennant.

May it please your Honours.

I hope I have rendred a faithfull accompt of what is commanded to mee, that is to give satisfaction to those votes, and what Greivances did remaine upon their spiritts.

Collonel Sheffeild.

Truly I beleive that Captaine Rainborrowe's accompt doth not make mine otherwise.

Lieutennant.

This relation that Captaine Rainborrowe makes of Colonell Sheffeild's regiment upon my knowledge is true. Colonell Sheffeild and the Major[a] were there; they drew upp the severall troopes; they did read it particularly to every troope, and after they had done soe they signed them in the respective troopes, and there is brought upp by those souldiers [the desires of] at least 500 souldiers.

And if any other accompt be given the Regiment doth not owne it.

Collonel Sheffeild.

I wish that Gentleman would keepe to his duty, for I thinke I shall bee able to prove that hee hath nott. I humbly desire that when any officer doth doe anything that may make a breach in the performance of that duty, hee may be call'd to accompt for it.

Lieutennant.

Collonell Sheffield, what I doe [promise] I shall performe.

Wee desire that wee may not be misunderstood; there are many officers of the army that doe desire the good of our Souldiers as of our selves, and therefore wee desire that those papers that I delivered in may be heard read publiquely, that it may be knowne what wee have desired in the behalfe of our Souldiers.

Colonel Rich.

Sir I shall offer this to you; in what hath been delivered, you have a summary extract of what was the troubles of our souldiers. Though wee are not ambitious of what wee have done, or our way

[a] Richard Fincher.

of proceeding more then all the world, yet if any of themselves knowe their owne greivances to be soe plausible, and to carrie with them such a face of justice and equitie to any that shall heare itt, it will not be only a satisfaction but a courtesie [to hear them].

Captain Holcraft.

I did not speake any thing in reflection, but to satisfie you that, for very honest reasons, wee doe not judge it necessary to joyne in those things that other Regiments doe.

Major Scroope.

I have given you an accompt of that of Colonell Graves' Regiment, to give satisfaction to those that desire itt.

Major Gen. Skippon.

Major Scroope, I suppose the case with that is much the same in every regiment, and that wee did [in one] that wee will doe through every regiment.

Captain.

May it please your Honours I am here with a member of Colonell Lilburne's Regiment; my Collonell is commanded to waite upon the Houses at London, hee cannot be heere.[a]

His Major was here and received your Honour's command; hee was here on Fryday to give what accompt hee had then ready, but since hee is gone away to London hee hath left noe order to any to doe itt, but I thinke none can give soe just an accompt as my selfe; if your Honour please to take it from mee I shall as faithfully make the returne. Upon Wednesday last the Regiment was drawne to a Randezvouz to muster, and according to your Honour's command had the votes of Parliament communicated to them. The Collonell's orderly . . . . and soe consequently

[a] Colonel Robert Lilburne; his major was William Master.

the rest; but for those that saw nothing nor heard nothing of those votes communicated to the Souldiers, it being as they alleadge done privately . . . . . I knowe what was said in itt by the souldiers to whome I heard them read, and particularly two companies; they were inserted amongst those which are presented to your Honours.

Major General Skippon..

Are there any officers of the Regiments that have not yett spoken that have anything to speake?

Lievtennant Collonel Grimes.[a]

I said this, There was noe dissenting; you were pleased to say there was dissenting in the army, I knowe that the mindes of the officers are knowne to the Collonells.

Major General Skippon.

Wee speake of distempers.

Commissary General Ireton.

The question that is expected to be answered is an accompt of the desires of the regiments.

C——

According to my Colonell's command I went to the Regiment, and when they came to the Randezvouz, hee drew them together, and then I told them there were severall Votes which the Commissioners of Parliament delivered to be read to them; as for distempers there are none. I made[b] this answeare, first for the Act of Indempnitie, they should be very well content when they had itt; they thought a considerable summe was noe more then what was due to them. They said they were willing to any peace, they desired they might be presented to you which I have presented to the

[a] Mark Grime, of the regiment late Mountague's, now Lambert's.

[b] had.

Colonell. And as for Ireland, [they gave] that answeare that Collonell Rich made and some others, they did desire some satisfaction for what was herein, satisfaction for what was done there.

Lievtennant Colonel Jackson.

I desire to speake but one word, and then I shall have done in an instant.

Least there should be any hard thoughts of the officers of the Generall's Regiment, wee have dined together these two dayes; yesterday I shew[ed] to Captaine White the resolution of the souldiers for Ireland, and Captaine White himselfe, and Captaine Leigh also, who dined with us . . . . . that hee did all, that that was true which he had written, and much more which he desired to be spared, and that concerning the Irish bussinesse.

Collonel Whalley.

Gentlemen, our owne hearts and consciences tell us that upon this last bussinesse that the Commissioners have imployed us about in goeing to our severall regiments, wee have performed itt to the great and good service of the Parliament; yet wee may be out of doubt that there will be various representations, nay I may say misrepresentations, offered to the House of Commons of our acting and doings; itt is as good as already promised us. I shall therefore move you, whether it were not good for us all in a joint and sollicitous desire to request one or more of the Commissioners here to goe to London in our behalfes, to answeare what shall falsely be laid to our charge. and to give the Parliament a true sence of our doings heere.

Lievtenant Colonel Grime.

You will please to satisfie the Commissioners that there is not soe much dissenting as they speake of, for 7 or 8 men doe not make a dissent in the army.

Collonel Whalley.

I thinke there shall not neede to be any such thing.

Captain.

Every man is left to his owne freedome to subscribe that which hee does agree to. I suppose in the whole greivances there is delivered different things, but wee may assent to that which is wholly and perfect ours and noe more.

Collonel Whalley.

This I say further. If you doe approve of what I have now tendred to you, that it is your desire to have one or more of these gentlemen that are members of the House to goe upp, that you will [let] them heare.

Heere the officers generally cried out. Two.

Major Scroope.

Perhapps there may be an information given to the House, for they cannot goe yett.

Collonel Rich.

I most humbly offer this also, to take this along with you, concerning the Commissioners of Parliament of their going to London to serve you there and the kingdome, that it should be with submission to their judgment and reason it should be very well, but otherwise I doe not knowe whether it be soe well or noe, itt is our desire.

Lievtenant Chillenden.[a]

I shall desire that Collonell Whalley and the rest may goe.

[a] Edmund Chillenden, an account of whom may be found in the *Dictionary of National Biography*.

Lievtenant Generall.

Gentlemen, by the command of the Major Generall I will offer a word or two to you. I shall not not need to reminde you what the occasion of this meeting was, and what the bussinesse wee are sent down about: you see by what has past that it was for us to learne what temper the Army was in, and truly to that end were the votes of the Parliament communicated by us to you, that you should communicate them to the Army that soe we might have an accompt from you. That accompt is received, but it being in writing and consisting of many particulars, wee doe not yett knowe what the contents of those papers are. But this I am to lett you knowe: that wee shall deale very faithfully[a] through the grace of God with those that have imployed us hither, and with you also. The further consideration of these bussinesses will be a worke of time. The Major Generall and the rest of the Gentlemen thinke it not fitt to necessitate your stay here from your severall charges; but because there may be many particulars that may require further consideration in these papers that are heere represented, itt is desired that you would stay heere a field officer at the least of every regiment, and two Captaines. For the rest it is desired of you, that you would repaire to your severall charges, and that when you are there you would renew your care and dilligence in pressing [on] the severall souldiers under your commands, the effect of those votes that you have already read. That likewise you would acquaint them as particularly with those two things that the Major Generall did impart to you, which hee had in a letter from the Speaker of the House of Peers, to witt the addition of a fortnight's pay, a fortnight to those that are to goe for Ireland, and a fortnight to those that doe not goe, and likewise there is an act of Indempnitie very full already past the House of Commons. Truly, Gentlemen, it will be very fitt for you to have a very great care in the making the best use and improvement that you can both of the Votes and

[a] A note, evidently written in 1662, when these reports were transcribed, says: "Looke that Rogue's words was fidele, Ambo nebulones."

of this that hath been last told you, and of the interest which all of you or any of you may have in your severall respective regiments, namely, to worke in them a good opinion of that authority that is over both us and them. If that authoritie falls to nothing, nothing can followe but confusion. You have hitherto fought to maintaine that duty, and truly as you have vouchsafed your hands in defending that, soe [vouchsafe] now to expresse your industry and interest to preserve it, and therefore I have nothing more to say to you. I shall desire that you will be pleased to lay this to heart that I have said.

Cornewall.

Wee shall desire that though there are dissenters in few regiments yet appeare, that the like is in all regiments.[a] I presume most of us doe abhorre to engage against authority, and wee doe as equally abhorre the hindring the service of Ireland. You will find that the matter conteyned in any of the answeares is the sence of most of them.

Commissary Ireton.

Itt was told you that the Major Generall's result was, that there should stay here a feild officer of every regiment; but because there have been diverse officers that have seemed to presse some differences, the Major Generall offerrs it to your consideration, that it any other besides those shall stay from the regiments have occasion to attend, they may have liberty.

Officer.

May it please your Honours, I thinke there cannot be an exacter accompt given from some regiments, there being none given from Colonell Okey's Regiment, they haveing not had the votes.

[a] Colonel Whalley ? We shall desire you to say that though there are dissenters in a few regiments yet it appears that the like sense is in all regiments.

Major Disborow.

I shall offer only one thing to your Honours, the greivances have been presented [but] it hath not been as yett put to them whether it be with their consent, or for that purpose. Some may suggest that it is some private actings of some few of us, and therefore I desire that the question may be putt whether they doe consent or not.

Colonel Rich.

I shall humbly offer one word to you more in referrence to what Major Disbrowe gave an hint, and that is truly a thing that hath a little troubled mee, to see a dislike testified to some of us, as wee have thought have tended to serve the Kingdome, the Parliament, and the Army, and to contract the bussinesse that you are hereabout into as narrowe a compasse as the thing it selfe will beare, as such an unpleasing thing as the representation of greivances will admitt. I could heartily wish that as the unanimity of this Army Officers and Souldiers is very well knowne, [during the war] which God be thanked is not now in the Kingdome [it] might be soe exprest at our conclusion, and wee desisting from further engagement in another Kingdome [be united] as it hath been formerly. I hope though there may have been some extravagancies spoken by some Officers or Souldiers of the Army, that it shall not be represented to you, that those extravagancies are the acts of the whole Army; itt is fully acknowledged by all of us that there [are] weaknesses and imperfections in the best, but I professe it seriously that wee have, as wee shall answeare it to God and man, done our best endeavours to preserve our regiments from those things that the Parliament are pleased to call distempers amongst us, and to doe our utmost endeavours I say as may become us in our places, as may conduce to the further prosecution of the Parliament's affaires either in Ireland or England. I meane in England iff wee should goe on in our bussinesses, as wee have done, united in a body. If any shall say, because wee talke of arreares before wee disband wee doe not intend to disband before wee have them, I speake that for my owne part, I speake the sence of my owne, that it is not any immodest, irrationall thing that wee drive at: only that the Parliament will please to reassume into their consideration that thing of arreares, before they are pleased to send us home or elsewhere.

Major Butler.[a]

In that particular I thinke there are not any officers here butt will agree to make an application to the House in that humble and submissive way as Colonell Rich hath proposed, to be reassumed into their consideration; I speake in the behalfe of diverse who are free to itt.

Lievtenant Colonel Jackson.

Itt is my desire.

Captain Holcraft.

, But there are some particular exceptions of which wee doe not soe well approve, and some things wherein they are not at all concern'd; and therefore, upon those and other considerations, they desire to take that course apart; and as that cannot reflect upon any proceedings in the Army, soe they are very well satisfied in their consciences, that there is none can desire the peace of the Army more than they doe.

Colonel Hewson.

Major Disbrowes motion, as I understand, was to desire that you would knowe whether they did not desire Colonell Whaley and some other Gentlemen to accompany the Commissioners with their report to the House, that it may not be thought thatt it was of Colonell Whalley's particular act, or any others joyn'd with him,

[a] Colonel Butler ?

and [lest] that itt should be look'd upon to be their actings, and not the desire of the rest.

Major General Skippon.

For my part I thinke it was the desire of other Officers, though only Collonell Whalley mov'd itt.

All.

Noe. Noe.

Major General Skippon.

Let us understand things soberly, rationally, and freindly one from another. I say, I thinke there was none of us, though I beleive wee did not knowe of itt, nor it was not by order from us, yet I doe verely beleive that wee could not imagine that Colonell Whalley whome wee thinke to be a wise man and an honester man then to doe a thing of his owne head . . . . .

But that you should make this the unanimous concurrence of the Army whereas there are divers officers that doe say otherwise . . . . .

Colonell Whalley.

The thing is soe cleere as you cannot chuse but take notice of itt ; but in regard they doe heare of some that does almost threaten to send up such informations to the world as I may say are not true, therefore their humble request is, that two of the Members of the House of Parliament, you being all members, that you would be pleased to take the paines to goe up to London, that soe you may be able in their behalfe to represent their desires to the Parliament; and likewise to give the Parliament a cleare and true sence of what is their actings and doings here.

Collonel Sheffeild.

I humbly couceive that Collonel Whalley [is] speaking this as from himselfe, but if there be such a thing you all must knowe itt.

C[olonel] W[halley.]

Sir, I did soe, yet I am sure it is most of their mindes. Does your conscience accuse you ?

Major General Skippon.

I pray either speake with moderation or else be silent.

Cornett Joyce.[a]

The thing is thus, that letter which was sent out was communicated to the severall Regiments, and that answere was sent from ours; if you desire mee to justifie itt I am willing, and acknowledge what they did, and whatsoever hath been done, hath been done to the end in the relation come upp.

Commissary Ireton.

I conceive that by what is said that some officers doe take offence as taking more upon them then was fitt for them to doe. [I therefore conceive it fit] That before this meeting doe breake uppe that some officers be appointed to present the sence of the whole. I speake only to drawe that bussinesse to a conclusion soe you may be noe longer deteyned.

Colonel Hammond.

Sir I shall make a short motion to you. That you will appoint us to make a more full discovery, and [to take the names of] those that doe assent to the appointing of us.

Captain Holcraft.

The Major Generall hath already an accompt who wee are that doe dissent.

Colonel Hammond.

I hope you will rightly understand us in that point of division. That word dividing was spoken.

[a] George Joyce, cornet to Faurfax's life-guard.

Major General Skippon.

Gentlemen, I shall cover all in as good language as I can, and in as good earnist as I can, and in all faithfulnesse that I can. Put an end to this discourse. I thinke the papers that you have given in by the hand of Colonell Whalley will evidently mannifest who they are that dissent.

I thinke the papers on the other side will cleare itt; and therefore I beseech you in all earnestnesse that you doe nothing but what may tend to unitie, love and peace. And soe good night.

[A Declaration from the Agitation of eight regiments of Horse.]

Walden, May 17th.

Whereas some few Officers of this Army (dissenting from the Army) have not only declared their owne dissent, but pretended also to declare the dissent of a parte of the Souldiers under their command, and thereby have done as much as in them lieth to render the Army in a divided condition. Wee, whome our severall Regiments of Horse have made choice of to act in their behalfes, doe in their names attest to your Honours from our owne certaine knowledge, that whatever dissent there may be by any particular Officers, that there is not any the least appearance of any difference or dissent among the Souldiers from the greivances presented by our Officers to your Honours; and this wee will undertake to make more fully appeare, when wee shall be called to an accompt by your Honours, or any other having authoritie to doe it, and in the meane time protest against that action of those dissenting Officers.

Edward Sexby
Wm. Taylor } of the Generall's Regiment.

Wm. Allen
Sam. White[a] } of the Lievtenant Generall's Regiment.

[a] Should be probably Sam. Whiting.

Thomas Sheffeild[a] } Anthony Nickson } of Commissary Generall Ireton's.

William Prior } John Caseby } of Colonel Fleetwood's Regiment.

Thomas Kendall } Wm. Young } of Collonel Whalley's Regiment.

Tobias Box } John Willoughby } of Colonel Butler's Regiment.

John Brayman } Nicholas Lockyer } of Colonel Riche's Regiment.

Henry Gethings } Thomas Diggell } of Colonel Sheffeild's Regiment.

[a] Should be Thomas Shepherd, I believe.

Of the sixteen names appended to this, nine, or if the corrections suggested be accepted, eleven are also attached to the letter of April 28.

The subsequent history of some of the men signing this document is of interest.

John Brayman (or Breman) became a lieutenant in Colonel Rich's regiment and was cashiered in February 1655, on the charge of complicity in the plot for raising a rebellion amongst the army in Scotland, in which Major-General Overton was implicated (*Mercurius Politicus*, pp. 5052, 5165). In June 1659, he was restored to his place in the army with the rank of Captain, became major of Rich's regiment, and was arrested on April 13, 1660, for endeavouring to raise his soldiers in support Lambert's intended insurrection (Cal. State Papers, Dom. 1658-9, p. 289; *ibid.* 1660, pp. 202, 573). He was again arrested in May, 1662, and confined in the Tower and in Windsor Castle (Cal. State Papers, Dom. 1661-2, pp. 376, 456). He was imprisoned in 1682 on account of suspected complicity in the Rye House plot (*Luttrell's Diary*, i., 269, 286, 556.

William Prior's career was less distinguished. He was, however, arrested in January, 1655, for taking part in the plots of the levelling party against the Protector (*Mercurius Politicus*, p. 5050; Thurloe, iii., 35).

To General Fairfax.

May it please your Excellency,

I thought it my duty to give you an Accompt of what hath happned in the transaction of this waighty bussinesse committed unto the care of Major Generall Skippon &c. what has been done by them, and what by the Army, in order, and obedience to the Commands. Upon Fryday last many Officers, and almost from every Troope or Company one, conven'd at Walden, and brought them from every Regiment severall Particulars of those Greivances which the Souldiers were most sencible of; aud there by generall consent and desire of those Officers Collonell Hammond, Rich, Whalley, Okey, Major Disbrowe, Cowell and myselfe,[a] would extract out of the severall Papers sent from the Regiments those greivances which were most common to all, most probable to occasion the late distempers in the Army, and most seasonable to be presented to the Parliament, and compose out of them a forme and draught[b] in the name and behalfe of the whole Army; which although it was both troublesome and we might bring thereby an inconveniencie upon our selves, wee undertooke, as a thing which we might possibly doe the Parliament and Army reall service in;

[a] This letter was evidently written by Colonel Lambert, who expressed in the debate views exactly similar to those contained in this letter, (p. 42), and acted as spokesman of the ten office s authorised to draw up the grievances. The authority given to them ran as follows:—

"The Officers whose names are here underwritt doe declare, That they conceive the summary of the severall Representations of their respective Regiments read to them in the Church in Walden the 15th of May, 1647, to be the substance of the severall Representations, and doe desire that Collonell Whalley, Collonell Hammond, Collonell Rich, Collonell Lambert, Collonell Ingoldesby, Collonell Okey, Collonell Hewson, Major Desbrowe and Major Cowell may perfect and drawe upp our summarie to be delivered to Major Generall Skippon and the rest of the Officers sent from the Parliament:" (Worcester MS., vol. xli., f. 101 b.) The list of names which follows is practically the same as that printed in Rushworth, vi., 471.

[b] MS. "brought."

and accordingly went about it, but could not possibly perfect it in time against the appointed houre of tenn of the clock the next day, and therefore were forced to desire a longer time of the Commissioners, which was granted untill five a clock the next day in the afternoone. Against which time wee being prepared, deliver'd in by the hand of Collonell Whalley the summe of what we had composed; wherein we used as much moderation as possibly wee could with satisfaction to the Souldiers, who, though they remaine very high in their demaunds and expressions,[a] yet I am confident I have declined much which was in their hearts to have strongly insisted upon. A copie of which according to its last extraction, together with the Interduction and Conclusion, I could not in this short time procure to send unto your Excellencie, but doubte not but Mr. Rushworth's man[b] will send them in shorthand to the Secretary who may make them knowne unto you. After that wee had delivered this with the sence of the Army the Commissioners desired a more particular Accompt of what pass'd at the Randez-vouz's of every Regiment; which was accordingly done by the Collonell's Majors, or cheife Officer of every Regiment, and most of them was to this effect: That they for the present found their respective Regiments in very quiet condition, neverthelesse were sensible of some present and other approaching greivances, the Summe of which was delivered in to Collonell Hammond, Whalley, Rich, &c. and were very much the same which were delivered at that present to the Commissioners. There was return'd from your owne Regiment of Foot, two severall differring Accompts; one from the Lieutennant Collonell, the other from Captaine White and some other common Souldiers, whom the Regiment hath appointed to agitate in the behalfe of the whole Regiment. And likewise from Collonell Sheffeild's some differrences of the like nature, and also a somewhat lame and imperfect accompt from Collonell Graves' Regiment; but all the rest were intire and very

[a] MS. "expedition."

[b] Either Thomas Wragge or William Clarke.

full. Next to this [the] Major Generall desired an Accompt of what had been done in order to his designe of motioning the releife of Ireland; to which an answeare was given as from most of the Army, that they could find nothing of willingnesse or affection to that service, untill they had received some satisfaction in their greivances. And indeed, if the Parliament thinke to have helpe out of this Army for Ireland, they must goe another way then what they are in for the present. Collonell Sheffeild, Collonell Butler, Quarter Master Generall Fincher, and some few others, who indeed were not acquainted with our private debates by reason they have subscribed for Ireland, and therefore are not liable to most of these greivances, and by reason they had delivered in a Petition, the substance whereof was the great cause of trouble upon us, and were unsatisfied in what wee did, and have expressed their dislike in a Paper delivered to the Commissioners, the contents whereof for the present I knowe not.[a] Betwixt them, and [us] is something past of heat and animositie, especially betwixt Cols. Sheffeild and Whalley, but I hope will goe noe further.

Walden, 16° May, 1647.[b]

Lettre from Sexby[c] *to the Agitators.*

Gentlemen,

If these be not *s a presse gott into the Army wee shall be att a

[a] The protestation and vindication of Colonel Butler and the other dissenting officers, which are annexed in the MS., were printed in a pamphlet entitled "*A Vindication of a Hundred and Sixty-seven Commission Officers that are come off from the Army in Obedience to the Parliament Orders*," published July 1, 1647. See also Rushworth vi., 495.

[b] In the MS. this letter was originally dated 1662, for which date 1647 was afterwards substituted. This and an entry at the beginning of vol. lxvii. of these MSS. shows that these copies were made in 1662.

[c] Edward Sexby first appears in history as one of the presenters of the letter of the

losse. There wants nothing but money, therefore tell the Officers they must disburse the money.

The King will it is verily thought come and joyne with them, and that makes them soe high, therefore minde that by all meanes hasten the greivances away. There is a Committee to goe to Rainborrowes Regiment, *s will goe if you send him instructions, which doe by to morrowe night, and send two more to London to convey Newes. The generall will be with you on Thursday, Soe I rest

Your freind,

*

17° May, 1647.

agitators of the eight regiments to their General. He was a Suffolk man, and had served first in Cromwell's regiment of horse, and then in that of Fairfax. See his account of himself in Appendix B. He seems to have left the army after 1647, but happening to be present in Cromwell's army at the time of the battle of Preston (on some private business) was entrusted with a letter from Cromwell to the Speaker, announcing the victory. For this service the House of Commons voted him £100 (August 23, 1648, *Commons' Journals*, v., 680). In February, 1649, Parliament ordered the detention of the Scotch Commissioners, and they were arrested by Mr. Sexby at Gravesend, for which he was ordered £20 (February 28, *Commons' Journals*, vi. 152). He was also appointed Governor of Portland, is henceforth designated as Captain Sexby, and was more than once charged with commissions requiring dexterity and energy (Cal. State Papers, Dom. 1649-50, pp. 135, 155, 531). In June, 1650, he was, at Cromwell's suggestion, selected for employment in Ireland, and charged to raise a foot regiment, but on September 23, 1650, was ordered to march to Scotland instead, as Cromwell complained of the want of foot (Cal. State Papers, Dom. 1650, pp. 206, 332, 352). He took part with his regiment in the siege of Tantallon Castle, in February, 1651 (*Mercurius Politicus*, p. 621). In June, 1651, however, he was cashiered by court-martial, for what offence does not appear (*Letters of Roundhead Officers to Captain Adam Baynes*, Bannatyne Society, 1856, p. 27). This letter was evidently written from London to the agitators at Saffron Walden.

A letter to the Agitators.

Sir,

I kindly salute you, I have noe newes but this, That the House did order those that brought Ensign Nicholls prisenour 10[li]. a peece for their good service.[a] Thus you may see their proceedings. And lett mee tell you, this is in hand to divide us ; they intend to pay the private Souldiers all their Arreares and to abuse the Officers, and soe to divide the Souldiers from their Officers. This is the way they intend to doe as their last designe ; and therefore Gent.[lemen] you must use your dilligence to the severall Regiments, Troopes, and Companies to sett them right in this bussinesse, and to try them whether they will stick to their Officers, though they should be paid their Arreares and have securietie by an Ordinance to see whether they will have Justice done to. Their Officers have stuck to them, and it is expected in Honour and Justice they will stand to us. Therefore use your dilligence. I neede not say more to you. I have sent to you some of the

[a] Lieutenant Frances Nicholls, of Lilburne's regiment, was committed by the House of Commons on April 27, having been sent up from the army in custody on account of his opposition to the enlistment for Ireland (*Lords' Journals*, ix. 154; *Commons' Journals*, v. 155). The vote mentioned in the letter took place on May 14 (*Commons' Journals*, v. 175) and is thus referred to in a newsletter of 17 May, amongst the Clarke Papers :—

"The House of Commons voted those that brought upp Ensigne Nicholls 10[l]. and debated very much about discharging the Ensigne, and giveing him 10[l] towards his charges, but going by voices foure carried it in the Negative, the Ensigne was informed by the Sargeant, that if he pleased to Petition the House they would give him his release and a gratuitie besides perhaps of 20[l]. The reason why it was carried in the negative was because then it would be said they repented them of what they had done."

Cittizen's Petitions, and they doe much rejoyce in our unanimity. Therefore knowe I am

Your assured freind,

* [a]

May 18th, 1647.

Letter to the Agitators.[b]

These are to tell you that this day the Armie is to be disbanded by vote of the Commons House, and referred to the Committee of Derby House for manner, time, and place; and soe farr as I conceive, itt is upon good information, that they intend to disband the Foote first, and then the Horse, and that by Regiments, and they to be 40 miles asunder. Beleive itt my deare fellowes, wee must now be very active to send to all our severall Regiments of Horse and Foote and [let them] knowe that nothing but destruction is threatned. I pray you observe these severall directions and send to the severall regiments, to principle them by all meanes presently, and Sir . . . . . in the Commons House abuised the Generall as basely, they said "there was never Generall did like him, hee is now in Towne and courts Ladies, and itt is a shame for him that he should be now in Towne and his Armie in a distemper,"[c] and Mr. Hollis hath promised to deliver the Cittee's Petition though hee

[a] This letter is headed in the MS. "Letter from Lt. Cn." It is perhaps also from Sexby, who was undoubtedly the leading spirit amongst the agitators. In that case the heading may have been added by the copyist in 1662, and may mean Lieutenant-Colonel Sexby, giving him his later title. On the other hand, the expression "it is expected they will stand to us," seems to show that the author was an officer. Perhaps "Lt. Cn" signifies Lieutenant Edmund Chillenden of Whalley's regiment of horse, one of the two officers elected in June, 1647, to act as "agitator" for the officers of his regiment.

[b] There are two copies of this letter amongst the Clarke Papers, one of which gives it as a postscript to the preceding letter. It was evidently written on May 18, from the reference to the disbanding vote (*Commons' Journals*, v. 176).

[c] See *Fairfax Correspondence*, iii., 343.

himselfe is nominated to have justice done on him ;[a] what this will effect I knowe not but you shall heare by the first. I would you would tell that the Printer is taken and undone, and if it be not thought on to have a Presse in the Army wee are undone. Heere is one perfect and workmen :[b] Lett him therefore see what will be done amongst the Officers concerning itt, and, Sirs, you must be sure to send to the Foote, and tell them this, and be sure they doe not turne. Loving freinds, be active, for all lies at the stake. This is the stratagem that was spoken on the other night. I would intreat you to bestirr your selves, for the good of all the kingdome and their preservation is in your hands. In the name of God improve itt for the kingdomes happinesse.[c]

[a] A newsletter of 18 May says: "The petition of the well affected partie in the City should have been presented this day, but none can be found to present it though tendered at the House of Commons door. I understand that Mr. Hollis hath received the City petition, though himselfe is concerned in it, and hath presented it to the Speaker, with a promise to see it read to-morrow in the House."

[b] The advice about the printing press was followed. Hollis, in his Memoirs, § 66, describes the army as "countenancing and publishing seditious pamphlets, for which they had a press which followed the army." The printer of these pamphlets seems to have been a certain John Harris, who himself wrote several pamphlets under the name of "Sirrahniho." Harris printed, *inter alia*, the following pamphlets : "*A Declaration of Master William Lenthall, Speaker of the House of Commons, wherein is contained the reasons that moved him to absent himself from the service of the House on Friday, July* 30, 1647." The imprint it bears is "Oxford, printed by J. Harris and H. Hills, living in Pennifarthing Street, 1647." "*The humble address of the Agitators*, 14 Aug. 1647," is said to be printed at London, "for J. Harris, Printer to his Excellency Sir Thomas Fairfax," and also "*the Resolutions of the Agitators of the army*" "printed for John Harris, London, 1647." On September 30, 1647, Parliament passed a stringent ordinance against unlicensed printing, and, at the request of Fairfax, appointed Gilbert Mabbot, licenser. The political press in general thus passed under the control of the army, and there was no further need of Harris and his travelling press. *Old Parliamentary History*, xvi., 300, 309. About November, 1647, Harris printed a pamphlet entitled "*The Grand Designe or a discovery of that form of Slavery entended, and in part brought upon the free people of England by a powerfull party in the Parliament, and Lieutenant General Cromwell, Commissary General Ireton and others of that faction in the army.*" From this time he became closely associated with the Levellers, and published pamphlets for that faction.

Letter from the Agitators to the severall Regiments.

Gentlemen and Fellow Souldiers, wee greet you well.

These are to let you knowe, that wee have received Letters from London this day certifying, that still the dividing and soe the destroying designes are in hand. Before you were the Marke shott at without your Officers, and they loath to see you in such a condition designed to ruine they appeare now to speake and act for you; but noe sooner came they to speake on your behalfes, but they become the Marke instead of you. This is now the thing in hand to divide betweene you and them, and that is either propounding or giving you your arreares, and soe [to] take you from your Officers, thereby to destroy them, and then to worke about their designes with you also, which will make your money be but little usefull to you. As soone as you have it and you disbanded you may be prest away for Ireland, or hang'd in England, for prosecuting the Petition, or refusing to goe for Ireland; which wee question not but many of us shall be found guiltie of, some already saying if you be but disbanded, if you will not goe they will drawe you along like doggs. Fellow Souldiers, the summe of all this is, if you doe but stand, and not accept of any thing nor doe any thing without the concent of the whole Army, you will doe good to your selves, your Officers, and the whole kingdome. Stand with your Officers, and one with another you need not feare. If you divide you destroy all. Therefore once more, Fellow Souldiers, as you tender your owne wellfares and the welfares of us all, acquaint one another with these things, and resolve neither to take mônie, nor march from one another, but lett all your actions be joyn'd. And if any orders should come to your particular Regiments to march from the rest of the Army, march not while you have consulted with the rest of the Army. Be sure you take heed how you obey any such orders, untill you have acquainted and consulted with the rest of the Army. Be active and unanimous, the whole Army will assist you, if you doe but acquaint them with it. Doe nothing for your owne securitie, but what may secure your reall and faithfull Officers as well as your selves. Be assured they are yours, while you are theirs.

Yours and the Kingdomes faithfull servants,
choen to advise and consult in your behalfes.

EDWARD SAXBY.	ANT. GRAYES.
WM. ALLEN.	NICH. LOCKIER.
THOMAS SHEPHARD.	JOHN NEWSON.
THOMAS KENDALL.	ROBERT PRICHARD.
THO. JONES.	RO. MASON.
TOBIAS BOX.	THO. DIGGELLS.
JOHN NEWSON.	WM. LAUNDY.[a]

Bury : May 19, 1647.

For our assured freinds and fellowe
Souldiers that are of the Regiment
that was lately Collonel Herbert's.

[a] Agitators were first elected by the eight regiments of horse whose representatives signed the letter of April 28; see p. 33, and Appendix B. In May, in consequence of the mission of the four officers to enquire into the grievances of the army, the foot regiments also chose agitators (Rushworth, vi., 485). Each company is said to have elected two, out of whom two were selected to represent the regiment. A comparison of the names appended to the different declarations of the agitators shows that in this letter one man signs for each regiment. The signatures to this letter represented the eight regiments of horse above mentioned; Diggell belonged to Sheffield's regiment of horse, Mason to Sir Hardress Waller's foot regiment, Newson to Fairfax's regiment of foot, and the three others probably to regiments of foot then near Saffron Walden. The double mention of Newson is probably an error of the transcribers. The address of the agitators to Fairfax on May 29 (*Book of Army Declarations*, p. 16) is signed by the representatives of ten horse regiments (the two additional regiments being those of Pye and Graves), and by representatives of six foot regiments (those of Lambert, Harley, Lilburne and Hewson with the two before-mentioned).

Herbert's regiment is probably spoken of as lately Colonel Herbert's, because he had accepted the command of a new regiment to be raised for the Irish service, out of the volunteers for that object from the different regiments of the new model. His old regiment was given in June or July to Colonel Robert Overton.

[*Letter from the Agitators of Horse to the Horse in the North.*]

Honoured Gentlemen and Fellowe Souldiers wee greete you well.

Wee in this Army whereof you are a part haveing for these few weekes last past had it made our portion to be brought on the publique stage of the Kingdome as acting in the things which wee could wish had been more private, but necessitie hath noe law, fellow Souldiers, wee knowe, that these actions of ours have through the false suggestions of some been liable to misconstructions and misinterpretations which we well knew must be our portion before we began to act, but our comfort is, Wisedome is justified of her children, and we hope wee shall not be condemned by you; and to the end you may have right apprehensions of our candid intentions and actions wee present you with these following lynes, wherein we shall breifly give you the ground of the way and the end of our Proceedings. For the Ground it was this, Wee in this Army lying under many sore and pressing greivances, and being apprehensive of many more we were ere long like to be involv'd into if not prevented; for the prevention of which wee had an humble Petition with Representations annexed framed to be presented to the Generall and by him to the House, we conceiving this to be our undoubted right and priviledge whether considered as Souldiers or Subjects if wee have a right to any thing; but while this was only in intention, such was the haniousnesse of itt apprehended to be, according as it was represented by a Letter from an unknowne Officer of the Army who was not sparing in the Letter in the laying many odious aspersions both on itt and us, and suddenly after the receiving of this letter (unexpectedly and to our amazement) comes forth the Declaration against our Petition, declaring us enemies to the State and persisting and laying many heavy charges upon us as you may see in itt at large (to which wee referre you); this coming out from our professed Enemies, it sadned our spiritts that wee should be declared Enemies for going on in that way which they themselves had directed us to in case of Greivances, and the thoughts of this putt us upon drawing a vindication of our late Petition which wee beleive you have seene. The next thing was to thinke of framing of a Letter[a] to the Generall and Major Generall and Lieutenant Generall. Our end in that was thus, wee did not knowe but the Parliament might be pleased to heare them speake for us though they would not receive our Petition from us, but were pleased to condemne it to die before it was brought out to live. This Letter being presented to the persons to whome directed, it was conceived by Major Generall Skippon to have many things of great importance and dangerous consequence; soe it was presented to the House, and the messengers called in and examined and much debate about it, and the results were the dismissing of the messengers at present to attend them on the next summons, and this Letter according as wee conceive was the occasion of the Commissioners coming downe to take a view of the distempers reported in the Armie, which accordingly they did, and having conveen'd the Officers gave them order to repaire to their severall charges to receive the greivances of those under their commands, which was done accordingly and the greivances brought in to the Commissioners to be by them presented to the House, and wee have herewith sent you a coppie of them as they are in the abstract, though they would have been longer, but the severall Regiments being streightened in time they could not bring them in soe large as otherwise they would, which wee desire you to read and impartially to judge of our sad condition wee are in, and what just cause we have to doe what wee have done, and withall what little ground there is for all these loud clamours against us as is sounded abroad daily. Wee desire the just God and all just men to judge whether wee have deserved such hard measure from them

[a] April 28, 1647.

that wee [who] have not thought any thing too deare to part with for their sake, who have manifested our selves not to be enemies but reall freinds and soe knowne to be in the dayes of their adversitie, and did little thinke that this should have been our portion to be declared Enemies in the dayes of their prosperitie, but our God his will is done, and our worke is with him and our reward is before him. As to our ends [it] is to selfe preservation, which all creatures does, and Man, the cheife of creatures, cannot but doe, that soe when God hath made us instrumentall in saving a kingdome we might [not] be accessorie to our owne destruction, as we should be if wee should suffer our selves to be deprived of our just freedomes, which are ours in a double sence, first, as by the lawes of this Nation it hath been conferred upon us; and 2dly, as by many of our dearest blouds it hath been purchased by us, and whatsoever the false suggestions of men are to the contrarie, yet our ends, soe farre as wee knowe our own hearts, are noe other but in that we might live and enjoy that which the knowne lawes of this Nation allowe us to enioy, and the Parliament in many of their Declarations have oftentimes assured us wee should have; and wee shall never desire any to adheere to us any further or longer then wee are acting to this end. Thus you have our whole bussinesse before you. Read and consider, and God direct you. Thinke wee are prosecuting just things in a just way, and if from such thoughts of us you have a desire to joyne with us, these Gentlemen which are the bearers hereof will direct you in the way of doing itt, and our hearts will aboundantly reioyce in it, and wee shall not be wanting in the use of all lawfull wayes and meanes to assist you to the utmost of our power in the attainement of this our desired end; and wee question not but the just Lord who loves Justice will assist us all while Justice doth runne as a mighty streame amongst us. In the meane time wee hope to stand right in your apprehensions soe long as you shall discerne the the clearenesse of our intentions. Soe we leave you to God who wee hope will never leave you but will be to you a God of direction, and to you and us a God of Protection in all our warrantable undertakeings.

Yours and the Kingdomes humble Servants Adjutating for the severall Regiments whose names are hereto subscribed.[a]

Letter to the Agitators.[b]

Gent.

The great bussinesse of the House yesterday was a long debate upon the honest partie of the Citties Petition,[c] and likewise upon the great Petition that is gone out into the Kingdome, and in conclusion order'd them both to be burnt by the Hangman at the Exchange and Pallace Yard—a new way to answer Petitions and doubtlesse (might some have their wills) the Petitioners too should be burnt in Smithfeild. They committed one of the Citty Petitioners to Newgate, for telling a Parliament Instrument "if wee cannot be allowed to Petition wee must take some other course."[c] The expression indeed was too high but he knew him

[a] This letter is not dated and no signatures are appended. It was, however, 'evidently written immediately after the abstract of the grievances had been drawn up, *i.e.* about May 20. Several agitators are mentioned as being sent with it to the northern troops. The names of three agitators belonging to the southern army are appended to a subsequent declaration, viz. Richard Kingdom of Cromwell's regiment, Thomas Diggel, of Harrison's, late Sheffield's regiment, and John Caseby, of Fleetwood's. None of these signed the petition of May 29, but Diggel signed the letter of May 19, therefore their despatch to the north probably took place between 19th and 29th May.

[b] It is difficult to determine the authorship of this letter. It seems to have been written by some one officially employed at headquarters. The signature does not occur again.

[c] An account of the whole business of these petitioners is given in a pamphlet entitled *Gold Tried in the Fire*, 1647. British Museum, E. 392, (19). The petitioner committed to Newgate was one William Browne. *Commons' Journals*, v. 179; Rushworth, vi., 488.

not to be a Member, yet it was not soe high as both parties was that day in the House, for one of the parties said That they [that] had delivered and sent the letter to the Generall, Major Generall, and Lieutenant Generall were a companie of rascalls; and another said, That hee shall very willingly die with his sword in his hand though there be an Army of 30,000, in the Feild. Massie is sent downe to Gloucester (they say), from thence to secure Monmouth for feare of some insurrection in those parts. Sir Robert Pye is gone to his Regiment. The designe of the King's letter to settle Presbitry for three yeares, and the Militia for tenn, may be easily gues't at:[a] His Majestie hath a mind to please the Citty, and they him; they forgett that they are little lesse then 80 thousand pound arreare to this Army. His excellencie came hither this Evening. The Major Generall and some other Officers came to vissitt him (though they went not forth to meet him). Major Gooday saluted him with a pittiful complaint in a Letter from Lieutennant Collonell Jackson. That his Regiment would have meetings, and some of them come to the Head Quarters without orders, notwithstanding they had acquainted his Souldiers, with a desire which the Major Generall, Lieutennant Generall, &c. made Thursday before the Lieutennant Generall went to London, That the Officers would use their endeavours to prevent any meetings of the Souldiers. The Major Generall sett it home with Arguments of the inconveniences that might come by it, Mutinies, disorders, &c. It was moved that the Generall would send some command in writing, that the Major Generall and the rest had forborne it before, expecting his Excellencie's coming downe. There is noe order as yet given; if you have not that libertie

[a] A news-letter of May 18 says: "Things growe very high; the Lord moderate them or else we are like to have a very sad kingdome. It is thought that the House intends to send down propositions to the King; it is thought such propositions will be sent as the King will signe, and then they thinke the King's party and theirs will be hard enough for us. . . . . The great designe of the Parliament is to get the Magazine of Oxford into their hands upon pretence of the service of Ireland."

(carrying things discreetly and moderately) I knowe not what can be done to purpose. Our Enemies may worke and destroy us before wee are aware.

36

Walden, 20th May 1647.

Letter from the 4 Officers to Mr. Speaker.

Sir,

Upon the order you sent us of the 18th instant wee have herewith sent upp two of our selves (Lievtennant General Cromwell and Collonell Fleetwood) to give an accompt to the House of the bussinesse wee are imploy'd in here according to certaine heads by a Report here agreed upon for that purpose by us all who are

Your most humble servants,

PHIL: SKIPPON.
OL: CROMWELL.
HEN: IRETON.
CHARLES FLEETWOOD.

Walden, May 20th,
1647.

THE HEADS OF A REPORT TO BE MADE TO THE HONOURABLE HOUSE OF COMMONS BY LIEVTENNANT GENERALL CROMWELL AND COLLONELL FLEETWOOD IN THE NAME OF THEMSELVES AND THE REST OF THE OFFICERS IN THE ARMY AND MEMBERS OF THAT HOUSE LATELY SENT DOWNE TO THE ARMY WHOSE NAMES ARE SUBSCRIBED.

Agreed upon and sign'd by them all at Walden May 20th, 1647.

1. That according to the appointment (whereof wee have formerly

given accompt) the Officers mett here againe on Satturday last to returne an accompt of their proceedings and successes in communicating the Votes and improving the same together with their utmost interest and power for the satisfaction of the Souldiers and quieting of all distempers, as also to give a full accompt of the tempers of the Army in relation to the late discontent appearing therein.

2. That on Sunday Evening wee received a summarie accompt in writing agreed upon and signed by about 24 of the Officers, and presented to us by some of the cheife in the name and presence of the rest of the Subscribers which wee have now sent upp.[a]

3. That at the same time from the 8 Regiments of Horse and 8 of Foot now lying within the association the severall Cheife Officers present for the respective Regiments gave us accompt by word of mouth all of them to this effect. That they had communicated the Votes and done their endeavours according to order and doe find their Souldiers very quiet and in noe visible distemper at present, but having divers greivances sticking upon them, which (they said) were contained in the respective papers then given in by them, and all of them did also expressly declare, That the effect and substance of those their Greivances was contain'd in the said Summary then given in, except only those Officers whose distinct returnes for their severall charges given to us in writing are these following, which wee have likewise sent upp,[b] vizt.

1. One from three Officers of Collonell Lilburne's Regiment for the remaining soldiers of there three Companies only.
2. One from the Feild Officers and 5 Captaines of the Generall's Regiment of Foote.
3. One from Captaine Hall for the Life Guard.
4. One from Collonell Sheffeild, his Major and 2 Captaines.

[a] See *Army Declarations*, p. 17.

[b] These returns are amongst the Clarke Papers, Worcester MSS. vol. xli.

To that from the Generall's Regiment there was exception made by three Captaines and some other Officers of that Regiment, as also by 7 Souldiers chosen and intrusted by their fellowes of 7 Companies, who declar'd their greivances to be as in the Summarie and have given in a Paper to that purpose which wee have also sent upp.

To that from Collonell Sheffeild there was exception made by Captaine Rainborrow, and Captaine Evelyn's Lievtennant for their respective Troopes, and by private Soldiers for other Troopes of that Regiment chosen and intrusted by their fellowes, who brought the hands of all the Souldiers of the Regiment to attest their greivances, which because contain'd for substance within the Summarie wee doe not trouble the House withall. Colonell Sheffeild repli'd, That hee knew of noe such thing while hee stai'd with that Regiment, but the other averr'd it was publiquely agreed on upon the Randezvous after hee was gone.

That wee received also in writing other distinct accompts from some other Officers of Horse and Dragoones lying out of the Association, vizt.

One from two Lievtennants, two Cornetts and a Quarter Master of Collonell Graves's Regiment.

One from the Major and two Captaines of Dragoones of the three Troopes lying about Holdenby.

One from two other Captaines of Dragoones for their two Troopes lying in Shroppshire.

But wee find that these accompts were made by the respective officers without the imediate privitie of all their Soldiers or the other officers and Troopes of the same Regiments, and that they had not since the former meeting here had time to draw out their Troopes from the rest of those Regiments to acquaint them fully with the votes, or gaine a certain accompt of them, the great distance of all from those of their Quarters not admitting itt to be soe done within that time, and therefore wee have given order that the Votes, together with what is since added of the arreares, be effectually communicated to them all, and a certaine accompt to be returned from each as soone as may be.

5. That from Sir Robert Pies Regiment of Horse (we suppose for the same reason) we have had noe returne from any officer yet appearing, nor doe we yet heare whether they have received the Votes. The copie whereof for them was (in defect of any officer of that Regiment at the first meeting) delivered to an officer of Collonell Graves's Troope for both those Regiments.

6. Wee have also received some other Papers which at present wee thought not necessary to trouble the House withall.

7. That on Monday another Paper was delivered to us by Lievtennant Collonell Jackson, subscribed by himselfe and other officers that dissented from the rest to cleere themselves from mistake or misapprehensions in their said dissenting, which wee have likewise sent.

8. That since the said Generall meeting the Officers (who by consent of the rest had subscribed it) drew up and perfected the Summary, have shew'd us, and we have read over.

1. The particular returnes in writing from the 8 Regiments of Horse, and 8 of Foot lying in the association out of which the Summarie was extracted.
2. A Request of them in writing sign'd by the officers that brought in the same unto them, desireing that they would take the paines to frame and perfect the said Summary.

By all which wee find,

1. That those officers had good ground for what they did in the Summary, the said particular returnes of greivances being full to the heads of the Summary and many of them exceeding.

2. That whereas many of them for matter or expressions were brought confused and full of tautologies, impertinencies, or weaknesses answerable to Soldiers dialect, they drew the matter of them into some forme more fitt for view or judgment.

3. That whereas many of them for matter or expressions were such as might have given greater offence, they did, by their perswasions with the inferiour Officers and Souldiers that came with them (intrusted for the rest), bring them to lay aside many more offencive things, and to be satisfied in the heads of the Summarie, and therein endeavoured to bring them as low and to as much moderation as they could.

4. That their end and reason for going in that method and undertakeing the Summarie seems (most probably) to be to gaine the precedent effects, and to avoid further offence to the Parliament, soe as the Armies tendernesse towards the authorities and priviledges of the Parliament, and the Parliament's favourable construction and consideration of the Army might seeme to remove all discontents and prevent any more inconveniencie.

5. That the Officers thus joyning with the Souldiers againe in a regular way to make knowne and give vent to their greivances hath contributed much to allay precedent distempers, to bring off the Souldiers much from their late wayes of correspondencie and actings amongst themselves, and reduce them againe towards a right order and regard to their Officers in what they doe.

6. That the said severall Returnes doe generally expresse a pationate sense of the scandall concerning the petition to the King, protesting against the thing and the appearance of it amongst them in a great detestation thereof and importunitie for their clearing therein.

> 1. The same particular returnes themselves the said Officers that shew'd them to us desir'd they might keep, both for their owne justification in what they had done, and especially because the Officers and Souldiers that brought them being all satisfied in the Summary.
>
> > 1. It was their owne request the particular papers might not be produced in publique to discover the weaknesses or rashnesse of those that sent them, which they are very sensible of.

2. The Officers therefore conceiv'd it might be better (if the Parliament pleas'd) to take noe notice of them.

9. That though (in the charge to the Officers at their first meeting) wee exprest not, nor did intend to expect to have any such Returnes of Greivances, but only an accompt of what effect the Votes with the Officers endeavours had for quieting of distempers, and to knowe what distempers had been or should remaine, to the end wee might the better understand how to apply our selves to pay them, and give the better accompt to the House, yet now upon the whole matter wee humbly conceive, that the way it hath falne into, the course taken by the said Officers and admitted by us (being all upon a kind of necessitie as providence hath cast it for preventing of worse) hath hitherto proved for the best, and may (through the goodnesse of God with the wisedome of the Parliament) be turn'd to a good issue.

10. Lastly. That what hath been publiquely said or done by us in the transacting or prosecution of this great affaire hath been with the advice and unanimous consent or with the allowance and approbation of us all.

All which wee humbly submitt to the Parliament's better Judgment and the good pleasure of God.

PHILLIP SKIPPON.
OLIVER CROMWELL.
H. IRETON.
CHARLES FLEETWOOD.[a]

May 20, 1647.

[a] This report was presented to the House of Commons by Cromwell on May 21. *Commons' Journals*, v. 181; *Fairfax Correspondence*, iii. 348. It forms a sequel to the letters printed in Cary's *Memorials of the Civil War*, i. 205, 207, 214; and in Carlyle's *Cromwell*, Appendix, 10. The originals of those letters are amongst the Tanner MSS. in the Bodleian Library, but the MS. of this report is not amongst them. There are, however, amongst the Clarke MSS., copies of several letters which are in Tanner's collection, and the two frequently supplement each other. A news-letter amongst the *Clarendon Papers*, No. 2,520, says, "Lieutenant-General

[Letter to the Agitators.][a]

Gentlemen,

My best respects. I rid hard and came to London by 4 this afternoone. The House hath ordered and voted the Army to be disbanded, Regiment by Regiment. The General's Regiment of Foote on Tuesday next to lay downe their Armes in Chelmsford Church, and they doe intend to send you down once more Commissioners to doe it of Lords and Commons; they will not pay more then two months pay, and after we be disbanded to state our Accompts and to be paid by the Excise in course. This is their good Vote, and their good vissible securitie. Pray, Gentlemen, ride night and day; wee will act here night and day for you. You must by all meanes frame a Petition in the name of all the Souldiers, to be presented to the Generall by you the Agitators, to have him in honour, justice, and honestie, to stand by you, and to tell Skippon to depart the Army and all other Officers that are not right. Bee sure now be active, and send some 30 or 40 Horse to fetch away Jackson, Gooday, and all that are naught, and be sure to possesse his Souldiers, hee will sell them and abuse them; for soe hee hath done, hee engaged to sell them for 8 weeks pay. Gent. I have it from (59) and (89) that you must doe this, and that you shall expell [them] out of the Army; and if you doe disappoint them in the disbanding of this Regiment namely (68)

Cromwell on Friday last made his report from the army, that it will without doub disband, but they will not by any means hear of going for Ireland. The greatest difficulty, he said, would be to satisfy the demands of some (whom he had persuaded as much as he could possibly) but a great part of the army remitt themselves entirely to be ordered by the Parliament." Compare Hollis, *Memoirs*, § 87, Walker, *History of Independency*, ed. 1661, pt. i. p. 31.

[a] This letter is headed "Letter from Lt. C. to the Agitators:" see p. 85. The second sentence refers to the votes of the House of Commons on May 25: this letter was apparently written the same day. Of the cyphers some can be easily explained: 51 stands for London, 55, the army, 44, the agitators, 43, a rendezvous, 68, probably Fairfax.

you will breake the neck of all their designes. This is the Judgment of (59) and (89), therefore Gent. followe it close. The (52) are about (42) which Coppies I send you, and let mee tell you (41) and (52) in (54) are all very gallant; I pray God keep us soe too. Now, my Ladds, if wee worke like men wee shall doe well, and that in the hands of (52); and lett all the (44) be very instant that the (55) may be called to a (43) and that with speed; delay it not, by all meanes and be sure to stirre upp the Counties to Petition, and for their rights to make their appeale to (55) to assist them. You shall heare all I can by the next. Soe till then I rest.

Yours till death,
102.

From 51, 11° at night.

Sir,

As soone as the Generall came to Walden hee sent to the severall Regiments to acquaint them, that on Friday last the House had taken their greivances under consideration, and requir'd them to desist from their meeting; and because hee would be neere the Horse Quarters to prevent inconveniences he removed to St. Edmonds Bury in Suffolke, on Tuesday last. All Fryday hee was very ill, hee left his course of phissick too soone, but your commands were above phisick. This day the Regiments understand of the proceedings on Tuesday last, that as to vindication &c. nothing is to be done till after disbanding, and that only 8 weeks is ordered them at disbanding. Truly Sir, I am loath to expresse what their sense is of this. Tis in vaine to say any thing on their behalfe; I only dread the consequences, and desire that on all sides there may be more moderation and temper. I doubt the disobleiging of soe faithfull an Army will be repented of; provocation and exasperation makes men thinke of that they never intended. They are posses't, as farr as I can discerne with this opinion, That if they be thus scornfully dealt withall for their faithfull services whilst the Sword is in their hands, what shall their usage be when they are dissolved? I assure you that passionate and violent councell which is given thus to provoke the Army will in time be apprehended to be destructive, or my observation failes mee. It shall be my endeavour to keepe things as right as I can; but how long I shall be able I knowe not. Unlesse you proceede upon better Principles, and more moderate termes then what I observed when I was in London in the bitternesse of spirit in some Parliament men, Cittizens, and Clergie, and by what I perceive in the Resolution of the Souldiers to defend themselves in just things as they pretend—and truly many honest consciencious men much disobleiged by the Declaration—I cannot but imagine a storme. The Lord fitt all those that belong to him to heare[a] things with patience, and lett the Parliament see it is possible they may erre as well as the Army or any other State.[b]

25, May, 1647.

[a] beare ?

[b] The date above given can hardly be correct. Fairfax was ordered down to the army on May 18, and arrived at Walden on May 20 (ante p. 93, Rushworth, vi., 491). The letter "to the several regiments" is that of May 24, printed in Rushworth, vi., 495. The removal of the headquarters to Bury took place on Tuesday, May 25. The letter also refers to the votes of Parliament on May 25 "Tuesday last," as having this day become known to the soldiers, and was therefore probably written on Thursday, May 27. The Friday on which Fairfax was ill would then be May 21, the day after his arrival at the army; if it be taken to refer to Friday, May 28, this letter must have been written on May 29, and in that case the absence of any reference to the council of war fixed for that day is curious. The authorship of the letter is more difficult to determine. It was evidently written by some one in authority in the army, to some one in the Parliament. The author speaks of the vote ordering Fairfax to the army as "your commands," and says of the proceedings of Parliament, "unless you proceed," etc. It was very probably addressed to Cromwell. The author had been recently in London, and it was his business in the army to keep things as right as he could; it was probably one of the four commissioners sent down at the beginning of May, two of whom, Skippon and Ireton, were still with the army. From substance and style it seems more likely to have been written by the latter.

Letter from Collonell White to the Generall.[a]

May it please your Excellencie,

I am bold to send you such votes as the House hath passed in order to the disbanding of your Army, which being now resolv'd uppon I shall pray to God that it may be done peaceably, upon which I looke as that which carries in it the good and safetie of this Kingdome present and future. I knowe that some are of opinion that the Army being disbanded libertie is endangered, which I confesse—but withall doe clearely discerne, that if the Army shall continue it selfe against the authoritie of Parliament (for soe wee must conclude that which is passed by majoritie of Votes however contrarie to particular opinions) that there must inevitably follow the ruine and desolation of the Commonwealth, for this must needs occure to every eye (which looks forwards) to be the consequence: the Parliament being disobeyed and the Kingdome burthened with an Army voted unnecessary and to be disbanded, a force must be raised to compell obedience, and rather then faile the Scotts speedily call'd in, the issue of which (whosoever prevailes) must be the ruine of the Kingdome, and a sure stepp to the King and those that designe his ends either to bring him in (upon his owne termes) as the aire of these distempers, or to have opportunitie to raise a force such a one as may subdue and destroy both the other. On the contrarie, if it please God to dispose the Army to a quiet disbanding I am confident to say the Royall Designers have plotted in vaine, and their Councells how craftie soever are frustrated, for I am sure that if ever the King's interest appeare bare fact, without the masque of publique ease and zeale against hereticks, it will not have many to countenance it, few inclining to a confidence that the King is to be trusted with power

[a] Colonel William White, M.P. for Pontefract; see *Fairfax Correspondence*, iii., 42, 318, 342; Hollis, *Memoirs*, § 130.

over their lives or estates. Your Excellencie I confesse hath a most difficult game to play, your relations to Parliament and Army considered especially if there shall be opposition to the Parliament's command's (which God prevent) and if such be the sequell (which if reports be true wants not its simptoms), I beseech you pardon my boldnesse that I presume to offer you my humble advice. God hath made your Excellencie his great Instrument of good unto this Kingdome in subduing the Enemies thereof. The Parliament honours and esteemes your Person and services most highly—I say the Parliament, I dare not affirme it of every individuall person, vertue is alwaies the object of envy, and honour hath ever its emulations—as God hath made you successefull in their warrs to their advantage and your owne honour soe I may confidently say that your endeavours for quiet disbanding at there commands will add to their esteeme and love of you; for I doe assure your Excellencie, though some differ about the time and manner of disbanding, yet there are not many whose opinions are to continue more forces then the number of Horse and Dragoones voted to be under your Excellencie's command. If any disturbance (upon occasion of Disbanding) shall happen in the Army (which your Excellencie cannot speedily remeady) I beseech you foresee it in time, and write to the Parliament to give you leave so come upp to London to preserve them with your advice for the quieting thereof. I cannot see that your stay in the Army in any unquiet distemper (upon this occasion) can be for your safetie, nay I am sure it must be to your apparent danger. I leave your Excellencie to imagine the reasons, I know they are obvious to you. Pardon, I beseech you, this boldnesse and presumption, which is noe other then the reall effect of Duty to you and my Country, and of honour and faithfullnesse to your Excellencie, to whome I shall ever render my selfe upon all occasions.

Your Excellencies most faithfull and most humble servant

[William White.]

London, May 28, 1647.

Lettre from[a] *to the Agitators.*

May 28, 11 at night.

Send this to 92.[b]

Send to mee and you shall have powder enough and that in your owne Quarters, 500 Barrells, and it shall not cost a penny, and on Tuesday[c] I will informe you how and where.

Gent.,

There is 7,000li comming downe to Chelmsford, on Monday night it will be there. The Earle of Warwick, the Lord Dewan,[d] of the Commons, Mr. Annesley, Sir Gilbert Gerrard, Sir John Potts, Mr. Grimstone, all these are to come as Commissioners for to disband us, therefore Gent. you knowe what to doe. Collonell Rainborrow[e] is to goe to his Regiment, and it is by Oxford; and

[a] Headed as before, "Letter from Lieutenant C—— to the Agitators."

[b] 92 is perhaps Cornet Joyce.

[c] Tuesday, June 1. These three lines appear to be an enclosure, a message to be forwarded to the agitators. It is probably from some one at Oxford.

[d] Lord De La Warr.

[e] Colonel Rainborowe was appointed on May 25 to command the forces intended for the reduction of Jersey. On May 28 he was ordered to repair to his regiment with all speed and take course to stay it at the place he shall find it at his coming down. *Commons' Journals*, v., 184, 193. For the reasons of this order see Hollis, *Memoirs*, § 95. He found it quartered about Abingdon, and in a state of great disorder. Cary, *Memorials of the Civil War*, i., 221. The cause of Rainborowe's being ordered to his regiment is related by Hollis, *Memoirs*, § 95, and is thus stated in a royalist news-letter, "Friday last Colonel Rainsborough told the House of Commons 'that his regiment was marching, being thereto invited by the other regiments of the army who have persuaded them to participate in the fortune with the rest of the soldiery.' The said House asked the Colonel what that signified, he answered he knew not, that he had been three months past rather a sollicitor for the Colonel of that regiment, showing from time to time the wants of his soldiers, and that the country people, being injured by some of his necessitous soldiers, fell upon them, as he had formerly acquainted the House, in soe much that his regiment was constrained to dislodge, and was now marched towards Oxon." Clarendon MS. 2,522 The regiment had been quartered in Hampshire.

a Guard of Dragoones comes with the money and the Commissioners, but how many I knowe not. All the honest partie doe much rejoyce here at your courage, and the other partie doe much threaten and speake bigge; therefore I pray be carefull to have horse to apprehend and seize on the money and Commissioners before they come at the Foote; and if you can bannish Jackson and the rest out of that Regiment you will doe the worke, and be sure you doe what you can. Doe not let Jackson be there to goe to London, nor none of them of that Regiment, and you will doe well enough. Lett two horsemen goe presently to Collonell Rainborow to Oxford, and be very carefull you be not overwitted. Now breake the neck of this designe, and you will doe well, and you must now doe to make a Bolt or a shott, and not to dally, but a good partie of Horse of a 1,000, and to have spies with them before to bring you intelligence, and to quarter your Horse overnight, and to march in the night.

Soe God blesse.

I rest,

Yours,

102.

[*Sir Thomas Fairfax to Field Marshal Skippon* [a].]

Sir,

I understand this day there are Votes concerning the disbanding of the Army to beginne with my owne Regiment on Tuesday next; most of the Officers are here already, but in a bussinesse of soe great concernment, I desire your Advice and company this Sattur-

[a] Skippon was not present at the council of war; see list of persons present, *Army Declarations*, p. 15. On June 1, the House of Commons ordered him to return at once to London, and he was again in his place on June 4. *Commons' Journals*, v., 195, 198. The letter should be dated, Bury, May 29.

day morning if it be possible. I am sorrey the time is soe short but necessitie hath occasioned this suddaine desire of

Your very affectionate freind,

THO. FAIRFAX.

To the Honorable
Feild Marshall Skippon.

Walden, 28th May, 1647.

Lettre from Derby House to the Generall.

There is 7,000[l] appointed to be sent to Chelmesford towards the Disbanding of your Army, which is to be there on Monday night next; wee desire you to take care that the said monies may be there in safety, and therefore to give Order to your Life Guard, or such other or more forces as you thinke fitt to be at Chelmesford by Munday at noone, and that they goe forth to meet the money upon the way from London to Chelmsford,

Soe we rest,

Your very affectionate freinds and Servants,

WARWICK.	THOMAS WILLOUGHBY.
	E. MANCHESTER.
SUFFOLKE.	PH. STAPYLTON.
DENZILL HOLLIS.	GILBERT GERRARD.
WM. LEWIS.	WM. JEPHSON.
	JOHN CLOTWORTHY.
	JOHN TEMPLE.

Postcript.

Wee send you also herewith inclosed a copie of the Votes of the Houses whereby you may see their results concerning the time and manner of Disbanding your Army.

Satturday, May 29th, 1647.

His Excellencie this day communicated to his Councill of Warr the Vote of the House of Commons of the 25th of May,[a] and also a Petition lately presented to himselfe in the name of the Souldiers of 8 Regiments of Horse and five of Foote,[b] and left the same to their consideration, desireing their advice thereupon for the preventing of any inconvenience that might arise.

The said Votes and Petition were read and thereupon these severall Questions being debated, were propos'd to every officer, and resolv'd as followeth.

1st Question.

Whether upon the Reports come to the Army concerning the Votes of the House of Comons on Fryday sennight last and the Resolutions on Tuesday last you find such satisfaction in the Army in relation to the late greivances as that there be noe danger of any disturbances and inconveniences in the proceedings upon these Resolutions.

Resolved Negatively.

Vizt. Negatively 86 votes, affirmitively by 3: and 4 Votes were suspended upon their owne desires.[c]

2d Question.

Whether upon the satisfaction and danger implied in the last vote you thinke it needfull for preventing of inconveniencies, that

[a] These votes for disbanding were passed by the House of Commons on 25 May, on the report of the Derby House Committee, brought in by Hollis. They were agreed to by the Lords on May 28.

[b] "*The humble petition of the souldiers of the army*" is printed with the names of the agitators appended in the book of *Army Declarations*, published in 1647, p. 16, and without the names in Rushworth, vi., 498.

[c] A list of the names of the officers present is given in the book of *Army Declarations*, p. 15. A short account of the Councils in Rushworth, vi., 497.

the Quarters of the Army not fixed upon duty be imediatly contracted.

Resolved Affirmitively.

Vizt. 82 Votes Affirmitively. 5 voted Negatively, and 6 were absent at this vote.

Ordered By this Councill, That Commissary General Ireton, Collonell Whalley, Collonell Rich; Collonell Lilburne, Collonell Okey, Collonell Hewson, Lt. Collonell Jackson, Major Desbrow, or any 5 of them, shall drawe up a Representation of the effect of the precedent votes to the Generall, with the grounds and intention thereof according to the Debates past, and also of their humble desires to the Parliament for suspending the present proceeding upon their Resolutions on Tuesday last and the resumeing the consideration thereof, and this to be presented to the Councill of Warre at the next meeting for their approbation.

The Councill adjourned till 6 a clock afternoone.

The Councill accordingly mett at 6 a clock and there were present this afternoone which were not present in the morning

Col. Sir Hardresse Waller.	Capt. Leigh.
Major Rogers.	Ensigne Perth.
Major Saunders.	Ens: Nicholls.
Capt. Rainborrow.	

And upon Debate this Question was first putt.

3[d] Question.

Whether upon the dissatisfaction and danger implyed in the first vote at the meeting this morning you thinke it necessarie for preventing of inconveniencies That the Quarters of the Army being contracted as in the 2[d] vote there be a generall Randezvouz of that part of the Army whose Quarters shall be soe contracted.

Resolved Affirmatively.

Vizt. 84 voted for the Affirmative, 7 voted for the Negative, and 9 were absent.

After the passing this last vote the Officers appointed in the morning according to the last and precedent votes in the morning deliver'd in a Paper and upon reading and debating thereof into parts this Question was put, vizt.

4th Question.

Whether this paper drawne upp and brought in by the Officers appointed thereunto by this Councill, and now read and debated in parts, shall passe with the Amendments now made as the opinion and advice of the Councill of Warre to be presented to the Generall.[a]

Resolved Affirmatively.

Vizt. Voted Affirmatively by 82: Negatively by 4. 13 were absent, and one was suspended, Vizt. Sir Hardresse Waller's Vote upon his own desire, in regard of his long absence from the Army and Kingdome.

Here a Letter from the Earle of Manchester, Speaker of the House of Peeres, to his Excellencie together with the former Votes of Parliament, passed both Houses and signed by the Clerke of the Parliament,[b] were read, after which the Question was moved by the President to this effect, vizt. Whereas by the Votes of Parliament now read severall Regiments of Foote are appointed to be disbanded at severall times and places, That upon the drawing out of those Regiments for the contracting of Quarters the said Votes may

[a] "The opinion and humble advise of the Councell of Warre, convened at Bury, Saturday, 29 May, 1647." *Army Declarations*, p. 12; *Lords' Journals*, ix., 226; *Old Parliamentary History*, xv., 385.

[b] On May 28, Parliament ordered the votes to be sent to the General with a joint-letter from the Speakers of the two Houses. The letter is printed in the *Lords' Journals*, ix., 217; *Old Parliamentary History*, xv., 380. Fairfax's answer to Manchester, *Lords' Journals*, 226; *Old Parliamentary History*, 384; his reply to Lenthall, Rushworth, vi., 499; *Old Parliamentary History*, 390.

be communicated to them by their respective Officers at the head of every Regiment, to the end that if any of them appeare satisfied soe as to stay to be disbanded without disturbance or inconvenience those that shall be soe satisfied may continue at their present Quarters untill they shall be drawne out to be disbanded; and after some debate thereof this Question was put, vizt.

5th Question.

Whether the stating and determining of the Question last moved since the precedent Vote shall be laid aside for the present or noe?

Resolved Affirmatively. Nemine contradicente.

JO. MILLS, Advocate.

Letter of Intelligence,[a]

The Generall is at St. Edmunsbury. About 200 Officers have mett this day at a full debate. Upon reading the Votes of Parliament on Friday was sennight and Tuesday last, it was resolved by all except Lieutennant Collonell Jackson, Major Gooday, and two Officers more of the Generall's regiment, that they were all unsatisfied with those Votes; and that it would be as unsatisfactory to the Army to heare there were dayes of Randezvous appointed to disband, and yet their greivances to be unredressed. I assure you, Sir, the more they stirre to disunite us, the more wee are cemented. God shews their actions to be but foolish in what they attempt against us, for what ever they propose for their Ends does our's while we are at a stand. A Committee is appointed (Lords and Commons) to come down on Tuesday next to disband the Generall's Regiment; they may as well send them among soe many Beares to take away their whelps. I wish your good Lord

[a] The mention of the council of war gives the date of this letter to 29 May.

R——[a] be not one, hee will hardly returne with content. The Officers now owne the Souldiers and all that's done and doe beginne to bestirre themselves. I beleive before they depart this day they will agree to move the Generall for a Randezvouz, and if hee scruple itt, itt will be done however. All the honest People in the Citty and Country send to us to stand to them or they are undone; you will shortly heare of severall Counties Petitioning the Parliament that the Army may not be disbanded till things are settled, and that they may have their dearely earned wages, and not [be] scornefully cast off with 8 weekes pay as both Houses have now voted to be paid.[b] The House of Commons pass'd all Tuesday Votes unanimously (our freinds withdrawing). The Lords were divided 12 against us, 11 protested for us against every vote. Wharton was absent or else all had been equall. I hope in the Lord, if wee baffle these Maligoe [maligne?] Grandees in this their maine designe to divide us by disbanding Regiment after Regiment they will be put to new Councells, and court us to accept of Arrears (which they can easily pay us had they but will) if wee will demand noe further and accept of the Irish Service. The Citty Petitioned for 20,000 for to be imployed about the Lyne of the Communication, in order to make warre against us as we apprehend. Our drawing unto a Randezvouz upon it will undoubtedly put them into a military posture and great distractions. Oxford, where our Magazine is, wee have well secured. I wish things at Holdenby were as secure. Itt is incredible the Unitie of Officers and Souldiers except some few Officers who have put themselves in print in opposition to the Army, and now the Souldiers are Petitioning to cast them out or else they will doe it themselves. Sheffeild's Regiment hath begunne it already, dismounted their dissenting Officers, and seized their Horses and Armes.

[a] Robartes.

[b] According to the *Lords Journals*, ix., 207, only three Lords protested.

Saith Lieutennant Collonell Jackson to mee will the Foot do soe, I told him they would, for eight of his Companies had subscribed to stand with the Army and were resolved to cashier their Officers: the poore man sighed at it, but Mr. Edwards his Parishoner and Ghostly Father soe awes him hee dares not comply with the Army. Major Generall Skippon is quite lost in the Army by endeavouring to please both sides: hee will not gett any men with him, and I much feare if hee stay hee will be at a nonplus. Pye's Regiment and Graves' are all engaged with the Army. Sir Robert Pye drew his sword and another Captaine; the Souldiers hem'd them round, made them putt up and give present satisfaction, dismounted the Captaine, and beat him out of their Quarters. Graves look'd on and said never a word. All the Dragoones at Holdenby are come in upon Engagement to the Army; soe now they are all of a peice. I pray God the Souldiers gett not too much head; the officers must instantly close with them, or else there will be disorder.

[*Letter from the Committee at Derby House to Sir T. Fairfax.*]

Sir,

Wee received yours of the 30th of May[a] from Bury. The Commissioners are already on their way to Chelmesford, and being instructed for that service, we desire you to be with them at the place appointed; and whereas your letter seemes to imply that there are soe many Greivances to be further presented to the House from the Souldiers, the Houses have satt severall dayes upon that bussinesse, and have granted whatever they thought fitt for them to grant, or for the Army to desire, and wee are confident the Houses will expect a punctuall obediance in their disbanding according to their orders, And we desire you that if your Life Guard be not

[a] Fairfax's letter of May 30 is printed in the *Lords' Journals*, ix., 226.

yet come to Chelmesford. That you will order it to attend you there as soone as possible may be in this service. Soe we rest.

Your affectionate freinds and servants,

DENZILL HOLLIS, T. LINCOLNE,
PH. STAPYLTON, Ww. LEWIS,
WM. JEPHSON, WM. WALLER.

Derby House, 31 May, 1647.

For the Right Honorable, Sir Thomas Fairfax.

31 May, 1647.

At the Comittee for the affaires of Ireland at Derby House.

Ordered

That such of the Traine of Artillery and the Provisions thereunto belonging (apperteyning to the Army) as were either at Oxford[a] or Wallingford shall be brought up to London and put into the stores in the Tower, And that all the Ordnance and Ammunition that belong to the Garrison of Oxford be also brought up and put into the Tower.

That the said Traine and Provisions be brought from Oxford to

[a] Colonel Richard Ingoldsby's regiment was then quartered at Oxford. They were to be disbanded at Woodstock on June 14, and £3,500 was sent down to pay them, but recalled by vote of June 1. "The messenger being too slow, the money was got into Oxford before he could overtake it, and the soldiers, notwithstanding the Parliament's commands, were resolved not to part with it. The convoy of Dragoons who had guarded it from London attempted to have carried it back again, but the garrison soldiers fell upon them in the High Street by All Souls' College (where the money then stood), wounded several, and beat the rest so shamefully out of the city that they were glad not only to leave the money but a waggon and team of horses behind them." Wood, *Annals*, ii., 508. The agitators despatched Cornet Joyce and a body of horse to seize the magazine at Oxford, which was effected about June 1. Hollis, *Memoirs*, § 95; *Huntingdon's reasons for laying down his commission*, *Maseres Tracts*, i. 398. According to John Harris, whose statement is copied by Huntingdon and Hollis, the seizure of the magazine was approved by Cromwell, *The Grand Design*, 1647, p. 3.

Abbington by land, and from thence by water, together with that at Wallingford, to London.

That the Horses belonging to the Traine be brought by land to London and such other things as may best come by land as the Comptroller shall thinke fitt.

That the Officers and others belonging to the traine doe come to London to disband, and that they shall receive their two months pay as the rest of the Army receives upon their delivery of the Traine into the Tower.

That the Firelocks belonging to the Traine doe Guard the same to London.

That these Votes concerning the Traine be sent to Sir Thomas Fairfax, and a letter written to him to desire him to give order for the putting them in execution.

GUALTER FROST.

[*To Sir Thomas Fairfax from the Committee at Derby House.*]

Sir,

The House of Commons hath referred to this Committee to disband the Traine, and to bring the provisions belonging to it into the Tower, in prosecution of which wee have made the Votes which we send you inclosed, and desire you to give your Orders for the bringing the said Traine to the Tower according to those Votes. Soe wee rest,

Your very affectionate freinds and Servants

WM. WALLER, T. LINCOLNE,
WM. JEPHSON, DENZILL HOLLIS,
WM. LEWIS, PH. STAPYLTON.

Derby House, 31 May, 1647.

[*Sir Thomas Fairfax to the Committee at Derby House.*]

My Lords and Gentlemen

Having formerly written unto your Lordshipps concerning the former Letter about the disbanding of severall Regiments of Foote, and since that time having presented unto both Houses the result of the Councill of Warre concerning that bussinesse, I humbly desire I may not be thought to neglect your orders (considering the temper of the Army and my desires to prevent greater inconveniencies) if the Regiments be not drawne out at the time appointed; hoping speedily to receive the further pleasure of the Parliament herein, which I hope will tend to the prevention of further distraction, I remaine,

T. F.

Edmonds Bury, May 31, 1647.

[*News-letter from London.*[a]]

Sir,

I suppose from many you will understand how much the great Enemies of the Army lost ground yesterday, notwithstanding their motion of locking upp doores, and having an oath ready in case you [they?] should gett a decree for warr. The Lords being sent unto to sitt, and all out of a confidence to carry it by the end of the day; but when it came to the pull soe much sadnes, feare, and deadnesse was over their partie that they were ready to sinke with thoughts of it. I never saw mens lookes soe changed. Sir, in short, it was put off to this morning, when it's deem'd they will

[a] Undated, but pretty certainly written on June 2 from the references to the votes of the Commons of June 1, as to locking up the doors and sending to the Lords to sit. The end of the debate was a resolution "That this debate of this business concerning the army be laid aside for the present: and resumed the first business to-morrow morning; and nothing to intervene." *Commons' Journals*, v., 195.

find as little life to a new warr as yesterday. The great Citty of London having been privately felt, have noe minde to doe any thing further then redeeme publique faith and gett Brokeridg money ; its believed the combustion [conclusion ?] will be this, the going of the supernumerary to Ireland under their owne Officers, and there wee shall be put to it, the Lords having concurr'd to the Ordinance for those to be continued here according to the desire of the Comons as I am told.

[*News-letter from London.*]

London, 3 June, 1647.

All the talke in London is of your Army, some speake ill of you and many well ; for believe it you have a very considerable party in the Citty, they like well your proceedings and will stick by you. The Petitioners, who had a while agoe their Petition burnt, presented another Petition to the House of Commons on Wednesday last; itt was delivered in by Sir William Waller and read, but noe answeare given to it, and was carryed by some few votes to be laid aside; but the House that day insisted on one maine point desired in that Petition (but did it not in Relation to the Petition) about undue Elections, and voted out two of their Members for Wales, and were about nominating a Committee to receive Information about Members unduly Elected.[a] It is noe newes to tell you how the House was startled the day before when they understood from the Generall the Army would not disband, and how it was moved to send for the Generall, and to raise 10,000 men to assist or compell a disbanding ; but all that was laid aside, only the money sent for back againe, and the fortnight's pay to Colonel Rainsborrough's men, but the monies wee have news just

[a] See p. 92 ; this second petition was rejected by 128 to 112 votes, Hollis and Sir William Lewes being tellers for the majority. *Commons' Journals*, v., 195. Sir Richard Price's and Sir Philip Percival's cases were referred to a committee.

now is stop'd by the Souldiers at Woodstock. Itt had been well if that at Chelmesford had been the like.[a] I hope the Magazine at Oxford will be carefully looked unto. The Militia of London goe on bravely (as some suppose),[b] and have voted all the Godly party out of the Commission of the trayned Bands; butt this is not well rellished by many, and few of the Souldiers ('tis conceived) will be subject to the new Officers they intend to put over them; the new modell for the Guards is likewise disbanded, only 360 under new Officers to keepe the Guards.

[*A Letter from Cornet Joyce.*[c]]

Sir,

Wee have secured the King. Graves is runne away, hee gott out about one a'clock in the morning and soe went his way. Itt is suspected hee is gone to London; you may imagine what hee will doe there. You must hasten an answere to us, and lett us knowe what wee shall doe. Wee are resolved to obey noe orders but the

a See Cary's *Memorials of the Civil War*, i., 219-222, and Rushworth, vi., 499, 500, 502.

b See on the London Militia, Rushworth, vi. 648, 745.

c The question whether this letter is the famous letter addressed to Cromwell is discussed in the preface. There are reasons for believing that it should be dated June 3. It appears to have been written immediately after the events related in it. Joyce surrounded Holdenby on the night of Wednesday, June 2, and occupied it about daybreak on June 3. By eight the house was in his possession, and he was peacefully setting his guards. According to the letter of Lord Montague, one of the Commissioners, Colonel Greaves escaped before one of the clock on the Wednesday night, which agrees exactly with the statement in this letter. About one o'clock in the morning seems to refer to the morning of the day on which the letter was written, rather than the morning of the day before. By the morning of the 4th, Joyce had arranged to carry the King to Newmarket, and needed no instructions. His plans were made.

The best accounts of the seizure of the King are that in Rushworth, vi., 513, apparently written by Joyce himself, and those contained in the letters of Lord Montague, dated June 3rd and 4th. *Lords' Journals*, ix., 237, 240, 250.

Generall's; wee shall followe the Commissioners directions while wee are heere, if iust in our Eyes. I humbly entreat you to consider what is done and act accordingly with all the hast you can; wee shall not rest night nor day till wee heare from you.

Yours and the Kingdomes
faithfull Servant till death,
GEORGE JOYCE.

Holdenby this 4th of June
at 8 of the Clock in the
Morning.

[*A Letter from Cornet Joyce.*[a]]

There hath been a partie of Horse, about 500, at Holdenby, who

[a] As in the case of Joyce's first letter, there is no note of any name or address. It is possible however to deduce from the contents of the letter certain conclusions as to the person to whom it was directed. Joyce was now on his way to Newmarket, where the rendezvous of the army was to take place. The letter is evidently written to some person at Newmarket, near it, or on the way to it. He is asked to assist in conveying the King thither, by giving Joyce a party to help him, and by coming with his friends to meet the King. The person to whom the letter is addressed was apparently not in the plot himself. Joyce thinks it necessary to tell him that the King has been taken from Holdenby, that it is at the King's own desire that he is being conveyed to Fairfax, and he also thinks it necessary to protest the excellence of his own intentions. After telling him what has been done he urges him to make the best of it. These points suggest that Joyce was not writing to an accomplice but rather to a person whom he wanted to become one after the event. A suggestion based on these general conclusions may perhaps be ventured. Joyce purposed to go to Newmaket by way of Cambridge, as the fact that Whalley met him on the way the next day proves (*Lords' Journals*, ix. 248). His route from Huntingdon to Cambridge lay through the hundred of Papworth. On May 30, Major Adrian Scroope and that portion of the regiment of Colonel Graves which was not actually assigned to guard the King had been ordered to take up their quarters at once in Papworth hundred. (See Appendix C.) Had Scroope and his soldiers been so disposed they could have seriously hindered Joyce's journey to Newmarket. I suggest therefore that this letter was addressed to Major Scroope in general reliance on his sympathy and assistance. If so, Joyce in asking for "a partie" employs the word in the technical sense of a detachment of horse, and by "friends" probably means to ask Scroope to bring all the officers he can to meet the King.

have secured and taken his Majestie into their Custodie, and the King who doth desire to speake with Sir Thomas Fairfax.—— The King is now at Huntington Towne, and will be at New Markett to morrow. Persuade all the freinds you can to come and meet him, and endeavour to doe for the best. Certainly God hath appeared in a mighty manner, and therefore I shall wholly rely on you for what I desire, which is a partie to doe that which may be justifiable before God and Man. Hast, Hast, think on mee.

I rest,

GEORGE JOYCE, Cor^{tt}.

Huntington att 11 of the clock this night the 4th of June 1647.

---

[a] Read this inclosed, seale it upp, and deliver itt what ever you doe, that soe wee may not perish for want of your assistance. Lett the Agitators know once more wee have done nothing in our owne name, but what wee have done hath been in the name of the whole Army, and wee should not have dared to have done what wee have, if wee had not been sure that you and my best old friend had consented hereunto, and knew that I speak nothing but truth.[b]

[a] In the copy from which this letter is printed these lines are appended to the preceding letter as if they were a postscript to it. This appendix however is evidently not addressed to the same person as the letter. I take that letter to be itself the enclosure referred to, and this an endorsement appealing to some person to deliver it. The person to whom it was addressed was evidently in constant communication with the agitators. I should suggest that it was directed to some inferior officer, or possibly to some agitator belonging to the regiment of Colonel Graves, that he might deliver it to Scroope.

[b] There are two copies of this letter. In one, the last line runs, "I know that I speak nothing but truth." The reading given above is that of the earlier copy.

[A Letter from York.]

Sir,

Wee heare you have trustees engaging Souldiers heere, and not without successe, Collonel Pointz[a] beginnes to be much troubled, and writes to the Parliament this weeke of Colonell Boynton's[b] turning a Presbiterian out of Scarborow Castle. Hee hath desired of the Major and Aldermen that he may have an addition of men for the Tower; they answeared they have a Company of Cittizens which shall be ready for the publique service but will admitt noe strangers, according to your Order given them, which is to keepe the disposall of this place as much in their owne power as they can and out of the hands of one who will, it may be, be too forward to engage. Then I wish you Justice and us peace, for if wee beginne againe the second woe will be worse then the first. I wish your Army a repairation in point of honour, but, were there not w[e]ightier causes, that will be look'd upon as unequall

[a] A life of Poyntz is given in Sir John Maclean's *Historical and Genealogical Memoir of the Family of Poyntz*. Sydenham Poyntz, b. 1607, was the fourth son of John Poyntz of Reigate. Originally a London apprentice he took service in Germany and rose to high rank in the imperial army. On his return to England he entered the parliamentary service, and on May 27, 1645, was voted by the House of Commons the command of a regiment of horse and a regiment of foot in the north, and shortly after was nominated commander-in chief of the seven associated northern counties. *Commons' Journals*, iv., 248, 250. On September 24, 1645, he defeated the King's forces at Rowton Heath, near Chester. On March 13, 1647, he was confirmed by the Commons in the post of Governor of York, and Clifford's Tower was also placed under his command. He had some difficulty in getting control of Clifford's Tower. A news-letter written about this time says, "The northern general struts and looks big, and instead of true blue hath got a bundle of orange ribbon in his hat, much like a plume of feathers behind." The adherents of Fairfax wore blue ribbons in their hats, the Levellers adopted sea-green as their colour, and the Club-men in 1645 chose white ribbons. Lilburne, *An Impeachment of High Treason against Oliver Cromwell*, p. 41; Whitelock, *Memorials*, iii., 23, ed. 1854; Sprigge, *Anglia Rediviva*, p. 61, ed. 1854.

[b] Matthew Boynton, confirmed as governor of Scarborough, March 13, 1647. In the second civil war he sided with the royalists. Rushworth, vii., 1370.

to the hazard of new trouble, and they slack (?) doe well to dispence with it as much as they cann —— this very advice that the Generall be not engaged against the Parliament, and that it be not expected frcm him by the Army. For, in case an agreement come after a little busling, his joyning with them will robb the Kingdome of that employment of his from which wee expect much benefitt. And I hope the Army will be content that he carry faire to the Parliament.

J. B.

June 4th 1647.

[*Colonel Whalley to Sir Thomas Fairfax.*] [a]

Sir,

His Majestie about 5 of the clock this afternoone was pleased to be a little merry and laughingly told mee hee now perceived your Excellencie would not force him back to Holdenby, which I perceived hee tooke very well. I told him hee might rest confident you was very tender of his honnour, and would secure him in what you might, what your resolutions were, I knew not; hee desired to give order to his servants to prepare to goe to New Markett to morrow. I desired his Majestie to forbeare till I had acquainted you with his desires, and had orders from your Excellencie to that purpose. His Majestie longs to be there, and this night expects to heare from you, and to be answeared in his desires.

[a] On Friday, June 4, when Fairfax was at Kenford, near Bury, he received the news of the seizure of the King, and immediately sent Whalley and his regiment to march to Holdenby to take charge of the guard of the King and attend the Commissioners there. On the morning of Saturday, June 5, he learnt that Joyce had on the preceding day removed the King from Holdenby to Hinchinbrook, near Huntingdon, and sent Whalley further orders to guard the King back to Holdenby, despatching also two more regiments of horse to assist him. To his great surprise the King refused to return. See Fairfax's letters of June 4 and 7, *Old Parliamentary History*, xv., 400, 409; *Lords' Journals*, ix., 243, 248.

I doubt not but your Excellencie will take into serious consideration a bussinesse of soe high a nature; the Lord direct you, which is the prayer of

Sir,
Your Excellencies most faithfull
Servant,
EDW. WHALLEY.

[Sunday] June 6th 1647.

[*Letter from Collonell Whalley to Sir Thomas Fairfax.*[a]]

Sir,

I have acquainted his Majestie with your orders; hee seemes to be very well pleased. I told him from your Excellencie that your coach should be ready to waite upon him; hee thanks you and desires it may be sent hither to goe by him, in case it should raine hee may make use of itt. His Majestie intended to be upon his march presently after dinner, I suppose it will be betwixt one and two of the clock. I shall not faile further to advertise you, soe soone as hee shall be ready to mount I shall send presently to your Excellencie. His Majestie is resolued to goe through Cambridge, though last night he seem'd to be otherwise minded. I suppose having condescended soe much to him in a great bussinesse you will [not] crosse him in this; I shall take it for your pleasure if I receive not contrary commands from you. I cease not to be,
Sir,

Your most faithfull and humble servant,
EDWARD WHALLEY.

From the Court at Childersey.
June 7, 1647.

[a] Fairfax's answer to this letter is shown by a letter to Lenthal, June 8. Rushworth, vi., 551.

[*News-Letter from Newmarket.*[a]]

June 7th 1647.

This day the Generall, Lieutennant Generall, Commissary Generall Ireton, and Lt. Generall Hammond and divers Officers of the Army went to the [Lady] Cutts house where his Majesty was, according to his Majesties desire the day before. When they came there, they were according to the usuall manner received by the King with civilitie; after some generall discourse of things, the King went into the garden, and the Generall, his Officers, and the Commissioners went together and conferred upon the whole carriage of the businesse. The Commissioners seem'd to be much unsatisfied, whereupon the King coming up againe, the Generall and the Commissioners came to him and Cornett Joyce, who was the man that managed the bussinesse in secureing the King, was call'd before them all. The King charg'd him with saying hee had the Commission of the whole Army for what hee did, and by consequence had the Generall's, hee being the principall part of the Army. The Cornett replyed, and did avow hee told his Majestie hee had not the Generall's Commission when the King did particularly demaund it of him, and that [when] the King asked him by what Commission hee did come to secure him hee answered the King, if hee pleased to looke about hee might see by what authoritie, meaning the Troopers that were ready mounted. Whereupon the King publiquely said to the whole Company, that it was true indeed hee did say soe, and it was likewise true all the Gentlemen that were mounted on horseback did cry out giveing their approbation to what hee said, but saith the King I was notwithstanding perswaded that hee could not venture to attempt such a thing as to bring mee away but that hee had the councell of greater persons. Then Mr. Crewe, Sir John Cook extreamly prest against Cornett Joyce, that hee deserved to loose his head for what hee had done, that hee had injured the Parliament, the Generall, the Army, and the Commissioners intrusted with the King, and had brought them away without their

[a] An abridged version of this letter is given in Rushworth, vi., 549.

consent; whereupon Cornett Joyce replyed, That the King gave his consent to come, and that the Commissioners gave their consent to come, and told them hee would not bring them without their consent. I, sayth the King and the Commissioners, you told us wee should goe, and then it was in vaine for us not to consent, but sayth the King, now I am come, I had the promise of these Gentlemen to be conveyed to New Markett; I take them to be men of their words, and were I meere stranger mett upon the high way and stopt from going on, none in civilitie but would provide conveniencies for mee, here I have none, and therefore I doe expect to morrow to goe for New Markett, and desire Sir Thomas Farfax and his Officers [to] conferre together about it, for the Commissioners say they have noe power at all further to dispose of mee, for their power ended at Holdenby, and was limitted to that place, though the Commissioners be the same; whereupon the Generall and Officers withdrew and conferr'd together and afterwards returned to his Majestie, and told him, as they did at the beginning, hee was removed from Holdenby without their privitie, knowledge, or consent, yet notwithstanding since hee is unwilling to goe back, if the Commissioners present with them will condescend, the Generall would not be against his going to New Markett. Sayth the King, This is a perfect denyall.

[*John Cosens to Alderman Adams.*]

Newcastle, 7 June, 1647.

I am assured, That the present feare of a sudden change is better knowne to you, and more deeply considered by you, then my selfe, by how much neerer you are related to the publique trust of the Kingdome; but this storme threatening us (and you in us) to fall heere, both as suddenly and as heavily as upon any other place whatsoever, I could not forbeare to give you my present sence of our condition in this place. This Regiment[a] is betweene twelve

[a] Skippon's regimen

hundred and fouretcene hundred strong, the Commander whereof (which makes all our danger) absent, there being not one Officer of the whole Regiment of considerable command that I knowe of which standeth well affected to the Parliament and Government but one Captaine and Lieutennant; some of the rest of the Captaines have been lately at London, and this weeke unexpected came suddenly and hastily home, and as it is reported did not at all see their Commander in cheife the Feild Marshall, and since they came they spare not to speake their intentions of feighting freely. How they speake of the Citty you may guesse by their language in their Declaration, and how they talke of the Parliament many wonders to heare; to morrow they muster the Regiment, and a flying report goes that they will turne all the Scotts out of the Towne. On Satturday morning soe soone as the post came, and that the Major had returned his letters for the Deputy Governour, who then by reason of his sicknesse would not goe, but without question they doe now joyne Councells, and will when time serves joyne forces together also; as yet they come not to doe any thing vissible, but certainly as soone as they receive the word they will secure this Towne and the Castle of Tinmouth in a moment: for my part I looke for it every day. And I pray God there may be soe much time left as may admitt of a recovery and timely helpe; the only way will bee in my apprehension that the Feild Marshall doe post hither with all speed, soe may hee both save this Towne and his Regiment; another way I knowe not, only I seriously recommend it unto you and those in whose hands helpe lyeth, that that you would please to make it knowne unto them. Whether [were?] this Regiment out of the Towne and a Commission sent to any person here of trust together with a proportion of Armes, there were noe doubt but all would be well and the Towne kept safe by our owne inhabitants, for the body of the Commons of this Towne are right, and soe I thinke are the Common Souldiers of the Garrison, only the Commanders of both are to be doubted, and what may be the issue God only knowes; for my owne particular if they become

Masters, I expect noe more favour from them, nor lesse crueltie then from our last Enemies. But now, good Sir, for this Townes sake, for the Citties sake and for the Kingdomes sake, lay this to heart, and improve your power to rescue this soe desireable a Morsell from the mouth of the Adversary, and more I shall not say, the consequence thereof in relation to your Citty and the Kingdome being enough knowne unto you.[a]

To Alderman Adams, London.

[*Letter to Skippon from some one in the Army.*]

May it please your Honour,

Before the Parliament Commissioners came into the Army on the Heath there were read these ensuing Articles at the head of the severall Regiments, vizt.

1. That dureing the time of the Commissioners being at the Randezvous and the time of their speeches the Soldiers to be very silent and civill towards the said Commissioners.

2. That all Cinque Ports be presently seized on and secured, least the treasury should be conveyed out of the Kingdome.

3. That all Committeemen, Excisemen be presently seized on and secured untill they and every of them doe give upp their accompts from the begginning of this Warre.

4. That a Way be forthwith consulted for the speedy prevention of the Scotch Invasion to disturbe the Kingdome.

These or to the same effect with many more were read and applauded, but command was given that none should move any of these to any of your Members. Pardon I humbly beseech your

[a] From John Cosens. Rushworth, vi., 559; see also *Commons' Journals*, June 12, and two letters from Skippon on the subject. Cary, i. 229, 230.

Honour my presumption for this my troubleing of your Honour, it beeing out of a reall intention to the Kingdome's good from

Your humblest and most faithfull Servant.

June 10th, 1647,
at 7 at night.

Some Committees being at the Randezvouz and heareing it are gone aside for it I assure your Honour.

To the Honorable Field Marshall Generall Skippon at the Rose in Cambridge, These with my duty and humble service presented.

[*Letter from Major Twistleton to his Excellencie.*]

May it please your Excellencie,

By order from Major Generall Skippon [a] (at Newcastle) I drewe out of my Colonell's Regiment 150 Horse under the command of Captaine Anthony Markham, who were appointed to attend his Majestie to Holdenby as a guard, and to receive further Orders from Collonell Graves; where they accordingly continued untill Friday the 4th of this instant, when his Majestie was removed from thence by a partie of Horse under the command of Cornett Joyce, with whome parte of those of our Regiment are gone, the Officers and about 70 Souldiers are returned to the Regiment, [not] perceiving the Cornett nor any other to have any order from your Excellencie or other Superiour Officer to command them further. I thought it noe lesse then my duty herewith to acquaint your

[a] On June 15, the House of Commons voted that the General should deliver the person of the King to the Commissioners formerly appointed, that he should be placed at Richmond, and guarded by Colonel Rossiter's regiment. Twistleton was Major of Rossiter's regiment. His letter shows that a detachment of that regiment had before formed part of the King's guard. Further references to the subject are contained in the *Lords' Journals*, ix., 283, 287, 289. Twistleton succeeded Rossiter in the command of the regiment.

Excellencie, and humbly to crave your order whether to returne those to their former trust, or remaund the other from the Army to the Regiment. What in this or otherwise your Excellencie shall please to command shall be carefully and punctually obeyed by him who is

Your honour's most humble and faithfull servant,

PHIL. TWISLETON.

Lincolne, 11th June, 1647.

[*General Fairfax to Major Twistleton.*]

Sir,

I received your letter desiring my orders for the further disposall of that party which formerly was appointed out of your Regiment to attend upon the king to Holdenby; and in regard I perceive the occasion of the party soe dividing itselfe proceeded from the affection of some of your Souldiers who have seene and been fully possest of the reall and honest desires of the Army in order to the peace and libertie both of the Kingdome and themselves, have uninvited resolved to engage and stay with the Army in the lawfull prosecutions of the generall good, and therefore not doubting but all good men who understand us will joyne with us therein, I thought fitt to desire you to march upp with your Regiment to the Army, with all convenient speed; and least you or any else may be unsatisfied either in our proceedings, intentions, or present condition I have sent unto you Lieutennant Lloyd[a] of Collonell Fleetwood's Regiment, who is a faithfull man and one well knowne unto you, to give you a full Accompt of all our whole bussinesse.

[T. FAIRFAX.]

[a] Lieutenant Griffith Lloyd.

[Letter from Sir Thomas Fairfax to Collonell Whalley.]

Sir,

Having given orders for removing the head quarters to St. Alban's,[a] and the rest of the Army thereabouts, I send this to you to give you notice of it that you may order your bussinesse accordingly, not knowing whether the removing the Army that distance from you may not produce some inconveniency in refference to the safety of the king's person. I shall therefore committ it to you to take an especiall care of that your charge in useing all meanes tending to the securitie of his Majesty's person, not only in keeping strict guards, but also in sending out scouts into the Countries about you, especially into Norfolke, where I understand there hath been lately some kinde of disturbance as if they intended to rise. In case there shall appeare any such reall danger I desire you to secure his Majestie by bringing him towards the Army, and to send me timely notice thereof. Not doubting of your care herein, I remaine

[THOMAS FAIRFAX.]

Royston,
June 11th 1647.

[Letter intend[ed] to severall Counties concerning the Armies Engagements.]

Honoured Gentlemen and our Christian freinds,

Wee suppose you have received some information from our

[a] The headquarters were at St. Alban's on the night of June 12. Fairfax received on June 11 a petition from the peaceable and well-affected inhabitants of the counties of Norfolk and Suffolk. *Lords' Journals*, ix., 260, 261, 263; Rushworth, vi., 559.

printed papers concerning our late proceedings with the Parliament in relation to our affaires as Souldjers, we meane the bussinesse of Ireland, of our Arrears, the Declaration against us as Enemies after soe many experiences in bloud of our fidelitie to the Kingdome, and all these managed and carried on by a prevailing party who have abused and misledd the Parliament against their faithfull freinds and the Kingdomes interest in many particulars. As to these things wee have named we desire to referre you to our printed papers, and the declarations wee are setting forth; but the trueth is, whilst these things were in agitation, that greate designe of the prevayling partie against the Parliament and this kingdomes interest does discover it selfe in their transactions with us. We are unavoidably involved as subjects both respectively to our selves and the publique to keepe our swords in our hands. Wee hope within three or fowre dayes to publish a Declaration which wee are confident will give satisfaction to all honest and reasonable men of our proceedings. In the meane time wee thought fitt to give you this breife accompt, that we are come neere London without the least intent of giving occasion of a new warr, but hope fully to prevent it; wee seeke not our selves but the accomplishing those ends and obteyning those things which the Parliament held forth as arguments to invite us to undertake this warre, vizt., the recovery of the rights and liberties of the subject, the opposeing tyranny and oppression, the obteyning a firme and well grounded peace, and those other things which the Parliament held forth in their severall Declarations, without which wee had not engaged our selves; and now having through the good hand of God brought the warr to an end, wee would be loath the Kingdome should loose soe blessed a fruite and harvest of our labour, as we perceive some bad men are designing to defeate it of. Wee meddle not with matters of Religion or Church Government, leaving those to the Parliament. Wee desire as much as any to mainteyne the authority of Parliament, and the foundamentall government of the Kingdome. We seeke justice against those that have wronged us and the Kingdome.

To which wee desire the concurrence of you and all good men and rest

Your very affectionate Freinds.[a]

St. Alban's, June 13, 1647.

[*News-letter from London.*]

London: 13 June, 1647.

Our cheife news here is of your Army, and I can assure you wee have twenty stories in a day and scarce ever a true one; but your coming neere London I promise you put the Parliament and Citty into a shrewd fright. The Parliament satt hard at it Fryday and Satturday,[b] and soe did the Militia and Comon Councill; it was much urged to raise forces against you, nay and they would have done it if they could have found any way how. Many Officers Fryday and Satturday listed themselves at the Comittee at Derby House, and the Militia were consulting how to put the Citty into a posture, and to arme all, and have also listed some, but they find soe much difficulty in the manner they have laid all aside againe, and now intend to come to you with good words and are sending an answere to your letter by foure Aldermen and 8 Councill men. The Parliament have sent Sir Thomas Widdrington and Collonell White with additionall instructions. On Satturday morning things wrought after another manner, for upon the report of your being neere, all the Trayned Bands of London were commanded to rise on paine of death, and all the shopps to be shutt upp; and if this had taken, more pretty feates had been acted, the suspected party in London been secured, and they would have mett your Army (after you had been declared enemies) and done strange things; but this designe comes to nothing, for the trayned Bands would

[a] From the officers of the army, but apparently never sent. Compare the letter of June 10, given by Carlyle and Rushworth.

[b] Friday, June 11, and Saturday, June 12. See Rushworth, vi., 553, 557.

not budge, not 10 men of some companies appeared, and many companies none at all but the Officers; nay the very boyes in the streets jeered the drumms as they went about with their charge upon paine of death. The Westminster Regiment made a great appearance, and the Lord Mayor [a] was in person very active to compell the shopp keepers to shutt upp shopp, by which means most about the Exchange and Cornhill were shutt, but few in other places; and those that did shutt upp were of the right stamp, and these many of them, understanding upon what slight ground that command was and being laughed at by others, opened their shopps againe in the afternoone, when also the Trayned Bands were discharged, but stronger Guards kept then formerly.[b]

[*News-letter from London.*[c]]

Sir,

The game is hard that is plai'd but hee that hath ordered hitherto will still noe doubt for the best.

[a] Sir John Gayer, impeached for his share in the tumults of July. *Lords' Journals*, ix., 201.

[b] On June 11, a Committee of Lords and Commons was appointed to join with the Committee of the Militia of the City of London, with power to put London in a posture of defence, suppress insurrections, etc. The same afternoon the letter from Fairfax and the chief officers of the army to the city of London was communicated to the Parliament, and at the request of the city the army was ordered not to approach within 40 miles of London. On the 12th, hearing that the army was still approaching, the Mayor and Aldermen despatched a conciliatory answer to the letter and abandoned all intention of resistance. *Commons' Journals*, v., 206-209; Rushworth, vi., 554, 557; see also *Fairfax Correspondence*, iii., 355.

[c] Undated, but pretty clearly written early in June, as shown by the reference to the advice of the council of war of May 29 as recent; it was evidently written soon after the army declared its resolution not to disband, and before its political demands had been definitely set forth, *i.e.*, before the representation of the army of June 14. On 11 June, Parliament and City made preparations for fighting, on 12 June, the City gave way and sent a deputation to the army with a conciliatory answer to the letter of the officers of June 10. As that letter was written by Cromwell the statement about his speaking home must refer to it.

I perceive the purging the House is inclined unto here, for the Army to stand upon, and a Councell faithfully to transact martiall affaires (and the truth is there is noe safety without now, for that you have falce Elections, Members not capeable, such as have been corrupt and all to pay their debts will goe farre); and indeed this must be, and if possible the Lords and Commons sitt together, at least be declared joinctly the Supreame Judicature; and before theis severall particulars can be gone through, what time will be spent; if that a party to Ireland could goe, and the rest see the other done it were excellent. I like well your last results at Councell of Warr on pursuing the designes of disbanding. The truth is the Army may be now instrumentall of the greatest good that ever this Kingdome or any other tasted on, and it's cleere delivered from apparent ruine, which by these wretched instruments would have been brought upon it. Feare but the Citties, for to feare them is to conquer them, and feare hath done that; and now what say you to what I have ever told you, that the Citties being feared by the Parliament who had such an Army argued they were men of as much cowerdize as any in the world. O. Cromwell spake as gallantly and as home as if he had been charging his enemies in the feild.

[*News-letter from London June* 14.]

The House was this day informed, That about a thousand reduced Officers intended to addresse themselves to the Houses for their Arrears. It was thereupon ordered to send to the Militia for a stronger guard, which was speedily sent downe by a message to the House of Commons, and a Committee was appointed to goe to some of the cheife of the Petitioners and acquaint them with the ill sence the House had of this their publique meeting in the feild and to require them to disperse forthwith, and when all their Accompts were audited (which would be on Thursday next) the House would take speedy course for the payment of them. A Committee was then appointed to drawe a Declaration, That noe persons should upon paine of death gather themselves in a tumultuous way, and likewise what they have done in satisfaction of the Soldiers, and what they intend. A message came from the Lords; That their Lordshipps had appointed a Committee to drawe a Declaration to satisfie the Kingdome what the Houses had done, and what they would doe for the future, for the ease of the subjects, for the payment of the Souldiers, and for settleing the peace of the Kingdome.[a] The Commons named a Committee to joyne with the Lords for the drawing upp this Declaration. Another message came from the Lords desiring it might be referr'd to the same Committee that is appointed to drawe up the Declaration last mentioned to consider what place is fitt and convenient to have the person of the King brought unto, that soe hee may have the joynt applycation [of both kingdoms] for the settleing a safe and well grounded peace. Sir Phillipp[b] opened the bussinesse upon this message, pressing much for his Majestie to come on the South-side of this River, Mr. Sollicitour answered him, Mr. Hollis replied, Mr. Nathaniell Fienness answered, Sir William Lewis replied to him in a long and pithie speech; at last comes Sir Arthur Hazlerigg and spoiles all the play with a plaine and downeright answer. Soe that the House ordered to send their Lordshipps an answere by messengers of their owne. The further debate of this bussinesse concerning the King to morrow. Letters of intelligence from France was sent for from Derby House, which being read were laid aside. Here is great talke of a designe to bring the Scotts in againe, and that Lauderdaile is gone with a letter from his Majestie for the Prince, who is to come in the head of that Army.

I am,

Your Excellencies most humble servant,

June 14 1647.
10 at night.

O. C.[c]

[a] *Lords' Journals*, ix., 264.

[b] Sir Philip Stapleton.

[c] O. C. is not O. Cromwell. It is evidently written to Fairfax, and probably by some member of the House of Commons.

[*News-letter from London.*]

Sir,

Heere hath been this day the greatest tumults and insolencies raised upon the House of Commons that ever any yet heard of, some of their members (and by name Sir Henry Vane Jun[r]) threatned to be cutt in pieces, many others of them insufferably abused, and the whole House threatened, and I may truly say at this houre close block't up by common Souldiers clamouring for their pay, and vowing to lett noe member passe out till they be satisfied. Itt first begane in the Court of Requests, to whome Mr. Hollis, Sir Phillip Stapleton and others were sent to appease, with promiss of 10,000[l] more to be added to what was formerly given them; upon which promise those seemed to be quiett, but this latter and more dangerous one still continues and whether they be of the number of those who first rais'd itt, or some other discontented persons who now second it, the tumult and throng in the Hall is soe great that it cannot be knowne. I looke upon this as a very sad omen, fearing least under this colour the Parliament would be forced to drawe downe ths Citty Guards for their owne securitie, and by this the Army not only have some cause of jealousie ministred to them when they shall see the whole City in a posture of defence, which hath been soe often urged to be done and except under this colour would hardly be obteyned, but also those spiritts who soe much thirst after a second warre exceedingly encouraged and heightened, looking upon this as a handsome foundation to raise another Army upon.

London. June 14th 1647.[a]

[a] Dated in the MS. June 16, but apparently referring to the tumult of June 14. *Commons' Journals*, v., 209; Rushworth, 561, 571. One of the charges against the 11 members evidently refers to this tumult of June 14 described in this letter. See also the Army Declaration of June 23, and the *Fairfax Correspondence*, iii., 357, 358.

[*Letter from the Earle of Warwick to the Generall*].

Sir,

Your professions are soe large and soe cleere to the good and service of the publique as I cannot receive those feares that many take by your approach to this place, that the sword the publique hath trusted in your hand shall have any use but for the defence and advantage of the State and Parliament that you have soe faithfully and fortunately served. I am glad to find your expressions doe agree with my opinnion of your justice, goodnesse, and honour, which as it hath occasioned a great affection and desire in mee alwayes to serve your Excellencie, soe shall it continue me in a reall disposition to serve you as

Your Excellencies most faithfull and humble servant

WARWICK.

London: 14th June 1647.

[*The King to Sir T. Fairfax*].

Charles R.

The professions which you made to us at Childersley makes us hope, That albeit ye disavowed Cornett Joyce in bringing us forth from Holdenby yet you will not deny us those civilities which he (according to his power) did promise us; wherefore we desire, That the Duke of Richmond, Sir William Fleetwood, Doctor Shelden, and Doctor Hammond may be permitted to waite upon us to serve us in their severall places.[a] This being that which is soe necessary for our service, and not dissonant to your owne

[a] See Lord Montague's letter of June 27, 1647, and subsequent letters. *Lords' Journals*, ix., 299, 300. The commissioners of the Parliament complained on June 27 to Fairfax of his allowing these persons to have access to the King. They report, "the General tells us that it is very true that the King wrote to him about a fortnight since about those two chaplains, and he never gave him an answer; whereat the King was angry." In his letter to Parliament of July 8, Fairfax vindicated hi conduct in permitting Richmond and these chaplains to attend the King.

grounds, we cannot doubt but to have a satisfactory answere to these our letters. Att Newmarkett the 17th June 1647.

To Sir Thomas Fairfax, Generall.

Letter to the Gentlemen of severall Shires.

Gentlemen

You will understand by the bearer hereof the late proceedings with the present intentions and resolutions of my selfe and this Army in order to the good and peace of the Kingdome. The papers that have been published from the Armie will (I hope) satisfie you concerning our grounds and the occasions that have led us to what we doe. I desire that for preserving the peace of the Kingdome, (untill things may through the goodnesse of God come to a settlement) you would unanimously endeavour to putt your selves and the Country into such a posture as to prevent or suppresse any insurrections that may disturbe the peace of the country or the Kingdome, and that herein (without relation to different parties or interests) you would apply your self to such courses as may conduce to a generall composure, soe farr as may consist with the common right and liberties of the subject which we have hitherto fought for; and in prosecution heerof I shall acknowledge myselfe

Your very assured freind to serve you,

THO. FAIRFAX.

St. Albans.
19th June, 1647.

Letter to Collonell Whalley [*from Sir Thomas Fairfax.*[a]]

Sir,

I have received yours, and cannot but be very sencible of the great burthen which the confidence I have of your care and fidelitie

[a] Undated, probably written June 21, 1647. See Lord Montague's letter of June 20. *Lords' Journals*, ix., 283.

brought upon you, wherein I must needs say you have not now fayled my expectation, but have discharged your trust to the satisfaction of all and Honour to your selfe. I understand by Collonells Hammond and Lambert and also by your Letter, that the King, according to the Parliament's last letter, intended to beginne his journey towards Richmond upon Thursday next, and that he intends to ly the first night at Royston, according to which his resolutions I desire you to attend upon his Majestie thither, and with all possible care to pursue your former dilligence for the safetie of his person, and by a messenger to give all speedy intimation when you see hee is resolv'd his jorney, and second it by another when he takes Horse. and I shall take care that further orders shall meete you in good time at Royston. I heare of some jealousies of an intention to surprise the King to London, and though I need not be solicitous for your care, yet I thought it good to lett you knowe that I have received a caution thereof from other hands as well as your selfe. I shall say noe more, but, expecting as timely notice as you can, I rest,

[T. Fairfax.]

Tuesday the 22th of June, 1647.

To his Excellencie Sir Thomas Fairfax &c.

The humble Petition of the Adjutators of Collonell Rich his Regiment.

Humbly Sheweth,

That whereas it hath been this day debated by us the Adjutators of the severall troopes of Collonell Rich his Regiment and Officers of the respective troopes, in which wee are all satisfied and have joyntly concurr'd that Lievtennant Hooker, Lievtennant of that troope which was Captaine Nevill's, is noe freind but an enemy to the present iust proceedings of the Army: Wee therefore humbly Petition your Excellencie that hee may be suspended and discharged of that charge as Lievtennant of a Troope of Horse.[a] And your Petitioners shall as in duty bound ever pray &c.

JNO. BIDDLES JO. DOBER	Collonell's Troope
JON. BRADSHAW RICH. WILLIAMS	
OLIVER HARRIS THO. BUTTERY	
ROGER STURGIS WILLIAM ROOKE	
JOSEPH FOSTER TOBIAS HILL	
THOMAS COOKE RI. LOXTON	

Letter to Collonell Whalley from Barkhamsted.

Sir,

Having received yesterday's vote[b] from the House, which putts the Commissioners into the same capacitie that they were at Holdenby, we hold you free of all further charge, save to looke to your Guards that his Majestie make noe escape, and therein you must be carefull and more now than ever.

Dr. Hammond and the other of his Majestie's Chaplaines (soe much desired) went through this Towne this morning coming towards you; perhapps the Commissioners will put you upon it to keepe them from the King, see[c] you are exact only in faithfullnesse to your trust, and that dureing that only, for now you can be as civill as some others that pretend to be more. Lett such distrustfull

[a] Compare a paper printed at the end of the "*Solemn Engagement*" of June 5, 1647, entitled, "*Severall Reasons, why we Souldiers cast out our Dissenting Officers.*" British Museum, E., 392, 26.

[b] *Lords' Journals*, ix., 290, 292; *Commons' Journals*, v., 222.

[c] MS. "soe."

carriages be provided for by those Gent[lemen], who perhapps will incurre some difficulty in the way wherein you have been faulted. We commend our selves kindly unto you and rest

Your Affectionate freinds and Servants,

OLIVER CROMWELL.
JOHN HEWSON.

June 25th, 1647.

Prethee be very carefull of the Kings secureing; and although you have had some opportunity of putting all upon others that's unacceptable, yet be never a whitt more remisse in your dilligence.

[*News-letter from London to Sir T. Fairfax.*]

May it please your Excellencie,

The House of Commons this day made the inclosed order, to which the Lords have not yet assented; the House hath not yet received the motion made yesterday by 10 of the 11 Members,[a] the Recorder Glynn being not willing to joyne with the rest in that motion, but hopes for the protection of the Cittie. The neglect of this bussinesse makes delay which caused jealousies of some designes. The reduced Officers went to receive 10,000[li] at Christ's Church, which being denied to some of them because their Accompts were not audited, a tumult beganne which occasioned the Lord Mayor and Sheriffes to endeavour to raise the trained Bands, who fearing it was for some designe in opposition to the Army refused to stirre, though the Command was upon paine of death; the Cittizens shutt upp their Shopps, the Souldiers threatening to pull downe their Houses, whereupon said an eminent Cittizen, "how shall wee be able to oppose an Army when we cannot suppresse a small number of Officers." This last night the trayned Bands of Westminster about one of the clocke was

[a] See *Commons' Journals*, v., 224, 225. The ten members asked for leave to be absent, which was granted on the afternoon of June 26.

called out upon paine of death, but not one in 20 appeared. The Houses adiourned this day from 12 of the clock to 4 at which time they ordered to debate the Ordinance for putting the reduced Officers out of the Lines. I humbly thank your honour for your last and former favours to

Your Excellencie's humble servant.

26 Junii, 1647.

[*Letter from General Poyntz to his Officers*].

Gentlemen and fellow Souldiers,

I make noe question but you are sencible of the great distractions is like to befall these northerne parts who have already soe much suffered by these unfortunate warrs, and if not prevented are like to suffer much more, and that through the occasion of some discontented persons who seekes to sett the Army and Country in a great mutiny and uproare, and to draw them to dissobedience of the Parliament, my selfe, and all their Comanders, the issue whereof can produce nothing but ruine to these northerne parts. Now to give you the more satisfaction I thought fitt to write this lettre to you all that you might truly understand how things are carried on by such incendaries and disaffected persons who came into my quarters to intangle and draw my Souldiers from their obedience to the Parliament to whome you have alwaies been soe faithfull and done soe good service from the beginning of those unhappy troubles, and them which the Parliament looke more upon now then ordinarie for our civill comportment both to the Country and our Superiours, all which I make no doubt when time shall serve but wee shall reape both the benefitt and honour to perpetuall posteritie. Now I being informed that Major Lilburne with one or two more of such incendaries as hee is have had meetings within the West [riding] and with one Hodgson formerly a Mountebank's man and now a Chyrurgeon under the command of

Colonell Copley, who observing these parts to continue still in their obedience to the Parliament endeavoured to putt this Army into confusion and distraction, pretending they were sent with authoritie from Sir Thomas Fairfax, which I will assure you is false, for they neither doe nor can produce any such order from him. I know him to be soe much a Gentleman of Honour and a Souldier that if hee desired assistance of forces hee would have desired it of mee and not have imployed such mountebanks and illaffected persons. I am credibly informed by my owne Quarter Master who was with Commissary Ireton and Collonell Whalley within thes foure or five dayes, that some of them framed a letter as if it came from the Souldiers of these parts, that they would march to him if hee pleased; but hee utterly denyed their motion, and forbad them not to stirre. Now according to the rule and discipline of warre, that if any comes into anothers Quarters to inveagle or perswade Souldiers from their superiours hee is to be punnished with death; but I being unwilling to use my authoritie untill I first informe the Parliament of England therewith, and for answeare thereunto you may perceive by these inclosed Ordeynances[a] which I send you, which is soe much as I am confident will satisfie all honest and faithfull Souldiers. And truly, Gentlemen, you may all be assured that the Parliament does value you much, as may appeare by these inclosed Ordeynances; therefore I make noe question but you will continue in your wonted obedience to the Parliament, to mee, and your superiour officers as you have hitherto done, and if there be any of your fellow Souldiers that have unadvisedly engaged themselves with any such discontented persons, being misinformed, lett him returne to his Quarters and observe the commands of his commanders and all what hee hath

[a] In a letter dated June 17, Poyntz gave Parliament an account of the commencement of the disturbances amongst his soldiers. Cary, *Memorials of the Civil War*, i., 233, see also pp. 264-282. For the orders in question see *Lords' Journals*, ix., 288; *Commons' Journals*, v., 218, 219. The Major Lilburne referred to appears to have been Major Henry Lilburne.

done in this bussinesse shall be freely forgiven him and noe more thought upon. But in case these will not prevaile with such persons I will use my authoritie given mee by both Houses of Parliament. And these are to require you if any such incendaries or ill affected persons come into your quarters that then you apprehend them and bring them to mee with all speed. Having noe more at present, I rest,

Gentlemen,

Your loveing freind and faithfull
Commander in cheife
SEDNHAM POYNTS.

To all Captaines, L[ts], Cor[tts], Ensignes, and all other inferiour Officeres and Souldiers under my Comand.

Yorke. 28th June 1647.

[*General Poyntz to Col. Lionel Copley.*]

Honoured Sir,

I received yours of the 27th instant, and doe understand that those who pretend to be agitatours for the rest of some perticular Regiments doe continue in their obstinacy yet, and doe justifie their meetings without order from their Officers, and that they intend to make their just greivances knowne to his Excellencie. I would faine knowe why they should make their greivances knowne to Sir Thomas more now then they have done formerly. And why to Sir Thomas? they all knowing these forces are a distinct Army and not under the command of Sir Thomas, and that his Excellencie does utterly renounce their actions, as my Quarter Master [a] informes mee which came from the Army but some fower or five dayes since, and Commissary Generall Ireton and Collonell Whalley told

[a] Robert Newcomen. *Lords' Journals*, ix., 288; Cary, *Memorials*, i., 265.

him soe. As for their desireing to have a generall Randezvous to know result, all or in part, I thinke it not fitt, neither are my Officers or Souldiers to appoint any Randezvous without an expresse order from mee. A joynt Randezvous as they call it will be a great disturbance and oppression to the Country; neither can I conceive what they can have to demaund, consult, or act, being the Parliament have ordered them all their arreares and an additionall Act of Indemnitie, in summe all what Sir Thomas his Army has, as you may perceive by these inclosed Prints; but I and any man may plainely see what these disturbances ayme at. If any of these men have any greivances to make knowne that they have not full satisfaction of in these ordinances let them repaire to mee, who am their Commander in cheife, and alwaies have given redresse to all that ever complained to mee as yet; but [if] that they doe not come speedily in to mee, or forbeare to send out any more of their unlawfull orders, to appoint Randezvous or have any such unlawfull meetings which they pretend to be just, they shall see I will disturbe their next, for I believe by that time this Letter is come to your hands I thinke my orders are devulged throughout the Army. I have sent severall goods [?] into the Northerne Country to the same effect. I desire you will lett this Letter be sent to those fellowes which undertake to act for the rest. Sir, haveing noe more at present, I rest

Your servant,

SEDNHAM POYNTS.[a]

Yorke, 29th June,
1647.

[a] See p. 168, where this letter is made the the basis of the first charge of the agitators against Poyntz. Copley was impeached by the army in 1648. Rushworth, vii., 1354. Some other letters written by Poyntz at this period are in vol. 58 of the Tanner MSS. in the Bodleian Library. He invariably spells his own surname with a final "s," and his Christian name as above.

[*Fairfax to the Agitators of the Regiments of the Northern Association.*[a]]

Gentlemen,

I have received your letters, and doe perceive by them together with the Coppy of your intended Petition, Representation, and Declaration, how sencible you are both of your owne and our condition as Souldiers in referrence to our late greivances exprest in our severall papers and declarations, as also [of] the condition of the Kingdome now calling and pressing for a speedy settlement of their just rights and liberties with the peace thereof; as also your approbation [of the] proceedings of the Army in pursuance of our iust desires, soe that I cannot but well accept and approve of this your vnanimous and mutuall concurrence with this Army for the obteyning of their soe just and necessary concernments both to our selves and the Kingdome. And I doe give you this assureance that I looke upon you as the same with the Army more imediatly under my command, and shall in all things equally provide for you as God shall enable mee to provide for them, which I am the more engaged to doe because I cannot forgett the former labours and hardshipps which you under my command have soe willingly

[a] The petition and representation of eight regiments of the Northern Association is dated July 5, and was presented to Fairfax at Reading on July 15, and presented by him to Parliament on July 16. Rushworth, vi., 620-623. On June 25, Poyntz wrote to Fairfax informing him that several "gentlemen pretending dependence" on the southern army were causing disturbance amongst the northern regiments, and that in pursuance of the orders of Parliament he intended to arrest them. Fairfax's answer reached Poyntz, July 3. It was, "That if any officers or soldiers were come from his army into the northern army, and laboured to inform that army of the fair carriage of his, and that such demands as were desired were just, and that the reports cast upon himself and his army in disobeying ordinances of parliament were untrue, he had sent none such; but if any such were come from his army and had endeavoured to satisfy any of the truths aforesaid, he and the forces under him would countenance and protect such good instruments." *Fairfax Correspondence*, iii., 359, 363. Fairfax's answer was dated June 28, or 29. This letter was probably written about the same time.

undergone for the good and preservation of this Kingdome, and that upon as small and inconsiderable satisfaction as any forces in this Kingdome. I perceive by your inclosed papers that you intend some speedy addresse to the Parliament by way of Declaration to them, and therein to expresse your approbation of the Armies just requests both concerning themselves as soldiers and subjects of this Kingdome, and your resolution to associate with them in pursuance thereof, upon which intimation I though[t] fitt to lett you knowe that I shall be willing to all your desires [to] represent your just and modest desires in as effectuall a way as I have done for my owne Army; and for your desire of being exempted from any obedience to any other command which might occasion obstruction in the promoting of your iust desires, I shall assure you, though I cannot for the present answere your expectation, I shall not doubt but upon the returne of your representation &c. to be presented to the Parliament, to take such course and provide soe for you as shall both be for your owne satisfaction and of all those who singly desire the pease and quiet of the Kingdome.

[T. Fairfax.]

In his *Short Memorial* Fairfax says that he concurred with the Army against his will. "From the time they declared their usurped authority at Triploe Heath I never gave my free consent to anything they did; but being yet undischarged of my place, they set my name in a way of course to all their papers whether I consented or not" (p. 9). This and the other letters of Fairfax here printed seem to show that he acted more heartily with the Army than he was afterwards willing to admit.

PASSAGES THE FIRST DAY OF THE TREATY.

Wickham, July 2nd, 1647.

At a Treaty at Wickham then begunne at the Katherine Wheele,

Present,

Commissioners of Parliament.	Officers of the Army.[a]
The Earle of Nottingham.	Commissary General Ireton.
The Lord Wharton.	Sir Hardress Waller.
Sir Thomas Widdrington.	Colonel Rich.
Major Gen. Skippon.	Colonel Lambert.
Colonel White.	Major Desbrowe.
Sir Henry Vane.	
Thomas Povey, Esq.	
Thomas Scawen, Esq.	

The Instructions of the Commisssioners and severall votes of the House concerning the army read.

It was moved by the Commissioners of the Parliament That Mr. Marshall and Mr. Nye might be present at the Debate.

A long debate about that and whether the Agitators should be admitted to sitt there or noe.

Inclinable to neither for diverse reasons.

Inclinable only if they desired to be at any particular debate.

Reasons against admitting them.

A dissatisfaction and discontent to the Agitators.

For admitting them.

Query. That it should be proposed that our Commissioners should have two in liew of them.

[a] The Commission of Fairfax appointing these and other officers to negotiate is printed in the *Lords' Journals*, ix., 312.

A Paper read by Mr. Scawen with these Desires:

1. That the meeting shall from time to time, but at such places and at such times as shall be mutually agreed on by both parties.

Moved for the conveniencie of a meeting place at the head Quarters.

Desired the Quarter Master Generall may take notice of itt.

1. That the meeting of the Commissioners shall be from time to time, by the mutuall agreement of the Commissioners or upon the desires of either party respectively, at such place within the Head Quarters. . . . .

Colonel Lambert.

Query whither or noe they can debate upon what the Army shall now desire or according to what they have desired.

Sir Thomas Widdrington.

Iff wee propound some things at one meeting and then have others come at the next it will be a worke of labour.[a]

Wickham, Katherine Wheele, July 2nd, 1647.

At the Treaty (2nd meeting) in the afternoone.

First Paper delivered by our Commissioners (after the alteration made to the exception to the 2d offer).

Wee desire to treate first upon the first head in the representation of the Army concerning the purging of the Houses, in order to which wee propose:

1. That a speedy and effectuall course may be taken for the purging of the Houses of all such members as, for any delinquency

[a] The rest of the proceedings of the first day of the treaty are printed in the *Lords' Journals*, ix., 313; *Old Parliamentary History*, xvi., 58, 66; Rushworth, vi., 605.

in relation to the late Warre since his Majestie's setting upp his standard at Nottingham, ought not by Ordinance or Declaration of Parliament to sitt there, by laying some considerable penaltie upon any that being soe guilty shall continue to sitt there.

[*News-letter from London.*]

Sir,

Your removing further from London makes the cittizens smile: yet your freinds knowe not what to thinke on't, and some doubts there be that you are held in play with faire words only, till they be fitt to court you with other language. Wee know not what meanes the eager listing of Horse and auxilaries in London, under pretence to keepe the lyne, the Preists railing against you in their Pulpitts to purpose, and Mr. Ward Fast day before the House of Commons worse then Edwards his Gangrena.[a] "If the wheeles turnes thus," sayes Ward, "I knowe not whether Jesus Christ or Sir Thomas Fairfax bee the better driver;" gallant doctrine! The House gave him noe thankes for his sermon, nor (which hee better deserved) any cheque that I heare of. Fryday the generall expectation is that you gave in a particular charge against the members. If you strike not that home you will loose much of your creditt, or hardly at all be credited for the future. Sir John Maynard sweares you are all rebelles and traytors, and Mr. Recorder they say will plead with the innocentest and bring his accusers to shame. Collonell Massie's former gallantry will acquitt him before all the world, and Hollis and Sir Philipp Stapleton are men beyond your reach to deale withall: these and more are the comon discourses in London. I pray mind well the 9 heads to the King printed,[b]

[a] Mr. Ward's sermon was preached on June 30; Rushworth, vi., 596; *Commons' Journals*, v., 228. On incendiary sermons see the Earl of Leicester's Journal, 28 July, 1647, Blencowe, *Sydney Papers*, p. 26. *Gangraena* had been before complained of by the Army, *Army Declarations*, 1647, p. 19.

[b] See Rushworth, vi., 602; *Old Parliamentary History*, xvi., 61. Propositions falsely stated to be offered to the King by the Army.

something must speedily be done in vindication or you will suffer much.

London, July 3[d], 1647.

Reading, Generall's Quarters, July 5°, 1647.

Ordered by his Excellencye and the Councill of Warre that

Lieut. Generall Cromwell.	Capt. Carter.
Col. Lambert.	Col. Pride.
Col. Okey.	Col. Scroope.
Col. Hewson.	Lieut. Col. Bowen.
Col. Barkstead.	Lieut. Col. Goffe.
Col. Thomlinson.	Adjutant Gen. Deane.
Major Bethel.	Major Rainborow.
Capt. Berry.	Capt. Rolfe.
Capt. Clarke.	

with Mr. John Rushworth secretary, and 4 Souldyers Agitators, doe repaire to Colebrooke to meet the Lawyers about the charge and that they or any seaven or more of them (whereof 5 to be Captaines or of superiour quallitie), to agree upon the charge, and to appoint the persons, manner and time for the presenting of it to the House in behalfe of his Excellency and the whole Army.[a]

Col. Scroope.	Capt. Berry.
Col. Okey.	Capt. Clarke.
Col. Hewson.	Mr. Sexby.
Col. Pride.	Mr. Gethings.
Lieut. Col. Bowen.	Capt. Carter.
Lieut. Col. Goffe.	Capt. Rolfe.[b]

[a] The charge against the eleven impeached Members is reprinted in the *Old Parliamentary History*, xvi., 69, which also gives the answer, p. 117.

[b] This second list gives the names of the persons selected to present the charge which took place on July 16, *Commons' Journals*, v., 236.

Information given by Sir Francis Pile a member of the House to Lieutennant Colonel Bowen.

1. That there are 16000 listed for Souldiers in and about the Citty: 2000 of them being listed by a Lieutennant who was this afternoone inquired after and sent for to the House.

2. That the debate this afternoone was about sending out the Reformadoes into Kent, where it is thought the Scotts doe intend to land, and in case they doe not the Apprentices doe purpose to present a Petition in a tumultuous way to inforce them to it. And further they give out that they will have the King to London whether the Army will or noe, and also [prevent] the expulsion of the Members from the House.

That there are persons of quallitie sent into the country for the raising of forces.

July 6, 1647.

Certaine Informations and particular proofes of the late abuses committed by the present Militia of London.[a]

That about the beginning of May last Lieutennant Colonel Petit of Snow Hill being sumoned before the Comittee for the militia of the Citty of London, at which time Mr. Alderman Gibbs had the chayre, who declared unto him that the Committee had conferred the office of a Lieutennant Collonell upon him, and further told him that hee was to take notice hee must fight against all mallignants, sects and sectaries and all Godly persons that shall come to oppose the Citty; to which the Lieutennant Collonell replyed, Gentlemen, I thought you had all of you professed Godlynesse, for my part I doe, and therefore shall not engage against any godly man. Whereupon Mr. Alderman Gibbs or some

[a] Endorsed July 5.

other of the Militia then answered, that their meaning was, that if any out of pretence of Godlynesse should come to oppose them that hee should fight against such, or words to this effect.

Affirmed by LIEUTENNANT COLLONELL PETTITT.

About the 21th of June last Lieutennant Colonell Shambrooke was put out of his command by the Militia of the Citty of London upon these grounds that hee differ'd in judgment from them and that hee was of a particular Congregation; this Sir John Wolleston and Collonell West did affirme was the ground.

WILLIAM SHAMBROKE.[a]

About the time aforesaid Lieutennant Curtis of Walbrooke Ward was put out of his command for being an Independent, the Militia sayd they would have none of that judgment in comand.

Affirmed by CAPTN. COX.
MR. PARR.
MR. ROSIER.

In the month of June last, Alderman Adams having the chayre, divers Comanders of the Citty were summoned before the Militia, amongst whome was Major Abell, to whome it was propounded whether or noe they would all stand as one man for the safety of the Parliament and the Citty against all tumults and such as should come against them in a hostile manner, the said Major Abell affirming hee knewe of noe Army that would oppose the Parliament or Citty, notwithstanding hee could engage his life for the safetie of the Citty or the just priviledges of Parliament; this being said hee was dismist his Comand, noe cause being showne except for his difference in judgment.

Affirmed by EDWARD ABELL.

[a] Appointed Lieutenant Colonel of the Tower Guards in August, 1647; killed before Colchester in July, 1648; Rushworth, vii., 1179, 1181.

That the Comittee of the Militia for the Citty of London have put forth of the subcomittee for the Militia of Southwark divers persons of approved fidelitie and trust, only for difference in judgment, and have placed in their roomes such as were and still are looked upon as Malignants.

Witnessed by THOMAS COOPER and
MR. HIGHLAND.

That the aforesaid Committee did put out of Commission Captaine Thompson, a man of knowne fidelitie adventureing his life at the releife of Gloucester, and have put in his roome one Edward Walles, who being Lieutennant to the said Captaine Thompson laid downe his Commission refusing to goe forth to the releife of Gloucester, and since neither at home or abroad hath done anything for the service of the kingdome. And that the said Walles now being Captaine hath to his Lieutennant one Henry Hardcastle, who said hee would prove that Sir Thomas Fairfax was a Rogue, a Raschall, and base fellowe.

Witnes DOCTOR TRIGGE.
WILL JOLLY. PENNITENT PIGGOTT.
HENRY ROBINSON. NATHANIELL IBLE.
GIDION ROGERS.
JO: LEVETT.

That Captaine Wane, one who lately deserted this Army, being now put into Commission by the Militia in the Regiment of the blew Auxilleries to be a Captaine, did say there would not be soe much ware in their shopps if the Army came to London, and said to Will Pepiatt, Ensigne, that if hee would not fight against the Army hee should be noe officer of his; for, hee said, hee knew more of the Army then any there present.

Witnes ROBERT BURGIS, Lieut.
JO: FARDIN.

That the Comittee of the Militia did put out Colonell George Langham, a man of approved fidelitie in times of greatest difficulty, and put in his place Colonel Thomas Clarke, one that sayd that if the Army should come neere London, if other men were of his mind they should march through their blouds.

Witnes SAMUELL BLAIKLOCKS.
and E. P.

That by the aforesaid Committee one Captaine Maizy was put forth of his command for stopping and breaking open the Scotch Letters in May last, though the thing was approved and hee acquitted by the House of Commons; yet Alderman Bonch said it was a Jesuetticall plott to kepe him in.

FRANCIS MAZY.

That Captaine Wilkes, one whose fidelitie was approved, hee having twice adventured his life in the feild, but because hee was an Independant, Aldermann Bunch sayd itt was a Jesuetticall plott to keepe him in, therefore hee was voted out of his place by the Committee.

TYMOTHY WILKES.[a]

That upon Fryday the 2d of July there was order given forth by the Militia for the listing of all Prentices and others which were not of the trayned Bands, if fitt to beare armes.

JOHN BRAINE, Constable.

The names of those Members of the Committee of the Tower Hamletts that were putt out by the Comittee of the Militia of the Citty of London, which men were ever approved to be honest,

[a] Governor of Leith and Colonel of a regiment under Monk, 1654-1658; he was also one of the Commissioners appointed by Monk to treat with the English Army in November, 1659. *Baker's Chronicle*, ed. 1670, pp. 686, 694.

active men for the Parliament and faithfull to the state and Kingdome.

Captaine Tailor of Wappinge.
Mr. Townesend } of White Chappell.
Mr. Loton }
Capt. Gale.
Mr. Clarke.
,, Orbell.
Capt. White.
Mr. Tiler.
Mr. Fasson.
,, Saires.
Capt. King.
Mr. Waterton.
,, Hemings.
Capt. Hackwell.

In their places there are put in

Mr. Mempris of Mile End.
,, Silles of East Smithfeild.
,, Crowder } of Shoreditch.
,, Noble }

all of them disaffected men that never lent penny unto the publique but what they were forced unto.

Witnessed by JUSTICE HUBBORN.
COLL. WILLOUBY.
MR. WATERTON.

[*News-letter from London.*][a]

The Members came into the House this day, which some expected. The charge not touched upon, because our freinds expected

[a] *Commons' Journals*, v., 237-8.

that some of the members should begin to them. This afternoon the papers sent up from the Army prevented their debate upon the charge, and the House thus farr proceeded, and they have fully declared, that for the Reformadoes, or such as pretend to be such, that they shall be gone out of Town by the 15th of this instant upon penalty of loosing their Arrears, and 3 months imprisonment.

For Members of the House it's so prepared, that it's likely to pass to morrow morning the first business, with a sound penalty.

For the discharging the Soldiers assigned for Ireland, it's referred to Derby House to dispatch it, and those of that Committee withdraw this afternoon on purpose.

The charge to be taken into debate to morrow morning.

The Lords sent down a Letter to the Commons for their concurrence for removing the Chaplains, and to certify the reasons of the obstructions. This is sent to the Commissioners attending the King. Wee do believe that it's a design to sett us altogether by the ears, which honest men, out of passion are too apt to swallow; and your Letter to that business of the Chaplains &c. being not come to our hand, our freinds (tho' prepared by us according to the directions in Collonell Fleetwood's letter) did not think good to speak against it; some freinds that are temperate and most considerable do allow of the thing, but to be done without your Letter to the House.[a]

Wee can not but think that such is the influence of some persons in the Lords and Commons House, as they will never cease till they have brought you to declare, and so to break you upon one rock or another. 'Tis a good resolution must carry you through this and other difficultys, and in this our own principles give us a full encouragement.

We received your particulars this day and have consulted with

[a] Fairfax's letter of July 8, *Old Parliamentary History*, xvi., 101; *Lords' Journals*, ix.

your best freinds; if the Commons upon the full debate fall not upon suspition [?] the officers will move it in the name of the Army to morrow.

You must be more speedy in your business, and all men say, that if your dispatch be noe better you will run into infinite hazards.

Your trusty and good freind Lilburne is printing his [letter] against Rich and the Abbott and me, and saith in so many words (to Captaine White of the Tower) that he had rather cutt Sir Harry Vane's throate than Hollis's. It was in some bodys power to have quench'd this fire (we speak not as to our own particulars) while it was a spark, which perhaps in time may grow too great to be quenched.

London, Thursday night late [July 8].[a]

[*Letter from the Agitators into Wales.*]

Honoured and Noble Friends and fellow Soldiers,

It being a time of contest for the just libertys of this Kingdom and Dominion annexed, with those unjust persons by whom they have been endeavoured to be subverted, wee, conceiving you lying under many of the same pressures as we doe, and so have just cause

[a] Probably written by Scout-Master Leonard Watson. See Lilburne's *Jonah's Cry out of the Whale's Belly*, 1647, p. 8. In a letter to Cromwell Lilburne says: "Your scoutmaster-general Watson will never uprightly adventure the shaking of his finger either for God, his countrey, or for the Army, further than he may be thereby of the stronger side. As for Dr Stanes, whatever you may think of him, I averre he is a juggling knave . . . . . And as for Nat. Rich, you yourselfe knowe him to be a juggling paltry base fellow: remember what you told him to his face in his own chamber in Fleet Street before me and my wife and two more, at the time Manchester's treason was upon examination." Concerning Vane, Lilburne wrote to Cromwell on March 25, 1647, "O Cromwell thou art led by the nose by two unworthy covetous earthworms, Vane and St. John." *Ibid.*, p. 3.

of complaint, and if so as little hopes of being heard as we have had, whose just petitions have been obstructed and we declared against as enemys to the State, and our fellow subjects have had theirs burnt; all which shews how they and we have been slighted in our most humble addresses, which to us seems to be the highest infringment of our undoubted priviledges that ever was by any acted professing to maintain them; and when our most clear and fundamentall priviledges shall be deneyed us, what may wee or can we expect? And whether all our lesser rights may not and be not at the present, by the arbitrary acting of these men totally cutt off, we leave you to judge. Especially considering the time when this was done; even immediately after the dear redemption of those precious priviledges out of the hand of our former enemys, with the expence of so much blood and treasure; and that in this very juncture of time, when we were expecting to see and reap the fruit of all our weary travails, they by this should in effect tell us, and the Kingdom with us, we should never reap any of them, but that we who had fought to sett our Selves and a Kingdom free should now in the issue be more compleatly slaves than ever, not having so much liberty as to petition in case of greivances. And thus are we dealt with, and while an Army having power in our hands, and they occasion to make further use of us; therefore you need not wonder tho' you hear of such actings amongst us which at first view may seem strange, yet assure your selves that we are but acted by the very same principall we were at the first, by which we then endeavoured to keep our selves and the kingdom from being ruined by the exorbitant actings of prerogative Power, and shall still oppose the like power in any acting to the like ends; and this is all we aim at and are acting towards at this day, that the unjust oppressions lying upon the subjects of this Kingdom and other parts adjoyning might be removed, and that the just rights of all estates and persons therein might be restored, settled, and maintained, and this we desire and endeavour for every individuall person thereof. Which as soon as we have attained, according to the ends for which we were at first raised, we shall with all readiness and willingness lay down arms, or make use of them elsewhere, as the Parliament shall think fitt; but not till then can we in order to our own and the Kingdom's safety. And thus have we thought fitt to communicate our condition to you (dear Friends) that so you might rightly inform your selves and others to the end you might still, (as formerly to your honour you have had) a share in pleading and maintaining of the just freedom of the nation at such a time when they were so much in question; and (truly) then to come in to assert and defend them, when others were endeavouring to suppress them. It is that which will sett a badge of honour upon such a people to posterity, that you should have your part in redeeming the kingdom of England and Dominion of Wales from oppression and slavery, and your children yet unborn shall bless God for you; which if not, consider what a blott of infamy will lye on you and us to after ages, if we shall sitt still in such a time as this, when it shall be said by them lying under oppression, 'Our predecessors had a prize in their hands, and an opportunity offered to have freed us from it and have made us happy, but woe to us, through their neglects they have lett it slip, and left us in misery.'

Freinds, our earnest desire is that you would seriously weigh and consider things in the ballance of Judgement according to truth, and to that end take heed of all false representations of our persons or actions by the suggestions of any given in to you, and judge not according to appearance, but judge righteous judgement, and then doubt not but you shall have the assistance of a righteous God, who hath promised to do more for you than all the unrighteous men in the world are able to do against you, and also the concurrent assistance of all just and rational men; and we trust the appearances of God will be such upon us as we shall see those characters of himself engraven upon us, and amongst us, even judgement, truth, and righteousness; and the contrary to these (in his own time) removed, which both by you and us we hope shall be jointly endeavoured. In the doing of which the Lord direct us, in whom we bid you heartily farewell.

Yours to use, acting in behalf of the Army for the good of the Kingdom.

Cambridge,
12 July, 1647.

ROBERT KIRKBY Capt	RICH[d]. DEAN Capt.	DENNIS PUDMER.
HENRY CANNON Capt.	FRA: ALLEN Capt.	DANIEL HINCHMAN.
HENRY LLOYD Capt.	EVAN MORGAN.	EDWARD GARNE.
JOHN PATERSON.	W[m]. NEAL Capt.	NATH: FOTHERGILL.
FRANCIS WHEELER.	ABR. HOLMES Capt.	W[m]. JONES.
EDM[d]. CHILLENDEN Lieut.	J[no]. MERRIMAN Capt.	JOSEPH ADAMS.
STEPHEN SHIPMAN Lt.	JOHN CLARKE Capt.	JOHN COOK.
JO: WALLINGTON Lt.	EDW[d] SEXBY.	THO POND.
EDW[d]. SCOTTON Lt.	ARTHUR EVELIN Capt.	EDW[d]. TWIGG.
W[m]. YOUNG.	JOHN TAYLOR.	ROBERT MASON.
THO: KENDALL.	PHILL. EATON.	RICHARD COLEBROOK.
JOHN PLEIGH.	THO: BUTTERSEY.	RALPH PRENTICE.
TOBIAS BOX.	NICH: LOCKYER.	HERBERT FEILD.
JOHN DOVER.	CONS[t]. FOX Lieut.	
W[m]. SYMONDS.	HENRY ANDERSON.	
GEO. STANION.	ROB[t]. STALMAN.	
JOHN BREAMEN.	RICH[d]. SALTER.	
W[m]. WILKINSON.	BARTH: WILCOCK.	
EDWD[d]. VAUGHAN.	RICH[d]. CLARKE.	
	W[m]. CLARKE.	

To our Honoured Freinds our fellow Soldiers, and others of the well affected in North Wales. These.[a]

[a] Compare the letter from the Agitators to the Masters of Trinity House, June 18, 1647. *Cary, Memorials*, i., 237; *Lords' Journals*, ix., 284. There is also amongst the Clarke Papers a letter of the Agitators dated 6 July, printed as "*A Declaration from the Agitators in the name of the whole Army under His Excellency Sir Thomas Fairfax (to their fellow-soldiers) of their Representations*

[*Sir Thomas Fairfax to the Speaker of the House of Commons.*]

Sir,

I am informed from Bristoll, that Colonel Doyley being lately come thither, and having required the command of the Castle and Port there, hath thereby occasion'd some disturbance in that Citty, and distraction amongst the Soldiers, who have manifested their dislike of him, but have expressed their good affection to Colonel Rolph (who was left Deputy Governour of that garison by Major General Skippon [a]) with expectation of his return unto them impowered with that command; which also the Citty (from their experience of his faithfullness, worth, and sufficiency) do very much desire, as by their petition prepared to the Honse of Commons to that purpose may appear. I thought it necessary to acquaint you herewith for the present appeasing those distractions, and the settling that garison, and that you would please to take some speedy course for the supply of the Soldiers with moneys who are (as I am informed) 30 weeks in arrear. I remain

Your most humble servant,

THO: FAIRFAX.

To the Honorable W^m^. Lenthall Esq.
Speaker of the Honorable House
of Commons.
Reading, July 16, 1647.

---

and Desires," at the end of a pamphlet entitled "*The King's Majesty's most Gracious Letter to his son James, Duke of York*," 1647.

There are also some other papers relating to Wales, and threatened disturbances there, in vol. xli. of the Clarke MSS. A paper delivered to Fairfax at St. Albans by Dr. Basset, on the grievances of Glamorganshire; a letter from Colonel Laugharne to Fairfax, June 18, 1647; the grievances of the County of Pembroke, articles against Colonel John Poyer, etc.

[a] Lieutenant-Colonel William Rolfe, Deputy Governor of Bristol (Skippon's son-in-law), was given leave to come to London on May 28, 1647. *Commons' Journals*, v., 121. The dispute between Doyley and Captain Latimer Sampson, governor in Rolfe's absence, is narrated in one of Rushworth's letters. *Fairfax Correspondence*, iii., 370. Doyley had got a commission from Holles and his party.

[*News-letter from York.*]

Thursday morning[a] our General was taken out of his quarters by a small party, and carryed to Pontefract, where he is now, [and] hath all accomodations, tho' at his going out of town to Pontefract he had a wett doublett not a wett coat; this business hath putt for the present things to stand things at adventure. The Committee sat this afternoon, and have agreed to write to the General to move for a Commander in cheif for their forces. I understand that General Poynts is to be sent to the Generall and it had been base to send him without his tackling, which came so late to my knowledge that these few lines against him, which I sent there inclosed, were prepared. Your Agitators have putt forth a vindication concerning the takeing of them, which I sent therewith. You may be confident this Army is fixed to your[s] great dispute now about the Tower at York, whether Lt. Col. Fairfax or my Lord Mayor commands there; both have sent to the General about it. Accidentally I mett with this enclosed from Lyonell Coply. You may perceive how good a freind he is. I see an order from Darby House to a Colonel dated the 7th July instant wherein the Colonel is required to draw his Regiment with those that were remaining in Cumberland and Westmoreland together, and ship them for Ireland. Be assured they will be in parte . . . under that pretence against you; all the officers came post from London last night, they are all creatures of the accused, especially to Massy. Your remonstrances still are called for, and many were required to the Army there but . . . . I can gett nothing done for the Generall yet by reason of this business; it is fitting to be ashured there are many enemys against the Army. Sir, It is very much desired that the town of York be putt into some command; it is

[a] July 8, 1647. See Cary, i., 293, 298, 300.

under a dispute between Lt. Col. Fairfax and the Major. It were well to be speedily resolved on.[a]

[*Letter from the Agitators in Yorkshire to Fairfax.*]

May it please your Excellencie,

Whereas we have had sufficient experience, and the Kingdom's welfare at this day both do certifye, next under God, Your Excellency's care for the preservation and satisfaction both of soldiers and subjects, which every one will acknowledge who hath not shown himself an enemy to the wellbeing of the Nation—yet there remain some obstinate spirits, unwilling to be partakers of the common good, and to this end are not wanting in their endeavours to deprive others of the freedom of the Nation, because their own irregular judgments censure the same as a homage, and as we conceive it is because their wills are not made so predominant—as to acquaint your Excellency that something to this purpose hath been lately acted in the garrison of Clifford's Tower at York, the whole condition of the same standing thus: Whereas your Excellency was pleased to appoint Lieutenant Colonel Fairfax as Governor of the aforesaid garrison, a man of known integrity, he upon some just occasions being absent from the same, in the mean time Colonel General Poynts dispossessed his officers and soldiers of the garrison, and introduced such officers and soldiers as he thought fitt to accomplish his own designs; and the said Lt. Col. Fairfax being now returned to his former command, We humbly desire your Excellency that you would be pleased to issue forth the orders to those officers and soldiers, that were since introduced, that they quitt the garrison, and such officers and soldiers may be entrusted with the same as were formerly belonging to the garrison,

[a] This and the following letters relating to the disturbances in the Northern Army are all undated, but evidently written between 9-16 July, It was therefore thought better to put them together.

under the command of Lt. Col. Fairfax. This wee humbly tender to your Excellency as especiall means for the prevention of the future dangers, and without which we humbly conceive the garrison can not be safe. In the mean time we recommend our selves to your Excellencie's favour, and shall ever remain

Your Excellency's and the Kingdom's Servants as acting in the behalf of several Regiments.[a]

[*Letter from the Agitators in the Northern Army to Fairfax.*]

May it please Your Excellency,

Whereas we whose names are under subscribed were sent down to inform these forces of the proceedings of your Excellency and the Army more immediately under your command, We humbly tender unto your Excellencies consideration the relation of such things as have lately intervened to us. Your Excellency being pleased to appoint Lt. Col. Fairfax to come into these parts, and according to his commission to take charge of Clifford's Tower in York, Colonel General Poynts resigned over the command of the Tower to the Lord Mayor, which he accordingly took charge of altho without commission. Now the condition standing so that Colonell Generall Points had been induced to this garrison, the citty only upon a vote which passed the Honorable House that he should be Governor of Clifford's Tower after this . . . . and that he might the better effect what he desired (while Lt. Col. Fairfax was absent) drew forth those officers and soldiers out of the Tower which did belong to Lt. Col. Fairfax, and entrusted such of his own officers and soldiers with the Tower as might comply with him, but at last Col. General Poynts having layd down his commission desired the Lord Mayor to take charge of the Tower, altho Lieut. Col. Fairfax was there, and had com-

[a] Unsigned.

mission for the government of it; but since Colonel Poynts's departure from York the Lord Mayor hath done as much as in him lies to recover the Government of the Tower into his hands, and to this end hath written to Sir William Allison and Alderman Hoyle, burgesses of the Citty of York, who accordingly [press], as we are credibly informed, the Lord Mayor might be Governor of it, and in the mean time he endeavours to disswade the soldiers from adhering to Lt. Col. Fairfax, giving them money and promising them more to cleave to him; he hath also presumed to countermand Lieut. Col. Fairfax, and the officers here are very reverse unto your Excellencies proceedings, but it is humbly conceived that the reason is because they are and have been so much Sir Phillip Stapleton's. The soldiers have lately petitioned the Committee for some subsidies, but are deney'd and in great distress for want of pay. We humbly request your Excellency that both they and the garrison may have a place in your Excellencie's care. Colonel Overton desired to recommend his service to your Excellencie's command humbly requesting some [speedy] course for the payment of his garrison, and that a Captain and 2 Lieutenants may be accommodated with commands correspondent either in that army or amongst these forces, and he will wait on your Excellency very shortly. We at present request, and crave leave to remain

Your Excellencies humble Subservients

Richard Kingdom { Lt. Generall's Regiment.

Thomas Diggell—Colonel Harrison's Regiment.

John Caseby—Colonel Fleetwood's Regiment.

[*Letter from Fairfax to the Lord Mayor and Aldermen of York.*]

My Lords and Gentlemen,

I take this your acquainting me with the business of Clifford's Tower as your care to the City and the publick, and from the experience I have of your good affections to the Kingdom I shall very willingly meet your desires in letting the command of that place rest in your hands, knowing how faithfully you have expressed your selves in things of publick concernment; and I shall remain assured in confidence of those publick dispositions in you, that you will not suffer that place to be an occasion or encouragement to the begetting of new troubles; and therefore I desire, that you my Lord Mayor will take into your care the secureing of that place, for the peace of this City, and those parts of the Kingdom, till there be a further settlement of affairs. I am glad that I have this occasion from your selves to write to you. I hope you are no strangers to our papers and proceedings with the Parliament, and how the same necessitys that engaged us all at first hath continued us in pursuit of such things as concern the good and peace of this Kingdom, and that we are the same we ever were to the interest of the Parliament and Kingdom; and I question not but such hath been the transactions of things that you are not to be satisfy'd now in the justice of our proceedings. We shall desire the concurrence of our selves and the Kingdom no farther than we continue faithfull to the peace and safety of this Kingdom; and whatsoever is done by us by and relating to the King, who is now amongst us, is but in order to the first engagements, and to the peaceable settling of that publick affair.

To the Lord Mayor [a] and Aldermen of York.

[*Articles against General Poyntz.*]

The charge against Generall Poynts in reference to what he hath acted against his Excellency Sir Thomas Fairfax, and his Army in the South, and against the Northerne Association now under his Excellencie's command.

1st. That Colonell Generall Poynts did very much endeavour to

[a] Thomas Dickenson, Lord Mayor of York, was voted by the House of Commons on 13 July, 1643, to have the custody of Clifford's Tower. *Commons' Journals*, v., 243.

render his Excellency's person and authority contemptible and insufficient for the managing of those affairs which the Honorable Houses have intrusted him withall. Witness the letter written June 27th to Colonel Copley, wherein he repeats his Excellency's name double in a very scornful way, and deneys that the soldiers of those parts are under the command of his Excellency.

2ly. He labours to render the Army more mediated under your Excellency's command, under the notions of mutineers and necessary arrears, and rebellious Army,[a] as it appears by his letters written from York to Colonel Copley June 6th. Another letter written to his officers to be read in the head of each troop, in which he terms some that were sent from the South, with some of our agents, Incendiaries, and that they endeavoured to withdraw these forces from their obedience to the Parliament with other scandalous reproaches to be read in the head of each troop, in reproach and disdain of that Army.

3ly. That he endeavoured to reimbroyle this Kingdom in a 2d warr, and to this end laboured to exasperate the spirits of the soldiers in the [north] against that Army as evidently appears; for upon his journey last from London to York, he reported he was come post to draw up his army, to quell the rebellious Army of Sir Thomas Fairfax; and did also endeavour to accomplish his sinister ends to gett into his power places of strength; and caused the Tower of York to be putt in a condition of present resistance meerly against the Army; to this end also he gave special order for the drawing his forces together, putting them in a posture for action against the Southern Army, having no order from the Parliament, as particularly at Selby, Tadcaster, Cawood, and Ferry Bridge, keeping guard for the apprehending of any that should come as he pretended to distemper the Northern Army.

4ly. He threatned the Agitators from the Army with ours, to hang them if he could meet with them.

5ly. He endeavoured to justify the 11 accused Members and

[a] So in MS. These papers are from very corrupt transcripts.

kept correspondency with them, received divers letters from them, and wrote to them, acting what he did from their principles, and by their advice; for he can not deney, but that Sir Philip Stapylton desired him to keep his army in a posture ready for action till they should have occasion for them, which he did accordingly.

6[ly]. His arbitary committing some officers for speaking in the behalf of the Army, and hanging one soldier without a councill of warr.

7[ly]. His arming of a reduced company under Captain Peppar, who refused any engagement save against the Army.

8[ly]. That he used all means possible to make both the Army and their Officers odious, as appears by his printed papers, which was not only to be read at the head of every troop, but likewise by his order putt upon many posts in marketts, rendring us and the Army unparalleld men, in taking the King by force, and likewise falsely reporting therein, that his Majesty was so farr from complyance with the Army, that he struck both his Excellency, Cromwell, and Whaly. This he printed at York purposely to divide us, and to make us odious to the whole Kingdom.

9[ly]. That he threatened to disturb our nests, if we did continue to associate our selves with his Excellencie's Army, and that he would use the Parliaments power in the apprehending of us.

JOHN HOBGSON
W[m]. BEGYTS } Colonel Copley's Regiment.

JOHN DRAKE
JOHN MARK } Colonel Bright's Regiment.

JOHN PENNINGTON
ROBERT MORRIS } Colonel Overton's Regiment.

THO: ARTHUR
THO: WHALERTON } Colonel Ponsonby's Regiment.

ROBERT SHARBY
THO: MALLETT } Colonel Collingworth's Regiment.[a]

[a] Poyntz was brought under a guard to Fairfax's headquarters at Reading, and was immediately released by the General. The Agitators presented a charge

Representation of the Agitators presented at the Generall Councill of Warr July 16, 1647.

To his Excellency Sir Thomas Fairfax Knight Captain General of all the Forces raised and to be raised for the defence of the Kingdom, and to his Councill of Warr assembled at Cambridge July 16, 1647.

The humble petition and representation of the Agitators of Your Excellencies Army,

Humbly Sheweth

That your petitioners out of their deep sence of the sad and heavy pressures, great distractions, continual fears, and eminent dangers, under which this poor and bleeding Kingdom groans, expecting to be delivered and eased, whose peace, safety, and freedom from oppression, violence, and tyranny we tenderly and earnestly desire even above our own lives, are enforced to present these our humble requests in the name of the whole Army as their sence and desire, unto Your Excellency and this Honourable Councill, to be considered of, (if need be) corrected, and forthwith exhibited to the Parliament; And that for the reasons annexed to these ensueing desires, the Army may be immediately march'd to or near London, thereby to enable and assist the Parliament acting for the Kingdom's ease and preservation, and to oppose all those that shall act the contrary.

For the accomplishment whereof we are fully resolved (by the assistance of God and his strength with Your Excellency and Your Councill of Warr's concurrence) to putt a speedy period to these present distractions.

1st. That by Order of the House the 11 Members by his Excellency and his Army impeached, and charged of high mis-

against him which is evidently that here printed. Cary, i., 306, 308; *Fairfax Correspondence*, iii., 370. Compare the papers from the Northern Army, printed by Rushworth, vi., 620-625.

demeanors be forthwith sequestred, and disenabled from sitting in the House.

2[ly]. That the Militia of the City of London be immediately returned into the hands of those in whom it lately was, who did approve themselves faithfull to the Kingdom and Citty in times of greatest dangers, an answer whereof we expect within two days.

3[ly]. That there be an effectual Declaration forthwith published to the whole Kingdom, against the inviteing or coming in of forreign, or raising of intestine forces under any pretence whatsoever, except such as shall be by the Parliaments appointments, receive their commissions are and be at the disposall and command of his Excellency Sir Thomas Fairfax,[a] upon pain of being proceeded against as enemies and traitors to the State, disturbers of the publick peace, and invaders of this Kingdom.

4[ly]. That all Prisoners who have been illegally committed in any part of the Kingdom of England or Dominion of Wales, may be forthwith sett at liberty, and reparation given them for their false imprisonment, as namely:—Lieutenant Collonel John Lilburn, Mr. Musgrave, Mr. Overton's wife and brother, Mr. Larner, his two Lieutenants, Mr. Tew, Mr. Prest, and all others which have been in like manner wrongfully imprisoned; and for a more speedy effecting thereof there may be a Declaration published to the whole Kingdom and Dominion of Wales thereby commanding all Judges of Assizes, of Oyer and Terminer, Justices of Coram, and of the Peace, Mayors, Sheriffs, Bayliffs, and all other Officers and Ministers of State whatsoever (upon pain of severest punishment if they shall neglect to putt the same in execution) for the freeing of such as are in prison, and preventing the like for the future, upon the meanest subjects of the Kingdom.[b]

5[ly]. That we may be speedily pay'd up equall with the Deserters

[a] "Except such as shall by the Parliament's appointment receive their commission from, and be at the disposal, etc.?"

[b] An earlier paper on the subject of the release of these prisoners had been presented by the Agitators on July 6. Clarke MSS. xli.

of the Army, according to the Parliaments former Votes, whereby the Army may not be so burthensome and oppressive to the Country. And for the more speedy performance hereof, [that] the House of Peers would without delay concurr with the desires of the House of Commons for the reviving of the Committee of the Army, so many times urged by them to be done, that so the arrears of the Citty, which as we are credibly informed is 120,000[l] or more, besides what is in several countys, may be by their authority gathered up; and all this to be done within 4 days for these reasons following viz[t]:—

1st. Because nothing hath been done in reference to what we have proposed and they promised, but two or three votes; which if the latitude thereof be fully understood and their little endeavours weighed for the fullfilling of them hitherto, may give us just grounds to believe that we by them are little regarded, nor these never to be performed.

2[ly]. Because all those are countenanced, and some of them intrusted with places of preferment who have deserted the Army, and also summs of money to them pay'd; notwithstanding their votes to pay us up equall with those that deserted that we are left unpay'd, and thereby become burthensom to those whose burthens we desire earnestly to remove.

3[ly]. Because that those that were by the Army impeach'd and charged, (both which impeachment and charge was by the House so accepted) yet are they still countenanced, and large summs of money since then for some of them not only by the House voted, but also fully pay'd; whereby they are fully enabled to manage their designs, and do the Kingdom greater disservice.

4[ly]. Because that we by protracting of time impoverish the Country, which may alienate their affection from us, being the design of the obstructors of justice, thereby to destroy us and secure themselves.

5[ly]. Because by delays we give them advantage to improve all their interest in raising of forces, to the disturbance and involving the poor Kingdom in a new and more bloody warr.

6ly. Because this is the only expedient to know assuredly whether they will do what they have pretended and also promised, or otherwise all men may see and judge what they have intended and do endeavour.

7ly. Because we see justice more perverted now than ever, and violent illegall proceedings of corrupt magistrates, against the most cordiall and well affected people in the Kingdom, who are wrongfully imprisoned, fined, &c., and as yet left remedyless.

These recited grounds and reasons with the additionals annexed being seriously considered, we can not but earnestly and submissively desire Your Excellency and this Honourable Councill so to dispose of the Army as may conduce to the accomplishment of those our humble requests, which we conceive will greatly advantage the Army and Kingdom.

DANIEL ABBOT (Major).
JOHN CLARKE, Capt.
EDMd. ROLF, Capt.[a]

Additional Reasons more fully explaining our desires for a speedy march towards London.

1st. The Armys removal to this distance from London hath given liberty and opportunity to an adverse party in that City to scandalize our persons and actions by pamphletts and otherwise, whereby they prejudice the spirits of many against us, they being depriv'd of opportunitys to understand personally from our selves both our actions and intentions by reason of our distance from them.

[a] Edmund Rolfe was Captain in Hammond's regiment, and accused in 1648 of a design against the King's life. The papers respecting this accusation are printed at length in the *Lords' Journals*, in Rushworth, and in *Cary's Memorials*. A petition of Rolfe's is in Cal. State Papers, Dom. 1654, 352.

2ly. Our adversarys by our removal farr from them have taken advantage to induce many thousands to list themselves (under such new Commanders as the new committee for the Militia hath judged fitt to prosecute their ends), under pretence of being auxiliary forces to the Trained Bands ; And tho pretences may be specious, yet, considering that the principles of the actors have a natural tendency to oppose the Army, and that those whose principles did not concurr with theirs were displaced in order to these proceedings, who can imagine that any reason of such preparations, when no visible power appears against them, unless their thoughts and intentions be to oppose this Army? And indeed some lately have boasted that they have many thousands ready to fight with this Army, if they were commanded.

3ly. Upon the Army's drawing back from the Citty, the Parliament's proceedings for the good of the people and Army hath been slack'd. Whilst the Army was drawing near, the Excise was lessened and eased, the injuries done to the Army considered, some moneys provided for them; but since its drawing back no moneys have been allowed them to pay their Quarters for the peoples ease and the Army's content, there hath been no care to prevent the scandalizing of us, no discountenance of those that by pamphletts asperse as with mutinying, treason, and rebellion. And whether these neglects of us may not proceed from their confidence in those pretended auxiliaries, we leave to your wisdom to judge.

4ly. The Votes of Parliament whereupon we drew back appear to have been intended to delude us, as:

1. Tho' they declared that none should desert the Army from that time being they owned the Army, yet their first declaration that invited to desert the Army and promised their Arrears to those that should desert, it is not recalled; and tho' the last seems to cross the first yet there is no penalty in their last vote putt upon those that shall desert us, and a promise is made in the first to those that shall desert it, and which of these discover the affections and intentions of the Parliament we must leave to their wisdom to determine.

2. Nothing hath been done to shew the mistake and error of those that did desert us, or to dissipate or discountenance them, tho' it hath been much pressed since those votes.

3. They voted that the Army should be payd equally to those that deserted it, yet it was only when money could be raised conveniently; whereas they could find present moneys to pay them, on purpose to preferr them to us, and to abett and encourage them.

4. The Vote by this means is but a snare, seing they shall intimate to the Kingdom, that they are necessitated to tax them farther for our satisfaction.

5. They have since payd the Arrears of one of the impeach'd Members by 2000ł at once, altho' the House was inform'd that he was in debt to the State 15000ł.

The removal of the Army to this distance necessitates such delays, as give further opportunity to the adverse party to make overtures of plausible advantage to the King's party, and also to insinuate that our principles are against civil government; and certainly these endeavours may be well presumed by the overtures made to the Queen and Prince, and by the Parliament's not declaring against all invitations of forreign force, after intelligence given of this design.

6. The removal of the Army to such a distance from London hath much dissatisfyed the well affected Commons throughout the Kingdom, especially because nothing was insisted upon for the present ease of the oppressed Commons, as expedient to be done before their drawing back, which considered together with the present delays and the thoughts of the delatory Treaty, hath abated their expectations in some measure of that precious freedom that they hoped should be the issue of the Army's endeavours. And we cannot but observe that no country hath made their addresses to the Generall since their drawing back.[a]

[a] On the petitions presented to the General and Army see *Whitelock's Memorials*, ed. 1853, ii., 164; *Holles, Memoirs*, § 110.

Att a Generall Councell of Warre held att Reading. July 16, 1647.

Present.

His Excellency Sir Thomas Fairfax.

Lt. Gen. Cromwell.
Com̃. Gen. Ireton.
Lt. Gen. Hamond.
Col. Whalley.
Col. Rainborow.
Col. Lambert.
Col. Sir Hardresse Waller.
Col. Okey.
Col. Scroope.
Col. Tomlinson.
Col. Fleetwood.
Col. Harrison.
Col. Pride.
Col. Barkestead.
Col. Horton.
Col. Rich.
Adjutant Generall Deane.
Lt. Col. Bowen.
Lt. Col. Cowell.
Lt. Col. Goffe.
Major Disbrow.
Major Huntington.
Major Gregson.
Major Rainborow.
Major Abbott.
Adj. Gen. Evelyn.

Adj. Gen. Tulidah.
Major Waade.
Qr. Master Gen. Grosvenor.
Major White.
Capt. Blackwell.
Capt. Pretty.
Capt. Kirkby.
Capt. Lloyde.
Capt. Merriman,
Capt. Neale.
Capt. Rolf.
,, Orpin.
,, Clarke.
,, A. Younge.
,, Wolfe.
,, Deane.
,, Miller.
,, Laighton.
,, Hodden.
,, Audley.
,, Lagoe.
,, Rawlinson.
,, Watson.

Lt. Chillenden,
,, Scotton.

Lieut. Generall.

Moved for a Committee, many thinges then nott being fitt for debate, and the Councill of Warre to bee adjourn'd till the afternoone.

Lt. Chillenden.

Answered and gives the consideration which moved them to every proposall or desire.

Commissary Ireton.

Objects, that itt's desired this paper should be sent to London.

Answer. This paper first consider'd, and when consider'd noe body found that the paper should goe uppe to London, that thinges may bee had.

Col. Harrison.

That itt bee resolved whether to have a present debate or noe.

Comiss. Ireton.

That the end of the meeting was nott to have a paper brought in and read, when most of those that heare itt are the presenters.

I would wee were once cleare to consider in what condition wee stand as to that point.

I am, as all are, ready for the consideration of that, soe farre as my owne opinion serves, and soe every man heere may bee.

Delays, as they are hurtfull in bussinesse and soe most prejudiciall to those that are most hasty, so delusive, and I would nott have any such tendencie towards a Delusion as a delay; [a] therfore I desire wee may consider whether the Army should march to London in order to those thinges.

[a] *i.e.* As delays are prejudicial so haste is delusive, I wish to avoid both.

Major Tulida.

That all center in one thinge, that all the proposalls [will] bee of noe effect without a march to London.

Comptroller.

If any man bee satisfied in what hath bin [proposed] others heere are nott.

Lieut. Gen.

Marching uppe to London is a single proposall, yett itt does not droppe from Jupiter, as that itt should bee presently received and debated without considering our Reasons. For I hope this [temper] will ever bee in the Agitators, I would bee very sorry to flatter them, I hope they will bee willing that nothing should bee done butt with the best Reason, and with the best and most unanimous concurrence. Though wee have this desire back't with such reasons, certainly itt was nott intended [to say] wee had noe reason to weigh those Reasons ; for I thinke wee shall bee left to weigh these Reasons. All this paper is fill'd with Reasons: the dissatisfaction in particulars; the dissadvantages of removall from London; the advantages of marching towards London. You are ripe for a Conclusion, and gett a Conclusion ; but lett this bee offer'd to the Generall and Councill of Warre.

Col. Rainborow.

That what hath bin spoken to the votes if other Gentlemen are not satisfied, itt is growne very hard if one will nott beleive another, and [will] adde much delay to our businesse, and therfore I am nott uppon intending of the Debate till 5 or 6 a clock upon that ground too.[a] That other ground in a bussinesse of such weight as this is, that if there can bee more reasons given, action will bee soe much the better accepted. Therfore I doe humbly move that

[a] *i.e.* I am not in favour of beginning the debate till——

since itt is a businesse of that consequence, privately and for our owne satisfaction, wee may have some little time to satisfie our judgements in itt, and to come prepar'd to give other Reasons in itt.

Com: Gen:

Wee act as if wee did [would?] gett the power into our owne hands.

To give the Kingdome satisfaction in the thinges that wee desire, itt is not the getting power into one man's hands more then another, butt it is the setling and securing their liberties in order to a peace; though, as that Gentleman said, That noe body should withstand. There are some thinges prepared for that purpose if any know any particulars to bee added.

Before we doe bring ourselves into scandall and dishonour by putting it upon new Puntillios and quarrelling more, one is what itt is that wee intend to doe with that power when we have it.[a]

Lieut. Gen.

I desire we may withdraw and consider. Discourses of this nature will I see putt power into the hands of any that cannot tell how to use it, of those that are like to use it ill.[b] I wish itt with all my heart in better hands, and I shall be glad to contribute to gett itt into better hands. If any man or companie of men will

[a] The confused report of Ireton's speech may be thus paraphrased :—

"We act as if we sought only to get power into our own hands. It is not getting power into one man's hands more than another's, but the settling and securing the liberties of the kingdom, we ought to seek. Before we bring ourselves into scandall and dishonour by raising new points of dispute and quarrelling more, the one thing necessary is to satisfy the kingdom what it is we want, and what we intend to do with that power when we get it. Some particulars have been prepared by me for that purpose, etc."

[b] Cromwell's remarks may be thus paraphrased : "Let us withdraw and consider. Discourses of this kind serve no useful purpose. I see power put in the hands of many that cannot tell me how to use it, of those that are likely to use it ill ;" meaning the London Militia Commissioners.

say that wee doe seeke ourselves in doing this, much good may it doe him with his thoughts. Itt shall nott putt mee out of my way.

The meeting att 6 a clock. Itt is nott to putt an end to this businesse of meeting, but I must consult with myself before I consent to such a thinge,[a] butt really to doe such a thinge [I must consult] before I doe itt. And wheras the Commissary does offer that these thinges were desired before satisfaction bee given to the publique settlement,[b] there may bee a conveniencie of bringing in that to the Councill of Warre next sitting, if itt bee ready, and thought fitt to be brought in. If these other things bee in preparation wee may bringe them in, that wee may nott bee to seeke for a Councill of Warre if wee had our businesse ready.

Capt. Clarke.

I humbly conceive that the sence of these Gentlemen present is noe other then what is for the good of the Kingdome, and that none of us have an intention to begin a new Warre. The [causes of] Warres in parties are noe other then the misplacing of the power of the Kingdome, and wee have as much reason as them, if itt bee misplaced, to misplace itt.[c]

Mr. Allen.

I wish that while wee have bin propounding of that which does tend to preservation, and the avoiding the Destruction that wee are confident is intended to the Kingdome and Army, that while wee are acting unto that end wee should take power out of men's hands, and doe what wee may that wee may nott soe longe stand. Instead of getting a power to quarrell wee may nott doe any thinge that

[a] *i.e.* marching on London.

[b] *i.e.* that satisfaction be given as to the public settlement before these new things are desired.

[c] *i.e.* to place it in better hands.

is our duty to doe. Itt is the desire of those that have the power, or the greatest parte of itt, in their hands to carry on thinges that they may have power.[a] Whether this bee a picking a quarrell I shall leave itt to your consideration.

Mr. Lockyer.

Itt is the great dissatisfaction of all the well-affected in the Kingdome [to see power in the hands of men] who have indeavoured to their utmost against us.

Com: Ireton.

Itt was partly intimated by the Gentleman that sitts neere your Excellency, and uppon that occasion itt is further apprehended by a Gentleman that sitts on that side, as if there were an expression to that purpose, that this was done[b] with an intent to pick a Quarrell. I hope itt is nott, butt I neither know other men's intents neither will I sweare for them. I must tell you againe, that I doe verily believe that all in this Companie heere have heard of some designes of the Enemy, to sett men a worke amongst themselves, some to worke one way and some another.[c] If there bee any such men thrust in amongst them, or any that are soe wrought uppon, which is a possibility, itt may bee suggested from them by precipitancie, nott uppon such a thinge.[d] I am farr from beleiving that itt is in the hearts or

[a] Allen's argument seems to be: "I wish, do whatever we may, that we may not stand idle while we are propounding these proposals for the preservation of the kingdom, etc. While we are making these preparations we must take power out of the hands of these men. It is not a case of quarrelling to get power, but doing a thing that it is our duty to do. The people now in power desire so to carry things that they may have power to destroy us and the kingdom. Whether to deprive them of that power be picking a quarrell, etc."

[b] *i.e.* this paper presented.

[c] Several words are here omitted.

[d] For such a design.

intentions of the generality, or for ought that I know, of any of these Gentlemen, to picke a Quarrell. My meaning is, itt carries the appearance of picking a Quarrell; and I thinke itt is a Rule of concernement to this Army, that, as we are just in our intentions, and doe nott intend knavery, soe wee should nott act like knaves, or any appearance of that nature.

[We should give the kingdom first] some reall tast of that which wee intend for the satisfaccion of the Kingdome, and what wee would doe with that power if we had itt in our hands [after] the putting of itt out of soe many hands. I have mov'd itt, and soe must again. Butt whether itt should bee putt out of these men's hands [or not], itt should bee putt into those hands uppon whome in the matter they intend . . . . . .

Cornett Joyce.

The Commissary Generall speakes of things which hee gives as lawes to the Kingdome. Itt is too hard for us to give out lawes before the Kingdome is in a possibility of being setled, and itt is a great disadvantage for us to prescribe lawes when wee know not whether ever [we shall be able] to accomplish [a settlement].

Col. Harrison.

Names severall Committees to propose what thinges may bee answer'd, and what nott; and the rest of the thinges offer'd to bee consider'd by that time, to give some reasonable answer to that that is proposed to you.

Col. Rainborow.

That thinges might be manag'd as to your wisedomes shall bee thought fitt. For my parte I shall bee weary of the Meeting.

Committee appointed to looke over Engagements.

Lt. Generall	Col. Scrope.	Mr. Sexby.
Com̃. Generall.	,, Thomlinson.	,, Allen.
Col. Rainborow.	,, Overton.	,, Lockyer.
Sir Hardresse Waller.	,, Okey.	,, Clarke.
Col. Rich.	,, Titchborne.	,, Stenson.
Adj. Gen. Deane.	Lieut. Gen. Hamond.	,, Underwood.

Afternoone.

Lieut. Gen.

If you remember there are in your paper 5 particulars that you insist uppon. Two of them are thinges new, that is to say, thinges that yett have nott bin at all offer'd to the Parliament or their Commissioners, that is the 2[d] and the 4th.[a] The 2[d], which concernes the Militia of the Citty, and the 4th, which concernes the Release of those prisoners that you have named in your paper, and those that are imprisoned in the severall parts of the Kingdome, of whome likewise you desire a consideration might bee had now the Judges are riding their circuites.

To the first [we give you] this Account: That upon your former paper delivered,[b] and uppon the weight and necessity of the thinge, there has bin a very serious care taken by the Generall, hee having, as I told you to day, referr'd the preparing of somewhat for the Parliament concerning that to Col. Lambert and myself; and an account of that has bin given to the Generall att our meeting in the inner Roome; and, if itt please you, that which has bin in preparation may be read together with the Reasons of itt.

[a] See p. 171.

[b] The paper on the London Militia presented on July 6.

That paper that now itt is desired may bee read to you is parte of itt an answer to a former paper that was sent to the Commissioners concerning the excluding of the Reformadoes out of the lines of communication, and the purging of the House of Commons, and the discharging or sending away into Ireland the men that had deserted the Army. The Generall did order a paper to that purpose to bee sent to the Commissioners; and that paper, that now is to bee read to you of a reply to the Commissioners; and there is an addition of this businesse concerning the Militia with the Reasons to inforce the desire of itt.

The papers read.[a]

Lieut. Gen.

Care taken of all them only two, which are concerning the suspending of the 11 Members and the discharging of prisoners.

I am commanded by the Generall to lett you know in what state affaires stand betweene us and the Parliament, and into what way all thinges are putt. 'Tis very true, that you urge in your papers concerning that effect that an advancing towards London may have, and of some supposed inconveniences that our drawing back thus farre may bringe uppon us; butt I shall speake to that presently. Our businesses they are putt into this way, and the state of our businesse is this: Wee are now indeavouring as the maine of our worke to make a preparation of somewhat that may tend to a generall settlement of the peace of the Kingdome and of the rights of the subject that Justice and Righteousnesse may peaceably flow out uppon us. That's the maine of our businesse. These things are butt preparatory thinges to that that is the maine; and you remember very well that this, that is the maine worke of all,

[a] *Army Declarations*, p. 77, paper entitled *An Answer of the Commissioners of the Army to the Paper of the Commissioners of Parliament about a speedy proceeding*. Cf. *ibid.*, p. 49, paper of July 15.

was brought to some ripenesse. The way that our businesse is in is this: for the redressing of all these thinges, itt [is] a Treaty, a Treaty with Commissioners sent from the Parliament downe hither to the end that an happy issue may be putt to all these matters that soe much concerne the good of the Kingdome, and therein our good is soe that they must bee finished in the way of a Treatie. The truth of itt is, you are all very reasonably sensible, that if those things were nott removed that wee thinke may loose us the fruite of a Treaty, and the fruite of all our labours, itt's in vaine to goe on with a Treaty, and its dangerous to bee deluded by a Treaty. And therefore I am confident of itt, that lest this inconveniencie should come to us, lest there should come a second warre, lest wee should bee deluded by a longe Treatie, your zeal hath bin stirr'd uppe to expresse in your paper that there is a necessity of a speedy marching towards London to accomplish all these thinges. Truly I thinke that possibly that may bee that that wee shall bee necessiated to doe [in the end]. Possibly itt may bee soe; but yett I thinke itt will be for our honour and our honesty to doe what wee can to accomplish this worke in the way of a Treaty; and if I were able to give you all those Reasons that lie in the case, I thinke itt would satisfie any rationall man heere. For certainly that is the most desirable way, and the other a way of necessity, and nott to bee done butt in [a] way of necessity. And truly, instead of all reasons lett this [one] serve: that whatsoever wee gett by a Treaty, whatsoever comes to bee setled uppon us in that way, itt will be firme and durable, itt will bee conveyed over to posterity, as that that will bee the greatest honour to us that ever poore creatures had that wee may obtaine such thinges as these are which wee are now about. And itt will have this in itt too, that whatsoever is granted in that way itt will have firmenesse in itt. Wee shall avoide that great objection that will lie against us, that wee have gott thinges of the Parliament by force; and wee knowe what itt is to have that staine lie uppon us. Thinges, though never soe good, obtain'd in that way, itt will exceedingly weaken the thinges, both to our selves and to all posteritie; and therefore I say, uppon that consideration, I wish wee may bee well advis'd what to doe. I speake nott this that I should perswade you to goe about to cozen one another, itt was not in the Generall's, nor any of our hearts.

For the other two thinges that they yett take noe care of, that's the members impeached [and the prisoners], these are two additionall which will bee likewise taken care of to be considered, and answered nott with words and votes, but with content and action. In effect there hath bin consideration had of the matters in your papers, for there needs no more of our representing of them than these papers that have bin read. I believe that wee that are Commissioners should bee very positive and peremptory to have these thinges imediately granted, within the compass of time which your papers mention, within so many days. And if these be not granted in a convenient time, and answer given by the way proposed, you are yett putt in such a way in taking such a course of doing things as you have proposed sooner then that wee could nott have putt ourselves into a posture of doing.[a]

I hope in God that if wee obtaine these thinges in this way wee propose to you, and [in] this convenient time, that wee shall thinke our selves very happy that wee have nott gone any other way for the obtayning them. That which wee seeke [is] to avoide the having of a 2[d] warre and the defeating of those [things] that are soe deare to us, whose interest ought to bee above our lives to us. If wee finde any thinge tending that way to delay us or disappoint us of those honest thinges wee are to insist uppon, I hope itt cannott nor shall nott bee doubted that the Generall nor any of us will bee backward for the accomplishment of those thinges wee have proposed. It remaines that you have some short account as the time will beare of that that has bin soe longe in preparation, which is that that tends to the Generall Settlement; and the Generall hath

[a] In this paragraph the order of the clauses as given in the MS. has been altered, excepting in the case of the last three lines, which are past mending.

commanded the Commissary to lett you have a breif state of that.

Capt. Clarke.

I only offer this to your Excellency, whether the presenting of those thinges by way of Treaty will nott bee more dilatorie, and wanting of that virtue and vigour, than when itt comes from the hands of the Army more imediatelie, which though itt bee [from the Army] by way of Treatie [is] yett nott soe imediatlie [from it] ?

And further, whether those propositions [a] in order to the rights and liberties of the subject may nott prove in some measure obstructive to our present proceedinges, when they shall propose such thinges as the Kingdome shall nott bee satisfied in, or [not] soe necessary as these particulars which are very necessary in order to itt ? For my owne parte I conceive thus much, that wee have very good and wholesome lawes already, if wee had butt good and wholsome Executors of them ; and that's the thinge wee insist uppon, to remove such persons that are most corrupt out of power and trust, and that such persons as are of knowne integritie may bee plac't in their roomes. And wheras the Lieutennant Generall was pleased to move, that itt was the best way to compose the differences betweene the Parliament and Army by way of Treaty, I presume to say in the name of these Gentlemen, they likewise wish itt might bee soe. Butt truly, Sir, wee have great feares and jealousies that these Treaties, managed by a power soe adverse [?] to us, will prove rather destructive and delusive to us then any wayes certaine for our security and [for] the settlement of the Kingdom. If your Excellency please wee are very desirous that the paper presented to you might bee represented [to Parliament] as imediately from us and from this honourable Councill, and by the Agitators, which wee conceive will putt vigour and strength

[a] MS. "preparations."

to the businesse, and wee hope effect that which [is] soe earnestly desired.

Lieut. Gen.

I may very easily mistake that which the other Officer offer'd to your Excellency. Two particulars which might receive retardement or obstruction by carrying them on in a way of Treatie, I mentioned indeed, particulars which were that of the 11 Members and that of the prisoners, and meant that those[a] should goe as the sence of the whole Army. Hee conceives itt will adde vigour and strength to the desire and make our desires more easily granted [to] present not only those but all the rest [as the sense of the whole Army.]

If it bee soe all the rest will bee obstructed if they goe by way of Treatie. There may bee perhaps some mistake or forgetfulnesse in that which I offer'd to you. I thinke truly there is no objection lies in that which is said. For, soe farre as I know and discerne of these thinges and the way of management of them, if wee convey [this paper] to the Commissioners and by them to the Parliament as the sence of the whole [Army] represented by the Agitators to the Generall and assented to by the Councill of Warre, and [it] soe becomes the sence, nott only of the Armie that is the offended parte butt alsoe [of] the commanding parte of itt; and [if] wee represent itt to them with that positivenesse that hath bin spoken of, to be sent up to London, to which we desire an answer, and expect an answer within some few days, that is to say, within so short a time as they can have itt consulted, wee may call this a Treaty, butt I thinke itt signifies nothing else butt what that Gentleman speakes of.[b] Therefore for my parte I think they[c] differ in nothing but in words, and not in substance.

[a] MS. "means by those that."

[b] The report is here very confused and I have altered the position of several clauses to make the sense clearer.

[c] Our proposals.

I suppose there are resolutions nott to enter uppon a further Treaty till wee have an answer to these thinges, and if you have patience to heare that which is offer'd you to bee acquainted with from the Commissary Generall, I suppose that businesse may bee soe disposed of.[a] Therefore I shall desire that if itt please the Generall, that you may[b] have an account of that other businesse by the Commissary Generall.

Mr. Allen.

May itt please your Excellency, I desire to offer one word. The Lieut. Generall hath bin pleased to give us an account that your Excellency together with your Councill have travel'd hard in the transacting and managing of thinges in order to the weale both of the Kingdome and Army, in which I hope wee are satisfied as concerning your care and fidelity therein. Butt truly wee cannott bee soe fully satisfied in the apprehension of your care in the managing and transacting of thinges for us, butt wee are as much sadded that those[c] with whome you are transacting and endeavouring to manage these great affaires for us are taking soe little care of us while you in transacting are soe carefull of them, soe little care either to save your expence [of labour] or ours. Truly [as to] that which the Lieutennant Generall hath spoken, to conclude thinges in the way of Treatie, you conceive itt would bee singularly honourable to conclude them soe if possible. Itt hath bin our thoughts soe too, and therfore [we] have waited longe that wee might if possible have thinges ended in such a way; butt truly wee have waited soe longe as our patience is expended. The Lieutennant Generall hath exprest, that if things bee not ended in such a way then there is a ground to goe on in some other way.

[a] Here follows in the MS. "As that it may be seen to all the world that itt is an effectuall meanes to procure these things to bee granted as marching to London would doe." This sentence evidently belongs to the end of the preceding paragraph

[b] MS. "that the Commissioners General may by you."

[c] *i.e.* the Parliament.

How farre that way hath falne short, and how farre that has[a] presented us with a cleere ground to proceede in further, I shall leave itt to this honourable Councill to judge. And truly itt is that which is in most of our thoughts, that those who have bin treating with us are nott intended to conclude thinges in such a way. That when wee see God soe carried forth, or soe suffering mens spiritts to bee acted, that they shall refuse those peaceable thinges desir'd, that is the great thing observed by us.[b] And whether or noe proved once [God] hath nott pointed out some other way to us?[c] I thinke itt is most of our thoughts that hee has. And whether or noe nott such a way as this, namely, the proposall of these desires, those new ones, and those former that hath bin presented to them, [but] nott by them yet answered?[d] That which hath encouraged them rather nott to grant them hath bin our distance from them which our advancing towards them [will remove]. Itt is our thoughts that the proposall of these to them, and our speedy advance towards them, would be a preparation to attaine a speedy and a most effectuall answer to those thinges which wee desire, [in] which (if nott such a course taken) wee doe extreamely question that wee shall have nothing done. That now wee see delayes prove soe dangerous that they are almost every day expected to run into confusion, which [it] is the desire of you and of us to prevent, and wee have named those thinges that they may bee offer'd to the House, and that wee may march in order to a speedy procuring of an answer to them.

Lieut. Gen.

If that that I say of the Treaty bee applyed to one thinge which

[a] MS. "was."

[b] Clause transposed.

[c] Proved once, *i.e.* when this is once proved.

[d] The speaker's meaning seems to be that God has purposely prevented the parliament from accepting the terms of the army and thus pointed out to the army the necessity of using another way to obtain them.

I meane of another, then there may haply[a] bee a very great misunderstanding of mee; butt that which I speake of Treaty, that relates to those thinges that are prepared for a generall Settlement of the Kingdome, bee applyed to the obtayning of these thinges which are to precede a Treaty, is that that I have said to you hath bin mistaken throughout, and instead of giving mee satisfaction of that point which stickes on so with every one of danger and delay butt that which I say of Treatie in answer to that is offer'd in your paper that wee should obtaine these by positive demand within a circumscribed time and going of the Commissioners. Yett using the name will nott offend if wee doe nott the thinges, that is [if] wee doe nott treate of those thinges.[b]

Give mee leave to offer one thinge to your consideration which I see you make to bee your ground of marching towards London; because itt came in my minde, I am sorry I did itt, butt this came in my minde, and I would nott offer itt to you butt because I really know itt is a truth. Wee are, as our friends are elsewhere, very swift in our affections and desires; and truly I am very often judged for one that goes too fast that way, and itt is the property of men that are as I am to bee full of apprehensions that dangers are nott soe reall as imaginary, to bee alwayes making hast, and more some times perhaps then good speede; wee

[a] MS. "happily."

[b] Though the reporter has irreparably confused Cromwell's actual words his meaning is plain enough.

"That which I speak of the advantages of a treaty relates only to the propositions for a general settlement of the kingdom. What I said to you on that point has been mistaken throughout if it be applied to the obtaining of the things which are to precede a treaty. You keep on misapplying that instead of giving me satisfaction as to the question of the danger of delay. That which I say in answer to the proposal in your paper is that we should obtain these things by a positive demand, and within a circumscribed time, forwarding them through the Commissioners the Parliament has appointed to treat. There is no harm in nominally using the Commissioners for this purpose if we do not treat with them, but merely turn them into messengers."

are apt to misapprehensions that wee shall bee deluded through delay, and that there are noe good intentions in the parliament towards us, and that wee gather from the manifold bearing [?] of those words that wee have represented to them. Give mee leave to say this to you, for my owne parte perhaps I have as few extravagant thoughts, overweaning [thoughts] of obtaining great thinges from the Parliament as any man; yett itt hath bin in most of our thoughtes that this Parliament might bee a reformed and purged Parliament, that wee might see [there] men looking att publique and common interests only. This was the great principall wee had gone uppon, and certainly this is the principle wee did march uppon when wee were att Uxbridge, and when wee were att St. Alban's, and surely the thing was wise, and honourable, and just, and wee see that providence hath led us into that way. Itt's thought that the Parliament does nott mend—what's the meaning of that? That is to say, that company of men that sitts there does nott meane well to us. There is a partie there that have bin faithfull from the sitting of the Parliament to this very day; and wee know their interests, and they have ventured their lives through soe many hazards, they came nott to the House butt under the apprehension of having their throats cutt every day. If wee well consider what difficulties they have past that wee may not run into that extreme of thinking too hardly of the Parliament. If wee shall consider that their businesse of holding their heads above water is the common worke, and every other day ['s work] and to day that which wee desire is that which they have strugled for as for life, and sometimes they have bin able to carry itt, others nott, and yett daily they gett ground.

Iff wee [wish to] see a purged Parliament, I pray lett mee perswade every man that hee would be a little apt to hope the best; and I speake this to you as out of a cleare conscience before the Lord, I doe thinke, that [that part of] the Parliament is uppon the gaining hand, and that this worke that wee are now uppon tends to make them gaine more; and I would wish that wee might remember this alwayes, that [what] wee and they gaine in a free way, itt is better then twice so much in a forc't, and will bee more truly our's and our posterities; and therfore I desire nott to perswade any man to bee of my minde, butt I wish that every man would seriously weigh these thinges.

Mr. Allen.

May itt please your Excellency and this honourable Councill, I suppose your Honour hath att this time spoke those good hopes and thoughts that you have of the Parliament; and truly they are the same thoughts and hopes that wee have longe had, and are loath to lay downe or to deviate from, did not too visible testimonie take us off, or wee would willingly see, and itt would bee the rejoicing of our spiritts to see, as possibly might be,[a] a Parliament soe reformed as might back this present power, and that power and aucthority might goe hand in hand to carry on that great worke in order to the Kingdomes welfare; which could they doe, I thinke itt would much facilitate your carrying of itt on. Your Honour is pleased to tell us (I suppose speaking your hopes therin) that the Parliament or the prevailing parte of itt is a gaining parte, and like to gaine more. Truly I could wish wee could say soe too; butt soe farre as wee are able to judge of ourselves wee must speake our feares. That wee conceive they[b] are a loosing partie, and loosers rather then gainers. I think very few of us [believe] that they are at the present gainers, or like to be gainers. Whether our marching towards London may nott conduce to such an end, namely to the quelling of the spiritts of those who are acting as much as in them lies to make them and us and the kingdome be loosers? That they are loosers, and truly, if such a course bee nott taken to suppress those persons, that I fear itt will

[a] Clause transposed.

[b] Our friends in the Parliament.

bee past our recovery to make them gainers, if wee lett them go on.[a]

Coñ. Generall.

I suppose this debate depends uppon these two thinges; First, whether those desires read bee likely soe effectually to bee sent uppe to London in the way as they are, or in the other deliver'd in to day; and the other [thing] is, whether itt bee nott fitt, whether you send [them] the one [way] [b] or the other, to resolve uppon a marching of the Army towards London. I conceive [c] the effect of what was said to your Excellency last was, to my understanding, butt meerly an answer of one reason that seem'd to have bin urg'd against the marching of the Army towards London.

And first I cannott butt take notice of what was said uppon that point, soe as to give the Gentleman that hath spoke and the rest some satisfaction too, or att least to shew how little reason they have to bee unsatisfied. Itt is suppos'd that those who appeare, who wee account to bee friends of the Commonalty, as to the Kingdome, and of Justice and righteousnesse, which do professe as wee to [d] seeke after itt, itt is suppos'd they are rather of the loosing then of the gaining hand; and I expected to have had some reasons why wee should thinke soe; butt the maine [reason given] was, that they didd nott soe fully nor soe wholly comply with this Army in all the thinges that they desire [as we think they ought to do].

I cannott blame [them] nor cannott see [how] any man [can] that walkes by that rule of doing to another as hee would bee done to, which is the only rule of justice. I doe nott understand how wee can thinke that of necessity they must satisfie us in all these thinges wee desire, and those [things] tending still to putt power

[a] The report is here amended by transposing several clauses.
[b] MS. "partie." [c] MS. "perceive." [d] MS. "as wee professe doe."

into our hands, and to put all power too out of any other hands; I cannott expect itt reasonably from men. For what reason have I to expect that other men should trust mee more then I should trust to them? or that I should give them better testimonie of my fidelitie to them then they of their's to mee, and especially of the fidelity and clearnesse of my intentions? Truly I thinke wee have some intimations[a] that they are rather of the gaining hand, though I shall offer some [more]. You cannot but see they have prevail'd. We heare [that] there are daily uppon those votes many that doe discover themselves, and others that are discovered by others, that doe leave the House; and unlesse wee should thinke that those men of injustice and pusillanimity[b] may bee better friends to us then those that stay behinde, I cannott see how wee should thinke otherwise but *they* must needs bee by that of the gayning hand—I meane those that are friends to our interest, for the going against which, or betraying of which these men are cast out—and therfore I thinke that parte that was used of their being of the gaining hand, together with the consideration of the difficultie by which they doe carry these thinges daily—and att present they are strugling and striving with a partie that would carry all thinges with the worst to the Kingdome—I thinke [that consideration] ought to bee of [such] weight with us that wee should have some love towards them, as wee would expect that others should have the like towards us, if wee were in the like case.

I shall proceede to speake concerning the marching of the Army towards London for the inforcing of these desires, and concerning the way of sending uppe these desires of the Army. I cannott butt deliver my opinion, that itt would bee more effectuall if itt doe come as a paper agreed uppon by your Excellency, by your Councell of Warre, and by all the Agitators. [It] cannott butt bee more effectuall, then iff itt came in by the

[a] MS. "intentions."

[b] Clause transposed.

Commissioners that are appointed to treate, and soe I hope itt will bee satisfactory to them; and truly when wee have any thinge to say to the Parliament, and [it is] nott deliver'd [directly] to them, I thinke itt is a great incivility. Sir, I shall speake but a word or two concerning those apprehensions that I perceive there are of after troubles. For my owne parte I expect noe great matter, nor [do I desire] to putt much uppon the way of the Treaty; I should rather desire to shorten the worke, and if men doe understand your Excellency they may know that that which only hath occasioned the hope of any thinge in the Treatie is that wee would nott goe soe much in the way of Treatie, but the rather thinke of another way to drawe out all thinges out of our own proposalls;[a] and soe to make a short worke of itt without any longe proposall by way of debate. And wheras itt hath bin said, by any way of Treatie at all, there is little hopes expected, [but] if any[thing] discouragement,[b] because itt hath continued soe longe, and soe little done, I must deale freely and cleerly in that particular, that there is noe cause that I can apprehend for the starting of itt. Wee have noe reason to blame the Commissioners of Parliament, because they have still called uppon us to goe on in that Treatie, and they have sat still and bin content because wee have putt little into their hands.[c] And I must desire all these Gentlemen to consider that [in] the concluding of this by way of Treatie in order to the Settlement of the Kingdome, if there bee any delay, the fault of itt, if there bee any fault, itt lies wholly amongst our selves whatever itt bee; and I thinke much fault hath bin in none, [but there hath bin] a

[a] To draw out our own proposals of all things.

[b] Two clauses transposed.

[c] See the letters of the Parliamentary Commissioners dated July 6, July 8, July 10, and July 18, and the paper delivered by them to the Commissioners of the Army on July 7, in which they complain that the proceedings of the Army Commissioners in the treaty have been very slow. *Old Parliamentary History*, xvi., pp. 93, 95, 97, 107, 115; printed also in the *Lords' Journals*, and in the *Collection of Army Declarations*.

choice rather to present all thinges for the settlement of the Kingdom [together]. The other [reason] was because itt was nott [thought] soe fitt to proceede in itt till some other thinges for present securitie were satisfied, soe that there is noe reason indeed that those that have bin imployed in the Treatie should bee blam'd for itt as att this time; and I cannot butt adde one word more, that those Gentlemen that seeme to bee unsatisfied have little reason to blame any att all.

This preparation of an entire proposall of particulars they have bin desir'd, and I shall appeale to as many as have spoken to mee if I have nott made itt knowne that wee were uppon this worke of drawing all thinges for a proposall to the setling of the Kingdome.[a] Therfore [it was desired that] any man that had leasure and freedome and a minde to further the worke would thinke of any particulars to give in to my self and another that was sequestred or sett apart for that worke; and truly Sir, I thinke if noe man else hath prepared any other particulars, I thinke those that have prepared some particulars [deserve thanks]. Wee propose thus. Wee doe thinke that the settlement of peace is by having a settlement of itt in our hands; if ever itt doe come to settle, itt must bee by setting downe some thinge that may bee a rule to lay a foundation for the common rights and liberties of the people, and for an established peace in the Nation. I know nott [that] any of those Gentlemen that seeme to bee sensible of delayes, that any of them have tendred any thinge to the Commissioners that have satt, or have proposed[b] any termes wherin the settlement is.

I shall say no more to these, but [speak] to one [thing only] as to drawe the Army towards London. Truly Sir I should bee

[a] On the history of the drawing up of the Heads of the Proposals agreed on by the Army, see *Memoirs of Sir John Berkeley*, Maseres, *Select Tracts*, i., 353, and Wildman's *Putney Projects*, 1647, p. 13. The other person mentioned as set apart for that work appears to have been Lambert, v. post. p. 212, and Whitelock, ii., 163 ed. 1853.

[b] MS. "of proposing." The order of the sentences in this paragraph is evidently wrong.

against it altogether, unlesse wee had proposed those thinges for setling the peace of the Kingdome, and doe finde a profest preparation against you. Butt I am the more against you because those thinges are not proposed, and nott the more because att present you propose such a thinge which may justly receive a deniall, I meane to those whom you do nott give such a full satisfaction in. I do not knowe that there is a thinge agreed upon to bee propos'd, I mean the proposall of the Militia in those hands.[a] I am concluded by the Councell soe farre as nott to speake any thinge att all against itt, only soe farre as nott to that wee should nott faile for that as to march uppe to London,[b] and I wish when wee doe itt wee should have a more reasonable thinge then for that. And, Sir, I shall say noe more to itt, but adde some inforcement, and that is, the consequence of seeking to gaine such thinges as these are by force. Truly I know nothing that can make any man to scruple the weight of that, except itt bee that hee thinkes there hath bin force offer'd already, and [that] therefore wee shall thinke of nothing heerafter butt force, and nott make account of any thinge that can bee obtain'd any other way. If a man hath nott that apprehension this argument must bee a very weighty one.[c] I should butt desire to minde that which is visible and apparent in the papers, which was the only appearance of any kinde of threat-

[a] The last two sentences should probably run thus, "But I am the more against you because those things are not proposed—I do not know that there is a thing agreed upon to be proposed—and not the less because at present you propose to those to whom you do not give such a full satisfaction a thing which may justly receive a deniall. I mean the proposal of returning the Militia into the hands of those in whom it lately was." On the Militia, v., pp. 152, 171, 174.

[b] This may be thus paraphrased and emended, "I am bound by the opinion of the rest of the Councell so far as not to speak anything against that proposal itself, but I may go so far as to say that I would not have you for that fall to march up to London."

[c] Ireton's words perhaps were as follows: "I should but desire to remind you that that which is visible and apparent in your papers now is only the appearance of a kind of threatening."

ning. And I say yett, my ground then[a] was that this Army stood as it were proscrib'd; you stood butt as outlawes, all that were amongst you were invited to come away from you, and you were putt out of protection, and noe body owning of you as their Army. That was one Reason. Another Reason [was that those] who were the profest, open, knowne Enemies of the Army, who had (according to those thinges wee have impeached them for) indeavoured to engage in a Warre, they had place in Parliament, and such place and power in all Committees of Parliament as did give them a cleere advantage openly and aboveboard to carry on thinges for a Warre, and we saw very visible effects of that. Truly from that time [we have] seene an alteration as to that, and that is first of all that they are withdrawne from the House, and they are nott suffer'd to appeare that I can heere upon action as members of the House. There is nothing wanting butt a positive order for the sequestring of them the House, and that I thinke there is a greate deale of Justice to demand, and to demand with a further inforcement.

I speake all to this purpose, that wee had uppon our former march to London better grounds, and now wee have nott any left us. Wee were in all probability butt as ruin'd men, under noe acknowledgement nor own'd by noe body, by noe aucthoritie in the Kingdome. In that the case is very clearly alter'd, and for my owne parte I doe nott understand how we can have the same ground to goe agen now; but I apply all to this conclusion, that before wee had such a cleare ground for our going uppe that all might conclude that wee had reason to doe that, or else to have wholly laid downe our armes, and deserted the cause and interest wee have taken, for wee could nott continue in armes till that were done.

Mr. Allen.

The Commissary Generall's discourse hath bin large, and truly

[a] When the Army first marched on London early in June, 1647.

my memory and the time is something short. I shall nott speake butt only to one particular, and that the last, because itt is most fresh in my memory, and perhaps some heere have had thoughts of the former. Concerning our marching uppe to London, I take itt itt is waiv'd uppon this ground, that wee have nott now that reason as formerly wee had when wee did before march uppe towards itt; and the reason that then wee had was this, wee lay as a disown'd Army and wee had a House unpurg'd. Truly to that I shall only breiflie reply, that I doe confesse wee are own'd in name, butt I doubt nott in nature, to bee the Parliaments Army. And truly I will only hinte att some thinges in order to that, that give mee some grounds soe to suspect that we are nott own'd as their Army. Meerly the reason is, if wee were they would never suffer us to bee traduc't, revil'd, and rail'd uppon both in pulpitts and presses continually as wee are, butt itt would bee a little laid to heart by a Parliament owning us as their Army, and itt would reflect uppon their honour as well as ours. I conceive that they ought to doe some thinge in vindication both of our owne and their Honour in that particular; butt seing them silent and all this while wee should lie under itt, and I feare this is only that that they would putt upon us that wee are in name the Parliament's Army. Butt I will say noe more to that. As to the purging of the House [it is said that] there have been great thinges done. The Members[a] they are att present debarr'd of sitting there, and there wants butt an ordinance or something to that purpose—which is almost all—to the sequestring of them wholly. I feare yett they are in a capacitie of doing too much, and till they shall more fully declare themselves as to that, I question if wee looke nott uppon thinges in a multiplying glasse. And truly as those were the reasons uppon which the weight of our marching laid, as that our intentions might bee made knowne to the Kingdome that soe wee might have

[a] The eleven impeached members.

a cleare and undoubted way to gett swords out of mens hands that will cutt our throates with them. To mee itt seemes strange that this should bee a sufficient ground. I wish that while wee are laying to our selves a full ground, by a full foundation for a large structure, some body does nott interpose betweene us. If when we have presented ourselves and mindes to the view of the Kingdome as intending to satisfaction to satisfie, whether or noe this is nott that which wee expected and wee know what they doe intend, wee'll seeke to helpe our selves in another, and soe the other and the other way, and truly if you have noe power in your hands, why truly of what a consequence such a thinge may bee I leave itt to you to judge.[a]

Lieut. Gen.

This I wish in the generall, that wee may all of us soe demeasne our selves in this businesse that wee speake those thinges that tend to the uniting of us, and that wee doe none of us exercise our parts to straine thinges, and to lett in thinges to a longe dispute, or to unnecessary contradictions, or to the stirring uppe of any such seede of dissatisfaction in one anothers mindes as may in the least render us unsatisfied one in another. I doe nott speake this that any body does doe itt, butt I say this ought to *become* both you and mee, that wee soe speake and act as that the end may bee union and a right understanding one with another.

[a] The minor speakers are not so well reported as the more important ones Allen's argument appears to be, "As for the reasons on which the weight of the argument against our immediate marching is laid, viz., that we might make our intentions known to the kingdom, etc.—it seems strange to me that these should be thought sufficient grounds. I fear that while we are preparing our scheme for a settlement some one may step in between us and the settlement of the kingdom. What if when we have presented our heads of a settlement to the people, as intending to satisfy them whether they will or no, we fail to satisfy them? What if they say 'this is not what we expected, now we know what they mean we'll help ourselves some other way,' and so some take one way, some another way? If in such confusion you have no power in your hands what will the consequences be?"

Truly, if I thought that which was last spoken by Mr. Allen had bin satisfactory to that end for which hee spake itt, I should nott have said any thinge to you. Butt for that [answer] which hee made to the Commissary [General's argument] of the Parliament's owning of us, and what a thinge that was to us, and how much tending to the settlement of the peace of the Kingdome, to say or to thinke 'itt is butt a titular thinge that, and butt in name only that they doe owne [us,]' I thinke is a very great mistake. For really itt did att that time lay the best foundation could bee expected for the preventing an absolute confusion in this Kingdome; and I thinke if wee had nott bin satisfied in that, wee should nott have bin satisfied in any thinge. And [it is a very great mistake] to thinke that this is any weighty argument, 'itt is butt titular, because they suffer scandalous bookes flock uppe and downe,'—I would nott looke they should love us better then they love themselves, and how many scandalous bookes goe out of them. Wee have given them and the Parliament more to doe then attend [to] scandalous bookes. I hope that will not weigh with any man; and I desire wee may putt this debate to a conclusion, or else lett us answer those thinges that are really and weightily objected, as truly that was [not]. They have given us as reall a testimonie that they cannott give more. They cannott disowne us without the loosing of all rationall and honest people in the Kingdome; and therfore lett us take itt as a very great and high owning of us; lett nott us disown that owning. If any man would by that which was objected wee would have peace, a perfect settlement of all wee seek and we would march to London to say wee forc't them.[a]—Really, Really, Have what you will have, that you have by force I looke uppon itt as nothing. I doe nott knowe that force is to bee used, except wee cannott gett what is for the good of the Kingdome without force. All the arguments must tend to this, that itt is necessary to use force, to

[a] May be paraphrased thus, "If any man urges, we would have a perfect settlement of all we seek, and would therefore march to London. Say we did force them to grant what we ask."

march uppe with the Army, and nott to tarry 4 dayes. [Was not the argument thus][a] wee shall bee baffled, denied, and shall never march uppe, butt still bee patient and suffer, even to have the ruine of the Kingdome as hath bin imagin'd [if we do not march within four days]. Expect a speedy answer which hath bin offer'd, and to make that criticall to us whether they owne us or intend to perfect the settlement as wee expect. The Kingdome would bee sav'd [even] if wee doe not march within 4 dayes, if wee had these thinges granted to us. If these thinges bee granted to us wee may march to Yorke. I wish wee may respite our determination till that 4 or 5 dayes bee over, till wee see how thinges will bee, except you will urge reasons to show itt to bee of absolute necessity to all those ends to determine just now that wee will march uppe to London to morrow or next day. I am sorry that wee bee nott satisfied with that which hath bin propos'd as to this very thinge, and [hope] that[b] having had assurance these thinges were putt into such a way as hath bin offer'd to you that you will rest contented with this as att this time, except you will show us some absolute reasons.

Major Tulida.

The Lieutennant Generall hath putt itt to a good issue, for the weight of the businesse lies heere. That those proposalls presented to your Excellency to day, and those thinges wee all doe conclude on to be necessary, but there seems a difference in the way.[c] I cannot butt adde that there is a great deale of faith in this, that wee doe [all] conclude our owne [way] as the accomplishing of the thinges. Whether you should represent that wee canncott probably obtaine them? And really Sir to my apprehension the

[a] MS. "if the argument was not thus." This clause is transferred from the line below.

[b] MS. "if.

[c] Clause transposed from two lines below.

representation of a swete and honourable way of Treating is as much wish't and desir'd by mee as by any. If I shall cast my eye on[a] what is represented by these Treaties, and by the consequence of them, I should stand att a distance from them. I shall nott putt the fault uppon the Commissioners [of the Parliament] or uppon those that were your Excellencie's Commissioners, butt in the conclusion wee are noe further then where wee were att Uxbridge; nay, nott soe farre, and the same thinges press[b] uppon us. And therfore ——, though some have mentioned [as] to the Parliament, that wee should [not] expect from them any thinge that they could nott accomplish, —— therefore, Sir, as our advancing to Uxbridge putt them into [such] a way that they had liberty to speake, if our advance to Uxbridge sett them on the legges, nothing will expedite them to putt them into the same [way] of boldly speaking for the Kingdomes interest [like our advance] towards the City.[c] Wee seeme to bee startled att the expression of forcing thinges—Doe wee force, or doe wee desire by forcing [anything] butt that with [once] forcing there should bee noe more forcing? That by the sword wee may take the sword out of those hands that are enemies to justice, to equity? Itt was by forcing this, and soe wee conceiving the emergent necessity that without an advance to London wee cannott have any other accomplishment to these proposalls I desire that all may bee putt to this issue. As to the thinge propounded by the Lieutennant Generall, I doe nott know that wee can promise our selves soe as that wee can have itt,[d] when they doe nott owne us to bee their Army; and for the Militia of London there is

[a] MS. "in."

[b] MS. "prest."

[c] Clause transposed.

[d] MS. "I do not know as to the thing propounded by the Lieutenant General, I do not know that wee cannot promise ourselves soe as that wee cannot have it, nor then."

as great necessity for us to advance to London. Wee cannott have any thinge unlesse by the way of advancing to London.

Lieut. Gen.

Truly the words spoken by Major Tulidah were [spoken] with affection, butt wee are rationall [men]. I would faine know with what reason or colour of reason hee did urge any reason but only with affirmation of earnest words. For that Declaration of the Parliament, the Parliament hath own'd us, and taken off that that any man can loyally or rationally charge us with. If uppon his apprehensions or any man's else, wee shall quarrel with every dogge in the streete that barkes att us, and suffer the Kingdome to bee lost with such a fantasticall thinge? I desire that nothing of heate or earnestnesse may carry us heere, nor nothing of affirmation, nor nothing of that kinde may lead us, butt that which is truly reason, and that which hath life and argument in itt.

To that which was alledged that by our marching [a] to Uxbridge wee open'd those honest mens mouthes to speake for us. This is nott to be answer'd with reason, butt this is matter of fact, and better knowne to some of us then itt is to Major Tulida or any of you. 'Tis true there was [a] feare and an awe uppon the Parliament by our marching to Uxbridge, there was some thinge of that, for those 11 Members were afraid to bee in the House. If you will beleive that which is nott a fancie, they have voted very essentiall thinges to their owne purging, and I believe this, iff we will believe that which is the truth in fact,[b] uppon that very one vote that

[a] MS. "By that which was alleged of our marching."

[b] On July 5 a vote was passed that no persons who had been in actual war against the Parliament, or accepted pardons from the King, or taken any part in bringing about the cessation or otherwise assisting the Rebellion in Ireland, or were sequestered by Parliament for delinquency should presume to sit in the House of Commons. *Commons' Journals*, v. 233. Those who infringed this order were by a second vote of July 9 to be liable to the penalties imposed in the Newcastle propositions on those who had sat in the Oxford Parliament, *i.e.*, to be guilty of high treason and their estates to be sequestrated (*ibid.*, p. 238; Gardiner, *Constitutional Documents*, p. 217).

was pas't,—concerning the putting a fine or penalty [on those] that knew themselves to bee guilty, and that if they did nott goe out should accuse themselves to bee liable to sequestration[a]—I believe there will goe 20 or 30 men out of the House of Commons. And if this bee [not] an effect and demonstration of the happy progresse, [they have made] and that by use of that libertie that they have had by our [not] drawing neere, I appeale to any man? And if they shall, as I said before, disowne us, and wee give them noe cause to doe itt, butt pressing only just, and honourable, and honest thinges from them, judge you what can the world thinke of them and of us? Butt [what can the world think if] wee shall doe that, whilest wee are uppon the gayning hand, that shall really stoppe their mouthes, to open their mouthes in a title for us. That whilest they are, as fast as they can, gayning the thinges wee desire, if wee shall bee soe impatient that whilest they are strugling for life that they are unable to helpe us and gain'd more within these 3 dayes then in 10 dayes for aught I know wee may by advancing stoppe their mouthes.[b] They will nott have wherwithall to answer that middle partie in the House who is answer'd with this reason, "you see the Army is contented to goe backward, you see the Army is willing, to make faire representations[c] of that they have from us." I professe, I speake itt in my conscience, that if wee should move untill wee had made these proposalls to them, and see what answer they will give them, wee shall

[a] The report is here very confused. What Cromwell said was probably this, "If we will believe that which is the Truth in Fact, not that that which is a fancy, they have voted very essential things to their own purging."

[b] Cromwell's argument seems to be this: "Shall we do that whilst they are upon the gaining hand in order to open their mouths in a title for us, that shall really stop their mouths? If we shall be so impatient—and that whilst they are as fast as they can gaining us the things we desire and have gained us more in the last 3 days than in 10 days whilst they were struggling for life and could not help us—for aught I know we may by advancing stop their mouths." 'In a title' should perhaps be in a 'tittle' or may refer to the proposed declaration against foreign forces.

[c] MS. "fancie representations."

nott only disable them butt divide among our selves; and I as much feare that as any thinge; and if wee should speake to your satisfactions you must speake to our satisfactions though there bee great feares of others I shall very much question the integritie of any man, I would nott have itt spoken.[a]

Cornett Joyce.

What I shall speake is nott against that which is prepared and are to be presented to the House, butt I should thus offer [this] unto the Lieutennant Generall and likewise to the Commissary Generall; whether or noe when the Parliament did vote or declare us to bee their Army [they] did owne our act in fighting of the Kinge? Againe, if in case they have left out that, and doe nott owne that, there may bee some thing that may cause a . . . . to neglect this Army.

Mr. Sexby.

To mee this seemes very cleare, and I cannott see yet any satisfaction to itt. I conceive that what the Parliament has done in reference to their declaring us their Army was uppon this ground, that they did [it] rather out of feare then love. My reasons are these: first, because to this day those that deserted us are [better] look't uppon, countenanc't, and abundantly better paid then wee. 2ndly. Because as yett they looke uppon us as Enemies for this reason, that they send to treate with us; for truly Parliaments or Armies never treate with friends butt Enemies, and truly wee cannott butt looke uppon our selves soe.

Major Disbrow.

Soe farre as I understand, a great deale of this last is farre from the businesse in hand. Most men cry out for expedition, and this

[a] This might be rearranged thus: "And though there be great feares of other things I fear dividing as much as anything, and I shall very much question the integrity of any man that does not. I would not have the word spoken."

is nott the way to itt. One [point] that the Commissary Generall answer'd them fully in [was] the manner of presenting this paper. Another was a speedy marching, ... and to itt many have rather offer'd their owne fancies then any expedient. Some for a speedy marching and others to march within 4 dayes. I humbly offer this, that if there were reason to resolve now to march to London, [whether] preparations would nott last soe longe [as four days] ? I conceive this, that the chief ground of difference [is] of marching to London or nott marching to London ; and itt is prest uppon this consideration, because there is noe expectation of [obtaining] what is propounded without the Army goes to backe itt. I only offer this to all reasonable men, whether itt bee nott an unreasonable way ? Itt hath bin often agen and agen moved that there may bee an answer [obtained] by Munday night or Tuesday morning; and truly you could nott sett forward a march before; and therefore I offer itt to your Excellency that wee might nott take pleasure in speaking our own [fancies] butt to minde the businesse in hand, if any man hath any thinge to speake.

Lieut. Scotton.

One of the great ones was,[a] since wee see that your Excellency and the Councill of Warre hath bin pleas'd to take itt into consideration as to proceede to a Treaty, and truly I hope that reason that I have heard observ'd. Wee are soe farre satisfied to bring our desires about and waive the marching to London. I have one word [to say] that it does lie uppon our spiritts that there may bee a reall and effectuall course taken that [Lt.-Col. Lilburne] is freed.

Cornett Spencer.

I am now come from the Citty. There is this day many Officers of the Militia to take the names of every Apprentice and to cause

[a] One of the greatest reasons for marching was removed.

them to bee ready uppon an houres warning. That yesterday uppon the Kinges coming to Maidenhead.[a] That you and all of your Army I thinke wee may as well goe alonge with them as with our Army, as the Scotts did, and were justified, and therefore if wee bee right ——

Lieut. Gen.

Truly Sir I thinke neither of these 2 thinges that Gentleman spoke last are any great newes. For the one of them, the listing of Apprentices, I doubt they have listed them twice over ; I am sure wee have heard [it] more then twice over. For the other [that our friends in London] would rejoice to see us come uppe, what if wee [be] better able to consult what is for their good then themselves ? Itt is the generall good of them and all the people in the Kingdome [we ought to consult]. That's the question, what's for their good, nott what pleases them. I doe nott know that all these considerations are arguments to have satisfaction in these things that wee have in proposition. If you bee in the right, and I in the wronge, if we wee bee divided I doubt wee shall all bee in the wronge. . . . Whether of them will doe our worke, lett them speake without declaring.[b] Lett us nott thinke that this is a greater argument that they love those that deserted, that they have paid them and nott us, which was Mr. Sexbye's argument, which if itt had weight in itt I should have submitted to itt. The Question is singly this : whether or noe wee shall nott in a positive way desire the answer to these thinges before wee march towards London, when perhaps wee may have the same thinges in the time that wee can march. Heere is the strictnesse of the Question.

[a] Spencer refers to the King's coming to Maidenhead to meet the Duke of York, July 15. Rushworth, vi. 625. His argument seems to be, "Our friends wished we had come with the King and would march up to London with them."

[b] Cromwell's meaning appears to be : "Let us call on the Parliament to declare without delay whether they will do our work or not."

Major Tulida.

That if any thinge bee spoken, to say itt is out of zeale, that wee should abound in our sence —— I humbly desire there may bee libertie to speake, and that a providence may carry thinges, and nott that way.

Col. Rich.

There has bin a longe debate. There are only two thinges in Question: whether the paper and 5 particulars should goe as they are, or that this paper should bee first insisted uppon? and then whether this paper should bee presented to the Commissioners [of the Parliament] heere as from the Councill [of the Army] or from the Commissioners [of the Army]? Itt is well that itt should goe as from this Councill. The second is for the march to London. As for our marching to London the Lieut. Generall putts itt uppon this issue; whether wee shall march now or stay 4 dayes? To decide itt with a Question whether wee shall march to London, or noe.

Lieut. Chillenden.

That that proposall which my Lieutenant Generall propos'd to your Excellency concerning the proposall of this, for my parte to mee itt gives great satisfaction in my spiritt for to see itt, and I hope there will bee the like uppon my parte. And alsoe for the other concerning the prisoners, itt lies soe weighty uppon my spiritt, and truly I hope your Excellency and this Councill of Warre are those [that will insist upon it] . . . . . [But] that att this juncture of time the Judges are going the Circuites I should nott trouble your Excellency and this Councill of Warre concerning itt. That that paper may goe concluding all thinges in itt.

Commissary Gen.

That hee would have the 5 particulars in itt goe, butt nott the paper [itself], for [in] that itt is propos'd the Army should march towards or to London. If wee have friends in the Parliament or Citty that wish well to the Army or Kingdome, I could nott butt expect to loose them by itt, if they should butt see such a spiritt in this Army that they putt [force uppon] them . . . . . uppon such thinges [to] which some of them were never oppos'd.

Another expression, 'that they should nott only bee sequestred butt disabled.' I confesse I doe nott understand the justice of that ground, and I pray God this Army may avoide itt.[a]

Att a Generall Councill of Warre att Reading. July 17, 1647.

Commissary Ireton.

That those papers[b] doe nott concerne the Army in particular butt the whole Kingdome in generall.

Lieut. Gen.

That all prejudices might bee removed.

Coñ. Ireton.

There could bee butt 2 wayes: either by Treatie, or else to have such an intire proposall of particulars prepared, as might neede the lesse delay in way of Treatie. The Commissioners are those that your Excellency was pleased to appoint. Itt was offer'd to us by the Commissioners of the Parliament parte, whether wee would draw out particulars, or [make] an intire proposall of all together? Though there was noe publique proposall [ready], yett wee did satisfie our selves how longe and teadious itt would have

[a] Referring to the case of the eleven impeached members.

[b] The papers in question are the heads of the Army's proposals.

bin to draw out particulars by way of debate by the Commissioners there; and therefore truly I was, with the consent of your Excellency and the rest of the Commissioners, sequestred from that imployment of the Treatie to make some preparation of particulars fitt to tender to your Excellency and the Army as were declared in itt.[a] That if any body could thinke of any other particulars that concern'd the Kingdome every man was as free to doe as my selfe or any other, and would have bin as well accepted; and for my owne parte I should have bin glad that any other would have sett himselfe on worke as I did.

One thinge, the Parliament have sent propositions to the Kinge; wee have nott had any from them.

The propositions read.[b]

Lieut. Gen.

Butt you would nott have a Parliament dissolved without the consent of the Houses in 120 dayes?

Col. Lambert.

[They may sit] longer then that, that except the Councill of State, and the Kinge shall thinke fitt; if you involve themselves in itt if they may sitt without the consent of both Housses.

Lieut. Gen.

They may bee adjourn'd if the King and Councill of State thinke fitt; itt may bee as convenient to have a Parliament continued as to [have it] out itself whether it will or noe.

[a] The last words seem to belong to the next sentence. "That as was declared in the vote appointing me, if anybody, etc."

[b] The propositions are printed in Rushworth, vii., 731. *Old Parliamentary History*, xvi., 212; Gardiner, *Constitutional Documents*, p. 232. The present discussion is on the second clause of the first head. Parliament might sit 240 days at the outside, and must sit at least 120 days.

If itt does nott conclude itt publique, as that itt bee heare read or noe. If there bee any thinge afterwards that shall bee desired to bee offer'd for any addition the Councill of Warre will meete, and the Agitators [may] send soe many as they shall select to gett any alteration ; butt itt would nott bee read heere butt that itt bee passed by with silence.

Com̃. Ireton.

For either the passing those particulars heere read or such a particular as you last offer'd without a further weighing or consideration itt might bee inconvenient; and therefore I shall desire, that though there is noe man that findes anythinge of exception against any parte of the thinge that is read, yett that it may be referred to a less number that may weigh or consider all things.[a]

[These particulars are offered] nott for a present conclusion butt consideration ; for I cannott say the thinges have bin soe consider'd as to satisfie my self in them.

Mr. Allen.

I shall only offer one worde. I thinke that the thinges in hand hee names are things of great weight, having relation to the setling of a Kingdome, which is a great worke; truly the worke wee all expect to have a share in, and desire that others may alsoe. I suppose itt is nott unknowne to you that wee are most of us butt young Statesmen, and nott well able to judge how longe such thinges which wee heare now read to us may bee to the ends for which they are presented; and for us out of judgment to give our assents to itt must take uppe some time that wee may deliberate uppon itt; and therfore I shall desire that wee may nott only name them [*i.e.* a committee] now, butt spend some time [in debate], when wee heare thinges unsatisfactory to the ends for which they are proposed.

[a] Clause transposed.

Com̃. Ireton.

If that debate or consideration that is intended or desired [be that] that is most requir'd in such a Councill as this, I thinke itt cannott bee with soe much conveniencie butt when all men have heard [them] read, and had time to weigh them in their thoughts. I think that when we are never so well satisfied in the matter, such a select number are requisite for the perfecting of them in order and forme, soe as they may bee tendred for the service of the Kingdome.

Itt is proposed heere in order to a Councill of State, that there should bee a Councill of State to have the cheif command, both to have the command of the standing forces and of the Militia by sea or the Navy. Butt this Councill of State which commands them all to have noe dependancy of any of them by way of appointing officers. For the standing Militia of the Kingdome the [county] Committee[s are] to have power to name officers over them. Likewise for the Navy. The Councill of State [is to] have power to command the Navy, butt there are particular Commissioners to bee appointed for the *ordering* and regulating of itt, and appointing officers for the severall parts of the Navy.[a]

[*News-letter from head-quarters.*]

Reading, 17th July, 1647.[b]

Yesterday there was a great Councill of Warre call'd, it held till 12 a clock at night, consisted of above 100 Officers, besides Agitators, who now in prudence we admitt to debate; and it is not more than necessary they should be, considering the influence they have upon the souldiers, and the officer we hope hath such interest in

[a] At this point the report of the debate ends abruptly. The particular parts of the Army proposals referred to in Ireton's last remarks are—Head III., clauses 1—6.

[b] This letter is probably by John Rushworth. At least it very much resembles those from him to Lord Fairfax, dated July 13 and July 20. *Fairfax Correspondence*, iii., 367-371.

them, as if any of more fierce disposition amongst them moderate not their reason, the officers can command it; and I assure you, it is the singularest part of wisdom in the General and the officers so to carry themselves considering the present temper of the Army, so as to be unanimous in Councills, including the new persons into their number. It keeps a good accord, and obtains ready obedience, for to this hour never any troop or company yet mutiny'd, and if a man consider the alterations of officers that are now admitted, and interests of officers that are gone, it is the greatest wonder, that there is that unanimity still. It is the hand of God that doth it, I hope for a good end. It is not proper to relate particular debates yesterday, yet accept of a word in general, and think it not strange, if it should be advised to march nearer to London, as an expedient to obtain satisfaction in those particulars, which have been long desired by the Army of the Parliament, as in particular declaring against forreign forces coming in, the putting reformado's out of the line, and suspending the 11 Members, but more especially to desire the Parliament to putt the Militia of the Citty of London into the same hands it was before, without which we can not hold our selves secure in proceeding to treat, but that those persons being still in power who granted commissions to Dalbeere and such kind of soldiers of fortune may upon any encouragement from the designing parte be apt to doe the like again. Tho' this was much prest with reasons and earnestness by the Agitators, yet the Generall and the Officers after many hours debate so satisfyed them with arguments and reasons to the contrary, that they submitted it to the Generall and Officers, no man gainsaying it; and so it is resolved to send to the Parliament to desire these particulars, especially the Militia, and receive a positive answer within 4 days. These thinges being granted, the Treaty, all things being prepared to be debated on, will proceed; but till the Parliament be thoroughly purged, which is in a way, and the city Militia altered as aforesaid, we expect nothing but delays upon results of the Treaty, when ever they send them. And be assured you will find by those propositions that came from the Army, they take care for the Parliament and the interest of their party in a sufficient manner, and yet in order to the speedy settlement of the Peace of the Kingdome, make it their humble desires for some way of mediation for the King and his party, but so as not to prejudice the subjects liberty. Monarchy may be so settled, but not to be hurtfull as formerly. The King's party do flock from London hither, not to be entertained in the Army, for I assure you there is not a man of that party suffered to be listed, but they come to see the King, and that civility is connived at, but that party not comply'd with. When the Army was in their greatest glory, and the enemy under their foot, yet we were ever humane and Christian to them, and now being so near a reconciliation, we should not shew any aversion or indisposition. Besides it does begett more confidence in the King than before that we are those that mean to make good our selves, and I hope he is so assured of it as he will not much stop at what shall be propounded for the peace of the Kingdom. It is now our resolution to follow the bussiness day and night, till there be a speedy end putt to this great affair of finishing a peace so much expected by the Kingdom; and indeed it must not be delay'd, for else the odium will lye as much upon the army as it hath of late upon others. Quartering is burthesome to the country and the more where the soldiers are uncivill and rude, which in so great an army doth sometimes happen, especially where we have but one months pay in 18 weeks, and how we shall do to order things well without money will go hard with us, the 200,000ł being all expended, no man knows how.

[*Order appointing certain Officers to perfect the proposals of the Army.*]

I do appoint Commissary Generall Ireton, Collonel Fleetwood, Collonel Rich, Collonel Harrison, Collonel Horton, and Major Disborow of the Horse Officers, and Collonel Rainborow, Collonel

Hammond, Sir Hardress Waller, Collonel Lambert, Lieutenant Collonel Cowell, and Adjutant General Deane of the Foot Officers to meet, consult, and proceed with the 12 Agitators according to the appointment made at the General Councill of Warr yesterday, for the perfecting of the proposals then read, in order to the settling of the Liberties and Peace of the Kingdom; and to adjourn from time to time, and place to place, till the same be perfected, and Lieutenant Generall Cromwell to be present with the said Councill when he can. Given under my hand and seal at Reading the 18th day of July, 1647.

T. FAIRFAX.

[*Order for appointing a Committee of Officers.*]

I do appoint Lieutenant Generall Hammond, Collonel Thomlinson, Collonel Scroop, Collonel Pride, Lieutenant Collonel Goffe, and Lieutenant Collonel Read to attend dayly at my Quarters to advise upon all emergencys of the affairs of the Army. Given under my hand and seal at Reading the 18th of July 1647.

T. FAIRFAX.

[*Letter from London, July*, 26.]

Sir,

Since the writeing of my former Letter, attending neere Westminstere and some scouts abroad, wee are informed the Comon Councill (all pure Malignants) are gone back from Westminster without any answere, leaving the managment of their bussinesse to the Apprentice Petitioners, and they have soe well followed it that the House of Peeres past a vote [a] to recall the Declaration against them and to crosse it out of the Journall Booke; and that the more Creditt might be given to it, caused one of their Clerkes to read the order of their house publiquely in the Painted Chamber, the Clerke

[a] July 26. *Lords' Journals*, ix. 355 ; Whitelock, *Memorials*, ii. 182, ed. 1853.

standing upon the Table whilst he read it. Upon this they left the Lords house and fell more close then before to the Commons house, the Lords in the meane time quietly riseing 5 at night. The Comons still are close prisoners, and a private message being sent to the Collonell Campfeild[a] to assist the Guard at the Commons House, that the Members might have libertie to goe out, his Lieutennant in the Collonell's absence keeping the Guard at the Pallace, returned a slight answere, that the carriage of the Apprentices was more warrantable then the House's. I cannott forgett to tell you that just now Scout Master Generall Watson[b] was seized on by the Apprentices and some Reformadoes, and is in the charge of Captaine White and his Company; 'tis said the cause of his Committment was for that upon discourse he told some of the Petitioners, that if they held this course they would bring upon them the Plundering of the Citty. There is a pretty storie of one of them who said he had been one of your Army, and in that time hee was much against the Common Prayer Booke, and he had with his owne hands torne some of them, but that if it were to doe againe hee would rather have his hand cutt off. This was soe well taken that they prevailed with him to make this Recantation aloud in the head of the Hall at the King's bench, which he did accordingly standing aloft. As I am writeing theis Lynes downe comes the Shereiffes of London on Horseback to Westminster and many Halberteers with them to allay the tumult.[c]

[*Speaker Lenthall to Sir Thomas Fairfax.*]

May it please your Excellence

Sir Arthur Haslerigg can informe you of my condition. I found the many inconveniencies I was like to have falne into, not in

a One of the London Militia Committee. Rushworth, vi. 472.

b Leonard Watson, see *Fairfax Correspondence*, iii., 381.

c Unsigned and undated, probably written by Gilbert Mabbot, certainly July 26.

respect of my selfe, but in regard of the Kingdome's Co . . of your Army. I am assured it will be strange to your Excellencie to heare of my being at Windsor where I intend to stay untill I find the Parliament in a better condition, if in case it be my fortune to sitt any more. I pray God blesse your Excellencie and all the rest there, that you may be, under God, the Saviour of the Parliament and people's libertie, which I wish may be perfected by your selfe, which hath always been soe wished by

Your Excellencies humble servant

Wm. Lenthall.

[July 29 ?.] [a]

[a] This letter was obviously written between July 26 and August 4, 1647. On the former day the House of Commons adjourned till July 30, and on July 30 it was informed that Lenthal had left London on the morning of the 29th. The engagement of Lenthal, Manchester, and other members of Parliament to live and die with the army was dated August 4. According to Holles this was done "upon pretence of a force and violence that had been offered to the Parliament, but in truth, by a conspiracy with the Army, designed and laid principally by Mr. St. John, the solicitor; as appears by a letter sent from Rushworth (Sir Thomas Fairfax's Secretary) to the Speaker, with no name on it, but the latter part of it written with his own hand, advising him not to appear at the House on Friday morning, but to take counsel of Mr. Solicitor, who would tell him what was fit to be done, assuring him that the Army would all lie in the dirt, or protect them who were their friends. This, as I remember, was the purport of the letter yet remaining in one of the Houses: which no doubt came from Sir Thomas Fairfax, and Mr. Cromwell and the rest of those governors," etc. (Holles, *Memoirs*, § 144). Ludlow says "we resolved to betake ourselves to the Army for protection, Sir Arthur Haselrig undertaking to persuade the Speaker to go thither, to which he consented with some difficulty" (*Memoirs*, i., 207). Lenthal's reasons are given in his own declaration, printed at the time at Oxford and London, and reprinted in the *Old Parliamentary History*, xvi., 196. He complains of the violence offered to the Parliament and himself on Monday, June 26, and that there has been no effectual course taken to prevent the like for the future. "But on the contrary, it is generally voiced in the town, that there will be a far greater confluence of apprentices, reformadoes, and others on Friday at the Parliament doors; and particularly notice was given to me that after they had made the House vote what they pleased they would destroy me." See also Walker's *History of Independency*, ed. 1661, pt. i., p. 41.

[*News-letter from the Army.*]

Thistleworth, 5 August, 1647.

After a longe threatned storme to engage us in a new and bloody warre by Reformadoes and Cittizens,[a] God hath soe blest our indeavours in the preventing soe wicked a designe as to bringe the wicked designers and contrivers uppon their knees, and the great ones are fled. The Citty this day delivers uppe to us the forts which were to be possesst by our armes. The forts in Southwarke were yesterday deliver'd uppe to Col. Rainborow. The Army marches in to guard the Earle of Manchester and Mr. Lenthall, Speakers of both Houses, and the Earle of Northumberland and some 14 Lords more of the House of Peeres, and all those of the House of Commons who were enforc't to flie by reason of the tumults, and to guard them uppe to the Parliament to see their Speakers sett in the chaire and the Parliament sett free; which was the acclamation of all the souldiers, horse and foote, uppon Tuesday att the Randezvous on Hounsloe Heath,[b] when the Generall, Lords, and Commons rode through the army, being a mile and a half in length putt in Battalia, every man cried out, "Lords and Commons and a free Parliament," expressing their willingnesse and Resolution to lay downe their lives butt to sett the Parliament free. Wee have demanded of the Citty the delivery uppe of the 11 members, whose

[a] A news-letter amongst the Clarke Papers gives the following note on the designs in the city. "The Militia of the Citty have given forth double commissions to the same officers, the one in parchment very moderate, the other in paper very high and furious, to force, kill, slay, and destroy, etc. On Friday night last my Lord Mayor came from the Common Council into the Militia then sitting, and said, "how now gentlemen, be of good courage, I will be your Captain and stand by you," or words to that effect . . . . Presently Ryley, the City scoutmaster came in and spoke encouraging words to the same purpose, and told them that he had received good intelligences that 30,000 Scots were upon their march for their assistance, that Morgan was their friend and was gone down to raise forces, and that he doubted not but that shortly considerable strength would be upon the back of the Army."

[b] Rushworth, viii., 750.

actions have now made good the charge against them of indeavouring to raise a new warre, butt wee heare they are all fled. Wee have sent to all the ports in Kent and Sussex to seize uppon them, if they come that way. There is Major Generall Poyntz,[a] Col. Wiltshire, and divers other Reformadoes and others are likewise demanded; Poyntz gott away yesterday. Such is the suddaine turne of affaires in the Citty that they who before threatned nothing butt ruine to the army and to the Kingdome, by putting the sworde into bloudy minded mens hands and ungodly wretches, doe now begin to repent, nay are ashamed to show their heads, or to owne the least action, and have recalled their Declaration in the Common Counsell against the Army. Happy is that Commander that laid downe his commission butt two dayes since, hoping itt will save his stake, as Col. Campfeild and others. When the Parliament sitts this day, I suppose you will heare what great ones in the Citty they will demande, beginning with my Lord Mayor, Alderman Bunce &c., butt that's more proper for the Parliament who received the affront of the Citty to take cognizance of then for the Army, otherwise itt had nott bin omitted in the demands yesterday. In breif wee may have what wee will desire, soe hath God humbled them and brought them downe, and be assured the crushing of this horrid designe in the egge will have [no] little influence uppon any parte of the Kingdome where itt was intended to have had a correspondence. The first worke will bee now to bringe to justice offenders, and to settle the Militia of the Citty in such hands as our friends may for the future remaine secure, and then the army may back and apply ourselves for the relief of Ireland. Our Declarations and proposalls now in print will satisfie you more particularly of our proceedinges. I hope when Charles D'oyley and those which are dissaffected to the army, heare how their freinds in London are fled, they will nott bee very apt to stirre in the Country; and if [you light upon] any of the impeached

[a] Rushworth, viii., 741, 765, 774

Members or Reformadoes that you can learne have had an hand in the tumults against the Parliament or the killing the Cittizens att Guildhall, that you [will] make stay of them. Our freinds in London all yesterday went about to gett the well-affected apprentices together to seize uppon as many of the most active Reformadoes as they could light uppon; an example of these and some Cittizens must bee made in time. Wee shall speedily soe disperse our horse into the Westerne parts as that there will bee noe neede for the well affected in the Country any longer to continue together.

[*The Earl of Warwick to Sir T. Fairfax.*]

I received your Excellencie's letter, dated the 2d of this instant, this day, wherein you expresse the great sence you have of the indignity offer'd to the Parliament on Monday sennight last, which must needs oblige us the members of that body for your great care of the safety and honour of the houses; and lett these assure you for my particuler I shall ever bee ready to contribute all assistance I may to the vindication of their privileges and honour of the House. The metinge [of] Liftenants held not by reason of a miscaridge of my letter sent to somon them, which I did by the Clerke of the peace of the County, and he being from home my letter came not to his hand till the same daye; so as very few mett, and those I beleve have given your Excellencie an account of their metting. I myselfe, being on my journey towards you, was stayed on the way towards London by some of my Deputy Liftenants that duell in the Citty, who informed mee of some malignants and souldiers that were come downe into our Contrey and they feared might breed some disturbance in their parts neare Loundon, and desired my presence in the Country for a few dayes, that, if need had bin, I might have bin in some posture to have resisted those that would have disturbed the peace of this County. Sir, I doubt not but as this County hath allwaies been most forward to serve the Parliament in their best assistances, so they will be most ready to vindicate their honor whensoever their is occasion; and for my selfe I shalbe ever ready to pay that due respect to your merritt which you deserve by being instrumentall under God to protect the Parlement, and for your favoures to me I shall remaine

Your Excellencies humble servant,

WARWICKE.[a]

Leez this 5 of August
1647.

Putney, August 29
1647.

Commission for the Generall's Committee of Officers.

To Lieutenant Generall Cromwell, Lieut. Generall Hamond, Commissary Generall Ireton, Colonell Rainborow, Colonell Fleetwood, Colonell Hamond, Colonell Sir Hardresse Waller, Colonell Rich, Commissary Generall Stane, Scout Master Generall Watson, Quartermaster Generall Ireton, and Adjutant Generall Deane.

I doe heerby appoint you or any three or more of you; whereof Lieutenant Generall Cromwell, Lieut. Generall Hammond, Com-

[a] Rushworth, quoting the "Perfect Diurnal," notes under Aug. 2, that "the Earl of Warwick and Earl of Manchester sent to the General intimating that they had quit the Houses as most of the members likewise had; for that there could be no free parliament as things went; and that their Lordships were retired unto Essex, and intended, as there should be occasion, to wait on the General, casting themselves upon his protection," Rushworth, viii. 742. Sir William Waller gives an account of the consultations of the Lords who thus joined the Army, and of the origin of the engagement of Aug. 4. *Vindication*, pp. 191-5. In addition to these preparations to assist the Army in Essex, the counties of Hertford and Kent also sent their trained bands to support it. (Rushworth, viii. 755, 772; *Tanner MSS.*, lviii. p. 435. *Draught of a Letter from the Speaker* (*Pelham*) *to the Commissioners of the County of Herts.*)

missary Generall Ireton, or Colonell Rainborow to bee one, to bee a Generall Committee to receive and take into consideration all Businesses which shall by mee bee referred or shall otherwise bee tendred unto you, that are of publique and common concernement to the Army or Kingedome, or any considerable partie therin, or to any Garrisons or Fortes of this Kingedome, or to the affaires of Ireland.

And of all such Businesses soe receiv'd to consider whether they bee fitt for my cognizance or to bee intermedled in by my self and the Army or noe; and (if they be), then to consider of, and propose to mee, what you conceive may bee fitt to bee done uppon the same; and what you have nott time soe to consider of your selves, you are to transmitt to some such particular Committee as is heerafter mentioned to bee by them considered of. And for that purpose you the said Generall Committee or any three or more of you (whereof Lieut. Generall Cromwell, Lieut. Generall Hamond, Commissary Generall Ireton, or Colonell Rainborow to bee one), are heerby enabled out of the Officers or Agitators that doe or shall attend the Head Quarter to appoint such particular and severall Committees for severall businesses, as there shall bee occasion; every such Committee to consist of three persons or more as the matter shall deserve, (whereof one to bee named of the Quorum), and to have power to consider of such Businesses as shall by you bee transmitted to them as before, and to resolve what they conceive may bee fitt to bee done thereuppon, an Account whereof they are from time to time to returne to you the said Generall Committee, to bee tendred and proposed unto mee with your approbacion, if you shall approve of the same.

And you are to appoint a Clarke to keepe Account of the respective businesse, soe receiv'd, or to bee receiv'd, and of the Resolutions or proposalls thereuppon. Given under my hand and seale att Putney the 30th day of August, 1647.

THOMAS FAIRFAX.

I doe appoynt Colonell Fleetwood, Sir Hardresse Waller and Colonell Rich to be of the Quorum in pursuance of the afforesaid Comission, this 3d September, 1647.

THOMAS FAIRFAX.[a]

[*Major Huntington to Sir T. Fairfax.*]

May itt please your Excellency,

Uppon the deliverie of his Majesty's answer[b] to the propossisions of both kingdoms sent by Commissioners on Tewsday last, this afternoone, his Majestie layd his commands on mee to speed away this inclosed to yourselfe (which is the same delivered to the Commissioners in answer to the propossicions brought by them), with these words, that hee was engaged to bee soe civell to the Generall as to send his answere to the propossicions to him at the same tyme hee delivered them to the others, sayeing that in them he had put a great trust upon the army, not doubteing but that the Generall would stand by him in procureing a personall treaty with his two houses. This is all which is to be offered to the knowledg of your Excellencie by the meanest of

Your Excellencies servants
ROBT: HUNTINGTON.

Hampton Court, Sept. 9°, '47.

[a] The proceedings of this Committee from August 29 to November 11, 1647, are contained in vol. lxvi. of the Clarke MSS. at Worcester College. Questions concerning the movement of troops, military discipline, promotions, and the pay of the Army came under their jurisdiction. The cases of persons claiming the benefit of capitulations made with the Army were considered by them; see for instance the reports on the cases of Sir John Munson and Peter Scot under October 6, and October 22.

[b] Huntington states in his "Reasons for laying down his Commission," that the King's answer to the propositions was shown privately to both Cromwell and Ireton "in a garden-house at Putney, and in some part amended to their own minds." Berkeley says that Charles "followed the advice of all the leading part of the Independent Party both in the Parliament and the Army, by refusing the articles and desiring a personal treaty;" adding "we gave our friends in the Army a sight of this the day before it was sent, with which they seemed infinitely satisfied." (Masere's *Tracts*, i., 372, 403.)

Att the Generall Councill of Officers att Putney. 28 October, 1647.

The Officers being mett, first said,

Lieutennant General Cromwell.[a]

That the Meeting was for publique businesses. Those that had anythinge to say concerning the publique businesse might have libertie to speake.

Mr. Edward Sexby.

Mr. Allen, Mr. Lockyer, and my self are three.

They have sent two Souldiers, one of your owne Regiment and one of Col. Whalley's, with two other Gentlemen, Mr. Wildman and Mr. Petty.

Commissary General Ireton.

That hee had nott the paper of what was done uppon all of them.

Itt was referr'd to the Committee, that they should consider of the paper that was printed, "The Case of the Army Stated," and to examine the particulars in itt, and to represent and offer somethinge to this Councill about itt.[b] They were likewise appointed

[a] Fairfax was not present, "being not well, and at Turnham Green" (Rushworth, viii. 857).

[b] "The case of the Army truly stated, together with the mischiefes and dangers that are imminent, and some suitable remedies, and humbly proposed by the Agents of five Regiments of Horse, to the respective Regiments and the whole Army." This paper (filling twenty pages of a quarto pamphlet) is dated Guildford, October 9, 1647, and signed by agents representing the regiments of Cromwell, Ireton, Fleetwood, Rich and Whalley. It is accompanied by a letter from the agent to Fairfax, dated October 15, and was presented to the General on October 18. It is stated on the last page that "Upon the presentation to, and serious perusal thereof by his Excellency, the sum of his answer was to this effect. That he judged their intentions were honest, and desired that everyone of publique spirit would be acting for the publique, and that for his part he had freely ventured his life for common right and freedome, and should freely engage it againe, adding further that he

to send for those persons concern'd in the paper. The Committee mett according to appointment that night. Itt was only then Resolv'd on, That there should bee some sent in a freindlie way (nott by command, or summons) to invite some of those Gentlemen to come in with us, I thinke.

Mr. Sexby.

I was desired by the Lieutennant Generall to [let him] know the bottome of their desires. They gave us this answer, that they would willinglie draw them uppe, and represent them unto you. They are come att this time to tender them to your considerations with their resolutions to maintaine them.

Wee have bin by providence putt upon strange thinges, such as the ancientist heere doth scarce remember. The Army acting to these ends, providence hath bin with us, and yett wee have found little [fruit] of our indeavours; and really I thinke all heere both great and small (both Officers and Souldiers), wee may say wee have lean'd on, and gone to Egypt for helpe. The Kingdomes cause requires expedition, and truly our miseries with [those of] our fellow souldiers' cry out for present helpe. I thinke, att this time, this is your businesse, and I thinke itt is in all your hearts to releive the one and satisfie the other. You resolv'd if any thinge [reasonable] should bee propounded to you, you would joyne and goe alonge with us.

The cause of our misery [is] uppon two thinges. We sought to satisfie all men, and itt was well; butt in going [about] to doe itt wee have dissatisfied all men. Wee have labour'd to please a Kinge, and I thinke, except wee goe about to cutt all our throates,

thought it meet it should be presented to the Generall Councell." See also Rushworth, viii., 845, 849, 850, 857. In the meeting of the General Council of the Army on October 22 the paper was discussed, and a committee appointed to meet the next day, to consider the case of the Army and present their conclusions to the next General Council on October 28. In the meantime the agitators put forth a new paper vindicating themselves from the charge of dividing the Army. (Rushworth, viii., 845, 849, 850, 856, 857; Godwin, *Commonwealth*, ii. 445-451).

wee shall nott please him ; and wee have gone to support an house which will prove rotten studds,[a] I meane the Parliament which consists of a Company of rotten Members.

And therfore wee beseech you that you will take these thinges into your consideration.

I shall speake to the Lieut. Generall and Commissary Generall concerning one thinge. Your creditts and reputation hath bin much blasted uppon these two considerations. The one is for seeking to settle this Kingdome in such a way wherein wee thought to have satisfied all men, and wee have dissatisfied them—I meane in relation to the Kinge—The other is in referrence to a Parliamentarie aucthoritie (which most heere would loose their lives for), to see[b] those powers to which wee will subject our selves loyally called. These two things are as I thinke conscientiously the cause of all those blemishes that have bin cast uppon either the one or the other. You are convinc't God will have you to act on, butt [ask] onelie to consider how you shall act, and [take] those [ways] that will secure you and the whole Kingdome. I desire you will consider those thinges that shall bee offer'd to you ; and, if you see any thinge of reason, you will joyne with us that the Kingdome may bee eas'd, and our fellow souldiers may bee quieted in spiritt. These thinges I have represented as my thoughts. I desire your pardon.

[a] "Studds," *i.e.* the upright in a lath and plaster wall. Halliwell quotes the following passage from Harrison's *England.* "Our houses are commonly strong and well timbered, so as in many places there are not above four, six, or nine inches between stud and stud."

Major Francis White had used a similar metaphor in describing the intended agreement with the King. "Being at the convention, I spoke some words which gave distrust, that they were repairing an old house, and that when they were laying the top stone it would fall about their ears."

The Copy of a Letter sent to his Excellency Sir T. Fairfax, by Francis White, Nov. 1647. British Museum, E. 413, 17.

[b] MS. "bee."

Lieut. Generall.

I thinke itt is good for us to proceede to our businesse in some order, and that will bee if wee consider some things that are latelie past. There hath bin a booke printed, called, "The Case of the Armie Stated," and that hath bin taken into consideration, and there hath bin somewhat drawne uppe by way of exception to thinges contayn'd in that booke; and I suppose there was an Answer brought to that which was taken by way of exception, and yesterday the Gentleman that brought the Answer hee was dealt honestly and plainly withall, and hee was told, that there were new designes a driving, and nothing would bee a clearer discovery of the sincerity of [their] intentions, as their willingnesse that were active to bringe what they had to say to bee judg'd of by the Generall Officers, and by this Generall Councill, that wee might discerne what the intentions were. Now itt seemes there bee divers that are come hither to manifest those intentions according to what was offer'd yesterday, and truly I thinke, that the best way of our proceeding will bee to receive what they have to offer. Onely this, Mr. Sexby, you were speaking to us two. [I do not know why you named us two,] except you thinke that wee have done somewhat or acted somewhat different from the sence and resolution of the Generall Councill. Truly, that that you speake to, was the thinges that related to the Kinge and thinges that related to the Parliament; and if there bee a fault I may say itt, and I dare say, itt hath bin the fault of the Generall Councill, and that which you doe speake both in relation to the one and the other, you speake to the Generall Councill I hope, though you nam'd us two, Therfore truly I thinke itt sufficient for us to say, and 'tis that wee say—I can speake for my selfe, lett others speake for them selves—I dare maintaine itt, and I dare avowe I have acted nothing butt what I have done with the publique consent, and approbation and allowance of the Generall Councill. That I dare say for my self, both in relation to the one, and to the other. What I have acted in Parliament in the name of the Councill or of the Army I have had my warrant for from hence. What I have spoken in another capacitie, as a Member of the House, that was free for mee to doe; and I am confident, that I have nott used the name of the Army, or interest of the Army to anythinge butt what I have had allowance from the Generall Councill for, and [what they] thought itt fitt to move the House in. I doe the rather give you this account, because I heare there are some slanderous reports going uppe and downe uppon somewhat that hath bin offer'd to the House of Commons [by me], as being the sence and opinion of this Armie, and in the name of this Army, which, I dare bee confident to speake itt, hath bin as false and slanderous a report as could bee raised of a man. And that was this; That I should say to the Parliament and deliver itt as the desire of this Armie, and the sence of this Armie, that there should bee a second addresse to the Kinge by way of propositions. I dare bee confident to speake itt, what I deliver'd there I deliver'd as my owne sence, and what I deliver'd as my owne sence I am nott ashamed of. What I deliver'd as your sence, I never deliver'd butt what I had as your sence.[a]

[a] This must refer to the debate of September 23, 1647, on which day the House of Commons resolved "that the House will once again make application to the King, for those things which the Houses shall judge necessary for the welfare and safety of the Kingdom." (*Commons' Journals*, v. 314.) Cromwell and Rainborough were both present on September 22, when the question of "the whole matter concerning the King was discussed in a Committee of the whole House, and they told against each other on the proposal to resolve the House into a Committee for that purpose. (*Ib.* v. 312.) September 23 was a Thursday, on which day the general council of the Army usually met, which explains the absence of Cromwell and Rainborough. Of Cromwell's speeches in this debate news-letters give the only record. One of September 27 (*Clarendon MS.* 2602) says "The last week his Majesty's answers to the propositions being considered of in the House was voted to be a denial, and that the King's drift therein was to put a difference between the Parliament and the Army, and between the English and Scottish nation; whereupon a sharp debate grew whether the King should be sent unto any more, or whether they should forthwith proceed to the settlement of the kingdom; to the latter most of the orators inclined, and in likelihood would have led the house that way, but that it was opposed by Cromwell and Ireton, who said it was no fit time to proceed with such vigour, the King having gotten so great a reputation in the Army, and therefore advised them to proceed in

Col. Rainborow.

For this the Lieutennant Generall was pleas'd to speake of last,

a way towards the satisfaction of the kingdom and army; and so they went to review the propositions, having first voted that they should be carried to the King as ordinances, not as propositions. There have been in the prosecution of this business some desperate motions; as, that the King, in regard that many who give him ill counsel and are professed enemies to the Parliament resort unto him, should be restrained; that they should think no more of the King, but proceed as if there were no such thing in the world; for that he is always an impediment to all good resolutions; some calling him Ahab, others Coloquintida. But all those speeches have been stopped by Cromwell and Ireton, whose civilities are visible, but the reality of their intentions not clearly discerned."

Sir Edward Ford writes on 28 September: "It was moved earnestly in the House that the malignants might be removed from Court, and also that the King might be removed further off from the headquarters because of the confluence of people to him. . . . . might beget an ill influence and danger in the Army, but it was opposed by Cromwell and Ireton; of late they have spoken much in the King's behalf, seconded by young Harry Vane, Mr. Solicitor, and Mr. Fiennes. Cromwell, applying himself to the Speaker, told him that it was worth his consideration, how that there was a party in the army labouring for the King, and a great one; how the City was endeavouring underhand to get another party in the Army; and that there was a third party who was little dreamt of, that were endeavouring to have no other power to rule but the sword." (*Clarendon MS.*, 2604.) A news-letter addressed to Sir Richard Leveson, September 27, 1647, adds: "There has been snapping lately in the House between some of the root-and-branch men and the officers of the Army that are members. Ireton, moving the Army's proposals might be considered there, and sent to the King, gave occasion to one Scot (an insolent fellow and enemy to the proposals, as all of that spirit are) to let the House know there had been underhand treaties between the officers of the Army and the King, to which end Ashburnham and Sir John Berkeley were continually at the headquarters, agents for the King, which he desired might be examined; to which Cromwell by way of reply took occasion to vindicate his own innocency and to declare his readiness to obey the Parliament's commands, but if the House should think fit to examine that business, he desired it might be examined withal, which members of the House had been at head-quarters likewise, endeavouring to debauch the Army and seduce them from their principles" (*Fifth Report of Hist. MSS. Comm.* p. 173; *cf.* p. 179.) Scot was arrested by Fairfax on November 15, 1647, for inciting the soldiers to mutiny at the rendezvous at Corkbush-field, near Ware, for which he was suspended from sitting in the House of Commons. (Rushworth, viii. 875; *Commons' Journals*, v. 362.) He was member for Aldborough in Yorkshire, and should be distinguished from Thomas Scot, the regicide, member for Aylesbury. Scot, the leveller, died in January, 1648. (*Cal. Clarendon Papers*, i. 408.) It is probable that he was a royalist agent. (*Clarendon MS.* 2,534.)

itt was moved, that day the propositions were brought in. That itt was carried for making a second addresse to the Kinge, itt was when both the Lieutennant Generall and my selfe were last heere, and where wee broke off heere, and when wee came uppon the Bill itt was told us, That the House had carried itt for a second addresse; and therfore the Lieutenant Generall must needes bee cleare of itt. Butt itt was urged in the House that itt was the sence of the Army that itt should bee soe.

Com̃. Gen. Ireton.

I desire nott to speake of these thinges, butt onely to putt thinges into an orderly way, which would lead to what the occasion is that hath brought these Gentlemen hither that are now call'd in; yett I cannott butt speake a worde to that that was last touch't uppon.

If I had told any man soe (which I know I did nott) if I did, I did tell him what I thought; and if I thought otherwise of the Army, I protest I should have bin ashamed of the Armie and detested itt; that is, if I had thought the Army had bin of that minde, they would lett those propositions sent from both Kingdomes bee the thinges which should bee [final] whether peace or noe, without any farther offers; and when I doe finde itt, I shall bee asham'd on't, and detest any dayes condescention with itt. And yett for that which Mr. Sexby tells us hath bin one of the great businesses [cast] uppon the Lieutennant Generall and my self, I doe detest and defie the thought of that thinge, of any indeavour, or designe, or purpose, or desire to sett uppe the Kinge; and I thinke I have demonstrated, and I hope I shall doe still, [that] itt is the interest of the Kingdome that I have suffer'd for. As for the Parliament too, I thinke those that know the beginninges of these principles, that wee [set forth] in our Declarations of late for clearing and vindicating the Liberties of the people, even in relation to Parliament will have reason [to acquit me]. And whoever doe know how wee were led to the declaring of that point as wee have, as [a fundamental] one, will bee able to acquitt mee that I have bin farre from a designe of setting uppe the persons of these men, or of any men whatsoever to bee our Law Makers. Soe likewise for the Kinge; though I am cleare, as from the other, from setting uppe the person of one or other, yett I shall declare itt againe; I doe nott seeke, or would nott seeke, nor will joyne with them that doe seeke the destruction either of Parliament or Kinge. Neither will I consent with those or concurre with them who will nott attempt all the wayes that are possible to preserve both, and to make good use, and the best use that can bee of both for the Kingedome; and I did nott heare any thinge from that Gentleman (Mr. Sexby) that could induce or incline mee to that resolution. To that point I stand cleare as I have exprest. Butt I shall nott speake any more concerning myself.

The Committee[a] mett att my lodginges assoone as they parted from hence; and the first thinge they resolved on hearing there was a meeting of the Agitators [was, that] though itt was thought fitt by the Generall Councill heere they should bee sent for to the Regiment[s], yett itt was thought fitt to lett them know what the Generall Councill had done, and to goe on in a way that might tend to unitie; and [this] being resolved on wee were desired by one of those Gentlemen that were desired to goe, that least they should mistake the matter they went about, itt might bee drawne in writing, and this is itt:

That the Generall Councill, etc. [*blank*].

This is the substance of what was deliver'd. Mr. Allen, Mr. Lockyer, and Mr. Sexby were sent with itt, and I thinke itt is fitt that the Councill should bee acquainted with the Answer.

Mr. Allen.

As to the Answer itt was short (truly I shall give itt as shorte).

[a] A brief account of the proceedings of the Committee is given in Rushworth, viii., 849, 850.

Wee gave them the paper, and read itt amongst them, and to my best remembrance they then told us, that they were nott all come together whome itt did concerne, and soe were nott in a capacitie att the present to returne us an Answer; butt that they would take itt into consideration, and would send itt as speedily as might bee. I thinke itt was neare their Sence.

The Answer of the Agitators read.[a]

Com̃. Generall.

Wheras itt was appointed by the Councill and wee of the Committee did accordingly desire, that these Gentlemen, being Members of the Army and engaged with the Army, might have come to communicate with the Generall Councill of the Army and those that were appointed by them for a mutuall satisfaction: by this paper they seeme to bee of a fix't resolution, setting themselves to bee a divided partie or distinct Councill from the Generall Councill of the Army, and [seem to say] that there was nothing to bee done as single persons to declare their dissatisfaction, or the grounds for informing themselves better or us better, butt that they as all the rest should concurre soe as to hold together as a form'd and setled partie distinct and divided from others; and withall seem'd to sett downe these resolutions to [as things] which they expect the compliance of any others, rather then their compliance with others to give satisfaction. Butt itt seemes uppon some thinge that the Lieutennant Generall and some others of that Committee did thinke fitt [to offer] the Gentlemen that brought that paper have bin since induced to descend a little from the heighth, and to send some of them to come as agents particularlie, or Messengers from that Meeting or from that Councill, to heare what wee have to say to there, or to offer somethinge to us relating to the matters in that paper. I beleive there are Gentlemen[b] sent with them that though

[a] A portion of an answer of the agitators to the charge of attempting to divide the Army is given by Rushworth, viii., 857.

[b] Wildman and Petty.

perhaps the persons of them that are Members of the Army may nott give the passages in itt they may bee better able to observe them; and therefore if you please that they may proceede.

Buffe-Coate.

May itt please your Honour, to give you satisfaccion in that there was such a willingnesse that wee might have a conference, whereuppon I did engage that interest that was in mee that I would procure some to come hither both of the souldiers and of others for assistance; and in order thereunto heere are two souldiers sent from the Agents, and two of our freinds alsoe, and to present this to your considerations, and desire [a] your advice. [We believe that] according to my [b] expectations and your engagement you are resolved every one to purchase our inheritances which have bin lost, and free this Nation from the tyranny that lies uppon us. I question nott butt that itt is all your desires: and for that purpose wee desire to doe nothing butt what wee present to your considera-tion, and if you conceive itt that itt must bee for us to bee instru-ments, that wee might shelter our selves like wise men before the Storme comes. Wee desire that all carping uppon words might bee laid aside, and [that you may] fall directly uppon the matter presented to you.

Wee have heere met on purpose [c] according to my Engagement that whatsoever may bee thought to bee necessary for our satis-faction, for the right understanding one of another [may be done] that wee might goe on together. For, though our ends and aimes bee the same, if one thinkes this way, another another way—butt that way which is the best for the subject [is] that they [both] may bee hearkned unto.

a MS. "desiring."
b MS. "your expectations and my engagements."
c MS., two lines below, gives "we have here men on purpose."

The Answer of the Agitators, the 2[d] time read.[a]

Buffecoate.

I thinke itt will bee strange that wee that are souldiers cannott have them [for] our selves, if nott for the whole Kingedome; and therfore wee beseech you consider of itt.

Lieut. Generall.

These thinges that you have now offered they are new to us; they are thinges that wee have nott att all (att least in this method and thus circumstantially) had any opportunity to consider of them, because they came to us butt thus as you see; this is the first time wee had a view of them.

Truly this paper does containe in itt very great alterations of the very Governement of the Kingedome, alterations from that Governement that itt hath bin under, I beleive I may almost say since itt was a Nation, I say I thinke I may almost say soe, and

[a] The answer of the agitators here mentioned is evidently the document known as "the Agreement of the People," as the contents of Cromwell's speech prove, and the reference made to it by name by Ireton on p. 244. It is printed in Rushworth, viii., 859. It demands, (1) Equal electoral districts. (2) The dissolution of the Long Parliament on September 30, 1648. (3) Biennial Parliaments to be elected every March and sit for five months. (4) The limitation of the powers of future parliaments so as to guarantee complete toleration; a full indemnity for acts done during the late public differences, and good and equal laws. In one point it attacks the privileges of the peerage, demanding "That in all laws made, or to be made, every person may be bound alike, and that tenure, estates, charter, degree, birth, or place, do not confer any exception from the ordinary course of legal proceedings, whereunto others are subjected." In conclusion it protests against the proposed treaty with the King. "These things we declare to be our native rights, and therefore are agreed and resolved to maintain them with our utmost possibilities, against all opposition whatsoever; being compelled th reunto, not only by the examples of our ancestors, whose blood was often spent in vain for the recovery of their freedoms, suffering themselves, through fraudulent accommodations, to be still deluded of the fruit of their victory, but also by our own woful experience, who having long expected, and dearly earned the establishment of those certain rules of government, are yet made to depend for the settlement of our peace and freedom upon him that intended our bondage, and brought a cruel war upon us."

what the consequences of such an alteration as this would bee, if there were nothing else to be consider'd, wise men and godly men ought to consider. I say if there were nothing else [to be considered] butt the very weight and nature of the thinges contayn'd in this paper. Therfore, although the pretensions in itt, and the expressions in itt are very plausible, and if wee could leape out of one condition into another, that had soe specious thinges in itt as this hath, I suppose there would nott bee much dispute, though perhaps some of these thinges may bee very well disputed—How doe wee know if whilest wee are disputing these thinges another companie of men shall gather together, and they shall putt out a paper as plausible perhaps as this? I doe nott know why itt might nott bee done by that time you have agreed uppon this, or gott hands to itt, if that bee the way. And not onely another, and another, butt many of this kinde. And if soe, what doe you thinke the consequence of that would bee? Would itt nott bee confusion? Would itt nott bee utter confusion? Would itt nott make England like the Switzerland Country, one Canton of the Switz against another, and one County against another? I aske you whether itt bee nott fitt for every honest man seriouslie to lay that uppon his heart? And if soe, what would that produce butt an absolute desolation—an absolute desolation to the Nation—and wee in the meane time tell the Nation, "It is for your Libertie, 'Tis for your priviledge," "'Tis for your good." Pray God itt prove soe whatsoever course wee run. Butt truly, I thinke wee are nott onely to consider what the consequences are (if there were nothing else butt this paper), butt wee are to consider the probability of the wayes and meanes to accomplish: that is to say [to consider] whether,[a] according to reason and judgement, the spiritts and temper of the people of this Nation are prepared to receive and to goe on alonge with itt, and [whether] those great difficulties [that] lie in our way [are] in a likelihood to bee either overcome or removed. Truly, to anythinge that's good, there's noe doubt on

[a] MS. "that."

itt, objections may bee made and fram'd; butt lett every honest man consider, whether or noe there bee nott very reall objections [to this] in point of difficulty. I know a man may answer all difficulties with faith, and faith will answer all difficulties really where itt is, but[a] wee are very apt all of us to call that faith, that perhaps may bee butt carnall imagination, and carnall reasonings. Give mee leave to say this, There will bee very great mountaines in the way of this, if this were the thinge in present consideration; and therfore wee ought to consider the consequences, and God hath given us our reason that wee may doe this. Itt is nott enough to propose thinges that are good in the end, butt suppose this modell were an excellent modell, and fitt for England, and the Kingedome to receive, itt is our duty as Christians and men to consider consequences, and to consider the way.[b]

Butt really I shall speake to nothing butt that that, as before the Lord, I am perswaded in my heart tends to uniting of us in one to that that God will manifest to us to bee the thinge that hee would have us prosecute; and hee that meetes nott heere with that heart, and dares nott say hee will stand to that, I thinke hee is a deceivour. I say itt to you againe, and I professe unto you, I shall offer nothing to you butt that I thinke in my heart and conscience tends to the uniting of us, and to the begetting a right understanding amonge us, and therefore this is that I would insist uppon, and have itt clear'd amonge us.

Itt is nott enough for us to insist uppon good thinges; that every one would doe—there is nott 40 of us butt wee could prescribe many thinges exceeding plausible, and hardly anythinge worse then our present condition, take itt with all the troubles that are uppon us. Itt is nott enough for us to propose good thinges, butt itt behoves honest men and Christians that really will approve themselves soe before God and men, to see whether or noe they bee in a condition, [to attempt] whether, taking all thinges into consideration, they may honestly indeavour and attempt that that is fairly

[a] MS. "and."

[b] Clause transposed.

and plausibly proposed. For my owne parte I know nothing that wee are to consider first butt that, before wee would come to debate the evill or good of this [paper], or to adde to itt or substract from itt;[a] which I am confident, if your hearts bee upright as ours are—and God will bee judge betweene you and us—if wee should come to any thinge, you doe nott bringe this paper with peremptorinesse of minde, butt to receive amendements to have any thinge taken from itt that may bee made apparent by cleare reason to bee inconvenient or unhonest. This ought to bee our consideration and yours, saving [that] in this you have the advantage of us—you that are the souldiers you have nott—butt you that are nott [soldiers] you reckon your selves att a loose and att a liberty, as men that have noe obligation uppon you. Perhaps wee conceive wee have; and therfore this is that I may say—both to those that come with you, and to my fellow officers and all others that heare mee—that it concernes us as wee would approve our selves [as honest men] before God, and before men that are able to judge of us, if wee doe nott make good engagements, if wee doe nott make good that that the world expects wee should make good. I doe nott speake to determine what that is, butt if I bee nott much mistaken wee have in the time of our danger issued out Declarations; wee have bin requir'd by the Parliament, because our Declarations were generall, to declare particularly what wee meant; and having done that how farre that obliges or nott obliges [us] that is by us to bee consider'd, if wee meane honestly and sincerely and to approve our selves to God as honest men. And therfore having heard this paper read, this remaines to us; that wee againe review what wee have engaged in, and what wee have that lies uppon us. Hee that departs from that that is a reall engagement and a reall tye uppon him, I thinke hee transgresses without faith, for faith will beare uppe men in

[a] May be paraphrased, "which paper I am confident if your hearts be upright as ours you do not bring with peremptoriness of mind, etc." The words "if we should come to anything" seem to belong to the previous clause.

every honest obligation, and God does expect from men the performance of every honest obligation. Therefore I have noe more to say butt this; wee having received your paper shall amongst our selves consider what to doe; and before wee take this into consideration, itt is fitt for us to consider how farre wee are obliged, and how farre wee are free; and I hope wee shall prove our selves honest men where wee are free to tender any thinge to the good of the publique. And this is that I thought good to offer to you uppon this paper.

Mr. Wildman.

Being yesterday att a Meeting where divers Country-Gentlemen, and souldiers and others were, and amongst the rest the Agents of the five Regiments, and having weigh'd their papers, I must freely confesse I did declare my agreement with them. Uppon that they were pleas'd to declare their sence in most particulars of their proceedinges to mee, and desir'd mee that I would bee their mouth, and in their names to represent their sence unto you; and uppon that ground I shall speake something in answer to that which your Honour last spake.

I shall nott reply any thinge att present till itt come to bee further debated, either concerning the consequences of what is propounded, or [the contents] of this paper; butt I conceive the cheif weight of your Honour's speech lay in this, that you were first to consider what obligations lay uppon you, and how farre you were engaged, before you could consider what was just in this paper now propounded; adding, that God would protect men in keeping honest promises. To that I must only offer this, that according to the best knowledge [I have] of their apprehensions, they doe apprehend that what ever obligation is past must bee consider'd afterwards, when itt is urged whether itt were honest or

just or noe; and if [the obligation[a]] were nott just itt doth nott oblige the persons, if itt bee an oath itt self. Butt if, while there

[a] MS. "it."

is nott soe cleare a light, any person passes an Engagement, itt is judged by them, (and I soe judge itt), to bee an act of honesty for that man to recede from his former judgement, and to abhorre itt. And therfore I conceive the first thinge is to consider the honesty of what is offer'd, otherwise itt cannott bee consider'd of any obligation that doth prepossesse. By the consideration of the justice of what is offer'd that obligation shall appeare whether itt was just or noe. If itt were nott just, I cannott butt bee confident of the searinges of your consciences. I conceive this to bee their sence ; and uppon this account, uppon a more serious review of all Declarations past, they see noe obligations which are just that they contradict by proceeding in this way.

Commissary Gen. Ireton.

Sure this Gentleman hath nott bin acquainted with our Engagements, for hee that will cry out of breach of Engagement in slight and triviall thinges, and thinges necessitated to, that is soe tender of an Engagement as to frame or concurre with this Booke [a] in their insisting uppon every punctilio of Engagement, I can hardly thinke that man [b] can bee of that principle that noe Engagement is binding further then that hee thinkes itt just or noe. For itt hintes that, if hee that makes an Engagement (bee itt what itt will bee) have further light that this engagement was nott good or honest, then hee is free from itt. Truly if the sence were putt thus, that a man that findes hee hath entred into an engagement and thinkes that itt was nott a just Engagement, I confesse some thinge might bee said that [such] a man might declare himself for his parte to suffer some penalty uppon their persons, or uppon their partie.

[a] The text should probably run, "as to concur with the framers of this book."

[b] In "The Case of the Army" it was asserted "that the Army's Engagement, Representations, Declarations, and Remonstrances, and promises in them contained, are declined, and more and more dayly broken, and not only in some smaller matters wherein the Army and Kingdom are not neerly concerned, but in divers particulars of dangerous consequence to the Army and the whole nation." Ten points in which these engagements had been broken were then enumerated.

The question is, whether itt bee an Engagemeut to another partie. Now if a man venture into an Engagement from him [self] to another, and find[a] that Engagement [not] just and honest, hee must apply himself to the other partie, and say "I cannott actively performe itt, I will make you amends as neere as I can." Uppon the same ground men are nott obliged to [be obedient to] any aucthoritie that is sett uppe, though itt were this aucthority that is proposed heere, I am nott engaged to bee soe actively to that aucthority. Yett if I have engag'd that they shall binde mee by Law, though afterwards, I finde that they doe require mee to a thinge that is nott just or honest, I am bound soe farre to my Engagement that I must submitt and suffer, though I cannott act and doe that which their Lawes doe impose upon mee. If that caution were putt in where a performance of an Engagement might bee expected from another, and hee could nott doe itt because hee thought itt was nott honest to bee performed; if such a thinge were putt into the case, itt is possible there might bee some reason for itt. Butt to take itt as itt is deliver'd in generall, whatever Engagement wee have entred into, though itt bee a promise of somethinge to another partie, wherin that other partie is concerned, wherin hee hath a benefitt, if wee make itt good, wherin hee hath a prejudice if wee make itt nott good [that we are free to break it if it be not just]: this is a principle that will take away all Commonwealth[s], and will take away the fruite of this Engagement if itt were entred into; and men of this principle would thinke themselves as little as may bee [obliged by any law] if in their apprehensions itt bee nott a good Law. I thinke they would thinke themselves as little obliged to thinke of standing to that aucthority [that is proposed in this paper].

Truly Sir I have little to say att the present to that matter of the paper that is tendred to us. I confesse there are plausible thinges in itt, and there are thinges really good in itt, and there are those thinges that I doe with my heart desire, and there are

[a] MS. "finding."

those thinges for the most parte of itt [that] I shall bee soe free as to say, if these Gentlemen, and other Gentlemen that will joyne with them can obtaine, I would nott oppose, I should rejoice to see obtayn'd. There are those thinges in itt, divers [of them]; and, if wee were as hath bin urged now, free; if wee were first free from consideration of all the dangers and miseries that wee may bringe uppon this people, [the danger] that when wee goe to cry out for the libertie of itt wee may nott leave a being [in it], free from all [those] Engagements that doe lie uppon us, and that were honest when they were entred into, I should concurre with this paper further then as the case doth stand I can. Butt truly I doe account wee are under Engagements; and I suppose that whatsoever this Gentleman that spoke last doth seeme to deliver to us, holding himself absolved from all Engagements, if hee thinkes itt, yett those men that came with him (that are in the case of the Armie,)[a] hold themselves more obliged; and therfore that they will nott perswade us to lay aside all our former Engagements and Declarations, if there bee any thinge in them, and to concurre in this, if there bee any thinge in itt that is contrary to those Engagements which they call uppon us to confirme. Therfore I doe wish that wee may have a consideration of our former Engagements, of thinges which are the Engagements of the Army generallie. Those wee are to take notice of, and sure wee are nott to recede from them till wee are convinct of them that they are unjust. And when wee are convinc't of them that they are unjust, truly yett I must nott fully concurre with that Gentleman's principle, that presently wee are, as hee sayes, absolv'd from them, that wee are nott bound to them, or wee are nott bound to make them good. Yett I should thinke att least, if the breach of that Engagement bee to the prejudice of another whome wee have perswaded to beleive by our Declaring such thinges [so] that wee made them and led them to a confidence of itt, to a dependance uppon itt, to

[a] *i.e.*, "The soldier agitators contrasted with those who did not belong to the Army."

a disadvantage to themselves or the loosing of advantages to them, though wee were convinc't they were unjust, and satisfied in this Gentleman's principle, and free, and disengag'd from them, yett wee who made that engagement should nott make itt our act to breake itt. Though wee were convinc't that wee are nott bound to performe itt, yett wee should nott make itt our act to breake [it]. And soe uppon the whole matter I speake this to inforce. As uppon the particulars of this Agreement; whether they have that goodnesse that they hold forth in shew? or whether are nott some defects in them which are nott seene? that if wee should rest in this Agreement without somethinge more [whether] they would nott deceive us? and whether there bee nott some considerations that would tend to union? And withall [I wish] that wee who are the Armie and are engag'd with publique Declarations may consider how farre those publique Declarations, which wee then thought to bee just, doe oblige, that wee may either resolve to make them good if wee can in honest wayes, or att least nott make itt our worke to breake them. And for this purpose I wish—unlesse the Councill please to meete from time to time, from day to day and to consider itt themselves—to goe over our papers and declarations and take the heads of them, I wish there may bee some specially appointed for itt; and I shall bee very glad if itt may bee soe that I my self may bee none of them.

Col. Rainborow.

I shall crave your pardon if I may speake something freelie, and I thinke itt will bee the last time I shall speake heere, and from such a way that I never look't for. The consideration that I had in this Army and amongst honest men—nott that itt is an addition of honour and profitt to mee butt rather a detriment in both—is the reason that I speake somethinge by way of apologie. I saw this paper first by chance and had noe resolution to have bin att this Councill nor any other since I tooke this imployment uppon mee, butt to doe my duty.[a] I mett with a Letter (which truly was soe strange to mee that I have bin a little troubled, and truly I have soe many sparkes of honour and honesty in mee) to lett mee know that my Regiment should bee imediately disposed from mee. I hope that none in the Army will say butt that I have perform'd my duty, and that with some successe, as well as others. I am loath to leave the Army with whome I will live and die, insomuch that rather then I will loose this Regiment of mine the Parliament shall exclude mee the House, [or] imprison mee; for truly while I am [employed] abroad I will nott bee undone att home. This was itt that call'd mee hither, and nott any thinge of this paper. Butt now I shall speake somethinge of itt.

I shall speake my minde; that whoever hee bee that hath done this hee hath done it with much respect to the Good of his Country. Itt is said there are many plausible thinges in itt. Truly, many thinges have engaged mee, which, if I had nott knowne they should have bin nothing butt Good, I would nott have engag'd in. Itt hath bin said, that if a man bee Engag'd hee must performe his Engagements. I am wholly confident that every honest man is bound in duty to God and his Conscience, lett him bee engag'd in what hee will, to decline itt when hee is engag'd and clearly convinc't to discharge his duty to God as ever hee was for itt;

[a] Rainborowe had been added to the Committee of the Navy on 9 September, 1647, and appointed Vice-Admiral on September 27. (*Commons' Journals*, v., 297, 318.) On October 2 the Commons voted that he should be at once despatched to sea, and on October 8 that he should be commander-in-chief of the ships appointed for the winter guard. (*Ibid.*, 324, 328.) On September 29 the committee of general officers voted that Deane should succeed to the command of Rainborowe's regiment when the latter went to sea, which seems to be one of the causes of the discontent shown in Rainborowe's speech. Cromwell and Rainborowe had before this fallen out on the question of treating with the King. A news-letter of September 20 (*Clarendon MS.* 2577) says, "The Parliament is not well pleased with the Army's proposals, and the Army is as much displeased with them for disliking them; and upon Thursday last there was a resolution amongst them to send to the Houses that they should treat with the King upon the proposals. High language passed at the Council of War between Cromwell and Rainsborough, so high that Rainsborough told him that one of them must not live."

and that I shall make good out of the Scripture, and cleare itt by that if that bee any thinge. There are two objections are made against itt.

The one is Division. Truly I thinke wee are utterly undone if wee devide, butt I hope that honest things have carried us on thus longe, and will keepe us together, and I hope that wee shall nott devide. Another thinge is Difficulties. Oh unhappy men are wee that ever began this warre; if ever wee [had] look't uppon difficulties I doe nott know that ever wee should have look't an enemy in the face. Truly I thinke the Parliament were very indiscreete to contest with the Kinge if they did nott consider first that they should goe through difficulties; and I thinke there was noe man that entred into this warre that did nott engage [to go through difficulties]. And I shall humbly offer unto you—itt may bee the last time I shall offer—itt may bee soe, butt I shall discharge my conscience in itt—itt is this; that truly I thinke that lett the difficulties bee round about you, have you death before you, the sea on each side of you and behinde you, are you convinc't that the thinge is just I thinke you are bound in conscience to carry itt on; and I thinke att the last day itt can never bee answer'd to God that you did nott doe itt. For I thinke itt is a poore service to God and the Kingedome to take their pay and to decline their worke. I heare itt said, "Itt's a huge alteration, itt's a bringing in of New Lawes," and that this Kingedome hath bin under this Governement ever since itt was a Kingdome. If writinges bee true there hath bin many scufflinges betweene the honest men of England and those that have tyranniz'd over them; and iff itt bee [true what I have] read, there is none of those just and equitable lawes that the people of England are borne to butt that they are intrenchment altogether.[a] Butt if they were those which the people have bin alwayes under, if the people finde that they are [not] suitable to freemen as they are, I know noe reason

[a] *i.e.*, "All the good laws we now enjoy were innovations once, and intrenchments on the rights of the King or the Lords."

should deterre mee, either in what I must answer before God or the world, from indeavouring by all meanes to gaine any thinge that might bee of more advantage to them then the Governement under which they live. I doe nott presse that you should goe on with this thinge, for I thinke that every man that would speake to itt will bee lesse able till hee hath some time to consider itt. I doe make itt my Motion, that two or three dayes time may bee sett for every man to consider, and all that is to bee consider'd is the justnesse of the thinge—and if that bee consider'd then all thinges are—that there may bee nothing to deterre us from itt, butt that wee may doe that which is just to the people.

Lieut. Generall.

Truly I am very glad, that this Gentleman that spoke last is heere, and nott sorry for the occasion that brought him hither; because itt argues wee shall enjoy his company longer then I thought wee should have done.

Col. Rainborow.

If I should nott bee kick't out.

Lieut. Generall.

And truly then I thinke itt shall nott bee longe enough. Butt truly I doe nott know what the meaning of that expression is, nor what the meaning of any hatefull worde is heere. For wee are all heere with the same integrity to the publique; and perhaps wee have all of us done our parts nott affrighted with difficulties, one as well as another; and I hope have all purposes henceforward, through the Grace of God, nott resolving in our owne strength, to doe soe still. And therefore truly I thinke all the consideration is, That amongst us wee are almost all souldiers; all considerations [of not fearing difficulties] or wordes of that kinde doe wonderfully please us, all words of courage animate us to carry on our businesse, to doe God's businesse, [and] that which is the will of

God. I say itt againe, I doe nott thinke that any man heere wants courage to doe that which becomes an honest man and an Englishman to doe. Butt wee speake as men that desire to have the feare of God before our eyes, and men that may nott resolve to doe that which wee doe in the power of a fleshly strength, butt to lay this as the foundation of all our actions, to doe that which is the will of God. And if any man have a false deceit—on the one hand, deceitfulnesse, that which hee doth nott intend, or a perswasion on the other hand, I thinke hee will nott prosper.

Butt to that which was mov'd by Col. Rainborow, of the objections of difficulty and danger [and] of the consequences, they are nott proposed to any other end, butt [as] thinges fitting consideration, nott forged to deterre from the consideration of the businesse. In the consideration of the thinge that is new to us, and of every thinge that shall bee new that is of such importance as this is, I thinke that hee that wishes the most serious advice to bee taken of such a change as this is,—soe evident and cleare [a change]—who ever offers that there may bee most serious consideration, I thinke hee does nott speake impertinently. And truly itt was offer'd to noe other end then what I speake. I shall say noe more to that.

Butt to the other, concerning Engagements and breaking of them. I doe nott thinke that itt was att all offer'd by any body, that though an Engagement were never soe unrighteous itt ought to bee kept. Noe man offer'd a syllable or tittle [to that purpose]. For certainly itt's an act of duty to breake an unrighteous Engagement; hee that keepes itt does a double sin, in that hee made an unrighteous Engagement, and [in] that he goes about to keepe itt. Butt this was onely offer'd; and I know nott what can bee more fit, that before wee can consider of this [paper] wee labour to know where wee are, and where wee stand. Perhaps wee are uppon Engagements that wee cannott with honesty breake, Butt lett mee tell you this, that hee that speakes to you of Engagements heere, is as free from Engagements to the Kinge as any man in all the world ; and I know that [a] if itt were otherwise I believe my future actions would provoke some to declare itt. Butt I thanke God I stand uppon the bottome of my owne innocence in this particular; through the Grace of God I feare nott the face of any man, I doe nott. I say wee are to consider what Engagements wee have made, and if our Engagements have bin unrighteous why should wee nott make itt our indeavours to breake them. Yett if unrighteous Engagements[b] itt is nott a present breach of them unlesse there bee a consideration of circumstances. Circumstances may bee such as I may nott now breake an unrighteous Engagement, or else I may doe that which I did scandalously, if the thinge bee good.[c] If that bee true concerning the breaking of an unrighteous Engagement itt is much more verified concerning Engagements disputable whether they bee righteous or unrighteous. If soe, I am sure itt is fitt wee should dispute [them], and if, when wee have disputed them, wee see the goodnesse of God inlightening us to see our liberties, I thinke wee are to doe what wee can to give satisfaction to men. Butt if itt were soe, as wee made an Engagement in judgement and knowledge, soe wee goe off from itt in judgement and knowledge. Butt there may be just Engagements uppon us such as perhaps itt will bee our duty to keepe; and if soe itt is fitt wee should consider, and all that I said [was] that wee should consider our Engagements, and there is nothing else offer'd, and therefore what neede anybody bee angry or offended. Perhaps wee have made such Engagements as may in the matter of them nott binde us, in some circumstances they may. Our Engagements are publique Engagements. They are to the Kingedome, and to every one in the Kingdome that could looke uppon what wee did publiquely declare, could read or heare itt read. They are to the

[a] MS. "itt."

[b] *i.e.*, "if our engagements are unrighteous."

[c] Perhaps Cromwell means "though the engagement may be unrighteous, and it may be good in the abstract to break it, circumstances may render it scandalous to do so now."

Parliament, and itt is a very fitting thinge that wee doe seriously consider of the thinges. And shortly this is that I shall offer: that because the Kingedome is in the danger itt is in, because the Kingdome is in that condition itt is in, and time may bee ill spent in debates, and itt is necessary for thinges to bee putt to an issue, if ever itt was necessary in the world itt is now, I should desire this may bee done.

That this Generall Councill may bee appointed [to meet] against a very short time, two dayes, Thursday, if you would, against Saturday, or att furthest against Munday: that there might bee a Committee out of this Councill appointed to debate and consider with those two Gentlemen, and with any others that are nott of the Army that they shall bringe, and with the Agitators of those five Regiments: that soe there may bee a liberall and free debate had amongst us, that wee may understand really as before God the bottome of our desires, and that wee may seeke God together, and see if God will give us an uniting spiritt. Give mee leave to tell itt you againe, I am confident there sitts nott a man in this place that cannott soe freely act with you, but if hee sees that God hath shutt uppe his way that hee cannott doe any service hee will bee glad to withdraw himself, and wish you all prosperity in that way as may bee good for the Kingedome.[a] And if this heart bee in us, as is knowne to God that searches our hearts and tryeth the reines, God will discover whether our hearts bee nott cleare in this businesse. Therefore I shall move that wee may have a Committee amongst our selves [to consider] of the Engagements, and this Committee to dispute thinges with others, and a short day [to be appointed] for the Generall Councill. I doubt nott butt if in sincerity wee are willing to submitt to that light that God shall cast in amonge us God will unite us, and make us of one heart and one minde. Doe the plausiblest thinges you can doe, doe that which hath the most appearance of reason in itt that tends to change, att this conjuncture of time you will finde difficulties. Butt if God satisfie our spiritts this will bee a ground of confidence to every

[a] Clause transposed.

good man, and hee that goes uppon other grounds hee shall fall like a beast. I shall desire this, that you or any other of the Agitators or Gentlemen that can bee heere will bee heere, that wee may have free discourses amongst our selves of thinges, and you will bee able to satisfie each other. And really, rather then I would have this Kingedome breake in pieces before some company of men bee united together to a settlement, I will withdraw my self from the Army tomorrow, and lay downe my Commission; I will perish before I hinder itt.[a]

Bedfordshire Man.

May itt please your Honour,

I was desired by some of the Agents to accompanie this paper, manifesting my approbation of itt after I had heard itt read severall times, and they desir'd that itt might bee offer'd to this Councill, for the concurrence of the Councill if itt might bee. I finde that the Engagements of the Army are att present the thinges which is insisted to bee consider'd. I confesse my ignorance in those Engagements, butt I apprehend, att least I hope, that those Engagements have given away nothing from the people that is the people's Right. Itt may bee they have promised the King his Right, or any other persons their Right, butt noe more. If they have promised more then their Right to any person or persons, and have given away any thinge from the people that is their Right, then I conceive they are unjust. And if they are unjust [they should be broken], though I confesse for my owne parte I am very tender of breaking an Engagement when itt concernes a particular person—I thinke that a particular person ought rather to sett downe and loose then to breake an Engagement—butt if any man have given away any thinge from another whose Right itt was to one or more whose Right itt was nott, I conceive these men may [break that engagement]—at least many of them thinke themselves

[a] Cromwell's dread of division is commented on in Berkeley's *Memoirs*, *Masere's Tracts*, i., 364.

bound nott onely to breake this Engagement, butt to place [a] to give every one his due. I conceive that for the substance of the paper itt is the peoples due; and for the change of the Governement which is soe dangerous, I apprehend that there may bee many dangers in itt, and truly I apprehend there may bee more dangers without itt. For I conceive if you keepe the Governement as itt is and bringe in the Kinge, there may bee more dangers then in changing the Governement. Butt however, because from those thinges that I heard of the Agents they conceive that this conjuncture of time may almost destroy them, they have taken uppon them a libertie of acting to higher thinges, as they hope, for the freedome of the Nation, then yett this Generall Councill have acted to. And therefore as their sences I must make this motion; that all those that uppon a due consideration of the thinge doe finde itt to bee just and honest, and doe finde that if they have engaged any thinge to the contrary of this itt is unjust and giving away the people's Rights, I desire that they and all others may have a free libertie of acting to any thinge in this nature, or any other nature, that may bee for the peoples good, by petitioning or otherwise; wherby the fundamentalls for a well-ordered Governement for the people's Rights may bee established. And I shall desire that those that conceive themselves bound uppe would desist, and satisfie themselves in that, and bee noe hinderances to hinder the people in a more perfect way then hath bin [yet] indeavour'd.

Capt. Awdeley.

I suppose you have nott thought fitt, that there should bee a dispute concerning thinges att this time. I desire that other thinges may bee taken into consideration, delayes and debates. Delayes have undone us, and itt must bee a great expedition that must further us, and therfore I desire that there may bee a Committee appointed.

[a] The sense requires, "to replace it by a new engagement."

Lieut. Col. Goffe.

I shall butt humbly take the boldnesse to put you in minde of one thinge which you moved enow.[a] The Motion is, that there might bee a seeking of God in the thinges that now lie before us.

I shall humbly desire, that that Motion may nott die. Itt may bee there are or may bee some particular opinions amonge us concerning the use of ordinances and of publique seeking of God. Noe doubt formes have bin rested uppon too much; butt yett since there are soe many of us that have had soe many and soe large experiences of an extraordinarie manifestation of God's presence, when wee have bin in such extraordinarie wayes mett together, I shall desire that those who are that way [inclined] will take the present opportunity to doe itt. For certainly those thinges that are now presented, as they are, are well accepted by most of us; and though I am nott prepared to say any thinge either consenting or dissenting to the paper, as nott thinking itt wisedome to answer a matter before I have consider'd, yett when I doe consider how much ground there is to conceive there hath bin a withdrawing of the presence of God from us that have mett in this place—I doe nott say a totall withdrawing; I hope God is with us and amongst us. Itt hath bin our trouble night and day that God hath nott bin with us as formerly, as many within us soe without us [have told us], men that were sent from God in an extraordinarie manner to us. I meane [that though] the Ministers may take too much uppon them, yett there have bin those that have preached to us in this place, [in] [b] severall places, wee know very well that they spake to our hearts and consciences, and told us of our wandringes from God, and told us in the name of the Lord, that God would bee with us noe longer then wee were with him. Wee have in some thinges wandred from God, and as wee have heard

[a] enow. Halliwell gives "enow" as meaning even now and "anowe" as "now."

[b] Goffe perhaps was referring to what took place on October 7, when the Council "gave audience to an High German, who pretended to be a prophet, and would prescribe a way for the settling of a firm and lasting peace." Rushworth, viii., 836.

this from them in this place, soe have wee had itt very frequently prest uppon our spiritts [elsewhere], prest uppon us in the Citty and the Country. I speake this to this end, that our hearts may bee deeply and throughly affected with this matter. For if God bee departed from us hee is some where else. Iff wee have nott the will of God in these Councills God may bee found amonge some other Councills. Therfore I say, lett us shew the spiritt of Christians, and lett us nott bee ashamed to declare to all the world, that our Councills, and our wisedome, and our wayes they are nott altogether such as the world hath walked in; butt that wee have had a dependancie uppon God, and that our desires are to follow God (though never soe much to our disadvantage in the world) if God may have the glory by itt. And I pray lett us consider this: God does seeme evidently to bee throwing downe the glory of all flesh; the greatest powers in the Kingedome have bin shaken. God hath throwne downe the glory of the Kinge and that partie; hee hath throwne downe a partie in the Citty; I doe nott say, that God will throw us downe—I hope better thinges—butt hee will have the glory; lett us nott stand uppon our glory and reputation in the world. If wee have done some thinges through ignorance, or feare, or unbeleif, in the day of our straights, and could nott give God that glory by beleiving as wee ought to have done, I hope God hath a way for to humble us for that, and to keepe us as instruments in his hand still. There are two wayes that God doth take uppon those that walke obstinately against him; if they bee obstinate and continue obstinate hee breakes them in pieces with a rod of iron; if they bee his people and wander from him hee takes that glory from them, and takes itt to himself. I speake itt I hope from a divine impression. If wee would continue to bee instruments in his hand, lett us seriously sett our selves before the Lord, and seeke to him and waite uppon him for conviction of spiritts. Itt is nott enough for us to say, "if wee have offended wee will leave the world, wee will goe and confesse to the Lord what wee have done amisse, butt wee will doe noe more soe.'

Aaron went uppe to Hur and died, and Moses was favour'd to see the land of Canaan, hee did nott voluntarily lay himself aside. I hope our strayings from God are nott soe great, butt that a conversion and true humiliation may recover us againe; and I desire that wee may bee serious in this, and not despise any other instruments that God will use. God will have his worke done; itt may bee wee thinke wee are the onely instruments that God hath in his hands. I shall onely adde these two thinges. First, that wee bee warie how wee lett forth any thinge against his people, and that which is for the whole Kingedome and Nation. I would move, that wee may nott lett our spiritts act too freely against them till wee have throughly weighed the matter, and considered our own wayes too. The second is to draw us uppe to a serious consideration of the weightiness of the worke that lies before us, and seriously to sett our selves to seeke the Lord; and I wish itt might bee consider'd of a way and manner that itt should be conveniently done, and I thinke to morrow will bee the [best] day.

Lieut Generall.

I know nott what Lieut. Col. Goffe meanes for to morrow for the time of seeking God. I thinke itt will bee requisite that wee doe itt speedily, and doe itt the first thinge, and that wee doe itt as unitedly as wee can, as many of us as well may meete together. For my parte I shall lay aside all businesse for this businesse, either to convince or bee convinc't as God shall please. I thinke itt would bee good that to morrow morning may bee spent in prayer, and the afternoone might bee the time of our businesse. I doe nott know that these Gentlemen doe assent to itt that to morrow in the afternoone might bee the time.

Lieut. Col. Goffe.

I thinke wee have a great deale of businesse to doe, and wee have bin doing of itt these ten weekes. Itt is an ordinance that

God hath blest to this end. I say goe about what you will, for my parte I shall nott thinke any thinge can prosper, unlesse God bee first sought.

If that bee approved of, that to morrow shall bee a time of seeking the Lord, and that the afternoone shall bee the time of businesse, if that doth agree with your opinion and the generall sence, lett that bee first order'd.

Com̃. Gen. Ireton.

That which Lieut. Col. Goffe offer'd hath [made] a very great impression uppon mee; and indeed I must acknowledge to God through him, that, as hee hath severall times spoke in this place, and elsewhere to this purpose, hee hath never spoke butt hee hath touched my heart ; and that especially in the point that hee hintes. That one thinge is, that in the time of our straights and difficulties, I thinke wee none of us—I feare wee none of us—I am sure I have nott—walked soe closely with God, and kept soe close with him, [as] to trust wholly uppon him, as nott to bee led too much with considerations of danger and difficulty, and from that consideration to waive some thinges, and perhaps to doe some thinges, that otherwise I should nott have thought fitt to have done. Every one hath a spiritt within him—especially [he] who has that communion indeed with that spirit that is the only searcher of hearts—that can best search out and discover to him the errours of his owne wayes, and of the workinges of his owne heart. And though I thinke that publique actinges, publique departings from God are the fruites of unbeleif and distrust, and nott honouring God by sanctifying him in our wayes; they doe more publiquely engage God to vindicate his honour by a departing from them that doe soe, and if there bee any such thinge in the Army that is to bee look't uppon with a publique eye in relation to the Army.[a] I thinke the maine thinge is for every one

[a] The sentence should probably read thus: " Public departings from God (if there be any such thing in the Army that is to be looked upon with a public eye in relation

to waite uppon God, for the errours, deceits, and weaknesses of his owne heart, and I pray God to bee present with us in that. Butt withall I would nott have that seasonable and good Motion that hath come from Lieut. Col. Goffe to bee neglected, of a publique seeking of God, and seeking to God, as for other thinges soe especially for the discovery of any publique deserting of God, or dishonouring of him, or declining from him, that does lie as the fault and blemish uppon the Army. Therfore I wish his Motion may bee pursued, that the thinge may bee done, and for point of time as was moved by him. Onely this to the way; I confesse I thinke the best [way] is this, that itt may bee only taken notice of as a thinge by the agreement of this Councill resolv'd on, that tomorrow in the morning, the forenoone wee doe sett aparte, wee doe give uppe from other businesse, for every man to give himself uppe that way, either in private by himself, though I cannott say not in public. For the publique Meeting att the Church, itt were nott amisse that itt may bee thus taken notice of as a time given from other imployments for that purpose, and every one as God shall incline their hearts, some in one place, and some another, to imploy themselves that way.

Agreed for the Meeting for Prayer to bee att Mr. Chamberlaine's

Lieut. Gen.

That they should nott meete as two contrary parties, butt as some desirous to satisfie or convince each other.

Mr. Petty.

For my owne parte, I have done as to this businesse what was desired by the Agents that sent mee hither. As for any further

to the Army) are the fruits of unbelief and distrust; and though I think that public actings (*i.e.* public prayer meetings) do more publicly engage God to vindicate his honour by a departing from them that do so, still I think the main thing is," etc.

Meeting to morrow or any other time I cannott meete uppon the same ground, to meete as for their sence, [but only] to give my owne reason why I doe assent to itt.

Coñ. Ireton.

I should bee sorry, that they should bee soe suddaine to stand uppon themselves.

Mr. Petty.

To procure three, four, or five more or lesse to meete, for my owne parte I am utterly unconcern'd in the businesse.

Buffe-Coate.

I have heere att this day answer'd the expectations, which I engaged to your Honours; which was, that if wee would give a Meeting you should take that as a symptome, or a remarkeable testimonie of our fidelitie. I have discharged that trust reposed in mee. I could nott engage for them. I shall goe on still in that method. I shall engage my deepest interest for any reasonable desires to engage them to come to this.

Lieut. Generall.

I hope wee know God better then to make appearances of Religious Meetings as covers for designes for insinuation amongst you. I desire that God that hath given us some sinceritie will owne us according to his owne goodnesse, and that sincerity that hee hath given us. I dare bee confident to speake itt, that [design] that hath bin amongst us hitherto is to seeke the guidances of God, and to recover that presence of God that seemes to withdraw from us; and our end is to accomplish that worke which may bee for the good of the Kingedome. It seems to us in this as much as anything we are not of a minde, and for our parts wee doe nott desire or offer you to bee with us in our seeking of God further then your owne satisfaccions lead you, butt onely [that] against to-morrow in the afternoone (which will bee design'd for the consideration of these businesses with you) you will doe what you may to have soe many as you shall thinke fitt to see what God will direct you to say to us. Perhaps God may unite us and carry us both one way, that whilest wee are going one way, and you another, wee bee nott both destroyed. This requires spiritt. Itt may bee too soone to say, itt is my present apprehension; I had rather wee should devolve our strength to you then that the Kingedome for our division should suffer losse.[a] For that's in all our hearts, to professe above any thinge that's worldlie, the publique good of the people; and if that bee in our hearts truly, and nakedlie, I am confident itt is a principall that will stand. And therefore I doe desire you, that against to morrow in the afternoone, if you judge itt meete, you will come to us to the Quartermaster Generall's Quarters, and there you will finde us [at prayer], if you will come timely to joyne with us; at your libertie, if afterwards [you wish] to speake with us.[b]

Mr. Wildman.

I desire to returne a little to the businesse in hand that was the occasion of these other motions. I could nott butt take some notice of some thinge that did reflect uppon the Agents of the five Regiments, in which I could nott butt give a little satisfaction to them; and I shall desire to prosecute a motion or two that hath bin already made. I observ'd that itt was said, that these gentlemen doe insist upon Engagements in "The Case of the Army," and therefore it was said to bee contrary to the principles of the Agents, that an Engagement which was unjust should lawfully bee broken.[c] I shall onely observe this; that though an unjust Engagement when

[a] After Cromwell quitted the Parliament, says Berkeley, "his chief dependence was on the Army, which he endeavoured by all means to keep in unity; and if he could not bring it to his sense, he, rather than suffer any division in it, went over himself and carried his friends with him into that way which the Army did choose." *Masere's Tracts*, p. 364.

[b] In this speech of Cromwell's the position of several clauses has been altered with a view to clearing the sense.

[c] The two halves of this sentence have been transposed.

itt appeares unjust may bee broken, yett when two parties engage [each that] the other partie may have satisfaccion, yett because they are mutually engaged each to other one partie that apprehends they are broken [is justified] to complaine of them ; and soe itt may bee their case, with which I confesse I made my concurrence. The other is a principle much spreading and much to my trouble, and that is this: that when persons once bee engaged, though the Engagement appeare to bee unjust, yett the person must sett downe and suffer under itt; and that therefore, in case a Parliament, as a true Parliament, doth anythinge unjustly, if wee bee engaged to submitt to the Lawes that they shall make, if they make an unjust law, though they make an unrighteous law, yett wee must sweare obedience.

I confesse to mee this principle is very dangerous, and I speake itt the rather because I see itt spreading abroad in the Army againe. Wheras itt is contrary to what the Army first declar'd: that they stood uppon such principles of right and freedome, and the lawes of nature and nations, wherby men were to preserve themselves though the persons to whome aucthority belong'd should faile in itt, and urged the example of the Scotts, and [that] the Generall that would destroy the Army they might hold his hands ; and therfore if any thinge tends to the destruction of a people, because the thinge is absolutely unjust and tends to their destruction, [they may preserve themselves].[a] I could nott butt speake a worde to that. The motion that I should make uppon that account is this.

[a] Wildman refers to the principles laid down in the *Declaration of the Army*, of June 14, 1647.

"And truly such Kingdoms as have, according both to the Law of Nature and Nations, appear'd to the vindication and defence of their just Rights and Liberties, have proceeded much higher ; as our Brethren of Scotland, who, in the first beginning of these late Differences, associated in Covenant, from the very same Grounds and Principles (having no visible Form either of Parliament or King to countenance them ;) and as they were therein justified and protected by their own and this Kingdom also, so we justly shall expect to be.

"We need not mention the States of the Netherlands, the Portugals, and others, all proceeding from the same Principles of Right and Freedom: And accordingly

That wheras there must bee a Meeting I could nott finde [but] that they were desirous to give all satisfaccion, and they desire nothing but the union of the Army. Thus farre itt is their sence. That the necessity of the Kingdome for present actinges is such that two or three dayes may loose the Kingdome. I desire in the sight of God to speake plainly: I meane there may bee an agreement betweene the Kinge [and the Parliament] by propositions, with a power to hinder the making of any lawes that are good, and the tendring of any good [lawes]. And therfore, because none of the people's greivances are redrest, they doe apprehend that thus a few dayes may bee the losse of the Kingedome. I know it is their sence. That they desire to bee excused that itt might nott bee thought any arrogancie in them, butt they are clearlie satisfied, that the way they proceede in is just, and desire to bee excus'd if they goe on in itt; and yett notwithstanding will give all satisfaccion. And wheras itt is desir'd that Engagements may bee consider'd, I shall desire that onely the justice of the thinge that is proposed may bee consider'd. Whether the chief thinge in the Agreement, the intent of itt, bee nott this, to secure the Rights of the people in their Parliaments, which was declar'd by this Army in the Declaration of the 14th of June to bee absolutely insisted on? I shall make that motion to bee the thinge consider'd: whether the thinge bee just or the people's due, and then there can bee noe Engagement to binde from itt.

the Parliament hath declared it no resistance of Magistracy, to side with the just Principles and the Law of Nature and Nations, being that Law upon which we have assisted you. And that the Soldiery may lawfully hold the hands of the General, who will turn his cannon against his Army, on purpose to destroy them; the Seamen the hands of the Pilot, who wilfully runs the Ship upon a Rock (as our Brethren of Scotland argued). And such were the proceedings of our Ancestors of famous Memory, to the purchasing of such Rights and Liberties as they have enjoyed, through the Price of their Blood, and we (both by that, and the later Blood of our dear Friends and Fellow-Soldiers, with the hazard of our own) do now lay claim to." Rushworth, vii., 565.

Com̃. Gen. Ireton.

Truly Sir, by what Lieut. Col. Goffe moved I confesse I was soe taken off from all [other] thoughts in this businesse that I did nott thinke of speaking any thinge more. Butt what this Gentleman hath last said hath renewed the occasion, and indeed if I did thinke [a] all that hee hath deliver'd bee truth and innocence—nay, if I did nott thinke that it hath venome and poyson in itt—I would nott speake itt.

First, I cannott butt speake somethinge unto the two particulars that hee holds forth as dangerous thinges,—indeed hee hath cleerlie yoak't them together, when before I was sensible of those principles and how farre they would run together—that is that principle of nott being obliged, by nott regarding what Engagements men have entred into, if in their future apprehensions the thinges they engaged to are unjust; and that principle on the other hand of nott submitting passively for peace sake to that authority wee have engaged to. For hee does hold forth his opinion in those two points to cleare their way; and I must crave leave on my parte to declare [that] my opinion of that Distinction doth lie on the other way. I am farre from holding, that if a man have engag'd himself to a thinge that is nott just—to a thinge that is evill, that is sin if hee doe itt—that that man is still bound to performe what hee hath promised; I am farre from apprehending that. Butt when wee talke of just, itt is nott soe much of what is sinfull before God, which depends uppon many circumstances of indignation to that man and the like, butt itt intends of that which is just according to the foundation of justice betweene man and man. And for my parte I account that the great foundation of justice betweene man and man, and that without which I know nothing of justice betwixt man and man—in particular matters I meane, nothing in particular thinges that can come under humane Engagement one way or other—there is noe other foundation of right I know of, right to one thinge from another man, noe foundation of

[a] MS. "I thinke if."

that justice or that righteousnesse, butt this generall justice, and this generall ground of righteousnesse, that wee should keepe covenant one with another. Covenants freely made, freely entred into, must bee kept one with another. Take away that I doe nott know what ground there is of any thinge you can call any man's right. I would very faine know what you Gentlemen or any other doe account the right you have to any thinge in England, any thinge of estate, land, or goods that you have, what ground, what right you have to itt? What right hath any man to any thinge if you lay nott that principle, that wee are to keepe covenant? If you will resort onely to the law of Nature, by the law of Nature you have noe more right to this land or any thinge else then I have. I have as much right to take hold of any thinge that is for my sustenance, [to] take hold of any thinge that I have a desire to for my satisfaction as you. Butt heere comes the foundation of all right that I understand to be betwixt men, as to the enjoying of one thinge or nott enjoying of itt; wee are under a contract, wee are under an agreement, and that agreement is what a man has for matter of land that a man hath received by a traduction from his ancestors, which according to the law does fall uppon him to bee his right. [The agreement is] that that hee shall enjoy, hee shall have the property of, the use of, the disposing of, with submission to that generall aucthoritie which is agreed uppon amongst us for the preserving of peace, and for the supporting of this law. This I take to bee [the foundation of all right] for matter of land. For matter of goods, that which does fence mee from that [right] which another man may claime by the law of nature of taking my goods, that which makes itt mine really and civillie is the law. That which makes itt unlawfull originally and radically is onely this: because that man is in covenant with mee to live together in peace one with another, and nott to meddle with that which another is posses't of, butt that each of us should enjoy, and make use of, and dispose of, that which by the course of law is in his possession, and [another] shall nott by violence take itt away from him. This is the foundation of all the right any man has to any thinge butt to his owne person. This is the generall thinge: that wee must keepe covenant one with another when wee have contracted one with another. And if any difference arise among us itt shall bee thus and thus: that I shall nott goe with violence to prejudice another, butt with submission to this way. And therefore when I heare men speake of laying aside all Engagements to [consider only] that wild or vast notion of what in every man's conception is just or unjust, I am afraid and doe tremble att the boundlesse and endlesse consequences of itt.[a] What you apply this paper to. You say, "If these thinges in this paper, in this Engagement bee just, then," say you, "never talke of any Engagement, for if any thinge in that Engagement bee against this, your Engagement was unlawfull; consider singly this paper, whether itt bee just." In what sence doe you thinke this is just? There is a great deale of equivocation [as to] what is just and unjust.

Mr. Wildman.

I suppose you take away the substance of the question. Our[b] [sense] was, that an unjust Engagement is rather to be broken then kept. The Agents thinke that to delay is to dispose their Enemy into such a capacitie as hee may destroy them. I make a question whether any Engagement can bee to an unjust thinge. [If] a man may promise to doe that which is never soe much unjust, a man may promise to breake all Engagements and duties. Butt [I say] this, wee must lay aside the consideration of Engagements, soe as nott to take in that as one ground of what is just or unjust amongst men in this case. I doe apply this to the case in hand: that itt might bee consider'd whether itt bee unjust to bringe in the Kinge in such a way as hee may bee in a capacity to destroy the people. This paper may bee applyed to itt.

[a] M.S. "What you apply to this paper."
[b] MS. "ours."

Com̃. Generall.

You come to itt more particularly then that paper leads. There is a great deale of equivocation in the point of justice, and that I am bound to declare.

Capt. Awdeley.

Mr. Wildman sayes if wee stay butt three dayes before you satisfie one another, and if wee tarry longe the kinge will come and say who will be hang'd first.

Com̃ Gen.

Sir, I was saying this; wee shall much deceive our selves, and bee apt to deceive others if wee doe nott consider that there is two parts of justice. There may bee a thinge just that is negatively [so], itt is nott unjust, nott unlawfull—that which is nott unlawfull, that's just to mee to doe if I bee free. Againe there is another sence of just when wee account such a thinge to bee a duty,—nott onely a thinge lawfull "we[a] may doe itt," but itt's a duty, "you ought to doe itt,"—and there is a great deale of mistake if you confound these two. If I engage my self to a thinge that was in this sence just, that's a thinge lawfull for mee to doe supposing mee free, then I account my Engagement stands good to this. On the other hand, if I engage my self against a thinge which was a duty for mee to doe, which I was bound to doe; or if I engag'd myself to a thinge which was nott lawfull for mee to doe, which I was bound nott to doe, in this sence I doe account this [engagement] unjust. If I doe engage my self to what was unlawfull for mee to engage to, I thinke I am nott then to make good activelie this Engagement. Butt though this bee true, yett the generall end and equitie of Engagements I must regard, and that is the preserving right betwixt men, the nott doing of wronge or hurt to men, one to another. And therfore if [by] that which I engage to, though the thinge bee unlawfull for mee to doe, another man bee prejudict in case I

[a] MS. "hee."

did not perform it—though itt bee a thinge which was[a] unlawfull for mee to doe, yett [if] I did freelie [engage to do it] and I did [engage] uppon a consideration to mee, and that man did beleive mee, and hee suffer'd a prejudice by beleiving—though I bee nott bound by my Engagement to performe itt,[b] yett I am [bound] to regard that justice that lies in the matter of Engagement, soe as to repaire that man by some just way as farre as I can; and hee that doth nott hold this, I doubt whether hee hath any principle of justice, or doing right to any att all in him. That is [if] hee that did nott thinke itt lawfull hath made another man beleive itt to his prejudice and hurt, and [made] another man bee prejudic't and hurt by that, hee that does nott hold that hee is in this case to repaire [it] to that man, and free him from [the prejudice of] itt, I conceive there is noe justice in him. And therfore I wish wee may take notice of this distinction when wee talke of being bound to make good Engagements or nott. This I thinke I can make good in a larger dispute by reason. If the thinges engaged to were lawfull to bee done, or lawfull for mee to engage to, then [I] by my Engagement am[c] bound to [perform] itt. On the other hand if the thinge were nott lawfull for mee to engage, or [if it were] a duty for mee to have done to the contrary, then I am nott bound positively and actively to performe itt. Nay I am bound nott to performe itt, because itt was unlawfull [and] unjust by another Engagement. Butt when I engage to another man, and hee hath a prejudice by beleiving, I nott performing itt, I am bound to repaire that man as much as may bee, and lett the prejudice fall upon my self and nott uppon any other. This I desire wee may take notice of to avoide falacie on that part. For there is an extremity to say on the one hand, that if a man engage what is nott just hee may act against itt soe as to regard noe relation or prejudice.

[a] "nott" is here omitted, and the words "in case I did not perform it" are transposed from four lines below.

[b] MS. "though I bee bound by my engagement nott to perform itt."

[c] MS. "are."

[There's an extremity] for a man to say on the other hand, that whatsoever you engage, though itt bee never soe unjust, you are to stand to itt. One worde more to the other parte which Mr. Wildeman doth hold out as a dangerous principle acting amongst us, that wee must bee bound to active obedience to any power acting amongst men.

Wildman.

You repeat not the principle right—"To thinke that wee are bound soe absolutely to personall obedience to any Magistrates or personall aucthoritie that if they worke to our destruction wee may nott oppose them."

[Ireton.]

That wee may nott deceive ourselves againe [by arguments] that are fallacious in that kinde I am a little affected to speake in this, because I see that the abuse and misapplication [a] of those thinges the Army hath declar'd hath led many men into a great and dangerous errour and destructive to all humane society. Because the Army hath declar'd, in those cases where the foundation of all that right and libertie of the people is, if they have any, that in these cases they will insist uppon that right, and that they will nott suffer that originall and fundamentall right to bee taken away; and because the Army when there hath bin a command of that supreame aucthority the Parliament have nott obeyed itt, butt stood uppon itt to have this fundamentall right setled first, and requir'd a rectification of the supreame aucthority of the Kingedome; for a man therfore to inferre [that] uppon any particular, you may dispute that aucthority by what is commanded what is just or unjust, if in your apprehension nott to obey, and soe farre itt is well, and if itt tend to your losse to oppose itt.[b]

[a] Clause transferred from the line below.
[b] Past amending.

Mr. Wildman.

If itt tend to my Destruction that was the worde I spoke.

Com̃. Gen.

Lett us take heede that wee doe nott maintaine [that] this principle leads to destruction. If the case were soe visible as those cases the Army speaks of, of a Generall's turning the cannon against the Army, the bulke and body of the Army; or [of] a Pylott that sees a rock [and] does by the advantage of the steering[a] putt the shippe uppon't; if you could propose cases as evident as these are, there is noe man butt would agree with you. Butt when men will first putt in those termes of destruction, they will imagine any thinge a destruction, if there could bee any thinge better [for them]; and soe itt is very easy and demonstrable that thinges are soe counted abhorred and destructive, that, att the utmost if a man should make itt out by reason, that man[b] would bee in a better condition if itt bee nott done, then if itt bee done. And though I cannott butt subscribe to, that in such a visible way I may hold the hands of those that are in aucthority as I may the hands of a mad-man; butt that noe man shall thinke himself [bound] to acquiesce particularly, and to suffer for quietnesse sake rather then to make a disturbance, or to raise a power if hee can to make a disturbance in the State—I doe apprehend and appeale to all men whether there bee nott more follie or destructivenesse in the springe of that principle then there can bee in that other principle of holding passive obedience? Now whatsoever wee have declar'd in the Armie [declarations] itt is noe more butt this. The Parliament hath commanded us [to do] this. Wee have said, noe. First wee have insisted uppon [the] fundamentall rights of the people. Wee have said wee desire [first] to have the constitution of the supreame aucthority of this Kingedome reduced to that constitution which is due to the people of this Kingedome, and reducing the aucthority to this wee will submitt to itt, wee will

[a] MS. "stearne." [b] MS. "men."

acquiesce, wee will cast our share into this common bottome; and if itt goe ill with us att one time, itt will goe well att another. The reducing of the supreame aucthority to that constitution, by successe or election as neere as may bee, wee have insisted uppon as an essentiall right of the Kingedome; and noe man can accuse the Armie of disobedience, or holding forth a principle of disobedience uppon any other ground.

Lieut. Generall.

Lett mee speake a worde to this businesse. Wee are now uppon that businesse which wee spake of consulting with God about, and therfore I judge it altogether unreasonable [a] for us to dispute the meritt of those thinges, unlesse you will make itt the subject of debate before you consider itt among your selves. The businesse of the Engagement[s] lies uppon us. They [b] are free in a double respect; they made none, and if they did, then the way out is now; and [it is a way] which all the members of the Army, except they bee sensible of itt [may take], and, att one jumpe, jumpe out of all [engagements], and itt is a very great jumpe I will assure you. As wee professe wee intend to seeke the Lord in the thinge, the less wee speake in itt [now] the better, and the more wee cast ourselves uppon God the better.

I shall onelie speake two thinges to Mr. Wildman in order to our Meeting. Mee thoughte hee said if there bee delay hee feares this businesse will bee determined, the propositions will bee sent from the Parliament, and the Parliament and Kinge agree, and soe those Gentlemen that were in that minde to goe on in their way will bee cutt off in point of time to their owne dissadvantage. And the other thinge hee said was, that these Gentlemen who have chosen Mr. Wildman, and that other Gentleman,[c] to bee their

[a] Transferred from a lower line.

[b] "They," *i.e.* the representatives of the five regiments and the agents of the Londoners.

[c] "Petty."

mouth att this meeting to deliver their mindes, they are uppon the matter engaged in what they have resolved uppon, and they come as engaged men uppon their owne resolution. If that bee soe, I thinke there neither needes consideration of the former, for you will not bee anticipated. If that bee soe, you [can] worke accordingly. And though you [do] meete us, yett having that resolution you cannott bee prevented in your way by any proposition, or any such thinge; though wee should have come hither, and wee should meete to morrow as a company of men that really would bee guided by God. If any come to us to morrow onely to instruct us and teach us, how farre that will consist with the libertie of a free[a] [debate] or an end of satisfaction I referre to every sober spiritted man to thinke of and determine.[b] I thinke itt is such a preengagement that there is noe neede of talke of the thinge. And I see then if that bee soe, things are in such an irrevocable way—I will nott call itt desperate—as there is noe hope of accomodation or union, except wee receive the Councills—I will nott call itt the commands—of them that come to us. I desire that wee may rightly understand this thinge. If this bee soe I doe nott understand what the end of the meeting will bee. If this bee nott soe, wee[c] will [not] draw any man from their Engagements further then the Light of God shall draw them from their Engagements; and I thinke, according to your owne principle, if you bee uppon any Engagement you are liable to bee convinc't unlesse you bee infallible. If wee may come to an honest and single debate, how wee may all agree in one common way for publique good; if wee [may] meete soe, wee shall meete with a great deale the more comfort, and hopes of a good and happy issue, and understanding of the businesse. Butt if otherwise, I despaire of the Meeting; or att least I would have the Meeting to bee of another notion, a

[a] MS. "the liberty of a free liberty."

[b] The last two words transferred from three lines before.

[c] MS. "that they," *i.e.* Cromwell and the Council. The reporter changes into oratio obliqua for a moment.

Meeting that did represent the Agitators of five Regiments to give rules to the Councill of Warre. If itt signifie this, for my owne parte I shall bee glad to submitt to itt under this notion. If itt bee a free debate what may bee fitt for us all to doe, with clearnesse and opennesse before the Lord, lett us understand that wee may come and meete soe and in that sincerity.[a] Otherwise I doe verily believe wee shall meete with prejudice, and we shall meete to prejudice—really to the prejudice of the Kingedome, and of the whole Army—if wee bee thus absolutely resolved uppon our way and engaged before hand. The Kingedome will see itt is such a reall actuall division as admitts of noe reconciliation, and all those that are enemies to us and freinds to our enemies will have the clearer advantage uppon us to putt us into inconveniency. And I desire if there bee any feare of God among us, I desire that wee may declare ourselves freely, that wee doe meete uppon these termes.

Col. Rainborow.

I wish, that the Motion of Lieut. Col Goffe might have taken effect, nott only to the time and place for Meeting [but] as hee desir'd. Butt, Sir, since itt is gone thus farre, and since I heare much of fallacie talk't of, I feare itt as much on the one side as the other. Itt is made a wonder[b] of that some Gentlemen without should have principles to breake Engagements, yett [it is made no wonder of] that some Gentlemen within should soe much insist uppon Engagements. I doe nott consider my self as jumping, butt yett I hope when I leape I shall take soe much of God with mee, and soe much of just and right with mee, as I shall jumpe sure. Butt I am more unsatisfied against [another of] those thinges that have bin said, and that is as to another Engagement. For all that hath bin said hath bin [as to engagements] betweene partie and partie, if two men should make an agreement and the like, and there were noe living one amongst another if those Engagements

[a] Four words transferred from the previous line.

[b] MS. "noe wonder."

were nott made [good], yett I thinke under favour that some Engagements may bee broke. Noe man that takes a wife butt there is an Engagement, and I thinke that a man ought to keepe itt, yett if another man that had married her before claimes her, hee ought to lett him have her and soe breake the Engagement. Butt whereas it is told us, this engagement is of another nature,[a] that the partie to whome wee make the Engagement relyed uppon [it], and becomes therby prejudic't, [and so] wee ought to take itt rather uppon ourselves then to leave itt uppon them,—this may serve in a particular case, if any men[b] heere will suffer they may; butt if wee will make our selves a third partie, and engage betweene Kinge and Parliament, [it is not a particular case] and I am of that Gentlemans minde that spoke, the Kinges partie would have bin about our eares if wee had nott made some considerations. Heere is the consideration now. As concerning them, doe wee nott engage for the Parliament and for the liberties of the people of England, and doe wee nott engage against itt? Wee have gott the better of them in the feild, butt they shall bee masters of our Houses. Never was Engagements broken more then wee doe. Wee did take uppe Armes with all that tooke parte with the Parliament and wee engag'd with them.[c] For my parte itt may bee thought that I am against the Kinge; I am against him or any power that would destroy Gods people, and I will never bee destroyed till I cannott helpe my self. Is itt nott an argument, if a

[a] MS. "butt this engagement is of another nature, but wheras it is told."

[b] MS. "man."

[c] Rainborow's argument may be thus paraphrased, though his actual words are hopelessly confused:

"I am of that gentleman's mind that said the king's party would have been about our ears if we had not made some considerations as concerning them, some engagement in their favour. This is the consideration, the concession we made in favour of the King's party. Did we not at first engage for the Parliament and for the liberties of the people, and against the King's party? Now though we have beaten them in the field they are by this proposed agreement to be made masters of our houses. By this new unlawful engagement we have broken our original engagements to the people and all who sided with the Parliament."

pylott run his shipp uppon a rock, or [if] a Generall mount his cannon against his Army, hee is to bee resisted? I thinke that this as cleare the very case as any thinge in the world. For clearly the Kinge and his partie could nott have come in uppon those termes that hee is come[to] in [on], if this very Army did nott engage for him; and I verily thinke that the House had nott made another addresse, if itt had nott bin said that itt was the desire of the Army, and the Army were engaged to itt. Therefore I say I hope men will have charitable opinions of other men. For my parte I thinke I shall never doe any thinge against conscience, and I shall have those hopes of others. That which is deare unto mee is my freedome. Itt is that I would enjoy, and I will enjoy if I can. For my owne parte I hope there is noe such distance betwixt these Gentlemen as is imagin'd, butt they will heare reason that may convince them out of itt. I doe verily beleive they are soe farre from a disunion that they will bee advis'd by this Councill in generall, or by any honest man of this Councill in particular. I have nott the same apprehensions that two or three dayes will undoe us, butt I thinke a very little delay will undoe us; and therefore I should onely desire, (itt may bee because I have spoken some other may answer mee) the lesse wee speake itt may bee the better. And as this Agitator whom [a] I never saw before, said that hee will use his interest, I hope that God will doe somethinge in that for our next Meeting to morrow, that when wee doe meete wee shall have a very happy union.

Buffe-coate.

That hee could breake Engagements in case they [were] proved unjust and that itt might [so] appeare to his conscience. That whatsoever hopes or obligations I should bee bound unto, if afterwards God should reveale himself, I would breake itt speedily, if itt were an 100 a day; and in that sence wee deliver'd our sence.

[a] MS. "whence."

Mr. Wildman.

Provided, that what is done tends to destruction, either self destruction or to [the destruction of] my neighbour especially. Unlawfull Engagements [are] Engagements against duty, and an Engagement to any person to bring him in such a way as hee may bee enabled to engage, itt is that which may tend to destruction.[a]

Lieut. Generall.

I thinke clearly you were understood to putt itt uppon an issue where there is clearly a case of destruction, publique destruction, and ruine; and I thinke this will bringe itt into consideration whether or noe our Engagements have really in them that that hath publique destruction and ruine necessarily following? or whether or noe wee may nott give way too much to our owne doubts or feares? and the issue will bee[b] whether itt bee lawfull to breake a covenant uppon our owne doubts and feares? I thinke [best] if wee agree to deferre the debate, to nominate a Committee.

Col. Rainborow.

One worde. I am of another opinion. Nott that the Engagements of the Army are look't uppon as destructive, butt the nott-performance of the Engagements of the Army is that which is destructive.

Com̃. Ireton.

I thinke Mr. Wildman's conclusion is, that they are destructive because they are destructive to our neighbours.

Mr. Wildman.

That if an Engagement were such itt does nott binde.

[a] Perhaps "to engage us to that which may tend to the destruction of others."

[b] Four words transferred from two lines below.

Com̃. Ireton.

Then if itt were a compliance, or such a Meeting nott for a Law butt for satisfaction, since wheras the only ground which the thinge seemes to mee to bee represented that these Gentlemen thinke that there owne agreement is soe cleare, soe infallibly just and right, that. I doe thinke those Gentlemen have nott soe much ground of confidence to each parte of that agreement as itt lies there, that whatever goes about to take itt from them, or whatever does nott agree to itt, is a thinge unlawfull, butt somethinge may bee seene in that if you come, in the Engagement of itt; and therfore in that relation, and nott your owne principalls that you would admitt of soe much conference as to question itt.[a]

Mr. Lockyer.

I have gather'd from two men's mouthes, that destruction is somethinge neere, and the cause of the destruction as they understand is the going of the proposalls to the Kinge. I thinke itt were very necessary that if itt bee true, as is suppos'd, the proposalls may bee brought hither when they doe goe, that wee may see what they are.

Lieut. Generall.

The Question is whether the propositions will save us, or [whether they will] nott destroy us. This discourse concludes nothing.

[a] The report is so fragmentary that it is difficult to follow Ireton's argument. It seems to me to be this. "If your compliance to the meeting we desire means a meeting for mutual satisfaction and not one in which you are to give us the law, we ought to discuss then the question whether our engagements are of the kind you say. But it seems to me that the only ground on which you base your demands is that your 'Agreement' is so clear, so just, and so right that there is no need to discuss it. However, if you will come to the meeting, we shall be able to examine into your 'Agreement,' and therefore I hope you will come and allow us to discuss it."

Capt. Merriman.

One partie feares, That the Kinge will rise by the proposalls, another that hee will loose.

I thinke that most mens eyes are open to see that they are like to prove a broken reede, and that your charriott wheeles doe move heavily, and that this Engagement which is the ground of most of your discourse.[a] You both desire a succession of Parliaments. The fundamentall businesse of itt is the desire of most of this Councill, to have this Parliament that itt might nott be perpetuated and I thinke when.

That this Oedipus riddle is un-open'd, and this Gordian knott untied, and the enemies of the same, and the spiritt of God are the same in both, and the principles of both are the same. You have both promised to free the people, which you may doe by taking off tythes and other Antichristian yoakes uppon them, and [to] give contents to the souldiers, and I hope that when you meete together itt will bee for good, and not for evill.

Buffe-Coate.

Wheras this Gentleman that wee have requested to come alonge with us hath declar'd some parte of their resolutions with us, and wee are resolved that wee will have the peace of the Kingedome if wee can, and yett notwithstanding if a furtherance[b] for the manner of procuring of itt is what God shall direct unto us, I would nott have you judge that wee will deny that Light, till that you know what wee will doe. Noe man can judge soe of any man. A man cannott bee called to bee [of] a peremptory will or self willed, and

[a] Merriman's argument seems to be something like this:

"And I think that when this Oedipus riddle is unopened and this Gordian knot untied, you will find that as to this engagement, which is the ground of most of your discourse, the fundamental business of it is the desire of most of this Council. You both desire a succession of Parliaments, and to have this Parliament that it might not be perpetuated, and the principles of both are the same, and the spirit of God the same in both, and the enemies of both the same. You have both promised to free the people, etc." "Engagement" seems to be a mistake for "Agreement."

[b] Probably should be "further answer" or "further guidance."

and come resolved nolens volens [till you know what he will do]. Wee desire that better thoughts may bee of us.

Lieut. Chillenden.

I hope that these Gentlemen of the Five Regiments their ends are good, and hope their hearts doe tend to peace ; and I shall move this, that they would willingly come to morrow, and joyne with us in our Councills together, and alsoe I shall humbly move, That after wee have sought God in the businesse, that God will make itt out to us, to see wherin wee have failed, and that their being with us, and our vigorous proceeding in itt, and these Gentlemen of the five Regiments they will manifest this by a sweete compliance in communicating Councils.

Lieut. Generall.

That which this Gentleman[a] hath moved I like exceeding well; hee hath fully declar'd himself concerning the freedome of their spiritt as to principles. In generall they aime att peace and safetie, and really I am perswaded in my conscience itt is their aime [to act] as may bee most for the good of the people, for really if that bee nott the supreame [aim][b] of us under God, (the good of the people) our principles fall. Now if that bee in your spiritts and our spiritts, itt remaines onely that God shew us the way, and lead us [in] the way, which I hope hee will. And give mee leave [to add] that there may bee some prejudices uppon some of your spiritts, and [uppon] such men that doe affect your way, that they may have some jealousies and apprehensions that wee are wedded and glewed to formes of Governement; soe that whatsoever wee may pretend, itt is in vaine for [you] to speake to us, or to hope for any agreement from us to you. And I beleive some such apprehensions as [that we are engaged to] some parte of the Legislative power of the Kingdome, where itt may rest besides in the Commons of the Kingedome. You will finde that wee are

[a] *i.e.* "Buffcoat."

[b] MS. good.

farre from being so particularly engaged to anythinge to the prejudice of this—further then the notorious engagements that the world takes notice of—that wee should nott concurre with you that the foundation and supremacy is in the people, radically in them, and to bee sett downe by them in their representations.[a] And if wee doe soe [concur, we may also concur] for that that does remayne, how wee may run to that end that wee all aime att, and therfore lett us onely name the Committee.

Lieut. Col. Goffe.

You were pleased to say that somethinge which should bee offer'd by these Gentlemen[b] gave you another occasion of the Meeting, if itt were onely design'd to lie uppon you. I hope that you did nott conceive, that any such ground did lie in my brest. I would speake this worde to the quickening of us to a good hope. I am verily perswaded if God carry us out to meete sincerely, as with free spiritts to open ourselves before the Lord, wee may bee found going on according to his will. I desire such prejudices may bee laid aside.

Mr. Allen.

A Meeting is intended to morrow; butt that wee may fully end, I would humbly offer to you whether these Gentlemen have a power to debate; and if they have nott, that they may have recourse to them that sent them, to see what [powers] they will give [them], that wee may offer our reasons and judgement uppon the thinge, and act[c] uppon that principle uppon which wee act[c] If wee unite and agree to itt, itt will putt on other thinges. An agreement formally[d] made, wee must bee serious in itt, and to that end that wee

[a] Some people believe we are engaged to maintain the authority of the House of Lords. Waller asserts that Cromwell and Ireton privately entered into an engagement to maintain the rights of the House of Lords in August, 1647, when the nine Lords joined the Army. Vindication, p. 192.

[b] Clause transposed.

[c] Agree?

[d] MS. "formerly."

may have a full debate in itt. Otherwise itt will bee uselesse and endlesse our meeting.

Lieut. Generall.

That Gentleman sayes hee will doe what hee can to draw all or the most of them hither to bee heard to morrow; and I desire Mr. Wildman, that if they have any freinds that are of a loving spiritt, that would contribute to this businesse of a right understanding [they would come with him]. And I say noe more butt this, I pray God judge betweene you and us when wee doe meete, whether wee come with engaged spiritts to uppehold our owne resolutions and opinions, or whether wee shall lay downe ourselves to bee rul'd [by Him] and that which hee shall communicate.

Col. Rainborow.

Hee did tell you hee would improve his interest, which is as full satisfaction to what Mr. Allen sayes as could bee, if they shall come nott to doe, butt I hope they will come to full power, nott to debate. I thinke there needes noe more.[a]

Names of the Committee.

Lieut. Generall.	Col. Okey.
Com̃. Generall.	,, Tichborne.
Col. Rainborow.	Mr. Sexby.
Sir Hardresse Waller.	,, Allen.
Col. Rich.	,, Lockyer.
Adj. Generall Deane.	,, Clarke.
Col. Scrope.	Lt. Generall Hammond.
,, Thomlinson.	Mr. Stenson.
,, Overton.	,, Underwood.

To conferre with the Agitators of the five regiments, and such gentlemen as shall come with them about the "Agreement" now brought in, and their own declarations and engagements.

[a] May be paraphrased: "I hope they will come, if they shall come, with full power not to debate only but to do."

Putney, October 29, 1647.

Att the Meeting of the officers for calling uppon God, according to the appointment of the Generall Councill, after some discourses of Commissary Cowling, Major White, and others.

Capt. Clarke.

Wee have bin heere as wee say seekeing of God, though truly hee is nott farre from every one of us; and wee have said in the presence of God, as out of his presence wee cannott goe, that wee have none in heaven in comparison of him, nor none wee have even in earth in comparison of him. I wish our hearts does nott give us the lie, for truly had that bin a truth, I meane a truth in our carriages, wee should nott have bin soe lost this day. Had wee given eare to the inspiring worde of Christ, and had nott given ourselves to the false prophett within us, certainly God would have kindled that light within us, and [we] should have gone [on] and submitted to his will; and should nott have bin troubled or harassed as wee are with troubles and amazements, butt must have gone with God as hee hath allotted to us. What is the reason that wee finde the light and glory of God eclypsed from our eyes this day? Truly wee may finde this silence within us the cause of every evil sought after;[a] and lett us butt search our owne spiritts with patience, and looke by the light[b] of God within us, and wee shall finde that wee have submitted the spiritt of God unto the candle of reason, whereas reason should have bin subservient unto the spiritt of God. Wee are troubled when our owne reasons tell us, that this is the way, and wee are careless to seeke the way, or that true light Christ in us which is the way. Wee are apt to say, all of us, that if wee seeke that[c] first, the later first, the first[d] will nott bee wanting; butt truly, wee have sought the first last, and therfore the first is wanting, and before this light can take place againe that darke-

[a] Clause transferred from three lines above.

[b] MS. "candle."

[c] *i. e.* "the way."

[d] *i. e.* "the light."

nesse must bee removed. And first within us our lust, that candle of reason,[a] which doth seduce and intice us to wander from God, must bee eaten out of us by the spiritt of God, and when there is noe place for lust, there is place enough for the spiritt of God. If wee shall with resolutions and humility of spiritt nott say, butt doe, as the children of Israell used to doe many times when they were in distresse—many times they cryed unto the Lord—if wee shall doe as wee professe before God this day, that is, lay downe our reason, lay downe our goods, lay downe all wee have att the feete of God, and lett God worke his will in us that wee may bee buried with God in our spiritts; I doubt nott butt the appearances of God will bee more glorious, and I doubt nott butt there will bee that contentednesse in spiritt. Wee should desire noe way, butt waite which way God will lead us. I say, wee should chuse noe way, butt if the spiritt of God lead us, wee should bee ready to submitt to the will of God. And therfore I desire, that, since this is in order to another meeting in the afternoone, wee may lay downe all att the feete of God, nott following our owne reasons, butt submitting unto that light which is lightened in us by his spirit.

After this Capt. Carter prayed.

Adj. Gen. Deane.

Motion for a Meeting att this place, the Quartermaster Generall's Quarters, to meete Monday, the Councill day, from 8 till 11, to seeke God, &c.

Lieut. Col. Goffe.[b]

That which I must now desire to expresse to you was partly occasioned by the thoughts that I had the last night, as being indeed kept awake with them a good while; and, hearing somethinge that did concurre with itt from one that spake since wee came to-

[a] M.S. "that candle of reason, and that first within us our lust."

[b] Goffe was one of the most enthusiastic of the Army leaders, and resembled the Fifth Monarchy men in his views.

gether, I feele some weight uppon my spiritt to expresse itt to you. That which was spoken enow [was] concerning the conjunction that is betweene Antichrist, or that mistery of iniquity in the world carried on by men that call themselves [the] church, that[a] certainly itt is with the conjunction of men in places of power or aucthority in the world, with kinges and great men. And truly my thoughts were much uppon itt this night, and itt appeares to me very clearly from that which God hath sett downe in his worde in the Booke of the Revelations,—which is that worde that wee are bid and commanded to study and to looke into, being the worde which God sent by his Angell to John to declare as thinges shortly to bee done. Now certainly this worke of Antichrist hath bin a worke of great standing, and, as itt was well observ'd, itt hath bin mixt with the church, and men that call themselves the church, the clergie, mixt with men of aucthoritie. Itt is said in the Revelation, that the kinges of the earth should give uppe their power unto the Beast, and the kinges of the earth have given uppe their power to the Pope. Butt some places that have seem'd to deny the Pope's supremacy, yett they have taken uppon them that which hath bin equivalent to that which the Pope himself holds forth. Truly I could bringe itt to this present Kingedome wherin wee are. 'Tis true the kinges have bin instruments to cast off the Pope's supremacy, butt wee may see if they have nott putt themselves into the same state.[b] Wee may see itt in that title which the kinge hath, "Defender of the Faith," butt more especially in that canonicall prayer which the clergie used, "In all causes, and over all persons as well Ecclesiasticall as Civill [supreme]." Certainly, this is a mistery of iniquity. Now Jesus Christ his worke in the last dayes is to destroy this mistery of iniquity; and because itt is so interwoven and intwisted in the interest of States, certainly in that overthrow of the mistery of iniquity by Jesus Christ, there must bee great alterations of states. Now the worde doth hold out in the Revelation, that in this worke of Jesus Christ hee shall have a

[a] MS. "yett."

[b] *i.e.* "into the place of the Pope."

companie of Saints to follow him, such as are chosen, and called, and faithfull.[a] Now itt is a scruple amonge the saints, how farre they should use the sworde, yett God hath made use of them in that worke. Many of them have bin imployed these five or six yeares. Yett whatsoever God shall imploy us in, I could wish this were laid to heart by us, that, as wee would bee called the chosen and faithfull that will follow Christ wheresoever hee goes, lett us tremble att the thought that wee should bee standing in a direct opposition against Jesus Christ in the worke that hee is about. Lett us nott bee twisted amongst such kinde of compartinges where there shall bee a mystery of iniquity sett uppe by outward power, and that wee should bee the instruments of giving any life or strength to that power. And I wish [we may lay this to heart], and I beleive itt may somewhat tend to the worke by the way; because wee are to hold out the will of God for the time to come, and to bee humbled for what wee have done against itt. Lett us inquire whether some of the actions that wee have done of late, some of the thinges that wee have propounded of late, doe nott crosse the worke of God in these particulars; because in our proposing thinges wee doe indeavour to sett uppe that power which God would nott sett uppe againe. Itt hath bin hinted already. I meane in our compliance with that partie which God hath ingaged us to destroy. Wee intended nothing butt civility, butt I wish they were nott in some measure compliances; and if I mistake nott there are ways which God hath laid open to us, wherby wee may lay aside that compliance.

Butt this is nott all that I would speake, because God hath called forth my spiritt to unity. What wee doe according to the will of God will nott tend to division. This I speake concerning compliance may bee thought to reflect uppon some particular persons more then other some, soe on the other hand I desire to speake somethinge that may concerne some persons that may stand, or att least may seeme to stand, in direct opposition to us; and truly I wish wee may bee very wary what wee doe, and lett

[a] See Revelation, chaps. xvii., xviii., xix., xx., especially chap. xvii., verses 13, 14.

us take heede of rejecting any of the saints of God before God rejects them. If God bee pleased to shew any of his servants that hee hath made use of as great instruments in his hand as those that God hath blest in them, that God hath blest them, and this hath bin the greatest instrument of the ruine of sin and corruption in this Army. Lett us bee wary and consider what wee have to doe in that kinde; and I spake this the rather because I was sensible of some personall reflections that did nott argue the workinges of God [so much] as the workinges of passions in us. Now the worke of the spiritt is, that wee doe pull downe all workes [not] of the spiritt whatsoever; and therfore I desire that as in the presence of God wee may take heede of all thinges which may tend to dissunion, and that wee may nott despise those who may have some thinges in their hands to contribute for the worke of God. And there is another thinge: if wee have lost the opportunity of appearing against enemies, lett us take heede, when wee bee sensible of God's displeasure, that wee doe nott run before hee bids us goe a 2[d] time. There is a place which is very remarkable, Numbers xiv., where the spies were sent to the Land of Canaan; and when they came back the hearts of the people were discouraged. God was displeased att this, and hee discover'd itt in some such way as hee did this day. Uppon a suddaine there was a partie that would goe uppe, and fight against the Amalekites; and att such a time when God would nott have them goe uppe. "Though you did sin against the Lord in nott going att first," sayes Moses, "yett goe nott now uppe, for the Lord is nott amonge you, that yee bee nott smitten before your enemies."[a] Yett they did goe uppe unto the Hill Toppe, and were discomfited. I thinke wee have sinned in that wee did nott shew our courage and faithfulnesse to God. Lett us nott now in a kinde of heate run uppe and say, "wee will goe now;" because itt may bee there is a better opportunity that God will give us. And that wee may a little helpe us by our owne experiences, lett us remember how

[a] Numbers, xiv., 41, 42.

God hath dealt with this Army in our late proceedinges. There was some heavinesse in our proceedinges before the Citty,[a] as was thought by some; and itt was said by many, "Goe uppe, Goe uppe quicklie, and doe our worke." Butt lett us remember that God found a better season for us, then if wee had gone att first. Lett us consider whether this bee the best juncture of time for us to declare, and to throw off some of our freinds, when that they would have itt discover'd whether[b] God goes alonge with us. Lett this bee consider'd, that soe wee may bee humbled on the one hand, and breake off all unlawfull compliance with the enemies of God, soe on the other hand wee may stay, and take the company one of another, or rather the presence of God, [alonge with us]. And soe for the worke of the day, I wish there may bee a day of union amongst us; for itt may bee itt is the will of God that wee should waite uppon him therin to see what will bee the issue of a businesse that is now transacted; and if wee can trust God in this strait wee shall see him straight before us, if wee can bee of one minde. I wish this may bee consider'd, and if there be anythinge of God in itt, itt may be received.

Mr. Everard.[c]

This honourable Councill hath given mee great incouragement. Though I have many impediments in my speach, yett I thanke you that you will heare mee speake. I engaged myself yesterday to bringe the men to have a debate, and for that purpose I have prosecuted these my promises, and I have bin with them as many as I can finde; butt the most of them are dispersed, soe that I lost that opportunity which I would have enjoyed; butt neverthelesse I hope you will take itt kindlie, that those that were there are

[a] Goffe refers to the debate of July 16, pp. 176-211.

[b] MS. "that."

[c] Everard was evidently the trooper before referred to as "buff-coat." Robert Everard of Cromwell's regiment was one of the signatories of the "Letter to the freeborn people of England," published with the agreement. There were several Everards in the Army, *v.* Reliquiae Baxterianae, p. 78.

come hither, and those two freinds that were with mee yesterday. Our ends are that wee desire yett once more a compliance in those thinges that wee propounded to you, butt if itt shall please God to open our eyes that wee can see itt, wee shall comply with you. For our desires are nothing butt (according to our first Declaration,)[a] to follow our worke to deliver the Kingedome from that burthen that lies uppon us. For my parte I am butt a poore man, and unacquainted with the affaires of the Kingedome, yett this message God hath sent mee to you, that there is great expectation of suddaine destruction; and I would bee loath to fill uppe that with words. Wee desire your joynct consent to seeke out some speedy way for the releif of the Kingedome.

Lieut. Generall,

I thinke itt would nott bee amisse that those Gentlemen that are come would draw nigher.

I must offer this to your consideration, whether or noe wee, having sett aparte this morning to seeke God, and to gett such a preparednesse of heart and spiritt as might receive that, that God was minded to have imparted to us, and this having taken uppe all our time, all this day, and itt having bin soe late this last night as indeed itt was when wee brake uppe, and wee having appointed a committee to meete together to consider of that paper, and this Committee having had noe time or opportunity that I know of, nott soe much as a meeting, I make some scruple or doubt whether or noe itt is nott better,—[I know] that danger is imagined [near at hand], and indeed I thinke itt is,—butt bee the danger what itt will, our agreement in the businesse is much more [pressing] then the pressing of any danger, soe by that wee doe nott delay too.—That which I have to offer [is], whether or noe wee are [as] fitt to take uppe such a consideracion of these papers now as wee might bee to-morrow. Perhaps if these Gentlemen, which are butt few, and that Committee should meete together, and spend their time

[a] The Army's Declaration of June 14, 1647.

together an houre or two the remainder of this afternoone, and all this company might meete about 9 or 10 a clock att furthest, and they [might] understand one another soe well, as wee might bee prepared for the generall meeting to have a more exact and particular consideration of thinges then [we can have] by a generall loose debate of thinges, which our Committee or att least many [a] of us have [not] had any, or att least nott many thoughts about.

Col. Rainborow,

Sir. I am sorry that the ill disposition of my body caused mee to goe to London last night, and [hindered me] from coming soe soone this morning as to bee with you in the duty you were about. Butt I hope that which hath bin said att this time, which I hope is a truth and sent from God, will soe worke uppon mee that I shall indeavour att least to carry my self soe that I may use all that interest I have to a right and quick understanding betweene us. And truly, Sir, to that present motion that hath bin made I confesse I have nothing against itt, butt onely the danger that lies uppon us; which truly (if wee may have leave to differ one from another) may in a moment overcome [us]. I hope wee shall all take one worde that was spoken to us by Lieut. Col. Goffe, and I thinke that nothing will conduce soe much [to union as] that wee may have noe personall reflections. I thinke itt would have bin well if the Committee had mett, butt since all this company, or the greatest parte of them that have bin heere, have joyn'd in that duty which was on the former parte of the morning, I thinke there is nott much inconveniency that they may spend the other parte of the day with us. [That] if wee were satisfied ourselves uppon debate, and there should bee one partie, or one sort of men that are of a contrary judgement present, or others that should come over to us, itt would heerafter cost some time to know the reasons of their coming over. Therfore I thinke itt an advantage that it should

[a] MS. "any."

bee as publique, and as many as may bee present att itt. The debating this thus publiquely may bee an advantage unto us, and if wee finde at [a] after the multitude of people that are heere (that have bin spoken to) if wee finde that inconvenient, I doe nott doubt butt the Committee, when this company breakes uppe, may have two houres time together. Therefore I should desire, that since the Gentlemen and you are mett together to such an end and purpose, that you will follow to that end.

Mr. Everard.

That itt is not [fit] as I conceive to dispute any thing touching particulars, for all as I conceive doe seeke the kingedome's good. Lett us goe about the work, noe question butt we shall goe together. Butt if wee stand disputing the worke, much business will be. I desire this honourable Councill will pardon mee to make out some speedy way for the easing of us. I beseech you that you will let us now consider uppon that. I believe wee shall jumpe all in one with itt. If wee doe nott fall upon some extraordinary wayes between—Some lawes with us that will prick us to the heart, wee must winke att them, nott that I desire that wee should seeke to ruinate any wholesome lawes, butt such as will nott stand with the wholesome peace of the Kingedome.[b]

Capt. Awdeley.

I shall desire to second that Gentleman's motion. That while wee debate wee doe nothing. I am confident that whilest you are doing you will all agree together, for itt is idlenesse that hath begott this rust, and this gangreene amongst us.

Lieut. Generall.

I thinke itt is true. Lett us bee doing, butt lett us bee united

[a] MS. "that."

[b] In the MS. Everard's speech is extremely confused, as fragments of different sentences are mixed together. Three clauses have been moved.

in our doing. If there remayne nothing else butt present action,[a] I thinke wee neede nott bee in Councill heere.[a] Butt if wee doe nott rightly and clearly understand one another before wee come to act, if wee doe nott lay a foundation of action before wee doe act, I doubt whether wee shall act unanimously or noe. And seriously, as before the Lord, I knew noe such end of our speech the last night, and appointing another Meeting, butt in order to a more perfect understanding of one another, what wee should doe, and that wee might bee agreed uppon some principalls of action. And truly if I remember rightly, uppon the delivery of the paper that was yesterday, this was offer'd, that the thinges [that] are now uppon us are thinges of difficulty, the thinges are therfore thinges that doe deserve consideration, because there might bee great weight in the consequences; and itt was then offer'd, and I hope is still soe in all our hearts, that wee are nott troubled with the consideration of the difficulty, nor with the consideration of any thinge butt this; that if wee doe difficult thinges wee may see that the thinges wee doe have the will of God in them, that they are nott onely plausible and good thinges but seasonable and honest thinges fitt for us to doe. And therfore itt was desir'd that wee might consider, before wee could come to these papers, in what condition wee stood in respect of former Engagements, however some may bee satisfied that there lie none uppon us, or none butt such as itt's duty to breake, itt's sin to keepe. Therefore that was yesterday premised [that] there may bee a consideration had of them—and I may speake itt as in the presence of God that I know nothing of any Engagements, butt I would see liberty in any man as I would bee free from bondage to any thinge that should hinder mee from doing my duty—and therfore that was first in consideration. If our obligation bee nothing, or if itt bee weake, I hope itt will receive satisfaction why itt should bee laid aside, that the thinges that wee speake of are nott obliged. And therfore if itt

[a] The MS. inserts after "action," "I meane doing in that kind, doing in that sort," and after "heere," "such kind of action, action of that nature."

please you I thinke itt will bee good for us to frame our discourse to what wee were, where wee are, what wee are bound to, what wee are free to; and then I make noe question, butt that this may conclude what is betweene these Gentlemen in one afternoone. I doe nott speake this to make obligations more then what they were before; butt as before the Lord. You see what they are,[a] and when wee looke uppon them wee shall see if[b] we have bin in a wronge way, and I hope itt will call uppon us for the more double diligence.

Col. Rainborow.

I shall desire a word or two before that. I did exceedingly mistake myself the last night that uppon what wee say now was determined.[c] I look't uppon the Committee as a Committee to looke over this paper, to see whether itt were a paper that did hold forth justice and righteousnesse, whether itt were a paper that honest men could close with. Butt truly I am of opinion that if wee should spend ten dayes time in going over that Booke, and debate what Engagements wee have broke, or whether wee have broke any or noe, or whether we have kept our Engagements, itt would nott come to the businesse, neither would itt prevent that evill that I thinke will overtake us before wee fall into the right way,[d] unlesse God in abundant manner prevent;—and I could give you reasons for itt which this day I have from very good hands, and which I think is not prudent to declare soe publicly as this is.—Lett us goe the quickest way to worke; and truly, Sir, I have thought that the wounds of the Kingedome, and the difficulties that wee are falne into, and our cure is become soe great that wee would bee willing all of us to heale the sore, and [not] to skin itt over butt leave itt unwholesome and corrupt att the bottome.

[a] Cromwell at this point seems to have produced the book of *Army Declarations*, printed by Matthew Simmons in September, 1647.

[b] MS. "that."

[c] *i. e.* "that which you say now was then determined upon."

[d] Transferred from two lines below.

Therefore for my parte I doe conclude in my spiritt, for my owne parte I [did] say this yesterday uppon another occasion, I will nott say positively that wee are to take the course prescribed in that paper att present, butt if wee doe nott sett uppon the worke— Since in order to that there is a thinge call'd an Agreement which the people have subscribed, and being that is ready to our hands, I desire that you would reade itt and debate itt, whether itt bee a way to deliver us yett or noe; and if itt bee . . . . [that you would accept it], and if nott that you would thinke of some other way.

Lieut. Generall.

I shall butt offer this to you. Truly I hope that wee may speake our hearts freelie heere; and I hope that there is nott such an evill amongst us as that wee could or would exercise our witts, or our cunning to vaile over any doublenesse of heart that may possibly bee in us. I hope, having bin in such a presence as wee have bin this day, wee doe nott admitt of such a thought as this into our hearts. And therfore if the speaking of that wee did speake before, and to which I shall speake againe, with submission to all that heare mee—if the declining to consider this paper may have with any man a working[a] uppon his spiritt through any jealousie that itt aimes att delay; truly I can speake itt as before the Lord itt is nott att all in my heart, butt sincerely this is the ground of itt. I know this paper doth contayne many good thinges in itt, butt this is the onely thinge that doth stick with mee, the desiring to know my freedome to this thinge. Though this doth suggest that that may bee the bottome of all our evills— and I will nott say against itt because I doe nott thinke against itt—though this doth suggest the bottome of all our evills, yett for all of us to see our selves free to this [so] as wee may unanimously joyne uppon this, either to agree to this, or to adde more to itt, [or] to alter [it] as wee shall agree, this impediment lies in our

[a] MS. "worke."

way, [even] if every man bee satisfied with itt butt my self. That this is the first thinge that is to bee consider'd, that wee should consider in what condition wee stand to our former obligations, that if wee bee cleare wee may goe off cleare, if nott wee may nott goe on. If I bee nott come off [clear] with what obligations are made, if I bee nott free to act to whatsoever you shall agree uppon, I thinke this is my duty: that I should nott in the least study either to retard your worke or hinder itt, or to act against itt, butt wish you as much successe as if I were free to act with you. I desire wee may view over our obligations and Engagements, that soe wee may bee free [to act together] uppon honest and cleare grounds, if this bee [possible].

My desire —— (Col. Rainborow offering to speake.)

Lieut. Gen.

I have butt one worde to prevent you in, and that is for imminent danger. Itt may bee possibly soe [imminent] that [it] may nott admitt of an houres debate, nor nothing of delay. If that bee soe, I thinke that's above all law and rule to us.

Col. Rainborow.

I would offer one worde, for I thinke this will bringe us to noe issue att all. Both yesterday and to-day, and divers times, wee have had cautions given us to have care of divisions. I doe speake itt to avoide devision; that wee may nott att this time consider the Engagements. If you, or any other Gentlemen, are of opinion that you have nott broke them, and then some others are of opinion that you have broke them, wee may fall into contests which may occasion devision. Butt if you reade this, and finde it not against the Engagement, that will bee the worke. If it be nott against the Engagement, you will finde that in itt which you will finde from your Engagements, and I have somethinge to say to the particulars in itt.

Com̃: Cowling.

I shall onely offer this, the necessity of expedition if the people shall consider the necessities that they and we are in. Wee live now uppon free-quarter, and wee have that against our wills.[a] Those that know what belonges to Armies well know, none are to quarter souldiers, butt those that are within soe many miles; and if soe bee too that the owner of the house should refuse to open his doores wee are prevented to pay our quarters by those that might have supplyed us. I have seene this paper, and uppon second reading of itt I sett my hand to itt, that wee may nott lie as drones to devoure their families. I am ready where I am called by my superiours. If nott, the Lord bee mercifull to mee.

Major White.[b]

I should offer one worde to this Councill: I thinke itt is in all our mindes to deliver the Kingdome; if there bee particular engagements wee must lay them downe to lay downe publique good.

Lieut. Generall.

I desire to know what the Gentleman meanes concerning particular Engagements; if hee meanes those that are in this Booke? If those that are in this booke [they are the engagements of the Army]. Butt if hee meanes Engagements personall from particular persons, lett every man speake for himselfe. I speake for myself, I disavowe all, and I am free to act, free from any such ——

Major White.

I conceive that [if] they bee such as are past by the Representative[c] of the Army, I thinke the Army is bound in conscience to goe on with them.

[a] See the *Case of the Army Truly Stated*, p. 9.

[b] Can hardly be Major Francis White, as he had been expelled from the Council.

[c] The Representative of the Army, *i. e.*, the General Council established in pursuance of the Engagement of June 5, 1647, consisting of those general officers who

Col. Hewson.

All the Engagements that have bin declar'd for have bin by the Representative of the Army, and whether or noe that hath nott bin the cause of this cloude that hanges over our heads. I thinke if wee lay our hands over our hearts wee may nott much mistake itt.

Mr. Pettus.

According to your Honours desires yesterday, I am come in heere to give in my reasons why I doe approve of this paper, this Agreement, [and] to receive reasons why itt should nott bee agreed to. For the particular Engagements of the Army I am ignorant of them, butt, if itt please this Councill to lett this bee read, that either the matter or manner of itt may bee debated; and when any of the matter shall come to touch uppon any Engagement so as to breake any Engagement, that then the Engagement may bee showne; and if that Engagement shall prove just, and this unjust, this must bee rejected, or if this just, and these Engagements unjust [then they must be rejected]. I desire all those that are free from itt in their spiritts may act farther; and those that thinke themselves bound uppe soe[a] to acquiesce in itt, as that they would bee pleased to rest satisfied in the actions of other men that are att libertie to act for the peace and freedome of the Kingedome.

Com̃. Generall.

Truly I would, if I did know of any personall, particular Engagements, if I were personally or particularly engaged myself, which I professe, as in the presence of God, I know nott for myself.[b] I myself am nott under any Engagement in relation to that businesse that the great Question lies uppon—I neede nott name itt—more then what all men know that have seene and read, and in the Armie

had concurred in that engagement together with two commission officers and two privates for each regiment.

[a] MS. "soe as to acquiesce in it."

[b] MS. "for I know nott myself."

consented to, those thinges that were published. Butt if I were under any particular Engagement, itt should nott att all stand in any other man's way. If I were under [any particular engagement] I say, that I could bee convinc't of was ill and unlawfull for mee to enter into, my Engagement should nott stand in any other man's way that would doe any thinge that I could bee convinc't of to bee better. And till God hath brought us all to that temper of spiritt that wee can bee contented to bee nothing in our reputations, [in our] esteemes, in our power—truly I may goe a little higher and say, till the reputation and honour of the Army and such thinges become nothing to us, nott soe as to [let] the consideration of them, to stand att all in the way to hinder us from what wee see God calling us to, or to prompt us on to what wee have nott a cleare call from him—wee are nott brought to that temper wherin I can expect any renewing of that presence of God that wee have sought. Therfore for my parte I professe first, I desire noe [particular] Engagements [may be considered]. If there were particular Engagements of any particular man whatsoever, as to the leading of the Army one way or other, I desire they may nott bee consider'd; butt lett that man looke to himself for what justice lies uppon him, and what justice will follow him. Neither doe I care for the Engagements of the Army soe much for the Engagements [a] sake, butt I looke uppon this Army as having carried with itt hitherto the name of God, and having carried with it hitherto the interest of the people of God, and the interest which is God's interest, the honour of his name, the good, and freedome, and safetie, and happinesse of his people. And for my parte I thinke that itt is that that is the onely thinge for which God hath appeared with us, and led us, and gone before us, and honoured us, and taken delight to worke by us. I say, that very thinge, that wee have carried the name of God, and I hope nott in shew butt in reallity, professing to act, and to worke, as wee have thought in our judgements and consciences, [with] God to lead us;

[a] MS. "Armie's."

professing to act to those ends that wee have thought to bee answerable and suitable to the minde of God, soe farre as itt hath bin knowne to us. Wee have professed to indeavour to follow the councells of God, and to have him President in our Councills; and I hope itt hath bin soe in our hearts. That wee have bin ready to follow his guidance; and I know itt hath bin soe in many thinges against our owne reasons, where wee have seene evidently God calling us. That wee have bin carried on with a confidence in him, wee have made him our trust, and wee have held forth his name, and wee have owned his hand towards us. These are the thinges I say which God hath in some degree and measure wrought his people in this Army uppe to, in some degree of sincerity; and this itt is, as I said before, that I account hath bin [the cause] that God hath taken delight in, amongst us, to dwell with us, to bee with us, and to appeare with us, and will manifest his presence to us. And therefore by this meanes, and by that appearance of God amongst us, the name and honour of God, the name and reputation of the people of God, and of that Gospell that they professe, is deeply, and dearly, and nearly concern'd in the good or ill manage of this Army, in their good or ill carriage; and therfore for my parte I professe itt, that's the onely thinge to mee. [It is] nott to mee soe much as the vainest, or lightest thinge you can imagine, whether there bee a kinge in England, or noe, whether there bee Lords in England or noe. For whatever I finde the worke of God tending to I should desire quietly to submitt to. If God saw itt good to destroy, nott only Kinge and Lords, butt all distinctions of degrees—nay if itt goe further, to destroy all property, that there's noe such thinge left, that there bee nothing att all of Civill Constitution left in the Kingedome—if I see the hand of God in itt I hope I shall with quietnesse acquiesce, and submitt to itt, and nott resist itt. Butt still I thinke that God certainly will soe leade those that are his, and I hope too hee will soe lead this Army that they may nott incurre sin, or bring scandall uppon the name of God, and the name of the people of God that are both soe neerly concern'd in what this Army does. And therfore itt is my wish, uppon those grounds that I before declar'd which made the consideration of this Army deare and tender to mee,[a] that wee may take heede, [that] wee consider first Engagements, soe farre as they are Engagements publiquely of the Army. I doe nott speake of particular [engagements] I would nott have them consider'd, if there bee any. And secondly I would have us consider of this: that our wayes and workinges and actinges, and the actings of the Army, soe farre as the Councills of those prevaile in itt who have anythinge of the spiritt of Jesus Christ may appeare suitable to that spiritt. And as I would not have this Army in relation to those great concernements (as I said before) the honour of God, and the honour and good name of his people and of religion, as I would nott have itt to incurre the scandall of neglecting Engagements, and laying aside all consideration of Engagements, and of jugling, and deceiving, and deluding the world, making them beleive thinges in times of extreamity which they never meant, soe I would nott have us to give the world occasion to thinke that wee are the disturbers of the peace of mankinde. I say, I would nott give them just occasion to thinke soe; nay I would have them have just cause to thinke that wee seeke peace with all men, and wee seeke the good of all men, and wee seeke the destruction of none that wee can say; and in generall I would wish and study, and that my hearte is bent to, that the Councills of this Army may appeare acted by that wisedome that is from above, which wee know how itt is charact'd. Itt is first pure, and then peaceable, and then gentle, and easie to bee intreated, and wee finde many characters of the same wisedome, and other fruites of the same spiritt that all still run clearlie that way. Therfore I say, I wish that wee may have noe otherwise a consideration of Engagements or any thinge of that nature. That which makes mee presse itt is cheiflie, that consideracion of the concernement of the honour of

[a] Two lines moved from the previous sentence, and several words omitted.

God and his people in the Army; and as I prize them soe I press[a] that in all things whatsoever, though wee were free and had noe Engagements, we doe act as Christians, as men guided by the spiritt of God, as men having that wisedome [that is] from above, and [is] soe characteriz'd.

To the method of our proceeding. Having exprest what I desire may bee all our cares, I cannott but thinke that this will bee clearest, because I see it is soe much prest and insisted uppon: nott [to go][b] to read what our Engagements are, butt [to] read the paper that is presented heere, and consider uppon it, what good, and what matter of justice and righteousnesse there is in itt, and whether there bee anythinge of injustice or unrighteousnesse, either in itt self, or in reference to our Engagements. Soe farre I thinke our Engagements ought to bee taken into consideration: that soe farre as wee are engaged to a thinge that was nott unlawfull to engage to, and I should bee sad to thinke them soe, wee should thinke ourselves bound nott to act contrary to those Engagements. And that wee may consider of the particulars of this paper, first, whether they bee good and just, that is, nott ill, nott unjust; and then further to consider whether they bee soe essentially due and right as that they should bee contended for, for then that is some kinde of checke to lesse Engagements; and for such thinges, if wee finde any, light Engagements [may] bee cast off and nott consider'd.[c] Butt if wee finde any matter in them that, though itt bee just, though itt bee good, is nott probable to bee soe beneficiall and advantageous, nott to few, butt to many, that withall wee may consider whether itt bee soe much a duty, and wee bee soe much bound to itt by the thinge itt self as that noe Engagement can take us from itt. And[d] if wee finde any thinges that, if they bee just or good, [are] yett nott soe obligatorie or of [such] necessity to the Kingedome, [but that] the Kingedome may stand without them, then I thinke itt being [so] nott absolutely lawfull to act for them.

[a] MS. "prize all wheresoever."
[b] MS. "going."
[c] The last sixteen words are transferred from six lines lower.
[d] MS. "but."

Major Rainborow.

I desire wee may come to that end wee all strive after. I humbly desire you will fall uppon that which is the Engagement of all, which is the rights and freedomes of the people, and lett us see how farre wee have made sure to them a right and freedome, and if any thinge bee tendred as to that. And when that Engagement is gone through then lett us consider of those that are of greater weight.

The Paper called the Agreement read.

Afterwards the first Article read by itt self.[a]

Commissary Ireton.

The exception that lies in itt is this. Itt is said: "The pecple of England" etc. . . . . they are to bee distributed "according to the number of the inhabitants;" and this doth make mee thinke that the meaning is, that every man that is an inhabitant is to bee equally consider'd, and to have an equall voice in the election of

[a] The first article is, "That the people of England, being at this day very unequally distributed by Counties, Cities, and Burroughs, for the election of their Deputies in Parliament ought to be more indifferently proportioned, according to the number of the Inhabitants; the circumstances whereof, for number, place, and manner, are to be set down before the end of this present Parliament."

The supporters of the Agreement, as the debate shows, advocated manhood suffrage. Ireton however, and those responsible for the "Heads of the Proposals of the Army," published in August, had merely advocated more equal electoral districts.

"That the Elections of the Commons for succeeding Parliaments may be distributed to all counties, or other parts or divisions of the Kingdom, according to some rule of equality or proportion, so as all Counties may have a number of Parliament Members allowed to their choice, proportionable to the respective rates they bear in the common charges and burthens of the Kingdome, or according to some other rule of equalitie or proportion, to render the House of Commons as near as may be an equall representative of the whole; and in order thereunto, that a present consideration be had to take off the Elections of Burgesses for poor, decayed, or inconsiderable townes, and to give some present addition to the number of Parliament Members for great counties, that have now less than their due proportion, to bring all at present, as neer as may be, to such a rule of proportion as aforesaid."

the representors, those persons that are for the Generall Representative; and if that bee the meaning then I have somethinge to say against itt. But if itt bee onely that those people, that by the Civill Constitution of this kingedome, which is originall and fundamentall, and beyond which I am sure noe memory of record does goe—(Nott before the Conquest).[a] Butt before the Conquest itt was soe. Iff itt bee intended, that those that by that Constitution that was before the Conquest, that hath bin beyond memory, such persons that have bin before [by] that Constitution [the electors], should be [still] the electors, I have noe more to say against itt.

Col. Rainborow.

Moved, That others might have given their hands to itt.

Capt. Denne.

Denied, That those that were sett of their Regiment that they were their hands.

Commissary Ireton.

Whether those men whose hands are to itt, or those that brought itt, doe know soe much of the matter, as [to know whether] they meane that all that had a former right of election [are to be electors], or [whether] those that had noe right before are to come in?

Commissary Cowling.

In the time before the Conquest, and since the Conquest, the greatest parte of the Kingedome was in vassalage.

Mr. Pettus.

Wee judge that all inhabitants that have nott lost their birthright should have an equall voice in Elections.

Col. Rainborow.

I desir'd that those that had engaged in itt [should speak] for

[a] I take these words to be the remark of some interruptor, probably Cowling.

really I thinke that the poorest hee that is in England hath a life to live as the greatest hee; and therfore truly, Sir, I thinke itt's cleare, that every man that is to live under a Governement ought first by his owne consent to putt himself under that Governement; and I doe thinke that the poorest man in England is nott att all bound in a stricte sence to that Governement that hee hath not had a voice to putt himself under; and I am confident that when I have heard the reasons against itt, somethinge will bee said to answer those reasons, insoemuch that I should doubt whether he[a] was an Englishman or noe that should doubt of these thinges.

Commissary Ireton.

That's [the meaning of] this [" according to the number of the inhabitants."]

Give mee leave to tell you, that if you make this the rule I thinke you must flie for refuge to an absolute naturall Right, and you must deny all Civill Right; and I am sure itt will come to that in the consequence. This I perceive is prest as that which is soe essentiall and due,—the right of the people of this Kingedome, and as they are the people of this Kingedome, distinct and devided from other people,—as that wee must for this right lay aside all other considerations; this is soe just, this is soe due, this is soe right to them. And that those that they doe thus chuse must have such a power of binding all, and loosing all, according to those limitations; this is prest, as soe due, and soe just as [it] is argued, that itt is an Engagement paramount [to] all others: and you must for itt lay aside all others; if you have engaged any others you must breake itt. [We must] soe looke uppon these as thus held out to us; soe itt was held out by the Gentleman that brought itt yesterday. For my parte I thinke itt is noe right att all. I thinke that noe person hath a right to an interest or share in the disposing or determining of the affaires of the Kingdome, and in chusing those that shall determine what lawes wee shall bee rul'd

[a] MS. " I."

by heere, noe person hath a right to this, that hath nott a permanent fixed interest in this Kingedome; and those persons together are properly the Represented of this Kingedome, and consequentlie are to make uppe the Representors of this Kingedome, who taken together doe comprehend whatsoever is of reall or permanent interest in the Kingedome. And I am sure I cannott tell what otherwise any man can say why a forraigner coming in amongst us—or as many as will coming in amongst us, or by force or otherwise setling themselves heere, or att least by our permission having a being heere—why they should nott as well lay claime to itt as any other. Wee talke of birthright. Truly [by] birthright there is thus much claime. Men may justly have by birthright, by their very being borne in England, that wee should nott seclude them out of England, that wee should nott refuse to give them aire, and place, and ground, and the freedome of the high wayes and other thinges, to live amongst us; nott [to] any man that is borne heere, though by his birth there come nothing att all to him that is parte of the permanent interest of this Kingedome. That I thinke is due to a man by birth. Butt that by a man's being borne heere hee shall have a share in that power that shall dispose of the lands heere, and of all thinges heere, I doe nott thinke itt a sufficient ground. I am sure if wee looke uppon that which is the utmost within man's view of what was originally the constitution of this Kingedome, [if wee] looke uppon that which is most radicall and fundamentall, and which if you take away there is noe man hath any land, any goods, [or] any civill interest, that is this: that those that chuse the Representors for the making of Lawes by which this State and Kingedome are to bee govern'd, are the persons who taken together doe comprehend the locall interest of this Kingedome; that is, the persons in whome all land lies, and those in Corporations in whome all trading lies. This is the most fundamentall Constitution of this Kingedome, which if you doe nott allow you allow none att all. This Constitution hath limitted and determined itt that onely those shall have voices in

Elections. Itt is true as was said by a Gentleman[a] neere mee, the meanest man in England ought to have [a voice in the election of the government he lives under]. . . . I say this, that those that have the the meanest locall interest, that man that hath butt fourty shillinges a yeare, hee hath as great voice in the Election of a Knight for the shire as hee that hath ten thousand a yeare or more, if hee had never soe much; and therfore there is that regard had to itt. Butt this still the Constitution of this Governement hath had an eye to —— and what other Governement hath nott an eye to this? Itt doth nott relate to the interest of the Kingedome, if itt doe nott lay the foundation of the power that's given to the Representors in those who have a permanent and a locall interest in the Kingedome, and who taken altogether doe comprehend the whole [interest of this kingdom]. If wee shall goe to take away this fundamentall parte of the civill constitution wee shall plainly goe to take away all property and interest that any man hath, either in land by inheritance, or in estate by possession, or any thinge else. There is all the reason and justice that can bee if I will come to live in a Kingedome being a forraigner to itt, or live in a Kingedome having noe permanent interest in itt—if I will desire as a stranger, or claime as one freeborne heere, the ayre, the free passage of highwayes, the protection of lawes and all such things, if I will either desire them, or claime them, I (if I have noe permanent interest in that Kingdome), must submitt to those lawes and those rules which those shall choose who taken together doe comprehend the whole interest of the Kingedome.[b]

Col. Rainborow,

Truly, Sir, I am of the same opinion I was; and am resolved to keepe itt till I know reason why I should nott. I confesse my memory is bad, and therfore I am faine to make use of my penne.

[a] Rainborow.

[b] *i. e.*, "the laws and rule of those;" or possibly "the laws and rule which those shall choose who taken together," etc.

I remember that in a former speech[a] this Gentleman brought before this, hee was saying, that in some cases hee should nott value whether [there were] a Kinge or noe Kinge, whether Lords or noe Lords, whether a property or noe property. For my parte I differ in that. I doe very much care whether [there be] a Kinge or noe Kinge, Lords or noe Lords, property or noe property; and I thinke iff wee doe nott all take care wee shall all have none of these very shortly. Butt as to this present businesse. I doe heare nothing att all that can convince mee, why any man that is borne in England ought nott to have his voice in Election of Burgesses. Itt is said, that if a man have nott a permanent interest, hee can have noe claime, and wee must bee noe freer then the lawes will lett us to bee, and that there is noe Chronicle will lett us bee freer then that wee enjoy. Something was said to this yesterday. I doe thinke that the maine cause why Almighty God gave men reason, itt was, that they should make use of that reason, and that they should improve itt for that end and purpose that God gave itt them.[b] And truly, I thinke that halfe a loafe is better then none if a man bee an hungry, yett I thinke there is nothing that God hath given a man that any else can take from him. Therfore I say, that either itt must bee the law of God or the law of man that must prohibite the meanest man in the Kingdome to have this benefitt[c] as well as the greatest. I doe nott finde any thinge in the law of God, that a Lord shall chuse 20 Burgesses, and a Gentleman butt two, or a poore man shall chuse none. I finde noe such thinge in the law of nature, nor in the law of nations. Butt I doe finde, that all Englishmen must bee subject to English lawes, and I doe verily beleive, that there is noe man butt will say, that the foundation of all law lies in the people, and if [it

[a] p. 296.

[b] A vote, the right of exercising his reason by electing a representative.

[c] Rainborow's argument seems to be, "God gave man reason that he might use it, and though the poorest man may have no property yet he has his reason and he was meant to use it. It may be a small right but it is something, and you are not justified in taking from him any right God has given him." See the same argument stated by the agitators. *Case of the Army stated*, p. 21.

lie] in the people, I am to seeke for this exemption. And truly I have thought somethinge [else], in what a miserable distressed condition would many a man that hath fought for the Parliament in this quarrell bee? I will bee bound to say, that many a man whose zeale and affection to God and this Kingedome hath carried him forth in this cause hath soe spent his estate that in the way the State, the Army are going hee shall nott hold uppe his head; and when his estate is lost, and nott worth 40s. a yeare, a man shall nott have any interest;[a] and there are many other wayes by which estates men have doe fall to decay, if that bee the rule which God in his providence does use. A man when hee hath an estate hath an interest in making lawes, when hee hath none, hee hath noe power in itt. Soe that a man cannott loose that which hee hath for the maintenance of his family, butt hee must loose that which God and nature hath given him. Therfore I doe [think] and am still of the same opinion; that every man born in England cannot, ought nott, neither by the law of God nor the law of nature, to bee exempted from the choice of those who are to make lawes, for him to live under, and for him, for ought I know, to loose his life under. Therfore I thinke there can bee noe great sticke in this.

Truly I thinke that there is nott this day raigning in England a greater fruite or effect of Tyranny then this very thinge would produce. Truly I know nothing free butt onely the Knight of the shire, nor doe I know any thinge in a Parliamentary way that is cleare from the heighth and fulnesse of Tyranny, but onlie [that]. As for this of Corporations itt is as contrary to freedome as may bee. For, Sir, what is itt? The Kinge hee grants a patent under the Broad-seale of England to such a Corporation to send Burgesses, hee grants to [such] a Citty to send Burgesses.[b] When a poore, base, Corporation from the Kinge['s grant] shall send two Burgesses, when 500 men of estate shall nott send one, when those

[a] Any fixed interest to entitle him to a vote.

[b] The position of the last two sentences has been altered.

that are to make their lawes are called by the Kinge, or cannott act [but] by such a call, truly I thinke that the people of England have little freedome.

Commissary Gen. Ireton.

I thinke there was nothing that I said to give you occasion to thinke that I did contend for this, that such a Corporation [as that] should have the electing of a man to the Parliament. I think I agreed to this matter, that all should bee equallie distributed. Butt the question is, whether itt should bee distributed to all persons, or whether the same persons that are the electors [now] should bee the Electors still, and itt [be] equallie distributed amongst them.[a] I doe nott see any body else that makes this objection; and if noe body else bee sensible of itt I shall soone have done. Onely I shall a little crave your leave to represent the consequences of itt, and cleare my self from one thinge that was misrepresented by the Gentleman that satt next mee. I thinke if the Gentleman remember himself hee cannott butt remember, that what I said was to this effect:[b] that if I saw the hand of God leading soe farre as to destroy Kinge, and destroy Lords, and destroy property, and [leave] noe such thinge att all amongst us, I should acquiese in itt; and soe I did nott care, if noe Kinge, noe Lords, or noe property, in comparison of the tender care that I have of the honour of God, and of the people of God, whose [good] name is soe much concern'd in this Army. This I did deliver [so] and nott absolutely.

All the maine thinge that I speake for is because I would have an eye to propertie. I hope wee doe nott come to contend for victorie, butt lett every man consider with himself that hee doe nott goe that way to take away all propertie. For heere is the case of the most fundamentall parte of the Constitution of the Kingedome, which if you take away, you take away all by that. Heere are men of this and this qualitie are determined to bee the

[a] See p. 299; and also the note. [b] See p. 296.

Electors of men to the Parliament, and they are all those who have any permanent interest in the Kingedome, and who taken together doe comprehend the whole interest of the Kingedome. I meane by permanent, locall, that is nott any where else. As for instance; hee that hath a freehold, and that freehold cannott bee removed out of the Kingedome; and soe there's a [freeman of a] Corporation, a place which hath the priviledge of a markett and trading, which if you should allow to all places equallie, I doe nott see how you could preserve any peace in the Kingedome, and that is the reason why in the Constitution wee have but some few markett townes. Now those people [that have freeholds] and those that are the freemen of Corporations, were look't upon by the former Constitution to comprehend the permanent interest of the Kingdom. For [firstly] hee that hath his livelihood by his trade, and by his freedome of trading in such a Corporation which hee cannott exercise in another, hee is tied to that place, his livelihood depends uppon itt. And secondly, that man hath an interest, hath a permanent interest there, uppon which hee may live, and live a freeman without dependance. These Constitutions this Kingedome hath look't att. Now I wish wee may all consider of what right you will challenge, that all the people should have right to Elections. Is itt by the right of nature? If you will hold forth that as your ground, then I thinke you must deny all property too, and this is my reason. For thus: by that same right of nature, whatever itt bee that you pretend, by which you can say, "one man [a] hath an equall right with another to the chusing of him that shall governe him"—by the same right of nature, hee hath an equal [b] right in any goods hee sees: meate, drinke, cloathes, to take and use them for his sustenance. Hee hath a freedome to the land, [to take] the ground, to exercise itt, till itt; he hath the [same] freedome to any thinge that any one doth account himself to have any propriety in. Why now I say then, if you, against

[a] MS. "a man."

[b] MS. "the same."

this most fundamentall parte of [the] civill Constitution (which I have now declar'd), will pleade the law of nature, that a man should, paramount [to] this, and contrary to this, have a power of chusing those men that shall determine what shall bee law in this state, though he himself have noe permanent interest in the State, [but] whatever interest hee hath hee may carry about with him. If this be allowed, [because by the right of nature], wee are free, wee are equall, one man must have as much voice as another, then shew mee what steppe or difference [there is], why by the same right of necessity to sustaine nature [I may not claim property as well]? Itt is for my better being [I may say], and possibly nott for itt neither, possibly I may nott have soe reall a regard to the peace of the Kingedom as that man who hath a permanent interest in itt. Hee that is heere to day and gone to morrow, I doe nott see that hee hath such a permanent interest. Since you cannott plead to itt by any thinge butt the law of nature, [for any thing] but for the end of better being, and [since] that better being is nott certaine, and [what is] more, destructive to another, if uppon these grounds you doe paramount [to] all Constitutions hold uppe this law of nature, I would faine have any man shew mee their bounds, where you will end, and [why you should not] take away all propertie?

Col. Rainborow.

I shall now bee a little more free and open with you then I was before. I wish wee were all true hearted, and that wee did all carry our selves with integritie. If I did mistrust you I would use such asseverations. I thinke itt doth goe on mistrust, and thinges are thought to be matters of reflection that were never intended. For my parte, as I thinke, you forgott somethinge that was in my speech, and you doe nott only your selves beleive that [we] [a] are inclining to anarchy, butt you would make all men

[a] MS. "men."

beleive that. And Sir, to say because a man pleades, that every man hath a voice [by the right of nature], that therefore itt destroyes [by] the same [argument all property]—that there's a propertie the law of God sayes itt; else why [hath] God made that law, "Thou shalt nott steale?" If I have noe interest in the Kingedome I must suffer by all their lawes bee they right or wronge. I am a poore man, therfore I must bee prest. Nay thus; a Gentleman lives in a country and hath three or fower Lordshippes as some men have—God knowes how they gott them—and when a Parliament is call'd hee must bee a Parliament man; and itt may bee hee sees some poore men, they live neere this man, hee can crush them—I have knowne an evasion to make sure hee hath turned the poore man out of doores; and I would faine know whether the potencie of men doe nott this, and soe keepe them under the greatest tyranny that was thought off in the world. Therefore I thinke that to that itt is fully answered. God hath sett downe that thinge as to propriety with this law of his, "Thou shalt not steale." For my parte I am against any such thought, and as for yourselves I wish you would nott make the world beleive that wee are for anarchy.

Lieut. Generall.

I know nothing butt this, that they that are the most yeilding have the greatest wisedome; butt really, Sir, this is nott right as itt should bee. Noe man sayes that you have a minde to anarchy, butt the consequence of this rule tends to anarchy, must end in anarchy; for where is there any bound or limitt sett if you take away this [limit], that men that have noe interest butt the interest of breathing [shall have no voices in elections]? Therfore I am confident on't wee should nott bee soe hott one with another.

Col. Rainborow.

I know that some particular men wee debate with [believe we] are for anarchy.

Com̃. Ireton.

I professe I must cleare my selfe as to that point.

I would nott desire, I cannott allow myself, to lay the least scandall uppon any body; and truly, for that Gentleman that did take soe much offence, I doe nott knowe why hee should take itt soe. Wee speake to the paper, and to that matter of the paper, nott to persons; and I hope that noe man is soe much engaged to the matter of the paper, I hope our persons, and our hearts, and judgements are not [so] pinn'd to papers, butt that wee are ready to heare what good or ill consequence will flow from itt.

I have, with as much plainesse and clearnesse of reason as I could, shew'd you how I did conceive the doing of this takes away that which is the most originall, the most fundamentall civil Constitution of this Kingedome, and which above all is that Constitution by which I have any propertie. If you will take away that, and sett uppe as a thing paramount whatever a man may claime by the law of nature—though itt bee nott a thinge of necessitie to him for the sustenance of nature—if you doe make this your rule, I desire clearlie to understand where then remaines propertie?

Now then, as I say, I would misrepresent nothing; the answer which had any thing of matter in itt, the great and maine answer upon which that which hath bin said against this rests, that seem'd to be:[a] that itt will nott make the breach of propertie: that there is a law, "Thou shalt nott steale." The same law sayes, "Honour thy Father and Mother"; and that law doth likewise extend to all that are our governours in that place where wee are in. Soe that, by that there is a forbidding of breaking a Civill Law when wee may live quietly under itt, and a Divine Law. Againe itt is said indeed before, that there is noe Law, noe Divine Law, that tells us, that such a Corporation must have the Election of Burgesses, or such a shire, or the like; and soe on the other side if a man were to demonstrate his [right to] propertie by Divine Law, itt would bee very remote. Our property as well as our right of sending Burgesses

[a] The order of the first few sentences of this speech has been changed.

descends from other thinges. That Divine Law doth nott determine particulars butt generalls, in relation to man and man, and to propertie, and all thinges else; and wee should bee as farre to seeke if wee should goe to prove a property in [a thinge by] Divine Law as to prove that I have an interest in chusing Burgesses of the Parliament by Divine Law. Truly under favour I referre itt to all whether there bee anythinge of solution to that objection that I made, if itt bee understood,—I submitt itt to any man's judgement.

Col. Rainborow.

To the thinge itt self propertie. I would faine know how itt[a] comes to bee the propertie [of some men, and not of others]. As for estates, and those kinde of thinges, and other thinges that belonge to men, itt will bee granted that they are[b] propertie; butt I deny that that is a propertie, to a Lord, to a Gentleman, to any man more then another in the Kingdome of England. Iff itt bee a propertie, itt is a propertie by a law; neither doe I thinke, that there is very little propertie in this thinge by the law of the land, because I thinke that the law of the land in that thinge is the most tyrannicall law under heaven, and I would faine know what wee have fought for, and this is the old law of England and that which inslaves the people of England that they should bee bound by lawes in which they have noe voice att all.[c] [So with respect to the law which says 'Honour thy father and thy mother.'] The great dispute is who is a right Father and a right Mother. I am bound to know who is my Father and Mother, and I take it in the same sence you doe, I would have a distinction, a character wherby God commands mee to honour [them], and for my parte I looke uppon the people of England soe, that wherin they have nott voices in the chusing of their Fathers and Mothers, they are nott bound to that commandement.

[a] *i. e.* "The franchise," see pp. 315, 316. [b] MS. "itt is."

[c] This part of Rainborow's speech is too fragmentary to follow his arguments, but his two speeches on pp. 315, 316, supplement it.

Mr. Pettus.

I desire to adde one worde, concerning the worde Propertie.

Itt is for somethinge that anarchy is soe much talk't of. For my owne parte I cannott beleive in the least that itt can bee clearlie derived from that paper. Tis true, that somewhat may bee derived in the paper against the power of the Kinge, and somewhat against the power of the Lords; and the truth is when I shall see God going about to throw downe Kinge and Lords and propertie then I shall bee contented. Butt I hope that they may live to see the power of the Kinge and the Lords throwne downe, that yett may live to see propertie preserved. And for this of changing the Representative of the Nation, of changing those that chuse the Represention, making of them more full, taking more into the number then formerly, I had verily thought wee had all agreed that more should have chosen, and that all had desir'd a more equall Representation then wee now have. For now those onely chuse who have 40s. freehold. A man may have a lease for 100l a yeare, a man may have a lease for three lives [but he has no voice]. Butt [as] for this [argument] that itt destroyes all right [to property] that every Englishman that is an inhabitant of England should chuse and have a choice in the Representatives, I suppose itt is [on the contrary] the onely meanes to preserve all propertie. For I judge every man is naturally free; and I judge the reason why men [a] when they were in soe great numbers [chose representatives was] that every man could nott give his voice; and therefore men agreed to come into some forme of Governement that they who were chosen might preserve propertie. I would faine know, if we were to begin a Governement, [whether you would say] 'you have nott 40s. a yeare, therfore you shall not have a voice.' Wheras before there was a Governement every man had such a choice, and afterwards for this very cause they did chuse Representatives, and putt themselves into formes

[a] MS. "the man when they are."

of Governement that they may preserve propertie, and therfore itt is nott to destroy itt [to give every man a choice].

Com. Generall.

I thinke wee shall nott bee soe apt to come to a right understanding in this businesse, if one man, and another man, and another man doe speake their severall thoughts and conceptions to the same purpose, as if wee doe consider where the objection lies, and what the answer is which is made to itt ; and therfore I desire wee may doe soe. To that which this Gentleman spake last. The maine thinge that hee seem'd to answer was this: that hee would make itt appeare, that the going about to establish this Government,[a] [or] such a Governement, is nott a destruction of propertie, nor does nott tend to the destruction of propertie, because the people's falling into a Governement is for the preservation of propertie. What weight there [is in it] lies in this: since there is a falling into a Governement, and Governement is to preserve property, therfore this cannott bee against property. The objection does nott lie in that, the making of itt[b] more equall, butt [in] the introducing of men into an equality of interest in this Governement who have noe property in this Kingedome, or who have noe locall permanent interest in itt. For if I had said, that I would nott wish that wee should have any inlargement att all of the bounds of those that are to bee the Electors, then you might have excepted against itt. Butt [what I said was] that I would nott goe to inlarge itt beyond all bounds: that uppon the same ground you may admitt of soe many men from forraigne States as would outvote you. The objection lies still in this. I doe nott meane that I would have itt restrained to that proportion [it is now], butt to restraine itt still to men who have a locall, a permanent interest in the Kingedome, who have such an interest that they may live uppon itt as freemen, and who have such an interest as is fix't uppon a place, and is nott the same every where equally. If a man bee an

[a] The constitution proposed in the "Agreement of the People."

[b] *i. e.* "The franchise."

inhabitant uppon a wrack rent for a yeare, for two yeares, or 20 yeares—you cannott thinke that man hath any fix't or permanent interest—that man if hee pay the rent that his land is worth, and hath noe advantage butt what hee hath by his land, that man is as good a man, may have as much interest, in another Kingedome as heere. I doe nott speake of not[a] inlarging this att all, butt of keeping this to the most fundamentall Constitution in this Kingedome, that is, that noe person that hath nott a locall and permanent interest in the Kingedome should have an equall dependance in Elections [with those that have]. Butt if you goe beyond this law, if you admitt any man that hath a breath and being, I did shew you how this will destroy propertie. Itt may come to destroy propertie thus: you may have such men chosen or att least the major parte of them [as have no local and permanent interest.] Why may nott those men vote against all propertie? You may admitt strangers by this rule, if you admitt them once to inhabite, and those that have interest in the land may bee voted out of their land. Itt may destroy propertie that way.[b] Butt heere is the rule that you goe by; for that by which you inferre this to bee the right of the people, of every inhabitant, that because man[c] hath such a right in nature, though itt bee nott of necessity for the preserving of his being, therfore you are to overthrow the most fundamentall Constitution for this, by the same rule shew mee why you will nott, by the same right of nature, make use of any thinge that any man hath necessary for the sustenance of men.[d] Shew mee what you will stoppe att, wherin you will fence any man in a property by this rule.

[a] MS. "an."

[b] The passage may be thus paraphrased: "But here is the great objection to the rule that you go by. By that rule by which you infer this to be the right of the people, of every inhabitant, you infer also that because every man hath such a right in nature—though it be not of necessity for the preserving of his life—that therefore you are to overthrow the most fundamental constitution of the kingdom for it. Now show me why, by the same rule, by the same right of nature, you will not claim the use of anything any man hath that is necessary for the sustenance of men."

[c] MS. "this man."

[d] MS. "mee."

Col. Rainborow.

I desire to know how this comes to bee a propertie in some men, and nott in others.

Col. Rich.

I confesse [there is weight in] that objection that the Commissary Generall last insisted uppon; for you have five to one in this Kingedome that have noe permanent interest. Some men [have] ten, some twenty servants, some more, some lesse. If the Master and servant shall bee equall Electors, then clearlie those that have noe interest in the Kingedome will make itt their interest to chuse those that have noe interest. Itt may happen, that the majority may by law, nott in a confusion, destroy propertie; there may bee a law enacted, that there shall bee an equality of goods and estate. I thinke that either of the extreames may be urg'd to inconveniencie. That is, men that have noe interest as to Estate should have no interest as to Election. Butt there may bee a more equall division and distribution then that hee that hath nothing should have an equall voice; and certainly there may bee some other way thought of that there may bee a Representative of the poore as well as the rich, and nott to exclude all. I remember there were as wee have heard many workinges and revolutions in the Roman Senate; and there was never a confusion that did appeare, and that indeed was come to, till the State came to know this kinde of distribution of Election. That the peoples voices were bought and sold, and that by the poore, and thence itt came that hee that was the richest man, and [a man] of some considerable power amonge the souldiers, and one they resolued on, made himself a perpetuall dictator. And if wee straine too farre to avoide monarchy in Kinges [let us take heed] that wee doe nott call for Emperours to deliver us from more then one Tyrant.

Col. Rainborow.

I should nott have spoken againe. I thinke itt is a fine guilded pill, butt there is much danger and itt may seeme to some, that there is some kinde of remedy, I thinke that wee are better as wee are. That the poore shall chuse many, still the people are in the same case, are over voted still. And therfore truly, Sir, I should desire to goe close to the businesse; and the thinge that I am unsatisfied in is how itt comes about that there is such a propriety in some freeborne Englishmen, and nott [in] others.

Com̃. Cowling.

Whether the younger sonne have nott as much right to the Inheritance as the eldest?

Com̃. Gen. Ireton.

Will you decide itt by the light of nature?

Com̃. Cowling.

Why Election was only 40s a yeare,[a] which was more then 40ł. a yeare now, the reason was [this], that the Commons of England were overpowr'd by the Lords, who had abundance of vassalls, butt that they might still make their lawes good against incroaching prerogatives, therefore they did exclude all slaves. Now the case is nott soe; all slaves have bought their freedomes. They are more free that in the common wealth are more beneficiall. There are men in the country .... there is a tanner in Stanes worth 3000ł, and another in Reading worth 3 horseskins.

Com̃. Gen. Ireton.

In the beginning of your speech you seeme to acknowledge [that] by law, by civill Constitution, the propriety of having voices in Election was fixt in certaine persons. Soe then your exception of your argument does nott prove that by civill constitution they have noe such propriety, butt your argument does acknowledge [that] by

[a] *i. e.* "Limited to possessors of freeholds worth 40*s*. a year. Cowling is giving his theory of the object of the statute of Henry VI. limiting the franchise to persons having free land or tenement to the value of 40*s*. by the year."

civill [constitution they have such] propriety. You argue against this law, that this law is nott good.

Mr. Wildman.

Unlesse I bee very much mistaken wee are very much deviated from the first Question. Instead of following the first proposition to inquire what is just, I conceive wee looke to prophesies, and looke to what may bee the event, and judge of the justnesse of a thinge by the consequence. I desire wee may recall [ourselves to the question] whether itt bee right or noe. I conceive all that hath bin said against itt will bee reduc't to this and another reason; that itt is against a fundamentall law, [and] that every person ought to have a permanent interest, because itt is nott fitt that those should chuse Parliaments that have noe lands to bee disposed of by Parliament.

Com̃. Genˡ. Ireton.

If you will take itt by the way, itt is not fitt [a] that the Representees should chuse the Representors, or the persons who shall make the law in the Kingedome, who have nott a permanent fix't interest in the Kingedome.

Mr. Wildman.

Sir I doe soe take itt; and I conceive that that is brought in for the same reason, that forraigners might come to have a voice in our Elections as well as the native Inhabitants.

Com̃. Ireton.

That is uppon supposition that these [b] should bee all Inhabitants.

Mr. Wildman.

I shall begin with the last first. The case is different from the

[a] The word "fitt" should perhaps be "fixt." "It is now fixed that the electors must not choose men to make laws who have no permanent interest in the kingdom."

[b] These, *i. e.* "these foreigners."

native Inhabitant and forraigner. If a forraigner shall bee admitted to bee an Inhabitant in the Nation, soe hee will submitt to that forme of Governement as the natives doe, hee hath the same right as the natives, butt in this particular. Our case is to bee consider'd thus, that wee have bin under slavery. That's acknowledged by all. Our very lawes were made by our Conquerours; and wheras itt's spoken much of Chronicles, I conceive there is noe creditt to bee given to any of them; and the reason is because those that were our Lords, and made us their vassalls, would suffer nothing else to bee chronicled. Wee are now engaged for our freedome; that's the end of Parliaments, nott to constitute what is already according to the just rules of Governement.[a] Every person in England hath as cleere a right to Elect his Representative as the greatest person in England. I conceive that's the undeniable maxime of Governement: that all governement is in the free consent of the people. If [so], then uppon that account, there is noe person that is under a just Governement, or hath justly his owne, unlesse hee by his owne free consent bee putt under that Governement. This hee cannott bee unlesse hee bee consenting to itt, and therfore according to this maxime there is never a person in England [but ought to have a voice in elections]; if as that Gentleman[b] sayes bee true, there are noe lawes that in this strictnesse and rigour of justice [any man is bound to] that are nott made by those who hee doth consent to. And therfore I should humbly move, that if the Question bee stated—which would soonest bringe thinges to an issue—itt might rather bee this: whether any person can justly bee bound by law, who doth nott give his consent that such persons shall make lawes for him?

Com̃. Gen: Ireton.

Lett the Question bee soe; whether a man can can bee bound to any law that hee doth nott consent to? And I shall tell you, that hee

[a] Should be, "to constitute, *i. e.* to legislate, according to the just ends of government, not simply to maintain what is already established."

[b] "That gentleman," *i. e.* Rainborow, see p. 304.

may and ought to bee [bound to a law] that hee doth nott give a consent to, nor doth nott chuse any [to consent to], and I will make itt cleare. If a forraigner come within this Kingedome, if that stranger will have libertie [to dwell here] who hath noe local interest heere—hee is a man itt's true, hath aire that by nature[a] wee must nott expell our Coasts, give him noe being amongst us, nor kill him because hee comes uppon our land, comes uppe our streame, arrives att our shoare. Itt is a peece of hospitality, of humanity, to receive that man amongst us. Butt if that man bee received to a being amongst us I thinke that man may very well bee content to submitt himself to the law of the land: that is, the law that is made by those people that have a property, a fixt property, in the land. I thinke if any man will receive protection from this people, this man ought to bee subject to those lawes, and to bee bound by those lawes soe longe as hee continues amongst them, though [neither] hee nor his ancestors, nott any betwixt him and Adam, did ever give concurrence to this Constitution. That is my opinion. A man ought to bee subject to a law that did nott give his consent, butt with this reservation, that if this man doe thinke himself unsatisfied to bee subject to this law hee may goe into another Kingedome. And soe the same reason doth extend in my understanding to that man that hath noe permanent interest in the Kingedome. If hee hath mony, his monie is as good in another place as heere; hee hath nothing that doth locally fixe him to this Kingedome. If this man will live in this Kingedome or trade amongst us, that man ought to subject himself to the law made by the people who have the interest of this Kingedome in us; and yett I doe acknowledge that which you take to bee soe generall a maxime, that in every Kingedome, within every land, the originall of power, of making lawes, of determining what shall bee law in the land, does lie in the people that are possess't of the permanent interest in the land. Butt whoever is extraneous to this, that is, as good a man in another land, that man ought to give such a respect to the property of men that live in

[a] Probably should be "hath a right by nature that." But see p. 303.

the land. They doe nott determine [that I shall live in this land], why should I have any interest of determining of what shall bee the law of this land?[a]

Major Rainborow.

I thinke if itt can bee made to appeare, that itt is a just and reasonable thinge, and that is for the preservation of all the free-borne men, itt ought to bee made good unto them. The reason is, that the cheif end of this Governement is to preserve persons as well as estates, and if any law shall take hold of my person itt is more deare than my estate.

Col. Rainborow.

I doe very well remember that the Gentleman in the window[b] [said], that if itt were soe there were noe propriety to bee had, because a fifth parte of the poor people [that] are now excluded and would then come in. Soe one on the other side said, that if otherwise then rich men shall bee chosen [there would be no propriety]. Then I say the one parte shall make hewers of wood and drawers of water of the other five, and soe the greatest parte of the Nation bee enslav'd. Truly I thinke wee are still where wee were; and I doe not heare any argument given butt only that itt is the present law of the Kingedome. I say still, what shall become of those many [men] that have laid out themselves for the Parliament of England in this present warre, that have ruined themselves by fighting, by hazarding all they had? They are Englishmen. They have now nothing to say for themselves.

Col. Rich.

I should bee very sorry to speake anythinge heere that should give offence, or that may occasion personall reflections that wee spoke against just now. I did nott urge any thinge soe farre as

[a] The meaning apparently is, "Why should I have any interest in determining what the law of a land shall be, if I am not obliged to live under it."

[b] Colonel Rich, p. 315.

was represented, and I did nott att all urge that there should bee a consideration [had of rich men only], and that [a] man that is [poor] shall bee without consideration, or that hee deserves to bee made poore and nott to live att all. All that I urged was this, that I thinke itt worthy consideration, whether they should have an equality in their interest. Butt however I thinke wee have bin a great while uppon this point, and if wee bee as longe upon all the rest, itt were well if there were noe greater difference then this.

Mr. Peter.

I thinke that this may bee easily agreed on, that is there may bee a way thought of. I thinke you should doe well to sett uppe all night, butt I would faine know whether that will answer the worke of your Meeting.[a] You will be forc't to putt characters uppon Electors or Elected, therfore I doe suppose that if there bee any heere that can make uppe a Representative to your minde, the thinge is gain'd. I think three or four might be thought of in this companie.[a] But the question is, whether you can state any one question for the present danger of the Kingedome, if any one question or noe will dispatch the worke.

Sir, I desire that some question may bee stated to finish the present worke to cement us wherin lies the distance, and if the thoughts of the Commonwealth, the people's freedome, I thinke that's soone cured. I desire that all manner of plainesse may bee used that wee may nott goe on with the lapwinge, and carry one another off the nest. There is somethinge else in that must cement us where the awkwardnesse of our spiritts lies.

Col. Rainborow.

For my parte I thinke wee cannott engage one way or other in the Army if wee doe nott thinke of the people's liberties. If wee can agree where the liberty and freedome of the people lies, that will doe all.

[a] The position of these two clauses has been changed, but the latter part of the speech seems hopelessly confused.

Com̃. Gen. Ireton.

I cannott consent soe farre. As I said before: when I see the hand of God destroying Kinge, and Lords, and Commons too, [or] any foundation of humane Constitution, when I see God hath done itt, I shall I hope comfortably acquiesce in itt. Butt first, I cannott give my consent to itt because itt is nott good. And secondly, as I desire that this Army should have regard to Engagements wherever they are lawfull, soe I would have them have regard to this as well, that they should nott bringe that scandall uppon the name of God, that those that call themselves by that name, those whome God hath own'd and appear'd with—that wee should nott represent ourselves to the world as men soe farre from being of that peaceable spiritt which is suitable to the Gospell, as wee would have bought peace of the world uppon such termes, wee would nott have peace in the world butt uppon such termes, as should destroy all propertie. If the principle uppon which you move this alteration, or the ground uppon which you presse that wee should make this alteration, doe destroy all kinde of property or whatsoever a man hath by humane Constitution [I cannot consent to it]. The law of God doth nott give mee propertie, nor the law of nature, butt propertie is of humane Constitution. I have a propertie and this I shall enjoy. Constitution founds propertie. If either the thinge itt selfe that you presse or the consequence [of] that you presse [do destroy property], though I shall acquiesce in having noe propertie, yett I cannott give my heart or hand to itt; because itt is a thinge evill in ittself and scandalous to the world, and I desire this Army may bee free from both.

Mr. Sexby.

I see that though itt [a] were our end, there is a degeneration from itt. Wee have engaged in this Kingdome and ventur'd our lives, and itt was all for this: to recover our birthrights and priviledges

[a] "Itt," possibly means "the liberty of the people," referring to Rainborow's speech.

as Englishmen, and by the arguments urged there is none. There are many thousands of us souldiers that have ventur'd our lives; wee have had little propriety in the Kingedome as to our estates, yett wee have had a birthright. Butt itt seemes now except a man hath a fix't estate in this Kingedome, hee hath noe right in this Kingedome. I wonder wee were soe much deceived. If wee had nott a right to the Kingedome, wee were meere mercinarie souldiers. There are many in my condition, that have as good a condition [as I have], itt may bee little estate they have att present, and yett they have as much a [birth-] right as those two[a] who are their law givers, as any in this place. I shall tell you in a worde my resolution. I am resolved to give my birthright to none.[b] Whatsoever may come in the way, and [whatsoever may] bee thought, I will give itt to none. If this thinge that with soe much pressing after—There was one thinge spoken to this effect—that if the poore and those in lowe condition. . . .[c] I thinke this was butt a distrust of providence. I doe thinke the poore and meaner of this Kingedome (I speake as in that relation in which wee are) have bin the meanes of the preservation of this Kingedome. I say in their stations, and really I thinke to their utmost possibility; and their lives have nott bin deare for purchasing the good of the Kingdome. Those that act to this end are as free from anarchy or confusion as those that oppose itt, and they have the law of God and the law of their conscience [with them]. Butt truly I shall only summe uppe in this, I desire that wee may nott spend soe much time uppon these thinges. Wee must bee plaine. When men come to understand these thinges they will nott loose that which they have contended for. That which I shall beseech you is to come to a determination of this question.

[a] "Those two," *i. e.* Cromwell and Ireton.

[b] If this Agreement be not accepted I will still not give up my birthright.

[c] Probably refers to the speech of Colonel Rich, that poor voters would sell their votes, or otherwise destroy the kingdom.

Com̃. Gen. Ireton.

I am very sorry wee are come to this point, that from reasoning one to another wee should come to expresse our resolutions. I professe for my parte, what I see is good for the Kingdome, and becoming a Christian to contend for, I hope through God I shall have strength and resolution to doe my parte towards itt. And yett I will professe direct contrary in some kinde to what that Gentleman said.[a] For my parte, rather then I will make a disturbance to a good Constitution of a Kingedome wherin I may live in godlinesse, and honesty, and peace and quietnesse, I will parte with a great deale of my birthright. I will parte with my owne property rather then I will bee the man that shall make a disturbance in the Kingedome for my property; and therfore if all the people in this Kingedome, or [the] Representative[s] of them all together, should meete and should give away my propertie I would submitt to itt, I would give it away. Butt that Gentleman, and I thinke every Christian ought to beare that spiritt in him, that hee will nott make a publique disturbance uppon a private prejudice[b]

Now lett us consider where our difference lies. Wee all agree that you should have a Representative to governe, [and] this Representative to bee as equall as you can. Butt the question is, whether this distribution can bee made to all persons equallie, or whether equallie amongst those that have the interest of England in them. That which I have declar'd [is] my opinion [still]. I thinke wee ought to keepe to that [constitution which we have now], both because itt is a civill Constitution, itt is the most fundamentall Constitution that wee have, and [because] there is soe much justice, and reason, and prudence [in it], as I dare confidently undertake to demonstrate, that there are many more evills that will follow in case you doe alter, then there can in the standing of itt. Butt I say butt this in the generall, that I doe wish

[a] *i.e.* Sexby.

[b] MS., "every christian spirit ought to bear that, to carry that."

that they that talke of birthrights—wee any of us when wee talke of birthrights—would consider what really our birthright is.

If a man mean [a] by birthright, whatsoever hee can challenge by the law of nature, suppose there were noe Constitution att all, supposing noe Civill law and Civill Constitution—that that I am to contend for against Constitution, you leave noe property, nor noe foundation for any man to enjoy any thinge. Butt if you call that your birthrights which is the most fundamentall parte of your Constitution, then lett him perish that goes about to hinder you or any man of the least parte of your birthright, or will doe itt. Butt if you will lay aside the most fundamentall Constitution, which is as good for ought you can discerne as anythinge you can propose—att least itt is a Constitution, and I will give you consequence for consequence of good uppon Constitution as you for your birthright [b]—and if you meerlie uppon pretence of a birthright, of the right of nature, which is onely true as for your better being; if you will uppon that ground pretend, that this Constitution, the most fundamentall Constitution, the thinge that hath reason and equity in itt shall nott stand in your way, [it] is the same principle to mee say I, [as if] but for your better satisfaction you shall take hold of any thinge that a man calls his owne,

Col. Rainborow.

Sir I see, that itt is impossible to have liberty butt all propertie must be taken away. If itt be laid downe for a rule, and if you will say itt, itt must bee soe. Butt I would faine know what the souldier hath [c] fought for all this while? Hee hath fought to inslave himself, to give power to men of riches, men of estates, to make him a perpetuall slave. Wee doe finde in all presses that goe forth none must bee pres't that are freehold men. When these

[a] MS. "men."
[b] Clause transposed from two lines above.
[c] MS. "all the souldiers have."

Gentlemen fall out amonge themselves they shall presse the poore shrubs[a] to come and kill them.

Com̃. Gen. Ireton.

I confesse I see soe much right in the businesse that I am nott easily satisfied with flourishes. If you will lay the stresse of the businesse [not] uppon the consideration of reason, or right relating to humane constitution, or anything of that nature, butt will putt itt uppon consequences, I see enough to say, that to my apprehensions I can shew you greater ill consequences to follow uppon that alteration which you would have by extending [voices] to all that have a being in this Kingedome then by this a great deale. That is a particular ill consequence. This is a generall ill consequence, and that is as great as this or any else; though I thinke you will see that the validity of that argument must be[b] that for one ill lies uppon that which now is, I can shew you a thousand uppon this. Give mee leave [to say] butt this one worde I tell you what the souldier of the Kingedome hath fought for. First, the danger that wee stood in was, that one man's will must bee a law. The people of the Kingedome must have this right att least, that they should nott bee concluded [but] by the Representative of those that had the interest of the Kingedome. Some[c] men fought in this, because they were imediately concern'd and engag'd in itt. Other men who had noe other interest in the Kingedome butt this, that they should have the benefitt of those lawes made by the Representative, yett [fought] that they should have the benefitt of this Representative. They thought itt was better to bee concluded by the common consent of those that were fix't men and setled men that had the interest of this Kingedome [in them], and from that way [said they] I shall know a law and have a certainty. Every man that was borne in itt that hath a

[a] Possibly a reference to the parable of Jotham, Judges, ix. Or perhaps one should read "scrub."

[b] MS. "lie."

[c] MS. "soe."

freedome is a denizon, hee was capable of trading to gett money and to gett estates by, and therfore this man I thinke had a great deale of reason to build uppe such a foundation of interest to himself: that is, that the will of one man should nott bee a law, butt that the law of this Kingedome should bee by a choice of persons to represent, and that choice to bee made by the generality of the Kingedome. Heere was a right that induced men to fight, and those men that had this interest, though this bee nott the utmost interest that other men have, yett they had some interest. Now why wee should goe to pleade whatsoever wee can challenge by the right of nature against whatsoever any man can challenge by Constitution?[a] I doe nott see where that man will stoppe as to point of property that hee shall nott use that right hee hath by the law of nature against that Constitution. I desire any man to shew mee where there is a difference. I have bin answer'd "now wee see libertie cannott stand without [destroying] propertie." Libertie may bee had and property nott bee destroyed. First, the libertie of all those that have the permanent interest in the Kingedome, that is provided for; and in a generall sence libertie cannott bee provided for if property bee preserved; for if propertie bee preserved—that I am nott to meddle with such a man's estate, his meate, his drinke, his apparell, or other goods—then the right of nature destroys libertie. By the right of nature I am to have sustenance rather then perish, yett property destroyes it for a man to have by the right[b] of nature, suppose there bee noe humane Constitution.

Mr. Peter.

I will minde you of one thinge. That uppon the will of one man abusing us, and soe forth.—Soe that I professe to you for my parte. I hope itt is nott denied by any man, that any wise discreete

[a] May be paraphrased, "Now let any man shew me why, if we should go to plead, &c., we should stop there?"

[b] MS. "light."

man that hath preserved England or the Governement of itt—I doe say still under favour there is a way to cure all this debate—I thinke they will desire noe more libertie—If there were time to dispute itt —I thinke hee would bee satisfied, and all will bee satisfied and if the safetie of the Army bee in danger—For my parte I am cleare the point of Election should bee amended.[a]

Lieut. Generall.

I confesse I was most dissatisfied with that I heard Mr. Sexby speake of any man heere, because itt did savour soe much of will. Butt I desire that all of us may decline that, and if wee meete heere really to agree to that which was for the safetie of the Kingdome, lett us nott spend soe much time in such debates as these are, but lett us apply ourselves to such thinges as are conclusive, and that shall bee this: Everybodie heere would bee willing, that the Representative might bee mended, that is, itt might bee better then itt is. Perhaps itt may bee offer'd in that paper too lamely. If the thinge bee insisted uppon too limitted, why perhaps there are a very considerable parte of copyholders by inheritance that ought to have a voice, and there may bee somewhat too reflects uppon the generality of the people.[b] If wee thinke to bringe itt to an issue this way I know our debates are endlesse; and I thinke if you doe [desire to] bringe this to a result itt were well if wee may butt resolve uppon a Committee.[c] I say itt againe,

[a] Only the first words of some sentences out of the speech of Hugh Peters are here given. He suggests apparently an arrangement such as the one finally accepted, by which men who had assisted the Parliament should be given votes. Cromwell takes up the suggestion of a compromise, and develops it rather further, proposing the extension of the franchise to copyholders by inheritance.

[b] Perhaps in that paper (*i. e.* in the "Heads of the Proposals," i., § 5) the amendment of the representative may be offered too lamely, and there may be some reflection upon the generality of the people, if the franchise be insisted upon to be limited to the present voters. "Why perhaps there are a considerable number of copyholders by inheritance that ought to have votes," etc. "This paper" referred to on p. 329 is the "Agreement."

[c] Clause transferred from the last lines of the speech.

if I cannott bee satisfied to goe soe farre as these Gentlemen that bringe this paper,I professe I shall freely and willinglie withdrawe myself, and I hope to doe itt in such a manner that the Army shall see that I shall by my withdrawing satisfy the interest of the Army, the publique interest of the Kingedome, and those ends these men aime att.

Col. Rainborow.

If these men must bee advanced and other men sett under foote, I am nott satisfied if their rules must bee observed, and other men that are in aucthority doe nott know how this can stand together.[a] I wonder how that should bee thought wilfulnesse in one man that is reason in another; for I confesse I have nott heard any thinge that doth satisfie mee, and though I have nott soe much wisedome or notions in my head, I have soe many that I could tell an hundred to the ruine of the people. I am nott at all against a Committee's meeting; and as you say, for my parte I shall bee ready, if I see the way that I am going and the thinge that I could insist on will destroy the Kingdome, I shall withdraw it as soon as any, and I thinke every Christian ought to do the same;[b] and therfore till I see that I shall use all the meanes, and I thinke itt is noe fault in any man [to refuse] to sell that which is his birthright.

Mr. Sexby.

I desire to speake a few words. I am sorry that my zeale to what I apprehend is good should bee soe ill resented. I am nott sorry to see that which I apprehend is truth, butt I am sorry the Lord hath darkened some soe much as nott to see itt, and that is in short [this]. Doe you [not] thinke itt were a sad and miserable condition that wee have fought all this time for nothing? All heere both great and small doe thinke that wee fought for something. I

[a] Rainborow directly attacks Cromwell and Ireton. His words seem to mean: "If their rules must be observed, if these men must be advanced and other men that are in authority set under foot, I am not satisfied, and I do not see how this council can hold together."

[b] Clause transferred from two lines above.

confesse many of us fought for those ends which wee since saw was nott that which caused us to goe through difficulties and straightes to venture all in the shippe with you. Itt had bin good in you to have advertis'd us of itt, and I beleive you would have fewer under your command to have commanded. Butt if this bee the businesse, that an estate doth make men capable to chuse those that shall represent them—itt is noe matter which way they gett it, they are capable—I thinke there are many that have nott estates that in honesty have as much right in the freedome [of] their choice[a] as any that have great estates. Truly, Sir,[b] [as for] your putting off this question and coming to some other; I dare say, and I dare appeale to all of them, that they cannott settle uppon any other untill this bee done. Itt was the ground that wee tooke uppe armes, and itt is the ground which wee shall maintaine. Concerning my making rents and divisions in this way—as a particular, if I were butt soe, I could lie downe and be troden there. [But] truly I am sent by a Regiment. If I should nott speake, guilt shall lie uppon mee, and I thinke I were a Covenant breaker. I doe nott know how wee have [been] answer'd in our Arguments, and I conceive wee shall nott accomplish them[c] to the Kingedome when wee deny them to our selves. I shall bee loath to make a rent and division, butt, for my owne parte, unlesse I see this putt to a question, I despaire of an issue.

Capt. Clarke.[d]

The first thing that I shall desire was, and is, this; that there might bee a temperature and moderation of spiritt within us; that wee should speak with moderation, nott with such reflection as was boulted one from another; butt soe speake and soe heare as that which may bee the droppinges of love from one another to another's

[a] MS. "in the freedome their choice as free."

[b] To Cromwell.

[c] *i. e.* our promises, our engagements.

[d] Compare Clarke's speech on p. 339, which appears to be merely a second version of this.

hearts. Another word I have to say is, the grand question of all is, whether or noe itt bee the property of every individuall person in the Kingdome to have a vote in election[s]; and the ground [on which it is claimed] is the law of nature, which for my parte I thinke to bee that law which is the ground of all Constitutions. Yett really properties are the foundation of Constitutions, for if soe bee there were noe property, that the law of nature does give a principall [for every man] to have a property of what hee has or may have which is nott another man's propertie. This is the ground of meum and tuum. Now there may bee inconveniencies on both hands butt nott soe great freedome. The greater freedome as I conceive that all may have whatsoever. And if itt come to passe that there bee a difference, and that the one doth oppose the other, then nothing can decide itt butt the sword which is the wrath of God.

Capt. Audeley.

I see you have a longe dispute, that you doe intend to dispute heere till the 10th of March. I see both att a stand, and if wee dispute heere both are lost. You[a] have brought us into a faire passe, and the Kingdome into a faire passe, for if your reasons are nott satisfied, and wee doe nott fetch all our waters from your wells you threaten to withdraw your selves. I could wish according to our severall protestations wee might sett downe quietly, and there throw downe our selves where wee see reason. I could wish wee might all rise, and goe to our duties, and see our worke in hand.

Lieut. Generall.

Really for my owne parte I must needes say whilest wee say wee would nott make reflections wee doe make reflections; and if I had nott come hither with a free heart to doe that that I was perswaded in my conscience is my duty I should a thousand

[a] "You" refers to "both," *i.e.* Cromwell and Ireton on the one hand, and Sexby and Wildman on the other, *vide* pp. 329, 330, 335.

times rather have kept myself away. For I doe thinke I had brought uppon myself the greatest sin that I was [ever] guilty of, if I should have come to have stood before God in that former duty, and if [I should not persevere in] that my saying which I did say [to you before], and shall persevere to say, that I cannott against my conscience doe anythinge. They that have stood soe much for libertie of conscience, if they will nott grant that libertie to every man, butt say itt is a deserting I know nott what—if that bee denied mee I thinke there is nott that equality that [is] profest to bee amongst us.[a] I said this, and I say noe more that make your businesses as well as you can, wee might bringe thinges to an understanding, itt was to bee brought to a faire composure, and when you have said, if you should putt this paper to the question without any qualifications I doubt whether itt would passe soe freely, if wee would have noe difference wee ought to putt itt, and lett me speake clearlie and freelie, I have heard other Gentlemen doe the like, I have nott heard the Commissary Generall answer'd, nott in a parte to my knowledge, nott in a tittle, if therefore when I see there is an extreamity of difference betweene you, to the end itt may bee brought neerer to a generall satisfaction,[a] and if this bee thought a deserting of that interest, if there can bee anythinge more sharpely said, I will nott give itt an ill worde. Though wee should bee satisfied in our consciences in what wee doe, wee are told wee purpose to leave the Armie, or to leave our commands as if wee tooke uppon us to doe itt in matter of will. I did heare

[a] Compare with these remarks about freedom of conscience a similar passage in Cromwell's third speech in Carlyle's *Cromwell*. The remainder of this speech is simply a chaos of detached phrases from different sentences. The argument seems to be, "If you claim liberty to follow your consciences, but will not grant me liberty to follow mine, there is no equality between us. Though we conscientiously believe that under certain circumstances we ought to resign our commands, you taunt us as if we were following our wills instead of our consciences, and accuse us of deserting the cause. Can anything be more harshly said?" In answer to Sexby's demand for an immediate vote (pp. 324, 330) Cromwell again proposes (as on p. 328) that the question should be referred to a committee to try to make a fair compromise.

some Gentlemen speake more of will then anythinge that was spoken this way, for more was spoken by way of will then of satisfaction, and if there bee nott a more equality in our mindes I can butt greive for itt, I must doe noe more.

Com̃. Gen. Ireton,

I should nott speake, butt reflections, as if wee who have led men into Engagements and services had divided from them because wee did nott concurre with them, doe necessitate, doe call uppon us to vindicate ourselves. I will aske that Gentleman [a] that spoke, whome I love in my heart, whether when they drew out to serve the Parliament in the beginning, when they engag'd with the Army att New Markett,[b] whether then they thought of any more interest or right in the Kingdome then this? Whether they did thinke, that they should have as great interest in Parliament men as freeholders had? Or whether from the beginning wee did nott engage for the liberty of Parliaments,[c] and that wee should bee concluded by the lawes that such did make Unlesse somebody did make you beleive before now that you should have an equall interest in the Kingedome, unlesse somebody doe make that to bee beleived, there is noe reason to blame men for leading [you] soe farre as they have done; and if any man was farre enough from such an apprehension that man hath nott bin deceiv'd. And truly, I shall say butt this worde more for my self in this businesse, because the whole objection seemes to bee prest to mee, and maintain'd by mee. I will not arrogate that I was the first man that putt the Army uppon the thought either of successive Parliaments or more equall Parliaments; yett there are some heere that know who they were putt us uppon that foundation of libertie of putting a period to this Parliament, that wee might have successive Parliaments, and that there might bee a more equall distribution of Elections. There are many heere

[a] Rainborowe.

[b] June 5, 1647.

[c] See the Army's Declaration of June 14, 1647.

that know who were the first movers of that businesse in the Army. I shall nott arrogate that, butt I can argue this with a cleare conscience: that noe man hath prosecuted that with more earnestnesse, and will stand to that interest more than I doe, of having Parliaments successive and nott perpetuall, and the distributions of itt [more equal]. Butt notwithstanding my opinion stands good, that itt ought to bee a distribution amongst the fix't and setled people of this Nation. Itt's more prudent and safe, and more uppon this ground of right for itt: itt is the fundamentall Constitution of this Kingedome now, and that which you take away for matter of wilfulnesse. Notwithstanding [as for] this universall conclusion, that all inhabitants [shall have voices], as it stands [in the Agreement], I must declare that though I cannott yett bee satisfied, yett for my parte I shall acquiesce. I will nott make a distraction in this Army. Though I have a property in being, one of those that should bee an Elector, though I have an interest in the birthright, yet I will rather loose that birthright, and that interest then I will make itt my businesse [to oppose], if I see butt the generality of those whome I have reason to thinke honest men, and conscientious men, and godly men to carry them another way. I will nott oppose though I bee nott satisfied to joyne with them. And I desire [to say this], I am agreed with you if you insist uppon a more equall distribution of Elections; I will agree with you, nott onely to dispute for itt, butt to fight for itt and contend for itt. Thus farre I shall agree with you. On the other hand those who differ their termes, I will not agree with you except you goe farther. Thus farre I can goe with you, I will goe with you as farre as I can. If you will appoint a committee to consider of some of that, soe as you preserve the equitable part of that, who are like to be freemen, and men not given uppe to the wills of others, keeping to the latitude which is the equity of Constitution, I will goe with you as farre as

[a] See the Army Declaration of June 14, and the "Heads of the Proposals of the Army," § 1.

I can. I will sit downe, I will not make any disturbance amongst you.[a]

Col. Rainborow.

If I do speak my soul and conscience I doe thinke that there is not an objection made butt that itt hath bin answer'd, butt the speeches are soe longe. I am sorry for some passion and some reflections, and I could wish where itt is most taken the cause had nott bin given. Itt is a fundamentall Constitution of the Kingedome there—I would faine know whether the choise of Burgesses in Corporations should nott bee alter'd. The end wherfore I speake is onely this, you[b] thinke wee shall bee worse then wee are, if wee come to a conclusion by a vote. If itt bee putt to the question wee shall all know one another's minde. If itt bee determined and the resolutions knowne, wee shall take such a course as to putt itt in execution. This Gentleman[c] sayes if hee cannott goe hee will sitt still. Hee thinkes hee hath a full libertie, wee thinke wee have nott. There is a great deale of difference betweene us two. If a man hath all hee doth desire, [he may wish to sit still]; butt [if] I thinke I have nothing att all of what I fought for, I doe nott thinke the argument holds that I must desist as well as hee.

Mr. Pettus.

The rich would very unwillinglie bee concluded by the poore; and there is as much reason, and indeed noe reason that the rich should conclude the poore as the poore the rich. There should bee an equall share in both. I understood your Engagement was, that

[a] The last ten lines of Ireton's speech are too confused for amendment. They may perhaps be paraphrased thus: "If you will appoint a committee to consider of some more equal distribution of that—so as you preserve the equitable part of that—keeping the franchise to men who are likely to be independent and not given up to the wills of others—thus far I shall agree with you. On the other hand, to those who say 'I will not go with you except you go further,' I answer, 'I will go with you as far as I can, and when I can go no further I will sit down; I will not make any disturbance among you.'"

[b] *i.e.* Cromwell.

[c] *i.e.* Ireton.

you would use all your indeavours for the liberties of the people, that they should bee secur'd. If there is a Constitution that the people are not free that should bee annull'd. Butt this Constitution doth nott make people free, that Constitution which is now sette uppe is a Constitution of 40s. a yeare.

Lieut. Generall.

Heere's the mistake, [the whole question is] whether that's the better Constitution in that paper,[a] or that which is. Butt if you will goe uppon such a ground as that although a better Constitution was offer'd for the removing of the worse, yett some Gentlemen are resolved to stick to the worse, there might bee a great deale of prejudice uppon such an apprehension. I thinke you are by this time satisfied, that itt is a cleare mistake; for itt is a dispute[b] whether or noe this bee better; nay, whether itt bee nott destructive to the Kingedome.

Mr. Pettus.

I desire to speake one worde to this businesse, because I doe nott know whether my occasions will suffer mee to attend itt any longer. The great reason that I have heard is [that this is] the Constitution of the Kingdome, the utmost Constitution of itt; and if wee destroy this Constitution there is noe propertie. I suppose that itt were very dangerous if Constitutions should tie uppe all men in this nature.

Com. Ireton.

First the thinge itt self were dangerous if itt were settled to destroy propertie. Butt I say the principle that leads to this is destructive to propertie; for by the same reason that you will alter

[a] "This," *i. e.* the constitution in that paper, in the "Agreement of the People."

[b] *i. e.* "it is disputable."

[c] *i. e.* "The constitution proposed by the 'Agreement,' if it were actually established."

this Constitution meerly that there's a greater Constitution by nature—by the same reason, by the law of nature, there is a greater liberty to the use of other men's goods which that property barres you of; and I would faine have any man shew mee why I should destroy that libertie, which the freeholders and Burgers in Corporations have in chusing Burgesses—that which [if] you take away you leave noe Constitution—and this because there is a greater freedome due to mee by the law of nature—more then that I should take another man's goods because the law of nature does allow me.

Col. Rainborow.

I would grant somethinge that the Commissary Generall sayes. But whether this bee a just propriety, the propriety sayes that 40^s. a yeare inables a man to elect[a]—If itt were stated to that, nothing would conduce soe much whether some men doe agree or noe.

Capt. Rolfe.

I conceive that as wee are mett heere, there are one or two thinges mainly to be prosecuted by us; that is especially unitie, [the] preservation of unity in the Army; and soe likewise to putt ourselves into a capacity therby to doe good to the Kingedome. Therfore I shall desire, that there may bee a tender consideration had of that which is soe much urged, in that of an equall as well as of a free Representative. I shall desire that [there may bee] some thoughts of a medium or a composure, in relation to servants or to forraigners, or such others as shall bee agreed uppon. I say then I conceive, excepting those, there may bee a very equitable sence resented to us from that offer in our owne Declarations wherin wee doe offer the common good of all, unlesse they have made any shippewrack or losse of itt.[b]

[a] *i. e.* "Whether this be a just constitution which says that 40^s a year property enables a man to elect? If the question were stated so, etc."

[b] See the Engagement of June 5, 1647, which concludes: "We shall study to

Lieut. Chillenden.

In the beginning of this discourse there were overtures made of imminent danger. This way wee have taken this afternoone is nott the way to prevent itt. I should humbly move that wee should putt a speedy end to this businesse, and that not onely to this maine question of the paper, butt alsoe that, according to the Lieutenant Generall's motion, a Committee may be chosen seriously to consider the thinges in that paper, and compare them with divers thinges in our Declarations and Engagements; that soe as wee have all profest to lay downe ourselves before God—If wee take this course of debating uppon one question a whole afternoone, if the danger bee soe neere as itt is supposed itt were the ready way to bringe us into itt. [I desire] that thinges may bee putt into a speedy dispatch.

Capt. Clarke.

I presume that the great stick heere is this: that if every one shall have his propriety itt does bereave the Kingedome of itts principall, fundamentall Constitution that itt hath. I presume that all people and all nations whatsoever have a liberty and power to alter and change their Constitutions, if they finde them to bee weake and infirme. Now if the people of England shall finde this weaknesse in their Constitution they may change itt if they please. Another thinge is this. If the light[a] of nature bee onely [followed] in this, itt may destroy the propriety which every man can call his owne. The reason is this, because this principall and light of nature[a] doth give all men their owne. As for example the clothes uppon my back because they are nott another man's. If every man hath this propriety of Election to chuse those whom [they think fit], you feare [it] may begett inconveniences. I doe

promote such an establishment of common and equal right and freedom to the whole, as all might equally partake of, but those that do, by denying the same to others, or otherwise, render themselves incapable thereof."

[a] I should suggest here "right of nature," and "principle of the right of nature."

nott conceive that any thinge may bee soe nicely and preciselie done, butt that itt may admitt of inconveniencie. If itt bee in that wherin itt is now there may those inconveniencies rise from them. For my part I know nothing butt the want of love in itt, and the sword must decide itt. I shall desire before the question bee stated itt may bee moderated as for forraigners.[a]

Sir Hardresse Waller.

This was that I was saying, I confesse I have nott spoken yett, and having heard so many speake I was willing to bee silent that I might learne too. Itt is nott easy for us to say when this dispute will have an end; butt I thinke itt is easie to say when the Kingedome will have an end. If wee doe nott breath out ourselves wee shall bee kick't and spurn'd of all the world. I would faine know how farre the question will decide itt, for certainly wee must nott expect while wee have tabernacles heere to bee all of one minde. If it bee to bee decided by a question, and all parties are satisfied in that, I thinke the sooner you hasten to itt the better. If otherwise we shall needlessely discover our dividing opinion, which as longe as itt may bee avoided I desire itt may. Therfore I desire to have a period [put to this debate].

Capt. Awdeley.

I chanc't to speake a worde or two. Truly there was more offence taken att itt. For my parte I spoke against every man living,—nott onely against your self[b] and the Commissary, butt [against] every man that would dispute till wee have our throates cutt—and therfore I desire I may not lie in any prejudice before your persons. I professe, if soe bee there were none butt you and the Commissary Generall alone to maintain that argument, I would

[a] I take this speech of Clarke's to be merely a second version of the speech on p. 330, not a new speech. It will be observed that Waller does not answer Clarke but Chillenden.

[b] To Cromwell, who was presiding in the absence of Fairfax.

die in any place in England, in asserting that itt is the right of every free borne man to elect, according to the rule, Quod omnibus spectat, ab omnibus tractari debet, that which concernes all ought to bee debated by all. Hee knew noe reason why that law should oblige when hee himself had noe finger in appointing the law-giver.

Capt. Byshopp.

You have mett heere this day to see if God would shew you any way wherin you might joynctlie preserve the Kingedome from itts destruction, which you all apprehend to bee att the doore. God is please'd nott to come in to you. There is a Gentleman, Mr. Saltmarsh,[a] did desire what hee has wrote may bee read to the Generall Councill. If God doe manifest any thinge by him I thinke itt ought to bee heard.

Commissary Generall.

That you will alter that Constitution in my apprehension, from a better to a worse, from a just to a thinge that is lesse juste, and I will nott repeate the reasons of that butt referre to what I have declar'd before. To mee, if there were nothing butt this, that there is a Constitution, and that Constitution which is the very last Constitution, which if you take away you leave nothing of Constitution, and consequently nothing of right or propertie, [it would be enough]. I would nott goe to alter that, though a man could propound that which in some respects might bee better, unlesse itt could bee demonstrated to mee that this were unlawfull, or that this were destructive. Truly therfore I say for my parte, to goe on a suddaine to make such a limitation as that [to inhabitants] in generall—if you doe extend the latitude [of it so far] that any man shall have a voice in Election who has nott that interest in this Kingedome that is permanent and fix'd, who hath nott that interest

[a] Rushworth, vii., 913, 944.

uppon which hee may have his[a] freedome in this Kingedome without dependance, you will putt itt into the hands of men to chuse, [instead] of men to preserve their libertie, [men] who will give itt away.

I am confident our discontent and dissatisfaction, if ever they doe well, they doe in this. If there bee any thinge att all that is a foundation of libertie itt is this, that those who shall chuse the law makers shall bee men freed from dependance uppon others. I have a thinge putt into my heart which I cannott butt speake. I professe I am afraid, that if wee, from such apprehensions as these are of an imaginable right of nature opposite to Constitution—if wee will uppon this businesse of that enlargement contend and hazard the breaking of peace, I am afraid wee shall finde the hand of God will follow itt. I thinke if wee from imagination and conceits will goe about to hazard the peace of the Kingdome, to alter the Constitution in such a point, wee shall see that that libertie which wee soe much talke of and [have so much] contended for shall bee nothing att all by this our contending for itt, by putting itt into the hands of those men that will give itt away when they have itt.[b]

Lieut. Generall.

If wee should goe about to alter these thinges, I doe nott thinke that wee are bound to fight for every particular proposition. Servants while servants are nott included. Then you agree that hee that receives almes is to bee excluded.

Lieut. Col. Reade.

I suppose itt's concluded by all, that the chusing of Representatives is a priviledge; now I see noe reason why any[c] man that is a

[a] MS. "leave this."

[b] Compare the reasons against the "Bill for a new Representative," given in Cromwell's first speech in Carlyle's *Cromwell*. In this paragraph the position of several clauses has been altered.

[c] MS. "every."

native ought to bee excluded that priviledge, unless from voluntarie servitude.

Mr. Pettus.

I conceive the reason why wee would exclude apprentices, or servants, or those that take almes, is because they depend uppon the will of other men and should bee afraid to displease [them]. For servants and apprentices, they are included in their masters, and soe for those that receive almes from doore to doore; butt if there bee any generall way taken for those that are nott [so] bound [to the will of other men] itt would doe well.

Mr. Everard.[a]

I being sent from the Agents of the five regiments with an answer unto a writing, the Committee was very desirous to inquire into the depth of our intentions. Those things that they had there manifested in the paper I did declare, and what I did understand as a particular person. It was the Lieutenant General's desire for an understanding with us, presuming those things I did declare did tend to unity; "and if soe [said he] you will lett it appeare by coming unto us."[b] Wee have gone thus farre, wee have had two or three meetinges to declare and hold forth whatt itt is wee stand uppon. [Wee stand upon] the principles of unity and freedome. Wee have declar'd in what wee conceive these principles doe lie. I shall nott name them all because they are knowne unto you. Now in the progresse of these disputes and debates wee finde that the time spends, and noe question butt our adversaries are harder att worke then wee are. I heard (butt I had noe such testimonie as I could take hold of) that there are meetinges daily and contrivances against us. Now for our parts I hope you will nott say all is yours, butt wee have nakedlie and freelie unbosom'd

[a] *Vide* pp. 226, 233, 258, 276, 285, 288.

[b] The clauses making up these three sentences have been transposed. Lines 15-30 on p .343, "It was told mee . . . manifest unto you," seem properly to belong to this portion of the speech.

ourselves unto you. Though those thinges have startled many att the first view, yett wee finde there is good hopes. Wee have fix't our resolutions, and wee are determin'd, and wee want nothing butt that only God will direct us to what is just and right. Butt I understand, that [in] all these debates if wee shall agree uppon any one thinge, [to say] "this is our freedome," "this is our libertie," "this liberty and freedome wee are debarr'd of and wee are bereav'd of all those comforts," [that even] in case wee should finde out half a hundred of these, yett the maine businesse is how wee should finde them, and how wee should come by them. Is there any liberties that wee finde ourselves deprived of—if wee have greivances lett us see who are the hinderances, and when wee have pitched uppon that way—I conceive—I speake humbly in this, one thinge that I conceive myself as a particular person—that these delayes, these disputes will prove little incouragement. Itt was told mee by [one of] these Gentlemen that hee had great jealousies that wee would nott come to the triall of our spiritts, and that perhaps there might happen [to be] another designe in hand. I said to his Honour againe, if they would nott come to the light I would judge they had the workes of darkenesse in hand. Now as they told mee againe on the other hand, when itt was questioned by Col. Hewson, on the other hand they told mee that these Gentlemen, nott naming any particular persons, they will hold you in hand, and keepe you in debate and dispute till you and wee [shall] all come to ruine. Now I stood as a moderator betweene these thinges. When I heard the Lieutennant Generall speake I was mervailously taken uppe with the plainesse of the carriage. I said, "I will bringe them to you," "you shall see if there hearts bee soe; for my parte I see nothing butt plainesse and uprightnesse of heart made manifest unto you." I will nott judge nor draw any longe discourses uppon our disputes this day. Wee may differ in one thinge, that you conceive this debating and disputations will doe the worke, [we conceive] wee must putt ourselves into the former priviledges which wee want.

Sir Hardresse Waller.

I thinke this Gentleman hath dealt very ingenuously and plainly with us, I pray God wee may doe soe too, and I for one will doe itt. I thinke our disputings will not doe the thinge. I thinke if we doe make itt our resolution that wee doe hold itt forth to all powers, Parliament or Kinge, or whoever they are, to lett them know that these are our rights, and if wee have them nott, wee must get them the best way wee can.

Lieut. Generall.

I thinke you say very well, and my freind att my back,[a] hee tells mee that [there] are great feares abroad, and they talke of some thinges such as are nott onely specious to take a great many people with, butt reall, and substantiall, and such as are comprehensive of that that hath the good of the Kingedome in it. Truly if there bee never soe much desire of carrying on these thinges [together], never soe much desire of conjunction, yett if there bee not libertie of speech to come to a right understanding of thinges, I thinke itt shall bee all one as if there were noe desire att all to meete. I may say itt with truth that I verily beleive there is as much reallity and heartinesse amongst us [as amongst you] to come to a right understanding, and to accord with that that hath the settlement of the Kingdome in itt. Though when itt comes to particulars wee may differ in the way, yett I know nothing butt that every honest man will goe as farre as his conscience will lett him, and hee that will goe farther I thinke hee will fall back. And I thinke when that principle is written in the hearts of us, and when there is nott hypocrisie in our dealinges, wee must all of us resolve uppon this, that 'tis God that perswades the heart; if there be a doubt of sincerity, itt's the Devill that created that effect; and 'tis God that gives uprightnesse, and I hope with such an heart that wee have all met withall; if wee

[a] Everard.

have not, God finde him out that came without itt; for my parte I doe itt.

Com. Generall.

When you have done this according to the number of inhabitants, doe you not thinke itt is very variable; for the number will change every day? I would have us fall to somethinge that is practicable with as little paines and dissatisfaction as may bee. I remember, that in the proposalls that went out in the name of the Army itt is propounded as a rule to bee distributed according to the rates that the Counties beare in the [burdens of the] Kingedome; and remember then you have a rule, and though this be not a rule of exactnesse, yett there was something of equality in itt, and itt was a certaine rule where all are agreed, and therefore wee should come to some settling. Now I doe nott understand wherin the advantage does lie from a suddaine danger, uppon a thinge that will continue soe long, and will continue soe uncertaine as this is.[a]

Sir Hardresse Waller.

'Tis thought there's imminent danger; I hope to God we shall bee soe ready to agree for the future that wee shall all agree for the present to rise as one man if the danger bee such, for itt is an impossibility to have a remedy in this. The paper sayes, that this Parliament is to continue a yeare, butt will the great burthen of the people be ever satisfied with papers [whilst] you eate and feede uppon them? I shall be glad, that [if] there bee nott any present danger, you will thinke of some way to ease the burthen that wee may take a course [to do it]; and when wee have satisfied the people that wee doe really intend the good of the Kingdome [they will believe us]—Otherwise if the four Evangelists were heere and lay free quarter uppon them, they will not believe you.

[a] On the rule referred to, see "Heads of the Proposals of the Army," i. § 5.

Col. Rainborow.

Moved,

That the Army might bee called to a Randezvous, and thinges setled.

Com̃. Ireton.

Wee are called back to Engagements. I thinke the Engagements wee have made and published, and all the Engagements of all sorts, have bin better kept by those that did nott soe much cry out for itt then by those that doe; and if you will [have itt] in plaine termes, better kept then by those that have brought this paper. Give mee leave to tell you that in one point, in the Engagement of the Army not to devide, I am sure that hee that understands the Engagement of the Army nott to devide or disband, [as meaning] that wee are nott to devide for quarters for the ease of the country, or the satisfaction of service—hee that does understand itt in that sence, I am nott capable of his understanding.[a]

[a] The Army in their Engagement of June 5 declared that they would not disband till they had such satisfaction for their grievances and desires as soldiers and such security for their rights as private men as should appear sufficient to the General Council of the Army then established. "Without such satisfaction and security we shall not willingly disband, nor divide, nor suffer ourselves to be disbanded or divided" (Rushworth, vi., 512). On this subject the following observations are made in the *Case of the Army stated*, p. 2.

"That the Armie's Engagement, Representations, Declarations, and Remonstrances, and promises in them contained, are declined, and more and more dayly broken, and not only in some smaller matters wherein the Armie and the Kingdome are not so neerly concerned, but in divers particulars of dangerous consequence to the Army and the whole Nation, as,

"First, In the Engagement, page five, the Army promised every Member thereof each to other, and to the Parliament and Kingdome, that they would neither disband nor divide, nor suffer themselves to be disbanded or divided untill satisfaction should be given to the Army in relation to their grievances and desires; and securitie that neither the Army nor the free borne people of *England*, should remaine subiect to such injuries, oppression, and abuse, as the corrupt party in the Parliament then had attempted against them.

"Secondly, The Traine of Artillery is now to be disbanded, before satisfaction of securitie is given to the whole Army in relation to themselves, or other the free borne people, either in respect to their grievances or desires. And when the strength

There was another sence in itt, and that is, that wee should nott suffer ourselves to bee torne into pieces—such a dividing as [that] is really a disbanding, and for my parte I doe nott know what disbanding is if nott that deviding. [I say that] the subscribers of this paper, the authours of that Booke that is called, 'The Case of the Armie,' I say that they have gone the way of disbanding. Disbanding of an Army is nott parting in a place, for if that bee soe, did not wee att that night disband to severall quarters? Did wee nott then send severall Regiments—Col. Scroope's Regiment into the West[a]—wee know where itt was first—Col. Horton's Regiment into Wales for preventing of insurrection there—Col. Lambert's [and] Col. Lilburne's Regiment[s] then sent downe for strengthning such a place as Yorke. And yett the authours of that paper, and the subscribers of them—for I cannott thinke the authours and subscribers all one—we all know, and they may know, that there's noe parte of the Army is dispersed to quarters further then that. Wherupon that outcrie is [made]. They goe to scandalise [us as breakers of the Engagement not to disband or divide].[b] Butt hee that will goe to understand this to bee a dividing that wee engaged against, hee lookes att the name, and nott att the thinge. That deviding which is a disbanding [is] that

or sinews of the Army be broken, what effectual good can be secured for themselves or the people in case of opposition.

"Thirdly, The Army is divided into quarters so farre distant that one part is in no capabilitie to give timely assistance to another, if any designe should be to disband any part by violence sodainly, although neither our grievances nor desires as Soldiers or Commoners are redressed or answered. And as we conceive this dividing of the Army before satisfaction on securitie as aforesaid, to be contrary to the Armies intention in their Engagement, at the said Rendezvous, so we conceive it hath from that time given all the advantage to the enemies, to band and designe against the Armie, whereby not only pay hath been kept from the Soldiers, and securitie for areers prevented, but the kingdom was indangered to have been imbroyled in blood, and the settlement of the peace and freedome of the Nation, hath been thus long delayed."

[a] Scroope's Regiment had been at Holdenby, where a part of it was employed in guarding the King.

[b] MS. "they goe to scandalise an engagement or to devide."

deviding which makes noe Army, and that dissolving of that order and government which is as essentiall to an Army as life is to a man—which if it be taken away I thinke that such a companie are noe more an armie than a rotten carcass is a man—and [it is] those [who have done this] that have gone to devide the Armie. And what else is there in this paper [but] that we have acted soe vigorously for [already? We proposed that this Parliament should end within a year at most]; they doe not propose that this Parliament should end till the beginning of September. When all comes uppon the matter itt is but a criticall difference, and the very substance of that we have declared before. For my part I professe it seriously that we shall find in the issue that the principall of that division, of [that] disbanding is noe more then this, whether such or such [men] shall have the managing of the businesse. I say plainly the way [they have taken] hath bin the way of disunion and division, and [the dissolution] of that order and Government by which wee shall bee enabled to act, and that by the deviding from that generall Councill, wherein wee have all engaged we should bee concluded, and the endeavouring to draw the soldiers to run this way; and I shall appeale to all men whether there can bee any breach of the Army higher then that breach wee have now spoken of. [As for] that word "deviding the Army," let it bee judged whether [when we said] wee will nott divide [but] with such [and such] satisfaction, whether that deviding were nott more truly and properlie this deviding in every man's heart wherin wee doe goe apart one from another, and consequently [whether] those that have gone this way have nott broke the Engagement; [and] whether that [other dividing] were a deviding, [or] a keeping of the Engagement: and those that doe judge the one I doe nott thinke that wee have bin fairely dealt with.[a]

[a] Throughout this speech of Ireton's the sentences in the MS. are so broken and confused that much re-arrangement was necessary to make the sense intelligible. Compare the "Remonstance of his Excellency, Sir Thomas Fairfax, and the Council of War, concerning the late discontent and distraction in the Army" (November 14, 1647). It was evidently based on this speech and was probably drawn up by Ireton.

Col. Rainborow,

I doe nott make any great wonder that this Gentleman hath sence above all men in the world, butt for these thinges hee is the man that hath undertaken them all. I say this Gentleman hath the advantage of us, hee hath drawne uppe the most parte of them ; and why may hee nott keepe a sence that wee doe nott know of? If this Gentleman had declar'd to us att first that this was the sence of the Armie in deviding, and itt was meant that men should nott devide in opinions—To mee that is a mistery. Itt is a huge reflection, a taxing of persons, and because I will avoide further reflections, I shall say noe more.

Agitator,

Wheras you say the Agents did itt, [it was] the souldiers did putt the Agents uppon these meetinges. Itt was the dissatisfactions that were in the Army which provoak't, which occasion'd those Meetinges, which you suppose tends soe much to deviding; and the reasons of such dissatisfactions are because those whome they had to trust to act for them were nott true to them.

Comm. Gen.

If this bee all the effect of your meetinges to agree uppon this paper, there is butt one thinge in this that hath nott bin insisted uppon and propounded by the Army heertofore all alonge.[a] Heere[b] itt is putt according to the number of inhabitants; there according to the taxes. This[b] sayes a period att such a day, the last of September, the other sayes a period within a yeare att most. The Agreement says that these have the power of making law, and determining what is law without the consent of

[a] Ireton compares "the Heads of the Proposals of the Army," published Aug. 1, 1647, with "the Agreement of the People," first as to the basis to be taken in the equalisation of the constituencies, secondly as to the date to be fixed for the dissolution of Parliament, thirdly as to the question of the powers of the House of Commons.

[b] *i.e.* the Agreement.

another.[a] 'Tis true the "Proposalls" said nott that, and for my parte, if any man will putt that to the question whether wee shall concurre with itt I am in the same minde,[b] if you putt itt in any other hands then those that are freemen; butt if you shall putt the question, and with that limitation that hath bin all alonge acknowledged by the Parliament, till wee can acquitt ourselves justly from any Engagement old or new that wee stand in to preserve the person of the Kinge, the persons of Lords, and their rights soe farre as they are consistent with the common right,[c] till that bee done I thinke there is reason that exception should continue which hath bin all alonge, that is, where the safetie of the Kingdome is concern'd, this they seeme to hold out. But where I see thinges would nott doe reall mischief I would hold to positive constitution. I would neither bee thought to bee a wronge doer or disturber; soe longe as I can with safetie continue a constitution I will doe itt.[d] And therfore where I finde that the safetie of the Kingedome is nott concern'd, I would nott for every trifling [cause] make that this shall bee a law, though neither the Lords who have a claime to itt nor the Kinge who hath a claime to itt will consent. Butt where this is concern'd[e]—Uppon the whole matter lett men butt consider those that have thus gone away to devide from the Army.

[a] Clause 4 of the Agreement: "That the powers of this and all future representatives of this Nation, is inferior only to those who chuse them, without the consent or concurrence of any other person or persons" (*i. e.* King or Lords).

[b] May be paraphrased: "If any man will put it to the question whether we shall concur with that, I am willing to concur with it, provided you put the question with that limitation that hath bin all along acknowledged by the Parliament, that is where the safetie of the kingdom is concerned. Till we can acquit ourselves justly from any engagement, new or old, that we stand in to preserve the persons and rights of the King and Lords so far as they are consistent with the common right—till that be done I think there is reason that exception should continue." The rest is too chaotic.

[c] In the Declaration of June 14 the words used are, "so far as may consist with the right and freedom of the subject and the security of the same for the future."

[d] The position of this clause has been altered.

[e] "I do agree," etc., as on p. 351.

Admitt that this Agreement of the people bee the advantage, itt may bee wee shall agree to that without any limittation. I doe agree, that the Kinge is bound by his oath att his coronation to agree to the law that the Commons shall chuse without Lords or any body else. If I can agree any further that if the Kinge doe nott confirme with his aucthority the lawes that the people shall chuse, wee know what will follow.[a]

Mr. Pettus.

I had the happinesse sometimes to bee att the debate of the Proposalls, and my opinion was then as itt is now, against the Kinges vote and the Lords. Butt nott soe as I doe desire,[b] since itt hath pleased God to raise a companie of men that doe stand uppe for the power of the House of Commons, which is the Representative of the people, and deny the negative voice of King and Lords. For my parte I was much unknowne to any of them, butt only as I heard their principles, and hearing their principles I cannott butt joyne with them in my judgement, for I thinke itt is reasonable. That all lawes are made by their consent,[c] wheras you seeme to make the Kinge and Lords soe light a thinge as that itt may bee to the destruction of the Kingedome to throwe them out, and without prejudice [to keep them in]. For my parte I cannott butt thinke that both the power of Kinge and Lords was ever a branch of

[a] The controversy between the King and Parliament as to the meaning of the King's Coronation Oath had been very bitter in 1642. It then turned chiefly on the interpretation of the word "elegerit."

The Levellers now sought to interpret the oath so as to deny the legislative power of the House of Lords. Wildman in criticising the "Proposals," complains: "A restriction to their usurpation of a negative voice to all the resolutions of the Commons, is not once named, or intimated; although Ireton himself hath confessed in their counsels, that the King by his oath is obliged to confirm such laws as the Commons should chuse; the word 'Vulgus' in the King's oath, signifying people, or folke, excludes the Lords totally from any right to intermeddle in the making of laws" (*Putney Projects*, p. 41).

[b] *i.e.* "I did not then desire it so much as I do now."

[c] *i.e.* The consent of the King and the Lords is now necessary to the making of all laws.

Tyranny, and if ever a people shall free themselves from Tyranny, cartainly itt is after 7 yeares warre and fighting for their libertie. For my parte, [I think that] if the Constitution of this Kingdome shall bee established as formerly, itt might rivett Tyranny into this Kingedome more strongly then before. For when the people shall heare that for 7 yeares together the people were plundered, and [that] after they had overcome the Kinge, and kept the Kinge under restraint, att last the Kinge comes in, then itt will rivett the Kinges interest; and soe when any men shall indeavour to free themselves from Tyranny wee may doe them mischief and noe good. I thinke itt's most just and equall, since a number of men have declar'd against itt, they should bee encouraged in itt, and nott discouraged; and I finde by the Councill that their thoughts are the same against the Kinge and Lords, and if soe bee that a power may bee raised to doe that itt would doe well.

Mr. Wildman.

Truly, Sir, I being desired by the Agents yesterday to appeare att Councill or Committees either, att that time, I suppose I may bee bold to make knowne what I know of their sence, and a little to vindicate them in their way of proceeding, and to shew the necessity of this way of proceeding that they have entred uppon. Truly, Sir, as to breaking of Engagements: the Agents doe declare their principle, that whensoever any Engagement cannott bee kept justly they must breake that Engagement. Now though itt's urg'd they ought to condescend to what the Generall Councill doe [resolve], I conceive itt's true [only] soe longe as itt is for their safetie. I conceive [itt's] just and righteous for them to stand uppe for some more speedy vigorous actinges. I conceive itt's noe more then what the Army did when the Parliament did nott only delay deliverance butt oppos'd itt; and I conceive this way of their appearing hath nott appear'd to bee in the least way anythinge tending to devision, since they proceede to cleare the rights of the people; and soe longe as they proceede uppon those righteous principles [for which we first engaged],[a] itt cannott bee laid to their charge that they are deviders. And though itt bee declared [that they ought to stand only as soldiers and not as Englishmen], that the malice of the enemies would have bereaved you of your liberties as Englishmen; therefore as Englishmen they are deeply concerned to regard the due observation of their rights, [and have the same right to declare their apprehensions] as I, or any Commoner, have right to propound to the Kingedome my conceptions what is fitt for the good of the Kingedome. Wheras itt is objected, how will itt appear that their proceedings shall tend for the good of the Kingedome? The matter is different. Wheras itt was said before itt was propounded, there must bee an ende to the Parliament, an equality as to Elections—I finde itt to bee their minds—When they came there, they found many aversions from matters that they ought to stand to as souldiers, and nott as Englishmen, and therfore I find it. Concerning the matter of the thinge, I conceive it to bee a very vast difference in the whole matter of proposalls. The foundation of slavery was rivetted more strongly then before. As where the militia is instated in the Kinge and Lords,[b] and nott in the Commons, there is a foundation of a future quarrell constantlie laid. However the maine thing was that they found by the proposalls propounded the right of the Militia was acknowledged to bee in the Kinge, before any redresse of any one of the people's greivances or any one of their burthens; and [the King was] soe to bee brought in as

[a] The three passages given in brackets are supplied from the *Case of the Army*, p. 20.

[b] Compare Wildman's *Putney Projects*, p. 40: "Although the Lords are the very offspring of the King's corrupt will; and were never so honoured by the people, as to have a trust committed to them to represent any county; yet those Proposals invest them with the highest authority only because of the King's Pattent. (1.) The Proposals allow them a power over the Militia, coordinate, and coequal, to the representative of all the nation, the Commons in Parliament; thus in the first and second property of the Second Proposal, the power of the Militia, etc. for ten years, to be disposed of by the Lords and Commons."

with a negative voice, wherby the people and Army that have fought against him when hee had propounded such thinges[a]— And finding [this] they perceived they were as they thought in a sad case, for they thought, hee coming in thus with a negative, the Parliament are butt as soe many cyphers, soe many round Os; for if the Kinge would nott doe itt hee might chuse, "Sic volo, sic jubeo," &c., and soe the corrupt party of the Kingedome must bee soe setled in the Kinge. The godly people are turn'd over and trampled uppon already in the most places of the Kingedome. I speake butt the words of the agents, and I finde this to bee their thoughts. Butt wheras itt is said, "how will this paper provide for anythinge for that purpose?" I say, that this paper doth lay downe the foundations of freedome for all manner of people. Itt doth lay the foundations of souldiers [freedom], wheras they found a great uncertainty in the proposalls: that they should goe to the Kinge for an act of indempnity, and thus the Kinge might command his Judges to hange them uppe for what they did in the warres; because the present Constitution being left as itt was, nothing was law butt what the Kinge sign'd, and nott any ordnance of Parliament. And considering this, they thought itt should bee by an Agreement with the people, wherby a rule betweene the Parliament and the people might bee sett, that soe they might bee destroyed neither by the Kinge's Prerogative, nor Parliament's priviledges.

[a] The *Case of the Army*, p. 6, observes :—

"In the declaration of June 14, p. 10, as in all other Remonstrances and Declarations, it was desired, that the rights and liberties of the people might be secured, before the King's businesse should be considered. But now the grievances of the people are propounded to be considered after the restoring him to that legall power, and that in such a way according to the proposalls, viz. with a negative voice, that the people that have purchased by blood what was their right, of which the King endeavoured to deprive them, should yet solely depend on his will for their relief in their grievances and oppressions; and in like manner the security for the Armie's arrears is proposed to be considered after the businesse of the Kinge be determined."

The same view is expressed in Wildman's *Putney Projects*, 1647, pp. 22, 23. As Ireton points out, Wildman was probably the author of the *Case of the Army*.

They[a] are nott bound to bee subject to the lawes as other men, [that is] why men cannott recover their estates. They thought there must bee a necessity of a rule betweene the Parliament and the people, soe that the Parliament should know what they were intrusted to, and what they were nott; and that there might bee noe doubt of the Parliament's power to lay foundations for future quarrells.[b] The Parliament shall nott meddle with a souldier after indempnity. Itt is agreed amongst the people, wheras betweene a Parliament and Kinge—if the Kinge were nott under restraint—should make an Act of Indempnity—wheras another Parliament cannott alter this—That these foundations might bee established.

[a] This refers to Parliamentary privilege, which is aimed at in the fourth clause in the Agreement: "That in all lawes made or to be made every person may be bound alike, and that no tenure, estate, charter, degree, birth, or place, doe conferre any exemption from the ordinary course of legal proceedings whereunto others are subjected." This is explained to mean, "That whereas now severall persons are by an usurped power exalted above the law and protected from due process at law, viz, Lords as Peers, although legally indebted, may not be touched with an arrest, nor be made subject to the censure of the law; whereby they have made little conscience when they have got men's estates in their hands, to return the same, but have stood upon their prerogative and thereby been protected, to the utter ruin and undoing of many of the free people of England." *The Grand Designe*, 1647, by John Harris.

[b] See the Letter of the Agitators, "For the noble and highly honoured, the Free born people of England," appended to the "Agreement of the People."

"We have therefore inserted it into this Agreement, that no person shall be questionable for anything done, in relation to the late publike differences, after the dissolution of this present Parliament, further then in execution of their judgment; that thereby all may be secure from all sufferings for what they have done, and not liable hereafter to be troubled or punished by the judgment of another Parliament, which may be to their ruine, unlesse this Agreement be joyned in, whereby any acts of indempnite or oblivion shall be made unalterable, and you and your posterities be secure. But if any shall inquire why we should desire to joyn in an Agreement with the People, to declare these to be our native Rights, and not rather petition to the Parliament for them; the reason is evident: No Act of Parliament is or can be unalterable, and so cannot be sufficient security to save you or us harmlesse from what another Parliament may determine, if it should be corrupted; and besides Parliaments are to receive the extent of their power and trust from those that betrust them; and therefore the people are to declare what their power or trust is, which is the intent of this Agreement."

That there might bee noe dispute betweene Lords and Commons, butt these thinges being setled, there should bee noe more disputes, butt that the Parliament should redresse the peoples grievances, wheras now all are troubled with Kinge's interests almost. And besides if this were setled, the Parliament should be free from those temptations—which for my owne parte I doe suppose to bee a truth, that this very Parliament, by the Kinge's voice in this very Parliament may destroy—wheras now they shall bee free from temptations and the Kinge cannott have an influence uppon them as hee hath.[a]

Com̃. Gen. Ireton.

Gentlemen, I thinke there is noe man is able to give a better account of the sence of the Agents; hee hath spoke soe much as they have in their Booke and soe readily and therfore I see hee is very well able to give their sence. I wish their sences had nott bin prejudiciall to other men's sences; butt I feare as itt will prove really prejudiciall to the Kingedome, how plausible soever it seemes to bee carried. That paper of the Case of the Armie doth soe abuse the Generall and Generall Councill of the Armie, that such and such thinges have bin done that made them doe thus and thus. First as to the materiall points of the paper. As to the businesse of the Lords you know the way wee were then in admitted noe other.[b] This Gentleman that speakes heere, and the other gentleman that spake before, when wee were att Reading framing the

[a] Wildman's argument is given in the *Case of the Army*, p. 12. "The Armies and their assistants' indempnity is propounded to receive its strength from the King's consent; whereas not only his signing of or consent to any act is wholly null and void in law because he is under restraint and our indemnity will be insufficient if it shall depend in the least on his confirmation." He proceeds to argue that an act of indemnity passed by one Parliament might be repealed by another, "whereas another Parliament cannot alter this." Moreover, this very Parliament might be so corrupted by the King as to nullify an act of indemnity passed by it.

[b] From 1645 onwards the legislative and judicial powers of the House of Lords had been subject to constant attacks. Edwards, in the third part of his *Gangraena*, 1646, pp. 148, 196—200, collects a number of the utterances of the Levellers and

proposalls did nott thinke of this way. I am sure they did not thinke of this way; and according to the best judgements of those that were intrusted by the Generall Councill to drawe uppe the prosposalls, itt was carried by a question clearlie, that wee should nott. In these proposalls our businesse was to sett forth particulars; wee had sett forth generall Declarations, which did come to as much in effect in this[a] The thinge then proposed was, that wee should nott take away the power of the Lords in this Kingedome, and itt was concluded that in the proposalls. Butt as to the Kinge wee were clear. There is nott one thinge in the proposalls, nor in what wee declar'd, that doth give the Kinge any negative voice; and therfore that's parte of the scandall amongst others. Wee doe not give the Kinge any negative, wee doe butt take the Kinge as a man with whome wee have bin att a difference, wee propound termes of peace. Wee doe nott demand that hee shall have noe Negative, butt wee doe nott say that hee shall have any. There's another thinge that wee have, as they say, gone from our Engagements in our Declarations in. [They say] that in the proposalls we goe to establish the

Sectaries against the House of Lords. "The speeches and writings of the Sectaries against the House of Peers within this last six months or thereabouts are fearful and strange, tending apparently to the total overthrow of the House of Peers and of having any Lords in this kingdom, denying them all legislative and judicial power, and giving it all to the House of Commons, or rather to that beast with many heads, the common people." The leaders of this attack were John Lilburne and Richard Overton. See *An Alarum to the House of Lords*, 1646, and Overton's *An Arrow against all Tyrants and Tyranny shot from the prison of Newgate into the Prerogative Bowels of the Arbitrary House of Lords*. On three separate occasions the privileges of the House of Lords seem to have been guaranteed: in 1645, on the passing of the self-denying ordinance (Rushworth, vi., 14); and in the summer of 1647 (*Vindication of Sir William Waller*, pp. 192-6); in January, 1648, after the passing of the vote of no further addresses to the King (Rushworth, vii., 967).

[a] The text may be paraphrased thus:

"According to the best judgments of those that were entrusted to draw up the Proposals it was decided that we should not take away the power of the Lords in this kingdom, and it was so concluded in the Proposals. That in the Proposals our business was to set forth particulars. We had set forth general declarations which had come to much the same thing."

Kinge's Rights before [taking away] the peoples Greivances.[a] In our Generall Declarations wee first desire a purging of this Parliament, a period [to be set for] this Parliament, and provision for the certainty of future Parliaments; and if the Kinge shall agree in these thinges and what [things] else the Parliament shall propound that are necessary for the safetie of the Kingedome, then wee desire his Rights may bee consider'd soe farre as may consist with the Rights of the people. Wee did soe [speak] in the Declarations, and you shall see what wee did in the proposalls.[a] In the proposalls, [we put first] thinges that are essentiall to peace, and itt distinguishes those from the things that conduce to our better being, and thinges that lay foundations of an hopefull Constitution in the future. When those are past, then they say, 'that these thinges having the Kinge's concurrence wee desire that his Right may bee consider'd.' There were many other greivances and particular matters which wee did nott thinke soe necessary that they should precede the setling of a peace, which is the greatest greivance of the Kingdome. Our way was to take away that [first]. Then itt says there, [after] propounding what thinges wee thought in our judgements are to bee essentiall and necessary to peace, 'yet wee desire that the Parliament would loose noe time from the consideration of them.'[b] These Gentlemen

[a] In the Declaration of June 14, it is said: "These things we desire may be provided for by Bill or Ordinance of Parliament to which the royall assent may be desired. When his Majesty in these things, and what else shall be proposed by the Parliament, necessary for securing the Rights and Liberties of the people, and for settling the Militia and peace of the Kingdom shall have given his concurrence to put them past dispute, we shall then desire that the Rights of his Majestie and his Posterity may be considered of, and setled in all things, so farre as may consist with the Right and Freedome of the Subject and with the security of the same for the future."

In the Proposals, § xiv., it is demanded "That (the things heretofore proposed, being provided for settling and securing the rights, liberties, peace and safety of the kingdom) His Majestie's person, his Queen, and royall issue, may be restored to a condition of safety, honour and freedom in this nation, without diminution to their personal rights, or further limitation to the exercise of the regal power than according to the particulars aforegoing."

[b] After Clause xvi., the Proposals continue: "Next to the proposalls aforesaid for

would say now wee have gone from our Declarations, that wee propose the setling of the Kinge [first, because] itt stands before those Greivances. Wee say those Greivances are nott soe necessary, as that the remedying of them should bee before the setling of the peace of the Kingedome. What wee thought in our consciences to bee essentiall to the peace of the Kingedome wee did putt preceding to the consideration of the Kinge's personall Right; and the concurrence of [the King to] those is a condition without which wee cannott have any Right att all, and without [which] there can bee noe peace, and [we] have named [it] before the consideration of the Kinge's Rights in the setling of a peace, as a thinge necessary to the constitution of a peace. That therfore [to say] wee should preferre the Kinge's Rights before a generall good, was as unworthy and as unchristian an injury as ever was done [by any] to men that were in society with them, and meerly equivocation. Butt itt was told you, that the Generall Councill hath seemed to doe soe and soe, to putt the souldiers out of the way. Itt is suggested, that the Engagement is broken by our deviding to quarters; and whether that bee broken or nott in other thinges, itt is said, that the Generall Councill hath broken the Engagement in this; that wheras before wee were nott a mercinarie Army, now wee are. Lett any man butt speake what hath given the occasion of that. Itt hath bin pres't by some men that wee should [not] have subjected [our propositions] to the Parliament, and wee would stand to the proposi-

the present settling of a peace, wee shall desire that no time may be lost by the Parliament for despatch of other things tending to the welfare, ease and just satisfaction of the Kingdom." A number of grievances are then specially enumerated In the Declaration of Aug. 2, special attention is called to this distinction. "To these proposalls which we here first tender as necessary to a peace . . . we cannot but add the further expression of our desires in some other particulars, which, though not so essential to peace, as necessarily to precede the settling of it, yet being matters of very public, and (most of them) of general grievance to the kingdom: we shall desire, that (the Parliament being set free) no time may be lost for a speedy consideration of them, so as the former things for the present settling of peace be not delayed thereby."

tions whatever they were; butt the sence of the Generall Councill was this, that, as they had sent their propositions to the Parliament, they would see what the Parliament would doe before they would conclude what themselves would doe; and that there was respect [to be had] to that which wee have hitherto accounted the fundamentall Councill of the Kingedome.[a] If all the people to a man had subscribed to this [Agreement] [b] then there would bee some security to itt, because noe man would oppose; butt otherwise our concurrence amongst ourselves is noe more then our saying our selves wee will bee indemnified. Our Indemnity must bee to somethinge that att least wee will uppehold, and wee see wee cannott hold to bee a conclusive authority of the Kingedome. For that [charge] of going to the Kinge for Indemnity, wee propose an Act of oblivion onely for the Kinges partie; wee propose for ourselves an Act of Indemnity and Justification. Is this the asking of a pardon? Lett us resort to the first petition of the Army wherin wee all were engag'd once, which wee made the basis of all our proceedinges. In that wee say, that [wee wish] an ordinance might bee past to which the Royall Assent might bee desired; butt wee have [since] declar'd, that if the Royall Assent

[a] The charges referred to are shown by the following passages from the *Case of the Army.* "The whole intent of the Engagement and the equitable sense of it hath been perverted openly by affirming and by sinister means making seeming determinations in the Council that the Army was not to insist upon or demand any security for their own or other the freeborn people's freedoms or rights, though they might propound anything to the Parliament's consideration; and according to that high breach of their engagement their actions have been regulated, and nothing that was declared formerly to be insisted upon hath been resolvedly adhered to, or claimed as the Armie's or the people's due."(p. 3.)

"In the Declaration of June 14, it is declared that the Army took up arms in judgement and conscience for the people's just rights and liberties, and not as mercenary soldiers, hired to serve an arbitrary power of the State. But the strength of the endeavours of many hath been, and are now, spent to persuade the soldiers and agitators, that they stand as soldiers only to serve the State, and may not as free Commons claim their right and freedom as due to them." (p. 4.)

[b] Heads of the Proposals Articles, vi., xvi.

could nott be had, wee should account the aucthority of the Parliament valid without itt.[a] Wee have desired in the Generall Councill, that for security for arreares wee might have the Royall Assent; and lett mee tell you though I shall bee content to loose my arreares to see the Kingedome have itts libertie—and if any man can doe itt unlesse itt bee by putting our libertie into the hands of those that will give itt away when they have done. Butt I say that I doe thinke that true in this, whoever talk't either of the indeavours of the souldiers, or of any other Indempnity by the sworde in their hands, is [for] the perpetuating of combustions, soe that worde cannott take place, and does nott suppose the setling of a peace, and by that aucthority which hath bin here by the legislative power of the Kingedome; and hee that expects to have the arreares of the souldiers soe, I thinke hee does butt deceive himself.[b] For my owne parte I would give uppe my arreares, and for my parte loose my arreares, if wee have nott settlement; noe arreares or want of Indempnity, nor any thinge in the world shall satisfie mee to have a peace uppon any termes, wherin that which is really the Right of this Nation is nott as farre provided for as can bee provided for by men. I could tell you many other particulars wherin there are divers grosse injuries done to the Generall and Generall Councill, and such a wronge as is nott fitt to bee done amonge Christians, and soe wronge, and soe false that I cannott thinke that they have gone soe farre in itt.

[a] Ireton refers first to the petition of the Army drawn up in March, 1647; secondly, to the desires of the Army in relation to themselves as soldiers, September 21, 1647. (*Book of Army Declarations*, p. 160.)

[b] This passage may be thus paraphrased: "I think it is true in this, that whoever talks of the soldiers endeavouring to secure themselves by the swords in their hands, or any other indemnity to be obtained by force, is for the perpetuating of combustions. Talk of that kind is inconsistent with a settlement, and does not suppose a settlement by the authority that has been hitherto acknowledged by us, by the legislative authority of the kingdom. Anyone who expects to get the arrears of the soldiers paid except through Parliament and through such a general settlement deceives himself. For my part, if I am to choose between the payment of my arrears, and the general settlement of the kingdom I would rather lose my arrears."

Mr. Wildman.

I doe nott know what reason you have to suppose I should bee soe well acquainted with the Case of the Armie, and the thinges proposed [in it]. I conceive them to bee very good and just. Butt for that which I give as their sence, which you are pleased to say are scandalls cast uppon the Army, that you propounded to bringe in the Kinge with his negative voice. The legislative power had bin acknowledged [hitherto] to bee in the Kinge with Lords and Commons, whereas you do now say the legislative power to be partly in him. Then considering that, I doe humbly propound to your consideration, [that] when you restraine the Kinges Negative in one particular, which is in restrayning unequall distributions, and say directly in these very words [the King] "shall bee restored to his personall Rights," you doe now say the Legislative power to bee now partly in him. And therfore I conceive if I have any reason the Kinge is proposed to bee brought in with his Negative voice.[a] And wheras you say itt is a scandall for [us to say that you propose] the Kinge to come in with his personall Rights [before the grievances of the people are redressed, it is said in the proposals] that the Kinge consenting to those thinges the Kinge [is] to bee restored to all his personall Rights.

There's his Restoration. Nott a bare consideration what his

[a] "Let the seventh particular in the first proposal be compared with the fourteenth proposall. In the seventh particular it is proposed 'that the orders and rules set down by the Commons in Parliament, for the freedom of election of Members and the right constitution of their own house, be as laws,' thus restraining the King's negative voice only in that one particular. And in the fourteenth proposal it is expressly desired, 'that there might be no further limitation to the exercise of the regall power, than according to the foregoing particular'" (*Putney Projects*, p. 32). Wildman also complains that "When the proposalls were first composed there was a small restriction of the King's negative voice; it was agreed to be proposed that whatever bill should be propounded by two immediate succeeding parliaments should stand in full force and effect as any other law, though the King should refuse to consent" (p. 14). He states that Ireton and Cromwell to please the King expunged this restriction. The position of two clauses in Wildman's speech has been altered.

Rights are before the peoples Greivances [are considered], butt a Restoration to his personall Rights these thinges being done. Is nott the Parliament to loose their Rights? And for that of [asking the King's consent to an Act of] Indempnity, I doe nott say itt was an asking of the Kinge pardon; itt is rendring us uppe, [because the King is under constraint], and therfore itt is null in Law.

Saturday, 30 October, 1647.

Att the Committee of Oficers att the Quartermaster Generalls.

Present.

Lieut. Generall.	Capt. Merriman.
Commissary Generall.	Lieut. Col. Cobbett.
Col. Rainborow.	Lieut. Chillenden.
Sir Hardresse Waller.	Mr. Allen.
Col. Lilburne.	,, Walley.
,, Rich.	,, Sexby.
Lieutennant Col. Goffe.	,, Whiting.
Major Rainborow.	,, Gayes.
Capt. Clarke.	,, Andrewes.

To consider of the papers of the Armie, and the paper of the People's Agreement, and to collect and prepare somewhat to bee insisted uppon and adheer'd unto for setling the Kingedome, and to cleare our proceedinges hitherto.

Putney, October 30, 1647.

Att the Committee of Officers appointed to consider of the Agreement, and compare itt with Declarations.

Agreed,

1. That there bee a period sett to this Parliament to end and bee

dissolved on the first day of September next ensuing att the furthest.

2. That secure provision may bee made for the succession, constitution, and clearing the power of Parliaments in future, as followeth:

1. For the certainty of their succession, that Parliaments shall biennially meete on the first Thursday in Aprill every second yeare from and after the ending of this Parliament, with such provision for the certainty therof as shall bee found needfull before the ending of this Parliament. The place of Meeting for each succeeding Parliament to bee where the Parliament last preceding shall appoint, unlesse the Councill of State heerafter mencioned, during the intervall shall finde emergent cause to alter the place, and in such case the Meeting for the next Parliament to bee where the Councill shall appoint, provided, that notice bee given therof to all the severall Divisions of the Kingedome for which Members are to bee chosen att least 30 dayes before the time of Meeting.

2. For the certainty of their sitting,

That each Bienniall Parliament shall certainly continue to sitt untill the last day of September next ensuing after the meeting therof, unlesse adjourn'd or dissolv'd sooner by their owne consent, butt uppon the said last day of September to dissolve of course.

3. That this Parliament and each succeeding Parliament, att or before Adjournement or Dissolution therof, shall or may appoint a Committee or Councell of State, and such other Committees to continue during the intervall with such powers as they shall finde needfull for such ends and purposes as are in these articles referr'd and left unto them.

4. That in the intervalls betwixt Bienniall Parliaments the

Kinge, without the advice and consent of the Councill of State may nott call a Parliament extraordinary; butt uppon the advice of the Councill of State, and uppon their warrant for that purpose a Parliament extraordinary shall be called, provided, that itt meete above 70 dayes before the next Bienniall day, and shall dissolve of course att least 40 dayes before the same, soe as the course of Bienniall Elections may never bee interrupted. Other circumstances about the manner and way of calling such Parliaments extraordinary are to bee sett downe by this Parliament before the ende thereof.

5. For the Constitution of future Parliaments.

1. That the Election of Members for the House of Commons in succeeding Parliaments shall bee distributed to all Counties, or other partes or Devisions of the Kingdome, according to some rule of equality of proportion, soe as to render the House of Commons as neere as may bee an equall Representative of the whole body of the people that are to Elect; and in order therunto, that all obstructions to the freedome and equalitie of their choice, either by petitions or charters or other prerogative grants, bee removed, and the circumstances of number, place, and manner for more equall distributions bee sett downe by the Commons in this present parliament before the end therof; and what they shall order therin, as alsoe what they or the Commons in succeeding Parliaments shall from time to time further order or sett downe, for reducing the said Elections to more and more perfection of equality in distribution therof, freedome in the Election, order and regularity in the proceeding therof, and certainty in the returnes, shall bee lawes in full force to those purposes.[a]

2. That the qualifications of the people that shall have voices in the Elections, as alsoe of those that shall bee capable of being

[a] This stipulation occurs also in the "Heads of the Proposals," (i. § 7), but is not so clearly stated.

Elected, bee determined by the Commons in this present Parliament before the end therof, soe as to give as much inlargement to Common freedome as may bee, with a due regard had to the equality [a] and end of the present Constitution in that point; wherin wee desire itt may bee provided, that all freeborne Englishmen, or persons made free denizons of England, who have served the Parliament in the late warre for the liberties of the Kingdome, and were in the service before the 14th of June 1645, or have voluntarily assisted the Parliament in the said warre with mony, plate, horse, or Armes lent uppon the Parliament's propositions for that purpose, brought in theruppon before the [b] day of 1642, shall uppon such certificates therof as by the Commons in this present Parment shall bee determined sufficient, or uppon other sufficient evidence of the said service or assistance, bee admitted to have voices in the said elections for the respective Counties or Divisions wherin they shall inhabite, although they should nott in other respects bee within the qualifications to bee sett downe as aforesaid; as alsoe that itt bee provided, that noe person who for delinquencie in the late warre or otherwise hath forfeited or shall forfeite his said freedome, and is or shall bee soe adjudged by the Commons in Parliament, either by particular judgement or otherwise, or according to generall rules or law for that purpose, whiles hee standeth or shall stand soe adjudged and nott restor'd, shall bee admitted to have any voice in the said Elections or bee capable of being elected. And for that purpose, that itt bee provided either by law or judgement in this present Parliament, that noe person whatsoever who hath bin in hostility against the Parliament in the late warre shall bee capable of having a voice

[a] Perhaps this word should be "equity," see p. 334.

[b] Probably before 29th November, 1642, when an ordinance was passed for assessing those who had not voluntarily contributed. The third clause of the Agreement of the People (Jan. 1649) suggests May, 1643.

or being elected in the said Elections or to vote or sitt as a Member or Assistant in either House of Parliament untill the 2d Bienniall Parliament bee past.

3. That noe Peers made since the 21st day of May, 1642, or heerafter to bee made, shall bee admitted or capable to sitt or vote in Parliament without consent of both Houses.

6. For clearing of the power of Parliament in future and the interest of the people therin.[a]

Putney, 1 November, 1647.[b]

Att the Generall Councill of the Army.

Lieut. Generall.

The Lieutennant Generall first moved, that every one might speake their experiences as the issue of what God had given in answer to their prayers.

Capt. Allen [c]

Made a speech, expressing what experiences hee had received from himself, and from divers other godly people: that the worke that was before them was to take away the Negative voice of the Kinge and Lords.

A report from Col. Lambert's Regiment that two Horsemen, Agitators, came and perswaded them to send new Agitators, for that the Officers had broken their Engagements.

[a] The substance of the remaining articles is given later, pp. 407, 408.

[b] Monday, November 1. See Rushworth, iv., part 2, p. 859.

[c] Francis Allen of Ingoldsby's regiment; Major Allen of Berkshire, Thurloe, iv., 285.

Capt. Carter [a]

Exprest his experiences; that hee found nott any inclination in his heart as formerly to pray for the kinge, that God would make him yett a Blessing to the kingdome.

Com̃. Cowling

Made a speech expressing, that the sworde was the onelie thinge that had from time to time recover'd our Rightes, and which hee ever read in the Worde of God had recover'd the Rights of the people: that our ancestors had still recover'd their liberties from the Danes and Normans by the sworde, when they were under such a slaverie that an Englishman was as hatefull then as an Irishman is now, and what an honour those that were noblemen thought itt to marry their daughters to, or to marry the daughters of any cookes or bakers of the Normans.

Lieut. Col. Lilburne.[b]

That hee never observed that the recovery of our liberties which wee had before the Normans was the occasion of our taking uppe armes, or the maine quarrell; and that the Norman Lawes are nott slaverie introduced uppon us, but an augmentation of our slaverie before. Therfore I doubt for those reasons I have given you what was by some offer'd was not of God.

Lieut Generall.

To that which hath bin moved concerning the Negative vote, or thinges which have bin deliver'd in papers, and otherwise may present a reall pleasing. I doe nott say that they have all pleas'd, for I thinke that the Kinge is Kinge by contract, and I shall say,

[a] John Carter of Hewson's regiment.

[b] Henry Lilburne, Lieutenant-Colonel of the regiment of his brother, Robert Lilburne, turned Royalist in 1648, and was killed at the re-capture of Tynemouth Castle, August 11, 1648.

as Christ said, "Lett him that is without sin cast the first stone;" and minde that worde of bearing one with another, itt was taught us to day. If wee had carried itt on in the Parliament and by our power without any thinges laid on [us of] that kinde, soe that wee could say that wee were without transgression, I should then say itt were just to cutt off transgressors; butt considering that wee are in our owne actions failing in many particulars, I thinke there is much necessity of pardoning of transgressors.

For the actions that are to bee done, and those that must doe them. I thinke itt is their proper place to conforme to the Parliament that first gave them their being; and I thinke itt is considerable[a] whether they doe contrive to suppresse the power by that power or noe. If they doe continue to suppresse them how they can take the determination of commanding men, conducting men, quartering men, keeping guards, without an aucthority otherwise then from themselves, I am ignorant of. And therfore I thinke there is much [need] in the Army to conforme to those thinges that are within their spheare. For those thinges that have bin done in the Army, as this of the Case of the Army truly Stated. There is much in itt usefull, and to bee condescended to; butt I am nott satisfied how farre wee shall presse [it]. Either they are a Parliament or noe Parliament. If they bee noe Parliament they are nothing, and wee are nothing likewise. If they bee a Parliament wee are to offer itt to itt. If I could see a visible presence of the people, either by subscriptions, or number [I should be satisfied with it]; for in the Governement of Nations that which is to bee look't after is the affections of the people, and that I finde which satisfies my conscience in the present thinge.

[Consider the case of the Jews]. They were first [divided into] families where they lived, and had heads of families [to govern

[a] Considerable, *i.e.* "to be considered of." The sense seems to be: "I think they ought to consider whether they intend to suppress the royalists (?) by the power of the Parliament."

them], and they were [next] under judges, and [then] they were under Kinges. When they came to desire a Kinge they had a Kinge, first Elective, and secondly by succession. In all these kindes of Governement they were happy and contented. If you make the best of itt, if you should change the Governement to the best of itt, itt is butt a morall thinge. Itt is butt as Paul sayes "Drosse and dunge in comparison of Christ;"[a] and why wee shall soe farre contest for temporall thinges, that if wee cannott have[b] this freedome wee will venture life and livelihood for itt. When every man shall come to this condition I thinke the State will come to desolation. Therfore the considering of what is fitt for the Kingedome does belonge to the Parliament —well composed in their creation and election—how farre I shall leave itt to the Parliament to offer itt. There may bee care—That the elections or formes of Parliament are very illegall, as I could name butt one for a Corporation to chuse two. I shall desire, that there may bee a forme for the electing of Parliaments. And another thinge as the perpetuity of the Parliament[c] that there is noe assurance to the people, butt that itt is perpetuall, which does [not] satisfie the Kingedome; and for other thinges that are to the Kinge's Negative vote as may cast you off wholly, itt hath bin the resolution of the Parliament and of the Army—If there bee a possibility of the Parliament's offering those thinges unto the Kinge that may secure us I thinke there is much may bee said for the[ir] doing of itt.

[a] Philippians iii., 8.

[b] MS. "yett if wee cannot have."

[c] Cromwell's argument may be thus summed up: "Leave the settlement of government to Parliament, but provide that Parliament be rightly constituted. There may be care taken that future Parliaments be well composed as to their creation and election. Elections to Parliament are sometimes illegal, as for instance for corporations to choose two. I shall desire that there may be a form for the electing of Parliament. Another thing to be provided against is the perpetuity of the same Parliament, there is no security at present that it shall not be perpetual." The policy advocated is that set forth in the Army Declaration of June 14. Compare Cromwell's remarks on pp. 328, 336.

As for the present condition of the Army I shall speake somethinge of itt. For the conduct of the Army I perceive there are severall Declarations from the Army and dissobligations to the Generalls orders by calling Randezvous and otherwise. I must confesse I have a Commission from the Generall and I understand that I am to doe by itt. I shall conforme to him according to the rules and discipline of warre, and according to those rules I ought to bee conformable; and therfore I conceive itt is nott in the power of any particular men or any particular man in the Army to call a Randezvouz of a troope, or Regiment, or [in the] least[a] to disoblige the Armie from those commands of the Generall. This way is destructive to the Armie and to every particular man in the Armie. I have bin inform'd by some of the Kinge's partie, that if they give us rope enough we will hange ourselves. [We shall hang ourselves], if wee doe not conforme to the rules of warre, and therfore I shall move what wee shall center uppon. If itt have butt the face of aucthority, if itt bee butt an hare swimming over the Thames, hee will take hold of itt rather then lett itt goe.[b]

Lieut. Chillenden.

That God hitherto hath bin pleased to shew us many mercies. The relation of God's providence in bringing us from our march to London.

Mr. Allen.

On Friday was a day for to seeke God for direction in this worke,

[a] MS. "att least."

[b] Cromwell's general meaning is plain enough, though the illustration he uses is difficult to understand. The Army, he argues, must have some civil authority to support it, therefore it ought to own the authority of the Parliament. He would lay hold of any commission from Parliament, any simulacrum of authority, anything that came from Westminster, from the other side of the Thames. Possibly the illustration was suggested by the story of the multitude of rats swimming over the Tweed, which is told in a news-letter of September, 1647. (*Clarendon, State Papers, II.*, Appendix, xxxix.)

and uppon Saturday many were giving in their thoughts concerning what God had given in to them to speake, as to a cure for a dying Kingdome. Truly amongst the rest my thoughts were att worke. Providentially, my thoughts were cast uppon one thinge which I had often seene before, yett if prosecuted may bee the meanes of an happy union amongst us. That which I hinte att, and which I spoke to was, the Case of the Armie Stated. I doe perceive, that there is either a reall or an apprehensive—or rather a missapprehensive dissunion amongst us; and truly in my heart there was somethinge providentially laid for a uniting, and that in that passage that those Agentes—att that very time of dissenting from us and when they were ripping uppe our faults to open view—came in the issue to lay us down [as] a rule, and that was [a thing] which before had bin laid downe as a rule, and we and they were to act according to itt; butt being laid downe by them againe I thinke itt is a twofold corde that cannott easily bee broken. They doe referre us to our three Declarations, that of 14 June, 21 of June, 18 of August; and their desires are, that those might bee look't uppon, and adheered unto; and if they bee our desires and their desires that wee should walke uppe to them, I thinke this will putt the businesse to a very faire issue. I did looke over for my parte all thinges [contained] in those three Declarations, and therfore I humbly desire that whatsoever there is in those Declarations we should persist in, wee may intend and pursue, as tending to that end wee all aime att, namelie the Kingdomes good.[a]

Lieut. Col. Jubbes.[b]

Truly I doe nott know how to distinguish whether the spiritt of

[a] "We propound: that whatsoever was proposed to be insisted on, either in the Declaration of June the 14, or the Remonstrance of June 23, and in the Remonstrance from Kingston, August 18, be adhered to resolvedly, so as not to recede from these desires, untill they be thoroughly and effectually answered." *Case of the Army*, p. 14. On Allen, see Appendix B.

[b] John Jubbes, Lieutenant-Colonel of Hewson's regiment, see p. 21. He drew up in the next year, an "Agreement of the People" of his own, entitled "*Proposals*

God lives in mee, or noe, butt by mercy, love, and peace; and on the contrary whether the spirit of Antichrist lives in mee, butt by envy, malice, and warre. I am altogether against a warre if there may bee a composure [so] that the Englishman may have his priviledges; I have a commission ready to deliver uppe whensoever I shall bee call'd.

Queries wherin Lieut. Col. Jubbes desireth satisfaction for the preventing of the effusion of bloud.

1. Whether or noe the Parliament may yett be purged of all such Members as assented to the late insurreccions and treason of the City, and still continue a House?

2. If itt may bee purged and an House still remayning, whether the major parte of the remainder bee such persons as are desirous of giving satisfaction to our or the Kingdome's just desires?

3. If the 2[d] bee assented unto, that they are such persons, whether then they may nott satisfie our just desires, and declare the Kinge guilty of all the bloudshed, vast expence of treasure, and ruine that hath bin occasioned by all the warres both of England and Ireland, and then for that hee is the Kinge of Scotland, and alsoe of Ireland as well as England, that therfore to receive him as Kinge againe for avoiding further warres?

4. Whether if the Parliament may adjourne and dissolve when in their discretions they shall finde cause or nott before—as att this present, even by law, God hath order'd itt—they may nott then reject the Kinge's Act of Oblivion, and take unto themselves that godly resolution to doe that justice unto the Kingdome which now they dare nott doe?

for Peace and Freedom;" and was probably the author of a second pamphlet called "*A Plea for Moderation in the Transactions of the Army, or weighty Observations upon the late Proposalls for Peace presented by the City of London to Comm. Gen. Ireton.* By Veritie Victor, gent., 1648.

Col. Rainborow

Mov'd that the papers of the Committee might bee read.

Lieut. Col. Goffe.

I thinke that motion which was made by the Lieutennant Generall should nott die, butt that itt should have some issue. I thinke itt is a vaine thinge to seeke God if wee doe nott hearken after his answer, and somethinge that was spoken by the Lieutennant Generall moves mee to speake att this time, and that was uppon this ground. Itt was concluded by the Lieutennant Generall uppon what was spoken by one heere, that that was nott the minde of God that was spoken by him. I could wish wee might bee warie of such expressions. "There was a lying spiritt in the mouth of Ahab's Prophetts. Hee speakes falselie to us in the name of the Lord."[a] I doe not speake this, that this was the minde of the Lord in any thinge; yett wee may nott breake abruptly of that what one spoke was the minde of the Lord, yett wee must consider whether somethinge was nott spoken by others which may bee the minde of the Lord. Truly I am very tender in this thinge; if wee shall waite for God, and if God shall speake to us [and we not hearken], wee shall bringe much evill uppon ourselves. God hath spoken in severall ages in sundry wayes. Then they sent to a Prophett, and hee comes and tells them uppon his bare worde, and hee tells them that hee received such a message from the Lord. Butt God hath [now] putt us uppon such a course which I cannott butt reverence, and God does nott now speake by one particular man, butt in every one of our hearts; and certainly if itt were a dangerous thinge to refuse a message that came from one man to many, itt is a more dangerous thinge to refuse what comes from God, being spoke by many to us. I shall adde this, that itt seemes to mee evident and cleare, that this hath bin a voice from heaven to us, that wee have sinn'd against the Lord in tampering with his enemies; and itt hath soe wrought

[a] I. Kings, xxii. 22; Jeremiah, xliii. 2.

with mee that [though] I cannott run præcipitately to worke, yett I dare nott open my mouth for the benefitt or uppeholding that power. I thinke that hath bin the voice of God, and whatsoever was contradicted was our præcipitate running on, our taking hold of an opportunity before itt was given;[a] and therfore I desire wee may nott præcipitately run on, butt waite uppon God, and that in the issue wee may[b] see [if] God hath [not] spoken to us; and if the Lord hath spoken to us I pray God keepe us from that sin that wee doe nott hearken to the voice of the Lord.

Lieut. Generall.

I shall nott be unwilling to heare God speaking in any; butt I thinke that God may [as well] bee heard speaking in that which is to bee read[c] as otherwise.

Butt I shall speake a worde in that which Lieut. Col. Goffe said because itt seemes to come as a reproof to mee, and I shall bee willing to receive a reproof when itt shall bee in love, and shall bee [so] given. That which hee speakes was, that at such a Meeting as this wee should waite uppon God, and [hearken to] the voice of God speaking in any of us. I confesse itt is an high duty, butt when any thinge is spoken [as from God] I thinke the rule is, Lett the rest judge![d] Itt is left to mee to judge for my owne satisfaction, and the satisfaction of others, whether itt bee of the Lord or nott, and I doe noe more. I doe nott judge conclusively, negatively, that itt was nott of the Lord, butt I doe desire to submitt itt to all your judgements whether itt was of the Lord or noe? I did offer some reasons which did satisfie mee, I know nott whether I did others. If in those thinges wee doe speake, and pretend to speake from God, there bee mistakes of fact—if there bee a mistake in the thinge, in the reason of the thinge—

[a] *Cf.* p. 284.

[b] MS. "that in the issue wee may not see that God hath spoken to us."

[c] The papers of the committee, which Rainborow had just moved to have read.

[d] I. Corinthians, xiv. 29.

truly I thinke itt is free for mee to shew both the one, and the other if I can. Nay, I thinke itt is my duty to doe itt: for noe man receives any thinge in the name of the Lord further then [to] the light of his conscience appeares. I can say in the next place—and I can say itt heartily and freely as to the matter he speakes—I must confesse I have noe prejudice, nott the least thought of prejudice, uppon that ground—I speake itt truly as before the Lord—butt this I thinke; that itt is noe evill advertisement to wish us in our speeches of righteousnesse and justice to referre us to any engagements that are uppon us, and [it is] that which I have learn't[a] in all [our] debates. I have still desir'd wee should consider, where wee are, and what engagements are uppon us, and how wee ought to goe off as becomes Christians. This is all that I aim'd att and I doe aime att. I must confesse I had a mervailous reverence and awe uppon my spiritt when we came to speake. [We said], lett us speake one to another what God hath spoken to us; and as I said before I cannott say that I have recived any thinge that I can speake as in the name of the Lord—nott that I can say that any body did speake that which was untrue in the name of the Lord—butt uppon this ground, that when wee say wee speake in the name of the Lord itt is of an high nature.

Lieutenant Col. Goffe made an apologie for what hee had said before.

Mr. Allen.

My desire is to see thinges putt to an issue. Men have bin declaring their thoughts, and truly I would crave libertie to declare mine. The difference betweene us I thinke is in the interest of Kinge and Lords, some declaring against the name and title of Kinge and Lords. For my parte [I think] clearly, according to what wee have engag'd wee stand bound; and I thinke wee should bee look't uppon as persons nott fitt to bee

[a] "learnt," *i. e.* taught.

called Christians, if wee doe nott worke up to them. As first, concerning the Kinge. You say you will sett uppe the Kinge as farre as may bee consistent with, and nott prejudiciall to the liberties of the Kingedome; and really I am of that minde [too]. If the setting uppe of him bee nott consistent with them, and prejudiciall to them, then downe with him; butt if hee may bee soe sett uppe—which I thinke hee may—[then set him up], and itt is not our judgement onely, butt [that] of those that sett forth the Case of the Army.

Col. Rainborow

Tooke occasion to take notice as if what Mr. Allen spoke did reflect upon himself or some other there, as if they were against the name of Kinge and Lords.

Mr. Sexby.

Truly I must bee bold to offer this one worde unto you. Truly heere was somewhat spoke of the workinges and actinges of God within them, I shall speake a worde of that. The Lord hath putt you into a state, or att least [suffered you] to run you[rselves] into such a one, that you know nott where you are. You are in a wildernesse condition. Some actinges amonge us singly and joyntlie that are the cause of itt. Truly I would intreate you to weigh that. Wee finde in the worde of God "I would heale Babylon, butt shee would nott bee healed."[a] I thinke that wee have gone about to heale Babylon when shee would nott. Wee have gone about to wash a Blackamore, to wash him white, which hee will nott. I think wee are going about to sette uppe the power which God will destroy. Wee are going about to sett uppe the power of Kinges, some parte of itt, which God will destroy; and which will bee butt as a burthensome stone that whosoever shall fall uppon itt, itt will destroy him.[b] I shall propose this to your

[a] Jeremiah, li., 9; xiij., 23.

[b] Zechariah, xii., 3. Matthew, xxi., 44.

Honours, to weigh the grounds, whether they bee right, and then you shall bee led in pleasant pathes by still waters, and shall nott bee offended. I thinke this is the reason of the straights that are in hand.

Lieut. Gen.

I thinke wee should nott lett goe that motion which Lieut. Col. Goffe made, and soe I cannott butt renew that caution that wee should take heede what wee speake in the name of the Lord. As for what that Gentleman spoke last (butt it was with too much confidence) I cannott conceive that hee altogether meant itt. I would wee should all take heede of mentioning our owne thoughts and conceptions with that which is of God. What this Gentleman told us [was] that which [he conceived] was our great fault. Hee alludes to such a place of Scripture. "Wee would have heal'd Babylon, butt shee would nott." The Gentleman applied itt to us, as that we had bin men that would have heal'd Babylon, and God would nott have had her heal'd. Truly though that bee nott the intent of that Scripture, yett I thinke itt is true, that whosoever would have gone about to heale Babylon when God had determined [to destroy her] hee does fight against God, because God will nott have her heal'd. Indeed when wee are convinc't that itt is Babylon wee are going about to heale, I thinke itt's fitt wee should then give over our healing; and yett certainly in generall itt is nott evill to desire an healing. Butt since I heare noe man offering nothing to speake to us as a particular dictate from God, I shall desire to speake a word or two.[a] I should desire to draw to some conclusion of that expectation of ours. Truly, as Lieut. Col. Goffe said, God hath in severall ages used severall dispensations, and yett some dispensations more eminently in one age then another. I am one of those whose heart God hath drawne out to waite for some extraordinary dispensations, according to those

[a] Several words transposed.

promises that hee hath held forth of thinges to bee accomplished in the later time, and I cannott butt thinke that God is beginning of them. Yett certainly [we do well to take heed], uppon the same ground that wee finde in the Epistle of Peter, where hee speakes of the Scriptures, as "a more sure word of Prophecy" then their testimonies was, to which, says hee, you doe well to take heede, as a light shining in a dark place.[a] If, when wee want particular and extraordinary impressions, wee shall either altogether sitt still because wee have them nott, and nott follow that light that wee have; or shall goe against, or short of that light that wee have, uppon the imaginary apprehension of such divine impressions and divine discoveries in particular thinges—which are nott soe divine as to carry their evidence with them to the conviction of those that have the spiritt of God within them—I thinke wee shall bee justly under a condemnation. Truly wee have heard many speaking to us ; and I cannott butt thinke that in many of those thinges God hath spoke to us. I cannott butt thinke that in most that have spoke there hath bin some thinge of God made forth to us; and yett there hath bin severall contradictions in what hath bin spoken. Butt certainly God is nott the Authour of contradictions. The contradictions are nott soe much in the end as in the way. I cannott see butt that wee all speake to the same end, and the mistakes are onely in the way. The end is to deliver this Nation from oppression and slavery, to accomplish that worke that God hath carried us on in, to establish our hopes of an end of justice and righteousnesse in itt. Wee agree thus farre. I thinke wee may goe thus farre farther, that wee all apprehend danger from the person of the Kinge, and from the Lords. All that have spoke have agreed in this too ; though the Gentleman in the windowe[b] when hee spoke [of] sett[ing] uppe, if hee should declare itt, did nott meane all that that worde might importe. I thinke that seemes to bee generall amonge us all, that if itt were free before us

[a] The Second Epistle of Peter, i. 19.

[b] Allen.

whether wee should sett uppe one or other, there is nott any intention of any in the Army, of any of us, to sett uppe the one [or the other]. I doe to my best observation finde an unanimity amongst us all, that wee would sett uppe neither.[a] Thus farre I finde us to bee agreed, and thus farre as wee sre agreed I thinke itt is of God. Butt there are circumstances in which wee differ as in relation to this. I must further tell you, that as wee doe nott make itt our businesse or intention to sett uppe the one or the other, soe neither is itt [our intention] to preserve the one or the other, with a visible danger and destruction to the people and the publique interest. Soe that that parte of difference that seemes to bee among us is whether there can bee a preservation [of them with safety to the kingdom]. First of all, on the one parte, there is this apprehension: that wee cannott with justice and righteousnesse att the present destroy, or goe about to destroy, or take away, or [altogether] lay aside both, or all the interest they have in the publique affaires of the Kingdome; and those that doe soe apprehend would straine somethinge in point of security, would rather leave some hazard—or att least, if they see that they may consist without any considerable hazard to the interest of the Kingdome, doe soe farre [wish] to preserve them. On the other hand, those who differ from this, I doe take itt in the most candid apprehension that they seeme to run[b] thus: that there is nott any safetie or security to the libertie of the Kingedome, and to [the] publique interest, if you doe retaine these at all; and therfore they thinke this is a consideration to them paramount [to] the consideration of particular obligations of justice, or matter of right or due towards Kinge or Lords. Truly I thinke itt hath pleased God to lead mee to a true and clear stating our agreement, and our difference; and if this bee soe wee are the better prepared to goe [on]. If this bee nott soe, I shall desire that any one that hath heard mee [will] declare [it], if hee doe thinke that the thinge is

[a] *i.e.* "neither King nor Lords."

[b] *i.e.* "argue."

mistated as to our agreement or difference; and I shall goe on, onely in a worde or two to conclude that wee have bin about. As to the dispensations of God itt was more particular in the time of the law [of Moses than in the time of the law] written in our hearts, that worde within us, the minde of Christ;[a] and truly when wee have noe other more particular impression of the power of God going forth with itt I thinke that this law and this [word] speaking [within us]—which truly is in every man who hath the spiritt of God—wee are to have a regard to; and this to mee seemes to bee very cleare what wee are to judge of the apprehensions of men to particular cases, whether itt bee of God or noe. When itt doth nott carry itts evidence of the power of God with itt to convince us clearlie, our best way is to judge the conformity or disformity of [it with] the law written within us, which is the law of the spiritt of God, the minde of God, the minde of Christ. As was well said by Lieut. Col. Jubbs, for my parte I doe nott know any outward evidence of what proceedes from the spiritt of God more cleare then this, the appearance of meeknesse, and gentlenesse, and mercy, and patience, and forbearance, and love, and a desire to doe good to all, and to destroy none that can bee sav'd;[b] and as he said of the spiritt of malice, and envy, and thinges of that nature, I cannot but take that to bee contrary to this law. For my parte I say where I doe see this, where I doe see men speaking according to that law, which I am sure is the law of the spiritt of life—And I thinke there is this radically in that heart where there is such a law as leads us against all opposition. On the other hand, I thinke that hee that would decline the doing of justice—where there is noe place for mercy—and the exercise of the wayes of force—for the saftie of the Kingedome where there is noe other way to save itt—and would decline these out of the

[a] Hebrews, viii., 10; I. Corinthians, ii., 16. So Cromwell elsewhere observes of certain things that they are "written in better books than those of paper; written, I am persuaded, in the heart of every good man." Carlyle's *Cromwell*, Speech II.

[b] Compare Speech I. in Carlyle's *Cromwell*.

apprehensions of danger and difficulties in itt, hee that leads that way on the other hand doth truly lead us from that which is the law of the spiritt of Life, the law written in our hearts. And truly having thus declared what wee may apprehend of all that hath bin said, I shall wish that wee may goe on to our businesse; and I shall onely adde severall cautions on the one hand, and the other.

I could wish that none of those whose apprehensions run on the other hand, that there can bee noe safetie in a consistencie with the person of the Kinge or the Lords, or their having the least interest in the publique affaires of the Kingedome, I doe wish them that they will take heede of that which some men are apt to bee carried away by, [that is] apprehensions that God will destroy these persons or that power; for that they may mistake in. And though [I] my selfe doe concurre with them, and perhaps concurre with them uppon some ground that God will doe soe, yett lett us, [not] make those thinges to bee our rule which wee cannott soe clearlie know to bee the minde of God. I meane in particular thinges lett us nott make those our rules, "that this is to bee done, [this] is the minde of God, wee muste worke to itt."[a] Att least [let] those to whome this is nott made cleare, though they doe thinke itt probable that God will destroy them, yett lett them make this rule to themselves, though God have a purpose to destroy them, and though I should finde a desire to destroy them—though a Christian spiritt can hardly finde itt for itt self—yett God can doe itt without necessitating us to doe a thinge which is scandalous, or sinne, or which would bringe a dishonour to his name; and therfore let those that are of that minde waite uppon God for such a way when the thinge may bee done without sin, and without scandall too. Surely what God would have us doe hee does nott desire wee should steppe out of the way for itt. This is the caution, on the one hand that wee doe noe

[a] *Cf.* Cromwell's speech on p. 185.

wronge to one or other, and that wee abstaine from all appearance of wronge, and for that purpose avoide the bringing of a scandall to the name of God, and to his people uppon whome his name is call'd. On the other hand, I have butt this to say : that those who doe apprehend obligations lying uppon them—either by a generall duty or particularly in relation to the thinges that wee have declar'd, a duty of justice, or a duty in regard of that Engagement—that they would clearlie come to this resolution, that if they found in their judgements and consciences that those Engagements lead to anythinge which really cannott consist with the libertie and safetie and publique interest of this Nation, they would account the Generall [duty] paramount [to] the other, soe farre as nott to oppose any other that would doe better for the Nation then they will doe. If wee doe act according to that minde and that spiritt, and that law which I have before spoken of, and in these particular cases do [a] take these two cautions, God will lead us to what shall bee his way, as many of us as hee shall incline their mindes to, and the rest in their way in a due time.

Capt. Byshopp.

I shall desire to speake one word and that breiflie. What's the reason that wee are distracted in Councill, and that wee cannott as formerly preserve the Kingedome from that dying condition in which itt is? After many inquiries in my spirit I finde this answer, and the answer which is to many Christians besides amongst us. I say [it is] a compliance to preserve that Man of Bloud, and those principles of tyranny which God from Heaven by his many successes hath manifestly declar'd against, and which I am confident may bee our destruction [if they be preserved]. I say nott [this] in respect of any particular persons. I onely speake this [as] what is uppon my spiritt, because I see you are uppon inquiry what God hath given in to any one which may tend to the preservation of the Kingedome.[b]

[a] MS. "to."

[b] The position of several clauses has been altered.

Mr. Wildman.

I observe that the worke hath bin to inquire what hath bin the minde of God, and every one speakes what is given in to his spiritt. I desire as much as is possible to reverence whatsoever hath the spiritt or image of God uppon itt. Whatever another man hath received from the spiritt, that man cannott demonstrate to mee butt by some other way then meerlie relating to mee that which hee conceives to bee the minde of God. Itt is beyond the power of the reason of all the men on earth to demonstrate the Scriptures to bee the Scriptures written by the spiritt of God; butt itt must bee the spiritt of faith that must make him believe whatsoever may bee spoken in spirituall matters; yett in civill matters wee cannott finde anythinge in the worde of God what is fitt to bee done in civill matters. I conceive that onely is of God that does appeare to bee like unto God, justice and mercy, to bee meeke and peaceable. I should desire therfore that wee might proceede onelie in that way. If itt please this honourable Councill to consider what is justice and what is mercy, and what is good, and I cannott butt conclude that that is of God. Otherwise I cannott thinke that any one doth speake from God when hee sayes what hee speakes is of God.

Butt to the matter in hand, I am clearly of opinion with that Gentleman that spake last save one, that itt is nott of God [to decline the doing of justice] where there is noe way left of mercy; and I could much concurre that itt is very questionable whether there bee a way left for mercy uppon that person that wee now insist uppon. Whether itt is demonstrable by reason or justice [that it is right] to punish with death those that according to his command doe make warre, or those that doe butt hold compliance with them, and then [to say] that there is a way left for mercy for him who was the great actor of this, and who was the great contriver of all? Butt I confesse because itt is in civill matters I would much decline that, and rather looke to what is safetie, what the minde doth dictate from safetie, what is the safetie I know itt cannott bee the minde of God to goe contrary to; butt for what particulars that Gentleman speakes of the differences betweene us, I thinke they are soe many as nott easily to bee reckoned uppe. That which hee instanc't was that some did desire to preserve the person of the Kinge and person of the Lords, soe farre as itt was [consistent] with the safetie or the good of the Kingedome, and other persons doe conceive, that the preservation of the Kinge or Lords was inconsistent with the people's safetie, and that law to bee paramount all.

Com̃. Ireton.[a]

Sir, I did not speake of the destroying of the Kinge and Lords—I have nott heard any man charge all the Lords soe as to deserve a punishment—but [of] a reserving to them any interest att all in the publique affaires of the Kingdome.

Mr. Wildman.

Then Sir, as I conceive, you were saying the difference was this: that some persons were of opinion that the preservation of the power of Kinge and Lords was paramount to all considerations, and might keepe them from any giving them what was due and right.

Com̃. Ireton.

I said, that some men did apprehend, that there might be an interest given to them with safetie to the Kingdome, others doe thinke, that noe parte of their interest could bee given without destruction to the Kingedome.

[a] Wildman spoke in answer to the gentleman "who spoke last save one," referring obviously to the long speech here attributed to Cromwell. The difficulty is that Ireton hereupon answers Wildman as if he were the speaker referred to. On the other hand the MS. distinctly attributes the speech to Cromwell, and in many points it is distinctly Cromwellian in style and ideas. Possibly the two brief speeches on this page should be attributed to Cromwell instead of Ireton.

Mr. Wildman.

For the matter of stating the thinge in difference, I thinke that the person of Kinge and Lords are nott soe joyn'd together by any; for as your self said, none have any exception against the persons of the Lords or name of Lords. The difference is whether wee should alter the old foundations of our Governement soe as to give to Kinge and Lords that which they could never claime before. Wheras itt's said, that those that dissent [a] looke after alteration of Governement, I doe rather thinke that those that doe dissent doe indeavour to alter the foundation of our Governement, and that I shall demonstrate thus. According to the Kinges oath hee is to grant such lawes as the people shall chuse, and therefore I conceive they are called lawes before they come to him. They are called lawes that hee must confirme, and soe they are lawes before they come to him.[b] To give the Kinge a legislative power is contrary to his owne oath att his Coronation, and itt is the like to give a power to the Kinge by his negative voice to deny all lawes. And for the Lords, seeing the foundation of all justice is the election of the people, itt is unjust they should have that power.

Therfore I conceive the difference only is this, whether this power should bee given to the King and Lords or noe?

For the later parte of that noble Gentleman's wordes this may bee said to them, whether this consideration to give them [c] what is their due right may [not] bee paramount to all engagements?

Com̃. Ireton.

The Question is nott whether this should bee given to Kinge and Lords, or noe, but the Question is, whether that interest that they have in this, (if they have any) whether itt should bee now positively insisted uppon to bee clearly taken away.

[a] Apparently means those who subscribe the "Agreement of the People" as opposed to the officers who dissent from it. For the first "dissent," "assent" should probably be substituted.

[b] The position of this clause has been changed.

[c] "Them" *i. e.* "the people."

Mr. Wildman.

Sir, I suppose that the interest they have if they have any—if (for that supposition is very well put in)—for (as I said before) I conceive that neither Kinge, nor Lords according to the foundation of Governement ever had a right.

Com̃. Ireton.

I spake itt to you, and those that are of your minde, if you were satisfied nott to have an exception.[a]

Mr. Wildeman.

Then I say the whole tenour of the propositions or proposalls must bee alter'd, if any thinge bee in them [allowing the King a negative voice]. I conceive that not to expresse it because it hath bin usurp't is to confirme his usurpation of itt.[b] For many yeares this hath bin usurp't. Now, if after God hath given us the victory over them wee shall nott declare against them, wee give noe security for the peoples libertie.

Com. Ireton.

You speake parte to the point of justice and parte to the point of safetie. To the point of justice you seeme to speake this; that by the fundamentall constitutions of this Kingedome, neither Kinge nor Lords have rightfully a negative voice; and therfore to take itt away or to cleare itt that they have none is butt justice. I thinke that is itt, that [by] the fundamentall constitution, neither of them [have a negative voice].

You seeme to argue onely from the Kinges oath, and then you conclude, if as appeares by that they had itt nott before, though wee all bee satisfied wee would say nothing to give them itt, yett if wee doe nott expreslie take itt away, nay if wee doe send itt to any of them—wee doe leave to them a power to assent or dissent, and give them that which wee had before. Soe you well remember that that which

[a] Ireton says he made the exception to satisfy Wildman and his friends, not because he had any doubts of the fact himself.

[b] As the power has been usurped, not expressly to take it away is to confirm it.

you argue of the Kinge's Oath, and I know for my owne parte noe other [evidence] then an old Statute or two cited in the Declaration [a] wherin the Commons declare—

I remember I spoke itt, and I speake itt againe, and that that is the intent I doe verily beleive: that the originall sence and intention of the Oath of the Kinge's which is published in that Declaration of the Commons was, and is, and ought to bee, that the Kinge ought to confirme those lawes that the Commons chuse. Now whether this Kinge bee soe bound by his Oath, as that hee breakes his Oath if hee doe not confirme every law that they seeke, I conceive that depends uppon what hee did verily at his coronation make his Oath; butt I thinke that in the sence and intention of the people of the Kingedome their intention was that hee should confirme all the lawes that they should chuse. Butt you must take notice, that the Oath doth take them [as] lawes before hee should make them; itt calls them lawes, the lawes in Election, Quas vulgus elegerit. The Kinge promises that hee will by his aucthority confirme those lawes that the people shall chuse, soe that this showes clearly what use in the constitution of the Kingedome they made of the Kinge in the Commonwealth. The Commons are to chuse the lawes and the Kinge to confirme, they had this trust to the Kinge would confirme what they should chuse, and hee confirming them they were firme lawes. I doe really believe, that this was the Agreement that the people of England made with their Kinges; that is, they would have him give his consent to what lawes they should chuse and soe to have that implicite use. Butt this is most apparent, both by the Oath ittself, and by all the practice since—the sending of lawes to the Kinge—by all that itt is apparent, that they had some relation to the Kinge and to his consent in the making of a law.[b] This I am sure, if itt

[a] Remonstrance of May 26, 1642, and the King's answer: see Clarendon, *Rebellion*, v. 224-229, 292-305. See pp. 351, 399. The first part of this sentence seems to be really an interpolation of Wildman's: "Sir, you very well remember that which you argued of the King's oath," referring to Ireton's speech on p. 351.

[b] Several words omitted.

were never soe cleare in the Constitution that they were good lawes without itt, yett this is cleare—if that were true in the originall Constitution of this Kingedome this is cleare—that they have [been] sent still to him to bee confirm'd; as the word was to bee confirm'd or corroborated, Leges quas vulgus elegerit corroborandas.

I thinke if wee doe [take into] account all the sending of lawes heeretofore to bee corroborated by him, and if his denying of some of them—nott absolutely denying butt advising—if these have nott at all prejudic't [the right of] the people against his Negative voice, soe the sending of propositions now for his assent cannott prejudice the right of the people more then all their sending [laws to him] before. If wee should putt itt to the Kinge as his act—The Parliament have declar'd itt and asserted itt, that itt is their right that the Kinge ought nott to deny any [laws they offer to him]; itt is his Oath. They have gone thus much farther, that if hee did not confirme them they were lawes without him. Uppon this there hath bin a warre made. They have gone to make all lawes and ordinances that were needfull for the management of the affaires of the Kingedome without the Kinge. Itt is now come to a period. Soe that De facto itt is thus, they have made lawes, and held them forth to the Kingedome [as laws]. Now if the Kinge by his act doe confirme what the Parliament have done, and condemne all that have bin against the Parliament, whether hee doe nott acknowledge to all posteritie, that in case of safety, when the Parliament doth adjudge the safetie of the Kingedome to bee concern'd they are to make a law without him? For my parte I thinke there can bee nothing more cleare then this is. For my owne particular I doe apprehend that there is that generall right [in the Parliament] that the lawes [it shall pass] ought to bee confirm'd [by the King]; it[a] is my thoughts, that without anythinge of the Kinge's Declaration to that purpose, in point of safetie where they cannott dispense with the suspending of the Kinge, they are a law without him. This the Parliament

[a] MS. "that."

hath declar'd, and this is asserted in all the Declarations that have bin sent out, and [this is] the ground that I have proceeded [on] in those proposalls of the Armie. That "in a case of safetie" was provided for in those matters that I have spoke of. I account them materially and essentially provided for in those;[a] and if I had nott, for my parte I should never have rested or bin satisfied in that point, and in other points there might have bin a dispensation with a suspending. Notwithstanding the liberty of the Kingedome hath bin provided for in this, that there should nott bee any thinge done or lawes made without the consent of the people.[b]

Capt. Awdeley.

I thinke if soe bee that this business of the Negative voice bee all the dispute, wee shall all agree in itt; for itt appear'd by what you spake the other night that hee ought to have his Negative voice taken away.

Col. Hewson.

The Scotts have made provision, that hee should have noe Negative voice among them, and why should nott wee make the same provision with them?

Com̃. Ireton.

Those thinges that the Committee did prepare and they proceeded in last night will almost end us this dispute. Wheras itt

[a] Ireton seems to refer to the first thirteen articles of the "Heads of the Proposals," which contained the things "necessary for settling and securing the rights, liberties, peace and safety of the kingdom," the granting of which was to precede the King's restoration to his personal rights. This plan of taking away the King's veto with respect to certain specified subjects seems to have been substituted by Ireton for the scheme of giving him a merely suspensive veto which was suggested in the first draft of the "Proposals." See "*Putney Projects*," p. 15.

[b] See p. 407, resolution 2.

was desired that we should take into consideration the severall Heads to bee insisted uppon as fundamentall lawes that wee must stand [to] for the establishing of the Kingdome—They are still [things held to be necessary] in relation to the security of the Kingdome.

The Proposall read.[a]

Col. Rainborow.

That some thinges in the Agreement were granted there.

To Debate whether or noe when the Commons Representative doe declare a law itt ought nott to passe without the Kinge's consent.[b]

Com̃. Ireton.

Truly this is all; whether honour, title, estate, liberty, or life, [if] the Commons have a minde to take itt away by a law [they can do so]; soe that to say you are contented to leave them all, this [negative] being taken away, is as much as to say you are to allow them nothing. Consider how much of this dispute is saved, [by] this that is read to you. It gives the negative voice to the people, noe lawes can bee made without their consent. And secondly itt takes away the negative voice of the Lords and of the Kinge too, as to what concernes the people; for itt says that the Commons of England shall bee bound by what judgements and alsoe [by] what orders, ordinances, or lawes shall bee made for that purpose by them; and all that followes for the King or Lords is this, that the Lords or King are nott bound by that law they passe for their owne persons or estates as the Commons are, unlesse they consent to itt. Therfore what is there wanting for the good or safety of the Commons of England? [c]

[a] See p. 407.

[b] See articles 1 and 2, p. 407.

[c] See article 4, p. 407.

Col. Rainborow.

That if the Negative voice bee taken away, then if the Kinge or Lords were taking courses destructive how should they bee prevented ?

Com̃. Generall.

Itt is further provided if they will meddle in any other offices, as Officers of Justice or Ministers of State in this Kingdome, then they likewise are soe farre subject to the Judgement of the House of Commons. If they onely stand as single men, their personall interest and the like [is secured], and the right of being only judged by their peeres, and[a] their individuall persons [are not bound] by any law that they doe nott consent to.

Col. Rainborow.

If the Lords should joyne together by their interest in the Kingedome, and should act against the Commons, then the Commons had noe way to helpe themselves.

Com̃. Ireton.

Iff itt come to a breach of the peace itt will come to breake some law. That a Lord is subject to the common law. The Lords heertofore[b] [as] to the breaches of peace have bin subject to the common law; only for the matter of fact, whether guilty or nott guilty of the breach of such a law, they must bee tryed by their Peeres. Wee have stood very much for ourselves that wee should bee judged by our Peeres, and by our fellow Commoners; I would faine know this, how wee can take away that right of Peeres to bee tryed by their Peeres when that itt is a point of right for the Commons to bee tryed by their Peeres.[c]

[a] MS. "onely."

[b] MS. "heertofore have bin subject to the breaches of the peace, have bin subject to the common law."

[c] Position of several clauses altered.

Col. Rainborow.

That the lawes that binde the Commons are exclusive to the Lords.

Com. Ireton.

I would faine know this whether the High Sheriff in every County of the Kingedome [may not apprehend a Lord who breake the peace], and I am sure the law hath provided for the keeping of the peace. I know that there is noe law butt the chief justice of the Kinge's Bench, nay the Sheriff of a County, nay the Constable of any towne may seize uppon him.

Col. Rainborow.

If a Petty Constable or Sheriff shall apprehend a Peere of the Kingedome, whether hee can answer itt?

Com. Ireton.

That if a Lord shall bee accused, and by a Jury found guilty, hee will expect to bee tryed by his Peeres.

Mr. Wildman.

I would proceede to the thinges in hand. Though I protest I would nott widen a difference, yett I conceive the difference is as wide as ever; for in what's there provided the interest of the Kinge and Lords is given away which the Lord by a Judgement from heaven hath laid aside.[a] I conceive [that in] this [article] concerning the succession of Parliaments [it] is proposed positively that itt shall bee as Trienniall Parliaments were.[b]

Com. Ireton.

You did in your way propose a certainty or nott; if you did nott propose itt how farre—That which you propose is, the people

[a] The position of several words has been altered.

[b] For Wildman's criticisms see *Putney Projects*, p. 26; and the "Heads of Proposals" I. 1.

shall meete; you neither say where nor when. Wee say [with such provision] for the certainty of itt [as in the late Act made for Trienniall Parliaments]. That Act tells you particularly; butt because you must make a new provision for itt, since you must make a New Division and distribution of the Kingedome and a New Circuite, therfore itt sayes, "with such further provision as shall bee made for reducement [of it] to a certainty." [a]

Col. Rainborow.

That hee does take exception att [the provision] that noe man should bee chosen that hath nott 20^{ll} a yeare.

Com Ireton.

If Mr. Wildman thinke fitt to [let me] goe on without taking an advantage to every particular as itt is read, [he may shew afterwards] what they are that doe render these propositions soe destructive, and give the King and Lords such an interest as they never had before, if hee will take them uppon his memory, and by the way. I hope Mr. Wildman will nott offer such an assertion butt hee hath arguments to make itt good.

Mr. Wildman.

I onely affirme that itt doth establish the Kinge's and Lords' interest surer than before.

Com, Ireton.

Wee doe agree that all the Commons of England are bound, [by whatever laws the House of Commons shall pass;] butt the Kinge and Lords as to their persons are nott bound; butt if any of them bee an officer or Minister of State then hee is to bee subject [to the judgment of the House of Commons].

[a] Ireton again refers to the "Agreement of the People," Clause 3, and compares it with the first two clauses of the "Proposals of the Army."

Col. Rainborow.

How does itt reach the Kinge and nott a Lord?

Com. Ireton.

Every Lord is nott a Minister of Justice, butt if there bee any other difference they are tryed by their Peeres.

Col. Rainborow.

Itt is offer'd to make them capable of being chosen.

Com. Ireton.

Every Baron by the other exception may bee chosen.

Col. Rainborow.

Is itt nott soe in Scotland?

Com. Ireton.

In Scotland every Lord hath his place as Burgesse.[a]

Col. Rainborow.

Why should nott the Lords have the same priviledge? [b]

Com. Ireton.

I should thinke that [w]as the directest interest to the Kingedome in the world, for that for soe many persons to bee the permanent interest in the House, every two yeares——

[a] Unfortunately the article concerning the qualifications of persons to be elected Members of Parliament is not given, but it seems from this debate and from p. 394 that a member was to possess a property qualification of £20 a year, and that a peer might sit in the Lower House if elected, as indeed subsequently took place under the Commonwealth.

[b] Rainborow asks why the Lords and Commons should not sit together, in one House; and Ireton replies that it would be dangerous to admit so large a permanent element. See p. 397. The position of this question and answer has been changed. In the MS. they follow Ireton's answer about the trial of Lords by their Peers.

Col. Titchburne.[a]

I was speaking to this of the Negative. I doe remember on Saturday last wee were att this pitch, and there I did leave itt; itt did concurre with my sence, and that was this: that all the power of making lawes should bee in those that the people should chuse, the Kinge and Lords should serve onely to this end, that lawes should bee presented to them, that if they would doe the Commons that right as to confirme those lawes they should doe itt; butt if they should nott thinke fitt to signe them, itt should begett a review of that by the House of Commons; and if after a review the House of Commons did declare that was for the safetie of the people, though neither Kinge nor Lords did subscribe, yett itt was a standing and binding law; and therfore wee shall nott neede to feare to take a shadow when they can doe us little hurt. This was what I did then suppose agreed uppon.

Com̃. Ireton.

'Tis true, Saturday night wee were thinking of that, butt wee

[a] Robert Titchburne had been appointed by Fairfax, Lieutenant of the Tower, in place of Colonel Francis West (Rushworth, vii. 761). A contemporary thus speaks of Titchburne: "I will not call him Colonel, his commission being illegal, and he fitter for a warm bed then to command a regiment or citadel; one that not above a month before he was chosen Lieutenant of the Tower held an opinion that it was not lawful for men to fight or kill men, [not] thinking that fighting would be in fashion again. And indeed when he was first made Lieutenant-Colonel of the Auxiliaries in London, if he durst have marched down only for a guard of three or four pieces of battery to Basinghouse before it was fortified, he had saved many a thousand men's lives; but he loved then nothing tending to fighting, and therefore he discouraged his soldiers and took a journey himself under a colour to Brainford, and then came home in triumph that he might pray that the walls of Basinghouse might fall down like the walls of Jericho. . . . . But Colonel West is faithful, honest and valiant, and one that stood as well to his regiment as he hath done since to his principles: witness Gloucester expedition, where if the Newbery ground could speak, it would say his body was turned into a rock in the face of his enemy." (*The Honest Citizen or Faithful Counsellor to the City of London*, p. 7). Titchburne was one of the Sheriffs in 1650, and Lord Mayor in 1656. Noble gives an account of Titchburne in his "*Lives of the Regicides*," ii. 272. See also Heath's *Chronicle*, ed. 1663, p. 309.

had an eye to that of safetie, that is provided for by the Commons. Noe mony can bee raised, noe warre raised, butt by those that the Commons shall chuse. Butt that which was questioned in the name the safety and securing of safety that thought itt fitt that they should have a liberty to preserve one another, and soe wee thought to putt itt to consideration. That the Commons should make soe much use of the Lords in all affaires, they might occasion a review, butt if the Commons should uppon that review thinke itt fitt, itt should bee look't uppon as a law; but instead of that the Committee voted last night—That whether the Commons of England should bee bound by all the lawes past in the House of Commons, or whether itt should bee valid in the case of safetie, that which you speake of will follow. If there doe butt continue such a thinge as Lords, and they doe nott sitt joynctlie with the House of Commons, then the Lords will agree, or otherwise the Commons will doe itt presently themselves.[a]

[a] The absence of the text of the article discusssed, and the defects of the report make it difficult to decide the exact question at issue, but it seems to be this. On Saturday, October 30, the Committee had agreed to give the Lords a suspensive veto. Then, apparently at Ireton's instigation, they decided that the Lords should possess no veto of any kind with respect to laws where the Commons declared the safety of the kingdom to be concerned. Instead of that they should possess, in case of laws affecting their persons and estates merely, a power of exempting themselves from the operation of such laws, and so securing their personal rights, by refusing their consent. Thus, instead of a general suspensive veto they would get a simple power of nullifying certain particular laws so far as they affected themselves. Ireton's speech is very confused, but may be thus paraphrased and re-arranged: "'Tis true on Saturday night we thought of that, viz., that the Commons should make so much use of the Lords in all affairs that their refusal to pass a law should occasion a review, but that if the Commons should after that review think fit to persist, it should be looked upon as a law without the consent of the Lords: but that resolution was questioned in the name of safety. Instead of that the Committee voted last night, that the Lords should have a liberty to preserve one another, and we thought fit to submit a provision for that to your consideration. We had an eye also to that point of the safety of the kingdom. It is provided for in the clauses respecting the rights of the Commons, etc."

Col. Rainborow.

If they bee injur'd they have nott a remedy.

Com̃. Ireton.

That's all that can bee said. The Question is whether there bee soe much neede of giving them a power to preserve themselves against the injuries of the Commons. They are nott capable of Judgement as to their persons unlesse itt bee as they are Officers of State. Onely the truth of itt is, there is this seemes to bee taken away [by taking away their judicial power]. If a man doe come and violently fall uppon them in the Court, or doe any such thinge, they have noe power to preserve themselves, and all their way will bee to complaine to the House of Commons.[a]

Mr. Wildman.

I conceive that whilest wee thus run into such particulars there is very little probability of coming to satisfaction. The case as there itt is stated in the Agreement is generall; and itt will never satisfie the godly people in the Kingedome unlesse that all Governement bee in the Commons, and freely. Truly I conceive that according to what is there propounded the power of the House of Commons is much lessen'd--from what itt is of right, nott [from] what itt is now by usurpation of Kinge and Lords. Wheras itt's said, that noe law shall bee made without the consent of the Commons, itt doth suppose some other law makers besides the Representative of the Commons. Wheras itt is said, that the Lords in some cases should sitt as an House of Parliament to consent to lawes, doth give them that power which they never had before the Warres; for as your self said of the Kinge's Oath, itt sayes, that the King shall consent to such lawes as the people shall chuse, butt the Lords have noe power. If there bee a liberty to the Kinge to

[a] See. 407, resolution 2.

give them a title of honour they ought to bee under all lawes, and soe they ought to concerne them as well as all others; which I conceive is diminished in those particulars. Besides the generall current of the whole offer runs that nothing shall bee declar'd against that usurpation in the Kinge formerly, nor in the Lords formerly, and soe itt remaines perpetually dubious. They shall say, though itt does nott concerne mee in my private yett itt does in my politique; and noe law can bee made butt itt must bee sent to the Kinge and Lords, and that must occasion a review; and soe they must have recourse to the unrighteous for righteousnesse, and soe longe as itt is nott clearly declar'd that hee hath noe power to deny itt, and that they neede nott addresse themselves to him, the Kingedome cannott bee in safetie, butt his owne partie may gett uppe, and doe what hee will.[a]

Com̃. Ireton.

This businesse is much heightned. That I doe nott know by all that hath bin said that the Kinge or Lords are more fastened then before. Wee heere talke of lawes by ancient Constitution, and by usurpation, and yett I doe nott finde that the gentleman that speakes of them doth shew [any evidence] what was the ancient Constitution, nor of [that] usurpation, butt onely [the evidence] of the Kinge's Oath; and that is drawne as taking itt for granted that by ancient Constitution there were lawes without the Kinge's consent. For that [question of the oath] I did before cleare [it] sufficiently by comparing that with other evidence; for if wee could look uppon that as an evidence paramount to all, that needed nott bee soe much insisted uppon. If this Gentleman can finde noe law in being in this Kingedome which hath nott Lords to itt, and Kinge to itt, expreslie, and, "Bee itt ordain'd by the Kinge, Lords, and Commons"—if itt alwayes have gone soe, and

[a] For Wildman's general views on the rights of the Lords as affected by the "Heads of the Proposals" see *Putney Projects*. He now criticises article 2 on p. 407.

noe interruption and noe memory of any kinde of proceeding to the contrarie, but that all lawes past by the Commons have bin sent to the Lords for their concurrence—The Lords have [made amendments and] sent downe [to the Commons] for their concurrence, they have had conferences, and when they could nott agree, the Commons have lett itt rest and nott insisted uppon itt. Wee must look uppon these together with that testimonie of the Kinge's Oath as evidences of what is Constitution. But, wheras those other thinges that are numerous and cleare evidences doth in expresse termes relate to the Lords, when I doe consider the consequences of that Oath, I doe conclude either that the word 'vulgus' is concluded[a] to comprehend all Lords and Commons; or else itt is thus, that the two great powers of this Kingedome are divided betwixt the Lords and Commons; and itt is most probable to mee that itt was soe. That the judiciall power was in the Lords principally, and the House of Commons yett to have their concurrences, the Legislative power principally in the Commons, and the Lords' concurrences in practice to bee desired. Itt is a cleare and knowne thinge, that by the Constitution of the Kingedome, the House of Commons cannot make[b] an Oath, butt if they will have an Oath given they must resort to the Lords. Besides all the Judges of Common Law in the Kingedome sitt as assistants to the Lords. Uppon this the practice hath bin that in any private cause wherin unjust sentence hath bin past in another court a Writt of Errour may bee judg'd there.[c] Itt is beyond all record or memory. Soe that these two powers of the Legislative power and the judiciall have bin exercised betweene both Lords and Commons, and none of them to exercise the one or the other without mutuall consent. I desire this Gentleman, or any other that argues uppon the other parte [to] that wee are uppon—unlesse they

[a] MS. "included."

[b] MS. "take."

[c] MS. "heere." The position of several phrases in this sentence has been altered.

will produce some kinde of evidence of history uppon record by law—that they will forbeare arguments of that nature, calling such thinges usurpations from Constitution or from right, and insist uppon thinges of common safetie as supposing noe constitution att all.[a]

Com̃. Cowling.

Contrary to Resolution I must now speake, whether itt bee from the Lord, or noe I know nott. What foundation had the Commons of England to sitting (being 200 yeares in sitting), for in Kinge Henry the third's time when Magna Charta was finished (which by computation was 200 yeares) and this was granted to the Lords Spirituall [and] Temporall, and Edward the sonne was called to bee a witnesse, but when the Lords saw that they were nott stronge enough to sitt in that magnificence the Commons were drawne in, and that in that law the Kinges Oath should come in. Now had itt nott bin a fundamentall law the Commons should nott have bin drawne uppe, butt that they did drive uppe is cleare, and what will become of us if wee drive uppe to noe other purpose butt to support a Norman prerogative? The Lord knoweth, nott I.

Com̃. Ireton.

I thought this Gentleman had had some answer to this matter of History. As to the Norman Conquest, if subjection to a kinge bee a tyranny, [we had a King before the Norman Conquest]; the Question was betweene him and the Conquerour who had the right of the Crowne, soe as wee should nott seeme to derive all our tyranny from the Norman Conquest.[b] I cannott butt wonder att the strange inferences that are made. Hee tells us, that there is noe memory of the Commons having any interest in the Legislative power till Edward the First's time; and then [that] the Lords Spirituall and Temporall they found themselves not strong enough in King Henry the Third's time, and therfore they brought

[a] Order of words in this sentence changed.

[b] Order of clauses in this sentence changed.

them in; and yett would certainly have us to beleive, that the Commons had all the right before [the Conquest].

Com̃. Cowling.

In Alfred's time, the Commons had all the power, and the Kinge hang'd 43 in one yeare.[a]

Col. Rainborow.

That the Commissary Generall is willing to lay that of Constitution aside, and that of Custome aside, and to consider the equality and reasonableness of the thinge, and nott to stand uppon Constitution, which wee have broken againe and againe. I doe nott finde in all the reading that I have done, I doe nott know that ever the Commons made warre with the Kinge, the Barons did.

That besides the Oath hee found, that one of the maine Articles against Richard the Second [was], that hee did nott concurre with and agree uppon those wholesome lawes were offer'd him by the Commons for the safety of the people.[b] If that were soe great a right as did depose him, itt is in the Kingdome [still], and therfore lett us goe to the justice of the thinge. That justice and reason doth nott give to the major parte . . . .

Com̃. Ireton.

You would have us lay aside arguments of Constitution, and yett you have brought the strongest that may bee. I have seene the Articles of Richard the Second, and itt is strange that the Parliament should nott insist uppon that.

Col. Rainborow.

That is nott the thinge that I would consider of.

Com̃. Ireton.

I suppose noe man will make a Question, that that may bee

[a] Cowling probably refers to the story of King Alfred, "who caused 44 Justices in one year to be hanged as murderers for their false judgments." Andrew Horne's *Mirrour of Justice*, translated by W. H., 1646, p. 239.

[b] Rainborow appears to be wrong; see Stubbs, *Constitutional History*, vol. ii. § 269. and *Old Parliamentary History*, ii., pp. 12-29.

justice and equity uppon noe Constitution, which is nott justice and equitie uppon a Constitution. As for instance in the matter of a common &c.

I wish butt this, that wee may have a regard to safetie—safetie to our persons, safetie to our estates, safetie to our libertie. Lett's have that as the law paramount, and then lett us regard positive constitution as farre as itt can stand with safetie to these. Now therfore, thus for my parte I confesse itt, if I should have ever given a consent in my heart to propound any thinge that did nott consist with this, with regard to any Constitution whatsoever—butt for my parte I cannott see that any thinge butt safetie is provided for. Wheras Mr. Wildman sayes, that many godly men would nott bee satisfied with this that wee have read—which amounts to this: that the Commons have power to make lawes for all the Commons of England, that onely the person of the Kinge and persons of the Lords with their estates as persons are freed from them—I doe nott see they [a] are satisfied with anythinge without having a power over other men's liberties.

Mr. Wildman.

Wheras you are pleased to say I produced noe other evidence, Col. Rainborow brought another, because you did confesse the Lords had noe other power in making lawes.

Com̃. Ireton.

I never confest itt in my life, [otherwise] then [by] the recitation of that Oath "which the people shall chuse."

Mr. Wildman.

I could wish wee should have recourse to principles and maximes of just Governement [instead of arguments of safety] which are as loose as can bee.[b]

[a] "They," *i. e.* Mr. Wildman's godly men.

[b] Ireton's previous speech supplies the words given in brackets, and his speech on p. 404 shows that Wildman proceeded to argue that the first maxim of just

Com̃. Ireton.

The Governement of Kinges or of Lords is as just as any in the world, is the justest Governement in the world. "Volenti non fit injuria." Men cannott wronge themselves willinglie, and if they will agree to make a Kinge, and his heires, there's noe injustice. They may either make itt hereditary or elective. They may give him an absolute power or a limited power. Heere hath bin Agreements of the people that have agreed with this. There hath bin such an Agreement when the people have fought for their libertie, and have established the Kinge againe.

Mr. Wildman.

'Twas their superstition to have such an opinion of a Great Man.[a]

Com Ireton.

Any man that makes a bargaine, and does finde afterwards 'tis for the worse, yett is bound to stand to itt.

Mr. Wildman.

They were couzen'd as wee are like to bee.

Com. Ireton.

I would nott have you talke of principles of juste Governement when you hold that all Governements that are sett uppe by consent are just. [Argue instead that] such or such a way that can consist with the libertie of the people. Then wee shall goe to cleare reason. That's one maxime, that all Governement must bee for the safetie of the people.

Col. Titchborne.

Lett us keepe to that businesse of safetie. 'Tis uppon the matter

government was that all governments rested on the consent of the people; but the people never set up King or Lords, therefore the government of King and Lords was unjust.

[a] The order of these two interpolations of Wildman's has been changed.

solelie in the people. [By] what hath bin propos'd in that I give Kinge and Lords [opportunity] to doe mee a curtesie if they will—[a]

Mr. Wildman.
Noe Curtesie.

Col. Titchborne.
Itt is onely an opportunity—and shew themselves as willing as the Commons. Lett us nott fight with shadowes.

Com. Ireton.
Wee doe nott know what opportunity God will give us.[b] If God will destroy Kinge or Lords hee can doe itt without cur or your wronge doing. If you take away all power from them, which this clearlie does, butt [do nott] take away all kinde of destruction of them from other men, then you doe them wronge too. Their having a [security from] destruction from other men cannott doe us wronge. That you can doe to the utmost for the[ir] safetie is this, that a Lord or Kinge may preserve his owne person or estate free from the Commons. Now whether this can bee destructive to the Commons that soe few men should bee distinct from a law made by the Commons, especially when wee have lawes made as to the preserving of the peace of the Kingdome and preserving every man in his right? The King and Lords are suable, impleadable in any Court. The Kinge may bee sued and tryed by a Jury, and a Lord may bee sued and tryed per Pares onely, a Knight by Esquires. What needes more where there are such lawes already that the Kinge and Lords are soe bound?

Mr. Wildman.
I conceive that the difference does not lie heere, butt whether

[a] Titchborne argues thus: The right of making laws is expressly stated to be solely in the House of Commons. The formality of sending them to the King and Lords for their consent means nothing. Their consent is not necessary.

[b] I take this first sentence to be really another interpolation of Wildman's, and the rest of the speech Ireton's reply to it.

the Kinge shall soe come in, that the Parliament must make their addresses themselves unto him for [the confirmation of] every thinge they passe. Whether itt bee a shadow or noe, I thinke itt is a substance when nothing shall bee made but by addresse to the Kinge. This will bee very shamefull in future Chronicles, that after soe much bloud there should bee noe better an issue for the Commons.

Com̃. Ireton.

Doe you thinke wee have nott lawes good enough for the securing of [the] rights [of the Commons ?]

Mr. Wildman.

I thinke [that] according to the letter of the law, if the King will [he may] kill mee by law. Aske any lawiers of itt; by the letter of the present law hee may kill mee, and 40 more, and noe law call him to account for itt.[a]

Com̃. Ireton.

I thinke noe man will thinke itt, that when the Kinge stands thus bound with soe many Laws[b] about him, and all the Commons of England bound to obey what law [the House of Commons] doe make, lett any man guesse whether the Kinge, as hee is a single person, will hazard himself to kill this, or that, or any other man.

Mr. Wildman.

Itt will bee thought boldnesse in mee [not] to agree. If God will open your hearts to provide soe that the Kinge may nott doe mee injury I shall bee glad of itt. If nott, I am butt a single man, I shall venture myself and [my] share in the common bottome.

Resolved, That the Councill bee adjourned till to-morrow and soe from day to day till the proposalls bee all debated, and the same Committee to meete againe.

[a] Compare *Putney Projects*, pp. 19, 34.

[b] MS. "Lords."

November 2, 1647

Att the Meeting of the Committee.

Resolved,

1. That the power of this and all succeeding Representatives of the Commons in Parliament doth extend on the behalf and as to the whole interest of all the Commons of England to the enacting, altering, and repealing of lawes, to the conclusive exposition and Declaration of law, and to finall[a] judgement without further appeale, and generally to all thinges concerning the Commonwealth whatsoever is nott by the represented reserved to themselves as is heerafter expressed. Nemine contradicente.

2. That noe law shall bee repealed, nor any new law or ordinance made to bind the Commons of England, nor any Parliamentary Judgement, triall, order, or other proceeding valid against any Commoner, without the particular concurrence and consent of the Agreed. Major Corbett;[b] noe.

[a] MS. "small."

[b] Major John Cobbett of Skippon's regiment, probably opposed the vote on the grounds stated by Wildman on p. 398. A pamphlet quotes "the saying of Ireton to honest Major Cobbett of Snowhill, who, for joyning with the agents of the Army, asked him if he were not deluded in his understanding, in joyning with the giddy-headed souldiers, and advised him not to run against the interest of himselfe and the officers" (*The Hunting of the Foxes, etc.*, *Somers Tracts*, ed. Scott vi., 52). Cobbett seems to have been concerned in the mutiny at Ware; was tried by court martial at Windsor in January, 1648, and sentenced to be cashiered (Rushworth, vii., 937, 940). Like others then sentenced he was forgiven and sent back to his regiment, then at Newcastle, and distinguished himself by his gallantry at the re-capture of Tynemouth Castle, August 11, 1648 (Rushworth, vii., 1226; *The Second Part of England's New Chains Discovered*, 1649, pp. 7, 11). He was made Adjutant-General of the Foot to the Army which invaded Scotland in July, 1650 (*Cromwelliana*, p. 84). After the battle of Worcester he was selected to bear Cromwell's despatch to the Parliament, with the commendation "that the person who is the bearer hereof was equal in the performance of his duty to most that served you that day" (Carlyle's *Cromwell*, Letter clxxxiii). Cobbett made a relation, and produced "a collar of SS., which was the King of Scots', and his garter, which the said Major Cobbett took in his quarters at Worcester." He was voted a

House of Commons, except in case of actuall violence or affront done by a Commoner to the House of Peeres as a Court; and in that case noe further proceeding to bee valid, butt by the House of Commons, saving to the securing or imprisoning of the offender's person till hee can bee tryed.

Agreed.

Nemine contradicente.

3. That noe Commoner of England shall be exempt from butt shall bee subject to and concluded by the power and judgement of the House of Commons without further appeale, as alsoe to and by all such orders, ordinances, and lawes, or expositions and Declarations of law, as shall bee made, past, and insisted on by that House, except in such fundamentall thinges as are by the people electing generally reserved to themselves, as is heerafter expressed.

Agreed.

Nemine contradicente.

4. That noe person whatsoever being an officer of Justice or Minister of State shall bee exempt from, butt shall bee accountable and subject to the same power and judgement of the House of Commons for any mal-administration of his place to the hurt or damage of the Commonwealth; butt the persons of peeres, otherwise then in such capacity as aforesaid, shall bee tryed and judged onely by their Peeres.

Agreed.

Nemine contradicente.

5. That noe person whatsoever soe adjudged by Parliament as before shall bee capable of protection or pardon from the Kinge, or to have their fines remitted, without the advice or consent of Parliament, nor such fines to bee disposed of otherwise then by the same judgement, advice, or consent shall bee directed.

gratuity of £100, and an annuity of £100 from forfeited lands in Scotland (*Commons' Journals*, vii., 13, 191). He seems to have died a Lieutenant-Colonel in 1656 (*Cal. State Papers, Dom.*, 1656-7, pp. 249, 301). He should be distinguished from Major Robert Cobbett, another leveller, who ended by becoming a contractor for army-clothing (*Cal. State Papers, Dom.* 1657-8, p. 118; Lilburne's *Legal Fundamental Liberties*, 1649, p. 40), and from the better known Colonel Ralph Cobbett.

6. That in all Elections of Representatives for the people these thinges following are by the people electing reserved to themselves, and soe generally to bee understood, to witt: Agreed. Nemine contradicente.

1. Matters of Religion and the wayes of God's worshippe, as to any positive compulsion there, are nott intrusted to any humane power.

2. That the matter of impresting or constrayning any free commoner of England to serve in the warres, any further or otherwise then for the imediate defence of this Kingdome and keeping the peace within itt, is likewise reserved.

3. That noe Commoner bee henceforth questioned for any thinge said or done in reference to or prosecution of the late warre or publique contests within this Kingdome, otherwise then by the judgement or with the concurrence of the present House of Commons, or in execution or prosecution of such judgement.

4. That the matter and effect of the preceding Articles, To witt, First, Concerning the certaine succession of Bienniall Parliaments.[a] Then the 2d Concerning the certainty of their sitting. Likewise the matter of the 6th, and the particulars under itt concerning the clearing of the power of Parliaments in future as to the interest of the people therin, and soe much of the intent of the 5th as concernes the equall distributing of future Representatives, are reserved by the people represented as their fundamentall rights nott to bee given away or abrogated by their Representatives.

Added to the Committee.

Lt. Col. Salmon.
Com̃. Cowling.
Cornett Wallis.

[a] The propositions referred to are summarised by Rushworth, vii., 861.

That the said Committee shall prepare such other particulars to bee presented to the Parliament as they shall finde necessary in relation to our former Declarations, and likewise to prepare a Declaration to bee sent with them to the Parliament and Kingedome, to bee tendred to this generall Councill for their consideration att the next Meeting.

And if there appeare any likelihood, that the Parliaments propositions for peace may bee sent to the Kinge before the said Declaration and particulars can bee sent from the Army to the Parliament, then the said Committee are to move the Generall that the Parliament in the name of this Councill may bee desired to suspend the sending of their propositions to the King untill some thinges that wee have to offer shall bee tendred to them, which wee hold essentiall to the liberty and peace of this Kingedome.

Putney, 3° Novemb. 1647.

Att the Committee of Officers appointed by the Generall Councill.

A story about the Generall wearing the Kinge's Colours.

The souldiers saying, Lett my Collonell bee for the Devill an hee will, I will bee for the Kinge.[a]

400 of Col. Lilburne's Regiment declar'd for the Kinge, uppon their coming back to Dunstable offer'd the Countrymen their armes, and they would take clubs, and bringe the Kinge to

[a] A newsletter in the *Clarendon Papers* (vol. ii., Appendix, xlix.) says under Nov. 15: "On Thursday last Sir Thomas Fairfax's regiment of foot were drawn to a rendezvous; and one White, the Major of the regiment, told the soldiers that the kingdom must be under another government (which he said, to see how they would like it). Whereupon the whole regiment threw up their hats and cried, 'A King, a King.' And thereupon White got to his horse and made some haste out of the field."

Whitehall. They would see what their Officers would doe, and then they would carry the Kinge away.

Debate concerning the Militia.[a]

That the Terme bee ten yeares, and the Declaratorie lawes to take place from thence.

Tythes nott to bee paid, but either a Land-rate to bee made in lieu of them, or sold att 14 yeares purchase for the use of the State, and they to make provision for the Ministers.[b]

Putney, 8 November,[c] 1647.

The Lieut. Generall

Spoke much to expresse the danger of their principles who had sought to devide the Army. That the first particular of that which they call'd The Agreement of the People did tend very much to Anarchy, that all those who are in the Kingedome should have a voice in electing Representatives.

Capt. Bray

Made a longe speech to take off what the Lieut. General said, and that what hee call'd Anarchy was for propriety.[d]

[a] Rushworth gives the result of the debate concerning the Militia.

[b] Compare Rushworth, vii., 862.

[c] On the proceedings of the Council of the Army between Nov. 3 and Monday, Nov. 8, see Appendix E.

[d] William Bray, Capt.-Lieutenant in Col. Robert Lilburne's regiment of foot, was a personage of some importance amongst the Levellers. In the mutiny of that regiment at Ware on Nov. 15, 1647, Bray was the only officer above the rank of a lieutenant who stayed with the soldiers. He was arrested on the charge of having led the regiment to rendezvous contrary to orders (Rushworth, vii., 875; *Old Parliamentary History*, xvi., 434). Bray's own account of his conduct, as delivered to the council of war which tried him, is printed in a pamphlet called *The Discoverer*, pt. 2, p. 52, 1649. He was tried by court martial at Windsor,

Lieut. Generall

Moved to putt itt to the Question,

Whether that the Officers and Agitators bee sent to their Quarters, yea, or noe.

Resolved uppon the Question,

That the Generall Council doth humbly advise his Excellency, that in regard the Generall shortly intends a Randezvous of the Army, and forasmuch as many distempers are reported to bee in the severall Regiments whereby much dissatisfaccion is given both to the Parliament and Kingdome through some misrepresentacions; to the end a right understanding may bee had, and the souldiers quieted, in order to their obedience to his Excellency for the service of the Parliament and Kingedome, itt is thought fitt to desire his Excellency that for a time the said Officers and Agitators

Dec. 1647, and finally on submitting and acknowledging his error dismissed, and sent back to his regiment (Rushworth, vii., 922, 937, 940, 943). Owing, as he states, to the hostility of his lieut-col., Henry Lilburne, he was again suspended from his command. In the summer of 1648 he raised a troop of volunteers in Kent to serve against the royalists, and attached it to the regiment of Col. John Reynolds. In March, 1649, he was expelled from the General Council of the Army and deprived of his command. On March 19 he presented to the House of Commons a printed statement of his grievances, entitled, "An Appeal in the humble claim of justice against Thomas Lord Fairfax," etc., which was voted scandalous and seditious, and Bray committed to Windsor Castle, during the pleasure of the House (*Commons' Journals*, vi., 167; "*Appeal*," pp. 11-15). He remained a prisoner at Windsor and Wallingford till Oct. 9, 1651 (*Commons' Journals*, vii., 31; *Cal. State Papers, Dom.*, 1651, p. 353). Two letters from Bray to Lenthal, petitioning for his release, are amongst the *Tanner MSS.*, lvi., 62; liii., 82; see also Cary's *Memorials of the Civil War*, ii., 141. and *The Englishman's Fundamental Appeal; or the Third humble petition and address of Capt. William Bray*, 1659. The first use Bray made of his freedom was to interrupt the proceedings of the Commissioners of Berkshire for underletting the estates of delinquents (*Tanner MSS.*, lv., 110). In 1659 he published a pamphlet entitled, "A plea for the people's Good Old Cause," and was recommended for employment as a sufferer for the true interest of the Commonwealth (*Cal. State Papers, Dom.*, p. 249).

resort to their severall commands and Regiments, to the ends aforesaid, there to reside untill the said Randezvouz bee over, and untill his Excellency shall see cause to call them together againe according to the Engagement.[a]

Committee.

Lieut. Generall.	Mr. Allen.
Com̃. Gen. Ireton.	Capt. Clarke.
Sir Hardresse Waller.	Mr. Lockyer.
Col. Okey.	Capt. Deane.
Col. Tichborne.	Col. Thomlinson.
Col. Hewson.	Lt. Col. Goffe.
Commissary Stane.	Major Rainborow.
Scoutmaster General [Watson].	Lt. Col. Cowell.
Col. Rich.	Com̃. Cowling.

This Committee to drawe uppe instructions for what shall bee offer'd to the Regiments att the Randezvouz, to consider of the late lettre sent to the Parliament, and what shall bee thought fitt further to bee propos'd to them.[b]

[*Desires of the Army.*]

1. Itt is desired, That six weekes pay if possibly itt may bee, if nott a monthes pay, bee presently sent downe to the Army.

2. That the arreares may bee voted to bee paid out of the remainder of Byshopps lands, Deanes and Chapters lands, to bee sold in the same manner as the Byshopps lands, reserving a competencie for those that have a legall interest therin, and have nott forfeited the same by delinquencie, and two thirds out of

[a] This resolution is given in Rushworth, vi., 866.

[b] See "A remonstrance from his Excellency Sir Thomas Fairfax and his Council of War concerning the late discontent and distraction in the Army, etc., November 14, 1647" (*Old Parliamentary History*, xvi., 340.) The engagement given at the end was evidently drawn up by this Committee.

delinquents compositions who have nott yett compounded and out of forrest lands.

3. Wee desire, that the House will bee pleased either to make provision, that when this monthes pay is out there shall bee constant pay to inable the souldiers to avoide the oppressing of the people by free quarter (then which nothing is more greivous unto us), or if the Parliament does finde the Countries will nott soe readily bringe in their monies wee shall undertake, if inabled therunto, soe to dispose of the Army and of the severall counties as that the monies shall be raised and the people punctually satisfied for their quarters, provided that there may be an increase of the said tax to an hundred thousand pounds a month for the payment of this Army, and the other forces concern'd in the Kingedome, and those that are to goe for Ireland, and the disbanding of those that bee supernumerary, untill the Parliament shall otherwise provide by excise or otherwise for easing the said taxes.

4. Lastly, wee declare that if this course bee taken, that as wee have engaged that none shall uppon paine of death take any thinge from any inhabitant in this Kingedome against his will, wherin wee shall bee punctuall and positive, soe alsoe wee shall give assurance that noe man shall bee forc't to bee quarter'd uppon against his consent, provided there may bee an allowance for lodging, firing, and candle, or the owners uppon whose houses quarters are assigned to bee had in other places to bee allowed to those that shall quarte r.

Putney, 9 November, 1647.

Generall Councill.

The Generall present.

This Committee is to take into consideration, the Engagement,

These requests were accompanied by a letter from Sir Thomas Fairfax to the Speaker dated November 8, the original of which is in the *Tanner MSS.*, vol. lviii., f. 570. It is printed by Cary (*Memorials of the Civil War*, i., 356), and also by Rushworth, vii., 867, and was read in the House of Commons on November 9 (*Commons' Journals*, v., 353). The last lines of the 4th desire should probably run "to be allowed to those that shall quarter in other places, or the owners upon whose houses quarters are assigned to be had."

Declarations, and papers of the Armie, and uppon them to collect a summarie of those thinges that concerne the good of the Kingedome, the liberties of the people, and interests of the army, and further to consider the Case of the Army stated, and a paper commonly call'd The Agreement of the People, and to consider how farre any thinge contain'd in the same are consistent with the said Engagements and Declarations and Interests aforesaid.

This summarie soe concluded by the major parte of the Committee to bee represented to the Generall.[a]

CORNETT WALLIS.
CAPT. LEIGH.
LT. GENERALL.
COM. GENERALL.
LT. CHILLENDEN.
SIR HARDRESSE WALLER.
CAPT. CARTER.
CORNETT TRACY.
COL. RICH.
LT. COL. GOFFE.
COL. THOMLINSON.
CAPT. DEANE.
,, DISNEY.
LT. COL. COBBETT.
CAPT. ALLEN.
COL. OVERTON.
MR. COLBRON.
MAJOR BETHELL.
CAPT. WATSON.
MR. UNDERWOOD.

COL. TITCHBORNE.
MR. WILDMAN.
COM. COWLING.

Added since.

MAJOR SAUNDERS.
COL. HARRISON.
CAPT. SPENCER.
MAJOR RAINBOROW.
,, BERRY.
COL. RAINBOROW.
CAPT. PALMER.
LT. COL. ASHFEILD.

The place.
Quartermaster Generall's
Quarters.

Adjourned till Thursday
come fortnight att the
Headquarters.[b]

[a] See Rushworth, vi., 868, where this sentence continues "to the Generall for his order to communicate the same to the several regiments at their respective rendevouz."

[b] Met November 25th, at Windsor.

If any by that letter bearing date 5th of November doe make any construction as if wee intended that wee were against the Parliaments sending propositions to the Kinge, Wee doe heerby declare, That itt was noe part of our intentions in the said letter, but that the same is utterly a mistake of our intention and meaning therin, our intentions being only to assert the freedome of Parliament.[a]

LIEUT. GENERALL.
SCOUTMASTER GENERALL.
COL. RICH.
COL. HEWSON.
COL. THOMLINSON.
SIR HARDRESSE WALLER.
COL. TITCHBORNE.
,, OKEY.
DR. STANE.
MAJOR AXTELL.
LT. SCOTTEN.
COM. COWLING.
LT. COL. COBBETT.
MAJOR COBBETT.
,, BERRY.
QUARTERMASTER GENERALL GROSVENOR.
COL. TWISLETON.
,, OVERTON.
CAPT. MICHILL.
,, YOUNGE.
COL. BARKESTEAD.
CAPT. CARTER.
,, PRICE.
,, BYSHOPP.
MR. ALLEN.
MAJOR BETHELL.
LT. COL. BOWEN.
MR. WHITING.
,, LOCKYER.
ADJ. GEN. BURY.
COR. WALLIS.
LT. COL. ASHFEILD.
LT. CHILLENDEN.
MR. EYTON.
LT. COL. JUBBS.
CAPT. COX.
MAJOR ABBOTT.
MR. CLARKE.
CAPT. DISNEY.[b]
,, ALLEN.

[a] The letter referred to is printed in Appendix E.

[b] The letter of the Agitators to their regiments, quoted in Appendix E., continues as follows, referring apparently to the meeting of November 9:

"The next day they still waved and refused the free debate of the aforesaid Question, and dissolved this Council for above a fortnight; and for a time resolved

Putney, 11 November, 1647

Att the 2[d] Meeting of the Committee of Officers appointed by the Generall Councill.

Col. Harrison

Made a narration concerning some thinges that lay uppon his spiritt in relation to the Kinge, Lords, and the Reserve. That the Kinge was a Man of Bloud, and therfore the Engagement taken off, and that they were to prosecute him. That if the Lords had right to have a Negative voice hee would nott goe against itt, butt iff nott, if they had usurp't [it] an 100, 200, or 1000 yeares, the greater was the wronge, and they to bee debarr' of that power.

Lt. Generall

Answer'd him by putting severall cases in which merther was nott to bee punished. As in the case if a man that had kill'd his sonne should gett into a garrison, whether hee might raise warre, or nott give conditions to that place. Stated the case of David uppon Joab's killing of Abner, that hee spar'd him uppon two prudentiall grounds: one that hee would nott hazard the spilling of more bloud in regard the sons of Zeroiah were too hard for him.

Com. Generall

Answer'd in the same case, and further urg'd this that wee are nott to sin, or to goe in any unlawfull way to doe that which is for bringing a delinquent to Judgement.

they would only prepare some faire Propositions to the Army, and about Arrears and pay, and sent to the Parliament for a moneths pay against a Randezvouz; But they declared they would divide the Army into three parts, to Randezvouz severally: and all this appeares to be only to draw off the Army from joyning together to settle those cleere foundations of Freedome propounded to you, and to procure your rights as you are Souldiers effectually, without any more delusions."

Lieut. Generall.

That wee doe the worke when itt is disputable, and the worke of others to doe itt, if itt bee as an absolute and indisputable duty for us to doe itt.

The Generall.

That wee doe butt secure the Kinge in the right of another, and that itt became them for to order thinges concerninge him.[a]

Com̃. Cowling.

Itt was his usurping power in the law that would have ruin'd us, and doe butt destroy that and lett his person alone, wee care nott for itt.

[*Letter to a Commander in the North of England.*]

Sir,

I just now receiv'd information, that his Majesty is gone from Hampton Court, hee went about nine of the clock this night, and was mist within half an hower after his departure. Whither hee should bee gone I cannott as yett understand, butt supposing itt nott improbable that hee may intend towards the North, I thought good to give you this advertisement, and shall desire you to use all possible care and diligence by setting guards uppon all passages, and by making what inquiry you can that if possible you may discover and stay his Majesty. If itt shall soe happen I desire you with all speede to advertise the Parliament and myself therof, and remayne,

[T. FAIRFAX.]

I shall desire your utmost care and diligence imediately to send to all the Port Townes in England.[b]

[a] MS. "them."

[b] November 11, 1647, probably addressed to Lambert, who was in command at York.

Nov. 28, 1647.

To the right honourable his Excellencie Sir Thomas Fairfax, knt. Captaine Generall of all the forces raised in the Kingdome of England.

The humble peticion of some of your Excellencies officers and souldieres under the custodie of the Marshall General,

Humblie sheweth,

That whereas theire are many misrepresentationes of thinges in the world by men of corrupte minds, who would make the end of all your noble and your armie's valiante atcheivements (under the power of God) fruitelesse, and would destroye iustice and righteousnesse from amongst men, and make a common good and equall distribucion of iustice to become a particuler personall selfish interest; and for to accomplish this unholy, this unwarrantable selfish end, they have blazed abroade that one should say itt was lawfull to murther the Kinge, and the person that reported itt was one Leiutenant Collonell Henry Lilburne; therefore seing itt is a derogateinge from the power of a true established representative of Commons, and seinge allsoe itt is most abominable in our eys and contrarie to our principles, Wee therefore desire that the said Leiut. Coll. Lilburne may bee speedily sent for to testifie upon oath (as in the presence of God,) whoe used those words, where these words were used, and when, and what in particuler the words were; that soe such a person may come under a publique cognizance, and your Excellencye's faithfull servants and souldiers may free themselves and others from such aspersions, and your peticioners shall ever pray, &c.

JOHN WOOD.	WILL: PRYOR.
WILL: BRAY.	WILL: EYRE.
WILL: THOMSON.	GEORGE HASSALL.
JOHN CROSMAN.	THO: BEVERLEY.[a]

[a] A copy of this petition printed in *England's Freedom Soldiers Rights*, 1647, p. 10, adds the name of Will Everard.

Letter from Col. Robert Hammond.

Carisbrooke Castle, 19 Dec., 1647.

The Kinge stands engaged in his worde nott to stirr, and doth protest this is the place hee first designed when hee apprehended it not safe to continue longer at Hampton Court, and that if hee were to chuse anie place within his three Kingdoms hee would not remove hence except to London upon a personall treaty. I have often asked that if hee bee not thought safe here hee may be removed, which is the thing most desirable to mee.

[Ro. Hamond.[a]]

[a] This was probably addressed to Lord Fairfax.

APPENDIX.

APPENDIX A.

Colonel Wogan's Narrative.

The following narrative is a continuation of a paper printed by Carte under the heading, "*The Proceedings of the new-moulded Army from the time they were brought together in* 1645 *till the King's going to the Isle of Wight in* 1647. Written by Col. Edward Wogan, till then an officer of that Army."[1] Carte unfortunately printed only half of Wogan's narrative, stopping short at the battle of Torrington in February, 1646; the remainder, beginning where Carte leaves off, is printed from the original in the Clarendon State Papers (No. 2607). A sketch of Wogan's life will help to determine the value of his statements. Of his early career little is known, but it may be safely assumed that he is the Captain Wogan of Okey's dragoons mentioned in the list of the New Model. In March, 1648, he deserted, and succeeded in marching to Scotland with the whole of his troop (Rushworth, vii., 1021-4, 1031). His surrender was vainly demanded by the Parliament (*ibid.* 1046, 1064-6). Clarendon, who devotes some pages to an account of Wogan, mistakenly places his desertion after the King's execution (*Rebellion*, xiv., 59-61). Later he joined Ormonde in Ireland, was appointed governor of Duncannon and successfully repulsed an attack by Ireton (Carte, *Ormonde*, ii., 97).

In December, 1649, when Col. Sankey defeated Lieut.-Gen. Ferrall, Wogan was taken prisoner, but escaped by corrupting his gaoler (Carlyle's *Cromwell*, Letter cxvii.; Whitelocke, *Memorials*, f. 426). Had he not escaped Cromwell intended to execute him as a renegade and traitor, "who did not only betray his trust in England but

[1] Carte, *Collection of Original Letters and Papers concerning the Affairs of England from* 1641 *to* 1660, 2 vols., 1739; vol. i., pp. 142.

counterfeited the General's hand (thereby to carry his men, whom he had seduced, into a foreign nation to invade England), under whom he had taken pay and from whose service he was not discharged; and with the same nation did invade England and hath since, contrary to the said trust, taken up arms here" (Carlyle's *Cromwell*, Appendix 16). In 1653 Wogan boldly landed in England from France, enlisted fifty or sixty men for the King's service, marched from London to Scotland pretending they were soldiers of the Commonwealth, and joined Middleton and the royalists who were holding out in the Highlands (*Cal. Clarendon Papers*, ii., 286, 288; *History of the Rebellion*, xiv., 59). Soon after joining Middleton he was severely wounded in an obscure skirmish, died for want of a good surgeon, and was buried at the Kirk of Kenmore in February, 1654 (*Military Memoirs of John Gwynne*, 1822, pp. 220, 224, 237, 239, 243, 248, 253).

" We were soone enformed of that from Ireland by a small frigott that came into Padstow that was sent by my Lord of Woster, with letters to the Prince. The frigate came in wth that confidence being assured the place was within the King's quarters, theire men came on shore without asking anything of the Inhabytantes who was quartered theire by chance; some of o[r] horsemen being in that towne examined the men and found them to be Ireish, w[ch] presently confessed they came from Waterford in Ireland, they seized upon the seamen and got abord, the frigott being run aground there, the[y] tooke one Captain Allen w[ch] had the command of the vessell, him with a packett was brought to Bodman to o[r] Generall. By those letters we understood that there was noe daunger of any Foote coming out of Ireland, for in those letters was mencioned the want of Shipping and moneys before any Foote could be had from thence, then there was noe other feare then that of France and to prevent that daunger there was order sent to Admirall Batten to hover from the Land's End to the Coast of Brittany; then o[r] Generall resolved to advance towards Trurowe; in o[r] march the first day from Bodman o[r] forlorne of Horse encountred wth a partie of the Enimies w[ch] were commanded by Major Generall Web, both parties mett and fought nobly. At last the King's partie being over numbred was forst to give ground and leave the field in some disorder; only the Major Generall himselfe charged wth an undaunted curage through all our partie and in charging back agayne his horse was killed and himself wounded in severall places wth all those that stuck to him either slayne or taken, he being at last after a long fight on foote forst to submitt. The second day we mett with theire Commissioners that came to treate which was very strange to us all, yet o[r] Generall would not heare of a Treaty till he came to Trewrowe where the King's Army then lay. First it was agreed that the King's Army should draw back westward from Trurow and that o[rs] should quarter there. Allsoe it was agreed that theire should be a seasasion of armes for six days, dureing w[ch] tyme the Commissioners of both Armies were to sitt att Trurow to agree upon the Articles; for all this o[r] Generall had noe greate confidence in this treaty feareing least the King's Army should slip by them as they might easily doe, but to prevent that daunger he sent some horse and Dragoones back agayne to Bodman wth an order that all the trees should be cut downe behind Bodman bridge and in all the Cuntry thereabouts to stopp the King's horse if they came that way, in two or three dayes. That doubt was cleared, for o[r] Commissioners and theires agreed thus: First that the King's Army should disband and theire Souldiers leaveing theire horse should retourne to theire severall homes, and the Officers to march to theire severall homes wth theire horses and armes. The King's Army were to lay downe theire armes by Brigade on severall dayes till theire was a Regement of o[r] horse that convoyed them away to theire severall cuntryes. When all the King's Army was disbanded there was nothing more for o[r] Army to doe in those partes; a Councell of Warr was called and it was thought fitt that the Army should march towards Exeter and that Collonel Fortesque should stay in that Cuntry with two Regements of Foote and 3 Troopes of horse for the takeing in of Pendenis and the Mount. O[r] Generall with the rest of the Army came before Exetter, the Governor thereof, which was Sir John Berkley, seeing o[r] Army come before it and knowing that the King's Army was disbanded with all the nessecity he was reduced unto for want of provisions and with all that they had noe hopes of releefe, hee was forst to surrender the Citty upon honorable condicions; soe was Bastable deliver'd upon the same condicions; all o[r] horse were sent towards Oxford under the command of Commissary Generall Ireton, our Generall with the Lieutenant Generall stay with all the foote at Exeter to refresh them awhile. The Commissary lay wth all the horse round Oxford and continually on duty, for the Kinge was then in the Cytty with Prince Rupert wth a considerable party of horse as we heard, who were resolved to fall out upon some of our quarters, w[ch] made us all every night to expect their coming.

After the generall had settled the businesse of the west he marched wth all the foote towards Oxford. Before he came within three or fower dayes march of that Cytty the Kinge gott out privately in the night only wth two or three persons wth him. It was told the Comissary generall that the Kinge was gone for London, and was invited thither by the Presbiterian party of the House and Cytty, and was encouraged to it by the Scotts army that lay then before Newarke. I knowe not whether that report was true or noe, but I am sure that was the first pretended cause of jelousey that was betwene the Independant and Presbyterian party, and to make the army the more assured of this report it was credibly said that the King came first to London and was conveyed from thence to the Scotts army. This bred noe small division betwixt the Presbiterian and Independant officers of the army. The generall came up with the foote before Oxford, and placed them as conveniently as hee could, as above the horse and Major Generall Massey's Brigade was to lye about Farington. We continued soe for the

April 27th, 1646.

space of a moneth and the foote entrencht Themselves a good distance from the Towne. Collonell Whaley wth his regim^t^ of horse and 2 regm^ts^ of foote was sente to block up Woster wth the assistance of Collonell Morgan the govern^r^ of Glossester. It was just at that tyme the black lyst was presented to the Leu^t^ Generall, wch was the names of all those officers in the army that were Presbiterians. It was brought privately and presented by Lieuten^t^ generall Wattson, wch was a most pernitious factious fellow. He was backed by many of the cheefest of the Army and partly[1] by the Comissary generall. The Generall was ignorant of it, and knew not what it meant when one Major Fincher Quarter Mr Generall of the Horse discovered it unto him, and told him of what daungerous consequence (*sic*) would be if this liste came to the knowledg of those officers whose names were written in it The generall made answer that for his par^te^ he made noe differance of theire opinions but was confident that all his offic^rs^ were faythfull to the Parliam^t^, and that the Lieu^t^ Generall as he conceived would not doe any thing to the prejudice of any man that wisht well to the Parliam^t^ or Army. The Q^r^ Mr Generall was noe way satisfied wth this answer but was resolved to acquaint his frends in the Parliam^t^ House, wth this liste and of the new order that was given out by the Leu^t^ Generall, wch was Liberty of Conscience as they caled it to all that pretend to have the guift of the spiritt in preaching or expounding. Both houses tooke this soe haynously that their was an order sente to o^r^ generall that none should preach or teach in the Army but those that are lawfully called to it by the Assembly of Divines. This order was no sooner come but executed, but to the greate greefe of the Leut. Generall and his faction; yet they desembled the matter soe well that they seemed to take noe notice of it at present. In the meane while the seige went on, and the towne being streightned for provisions yet obstinate would not surrender. There were not those wanting in o^r^ Army that spred abroade that the king wth the Scots army would releeve that Cytty, and that the Presbiterian party of the Houses of Lords and Commons would invite him to it. Many papers to this purpose were spred abroade amongst the soldyers, but to noe effect, for the Presbiterians had much the stronger parte in the army; beside Major Generall Massie's brigade would back them upon any ocasion to that purpose. Collonell Raynsburrow was sent wth two regm^ts^ of horse and two of foote to strengthen the seige of Woster that was but slightly blockt up before by Collonell Whaley. Whaly was called back to the seige of Oxford, he being then accounted a Presbiterian. At last necessity compelled the Cytty to treate. Comisson^rs^ were ordered on both sides: after long debate they agreed and the Cytty was surrendred upon honorable condicions, soe was Woster, Farington and Wallingford, and allsoe Ragland that was beseiged by foote of ours sente from the seige of Oxford: our army having then noethinge to doe were sent to quarters, some to Wales, some to the Associate Countyes, another p^te^ were quartered about Wostershere, Oxfordshere, and Herifordshere. Major Generall Massie's brigade were sente to Dorsetshere, Som^r^s^t^shere and Wiltshere to quarter. The first of

[1] Contracted for "particularly."

Crumwell's stratagems was to get the Major Generall's brigade to disband under pretence to ease the Kingdom, though they offered theire service to Ireland and would willingly have gone wth that moneys they had at theire disbanding, but Crumwell prevented theire desires and spoake openly in the House that he would carry as many of the new modled army to that Kingdom as the Parliam[t] thought fitt and that he would disband the rest if they pleased. This motion of his tooke off all jealousey from Crumwell and the rest of the army: presently order was given for Massie's men to disband, w[ch] was presently done. Presently after happened the suddayne death of the Earle of Essex, w[ch] Cromwell tooke soe much to hearte in his outward apperance that he was seene by some to cry and tear his hayre, though it was judged by many that hee contrived his death ; at this tyme the King was at Newcastle wth the Scotts, his frends dayly resorting thither, w[ch] gave greate cause of suspition of the Scotts and credibly confirmed in ou[r] army that the Scotts would declare for the Kinge. To prevent further danger there were two reg[mts] of horse and Oakey's dragoons sent to quarter all along upon the River Trent; and to examin all that came that way Northwards. At last we're freed from that feare, for the Scotts were resolved to deliver up the King as soone as they had received an hundred thousand pounds, and soe leave the kingdome. Theire money was conveyed downe to them by Colonell Graves; there went alsoe wth him Commission[rs] from both houses that went to receive the Kinge, and to pay the money to the Scotts. The King was dellivered to the custody of Collonell Graves: the Scotts marched for their owne cuntry, and the Kinge was brought to Holmeby, there kept wth a strong guarde about him and none of his old frends suffered to come unto him except those that had leave from o[r] Commission[rs]. The Commission[rs] made divers propositions to the King, but not pleaseing to him. Crumwell all this whille sate in the House, and both Houses ordered that the most parte of the army should disband or goe for Ireland except those that were to stay in the kingdome as a standing armie, w[ch] was to be all Presbyterians. Crumwell seemed to be as forward for this as any in the House ; o[r] head Quarters was then at Nottingham. Commissary Ireton all this while was not ignorant what the Parliam[t] was resolved to doe, and at councell of warr tooke ocasion to speake of this; how the Parliam[t] had noe good intentions towards the army, and that it was a sad reward for we many yeares service to be cast of w[t]hout any reward for their service or security for their persons after they were disbanded: likewise that the Parliam[t] was resolved to set upp the King agayne, that there would be noe liveing for any in that kingedome that had served in our army. All the offic[rs] that were present were much moved at this and besought the Commissary to advise them what they were to doe. He answered there was noe way but one to prevent this, w[ch] was that every officer should repayre to his respective command, and to send a trooper of each troope wth the grievances of the severall troopes to Saffron Walden, where the Generall was then goeing to receive the Commission[rs] of both Houses that were coming downe to disband the Army. The Parliament thought none soe fitt as Crumwell to be one of those Commission[rs]. The Commission^{rs} came to Saffron Walden ; all the offic^{rs} of the army were to meete there wth the names of all those that will engage for the service of Ireland: there likewise came a trooper of each troope wth theire severall greevances. When they were all come to towne, they were called privately together by Capt John Reynolds of Cromwell's Regiment and one his greatest favorete : when the troope mett together the Capt made them a long and plesant speech, told them how they were like to be cast of w^{t}hout any man^{r} of reward for theire greate services, and that they had noe courage nor hon^{r} that would be soe, and that for his p^{te} he and all his troope would sooner dye then disband wthout the utmost farthing of theire arreares. This speech tooke soe well wth these troopers that they highly comended his brave resolution and were all of his opinion. When the Capt. perceived that his speech found such good successe, desired them all to sitt downe and consider what they had to doe, and for his parte if they pleased he would sitt wth them and doe nothing wthout theire consent, wch they gladly accepted of, and gave theire Capt. the title of Chayreman. The first thing they did was to dispatch messengers to every regim^{t} and troope in the army to let thom know what the Parliament was resolved to doe and what they for theire p^{te} were resolved to propose to the Commisson^{rs} and further desired that every troope should owne what theire deputyes should propose to the Comission^{rs} to be theire sense and desire, wch was accordingly granted by allmost every troope in the army. Our generall comanded that all our office^{rs} should meete in the greate Church at Saffron Walden to heare what the Comisson^{rs} had to say unto us. The Generall wth the Commisson^{rs} came to the Church, wch was allmost full; the General made a shorte speech, tould us how much the Parliam^{t} and Kingdom were obliged to us for our faythfull services, and desired them that would goe for Ireland to give in theire names : and that they first should have security for theire arreares. Then Crumwell stoode up and made a long grave speech in the behalf of the Parliam^{t}, first to give the army thanks for theire never to be forgotten services, as allsoe what a greate care the Parliament had to please each particular man according to his particuler meritt, and that the Parliam^{t} would in tyme pay the arreares of those that were to stay in the Kingdom, and give security for the payment of those that were to goe for Ireland, and protested for his parte that if the Parliam^{t} would command him he would gladly trayle a picke in that war of Ireland, therefore desired us all to consider what a holy war that was, and that it were a noble thing for all us that were young men to engage for that kingdom. Just whilst he was thus speaking he was interrupted by one of the troopers that was of Raynolds his Councell, wch had newly called themselves Agitato^{rs} ; the fellow spoake boldly to the Leu^{t} Generall and told him that he was employed thither by the Army to acquaynt the Generall and the Comiss^{rs} of theire agreevance, and to that purpose p^{r}sented a remonstrance in the behalfe of the Army, wch startled the Commisson^{rs} and the Generall himselfe, and Crumwell tooke on like a madman, and declared openly in the Church that all those that had a hand in that remonstrance were enimies to the Parliam^{t}. Many of o^{r} Officers were surprised at his saying, but not the Chayreman of the Agitators, wch was Capt Raynolds. He seemed to be the more confident in his request. The remonstrance was soe unreasonable that the Comisson[rs] would not grant anything that was desired in it: the offic[rs] were all dismist to theire severall comands. Crumwell and the rest of the Comiss[rs] retorned to London to give the Parliam[t] an account. Crumwell in his pretended fury protested the ruen of all those that had a hand in that remonstrance. Ireton seemed to be a neuter and would not openly owne the remonstrance, nor seeme to contest w[th] the Parliam[t]. The Chayreman of the Agitators was not idle, but sent allwayes to the Troop[e]s to let them know what a sad condicion they were if they did not owne that remonstrance, and the proceedings of the Agitators. The Generall was ignorant of these contrivances and certaynely persuaded by Ireton that these that were called Agitators intended nothing to his prejudice nor to the dishon[r] of the army, yet the General, the Comissary Generall, and all the Offic[rs] of the Army disavowed the proceedings of the Agitators. Ireton designed the matter, what he would have the army to doe, and privately would send it to London to Crumwell Crumwell would with as much privacie send it back agayne to his Capt. Reynolds, the Chayreman Raynolds would present it to the Agitat[rs] as the greevance of the Army, they would declare it to the Parliament as the desire of the Army, soe that all things were done and acted in that Councell of what concerned the Army w[t]hout the Generalls order or any other Offic[rs] of the army. The Parliament was much ofended at this and writt to the generall to appease that mutinie as they called it, and to apprehend such offic[rs] as had a hand in that mutinie, that the Generall would be pleased to send up Cap[t] Reynolds to them, he being, as they conceived, the cheefe instrument of what was past. The Generall tooke this letter with consideracion and advised wth Ireton about it. Whilst the matter was in debate whether Reynolds should be sent or noe, the Kinge was taken away from Holmebey by a partie of five hundred horse under the comand of Cornet Joyce. Those that had the guarde of the King condecended to his takeing away, I meane all the comon sould[rs]. Collonell Graves that had the comand of the King at that tyme was forst to fly away privately, for all his whole regm[t] mutined ag[t] him. He and S[r] Robert Pye came post to London to advertise the Parliam[t] of what was happened, then o[r] Generall sent to the Parlem[t] to let them know how parte of the army tooke away the Kinge he then knew not where, and that the rest of the army would mutinie, and protested his inocency in the proceedings of the army and taking away the king. This put both Houses into a strange feare soe that they knew not what to doe or say in the matter. Now Crumwell foamed and stormed, vowed that if the Parliament would comand him he doubted not but in a shorte tyme he would destroy all the mutiners there. He protested before God openly before the Houses that he would never leave them nor forsake them whilst he lived. The House seemed much satisfied wth Crumwell's solemne protestation and began to consider how he might appease this mutiny. Crumwell, that very afternoone stole out of Towne and posted downe to the army. As soone as he came, the first thing he did was to owne what the Agitat[rs] had done and the takeing away of the king to be his design. Our Generall was amased at his sayings, but Crumwell and Ireton perswaded him that there was a nessesity for it, and that it was for theire owne safety. First they made it app^{e} to him that the Parliam^{t} had a designe to ruen the army, and that they would close with the King and leave the army in the lurch to theire greate dishon^{r} and utter ruen: by much adoe they perswaded the Generall to be of theire opinion and moreover perswaded him to send his declaracion to that purpose to the Parliam^{t}, which accordingly he did. The Parliament was astonished at it, and had they not been encouraged by the Cytty of London that assured them they would live and dye with them.[1] The Parliam^{t} set forth theire declaration against the army and declared all those to be traitors that had a hand in takeing away of the Kinge. They further declared that all those offic^{rs} and sold^{rs} that would come of from the army to London should have six moneths' pay in hand and security for theire arrers, and that they should continue in the standing army that should be in the Kingdom. This declaracion wrought soe much in the army that it brought of many both offic^{rs} and sould^{rs}, first Coll. Graves, Coll. Herbert, Coll. Fortescue, Sr Robt Pye, Coll. Sheffield, Coll. Buttler, Quarter Mr Generall Fincher, the Generall's Leu^{t} Collonell of foot and many Cap^{ts} and other Offic^{rs} and sould^{rs} came away upon this declaration to London; without doubt all the rest would have followed, had it not bene for Crumwells subtilty, wch was his outward good carriage to the King wch was then in the army. It was given out in the army by Crumwell's permission that as the Parliam^{t} would reinthrowne the King wthout making condicions for the sould^{rs} soe would the army reinthrowne the King wthout makeing condicions for the Parliament. It was at that very tyme the Presbiterians lost all theire interest in the army, by reason all those offic^{rs} they had most confidence in had now deserted the army and were gone to London, wch had they not done, Crumwell and Ireton could never have brought theire designe to passe, nor ever have gayned soe much interest in the army as presently after they had, by reason that all those that deserted the army their comands were voyd and given to the most factious that could be found. The Parliam^{t} were preparing of an army, the caviler party in London were joyneing wth them. On the other side Crumwell endevored to oblige all the Kings frends and thought i t the nearest way first to make the King his frende, wch he did by his great protestacions and oathes upon his knees privately before the Kinge that he and the whole army would declare for him; and to give the greater assurance of his faythfulnesse gave order that all those that were the King's old frends might freely com to him without any kinde of examining, that his old servants might attend him, that there should be noe distinctive mark betwene the army and those that were formerly of the King's and comanded all the offic^{rs} to entertayne as many of them as came to o^{r} army: the King was likewise without any guarde of the army, and suffered to goe for his pleasure wheresoever he desired. The King's frends at London could not well tell wch side to take; for the Parliam^{t} profest as much for the King as the Army could doe, but they haveing not much confidence in the Parliam^{t} sent downe a gen^{t} of quallity to the King to

[1] Something omitted.

receive his comands. The gent[t] that came to the Kinge, as I take it, was S[r] Marmiduke Langdon, who was sent back to London, wth command to those of the King's frends not to medle nor engage wth the Parliam[t] in London. The Presbiterians in London were quite dishartened when they saw the Kings' party leave them. The Cyty would not advance any money for the levying of a new army. The Parliament at that tyme had noe money in their treasury; our army came towards London and sent theire propositions to the Parliament, first to demaund eleven of theire members to put into the hands of the army; next that the Parliam[t] should own all the proceedings of the army. The Parliament thought themselves soe much undervalued in these unreasonable demaunds that they would by noe meanes condescend to anythinge that the army desired. Still the army came on, and the Parliam[t] not being provided to defend themselves, the Cytty not willing to engage in a new warr, as they conceived that to be, being much discouraged at the Speaker's stealeing away wth thirty Lords and Commons; presently after the Speaker of the House of Lords went away allsoe to the army, with divers of the principall cyttezens of London. Those of the Parliam[t] that stayd behind were all in a confusion, and knew not well what to doe by reason the Cytty gave them quite over, and would have noething to doe wth them, nor would not doe soe much as maynetayne theire lyne to make condicions for themselves, but suffered the army to march through the Cyty without any maner of opposition. When we came on the other side of the Cytty o[r] Generall demaunded the Tower w[ch] was presently given him. O[r] army marched to Croyden, the King was sent to Hampton Court wth a small guarde. When Crumwell was possest of the Tower, Guildehall and Whitehall, the first thinge he did was to command the Cyttyzens to pull downe all the lyne and fortefications about the Cytty, w[ch] was accordingly done wth greate humillity and reverence. Then the Parliam[t] sate agayne, I meane those members that came downe to the Army. The first thing they did after they sate was to owne all that the Parliam[t] did this tyme past, and ordered that the Army should have six moneths' pay payd them out of hand, w[ch] was borrowed of the Cytty, and presently payd to the sold[rs]. The army was then sent to quarters wth an order to disband all those amongst us that were of the King's party. Coll. Whaley was sent wth his Regim[t] to guarde the Kinge at Hampton Court. The Generall removed his quarters to Puttney where he stayed till the Kinge was cuningly jugled away to the Isle of Wight, and soe presently after I marcht away into Scotland wth my troope.

APPENDIX B.

The examination of the three troopers who delivered the letter of the soldiers to Major General Skippon, April 30, 1647.

[Tanner MSS. Bodleian Library, vol. lviii., f. 84.]

The Gentlemen that delivered the letter were call'd in, vizt.
Mr. Edw. Sexby.
Mr. Wm. Allin.
Mr. Tho. Shepherd.

They brought and delivered a letter to Major Generall Skippon, the like to the Lieutenant Generall, and the like to His Excellencie.

By what authoritie

The joynt and unanimous consent of the Eight Regiments of Horse, they having attested it by two of every Regiment. They mett at severall places.

They had noe Rendevous but what wee had by our Officers.

Brought by our Officers [sic] each Regiment to a Rendezvous.

The Proposicions for the service of Ireland read.

They did know the contents of the letter else they would not have subscribed it. It was read in each Regiment and each Troope and subscribed. The originall is with the Regiments. This but a faire copie. There was an originall with each Troupe.

Ordered,

That the Sergeant doe keepe these persons asunder upon their Examinacions and after they are examined.

Mr. Allen.

How long hee had been in the Armie, a twelve moneth. Bore noe Office. Warwickshire man, served in Lieutenant Generall Cromwell's Troupe. Hee heard it read and subscribed it. Severall t[imes?] read, cannot recollect the names of these persons that read it.

Demanded his opinion touching a Clause in the letter concerninge some that had tasted of soveraigne ie and had degenerated into Tyrants.

Answered that

As it was the joynt Act of the Eight Regiments to contrive it, they will joyntly answer it.

That hee shall give in his answer with the rest as it was the joynt act of the rest with him.

Hee did not saye, that it was read in any of the Regiments or Troupes when they were brought to a Rendezvous, but that it was read in many places which hee cannot recollect.

Mr. Allen againe.

Neere a twelve moneth since hee came to this Army.

In the Lord General Essex's Army served under Collonel Holles in his Regiment till hee was a prisoner at Brentford and served afterwards in Gen. Major Skippon's Regiment.

A prisoner in the Kinges Armie seaven dayes, condemned among seaventene others to bee hanged, by judgment of a Councell of Warre, then every tenth man drawen out to bee hanged, at last an oath putt to them and dismissed. Wounded at first Newberry fight. Tooke the oath at Oatlands.

After hee had taken the Oath hee listèd himselfe in Major Generall Skippon's Regiment, served under Captain Beton.

A felt maker by trade in Southw. Wounded againe at Henly, where hee received five shillings of Major Generall Skippon.

Mr. Sixby.

Suffolk man, trouper in the Generall's owne troupe, serv'd fower yeares, before hee serv'd the Generali hee serv'd the Lieutenant Generall in that troupe which is now the Generall's.

Ask't what hee mean[t] thaire?

Being the generall act of all hee can give noe answer being but one particular man.

Mr. Tho. Shepherd. Shropshire.

Served first under the Earl of Essex in the Earl of Bedford's Troupe of Cuirasseers.

Taken prisoner at Oxington coming from the relief of Gloucester. Prisoner 5 weekes, tooke noe oath, not exchanged, made his escape. Hee did heare it read, did subscribe it. Cannot remember whether hee read itt himselfe, about a weeke since hee heard it first read. Where? One of the Eight Regiments.

At what place. Hee does not remember. Demanded clause.

If it pleased this Honourable House to putt the Queries in writing the Eight Regiments whereof I am a Member whose joynt act it was will give an answer to them.

Endorsed :—

Answers.
Sexby.
Allen.
Shepherd.

30 April, 1647.

[The question whether William Allen, the agitator, mentioned here was the William Allen who subsequently became Adjutant-General of the Horse in the Irish Army is a question of some interest Ludlow, describing the presentation of the letter by the three troopers, affirms that Allen "was afterwards known by the addition of Adjutant-general" (ed. 1751, p. 73). Carlyle asserts that this is a blunder of Ludlow's. (1.) On the other hand this question of identity is a point on which Ludlow was likely to be right. He knew Allen personally, and they served together in Ireland (*Memoirs*, p. 145). Allen belonged to the political party which regarded Ludlow as their leader, and is described as specially commending him (Thurloe, iii. 140, 143). (2.) Allen, the agitator, states that he had served in the Parliamentary army since 1642. Allen, the adjutant-general, writing in 1655 talks of his thirteen years faithful service (Thurloe, iii., 140). (3.) Adjutant-General Allen in his tract published in 1659 (entitled, "*A faithful Memorial of that remarkable meeting of many officers of the Army in England at Windsor Castle in the year* 1648," *Somers Tracts*, vi., 499), speaks as if he had been present at the army councils in 1647, and directly affirms his presence at those in the spring of 1648. At the meetings described in this volume there seem to have been only two Allens present, viz. Captain Allen and Mr. Allen. Captain Allen was Francis Allen of Ingoldsby's regiment, Mr. Allen, William Allen, the trooper of Cromwell's own regiment. I believe the agitators were present at the meetings at Windsor in the spring of 1648, and if so William Allen was pretty certainly there. It may be objected that a man who was an ordinary trooper in 1647, would hardly have become adjutant-general in 1651. But the office of adjutant-general did not imply high regimental rank, and when Allen was first mentioned as adjutant-general of horse he was merely a captain. In 1647 and 1648 several privates, who had been agitators, obtained commissions, including Allen's companion Sexby. Allen's rise was not as rapid as that of Sexby, who was a lieutenant-colonel in 1651, but there is no improbability in the supposition that the former obtained a commission in 1648.

Of Adjutant-General Allen's later career more can be stated with certainty. He is spoken of as "Captain Allen, adjutant-general of the Horse" in Ireland in September, 1651, and was later one of the commissioners for the settlement of Ulster (*Mercurius Politicus*, p. 2523). He disapproved of Cromwell's assumption of the Protectorate, but wrote of the Protector himself: "As to the person in chief place, I confess I love and honour him, for the honour God hath put upon him, and I trust will yet continue, I mean that of uprightheartedness to the Lord, though this last change with his atendencyes hath more stumbled me than ever any did" (Thurloe, ii., 214, 215). Allen was arrested in Devonshire in January, 1655, for "multiplying dissatisfaction in the minds of men to the present government" (Carlyle's *Cromwell*, Letter cxcvii.). Thurloe's papers contain an interesting account of the charges against Allen, and a letter from Allen to the Protector vindicating himself. "I can say truly," he wrote, "if I have erred it hath been, I fear, in esteeming too highly of you." He denied any intention of acting against the Protector: "I durst not lift a hand against you nor join with or advise the doing of it" (Thurloe, iii., 141). Allen was allowed to return to his post in Ireland, where he gave Henry Cromwell some trouble, and at length, in November, 1647, resigned his commission (Thurloe, iv., 328, 433; v. 670). In 1659 the Rump nominated him to be colonel of a regiment of horse in Ireland. In addition to the "Faithful Memorial" published in 1659 he printed "A word to the Army touching their sin and duty, 1660." On April 13, 1660, Allen was arrested "for endeavouring to debauch some of the soldiers from their duty" (*Cal. State Papers, Dom.*. 1657-1660, p. 573). On June 19, 1661, he was ordered to be released from the Gatehouse on giving security for £1,000 that he would leave the kingdom within fifteen days (*Cal. State Papers, Dom.*, 1661-1662, p. 12). I can find no later mention of him.]

APPENDIX C.

A LETTER OF COL. RICHARD GREVIS TO SIR PHILIP STAPLETON.

[Though the name of Richard Graves, Greaves, or Grevis does not appear in the original list of the army under Essex, he served as colonel in his army from the winter after Edgehill (*Cal. State Papers, Dom.*, 1644-5, p. 464). He distinguished himself at the second battle of Newbury. In May, 1645, he commanded the cavalry in the detachment of the New Model sent by Fairfax to relieve Taunton (*ibid.* pp. 76, 488). On April 8, 1647, the House of Commons voted that his regiment should be one of those to be kept up (Rushworth, vi. 452). He belonged later to the Presbyterian section of the royalist party, and when Charles II. was in Scotland was one of the gentlemen of his bedchamber (*Clarendon State Papers*, ii., 491; Carte, *Original Letters*, ii., 29). Taken prisoner at the battle of Worcester he was for sometime a prisoner in the Tower, but released on bail during 1652 (*Cal. State Papers, Dom.*, 1651, pp. 422, 430; 1651-2, pp 32, 114, 229).

The following letter written from Holmby a day or two before Joyce seized the King shows the state of feeling amongst the soldiers under the command of Greaves, who formed the King's guard.]

COLONEL GREAVES TO SIR PHILIP STAPLETON.

Most honoured Sir,

I thought it necessarye to give you notice of the removal of mine and Sir Robert Pye's regiments by a late order, of which I have sent you a coppy in the margent, by which it appeareth it is thought they have been too long under my command hereabout and that by quartering them the nearer to the armye they may the better be wrought up to the now humour of it. I cannot indeed commend the greater number of them as they are at this present, but that they have been too readily infected with the taynt of disorder, meerly by that powerful persuasion that they shall obtayne the more money for it. Some there are I am certayne and not a few who will not forsake or disobey the Parliament upon any conditions. I pray God direct and counsell the Parliament to such a speedy course that they and all honest men may be drawne from such as have other villainous and destructive designes: in this I should account it my meat and drink to be instrumentall, and to be further actually serviceable in these commands; and particularly as I am abundantly obliged to appeare more and more

Your constantly faithfull & obedient servant,

RICH. GREVIS.

I beseech you present me in my real honouring of Mr. Hollis and Sir Will Lewes.'

The order enclosed runs as follows :—

Sir,

By order for the Generall upon the advice of a Generall Councell of Warre you are forthwith to march with the regiment (saving that part of it which is assigned for the guardes about Holdenbye) to quarter in Papworth hundred in the Countye of Cambrige and immediately upon receipt hereof you are to send two men of the regiment to the head quarters at Bury in Suffolke for further orders by whome you are to give mee notice what time the regiment is like to come to the said quarters.

Your humble servant,

H. IRETON.

For Major Scroope or the chief officer present with Coll. Grevis his regiment of horse.

[This order, or rather this copy of the order, is undated. A similar order of Quartermaster-General Gravener for moving a foot regiment is dated 30 May, and this must be of the same date (*Tanner MSS.*, lviii., p. 121). This fixes the date of the first letter, which is also undated.]

APPENDIX D.

A LIST OF THE AGITATORS ELECTED IN 1647.

[The following list is based on a loose paper amongst the Clarke MSS. The paper has unfortunately suffered greatly from damp, and is in some parts very difficult to read. I have supplemented it from the list of names appended to the printed declarations of

[1] *Tanner MSS.*, Bodleian Library, vol. lviii., f. 141

the agitators, and added where possible the Christian names of the persons mentioned. These additions are marked by brackets. This paper is headed: "A list of the Names of the [two] Commission Officers and two Soldiers of every regiment in the army intrusted for the several regiments according to the Engagement of the Army." It is dated October, 1647.

Of the Foot Regiments.

	The two Officers.	The two Soldiers.
Of the Generall's regiment.	Major [Francis] White. Capt. Lewis Audley.	[Edmund] Vaughan. ——— Wilkinson.
Major Generall's regiment.[1]		
Col. Rainborowe.	Capt. Flower. Lieut Shipley.[2]	Joseph Adams. Robert Gladman.
Sir H. Waller.	Capt. [John] Clarke.[3] Capt. [Richard] Hodden.	Robert Mason. Henry Anderton.
Col. Lambert.	Capt. [Matthew] Cadwell. Capt. Blewin.[4]	Rich. Colborne. John Miller.
Col. Hammond.	Capt. [Edmund] Rolfe. Capt. Wheeler.	Nath. Foxgill. Morgan Clarke.
Col. Lilburne.	Capt. [Abraham] Holmes.[5] Capt. [Richard] Deane.[6]	Jacob Somers. Robert Linsey.

[1] Skippon's regiment was quartered at Newcastle, and seems to have been represented solely by Major John Cobbet, v., p. 407.

[2] Should be Stephen Shipman.

[3] See pp. 32, 173, 180, 187, 280, 330, 339. In 1859 John Clarke was Colonel of a foot regiment in Ireland.

[4] "Blewin" should perhaps be "Blethen," as the name stands in another list.

[5] Captain, afterwards Major Holmes, was implicated in the Rye House plot, and executed in 1685 for his share in Monmouth's rising.

[6] Cousin of Richard Deane, the admiral.

	The two Officers.	The two Soldiers.
Col. Hughson.	Capt. [John] Carter.	Edmund Garne.[1]
	Capt. [Alexander] Brayfield.[2]	Richard Nixon.
Col. Barkstead.[3]	Capt. Young.	
Col. Pride.	Capt. [Waldine] Lagoe.[4]	Nic. Andrewes ?
	Capt. [John] Mason.[5]	Ralph Prentice.[6]
Col. Overton.	Capt. [William] Knolles.	Rich. Flower.
	Capt. [Edward] Orpin.	Stephen Combe.
The Traine.	Commissary Cowling.[7]	
	[Commissary Thomas] Robinson.	Tho. Mills.
Col. Ingoldesby.	Capt. [Francis] Allen.	Rich. Johnson.
	L[t] [Consolation] Fox.	John Radman.[8]

[1] Edmund Garner appears as a Lieutenant in Hewson's regiment in November, 1647.

[2] Lieutenant-Colonel Brayfield was cashiered by Henry Cromwell in Ireland in 1657 for sedition. Thurloe, vi., 505, 527, 549, 552, 563, 599 ; Ludlow, *Memoirs*, ed. 1751, p. 198.

[3] This was originally Colonel Fortescue's regiment ; the greater part of it had volunteered for Ireland, hence, probably, its imperfect representation.

[4] Lieutenant-Colonel Lagoe was appointed Adjutant-General of the Irish Army in 1659.

[5] Lieutenant-Colonel John Mason presented the protest of the officers against kingship in 1657, (Ludlow, p. 224). Governor of Jersey in 1659. *Cal. State Papers, Dom.* 1658-9, p. 375.

[6] Prentice became an ensign in this regiment in November, 1647.

[7] Nicholas Cowley, or Cowling, see the book of *Army Declarations*, p. 71. Cowling is officially described as "Commissary-General of Victuals," and Robinson as "Commissary of the Draught-Horse. Peacock, *Army Lists*, pp. 101, 106.

[8] The principal instigator of the mutiny of Ingoldsby's regiment at Oxford in September, 1649. See *The Moderate*, September 11-18, 1649 ; and a paper in *Proceedings of the Oxford Architectural and Historical Society*, 1884.

Regiments of Horse.

	The two Officers.	The two Soldiers.
The Generall's Regiment.	Lt. Empson.[1] Cornet [Peter] Wallis.[2]	Edw. Sexby. John Taylor.
Lt. General.	Capt. [Joseph] Wallington. Lt. [Edward] Scotton.	Will. Alleyne. Sam. Whiting. Rich. Kingdon.
Comm. General.	Capt. [Henry] Pretty.[3] Capt. [Robert] Kirkby.	John Wood. Tho. Shepheard.
Col. Fleetwood.	Capt. Lloyd. Capt.	Will. Somes. Edw. Twigge.
Col. Harrison.	Major [William] Rainborowe. Capt. Pecke.	Hen. Gittings.[4] Rich. Graunte.
Col. Whalley.	Capt. [Henry] Cannon. Lieut. [Edmund] Chillenden.	Timothy Thornborough. Will. Younge.
Col. Horton.[5]	Lieut. [Thomas] Ellis. Cornet [John] Phelpes.	Tobiah Box. John Willoughby.

---

[1] In letter clxii. in Carlyle's *Cromwell*, Oliver rebukes Colonel Hacker for styling Empson a better preacher than fighter. "He is a good man and a good officer," says Cromwell, "I would we had no worse." Earlier in the campaign in Scotland Empson had distinguished himself by rescuing Lambert when the latter was taken prisoner. *Ibid.*, letter cxxxv.

[2] Recommended as Colonel of the regiment late Henry Cromwell's in 1659. *Cal. State Papers, Dom.*, 1659-60, p. 13.

[3] Recommended as Colonel of a regiment of horse in Ireland. *Cal. State Papers, Dom.*, 1659-60, p. 13.

[4] Sometimes spelt Gethings. He was sentenced to death in February, 1648, for causing a mutiny in this regiment, but the sentence appears to have been remitted.

[5] Horton died in Ireland, in October, 1649. "He was a person of great integrity and courage," writes Cromwell, Letter cxii. On his services in 1648, see Phillips *Civil War in Wales*.

	The two Officers.	The two Soldiers.
Col. Scroope.[1]	Capt. Wolfe.	Rich [Salter].
	Capt. Watson.	George [Stenson].
Col. Thomlinson.[2]	Capt. Johnson.	Barth. Willocke.
	Capt. [Thomas] Rawlins.[3]	Rich. Clarke.
Col. Rich.	Capt. [John] Merriman.[4]	Nich. Lockier.
	Capt. [William] Weare.	Tho. Buttery.
Col. Okey.	Major [Daniel] Abbott.	Will. Hall.
	Capt. [Tobias] Bridge.[5]	Will. Underwood.
The Life Guard	Capt. Michell.	
Col. Twistleton.[6]	Lt. Izod.[7]	John Wilson.
	Lt. Sheirman.	John Wells
Col. Thornhaugh.[8]	Capt. [George] Palmer.	John Harte.
	Capt. [Richard] Creed.	Richard Farre.

---

[1] A life of Scroope is in Noble's *Lives of the Regicides*, 1798. He was executed October 17, 1660.

[2] Matthew Thomlinson, knighted by Henry Cromwell, sat as one of the king's judges, but did not not sign the warrant, escaped at the restoration. See his petition 7th Report of *Hist. MSS. Comm.*, p. 123

[3] Probably the Captain Rawlins recommended in Cromwell's letter of 4 June, 1645. See *Cal. State Papers, Dom.*, 1659–60, 12, 183, 189, 189, 198; also 1644-5, p. 53.

[4] On Merriman, see Rushworth, vii., 1051, 1361.

[5] Bridge was knighted at the Restoration, having adhered to Monck and taken part in the seizure of Dublin Castle (Ludlow, *Memoirs*, ed. 1751, pp. 298, 307). He had succeeded to the command of Okey's regiment in January, 1655, when Okey was cashiered.

[6] Late Colonel Rossiter's regiment, *Lords' Journals*, ix., 217.

[7] See *Cal. State Papers, Dom.*, 1659-60, pp. 299, 591.

[8] On Colonel Francis Thornhaugh, see the *Life of Colonel Hutchinson*. Thornhaugh was killed at Preston in 1648. This was a Nottingham regiment, and not one of the new-model regiments. Rushworth, vi., 623.

APPENDIX E.

Proceedings in the Council of the Army between Nov. 3 and Nov. 8, 1647.

Of the meetings which took place between Wednesday, Nov. 3, and Monday, Nov. 8, the Clarke papers unfortunately contain no record. Of Nov. 4 Rushworth says, "This day the council of the Army again sat at Putney and they considered of some alterations to be desired in the propositions of peace to be sent to his Majesty." The special work of the day seems to have been considering the propositions dealing with delinquents in relation to the late war (Rushworth, vii., 863). Of the debates of Friday, Nov. 5, and Saturday, Nov. 6, he simply observes, "The general council of the Army sat this day at Putney, and the general with them, and had much debate of the Heads of the Proposalls before mentioned. They sat also again about the same on Saturday, but have not yet finished them" (*ibid.*, 864). Fairfax, who had been ill and was mentioned as absent on October 28, seems to have first returned to his place on Nov. 5. It is probable that Cromwell was absent attending to his duties in parliament. On Nov. 5 the Commons discussed the propositions to be sent to the King, which were that day reported to it from a committee of the two Houses appointed to give them their final form. A circular letter from the Agitators to their regiments says, "Our friends obtained a generall Randezvous, and a Letter from the Councell to clear the Armie from any desire or intent of constraining the Parliament to send Propositions to the King."

"*A Copy of a Letter sent by the Agents of severall Regiments of his Excellencie's Army (that are resolved to the last drop of their blood to stand for the Liberties and Freedoms of the people of England) to all the Souldiers in the said Armie.*"

The letter is referred to in the *Commons' Journals*, Nov. 6, 1647, but not given there or in the *Lords' Journals*. It ran thus :

Mr. Speaker,

Whereas it is generally reported that the House was enduced to make another addresse to the King, by Propositions, by reason it was represented to the House as the desire of the Army, From a tendernesse to the priviledges of parliamentary actings, this night the Generall Councell of the Army declared, that any such representation of their desires was together groundlesse; and that they earnestly desire no such consideration may be admitted into the House's resolutions in that particular.

Signed by the appointment of the Generall
Councell of the Army,
WILLIAM CLERKE,
Secretary.

Putney, Novem. 5, 1647.

A newsletter in the Clarendon Papers, dated Nov. $\frac{8}{18}$, says: "Colonel Rainborough, at a council of war held at the headquarters, intimated that the army was not disposed to make any more addresses to the King, which produced the letter to the Speaker, now in print, to that effect, signed by William Clarke, dated the 5th of November from Putney. Ireton opposed the same all he could, and in testimony of his dissent left the council, protesting he could come no more there to be partaker of the high neglect and violation of reason and justice which he observed to reign amongst them. He hath been moved since to returr, but continues resolute." (*Clarendon State Papers II.*, Appendix xli.)

The letter of the Agitators does not expressly mention Ireton's presence at the debate of Nov. 5 and seems to place his withdrawal on Nov. 6. Speaking of the meeting on Monday, Nov. 8, they say "the day before Commissary Generall Ireton withdrew and protested he would act no more with them unless they recalled the letter."

Of the debates of Saturday, November 6, and Monday, November 8, the Agitators say:—

At the next meeting *a Declaration* was offered to the Councell, wherein the Kings corrupt interest was so intermixed, that in a short time, if he should so come in, he would be in a capacitie to destroy you, and the people. *Upon this wee desired onely a free debate of this Question; Whether it were safe, either for the Armie, or the people, to suffer any power to be given to the King:* and Lievtenant Generall *Crumwell*, and the rest, professed as before God, they would freely debate it; and munday last, a Generall Councell was appointed for that purpose; but when they met they wholly refused, and in stead of that spake very reproachfully of us and our Actions, and declared against that which was past the Councell before *Concerning the voyces of those in Election, which have not fortie shillings by the yeare free-hold, and against the Letter sent by the Councell to the Parliament,* and to prevent any further *debate, they would have dissolved the Councell for above a fortnight;* and thus our hopes of agreeing together to settle your and the peoples freedoms were then frustated, and though the chiefe of them had desired some of our friends, not above three dayes before, to goe on in their actings, *for they might come in when they should doe us more service then at that time,* yet then they made great outcries against us, and complaints of distempers in the Armie, which were nothing *but endeavours after their rights and freedoms.*

END OF VOL. I.

PREFACE.

THE papers contained in this, like those in the previous volume, are derived from the Clarke manuscripts in Worcester College Library, and are mainly from the volumes numbered xvi., lii., lxv., and cxiv. But single documents have also been taken from other volumes in the same collection. Moreover, while these selections were being printed, my attention was called to the fact that a certain number of Clarke's MSS. were in the possession of Mr. F. Leybourne Popham, of Littlecote, Wilts, and were being examined for the Royal Commission on Historical MSS. By the kind permission of the Commissioners, and of the owner, I was allowed to copy several papers for publication in this volume. The thanks of the Camden Society are also due to Mr. J. J. Cartwright, for his good offices in the matter, and for the liberality with which he facilitated the consultation of the MSS., and the copying of the selected papers.

Mr. Popham's papers are specially valuable as supplementing the meagre account of William Clarke's own life given in the preface to volume one. A letter from Robert Spavin, one of Rushworth's assistants during part of 1648 and 1649, and secretary to Cromwell, fixes the date of Clarke's marriage. Spavin, who had accompanied Cromwell's forces into Scotland, wrote to Clarke on November 2, 1648, to congratulate him and wish him joy. "Deare friend and Mr. Bridegroome, I am glad you have a little breathing time after your solemnityes to visit your poor friends with a line. . . . But sure if you had noe better choyse than we had in Scotland you would not be soe lusty." Cromwell had halted in his march southwards to summon Pontefract Castle, and Spavin proceeds to give some account of the siege. "Pomfret put a stop to us, being by the howse's order and the Committee of Yorkshyre's desire to take the care of the seidge, which will take us three weekes time to settle, and then I hope we shall draw towards you and leave Col. Bright to command." In conclusion he turns to consider the position of politics, is glad to hear that the southern army is beginning to act, and hopes soon to see an end of "that old jog-trot form of government of King, Lords and Commons." "Noe matter," he continues, "how or by whome, sure I am it cannot be worse if honest men have the managing of it, and noe matter whether they be greate or noe. . . . The Lord is about a greate worke, such as will stumble many meane principled men, and such as I thinke but few greate ones shall be honoured withall." Spavin himself was not honoured with any share in the management of the said great work, for having been caught forging Cromwell's hand and seal to passes and protections, he lost his post, and was sentenced by a council of war "to ride on horseback from Whitehall to Westminster, and thence through the City, with an inscription on his back and on his breast, written in capital letters, to signify his crime."[a]

This occurred in June, 1649, when Cromwell was about to leave for Ireland. Clarke did not accompany him thither, but remained at the headquarters in England. In two letters addressed to him about this time he is described as "one of the secretaries to his excellency the Lord Fairfax," and as "secretary unto the Council of War." In the following year he took part in the invasion of Scotland, and the officers of the invading army recommended him for the post of secretary to the Committee of the Army, no small

[a] *Cromwelliana*, p, 61

proof of his popularity and his usefulness.[a] (October 19, 1650.) The application was unsuccessful, and on August 19, 1651, Clarke requested Lenthall to appoint him keeper of the Scottish records, which had been captured in Stirling Castle, but the Parliament preferred to have them all removed to England.[b] Clarke's official gains were sufficient to warrant his buying from the State part of St. John's Wood, when the crown-lands were sold. However, as the purchase involved him in a lawsuit which lasted for some years, it can hardly have been profitable.[c] In his petition to the Commissioners of the Great Seal on this subject, he complains that "one Mr. John Collins" had unjustly laid claim to the land in question. This John Collins was Clarke's uncle, and was the author of a curious narrative of the Restoration which is amongst Mr. Popham's papers. Those MSS. contain also the following letter from Margaret, daughter of John Collins, to her cousin Clarke, written early in 1661, congratulating him on his recent knighthood.

"Honored Cozen,

"Give me leave (though late) to congratulate your attainment of that well deserved honour confferd upon you, as likewise that which you more esteem, the hopes God hath been pleased to give yourselfe and Lady, of being once againe blessed with a child, which I hope you will beleeve wee doe heartily rejoyce with you in. Although our present disturbance hinders us from tendring our respects in that gratefull maner which your own and deare Ladyes merits justly challenge from us, who very unhappily came to be concerned in this last troublesom bussines, in which although we are the greatest sufferers, yet I hope God and the world will acquit us from being any way way the procurers of this or other troubles of this kind, which may happen to us. And since it hath pleased God to strip us of that deare and carefull freind my mother, and leave us in a condition not soe well provided for as shee endeavoured and desired wee should, wee must now make it our request to you, Sir, that you would please to importune my father to setle somthing upon my sister and selfe, that soe wee might not bee left destitute how ever things goe with us, and

[a] See p. 224; cf. *C. S. P. Dom.* 1650, p. 351.

[b] Cary, *Memorials of the Civil War*, ii., 332.

[c] *See* p. 227. Other documents concerning the disputed property are amongst the MSS. at Worcester College.

that the trust of it may bee reposed in your hands, in whom wee doe put the greatest confidence of any freind livinge, and wee doe hope that if wee could gett this done wee should soe farr followe my mother's pattern of good huswifery and thrift as that wee should not bee burthensom or chargeable to any of our freinds. And thus Sir, havinge acquainted you with our desires, and presenting our most humble service to your selfe and Lady, beseeching God to send her a happy delivery, and make her once againe the gladd mother of a much promisinge sonn, I rest

"Sir,

"Your most affectionate and obliged kinswoman
and humble servant,
"MARGARET COLLINS.

"Stanmore,
March 22,
1660.

"Addressed to Sir William Clarke 'att his house in the Pell Mell neer St. Jameses.'

"Endorsed 'Couz. Margr. Colins, Lre of Congratulation.'"

What the origin of the relationship between the Clarke and Collins families was I have not succeeded in discovering, and Clarke's parentage and early history still remain obscure. Two letters from his brother-in-law Kympton Hilliard, also derived from Mr. Popham's MSS., are printed in this volume (pp. 225, 228). Other relatives mentioned incidentally in the same MSS. are two cousins of Clarke's, James Staresmore and Captain Thomas Sherman, and "brother William Carey," a goldsmith in London.

The papers contained in this volume are more miscellaneous in their nature than those printed in the first volume, and cover a larger period of time. From 1651 to 1660, Clarke was employed in Scotland, and nearly all his collections during that period relate solely to the government of Scotland or to questions of army administration. As a selection from the papers relating to Scotland is shortly to be published by the Scottish Historical Society, I have thought it best to exclude any dealing with that subject. But I hope to put together at some future date a small volume of papers concerning the Restoration and the revolutions of 1659.

At the beginning of 1648 there were signs all over England of the approach of a second civil war. Hardly had the Army and Parliament come to an agreement to settle the kingdom without the King, when the Royalists began to take up arms to restore him. The movement began in Wales, in February, 1648. Col. Poyer and afterwards Col. Laugharne declared for the King, but their forces were routed at St. Fagans on May 8 by Col. Horton. A newsletter describes the effects of this victory on the temper of the London Presbyterians (p. 6). In the north of England the preparations of the Scots to send an army across the border roused the cavaliers of Yorkshire and Cumberland to action. Berwick and Carlisle were seized by them at the end of April, and on June 1 they surprised Pontefract (pp. 1, 8, 20, 25 ; Appendix, p. 251). In London a serious riot took place on April 9; seditious placards against the Parliament were posted about the City, and plans were laid for a general rising (pp. 2, 5, 11). On May 16 the tumultuous presentation of a petition from the county of Surrey led to a fight at the very doors of the House of Commons, and a week later the Kentish-men seized the county magazines and declared for King Charles (pp. 13-17, 22). Fairfax defeated them at Maidstone on June 1, but the Earl of Norwich with a portion of the Royalist army crossed the Thames, and joined the Royalists of Essex. Three letters from Col. Whalley to Lord Fairfax illustrate the history of their march from Stratford to Colchester, and their pursuit by Fairfax's cavalry[a] (pp. 24, 26, 27). In Colchester, Norwich and his followers held out for eleven weeks, hoping vainly to be relieved by the advance of Hamilton and the Scots, and believing that their stubborn defence would give opportunity for the rest of the kingdom to act. An intercepted letter from Lord Capel to Sir Marmaduke Langdale explains the position of the besieged, and shows their willingness to sacrifice themselves for

[a] One of these letters I afterwards found to be printed in the *Fairfax Correspondence,* iv., 35.

the King's cause (p. 28). But Cromwell routed Hamilton at Preston on August 17, and ten days later hunger forced the defenders of Colchester to surrender. The town was given up on August 28, and on the afternoon of the same day Sir Charles Lucas and Sir George Lisle were executed by order of Fairfax's Council of War. Clarke's account of the death of Lucas and Lisle, printed on pp. 31-39, adds many details of great interest to the accounts published at the time. Then, as now, many people regarded their execution as a cold-blooded and treacherous murder; but though the equity of their sentence may be disputed, there can be no doubt that the execution was not a breach of the terms of the capitulation. The reasons which justified that sentence in the eyes of the men responsible for it are clearly stated by Ireton in his discussion of the question with Sir Charles Lucas (pp 35, 37).[a]

The Earl of Norwich and the rest of the Royalist prisoners who surrendered at Colchester were assured by Fairfax of quarter for their lives, and at their trials in February, 1649, the plea was put forward that this promise exempted them from any future proceedings in a civil court. This plea seems to have been first suggested by the Earl of Norwich, in a letter which he addressed to Speaker Lenthall on October 3, 1648, on learning that the House of Commons had passed an ordinance attainting him of high treason.[b] On October 6 the House read Goring's letter, and ordered that a letter should be written to Lord Fairfax "to desire his explanation of that clause of his letter of 29 September, 1648, that concerns the quarter given to the Lord Goring and the Lord Capel, and leaving them to the further justice and mercy of the Parliament." The answer of Lord Fairfax is well summarised in Rush-

[a] I understand that Mr. J. H. Round has recently treated the subject in a paper read to the Royal Historical Society, but as it is not yet published I can scarcely discuss his arguments.

[b] *Commons' Journals*, vi., 45; Cary, *Memorials of the Civil War*, ii., 26.

worth,[c] but as the letter itself has never been printed,[d] and because its precise phraseology is of some importance, it is now inserted here.

"Mr. Speaker,

"Though I cannot easily understand what itt is in that letter of mine you recite that should soe much neede a serious explanation (as to the point in question), yett supposing the scruple to bee, whether my assuring of quarter to the Lord Goring and the rest did intend or does imply to secure them from further question as to life before your owne or other civill judgement for the warre leavied by them, in obedience to your commands I returne this answer.

"That the quarter assured to his Lordshippe and others of that condition was nott by capitulation or agreement (as by the articles and explanation annex't may appeare), and therefore could ground [noe] more claime then common quarter to any enemy taken in a feild engagement or other action.

"Now for the sense and extent of common quarter given I have alwayes understood itt to bee an assuring of life against the immediate execution of the military sworde from any further execution therby without judiciall triall, but whether it imply to protect or exempt them from any judiciall triall or proceeding to life, either by the civill sword of that authority against which (being subjects) they rebell, or by the martiall power (as to persons and causes subject to its cognizance), having never soe understood itt nor knowne itt to bee soe I leave itt to your determination.

"And the same power of giving quarter every souldier also hath in his proper action, which is daily used by them (if they see cause) to all sorts of the enemy, and then (unlesse where particular command is beforehand to the contrary) alwayes allowed, whatever the parties prove, because nott understood to amount to further exemption then as aforesaid, and whether now itt should bee taken otherwise, and that the souldier granting quarter shall bee a full pardon (as to life), lett not my sense, but the generall sense and practise in all warres and of both parties in this warre give the determination; butt if itt were soe then nott only noe Rebell (by that civill Judicature to which hee stood a subject), butt alsoe noe revolter or deserter of his colours and trust (running to the enemy), nor any spie or the like (by the martiall power), after once taken uppon quarter should bee brought to a judiciall triall or execution for their revolt or treachery; and therefore Sir I doe not urge these thinges out of any perticular animosity to the Lord Goring, for were hee even an innocent person, or one for whome I would begge your pardon, yett I should nott by my opinion or silence bee guilty of staying your judiciall proceeding uppon such a ground the admission whereof would at once condemne soe much the just and

---

[c] Rushworth, vii., 1285, 1303.

[d] The letter is amongst Clarke's MSS. (vol. cxiv., f. 89); but was not noticed till it was too late to insert it in its proper place in the body of the volume.

necessary practices of the Parliament and other states, and alsoe preclude or prejudge your future proceedinges in publique justice against any person for rebellion, revolts, or treachery in warre, who after utmost extreamity against you could finde butt any souldier of yours to give him quarter.

T. F.

"St. Albans 13 October
1648."

The questions discussed in this letter were again argued in February, 1649, at the trials of Hamilton, Capel, Holland, and Norwich by the High Court of Justice. A volume amongst Clarke's MSS. (numbered Worcester MS. lxx.) gives a much completer account of these trials than any yet published, and the evidence then given by some of the witnesses against the Earl of Norwich deals with several of the points raised in the cases of Lucas and Lisle. But the account is too long to print *in extenso,* or even in an abridged form, in this volume, and it was thought better to leave it to be treated as a whole at some future time than to extract a few fragmentary passages from it. A debate in the Council of Officers on the case of Hamilton and others will be found on pp. 194-198.

Fairfax's capture of Colchester and Cromwell's defeat of the Scots set the army at liberty once more to intervene in politics. While the northern army under Cromwell was assisting to establish the supremacy of Argyle's party in Scotland (pp. 42-49), the southern army prepared to prevent the negotiations at Newport from ending in a treaty which would restore Charles to his throne. In October the soldiers began to present petitions demanding justice against all offenders without respect of persons, and on November 7 a Council of Officers met at St. Albans to formulate the desires of the army. On November 16 the "Remonstrance of the Army" was agreed to by the Council, and four days later it was presented to the House of Commons (p. 54). As to the history of the Remonstrance these papers supply no new information, but they do throw a great deal of light on the development of the design for the seizure of the king, and on the history of his removal from Carisbrooke to Hurst Castle (pp. 54, 55, 57, 59, 63, 65, 67). Charles was transferred to Hurst Castle on December 1, and Fairfax's troops occupied London on the following day. A newsletter, possibly written by Clarke himself, supplies an account of the occupation of London and of the forcible purgation of the House of Commons, which is supplemented by a letter from one of the excluded members to his constituents (pp. 67, 136). The Council of the Army next passed a vote to send for the King to Windsor Castle, "in order to the bringing of him speedily to justice" (December 15). The precautions to be adopted to prevent his escape, and the manner in which he was to be treated during his detention at Windsor, were minutely prescribed to the officers employed, and the instructions of the Council on these heads were further explained by private letters from Cromwell and Ireton (pp. 132, 133, 140-147). Concerning the King's trial Clarke's papers are silent. There are, however, certain orders issued to the troops quartered in London, forbidding either officers or soldiers to come to Westminster Hall, except such as were on duty there, and commanding the cavalry regiments to be ready for action both night and day until the trial ended (p. 186).

Whilst the King's trial was going on, and for some weeks before it began, the Council of Officers had been busily discussing the constitution of the future republic. The plan of defining by an "Agreement of the People" the rights which the people reserved to themselves, and the powers which they delegated to their representatives, originally put forward by the Levellers in the autumn of 1647, was revived again a year later. After a certain number of conferences between representatives of the Levellers, the army, and the leaders of the Independent party in and out of Parliament, it was agreed that a joint committee should be appointed to prepare a revised "Agreement of the People" (Nov. 29). The Levellers believed that the decision of this committee was to be final, and that the document drawn up by it was to be at once offered to the nation for acceptance.[a] When they discovered that it was to be submitted to the Council of Officers for discussion, and found that the Council insisted on altering and amending it in several important points, they regarded the army leaders as false to their pledges. They were still more disgusted when the Council, instead of circulating the "Agreement" for signature amongst the people, and compelling the Parliament to adopt it, simply presented it to the House with a request that they would take it into consideration and adopt so much of it as they thought proper. Lilburne had taken the alarm even before the Agreement was revised by the Council of Officers, and he published on December 15 the draft of that document upon which the joint committee had agreed, under the title of "Foundations of Freedom." He was anxious to enlist popular support in its favour, and prefixed to it the following appeal to his readers:—

"Dear Countryman,

"This Agreement having had its conception for a common good, as being that which contains those Foundations of Freedom, and Rules of Government, adjudged necessary to be established in this Nation for the future, by which all sorts of men are to be bound, I adjudged it a just and reasonable thing to publish it to the view of the Nation, to the end that all men might have an opportunity to consider the Equity thereof, and offer their Reasons against anything therein contained, before it is concluded; that being agreeable to that Principle which we profess, viz., to do unto you, as we would all men should do unto us, not doubting but that the Justice of it will be maintained and cleared, maugre the opposition of the stoutest Calumniator, especially in those clear points in the Reserve so much already controverted, viz., touching the Magistrates power to compel or restrain in matters of Religion, and the exercise of an arbitrary power in the Representative to punish men for state offences, against which no Law hath provided; which two things especially are so clear to my understanding that I dare with confidence aver,

---

[a] Gardiner, *Great Civil War*, iv., 239, 262. A history of the origin of this second Agreement, and of the negotiations and debates concerning it, is given by Lilburne in his "Legal Fundamental Liberties of the People of England," 4to, 1649. His narrative is so necessary to the understanding of the debates that I have inserted it in the Appendix (pp. 254-266).

That no man can demand the exercise of such a power, but he that intends to be a Tyrant, nor no man part with them, but he that resolves to be a slave. And so at present I rest,

"Thy true-hearted
"Countryman.

"Friday, Decemb.
15, 1648."

The debates of the Council, as recorded by Clarke, deal mainly with the first of the two points mentioned by Lilburne. On December 14, 1648, the portion of the Agreement which prohibited the magistrate from imposing any restrictions on the free exercise of religion, was discussed by the officers, assisted by representatives of the Levellers and by a number of Independent divines (pp. 73-132). These assistants, however, were allowed no vote in the final decision on the controverted clause (p. 139). The clause was referred to a committee, and it was decided by the Council on December 21, that in the general article reserving certain questions from the control of Parliament the original reservation concerning religion should not be included (p. 140). Instead of this it was resolved to insert a special article, the ninth in the Agreement when completed, to define the powers granted to the Government in religious matters, and the limits of religious freedom. Early in January this article seems to have been finally agreed upon and passed (pp. 171-174).

Lilburne and his partizans, angered by the refusal of the Council to adopt their scheme in its entirety, presented to Fairfax on December 28, 1648, a protest against the proceedings of the officers, printed under the title of "A Plea for Common Right and Freedom." They began by setting forth the satisfaction with which they had seen the adoption of their proposal for a new "Agreement of the People," and the hopes with which they had hailed the first steps taken to carry out the plan. Then they complained bitterly of the obstructions which had arisen "since the same hath been tendered to the consideration of your Council."

"The long time spent already therein, and the tedious disputes and contests held thereupon, and that in things so essential to our freedom, as without which we account the Agreement of no value: for what freedom is there to consciencious people where the magistrate shall be intrusted with a restrictive power in matters of religion? Or to judge and punish in cases where no law hath been before provided? Which are the points which yet remain in suspence, and about which most of the time hath been spent." They lamented that too many in the Council had supported the granting those unreasonable powers to the magistrate, that those who spoke for them had been countenanced, and those who spoke against them discountenanced; and that finally even the Presbyterian clergy "interests directly opposed to freedom of conscience in points of God's worship," had been consulted, and attempts made to satisfy their objections. In conclusion they demanded as a necessary preliminary to the production of "a full and ample Agreement for the people," the re-organisation of the Council, and laid down the principles upon which that body ought to be constituted and its debates conducted.

"1. To agree what certain number of officers, and no less shall make a Councel, which we humbly conceive ought not to be lesse than the major part of the Commission Officers at the head Quarters and adjacent thereunto, not excluding of others.

"2. That all persons in Councel may sit in a distinct orderly way, so as they may be observed by the President when they are inclinable to speak.

"3. That you will agree how many times any person may speak to a Question.

"4. That you will free your Determinations from all pretences of a Negative Voice, and from all discountenance and check by any Superior Officer. And being so regulated, 1. That you will consider and resolve, what is the most proper way for the advance of Officers, so as to preserve them entire to the interest of the People, and from a servile condition or necessary dependence upon the favour or will of any; and seriously to consider whether your Articles of Martial Law (as now they are) are not of too Tyranous a nature, for an army of Freeborn Englishmen, and to reduce the same to reason and an equal constitution.

"2. To take special care of the principles of any Officer to be admitted, that they be not tainted with those of Arbytrary power or of persecution for matters of Religion.

"3. That there be no disbanding of any sort of men, but by consent of the General Councel; nor admission or listing of any for Horse or Foot, but according to provision made by the said Councel, it being reported that very many of late are listed of bad and doubtful condition; by all which means, if conscionably observed, (and we trust you will not be the lesse sencible because we advise) the growth of any corrupt interest will be effectually prevented. And if it shall seem good or any way usefull unto you, we shall chuse and appoint four of our Friends always to attend and assist though not to Vote with you."

Fairfax naturally refused to listen to these demands. He was neither inclined to limit the power of the general officers over their subordinates, nor to take any steps which would have revived, under any form, the representative council of agitators and officers which had given him so much trouble in 1647. It is evident from reading the debates that Lilburne's third proposal was aimed at Ireton, of whose predominance in the Council he elsewhere speaks with great wrath (Appendix, p. 265). In the debate of December 14 Ireton made five speeches of considerable length, answering the Independent divines and the representatives of the Levellers with equal effect. His remarks on the origin of commonwealths, on the end of the state (p. 79), and on the extent to which biblical precedents could be applied in drawing up modern constitutions are of particular interest (pp. 113, 122, 128).

A curious scene in these debates, which throws a strange light on the religious fanaticism of the times, was the appearance of a woman in the Council of Officers, who announced that she had a message to deliver to them which had been revealed to her in a vision. She came twice: on December 29 to manifest to them the disease of the kingdom and its cure (p. 150), and again on January 5 to protest against the execution of the King (p. 163). The Council heard her with great gravity, and solemnly enquired into the nature of the evidence which proved that her message was a divine revelation. An anonymous Royalist pamphlet published in 1651 gives a strangely distorted version of the incident, attributing the whole affair to the contrivance of Cromwell.[a]

"Now that Cromwell might firmly unite the Councell of War to him, which consisted of a few able Head-pieces, to whom he laid himself open so far, as to shew them their profit and preferment in the designe, which united them fast to him, the other part, who were soft heads, and had a good meaning to do no evill, but to promote the Kingdome of Christ, and throw down Antichrist, and then according to their duty (as they were taught) to take possession of, and (as Saints) raign over the Kingdom; Cromwell provided fit food to feed such fantacies, for he had provided a monstrous Witch full of all deceiptfull craft, who being put into brave cloaths pretended she was a Lady that was come from a far Countrey, being sent by God to the Army with a Revelation, which she must make known to the Army, for necessity was laid upon her; this Witch had a fair lodging prepared for her in White-Hall where she was very retired.

This Witch had her lesson taught her beforehand by Cromwell and Ireton, by whose order she was entertained at White-Hall.

She desired audience at the Councell of Warre, for to them she said she was sent.

Cromwel and Ireton to beget the more attention and belief in the Officers in the Councell of Warre, began to extoll the excellency of Revelation, and conceived that this Prophetess being a precious Saint, and having much of God in her, ought to be heard, and that with all attention; because in such glorious days as these God did manifest himself extraordinarily: and especially to his Saints, in chalking out their way before them when they came into straights and difficulties; such as they were in at that time.

By this time the Witch was come to the door, and forthwith she had admittance; where the Officers all beheld her, and her strange postures, expressing high devotion.

Cromwel and Ireton fixing their eyes upon her in most solemn manner, (to beget in the rest of the Officers (who were ready to laugh) an apprehension of some extraordinary serious thing) fell both of them to weeping; the Witch looking in their faces, and seeing them weep, fell to weeping likewise; and began to tell them what acquaintance she had with God by Revelation, and how such a day, such an hour, after such a manner she had a Revelation, which she was to reveal only to them; and that was, that the glorious time of setting up Christ's Kingdom was near

---

[a] *A Brief Narrative of the Mysteries of State carried on by the Spanish Faction in England*, 4to, 1651 (printed at the Hague), p. 69.

at hand, and that Antichrist must be speedily thrown down, and that they were the Instruments that were by God ordained to throw him down, and how they were about that great work, and that if they would prosper in it, they must first remove the King out of the way, which they must do by proceeding first to try him, and then to condemn him, and then to depose him, but not to put him to death: with a great deal more such stuff which that weeks Diurnall printed at large, so open was this business. This relation I had from one that was strongly of the Armies party, but related this shamefull story with much indignation."

The last important debate on the subject of the Agreement took place on January 13, 1649. On that day it was finally passed by the Council, and a declaration was agreed upon to be presented to the Parliament, explaining the motives which had led them to draw it up and offer it to the House. Some members of the Council, and many of the friends of the Army out of doors, objected to the proposal that the Army should abandon the dictatorship it had assumed, and leave Parliament the task of carrying out the schemes embodied in the Agreement. In that sense the prophetess from Abingdon had spoken, urging the Council to "go forward and stand up for the liberty of the people," and not to surrender to others the power which the Lord had given into their hands (pp. 151, 163).

In a similar spirit Mr. Erbury now declared, that the Council, instead of drawing up a new constitution, ought to take in hand the removal of the oppressive burdens and unrighteous things which troubled the people. That would be the way to settle the Nation, and a dozen or twenty-four selected men could effect it in a shorter time than a Parliament of four hundred (p. 178). Captain Joyce added that Fairfax and the Council ought not to try to shift off on others the work which the Lord had called them to (p. 182). Ireton answered, that to clear up the dispute as to the question of sovereignty, which had originally caused the war, and to take away from future governments the power to oppress the people, were the likeliest ways to settle the nation. Harrison's speech was probably more effective, for he sympathised strongly with the view of the Fifth

Monarchy men, but argued that the day of the Lord, when the powers of this world should be given into the hands of his saints, had not yet come. And both Ireton and Harrison urged that the Army was pledged by its declarations, not to use the opportunity to perpetuate power in its own hands, but to give it back to the civil authority (pp. 175-183). Their views prevailed; the Agreement was presented to Parliament on January 20, and the attempt of the army to settle the nation by its own action was adjourned until 1653.

The last meeting of the Council of Officers recorded in this volume took place on March 24, but though Clarke does not record its further debates it certainly continued to assemble. For the three following years, however, it busied itself almost entirely with military affairs, and its next important intervention in politics was the presentation of the petition of August 13, 1652 (*Old Parliamentary History*, xx., 97). From January, 1653, to the expulsion of the Long Parliament in the April following, it met with great frequency, and discussed public affairs with great vigour. Unfortunately Clarke was at that time in Scotland, and excepting a few short notices amongst the newsletters in his MSS., there is no record of these most important debates (See the *English Historical Review*, July 1893, p. 527).

The action of the Council of Officers in January, 1649, had postponed for four years the final breach between the military and the Parliamentary sections of the republican party.

So long as the harmony between the leaders of the Army and the Parliament continued, the newly-founded republic was safe. But in the spring of 1649 so many dangers threatened the existence of the Commonwealth, that there was good ground for doubting if it could weather the storm. In Ireland the English interest was, in Cromwell's phrase, almost "rooted out." In Scotland there prevailed "a very angry hateful spirit" against the "army of sectaries" and its leaders. In England the Presbyterians and Royalists were making ready to co-operate with Scots and Irish in restoring Charles II. (pp. 203, 205). A more immediate and pressing danger was the spread of insubordination in the army, caused by the doctrines propagated by Lilburne and his followers. On February 22, 1649, the Council of the Army found it necessary to lay down regulations limiting the right of the soldiers to petition, and forbidding them to hold clandestine meetings for political purposes (p. 190). Nevertheless, on March 1, a petition was presented to the Council of Officers, demanding the re-establishment of the representative "General Council of the Army" which had existed in 1647 (p. 193). The discipline of the army had evidently become considerably relaxed, especially in some of the newly-raised regiments. Fairfax consequently issued stringent orders for the punishment of any soldiers guilty of plundering during their march for Ireland (p. 193), and Marten's regiment, which had earned an evil notoriety by its bad conduct, vanishes from the army lists (pp. 56, 213). One of the worst offenders of all, William Thompson, was the leader of the mutiny suppressed at Burford, and was killed a few days later (p. 199).

Several papers illustrate the history of the wilder sects to which so great a political and religious revolution had given birth. The little band of Socialists who termed themselves "Diggers," and attempted to found a settlement on St. George's Hill in Surrey, found themselves so hardly treated by the local authorities and by their neighbours, that they applied to Fairfax for protection. Their colony seems to have been broken up about the end of 1649. The song of the Diggers, doubtless written by their leader Winstanley, is extremely curious (pp. 209-212, 215-224). The doctrines and the preaching of the Fifth-Monarchy men are illustrated by the trial of John Erbury for blasphemy, which took place in 1652 (p. 233). Of the miscellaneous papers contained in this volume four letters illustrate the history of the navy (pp. 39, 42, 62, 138), whilst others will be of interest to the historians of

Cambridge (p. 28), Yorkshire (pp. 1, 8, 20, 25, 70), Cheshire (136), Hereford (p. 157), Lancashire (pp. 160, 187), and Jersey (p. 228).

On several important passages in Cromwell's life these papers shed fresh light. The most important and most characteristic of them all is the long letter from Cromwell to Hammond, printed on p. 49. Large extracts from it have been given by Mr. Gardiner, and it is sufficient to refer the readers of this preface to his admirable explanations of its political significance.[a] Two points the letter makes clear; the first is Cromwell's deep distrust of the King and of any attempt to treat with him; the second is his desire to see "union and right understanding" between Puritans of every sort, "Presbyterians, Independents, Anabaptists and all." The justification of the alliance with the Argyle party in Scotland expresses the views not merely of Cromwell himself, but probably of the majority of the superior officers of his army. Exactly the same sentiments are expressed in a letter from the headquarters in Scotland, printed in one of the pamphlets of the time.[b] It is signed J. L. only, but there can be little doubt that these initials designate John Lambert, Cromwell's second in command.

"Sir,

"The godly party in Scotland seem to be very sensible of the benefit they have lately reaped by the victory God gave to our Army, and say they hope never to forget those instruments which the Lord chose to work their deliverance; and check themselves for the hard thoughts they formerly had of the Army: And its very observable, that this Army which the honest party in Scotland looked upon as a bundle of Sectaries, not fit to be continued, and did many ways unjustly reproach, should now under God, be the onely authors of their deliverance. Some of the most eminent and honorable in Scotland have ingenuously confessed to me their error and rashness in charging the Army last year with rebellion unjustly, seeing now there is a necessity put upon them to tread in that very path: Nay, they acted now against a clearer authority, where was the concurrence of the three States, King, Lords, and Commons. I am much persuaded that the Lord hath a glorious work in Scotland as well as in England. The interest of the godly people in Scotland, as to the Civil,

[a] *Great Civil War*, 2nd edition, iv., 248.

[b] Good news from Scotland, being a true relation of the present condition of the army under the command of Lieut.-Gen. Cromwell, 1648, 4to.

was once different from that of the godly people in England, or at least acted as it had been different; but now the Lord hath been pleased to order the affairs of that Kingdom, as that the interest of the godly people there, is become the same with ours in England, and they and we must act upon the same grounds and principles: And I am persuaded that so much of their power as the Princes of the Earth have lent to the support of that Man of Sin, God hath and will suddenly break and destroy.

"I have no more at present, but that I am

"Your most affectionate friend,

"J. L.

"Mordington in Scotland,
Sept. 27, 1648."

Cromwell's friendship with Hammond, proved by this letter of November 6, and by many of those printed by Carlyle, is further illustrated by two other letters to Hammond printed here for the first time. Mr. Gardiner copied them from the MSS. of the Marquis of Lothian at Newbattle, and has been good enough to allow me to add them to those contained in this volume.

The first, which is not dated, was evidently written between January and April, 1648, and deals with the precautions to be taken by Hammond to prevent the King's escape from the Isle of Wight. The same subject is touched in letters lii. and lvii. in Carlyle's Collection.

Cromwell to Hammond.

"Deare Robin, am I forgotten?

"Thou art not, I wish thee much comfort in thy great businesse, and the blessinge of the Almighty upon thee.

"This intelligence was delivered this day viz. that Sir George Cartwright[a] hath sent 3 boates from Jersey, and a Barque from Sharbrowe,[b] under the name of Frenchmen, but are absolutely sent to bringe the Kinge (if their plott can take effect) from the Isle of Wight to Jersey, one of which boates is returned back to Jersey with newes, but it is kept very private.

"I wish great care bee taken. Truly I would have the Castle well manned, you

[a] Carteret. [b] Cherbourg.

know how much lyeth upon itt. If you would have any thinge more done lett your freindes know your minde, they are readye to assist and secure you.

"You have warrant now to turne out such servants as you suspect, doe itt suddenly for feare of danger, you see how God hath honored and blessed every resolute action of theise [?] for him, doubt not but Hee will doe soe still.

"Lett the Parliaments shippes have notice of Cartwrights designe that soe they may looke out for him.

"I have noe more but rest
"Your true servant
"O. CROMWELL.[a]

(Addressed):
"For Col. Robin Hammond
Governour of the Isle of Wight
theise att Carisbrooke Castle
hast post hast."

Hammond was removed from the government of the Isle of Wight at the end of November 1648, for refusing obedience to the orders of Fairfax concerning the securing the King's person, and during the Commonwealth neither held any military office, nor took any part in public affiairs. In 1651 however he again sought for employment, but had some doubts of the justice of the war with the Scots, and would have preferred to serve in Ireland. Cromwell thought him unfit for the work. "You must not expect," he said to his Parliament in 1656, "that men of hesitating spirits, under the bondage of scruples, will be able to carry on this work,"[b] and he wrote in the same spirit now to Hammond.

"Deare Cozen,

"I receaved yours for which I thanke you, I understand my cozen your wife is under some trouble of minde, but because you are not perticular, I can only say my poore prayers shalbe for her that it may bee sanctified to you both. I am glad to heere my aunt and you are agreed, I hope it's a mercye to you both. You mention some purposes to come and visitt us, which kindnesse deserves and hath a thankefull acknowledgment from your freindes heere, whoe retaine in some measure their ould principles, which are not unknowen to you.

"You doe expresse in your letter thatt its the desire of your soule that you may

[a] Holograph. [b] Carlyle's Cromwell, Speech v.

be ledd forth in some way wheerein you may have more enjoyment of God, and bee used to his glorye, findinge deadnesse.

"Truly Sir it's a favor from the Lord not to bee vallewed that hee vouchsafe to use and owne us, of the sweete whereof you have heeretofore tasted, and well it becomes you in remembrance of former experiences, to say, and thinke soe. Hee is a master whoe ownes every servant in the lowest station, and those whoe are in the heighest have nothinge to boast of but his favorable countenance and acceptance, the greater the trust the greater the account, there is not reioycinge simplie in a lowe or high estate, in riches nor povertye, but only in the Lord. Noe, nor cann wee fetch contentment from the securest, hopefullest condition wee cann choose for our selves, nor is the comfort and peace of the spirit annexed to the greatest retirements, but the winde bloweth where it listeth, and if wee bee found with the Lord in his worke, Hee will dispence what is needfull, and oftentimes exceede in bountye.

"You hint somewhat of a willingnesse to bee againe engaged, but with this that the worke in Ireland goes smoother with you then this. You will forgive mee if I wonder what makes the difference, is it not one common and complexed interest and cause acted in Ireland and Scotland ?

"You oppose a call to your beinge in a good and setled condition to your contentment. Truly if it bee the Lord's worke now in hand lett it bee of choyce to leave contentments for itt.

[a] "The Lord hath noe neede of you, yett Hee hath fitted you with abillityes for the present dispensation, your freindes heere iudge soe, and will heartily welcom you, but indeed I doe not thinke you fitted for the worke untill the Lord give you a heart to begg of him that Hee will accept you into his service. Indeed, I write not this but in deernesse of love, truth of heart, and feare of the Lord, to you. The Lord may lay us in the dust when Hee pleaseth, yett wee serve him—Hee is our master, this is our boastinge—to receave and welcom you with comfort into the fellowship of his service is not more desiered by any then by

"Your cozen and very affectionate freind
to serve you

"O. CROMWELL.

"May 13th, 1651.
My affection to my deere cozen,
and aunt Hampden."

In two letters to Lord Wharton, numbered by Carlyle cxlvi., and clxxxi., Cromwell refers to the similar scruples of Wharton and other old friends, and treats them in much the same way. Hammond's answer to Cromwell's letter has not survived, but on July 22, 1651, he wrote to Cromwell interceding for the life of Mr. Love,

[a] The remainder is autograph.

and incidentally saying that his wife's ill-health had prevented him from joining Cromwell in Scotland.[a] In 1654 the Protector appointed him one of the Commissioners for the Government of Ireland, but he died a few weeks after entering upon the post he had so long sought.

To return to 1648. The letter printed on pp. 49-53 shows Cromwell's deep distrust of the King and his objections to the treaty then in progress at Newport. These are further explained in the famous letter of November 25 to Hammond, printed by Carlyle (No. lxxxv.). He approved of the petitions of the northern army for the punishment of the King, and he approved also of the Army Remonstrance of November 20. His letters show this. On November 20, forwarding the petitions of his army to Fairfax, he wrote: "I find in the officers of the regiment a very great sense of the sufferings of this poor kingdom, and in them all a very great zeal to have impartial justice done upon all offenders. And, I must confess I do in all, from my heart concur with them, and verily think and am persuaded, they are things which God puts into our hearts." On November 25, referring to the Army Remonstrance, he added: "We have read your Declaration here, and see in it nothing but what is honest, and becoming christians and honest men to say and offer. It is good to look up to God, who alone is able to sway all hearts to agree to the good and just things contained therein."

On two important points however Cromwell though he accepted the responsibility of the acts done by the southern army, disagreed with the policy adopted by them. He agreed with the opinion which Ireton some months earlier had expressed to Ludlow, viz., that it would be best to delay the intervention of the army till the treaty between the King and the Parliament had been actually completed. "We could perhaps have wished," he wrote "the

[a] *Original Letters and Papers of State addressed to Oliver Cromwell,* edited by John Nickolls, 1743, folio, p. 77.

stay of it [*i.e.* the Remonstrance of the Army] till after the treaty, yet seeing it is come out, we trust to rejoice in the will of the Lord, waiting his further pleasure."

In the second place he evidently desired that the army and the parliamentary minority should imitate the proceedings of the Argyle party, and as he expressed it "make the parliament null and call a new one" (p. 53). On this question however, as Mr. Gardiner has shown, the army leaders were obliged to yield to their parliamentary allies, and to content themselves with purging the parliament instead of forcibly dissolving it. Had Cromwell been in London at the beginning of December, instead of in Yorkshire, it is possible that his influence might have won over the parliamentary republicans to the original plan. In that case the breach caused by the forcible dissolution of 1653 might have been avoided. On the other hand he was extremely anxious, in 1649 as in 1651, that the Parliament should be persuaded to dissolve themselves, without undue pressure or force from the army (pp. 170, 233).

Cromwell was summoned to London by Fairfax on Nov. 28, (p. 62) and arrived there on Dec. 6. Concerning his share in the trial of Charles I. these papers give less information than we might have expected. The two letters from Cromwell and Ireton jointly to Colonel Harrison, with the minute precautions for the King's safe keeping prescribed by them, prove that Cromwell was determined that Charles should be brought to trial, (pp. 140-144). Mr. Gardiner has shown that even after the King had been conveyed from Hurst Castle to Windsor, "Cromwell and his allies among the officers desired to save the King's life, if it was possible to do so without injury to the cause for which they had fought."[a] Discussions on the subject undoubtedly took place in the Council of Officers, but no record of these important debates has been preserved. No doubt Clarke was there and took shorthand notes as usual, but

[a] *Great Civil War*, iv., 283.

if so he probably destroyed them in 1662 when the notes of the other debates of the council were transcribed. A royalist newspaper gives the following account of the division of opinion amongst the officers.

"There is great talke at White-Hall of bringing the King to tryall, and on Christmas day, when they should have bin at church, praying God for that memorable and unspeakeable mercy, which he in that day showed to mankind, in sending his onely begotten son into the world for their salvation; they were practising an accusation against his Deputy here on earth; and Ireton declared, they had conquered the Kingdom twice; and therefore it was fit they should bring the King, the capitall enemy thereof, to speedy justice: there were six in the council that were very hot for justice; and Hugh Peters did very gravely shew the necessity of it; but Cromwell had more wit in his anger, and told them there was no policy in taking away his life, and shewed divers and more solid reasons than Hugh's were; whereof one was, that if they should at any time loose the day, they could produce the King, their stake; and by his means work their peace: so it was concluded, that His Majesties charge should be forthwith drawn up, and himself brought to a speedy tryall; and, being found guilty, they could proceed either to mercy, or justice, as they pleased."[a]

But if Cromwell had doubts as to the expediency of the King's execution, he had none as to its justice. Mr. Goldwin Smith erroneously states that Cromwell neither in his speeches nor letters touches on the King's death. Cromwell refers to it with satisfaction, as a warning and as an example, in one of his letters to the governor of Edinburgh Castle.[b] He refers to it again in his speech about the Irish expedition on March 23 1649. "God," he tells the officers, "hath brought the warre to an issue heere and given you a greate fruite of that warre, to witt—the execution of exemplary justice upon the prime leader of all this quarrell," (p. 202).

In the debates of the Council of Officers recorded in this volume, Cromwell took scarcely any part. Indeed, as the table of attend-

[a] *Mercurius Melancholicus.* Dec. 25-Jan. 1, 1649. For this reference I am indebted to Mr. Gardiner.

[b] Carlyle, letter cxlviii. Goldwin Smith, *Three English Statesmen*, 1868, p. 59.

ances shows, he was generally absent (p. 272). But as the discussions mainly concerned the question of liberty of conscience—a subject upon which his opinions are perfectly well known from the speeches in Carlyle's collection—this is less to be regretted. On the other hand the important speech of March 23, on the subject of the expedition to Ireland, throws a good deal of light on Cromwell's views about the Irish war (pp. 200-207). He regarded the reconquest of Ireland as forced upon the English republic, by the adoption of the cause of Charles II. in Ireland, and by the danger of a possible invasion of England from thence. His national pride revolted at the idea of a Stuart restoration by the arms of Irish Catholics, or indeed of Scotch Presbyterians. "I confesse I have had these thoughts with myself that perhaps may be carnall and foolish. I had rather be overrun with a Cavalierish interest than of a Scotch interest; I had rather be overrun with a Scotch interest than an Irish interest; and I thinke of all, this is most dangerous. If they shall be able to carry on their work, they will make this the most miserable people in the earth, for all the world knows their barbarism" (p. 205).

Equally characteristic is Cromwell's confidence in the triumph of his cause, and his firm assurance of divine assistance and protection. "All the rest of the world, ministers and profane persons, all rob God of all glory, and reckon it to be a thing of chance that has befallen them. If we do not depart from God, I am confident, we doing our duty and waiting upon the Lord, shall find he will be as a wall of brass round about us till we have finished that work that he has for us to do" (p. 204).

The last of these new documents relating to Cromwell is a letter directed to Lieut. Col. Timothy Wilkes, apparently written early in January 1655. Wilkes was one of the Protector's most devoted adherents, and to him Cromwell unbosomed himself with the greatest frankness, and expressed the grief which the divisions of his own party and the opposition of his former friends aroused in him.

It resembles in its tone the letters which Cromwell wrote to Fleetwood, and reiterates the same complaints. "Truly" he had written in August 1653,[a] "I never more needed all helps from my Christian friends than now. Fain would I have my service accepted of the Saints, if the Lord will;—but it is not so. Being of different judgments, and those of each sort seeking most to propagate their own, that spirit of kindness that is to them all, is hardly accepted of any. I hope I can say it, my life has been a willing sacrifice, and I hope for them all. Yet it much falls out as when the two Hebrews were rebuked: you know upon whom they turned their displeasure." And again, in June 1655:[b] "The wretched jealousies that are amongst us, and the spirit of calumny turn all to gall and wormwood. My heart is for the people of God: that the Lord knows, and will in due time manifest; yet thence are my wounds;—which though it grieves me, yet through the grace of God doth not discourage me totally. Many good men are repining at everything, though indeed many good are well satisfied and satisfying daily. The will of the Lord will bring forth good in due time."

The causes of the breach between the Protector and his former friends, and the motives which dictated the vehement opposition of the Fifth Monarchy men to his government are very clearly set forth in a long and interesting letter from Thurloe to Monk (p. 242). Two letters from Thurloe's MSS. in the Bodleian Library, omitted by the editor of the Thurloe papers, are added here in order to further elucidate this subject. They were either intercepted by the government, or found amongst the correspondence of some Fifth Monarchy man arrested by its orders. The originals were probably written in cypher.

"I account it as great a happiness, that I have opportunity either to receive from you or transmitte unto you. Since I received your letter it hath beene matter of

---

[a] Carlyle, letter clxxxix.

[b] Carlyle, letter cxcix.

refreshment to me and to all the (remnant) Saintes who have heard of it, that in the day of darknesse upon the world, there remains a spirit of vigour and resolution for the King of Saints amongst you, both in God's servants and handmaydes. It was no unusuall thing in former ages, for the handmaydes of the Lord to seek him apart upon any inferiour account, much less upon so glorious behalfe (as this day they are, in seaveral places of this Nation remote from each other) which is a notable testimony to me, that they are set at worke by the Lorde's owne Spirit, and that he is now formeing of that Little Stone (cut out of the mountains without hands) to set the Image upon its feet; which are part of iron and part of clay, partly strong and partly broken, which is so lame, that it would endeavour to mingle it selfe with the seed of men, whereby to maintain its brotherhood a little longer; but it is no other than for the moulding (if I may so say) of the Little Stone in purer mettall that when it cometh actually to strike, it may make thorrow work with the Image both civill and ecclesiastical, and not deal so spareingly with the Antichristian relations as those honest harts would have done in the late Little Parliament (so called) as many of them do acknowledge. But now the indignation of the Saints against Babylon is so heightened, that when they come to the Lorde's worke againe no less will serve then the utter eradication of all what is planted, or built by the Manne of Sinne. Surely notable havock will be made in England the next . . . . . as ever was since the world began, and trully the greatest thing that lyeth upon my hart at present is, that the Lord would make me fitte to follow the Lambe at that time, and give me such a spirit for the executeing of his judgments, and the rewarding of Babylon as she hath rewarded us, as he shall call for in such a day. Doubtless his motions will be very swift when he beginns againe to march visibly, and those who resolve to follow him had need to be redeemed from the earth, as well as from among men; and indeed to become virgins having no interest marryed unto them, besides the pure and honourable interest of Jesus Christ. The Remnant of Saintes (since you were here) are exceedingly raised in their spirits, to consider how they may beare their witnesse more effectually for Christ then hitherto they have done, many being strongly perswaded that the Lord looketh for more from his servants, then faith and prayer; and that God speaketh to them now as he did to Moses, "Why cryest thou unto me? Speak to the children of Israel that they goe forward." And several of the choicest saintes here have beene much before the Lord in their clossets in order to this concerne; also in our private meeteinges much time is spent in seeking for a cleere and sure call, that whether we live or dye we may be found in the worke of the Lord, which we know shall prevail, though it were but with Gideon's 300 men, if so many could be found of such a spirit as they were.

My perswasions are great that a terrible destruction will suddainely be brought upon Babylon's workes and workemen in England. There are . . . . . sent from us to Norfolke, where about 15 or 16 churches have mette to conferre together, and begge wisdome of the Lord how to beare their witnesse for him against the present powers and their wickedness. The last time they conveen'd was the 13th of this moneth, at what tyme they would come to a result, whether in print, or by word of mouth to the present superiors. What the conclusion is, wee cannot yet heare: our friendes did judge it would be by sending two members from every church to London, there to bear the testimony of their dissatisfaction and dislike of them, which will be about 30 men. However things goe the councell of the Lord shall stand, that the bloody city must be remembered with all hir inhabitants farre and neere; because strong is the Lord God who judgeth hir, to whom be Glory for ever. Amen.

"Wee should have writte to you in general from the whole meeting if wee had a safer way of conveyance then by the post, but wee are considering whether to send messengers to all parts of this nation and Wales to enquire how the Lord moves upon the spiritts of . . . . . .

. . . .

ere long to be cutte short of that also, when the great Revolter hath strengthened his Hornes a little more, if God suffers him. It will be more visibly knowne who indeed are the people that know their God, and shall do exploites.

"Your friend and bro. in Christ, etc.

"London 19°—10^{m}—1654."

Copy of another Letter from London,

Dated 21°—10^{m}—54.

"As for your desires concerning Anna Trapnell, it is (to be playne) to me a very strange dispensation, yet I am perswaded she hath communion with God in it, but under what sort to rank it, I am at some stand. The dispensation is strange, because rare, more strange, because to me there appeares no such amongst the Scripture records, as to the manner of it: for I cannot reckon it among the visions and revelations of the Lord, because in the things she utters (whether in verse or prose) its only what she hath been conversant in before, and had the knowledge of, as now she spoke much concerning the Windsor prisoner (which those that know not she had beene there would have thought she had by revellation) and of the young men and their meeting, which she is conversant in, and much taken with. If she did continue it, but for one or two dayes I should be apt to think she might do it when she would, in the strength of phansie [?] save for two things. First, she is so stiffned in her body that were she not warme one would thinke hir dead. Secondly, because (she saith) she cannot make a verse when she is herself. But it is strange to me she should continue for 8 dayes as she did now; and I am ascertain'd (from those I can believe as if I saw it my self) that she eat nothing all that time; no, nor drunk, save once in 24 houres a little (and but very little) small beere. And on the last day of the weeke she declared in my hearing that she would be the next morning at the young men's meeting, which I much doubted, seeing how she lay and had layne; so I went that morning on purpose, and found hir there, she taking me by the hand ere I was aware; she came out without eating or drinking save a little small beere, yet did not experience herself weak or faint. My Lady Roles heareing she was there, called hir to goe to Lambeth in her coach, with whome I went also, and though wee spent the whole day there, she refused to eat. In our converse she was full of affection, with what sweet enjoyment she had of God the whole weeke. I tould hir that it was the opinion of some, that what she delivered was from the strength of hir naturall memorie. She answered, no, but throwne in by the Spirit to hir. I have sometimes said, that I thinke God in this Dispensation doth teach his people that when our communion with him is enlarged a very little of the creature will satisfie us.

"John Simpson is come to London; and did preach the last first day with the congregation, and at Allhallowes on the second day, where he related his reasons why he submitted to their order of banishment, and why now he breaks it; one reason to this was, because he hath it from good handes that O. P. had said to them, that John Simpson might come to London if he would, and that the Order was of his owne procuring; he might come to the Church if he pleased, but had no mind to it. Whereupon he declared, after he heard the certaine truth of this, he thought he was bound in conscience to come, whatever it cost him.—O. P. hearing he was in the Citty, sent for him, desiring him to come and conferre with him as a brother and a christian, and to bring three or four of the Church along with him. It was put to the church, and by vote they resolv'd he should goe, but some said he went into a temptation he should have avoyded. He was at Whitehall the whole day; wee were together till six of the clock at night, at which time he was not returned, and since I have not had opportunity to know the event. Mr. Simpson did declare in the pulpit his sameness to what he ever was; and that he never in the least doubted of the goodness of his cause, in bearing witness against the last publique thinge, as a publique sinne against former vowes. [Mr. Sim]pson I apprehend not to be fully enlightned about the kingdome of Christ; and comeing home, as I conceive, may occasion further tryalls upon the spirits of the Church in some tyme. God is sifting all sortes.

"It is now I perceive much upon the Spirits of some choice Saintes, that the next tryal may very great: possibly O. P. closeing so farr as to do such thinges as (he thinkes) may please the Sectaries, take away tythes, and loppe the laws; and so deceive the minds of the simple, and enrage all the more against the non-complyers. This tryall some are prepareing for. A petition I understand is prepared in the Common Councell of this Citty to encourage the Parliament about settling Church Government, etc. And I have it from a good hand that O. P. sent for a certain citizen, desiring a sight of that Petition; which having read, he said, "I think wee must labour to have Collonel Pride's Common Councell again, for these will undo all." One answered, "You (my Lord) called that a Lev[elli]ng Common Councell, but wee shall never have so good againe?" He replyed, "Where shall wee have men of a Universall Spirit? Every one desires to have liberty, but none will give it."

"Collonel Okey hath layd downe his grounds so farre as is apprehended, they had him at advantage, and he wanted power to oppose them; they on the other side weresuspitious, and so were glad of his resignation. As for that friend, surely the Lord will be a Light in Darknesse to those that with a single heart cleave to him. I desire to present my service to them both, leaving them with the Lord, and desireing he may stand compleat in all the will of God. But I conceive the great ones have lost their opportunity. Surely they were once betrusted by God, and had power to have stood up for what they had engaged, and ought to have kept their watch better, and not have suffered themselves to be cheated of so good an interest through the deceits of men and cuning craftiness; and whether ever God may trust them againe I question. But let them in the meane time take heed of strengthning the handes of evildoers, and surely were but a few good spirits to appear for their old good cause in the strength of truth, the Appostates and revolters would soon flee with Adonijah and his followers, when that cry was made in Jerusalem, "God save King Solomon."

"I could now relate at large what passed between O. P. and Mr. Simpson and those with him; but it is too late. Yet in brief thus: They conferred together from 9 to 12, at what time O. P. was called to dine an Ambassador he had invited; when he went out he commanded six dishes of meat might be sent to Mr. Simpson and his friends, whom he tould he would again conferr with them, which he did from 3 or 7; they took not his dinner, but consulted together how to answere him, for he had challenged them to decla what vowes or declarations he had broken; and being met again they instanced: 1st, In his promise about tythes to be taken away before 3 September, to which he replyed, "He wist not whether he had said so or no? But he heard Mr. Jessey should report it of him, in which he had not done well; and for his part he could not do it, for he was but one, and his Councel alledge it is not fitt to take them away." There were further arguings about this. Another thing that he had sworne to maintain the just laws of the Land, but had contrary to law imprisoned J. S., and C. F. I cannot now write the answers. He sayd it was out of love to them to save their lives. They instanced further that he had vowed and engaged others to the Goverment without king or single person, and now by taking this Goverment had not only broken those vowes, but also an Act of Parliament that it should be treason soe to do. To which among other things he replied: "Well said, Simpson, thou art plain indeed; not only to tell me I have broken my vowes, but that I am in plain termes A Traitor." He concluded his answer with this, That the Goverment he had taken and would stand to maintain it. Againe that he had promised Liberty to the Saintes, but now by the Tryers they were thrust out of all publick liberty. Hee sayd the Tryers were set up only to keep out knaves, but should not be used against any Godly men. At parting he gave Mr. Simpson an exhortation to carry soberly, as that should be best for them. Upon the whole they came away very much disatisfied with his Spirit and words.

B. T."

In the beginning of Cromwell's letter to Wilkes he alludes to the collection set on foot for the town of Marlborough which had been almost entirely burnt to the ground by the great fire of April 28, 1653. Mr. Waylen in his *History of Marlborough* (pp. 257-269), gives a full account of the fire, but both in that work, and in his *House of Cromwell* (p. 319), omits to notice a circular letter from the Protector recommending to the charitable the relief of the sufferers. As it is not included in Carlyle's collection and seems to have escaped notice I have thought it worth reprinting in full at the close of this introduction.

"Loving Friends

"Whereas it pleased the Lord to lay his afflicting hand upon the Inhabitants of the Town of Marlebrough in the County of Wilts, on the 28 of April 1653, by a sudden and terrible Fire, which burnt and consumed (within the space of foure houres) the Church, Market-house, and 250 dwelling houses, besides divers barns, stables, and other out-houses, with most of their goods, to the losse of above 70,000£. as hath been made appeare by sufficient testimony, whereby many of the poore inhabitants were reduced to a low and miserable condition, even without hopes of a future subsistence, had not the Lord in mercy by his good hand of Providence enlarged the hearts of some good people to extend their charity towards the re-building the said Town, and relieving of the necessities of the poore inhabitants thereof: And yet (as we are credibly informed by persons intrusted with the distribution of the monies collected for that purposes) the monies so collected doe not amount to the sixt part of their said losses, so that many mens houses lie unbuilt, and divers who have begun building, are necessitated to give over in the midst thereof, being no way able to finish them, by reason of their yet extream want: We doe therefore make it our earnest desire, That you the Officers and Soldiers under our command in England and Scotland, would take the premisses into your serious consideration, cheerfully to impart something to be deducted out of your next months pay for the further reliefe of those poore distressed people, towards which our Army in Ireland hath already unanimously manifested large bowells of compassion: which we hope will be a good example for you to follow:

And the rather, for that the Town was the first in the West of England that declared for, and took up Arms in the defence of that Cause which the Lord hath so eminently appeared for, and hitherto carryed on, by which meanes they then sustained exceeding great losses both by fire and plundring: of which We need say no more, but shall conclude with that saying, 'He that giveth to the Poore, lendeth to the Lord,' and rest,

"Your Loving Friend

"OLIVER P.

"White-Hall, 20 Nov.
1654."

In conclusion it only remains to refer readers of this volume to the account of the nature and condition of the MSS. given at page lxxvi. of the preface to volume one. The papers printed are generally derived from copies, or, in the case of the debates, from notes made in shorthand at the time but not transcribed till many years later. Both contained in consequence a large number of clerical errors and other mistakes which it was necessary for the editor to correct. Corrections or alterations of any importance are printed out in the notes. For mistakes of his own the editor can only apologise beforehand, and plead that the exceptional difficulty of his task may be taken into account.

C. H. FIRTH.

May 29, 1894.

ERRATA.

VOL. I.

Page xxxiii., note a, for "*Lords' Journals*, vii." read "*Lords Journals*, ix."

Page 82, last line, for "if these" read "if there."

Pages 128, 129, for "Twistleton" read "Twisleton."

Page 150, line 18, for "gave" read "give."

Page 219, note a, line 23, for "June 26" read "July 26."

Page 226, note b, line 6, for "agent" read "Agents."

VOL. II.

Page 1, note a. "Cavalrie" is a word frequently used to denote the Cavaliers in general.

Page 49, note a. On this note Mr. Gardiner observes: "The letter at Newbattle is not in Cromwell's hand, but it had every appearance of being the letter actually delivered. The explanation which occurred to me when I saw it was, that to avoid suspicion if the letter fell into bad hands, Cromwell either dictated it or had his own handwriting copied."

Page 72, note a, for "vol. 67" read "vol. 65."

Page 89, note c, Mr. Gardiner points out that Peter refers to the Diotrephes mentioned in the third Epistle of St. John, verse 9: "Diotrephes who loveth to have the pre-eminence among them."

Page 169, note a, line 8, for "Cowell" read "Cowling."

Page 171, note c, for "Athenae Oxonienses, ii. 75" read "ii. 175."

Page 229, line 10, "St. Won's Bay," *i.e.* "St. Ouen's Bay."

Page 233, line 23, for "John Erbury" read "William Erbury."

THE CLARKE PAPERS.

Thomas Margetts to William Clarke.

My deare freind,

Besides the inclosed I have little this weeke. On Wednesday last there was a meeting in this Citty of divers of the Presbiterian Ministers of the County for the setling of that government; but I perceive no great progresse is made in it, they have onely begun some 3 or 4 Classes in the West Riding, tis thought it will goe on but slowlye. The high reports of the Scotts coming in makes a sower countenance in theis parts; the Cavaliers[a] denie it on tooth and nayle, and I feare they will quickly bee upon our backs, and whether our late disbanding heere were good service or no, judge. I told you when the Parliament first resolved it, it would give advantage against themselves and kingdome; but I desire my former feare and apprehensions may not happen, if it may not be against the will of God, who works all things for good. By a private gentleman lately come from Scotland wee understand that the moderate party are now the fewest, and that the generall resolution is to come into England. They are for the present preparing their way, and privately carry on their designe of making their entrance as plausible as they can, to preserve and gaine interest. Our forces heere are so disperst into quarters over all the Association that if they intend a sudden and private entrance, or surprizall

[a] MS. "cavalrie."

of Barwick &c., wee are neither in a posture of offence or defence. Our intelligence from thence is meere[ly] accidentall, not certaine; having no scoutmaster or other intelligences. I wish theis things were considered, and that wee might be as active in private actings for defence as they are for offence. Episcopacy was the roote of the former war. Presbyterianism you will find to be the roote of the succeeding. The lamb and the dragon cannot be reconciled, so a victory there must be, but I rest

Thine owne,

THO: MARGETTS.

York 8 Apr. 1648.

It was against my judgment to send the abstract of the Muster by an express, but it was the Major Generall's express command, in regard the Committee of the Army did so earnestly write for it, neither is such to be practised.[a]

[Addressed:—]
To his very loving freind Mr. William Clark
at the Head Quarters.

[*News-letter from London.*][b]

Queenstreete, 10 Apr. 1648.

To give you first the newes from Scotland: the Parliament hath yett return'd noe answer to the desires of the Commissioners of the Kirke of Scotland, butt seeme to be very angry that the Ministers still persist to crosse them in their designes, and they seeme to bee farre from agreement. The Parliament are resolved to proceede against them; a new modell of their army is agreed on, and great store of armes lately come thither from Holland. Sir Phil. Musgrave hath ingeniously confest uppon discourse with his freinds in Scotland, that the Cavaleers would nott joyne in a body with or

[a] Compare Rushworth, vii. 1054. Rushworth simply reprints the "Perfect Diurnal" in which a sentence or two of this letter is quoted.

[b] Headings enclosed in square brackets are added by the editor.

under the command of the Scotts, if they come into England, butt are confident to have opportunity and assistance to make a body of their owne partie to carry on their owne designe, and manage their owne interest.

And itt seemes their freinds in London had some intimation of this their intention, though they began to act something too soone, and engaged before the other could assist.[a] For, on Sunday last, there mett in Moorefeilds London some thousands of apprentices and others to sport, which being contrary to the ordinance of Parliament the Lord Major indeavoured to prevent, and sent one of the Trained bands to disperse them; butt such was the greatnesse of their number and their resolutenesse, that they pelted the Trained bands with stones and att last fell in upon them, and disarm'd divers of them, and tooke away their colours. This done, they thought their designe was now ripe, and that they were fitt for any enterprize; wheruppon they gave a generall shoute, and cryed, "Now for King Charles," and soe went shouting alonge; their numbers increased downe towards Whitehall, crying out "For King Charles", and [at] Whitehall intending to beate Col. Barkestead's men out from thence. In this manner they passed through Fleetstreete and the Strand, where they were animated and incouraged by divers Malignants, and their number made them about 3000, some with musketts, others with swords and clubbs. Butt notice therof coming to the Generall, and the Lieutennant Generall, and Commissary Generall, who were very neere surprizing by the multitude, having noe notice of itt till they were almost att the Mewes; butt before they could gett thither the Generall went to the Mewes, and the Lieut. Generall drew forth a partie of horse, fell uppon them, kill'd him who carried the colours, and one or two more were slaine, and divers of them cutt and hack't by the troopers, wheruppon they soone fled and were dissipated. This was

[a] Cf. *Old Parliamentary History*, xvii., 93; Rushworth, vii., 1051, 1055; Walker, *Independency*, pt. i., pp. 84, 90; Gardiner, *Great Civil War*, iv., 97; Collections of the Massachusetts Historical Society, 4th series, vii., 140.

about 8 att night. The troopers followed them and clear'd the streetes, and the Generall went in person to Ludgate, and soe into Smythfeild, giving charge to all to keepe within their houses. After this (though it thundred, lightned, and rained), all thinges appear'd quiett and serene, and noe appearance was found of any company. Butt the Generall had nott bin longe come in and in bed, butt about two in the morning, there came newes, that the rude rabble were againe mett, and had secur'd Ludgate and Newgate, and afterwards went to the Lord Mayor's house, and fell uppon some of the Trained bands there, kill'd 2 or 3, and tooke 2 drakes which hee had for the security of his house. These they drew downe towards the Gates. They alsoe went into Milkestreete, and broke open the Armorie there, and furnished divers of themselves with armes. Thus they continued till about 7 or 8 in the morning, their numbers nott much increasing, nor any of the Citty Trained bands appearing to oppose them. Att last the greatest parte of Col. Barkesteads regiment of foote and 4 or 5 troopes of horse being sent against them, they refused to lett them enter the Gates; wheruppon they went about to Mooregate, where they were lett in, and overtooke a great parte of the rabble as they were going to seize uppon some magazine in Leadenhall, fell uppon them in Gracious streete, charg'd them; they received the first charge butt were repulsed with the losse of 8 men, and divers wounded, none of the souldiers kill'd, butt only Capt. Merriman shott in the shoulder butt curable. After this they were driven like sheepe into Leadenhall, the cheif of them prisoners. Afterwards the horse and foote clear'd the streetes of them. The Generall continued all the morning att Whitehall.

This was the abortive issue of the designe of the Malignant partie. To prevent the like tumults, and that the Army may bee in a fitt posture, there is a randezvous of 5 Regiments of horse and 5 of foote (besides those already in the Citty) to bee shortly held within 10 miles of London, when something will bee done in order to a settlement of thinges.

The Examination of William Paradine.

That on Munday night being the first of May, 1648, according to a former engagement the Cavaleers and others were mett att the signe of the 3 Tuns in Newgate Market, to consult together to finde out a way to raise horse and foote, For God, the Kinge, and Citty. The number of Cavaleers, Apprentices, Innes of Court Gentlemen, and others were neere 30 persons, being all together in an upper roome 2 pair of staires high. Major Pilkington, formerly belonging to the Kinge, drew from his pockett 6 proposalls, consisting in 2 sheetes close written, to certifie unto their fellow plotters the lawfulnesse of their undertakinges (having bin advised in them by councell): which proposalls run to this effect, First what they intended to fight for (is) in the defence of the Kinge and his posterity. 2[ly] The ancient protestant Religion. 3[dly] The safety of the Citty. Further that they meete noe more att present all together, butt are appointed severally to list men in severall precincts, and to bringe in the names of those men they list to the signe of the Queenes-Armes in Lumbard streete, and that they have already listed neere 1500, wherof of them in Fanchur[c]h streeete and therabouts 700, and that they doe intend when they have perfected their designe to seize on all the Gates of the Citty, and to take all the horses they can light uppon. This is to bee done before the terme bee ended if possible, and when they have soe done they intend to send to the Lord Major, and Common Councill propositions to this effect: that they intend noe hurt to the Citty but their preservation.[a] After this was declar'd to the company,

[a] On this plot see *Lords' Journals*, x., 262, May 18, 1648. Rushworth, vii., 1119. An earlier plot of the same kind is mentioned in *Mercurius Dogmaticus*, Jan. 20-28, 1648: "There was a design of late . . . which was—One Major Clark, sometime a Vinter at the Miter in Bishopsgate Street, Lieutenant Corbet, and Richard Yates, formerly officers in the King's army, had contrived a way how to purchase themselves and the loyall partie of this kingdome a redemption from their cruell bondage; and for that purpose had given forth tickets to those whom they knew to

one objected, what shall wee doe for amunition? The Major answer'd 'I hope there is none heere soe poore butt are able to buy two or 3 shotts apiece, for (said hee) when once the Gates are secur'd wee will nott want for amunition.'

Signed,

WILLIAM PARADINE, &c.

[*News-letter from London.*]

12 May, 1648.

To observe the strange alteration the defeating of the Welsh hath made in all sorts is admirable.[a] The disaffected to the army of the religious Presbyterians now fawne uppon them, partly for feare of you, and partly in that they thinke you will keepe downe the Royall partie, which threatened them att their doores in the streetes to their faces with destruction, and putt noe difference

be cordially affected, exhorting them to make all the strength they could amongst their friends and allies; and when of considerable strength to divide themselves into three bodies, whereof the one was to seize upon the Tower, the other to surprise the men at Westminster, and the other to keep a court of guard at Temple Barre, to hinder the citizens from flocking to their rescue. . . . A Declaration was printed and dispersed abroad the heads whereof were these:

"'To all those that are faithfull to God, loyall to their King, and desire to be freed from their cruell bondage.

"'1. Wee declare our intentions to be onely for the preservation of His Majestie and ourselves from ruine and the restitution of His Majestie to His just rights, the knowne lawes to their due course, and ourselves to our ancient liberties.

"'2. To destroy all those who shall adhere to Sir Thomas Fairfax, in pursuance of his damnable Declaration for deposing the King.

"'3. To hang up all men at their own doores immediately who shall conceale any parliament-man in their house within the Citie, and not give present ncotie of him to the present governor of the Tower.'

"But this undetaking was blasted, even in the bud, for (as the Devill would have it) the Citie Marshall had notice given him of the place where these Loyalists resorted, who at the second search found and surprised them."

[a] Cf. Gardiner, *Great Civil War*, iv., 126.

betweene Presbyter and Independant. The Parliament men that went alonge with you because they supposed you would prevaile, and they should bee most secure in you, how doe they flagge, [they that] fawne[d] uppon the Citty, and whisper'd against you, beginning to say you had done thus and thus amisse, [are] now cordiall to you. When the lettres were read in the House of the defeate, how many Royalists hunge downe their heads, and went out, nott staying the conclusion; from all which you may see clearly how necessary itt is to bee alway in action with your army, and if nott heere, yett elsewhere. I finde the people have alway bin content to nott onely parte with mony, soe itt was fairely carried in raising and faithfully disposed of,[a] butt to bee taken with successes, and the noyse of victorie running in a ballad is matter for them to prate of; the more wise are putt into feare and conformity. This went alonge with all our victories and warres in France, though they exhausted never soe much. The City talke as if they would alsoe joyne with you against the Royall partie, butt trust them nott; for all that are nott fooles, unlesse your frends, are for Kinge and Byshopps. Our new Statesmen in the House of Commons are att a losse, nott knowing how to goe farther, either in setling the Kingdome, or in contenting the Scotts. The 2 chief Sco[tts] Officers came to some of our's for advice, who told them they lik't nott their foundation, and soe itt were indiscretion for them to give advice in the building. The Lords I doe verily thinke will nott parte with the Tower, nor give way to the Militia altering; for one of their selves told mee, if itt bee a truth, that the present state of itt hinders trade. 'Tis best to putt the Tower into such an hand as you may confide in and they bee pleas'd with, and soe now itt is, were they nott soe bent to basenesse. The Scotts honest partie declaring against the other very much stuns them heere, and putts them to their witts end. Now to declare never to receive the Kinge nor any of his, unlesse hee give satisfaction to the 4 Bills and what was soe presented:[b]

[a] Position of clause altered.

[b] By the letter of intelligence of May 8, Clarendon MS., 2778, it appears that the Independent leaders were even then reviving the negotiations.

that the Parliament shall sitt butt 3 monthes in the yeare, and confined to making lawes, giving mony, and righting those wronged in inferior courts : that then the[a] excise shall cease and soe much uppon the pound rent paid instead thereof : that noe man shall bee punished for discourse in any point of Religion, the same disturbing nott the civill peace: that none shall bee barr'd from trust for not taking the Covenant : and a way taken uppe for raising mony in this Kingdome to pay 10,000 Horse and 30,000 Foote for ever without tax: which may bee done, and to which all the Kingdome, a few excepted, will concurre in. I am confident you might nominate alsoe 21 for a Councill of State, and they would bee yielded unto.

[*News-letter from York.*][b]

Yorke, 12 May, 1648.

To relate unto you the true present condition of these parts is very difficult. In generall wee are all ever in a strugling, striving, fearing, hoping, marching, fighting posture. The late surprise of Barwick and Carlisle hath put . . . . the Cavaleers . . . . many high, proud and confid[ent] . . . . with them, ... and that they have plotted and hoped for, have they now oportunity to putt in execution, taking advantage of the paucity of our forces to resist, if they can but possibly gett into a body ; their number every where is soe great and the well affected so few, that the former are very highly incouraged even to confidence, and the latter are much discouraged even to differences, because they heare of no visible assistance approaching (which is soe much desired and would never bee more seasonable then now) to give a stop to their dayly confluence and engaging the country on their side, which they loose no time in, while the poore well affected are forced to leave their homes and flie for their lives. They are so high, that

[a] MS. "these."

[b] This letter is injured by damp, and in parts illegible. It is pretty certainly from Thomas Margetts, like that of April 8.

they cry out in every place "hay for King Charles againe," (and satyriacally) "what will become of the saintes now." Indulgence, I feare, hath whetted this knife to cutt our owne throtes; a hundred or six score of the well affected are fled out of Cumberland for feare of the enemy. All our forces are marched northward to endeavour all they can to prevent the enemies multipling, and dissipate their tender bodies before they grow too corpulent. By the inclosed, which is a coppy of the gentlemen's warrant under named, at Tor . . . . in this new rebellion, Major Cholmley's lettre, and the list of men's names enrolled, you will see the forwardness and cuningnes of the enemye. By that warrant they procured a great meeting of the Country to see what those new agents would propound to them. Sir Robert and Sir Thomas Strickland made large speeches to the poore ensnared country to [venture] lives and f[ortu]nes in this their present designe. [Enclosed] is a coppy of the list of those that gave in their names for it, which was taken by [one] Harrison, Clarke of the Peace for Westmerland. Their meting was on Saturday last, and at their dissolve they appointed the Tuesday following to perfect their resolves; but that Saturday night after their meeting Major Cholmely with his troope fell into some of their quarters, and apprehended some of them, which hath given a little hush to the people, and 'tis thought now upon the approach of our forces they will disperse. Among the rest Harrison the Clarke of the Peace was taken at Kendall, crying about the stretes "now high for King Charles," and had the list in his pocket. Hee and one Captain Ferrand were sent up to Yorke, and are comitted to Clifford's Tower, and some more are taken. Harrison conffesed ingenuously to mee that he did take the names upon a hill in the feild at the randezvous, upon the desire of Sir Henry Bellingham, and that it was a true coppy. Here in Yorke there hath bene a great feare of the enemies rising to surprise this towne,[a] and indeed not without ground, because they are so high and many, and doe indeed in plaine termes threaten and speake it, and terrifie the well

[a] Cf. Rushworth, vii., 1113.

affected as much as they can ; and on Wednesday night last about midnight runned in a party of horsemen, and disperst themselves, as is conceived, to severall malignants houses to lie there till an opportunity of setting themselves in a fitt equipage of putting themselves into action, insomuch as the well affected were sore-frighted and began to shift for themselves, and looke about them. This gave a great alarm to the Lord Maior and Aldermen, who presently under strict charge to looke well to the barrs and [H]ouse of C[apt] Spencer, who hath a Con . . . . . Clifford's Tower to suppress meeting[s] and insurrections in the Citty ; and p[resent]ly they sumoned a counsell, and tooke into consideration the raising of some volunteers for the defence and safety of themselves. While the Citty was in this confusion, comes in, providentially, and unlooked for, a troop of our horse that quartered in Darbysheire ; the Cavaleers seeing them cryed "Glenham was come, Glenham was come," and Quarter Master Diggles, who brought them in, hearing the Citty in that posture, drew uppe the troup in the heart of the Citty, and spake to them to make ready in case of present opposition, which they did, but nothing done ; onely this much discouraged the enemy, and incouraged freinds and gave life to the present motion of the Lord Mayor and Aldermen in raising men, who now though lately they would . . . . in the Citty, beg heartily that they would stay in the Citty, till they have raised and putt the Citty in a posture of defence and safety. I heare they have agreed to raise 2 Companies of Volunteers under Aldermen Dickenson and Alderman Gray, and some horse to ride about a nights to keepe downe the enemy. It was verily believed that the last night, had not that trouppe come in, the Cavaleers would all have beene up in armes, and possest themselves of the power of the Citty for the Enemy.

A Libell dispersed att Covent Garden.

On the Lords day May 14, 1648.[a]

Oyes, Oyes, Oyes!

If any manner of Man in citty, towne or country can tell any tidinges of a thanksgiving to bee kept the 17th day of this present month of May, by order of the Commons now assembled att Westminster, lett him come to the cryer, and hee shall bee hanged for his paynes.

God save Kinge Charles and hange all his Enemies.

[*Gilbert Mabbott to Lord Fairfax.*]

May it please your Excellencie.

I am comanded by Collonell Hewson, and some other officers of your Excellencies here in towne, to desire your Excellencie forthwith to give speedie orders for some considerable force that lies quartered neere this place, to advance hither, or neere Westminster. For that before the Surrey Petitioners would with-drawe they forced the Howse and the guards, which occasioned 2 more companies to bee speedily sent for from the Mewse, upon whose comeing, severall affronts were offered them, and shouting for about an houre together gathered about 2000 in a body, and then cryed "a King" "a King," some of them forceing upon the companies in the Pallace, which occasioned them to keepe of at pikes'-end, but getting one of the souldiers among them accidentally the Petitioners fell upon [him] with their swords and clubbs, whoe was runne through (and conceived dead by this time) before hee could bee releived. Upon which the troope of horse fell in upon them, and routed them; and then the companies

[a] Wednesday May 17. "This was thanksgiving day for the victory in Wales, which was punctually observed by the Houses, but very slightly in the City." Rushworth, vii., 1117.

pursued, and forced them through the Hall and out at King's Bridge. Not above 2 or 3 slaine, and many wounded, and some striped, about 20 odde of the cheife of them taken prisoners. The City gates are shutt up, and they stand upon their guard. I leave all to your Excellencies consideracion, resting,

Your Excellencies most humble servant,

G. MABBOTT.

16 May, 1648.

[*Col. Barkstead to Lord Fairfax.*]

May itt please your Excellency,

This day was a petition presented to the Commons from the County of Surrey[a] by neere 3000 Horse and Foote. They came to the House about 12 of the clock, and after they had staid about 3 houres they began to expresse much discontent that they had nott an answer, some of them saying, that they would have an answer, others that they would have such an answer as should please them. Att last they cried out with a loude acclamation, "For God, and Kinge Charles," and soe crowding towards the doore disarm'd and knock't downe some of the sentinells, indeavouring to have surprized the whole [guard], saying, "wee will pull them out by the eares." Butt I having a very watchfull eye over them, and being very unwilling to give them any just occasion, yett seeing their outrage went thus farre, I sent downe a partie of about 500, which came in very seasonably, for as they came, the petitioners had began to force the guard, att which began a present engagement with them, in which two of our men were kill'd, and 4 or 5 of the Enemy. The businesse was soone over. My Lord, I am informed by some that is amongst them this night, that they resolve to fall on those of

[a] On the Surrey petition see Rushworth, vii., 1116, and Walker, *History of Independency*, part i., Epistle. Mr. Gardiner enumerates the pamphlets written on the side of the petitioners and the side of the soldiers, and concludes in favour of the account given by the soldiers. *Great Civil War*, iii., 376.

Col. Harrison's regiment which quarter with them, by way of revenge. No more butt that I am and ever shall bee,

Your Excellencies most humble and faithfull servant,

Jo: Barkestead.

London.
May 16, 1648.

Sir John Rayney's Information concerning the insurrection in Kent.

Sir John Rayney of Wortham in the County of Kent, Bart. certifieth, That uppon the 22th of May instant hee being come to Rochester, uppon a summons for a generall meeting of the Deputy Lieutenants of Kent to bee there that day, found the gate uppon the bridge shutt, and about 20 musqueteers uppon the guard, and 2 peices of ordnance mounted uppon the bridge; and the gates being open'd unto him hee was followed by a musketeer to the inne called the Crowne, without being questioned att all, untill such time as this informant, perceiving the said souldier to follow him, did speake to the said souldier these or the like words, "Thou needest not to follow mee." Hee this informant supposing the said guard to have bin placed by the Deputy Lieutennants of the County, and demanded of the said souldiers and others what Deputy Lieutennants were there; wheruppon the said souldiers and divers others replyed, that there were none of the Deputy Lieutennants there, neither did they expect any of them. Wheruppon this informant answer'd, that there was a meeting of them appointed to bee there that morning; to which one amongst the rest replyed "the case is alter'd now," and that the Citty was for the Kinge, and should bee kept for him or words to that effect; and another of the said companie demanded whether this informant were nott for the Kinge, to which this informant jestingly replyed, "There is noe doubt of that." Uppon which one of the said companie, who had formerly bin this informants coachman, replyed in these or the like words, "I know that Sir John Rayney wisheth well to the Kinge," and offer'd to guard him out. To whome this informant replyed "you neede nott," and soe left them; and passing back through the maine streete found them all armed alonge the streetes in the manner of a court of guard att every doore, and att Margretts Church in his returne was againe stop't and questioned by a guard, demanding his name and whither hee went, and whether hee were for Kinge Charles; whome this informant did putt off with the like answer as before.

JOHN RAYNEY.

[*Sir Michael Livesey to Sir Anthony Weldon.*]

Sir,

Wee are glad your parts are soe quiett. Itt is otherwise with other parts of the County;[a] Rochester, Sittingburne, Feversham, and Sandwich all garrison'd for the Kinge. The County Magazines in those places, and as wee just now heard . . . . likewise seized, Mr. Box their prisoner att Sittingburne, and one John Swan though of their owne partie, and by themselves . . . What our indeavours are and present engagements wee shall att large acquaint you with att your coming, which we daily expect. In the meane time resting,

Your humble servant
MICHAELL LIVESAY.

Aylesford,
22 May. 1648,
past 9 att night.

Wee desire you to hasten the raising of all your horse and foote, and imediately to send away Capt. Skinner's troope to Aylesford, where they shall receive further orders.

For Sir Anthony Weldon Kt. att Swanscombe these.

[a] On the origin of the Kentish rising see Matthew Carter's *A true relation of the Honourable though unfortunate expedition of Kent, Essex, and Colchester.* He is particularly hostile to Livesey, pp. 7, 15, 96, 32.

[*To the Derby House Committee.*]

My Lords and Gentlemen

I send you this inclosed sent mee this morning, by which you may understand the constitution of this County. Never was the faire face of such a faithfull County turn'd of a suddaine to soe much deformity and uglinesse. If your Lordshippes doe thinke that by flinging water on our flame you shall extinguish all, believe mee itt will nott doe, butt make all parts in flame the more. I heare some Members of the honourable House of Commons are sent to appease the insolencies att Rochester . . . besides many already in the same posture, and noe question by that course all will follow. I cannott say more then I have to your Honours in my former lettre's postscript. You may cast away many gentlemen that have serv'd you formerly from the first beginning of these unhappy differences, butt where to finde such is nott easily to bee advised. For my parte I looke hourely to bee seized, which must cost the seizers or some of them their lives, for I shall nott bee their prisoner to bee led in triumph as poore Mr. Box. I shall nott say more, butt if you suffer us to perish for want of aide you shall wish aide had come in time.

Your humble servant

ANTHONY WELDON.

The 23th of
May, Swanscombe.

To the right honorable the Committee of Lords and Commons sitting att Derby House.

[*The Kentish Committee to the Speaker.*]

Mr. Speaker,

Perceiving the growing distempers of this County arising by a

Petition to the Parliament sett on foote by the malignant partie in this County, and by a generall randezvouz appointed for a tumultuous meeting att Blackheath, uppon pretence to carry uppe the same, wee raised a small partie of horse to preserve the peace of the County. Since which time uppon the rumours given out of the Princes landing att Sandwich, that towne with the ordnance belonging therto seized by a route, and the Malignants flocking thither from Canterbury and other parts, wee applyed our selves to all possible indeavours to raise forces to prevent the heading of that partie; in the very act wherof wee received the inclosed of the 21th instant from Capt. Leigh, Capt. Westrowe, and the Mayor of Rochester, which gave a stoppe to our proceedings. That very night the magazines of Sittingburne and Feversham were seiz'd, and those townes in armes declaring for the Kinge, and one there kill'd, Rochester that night forewarn'd the approach of our partie of horse towards them which wee had with us for preserving the Counties peace (as will appeare by the severall inclosed of the same date from Col. Newman, and one likewise from the Mayor and severall inhabitants of Rochester) the citty then standing, uppon their guard, and the next day openly declaring for the Kinge, as will appeare by the inclosed information of Sir John Rayney, one of the Deputy Lieutennants of the County. Since which that the like is done att Canterbury and Ashford, wee lately represented our position [a] to the honourable Committee of Lords and Commons att Derby House by our's of the 21th instant, together with our desires of their speedy care for a timely releif to this County by a considerable strength from the Army or the Citty out of hand; without which this County is in danger to bee wholly lost. What this dayes meeting of the Malignants att an horse race att Cox Heath will produce you will further heare. Wee have a small partie att Maidstone, and the parts adjacent, and are in hourely expectation what supply the Weild of Kent will or can afford us. What help may be had from the Army or Citty, wee shall againe

[a] MS. Commission.

humbly desire may bee speeded to us, and in the meane time to send us your further directions.

Your humble and faithfull servants,

MICHAELL LIVESAY.
AUGUSTINE SKINNER.
RICHARD BELL.
LAMBERT GODFREY.

Aylsford, the
23th of May.
1648.

For the honourable William Lenthall Esq.
Speaker of the honourable House of Commons.

[*An Anonymous Letter to Lord Fairfax.*]

May itt please your Excellencie,

I thought my self bound in duty and conscience to informe your Excellency that Sir Henry Vane Junr (uppon devision of the House of this day concerning the treaty with his Majesty) voted with the malignant partie against the honest partie, and therfore I shall humbly desire your Excellency nott in the least measure to confide in him. Some honest men were fearfull of his revolt of late, because Doctor Stane and Scoutmaster Generall Watson [a] had bin too conversant with him. I humbly begge your Excellencies secrecie and pardon heerin, and leave to subscribe myself,

Yours &c.

24 May, 1648.

[*The Derby House Committee to Lord Fairfax.*]

My Lord,

Uppon some propositions made to this Committee by the Earle of

[a] On Scoutmaster-General Leonard Watson and his intrigues with the royalists see Carte, *Original Letters*, 1739, i., 220.

Thanett about appeasing the tumults in Kent, which propositions were reported to the Houses, the inclosed instructions[a] were ther-uppon approv'd of to bee given to the said Earle of Thanett to proceede in that businesse, which wee thought fitt to send to your Lordshippe that you may see how farre the Houses have proceeded in itt, butt for that itt is of soe great concernement that this tumult bee speedily suppressed, wee desire your Lordshippe that noe opportunity may (uppon occasion of those instructions) bee lost to reduce them by force, if they shall nott conforme themselves to what is contayn'd in the instructions by Saturday morning next. Wee have desired Mr. Boyce Knight of the shire of Kent, and alsoe Sir Anthony Weldon and Mr. James Morice, who have bin very faith-full and active for the Parliament, to waite uppon your Lordshippe, who are able to give you a full information of the present state of that County.

Signed in the name and by warrant of the Committee of Lords and Commons att Derby House by
Your Lordshippes
very affeccionate freind and humble servant
WILLIAM SAY & SEALE.

Derby House,
25° May, 1648.

For the right honourable Thomas Lord Fairfax, Lord Generall.[b]

[*Lord Fairfax to the Derby House Committee.*]

My Lords and Gentlemen,

Having received the votes of the House of this day, by which I finde the regiments att the Mewes, Whitehall, and the Tower,[c]

[a] *Lords' Journals*, x., 282.

[b] This letter and that of the same Committee dated May 26, are calendared in Cal. S. P. Dom., 1647-9, pp. 79, 81.

[c] These 3 regiments were those of Cols. Rich, Barkstead, and Tichborne. Cf. Gardiner, *Great Civil War*, iv., 134.

to bee set free from their present duty, and left to your Lordshippes disposall for other service heerabouts, I thought good to represent to your Lordshippes the opinion of my self and the Officers heere, that itt is nott safe or adviseable to engage those regiments (or any parte of them) uppon any service by themselves, in relation to the present great insurreccions ; butt itt is our humble advice and desire that your Lordshippes would take order they may speedily bee drawne forth this way to morrow, in order to randezvous with the rest of our small bodie about Hounsloe Heath, that wee may once bee imbodied together; and then as wee shall bee more considerable for any service, soe wee shall bee ready with the whole to bee att your Lordshippes commands. To receive which in order to the managing and carrying on of the present businesse, I have, according to a lettre from the Speaker of the House of Commons (for the sending of some person to consult with the Committee att Derby House) appointed Col. [Hewson] to attend your Lordshippes for that purpose, having noe other whome I could att present spare; and there being likewise much neede of his speedy returne, I desire hee may receive a dispatch from your Lordshippes assoone as may bee.

T. F.

Windsor, 26° May, 1648.

[*The Derby House Committee to Lord Fairfax.*]

My Lord,

Wee have received your Lordshippes letter of the 25th instant from Windsor, and wee conceive the forces therin mencioned to bee much too short to provide against that danger which wee conceive the Parliament to bee in from this insurreccion in Kent, and the distempers that are in other places ; wee are inform'd that the Kentishmen will have a meeting att Black-heath on Tuesday next,

A letter from Fairfax to the Derby House Committee printed in the *Lords' Journals*, and reprinted in the *Old Parliamentary History*, xvii., 149, gives an account of the distribution of his forces.

and att the same time those of Surrey att Putney Heath, and those of Essex att Wanstead; wee therfore desire your Lordshippe to give order to as many forces as can bee timely had for the defence of the Parliament and the preservation of the peace of the Kingdome. Wee heare, that many of the inhabitants of Surrey are very unwilling that any forces should come into their County. Therfore, if your Lordshippe shall see the necessity to send any forces that way, wee desire your Lordshippe that they may take care to carry themselves inoffensively to the people of the County, and to their owne quartering that they may bee in safety. Since the lettre wee wrote this day Mr. Westrowe, a Member of the House, is come from Rochester, who will waite upon your Lordshippe to give you the state of the Country.

Signed in the name and by warrant of the Committee att Derby House by,

Your Lordshippes very affeccionate freind and Servant

WILLIAM SAY & SEALE.

Derby House.
26 May, 1648.

[*News-letter from Yorke.*]

May 27, 1648.

Affaires heere looke nott with soe plesant a countenaunce as by this time, if my Lord Generall had been heere, they would have done—the reason alleidged of his not coming satisfies not, but people now feare whether he will come or no, and say that discontent in the army, unwillingnes and dissatisfaccion in another engagement is the cause; notwithstanding the Cavaleers are not altogether soe high as lately, in regard their designes have not taken effect answerable to their desire. Langdale with all his forces in armes is confined onely to Westmorland and Cumberland, though sometimes they inrode into the Dales, but without any considerable act. Wee have given power and comission to the well-affected there to putt themselves into a posture of defence, and to rise and nott permitt the Cavaleers comming unto them, or through them into Yorkshire, which of them selves they are able and wee beleive will doo. The Enemy however strong reported, (and how strong they are our intelligence is so bad wee cannot certainly learne) yet they have acted nothing, but taken some well affected out of their houses and carried them away. One troup of ours lay farre from the rest even upon their borders, and yet they stired not to offend them. Nine of our tropes are in a body, and have laine at least 10 daies upon the borders of Westmorland, but no enemy hath appeared, onely a partee of ours lately tooke 5 of them with horses and armes to a good value, which hath much incouraged our souldiers. The Major-Generall came on Thersday night from the troupes which lay at Barnard Castle, and in regard no enemye appeared (though wee heare they were at Kirby Stephen) a partee of about 7 score were drawen out under the comand of active Major Cholmley, who had directions to march towards Kirby Stephen into their quarters, and if he saw cause or any advantage to engage, and Coll. Lilburne, who comands the trops in cheife in absence of the Major Generall, was to follow with the rest to second or secure him as occasion should bee. Wee expect every hower to heere of something to be done, for our men are in good case and ready, though they are 6 weekes pay behind the rest of the army. There hath been lately a treaty betwene the Cavaleers and Lancashire, and wee heare that County is newtrall, onely have agreed that they and the Cavaleers shall not hurt one another, soe that now wee thinke they will suddenly attempt Yorkshire. Coll. Harrison is invited out of Lancashire hither. Coll. Twisleton's regiment quartered last night at Otley, himself at York, and had discourse with the Major Generall. [If] those 2 regiments of horse ioyned with oures, which is intended, wee shall be able I hope to looke the enemy in the face; besides Yorkshire is in a pretty good posture, and [three] regiments of foote, vizt. one in East Riding [etc.], agreed to be raised, and one of horse. Col. Legard to comand the

East Riding Regiment, Col. Ch. Fairfax, uncle to the Lord Generall, the West, the North not yet named, and Coll. Bethell the horse.

T. M[ARGETTS].

[*Col. Barkstead to Lord Fairfax.*]

May itt please your Excellency,

The Enemy still continues att Dartford; they give out themselves to bee ten thousand butt the countrymen lessen every day; very many officers and souldiers that have formerly serv'd the Kinge come in hourely to them. The discourse among them is, that if the country will nott stand to them they will imediately possesse themselves of all the castles and stronge holds, and therby secure landing for the Irish, French, or Danes, of whose coming they fondlie flatter themselves and the malignant partie of the country. These countrymen that are come home doe extreamly cry out against the gentlemen that did engage them, looking uppon themselves as utterly undone, which is the onely cause of their coming home, hoping th[us] to keepe their neckes out of the halter. I have received order [from] your Excellency by Col. Rich, and accordingly have drawne the be[st part of] my regiment to Lambeth, 200 foote I have left uppon [the] passes att Southwarke townes-end with 3 troopes of Horse. [I] have nott more att present butt doe waite in expectation of your Excellencies farther orders, which shall bee punctually obeyed by him who is,

My Lord,

Your most humble and faithfull servant,

JO: BARKESTEAD.

Lambeth House,
the 29th of May
1648.[a]

[a] Cf. Gardiner, *Great Civil War*, iv., 137.

I had 2 scouts from them just now, who brought mee the inclosed pamphlett from amongst them. They report they hope to bee possest of Dover this night, and doe nott doubt of seizing of all the Navy, if your Excellency stay butt 2 or 3 dayes from them.

[*A letter from Carisbrook.*]

My letters have ever bin welcome to your hands, and soe I am assured this will doe the like, conveying such good newes as the happy prevention of the Kinges escape this last night, which was most graciously prevented. Mr. Dowsett the Clerke of the Kitchin, and one Osborne (gentleman usher and recommended by my lady Wharton, a truly soe seemingly pious and faithfull that we all tooke him for a very upright man) having corrupted the sentinells and Mr. Readinges man, a barber and butt newly entertain'd, had design'd to conveye the Kinge over the Castle wall at midnight, two of the Worseleys, gentlemen of this Isle, and Osborne had prepared horses and brought them to the counterscarpe of the line. The Kinge alsoe had cutt the toppe of a stronge iron barre in's chamber, and was ready to descend by a rope which Dowsett was to furnish. Now itt pleased God to move two of the 3 souldiers' hearts to reveale itt to the Governour, who lett the plott goe as farre as itt would, butt the rope failing, the Kinge attempted itt noe further then to bee ready when the signe should bee, which was the throwing a stone against the windowe. The 2 souldiers that discover'd itt have 10*li.* a piece given them, and deservedly, that others may bee incouraged to bee honest uppon all occasions. The designe is (att our request alsoe) examining, to the end that all false hearts may fully bee discover'd as God will give way, for truly itt is cause of joy and sorrow; joy that soe dangerous an attempt succeeded nott according to the craft of those villaines and the expectation of our enemies; sorrow that in soe small a family such perfidie should bee harboured and to throw a scandall uppon the honest partie who serve by principles of conscience and honour, and were itt nott unseemly to justifie my self I should say somethinge that your good opinion may bee continued where I hope 'tis fix't. Truly I appeale to the Governour what my diligence and care hath bin, without any mixture of other businesse, and to God as touching the integrity of my heart, which I hope will never faile mee, I pray heartily for itt, I shall indeavour itt to the utmost; and as I wish the false may have their reward proportionable to their demeritt, soe I pray God such as bee faithfull may nott bee discouraged. I am sure 'tis an unspeakeable joy to mee that God has vouchsafed us such a mercy.

Sir, your most affecionate humble servant,
T. H.[a]

Caresbrooke Castle,
May 29, 1648.

[*Col. Whalley to Lord Fairfax.*]

My Lord,

The Enemy hath quitt the towne and Stratford, left their guns and ammunition behinde them. They are betwixt two and 3000 foote and 100 horse. They are marching towards Rumford. I have sent a partie of neere 300 horse and dragoones in pursuite of them, which are as many as wee conceive can doe service in these narrow wayes. I remaine with the body att present att Stratford Langton till I receive further order from Your Excellency, which I desire may be hastened to,

My Lord,
Your most humble and faithfull servant
EDW: WHALLEY.[b]

Stratford Langton.

[a] Compare with this the letter of Hammond on the same subject, May 29, 1648. *Old Parliamentary History*, xvii., 191. Is T. H. Thomas Herbert?

[b] Cf. Gardiner, *Great Civil War*, iv., 145. This letter, which is not dated, immediately follows one dated June 4, and was probably written June 5 or 6.

[*News-letter from Yorke.*]

9 June, 1648.

Our affaires heere are in a very sad and dubious state, the Enemy very active, strong and cunning. Yow have I question not heard of the taking of Pontefratt Castle, being betrayed by a sergeant and a corporall that formerly served the Enemy, who were upon the guard. The Governour Major Cottrell, having left the keyes with them att that time (which hee never did before) till hee tooke a little rest about 6 or 7 a'clock in the morning, after his watching the whole night himself as hee used to doe. Hee was a man that all men iudged faithfull, how farre he may bee guilty in this I cannot tell, but hee refused to take quarter, and was shott in the thigh and cutt in the arme, but is living and like to recover. Lieutenant Coll. Morris, who once served the Enemy and delivered up Leverpoole to us, and since served the Parliament, was the maine actor, and is now Governour. Helmsley Castle was lately attempted to bee taken in the like manner, but the fidelity of the souldier they applyed themselves to (to whome was offered 100*li.* in hand and 500*li.* more upon bond, and to bee knighted) prevented it, for hee discovered the parties and apprehended them prisoners, and now they are in the dungeon att Helmsley Castle This I can assert for trouth having examined it upon oath. Langdale is in Westmerland, and wee heare is unwilling to fight if hee can prevent it, but our forces now are in a bodey, and are upon the edge of Westmerland about Bowes, waiting an oportunity to ingage him, though fewer in number. Tis thought hee will wheele about for Pontefratt if hee can possible, and misse fighting. Pontefratt is block'd up with about 800 horse and foote,[a] which is all can possibly be made here for the present; the Enemy there increases, and are as wee heare 250 horse and 400 foote, so that that partee canot lay close seige, and if our partee there or

[a] Cf. Surtees Society, *Miscellanea*, 1860, *Journal of the Siege of Pontefract*, p. 89.

those attending on Langdale received a worst, it will so highten the King's partee in theis parts (which I think are 20 for one,) that wee shall be in danger of loosing theis parts, except the good providence of God smile on us, as it hath on you in the southerne parts.

[T. MARGETTS.]

[*Col. Whalley to Lord Fairfax.*]

My Lord,

The Enemy hath quitt Chelmesford, march't to Lees, where as soone as hee came hee had 500 armes besides ordinance without resistance. Wee marched close in the reare of him, but he doth so overpower us with foote that wee cannott ingage in this close countrey, but with greate disadvantage, to the hazard of the brigade. Wee are indeavouring a conjunction with Sir Thomas Honiwood's forces, who is reported to bee 1200 horse and foote. Itt behoves you to hasten all the foot up you can, and to come your selfe; other wayes the Enemie will be suddenly formed into a considerable army, and will engage us. I shall neede to say no more to your Excellencye, but that I am,

My Lord, Your Lordshipps most humble and faythfull servant

EDWARD WHALLEY.

Much Walton, 5 miles from Chelmsford.
June 10th 1648.

Our frendes repourt the Enemy to bee 3000 horse and foote, and like a snowball increasing.[a]

My Lord, I desire to knowe which way and when your Lordshipp comes, that I may take care to secure you; doubtles the best way is by Gravesend.

My Lord,

Since the writing and sealing of theis, I received your expresse, and shall desire your Excellencies force may march by Gravesend to Tilbury, and so to Billericay.

EDW. WHALLEY.

[a] MS. "small increase." See Fairfax Correspondence, iv., 35.

[*Col. Whalley to Lord Fairfax.*]

My Lord,

After wee had falne uppon the enemies reare the last night att Lees they marched to Braintree, as itt is conceived with an intention to sett upon Sir Tho: Honywood's forces, soe they gave out, soe wee beleived; wheruppon I imediately sent Col. Scrope with his 3 troopes to their assistance, they being very stronge in foote and desir'd onely an addition of horse. I march't in reference to the safety of Coggeshall (uppon the conjunction of your Excellencies other forces assign'd for this service) for the better interposing betwixt the rebells and London, to Wittam, where I now lie and waite uppon the enemies motion. Hee hath laine still all this day till now, being one of the clock, butt by a spye that I sent amongst them I am inform'd that they beate their drums and have drawne out a great parte of their foote to Rayne Greene, which is towards London from Chelmesford. Therfore our purpose [is] for the better securing your Excellencies forces out of Kent, to draw somethinge back; and I desire your Excellency would send to Col. Ewer to march to Chelmesford, where I shall bee this night, because just now Sir Thomas Honywood sends mee worde, if I will but spare him 2 troopes more they shall bee sufficiently stronge to defend themselves against any attempt of the enemy made against them. Wee desire your Excellency would expedite your march, for wee cannott engage them heere without more foote, and the longer they are suffer'd the more numerous they growe:

I am, My Lord,
Your Excellencies most humble
and faithfull servant,
EDW. WHALLEY.[a]

Wittam,
11 June, 1648.

[a] Cf. Gardiner, *Great Civil War*, iv., 148; Rushworth, vii., 1150.

[*Mr. Rushworth to Col. . . . .*]

Sir, The Generall desires you to send a partie of 50 or 60 Horse into Sussex to Chichester to march to Lewis; for there is a beginning of a rising, and Col. Temple is confident that this party will give life to the honest partie to make head against the rest.

J. R[USHWORTH].

[*Extract from a News-letter.*]

His Excellency hath written to the Committee at Cambridge to authorise Major Blackley (?) for commanding 300 men. The well affected Schollers in Cambridge did chuse 2 out of each College to represent the rest, which gave uppe themselves to their results and counsells, which were soe prosperous that in lesse than the space of 24 howses there was 200 fighting Schollers, suitable armes and ammunition, with provisions for a week's space. They pitcht upon the most tenable place Queens Colledge, and in a civill manner requested the Fellows thereof that they might have itt, who gave them a peremptory deniall, and secretly caused the tutors of the engaged Schollers to summon them to their severall Colledges, soe that the company was forced to breake.

Leaguer before Colchester,
17 June, 1648.

Lettre intercepted going to Sir M. L[angdale] from the Lo: Capell.

10 July, 1648.

Sir,

Wee are advertised from soe many severall parts of your being att Lincolne, that wee cannot refuse the beleefe of it, and in con sideration that itt may advance his maiestyes service, I thought itt fitt to advertise you some what [of] our condition att Colchester. Fairfax hath beene for this month engaged heere att Colchester; I presume with the considerablest force that party can make, which I beleave exceeds not 3500 foote and 1200 horse. Hee had soe ill successe in his first adventure to storme us, and [in] the last, hee hath had 5, [and] of our ffoote by divers sallies hee relishes soe ill, that his endeavour is to surround us with a line and works att some distance, in which hee haith proceded not unsouldyerly. It is to bee doubted wee may soone want fodder for our horse. Neither the Enimy nor wee are idle, yet wee heere cõceive that our tying and obliging Fairfax to us is the best way of proceding for his Majesties service; for the rest of the Kingdome have the more scope to act their parts by it, and a disaster here would lett him loose, which is the reason wee hazard not more then needs must stande with our duty and honour, considering the advantage the enimy hath of us in numbers. If this findes you according to our expectation neere Cambridge, I conceive that if you march to Walden on the border of Essex, and Fairfax his army will not neerer attend your comming, and you are att your election to march directly to us, or to goe to London, [that you should act] as shall bee most requisite for the Kinge's service; though wee should bee glad to have that advantage by your comming to us to bee releived, and more liberty to encrease our numbers; and itt is to bee doubted when wee are driven to strayt[en] the provisions our men will nott bee kept well satisfied. By this much I doubt not but you will judge of our condition. Sir, I rest your most humble servant,

ARTHUR CAPEL.

July 10.
Colchester.

[*Extract from a News-letter to Lord Fairfax.*]

Your Excellency's answer to the letter of the House concerning the Earle of Holland gave much distaste to some, who moved that your Excellency's commission might bee taken from you; but this not carried, the House of Lords debated neere two houres this day for a generall cessation, butt laid aside for the present, butt will bee insisted on againe tomorrow, and then itt's thought will bee carried, and itt's feared the Commons will comply. The Citties listing goes on this day more violent than ever before. The Lord direct your Excellency for some speedy course in reducing Colchester, which done the rage of the enemies would cease, and till then much increase. . . . . Thinges are high, the designe will bee speedily putt in execution, if not prevented by a blow att Colchester or the North. I have writt to the Lieutenant-Generall by advice of some members to engage upon any condition speedily, else the Houses will vote an approbation of the coming in of the Scots Army.

London, 16 Aug. 1648.

Lettre from the Townesmen to his Excellency sent by Doctor Glissen.

Right honourable,

Wee returne your Lordshippe our most humble thankes for your Lordshippes lettres in answer of our petition, and for your condescention soe farre in granting of our desires; butt soe itt is that the Commanders in chief heere having bin made acquainted with the contents of the letters, they have absolutely declar'd their deniall in granting liberty to the Committee heere under restraint to passe hence, and have this day passed an order of their Councell of warre, that all such inhabitants within this towne as have noe provisions for the maintenance of themselves and families for 20 dayes to come are to depart the towne tomorrow in the forenoone, and have caused warrants to bee issued out to the respective constables of each parish to give notice of such their order. Your Lordshippe well knowes that itt is nott within the compasse of our power to inlarge those of the Committee kept heere; and therfore in the behalf of the inhabitants wee humbly renew our former petition to your Lordshippe, that you would be pleased (notwithstanding such the deniall of the Lords and other commanders heere) to grant your Honours lettres of libertie of all such as are nott excepted in your Lordshippes lettre to passe into the country for the preservation of their lives; and soe commending your Lordshippe with the issue of this businesse to God Almighty wee humbly take our leaves.

Your Lordshippes humble servants
William Cooke Major.
Robert Buxton.
John Furleigh.
John Shaw.

Colchester,
Aug. 21, 1648.

Postscript.

Your Lordshippe may perceive that this lettre was intended to have bin sent yesterday, butt wee could nott with convenience, and the commanders heere have now given licence for the sending itt by Doctor Glissen, and att the request of our selves and the Committee heere have respited the putting of their order in execution for turning out the poore people.

For the right honourable Thomas Lord Fairfax his Excellency these humbly present.[a]

An account of the death of Sir Charles Lucas &c., the originall of which, writt with my owne Fathers' hand, I gave Sir Thomas Clarges.

Colchester, 28 August, 1648. Sir Charles Lucas speech att his first comeing into the Castle yard.

There may be something that I may vindicate my self in. In order to my duty, I came to this place in the Prince's service, but

[a] Cf. Gardiner, *Great Civil War*, iv., 200; Rushworth, vii, 1235.

since I came hither, I am not guilty of wronging the least person the least soldier of this army.

God knowes I never intended my owne particular in my life, and if God Almighty had pleas'd as for my sins I doe justly deserve death, but for this God Almighty is the best judge ; yet I should have been very glad, that those [a] people that made themselves my judges had been pleas'd to have allow'd mee a longer time of repentance, for the best of us all hath not liv'd such a life but he does deserve a longer time of repentance then I have now.

Minister.

If it be true, it is as acceptable.

Sir Charles.

My sins are many, and Gods mercies are great that I doe expect.

All those that have either kindnesse for the King, or so much conscience for themselves, I shall desire that they would be pleased to let me have their prayers. For what God hath bestow'd upon mee in this life, I praise him, and pray for his mercy upon mee after this life. I doe not professe my self a rhetorician att all. I doe not know how it may be construed, but in the first place, I wish I could have liv'd longer, to have serv'd my Prince and my country, or at least [had] a larger time of repentance. But [since it] hath pleas'd . . . . to allow mee the means to receive the Sacrament, God make mee a worthy receiver, to my salvation, not my damnation ; and so God blesse you all, and send you peace and happinesse in the Kingdome.

Sir Bernard Gascoyne.

I would very faine take my leave of Sir Charles Lucas, for I care not how soon, when it shall please those God hath made my judges——

Sir Charles.

Farewell, Sir Bernard.

They embrace and kisse.

[a] M.S. "more."

Sir Charles.

I confesse the great obligation our country owes to you, for your service to our Prince.

Sir Bernard.

It is a very great consolation to mee for to die with such a companion. I did no man any hurt.

Sir Charles.

[To the minister.] If you have the means to see his Majestie present my duty to him, he is my Prince and Master. Bid my parents and friends they should not afflict themselves. Truly I think it is a great deal of happinesse to mee [to die thus]. God might have taken mee away without such a sense of my sins. They know my genius would not let mee die upon any base thing; bid them blesse God, that I die so happy for the service of my country, as I beleive I have, and have the honour of it.

[To the officers] What is the death that is pleas'd to be assign'd to my self and these worthy gentlemen? doe you know by what means?

Captain Packer.

That which is most proper to soldiers, to be shot.

Sir Charles.

With all my heart, shoote mee out of a cannon when they please.

To his Kinsman.

Present my duty to my father.

He and the minister retire aside and pray against the Castle wall.

Sir Charles.

Come, my heart, I need not cheer you up, I know your chearfulnesse by my owne, but here is my amends, I die for my Prince, and you die not soe.

Sir Bernard.

I thank God, I doe not fear death.

Sir Charles.

I will not say I do not apprehend death, but I can look him in the face now.

Sir Bernard.

I wish to die, and repent of my sins.

Sir Charles.

You have God's word for it, if I may speak a divines part in it, [that] at what time [soever] a sinner does repent. . . .

Minister.

Hee that repents truely and properly.

Sir Bernard.

I could say so, wheras you repent: from the bottom of my heart I have not found so sorrowfull as it need to bee.

Sir George Lisle.

Better late than never. Though I don't beleive in predestination, yet I beleive it is God's will, and truly I should have thought myself a happy person, if I could live to have a larger time of repentance, and to see the King my master in his throne again, whom I beseech God to send to all the happinesse which is due to so just, so good a man.

I was bid to goe my way, say divers people; but truely I was confident my innocencie in this action would have rendred mee very clear from any such punishment, especially so suddenly.

Sir Bernard.

My conscience is guilty of many things, but nothing this way.

I say that I have never in my life done any action which I will not acknowledge before all the world.

Sir George.

He will that his body remaine with my servant.

I will bear it with as much patience as I can, I should take it for a very great favour done to my poor soul to have a little more time, I have deserv'd it as much as an enemy can doe.

Sir Charles.

I should very willingly hear, if you would please to satisfy mee, by whom I am condemned, whether by my Lord Fairfax alone, or by a Councell of Warr; I beseech you to lett me know my judge.

Com̃. Ireton.

I may answer so far, as you were condemned by the Parliament, upon your owne actions. [The war] wherein you have so voluntarily a second time engaged, hath rendred you in their judgement in generall your whole party deserving death, and your self is in some particular exception.

Sir Charles.

Pray Gentlemen bee pleas'd to give a dyeing man leave to speak, I beseech you.

Com̃. Ireton.

Know, your self as all others that engage a second time against the Parliament are traitors and rebells, and they doe employ us as soldiers by authority from them to suppresse and destroy. Would you know our commission, itt's that. Sir, you were here in armes, (the head), one of the heads of a great party; you have not yet had quarter given, not any of those gentlemen yonder, but by the Generall's demands of you, and by your commissioners consent to it, you were to render your selves att mercy; and for yourself you can't but know, because your commissioner came in to acquaint you with it, that by mercy it was meant to be free in the Generall's breast, without any obligation to the contrary, to put some of you to the sword, if he saw cause. Now as to any matter of judgement; neither the Generall nor any censure of the Councill hath pass'd in this businesse; the judgement hath been in generall pronounced by the Parliament, for whom wee fight, and you being persons in hostility, that yet have had no assurance of quarter, for you it is only thus far resolv'd by the Generall, by the advice of the Councill of war in generall upon the businesse.

Sir Charles.

Sir, this is a very nice point to take away a man's life, when there is a law in the Kingdome, which truely I must plead; and look to it [lest] my blood be upon you. I doe plead before you all the lawes of this Kingdome. I have fought with a commission from those who were my soveraignes, and from that commission I must justifie my action. For yeilding to mercy, wee must needs yeild to those in whose power we were then. I must starve or yeild. That yeilding of ours, all the world knows, was meer constraint.

Com̃. Ireton.

Wee take it for no other.

Sir Charles.

If wee yeild ourselves unto you, if it be for our lives you should try us.

Com̃. Ireton.

If wee had taken it for any other then what you had voluntarily done upon confidence of the Generall's mercy.

Sir George.

I am confident I did it upon that ground.

Com̃ Ireton.

But now it is by constraint, and no otherwise. I did speak that that you may yet know there was no assurance of quarter given to any of you, and the Generall did expressly declare that he would be free to it.

Sir George.

Gentlemen, lay your hands seriously upon your breasts, you that were of the Council of Warr, and consider what it is to take away a man's life in this kind, that you may have nothing to rise against you hereafter.

Com̃. Ireton.

Sir, wee have nothing more to add to that. But to what you said before: you know it is a certaine rule, that among armes the lawes are silent, and had not you by armes stopt the lawes of the land, you and other men might have had the justice of the lawes of the land; but you and others, by pretence of the lawes of the land, have stopt the current of judgement and law which wee had. When you are mett in armes there is no more reason for you to plead it now then there hath been to many soldiers and officers of the Parliaments party, when they have mett some under your command, if they had pleaded the lawes of the land against them.

Sir Charles.

It was never knowne that men were kill'd in cold blood, before.

Collonel Whalley.

Sir, shall I answer you for that. You have given us a president before, where there was Major Wandstead [a] and about forty more, they submitted to mercy, and they hang'd up 14 of them.

Ensigne ———

May it please your Honour I will satisfy you.

Sir Charles.

If the Generall pleases, a man may be mercifull, and satisfy both his mercy, and the world besides, and justice. I doe here beseech the Generall that he will be pleased to looke upon mee in that nature as I am in his power, that he will excuse mee with my life, if I can but obtaine the General's mercy and favour [to me] and these gentlemen; and if it be not, God's will be done, I must submitt to it.

Com̃ Ireton.

I have no more to say to you, nor is there any other judgment that wee have received from the Generall, but you being persons who being in armes and hostility against the Parliament, he may as justly kill and give no quarter to you as ever any was in this warr. He having given you no assurance of quarter nor any of you, has only determined to yourselves in particular, that you are not in the compasse of quarter. Tis no more then if the soldiers mett you and shot you.

Sir Charles.

I am within the lawes of the Kingdome, for what I did is by commission, and quarter hath been given as the lawes of armes doth require elsewhere.

[a] Major Wansey and the garrison of Woodhouse in Wiltshire are referred to. Fourteen of the garrison were hanged by Sir Francis Dodington's orders, two by himself and twelve by Sir William St. Leger. Ludlow, *Memoirs*, i., 103.

Com̃ Ireton.

Sir, you are better acquainted with the lawes of armes. Is any body bound to give quarter where it is ask'd?

Two of the soldiers sayd, that at St[a] he came in rageing, and swore a great oath, 'why should they have any more quarter, then wee had at Cannon-Froome.'[b]

Com̃ Ireton.

You being a traitor——

Sir Charles.

I am no traitor, but a true subject to my King, and the lawes of the Kingdome. Sir, you ought to prove mee one, before you condemne mee to be a traitor.

Com̃ Ireton.

Wee tell you what judgement you are concluded by, and that is by the judgement of the Parliament.

Sir Charles.

I can say no more. I shall only desire that my life may satisfy for all the rest of these gentlemen, and these gentlemen may goe free.

Sir George.

I have given many hundred men quarter.

Sir Charles.

Give mee leave to pray with these gentlemen.

Retires with Sir George Lisle and Sir Bernard Gascoigne.

Gentlemen, I now die like a soldier, will you that these gentlemen shall looke upon mee?

They embrace and kisse.

[a] This word is unfinished. Probably Stinchcombe in Gloucestershire, a small parliamentary garrison near Berkeley Castle, taken by the troops of Rupert and Sir Charles Lucas in Aug., 1645. Twenty, or according to some stories forty, of the garrison are said to have been put to the sword in cold blood. Webb, *Civil War in Herefordshire*, ii., 214. *Report on the Portland MSS.*, i., 250.

[b] Stormed by the Scots in July, 1645. Vicars, *Burning Bush*, p. 203; Webb, *Civil War in Herefordshire*, ii. 378.

Sir Charles.

Remember mee to all my friends.

Sir Bernard.

I thank God I am no more troubled at it.

Sir Charles.

Remember me to all my friends, and tell them that I have died in a good cause; if I have offended any, I desire forgivenesse; I would have a decent buriall, and that I might be buried by my ancestours, and where they are. Their monuments are not only defac't, but their dead bodies remov'd.[a] Let us from henceforth lye in quiet.

Give mee leave to pray but a few words, and now I have done.

I pray God forgive you all, I pray God forgive you, gentlemen. Farewell, I pray God vengeance may not fall on you for it.

When I shall [fall] lay mee downe decently

One goeing to pull downe his cap, he said, stay a little.

Oh Father, Son, and Holy Ghost, receive my soule.

After this six dragoones with fire locks discharg'd att him; and after his falling, Sir George Lisle, having kissed him, was also shot to death.

[*The Earl of Warwick to the Derby House Committee.*]

My Lord and Gentlemen,

On Sabbath day last in the evening the fleete weighed from the Downes, and yesterday morning wee came to anchor off Goree, where calling a Councill of Warre, and finding the winde faire and the weather calme, wee resolved to goe into the harbour, and about 3 in the afternoone anchored off Gor[ee] towne. The revolted shippes about 13 in number being att anchor within 2 leagues of us off Helvoyett sluice, shortly after our coming to anchor wee

[a] See *Mercurius Rusticus*, No. 1; Carter, pp. 167, 234.

resolved on a summons, to the revolters, requiring amonge other thinges the taking downe of their standard, and contayning an offer of indempnity uppon the rendring of their shippes,[a] which I sent to the Admirall by a servant of my owne, who found aboard her Capt. Batten, Sir Henry Palmer, Capt. Jordan, Mr. Hamond, Capt. Bargrave, Capt. Fogge, and some others; to whome reading my message they declar'd, they bore the Standard by command, and in right of the Prince his Highnesse; without command from whence, or from his Majesty, they would nott take itt downe; butt gave noe reply to that of indempnity. My servant desiring their answer in writing they determined of Mr. Hamond to draw itt, who intimating unto them, that itt would bee fitt first to have some conference together, they did after a little retirement resolve of this answer: that the matter concern'd the Prince, that without communicating the paper to his Highnesse they could give noe positive answer, that they would send itt him early this morning (supposing itt would meete him uppon the way). They expected him to day aboard, and that this day I expect an answer with which my servant returnes. As yett I have nott heard further from the fleete, which when I doe I shall give your Lordshippes a further account of my message, and of the answer I shall theruppon receive. Last night and this day the weather hath bin very stormy, soe that our shippes could hardly correspond one with another, nor can wee as yett have any certaine intelligence of the revolters condition; what opportunities may bee taken for the publique service shall be faithfully improved, which is all I shall now trouble you with.

Your Lordshippes &c.
WARWICK.

Aboard the St. George riding att
Anchor off Goree, this 20th September, 1648.

[a] For a copy of Warwick's summons to the revolted ships and their answer see *Old Parliamentary History*, xvii., 496.

[*A Letter from Dr. Dorislaus.*]

My Lord

Uppon Tuesday night all the bloud-royall being att a play together about ten a clock att night, a boatswaine came with Sir John Minch,[a] and brought good newes from the Navy; being asked what good newes, hee said, Warwick was come with 20 shippes into Goree. The Prince of Wales asking agen, how hee could make this good newes, replyed, 'Because Warwick is come in to your Highnes, and to joyne his shippes with yours.' Itt caused a mighty discomposure in their merriment, and the rest of the night was spent in councill. Divers of their shippes are in the dock, or ashoare careening and the ordinance ashoare. The men in a mutinous disposition, disperst through all the neighbouring townes as farre as Roterdam riotting and drinking. In the morning itt was ordered, that the Prince of Wales' coach should bee ready by 6 a clock to goe for Helvoyett sluice, yett itt was one of the clock in the afternoone before hee went; with him went all that belonge to the partie, leaving a man scarce behinde in the Hague; and for to appease the wrath of the mariners which was especially fierce against Culpepper, for keeping from them (as they say) the money proceeding from their prizes, 4 small barrells of monie were carried alonge in their waggons. Some 3 or 4 houres after his Highnesse departure, the Prince of Orange and the Princesse Dowager came to the Hague. In the evening I spake with some of the States of Holland, to desire the same civilities towards the Lord Admirall of England which were showne to the Prince of Wales. They answer'd, they would keepe the neutrality, and afford equall respect to both parties, butt withall expect peacefull behaviour on all sides within their harbour.

In the morning Sir William Boswell gave in the paper in the Assembly of the States Generall, and the resolution was taken by

[a] *i.e.* "Mennes."

the States to send commissioners for to declare unto both parties the old resolution of neutrality taken A° 1643, and to charge them to keepe the peace within the States dominions; somewhat was afterward proposed about communicating with the Earle of Warwick the States inclination to mediate for peace in England att the time of the Treaty. I finde the partie itt self, and all their adherents in this nation full of despaire, giving this Navy utterly for lost, although for the present they may gett the mariners quiett againe by distributing of mony &c., and which concerneth the publique most, the reputation of England is fully secured in this Nation by their powerfull appearing att sea, and keeping now under a lock those haughty men which would brave the Kingdome butt a few dayes before. Since the Royall partie hath nott any other hope butt uppon the Treatie, uppon which they build great vast projects againe, and that soe the Kinge come butt in once they shall doe well enough, and since the Dutch adheering to that partie have soe great a desire to bee lett in agen into that mediatourshippe, your Lordshippes will doubtlesse [take] that course that the old censure of Philipp de Comines may nott bee laid to this age, 'That what was gott in a dozen yeares fighting was lost in 6 dayes treating.'

Your Lordshippes, &c.,

DORISLAUS.

Hague
21 September, 1648.

[*News-letter from Scotland.*]

Edinburgh, October 17, 1648.

The Committee of Estates have bin imployed for the most parte of this weeke uppon their forces, which they have now resolved shall bee onely 1,500 foote and 600 horse, the West being sure to them, the South under our reverence from Barwick and Carlile, and that force conceived sufficient att present to garrison and quiett the North and East. Other reasons indeed there are why they keepe uppe noe more, for they found the last army they so much stickled to keepe on foote to bee their greatest prejudice when an hower of temptation came, they turning head against them; they now finde much pressing to bringe in officers who (though without palpable exception) are nott throughly to bee confided in, and I beleive there is an eye of reflection, and the best ground of confidence is helpe from England, if there bee occasion. They have delayed J. R. (who brought the Kinges lettre) untill the Treaty bee near[a] towards an end; and though the lettre was intended to the malignant Committee of Estates, they that by providence are now invested in that power returning an answer, complayning of the miseries suffer'd by the late Engagement, declare how they are forced to rise in armes, what are the consequences of itt, and what their resolutions are since, for which they referre the Kinge to their agreement with Lanerick and their late declaration; and in conclusion they press[b] his Majesty att last to hearken to the advice of his Parliaments, in consenting to the propositions of both Kingdomes, and especially to those concerning the Covenant and Reformation of religion, which they finde to bee the points hee sticks att, and they in honour and interest are most obliged to stick to, and without which (they tell him) his throne cannott bee established in righteousnesse. They have alsoe writt to the Prince dehorting him from that course of opposition hee is in, and from attempting any acts of hostility against this Kingdome, butt the rather since all worldly policie and projects have failed, hee would apply his indeavour to mediate with his father to consent to the propositions of both Kingdomes, and especially the Covenant &c. (as before). Sir John Cheisley, who is this day on his way to London, is to communicate these to the Houses; then they are to bee sent, and with them two schooling lettres from the Assembly, and Commissioners of the Kirke, who can speake more plainly in the name of their master then the state can doe in their owne.

There is an additionall instruction for reparation of all losses of

[a] MS. "now." [b] MS. "promise."

horses, clothes or mony taken from our partie, bee made out of the estates of those that were in the late Engagement, and have nott consented or come in to the late agreement; and those that were intrusted to see itt done are uppon laying on the estates of Lanerke and Lauderdaile 100li a piece, which will pay all scores of that kinde if mony can bee had.

George Monroe, Coll. Diell, Coll. John Hamilton, and other desperadoes are yesterday and this day gone over the water into Fyff, where Crauford, Lanerke, Dury and other ringleaders of that partie were before. They give out itt is onely for a drinking bout att parting, Monroe and Hamilton having received passes from Generall Leven to goe to Sweden, butt knowing men apprehend some new mischief is brewing concurrent with some designe yett in reserve for the Kinge of England, and therfore the old Highland Regiment of Argyll's are speeded to Sterling, and some horse to St. Johnston's; and as all malignant designes will bee watched and opposed heere, soe itt's the wish and hearty prayer of many honest men, even of qualitie in this Kingdome, that they may bee soe there; and they particularly hope that your Excellency and your army will still bee instrumentall therin.

W. R.

The well-affected Lords and others desire that a strict hand may bee held over the great ones of this nation prisoners in England, having cause of jealousie that they will bee working some mischeife.[a]

[a] This letter is certainly from William Rowe. It is summarised in Rushworth, vii., 1304. William Rowe was in 1650 Scoutmaster-General, and evidently held that post (or some similar post) in the English army in Scotland in Oct., 1648. In the New Model the place had been held by Leonard Watson, who had now left the army. George Downing seems to have succeeded Rowe as Scoutmaster-General. Many of Rowe's letters of intelligence are amongst the *Letters and Papers of State addressed to Oliver Cromwell*, which were published by John Nickolls in 1743.

[*News-letter from Scotland.*]

Seaton, 24 October, 1648.

Our cheifest worke heere is to keepe downe the rising and tumultous humoures of the malignant partee, that the Committee of Estates may act securely till their forces be compleated, and 'tis conceved they will keepe us heere starving the most part of this winter till their Parliament sitt, which will not bee before Januery next.

Heere is one misery: wee stay to preserve a generation of men who call themselves the well-affected partee, till they seate and settle themselves, and their owne ends and interest, but doe feare it will be heere, as it hath been in other Kingdomes (and is the great politique fashion) the pulling downe of one power and partie by our countenance, and the setting up of another that may be as bad or worse then the other. This is our hope: that partee that is now downe wee are sure was [not] good, this for (ought wee know) may bee good; Providence may bring thinges about beyond our feares, thoughts, expectations; what ever the issue be, this is our comfort, wee are in the prosecution of our duty in love and peace.

Time lately was that the great expectation was out of the North. God did great thinges there by a fewe, even to admiration; the scene is now alterd, and the great expectation is now upon the Treaty.

The generall evill designe is the same still, and is acted in the latter by the same principles, though not by the same persons as the former; and though I canot well give iudgment of the presentt premises there at this distance, yet in the generall I am confidente that hee that overcame that great power of the common visible enemy in the feild, will alsoe bring to nought the great policy of those secret enemies in Insula Vectis. The mistery of iniquity is now discovering, tumults rising, feares &c. appeares, but hee is securd that sees God in every thinge. A man may guesse the temper of this Kingdome by the temper of the Clergy, who are the ringleaders, ductores et seductores, they are the supreame power both ecclesiasticall and civill, their height of glory is but fleshly, formall; cheifly of a double intrest, Presbiteriall and royall, and these pretty equally mixt, and for ought I perceive were wee gonne there would be another tugg who should be the greater, little striving who shall bee the better; formality in the one is little better than royalty in the other. I see butt little knowledge in the mistery of godliness, tis all confined to a forme and that called jure divino; and those that live above that forme are as great enemies as those that live belowe it, for they are iudged to bee equally evill, though in a different sence, because they sitt not upon that forme. If there be a composure called happy, that happines for ought I knowe either will be (or will be endeavoured to be) confined and have its center onely in that forme, which will certainly will be cryed up by the Clergy of both Kingdomes, that is their interest; and the slavish, ignorant people will as certainly make it their conscience to observe their lawes, though it be to their owne losse and mischeiff. England I think, are more above this forme then Scotland, perhaps our being in the schoole with them, and having had a little better learning, may iussle them up a little higher, and by degrees they may take out a new lesson and advance. When once the light brakes forth in this Kingdome, (and I thinke the sunne is neare rising) it will warme and heale apace, butt the cloudes must be broken first, the foundation of this ould fabrick must be shaken; and when the poore, blind, dead people shall see the light and feel the warmth of the sun (sweete liberty) to redeeme them out of their present slavery, then the strugglings of Scotland wilbe as great as those of England, which hath overcome a few of those, but not yet gotten to the top of its glory.[a]

[a] Part of this letter is printed in "The Moderate" for Oct. 31, Nov. 7, which has furnished me with one or two small corrections of the Clarke MS. copy. The Report on Lord Braye's MSS. (Hist. MSS. Comm. 10th Report, pt. vi, pp. 168-173) contains a series of letters written by Thomas Margetts to John Browne, Esq., Clerk of the Parliament, which help to complete those amongst the Clarke Papers. They are dated: Brancepeth, Sept. 14, 1648; Belford, Sept. 20;

[*News-letter from Scotland.*]

Edinburgh, 24° October, 1648.

In a late Declaration about the Covenant published heere (in the enumeration of errors and heresies) Independency is left out, which in former Declarations and papers alwayes brought uppe the reare. There is alsoe a printed Act for the leavies of their new modell (as they owne itt by that very name) in which there are severall observable thinges, for. 1. They lay all the whole charge and burthen uppon the Malignants, and exempt the well affected; 2. They trust the command to a number of new modell'd officers the most confiding they can picke out; 3. They lay out the best way their present constitution will admitt for the getting the honestest of the cominaltie for their souldiers; and for manage of publique affaires in the country they have new modell'd all Committees. By another Act they have discharged the Earle of Crawford Lyndsay, and all other officers belonging to the Treasury or Exchequer, from medling with the Kinges rents or the Exchequer affaires, and have appointed a Committee to manage the same.

On Friday last October 20, Sir James Stuart, Lord Provost of this Citty, warned all the Burgers therof to a Generall Convention, att which betweene 2000 and 3000 mett in a great roome by the Parliament House. After some preface to them hee desired them to joyne in prayer with him, and hee prayed; after which hee made a longe speech referring principally to the late Engagement of the loane of 40,000*lb.* Scotts (which is about 3000*lb.* sterling), which they without the consent or privity of the generallity of the Citty had furnished amonge themselves, and when Argyll's partie came

Mordington, Sept. 26; Seaton, Oct. 3; Dalkeith, Oct. 10; Seaton, Oct. 17; Broxmouth, Nov. 1. The letter of Oct. 17, summarised in the Report, is printed in full in Rushworth, vii., 1305, but wrongly dated. The letter printed above is obviously also from Margetts. He was attached to Lambert throughout the campaign, and Lambert was now remaining in Scotland to protect the establishment of the new government.

in they were leavying the same (for their reimbursement) uppon the Citty; uppon which account[a] hee requir'd that all who were privy or consenting, or that were for the same Engagement, should withdrawe, and they had then a free libertie to goe out, and all that had bin, or that now were against that sinfull engagement should stay. Nott a man going out, hee againe prayed with them, and after tooke every man's name, man by man as they went out, hee havinge guards, that suffer'd butt one att a time to passe by him and the bayliffs as they satt in the gate; this hath nott onely, putt all the loane monie uppon the Malignant Magistrates' shoulders, and freed the Citty of soe much charge, butt appearingly hath united them against the Malignant partie in further order, who run to. . . . . The former Clarke of the Citty (whose influence and power heere is nott inferiour to a Recorder of a Citty in England) is alsoe putt out, and Mr. Andrew Ker, Clerke to the Commission of the Kirke chosen in his roome.

Two ministers from the Presbytery and two officers from the souldiers of the Scottish Nation in the Province of Ulster came lately, instructed to move and presse some thinges there in order to the renewing of their interest as well in the townes they had by treatie and district garrisons (independant from Col: Monck) as[b] in the sole administration of Ecclesiasticall Government in that province; butt being by one or two of greatest power heere disswaded from itt, partly uppon the ground, that Ireland was indeed England's sole interest, and partly of unseasonablenesse, (att present att least) they are this day returned to Ireland, without soe much as proposing in publique anythinge concerning the same.

The Committee of Estates are now considering of the time for the Parliament's sitting downe, whiche they thinke to appoint about the middle of December, within a day or two after the time sett downe for renewing the Covenant, that after the recent impression thereof thinges may goe on the more cordiall and

[a] MS. "Act."

[b] MS. "butt."

orderly ; which in all probability they may, the best affected that could bee pick't out in all the quarters of the country being chosen [to] this next Parliament.

Lanerk is att Glencairne's house in the West Country; there is noe certainty of any number yett uppe in the North, though Malignants bragge soe.

Att a full meeting of the Committee of Estates this day [to] the number of above 60 persons, the papers and proceedings, from the first sending to Lieutenant Generall Cromwell to this day, were read and approved.

W[ILLIAM] R[OWE].

(*Cromwell to Col. Robert Hammond.*[a])

Dear Robin. Knottingley Novem[br] 6, 1648.

I trust the same spirit that guided thee heertofore, is still wth thee; looke to thy hearte, thou art where temptations multiply. I

[a] A copy of this letter is contained in vol. xvi. of the *Clarke Papers* at Worcester College, where it is signed "Heron Brother," and no indication is given of the person to whom it was sent. I concluded it from internal evidence to be written by Cromwell to Robert Hammond. Some letters from Cromwell to Hammond were mentioned in the Report of the first Historical MSS. Commission, p. 116, as being in the possession of the Marquis of Lothian. Mr. Gardiner at my request examined these letters last summer, and has kindly supplied me with copies of them. Two are now printed in the Preface. The third was identical with the letter in vol. xvi. of the *Clarke Papers*, but as the copy in the Newbattle MSS. gave an obviously better text I have printed it here in place of the copy given by Clarke. Differences between the two versions, simple variations in the spelling and punctuation excepted, are marked in the notes. The Newbattle version seems to me to be a copy also, and not an original. Compare with this letter Cromwell's letter of Nov. 25, 1648, to Hammond, letter lxxxv. in Carlyle's collection. Carlyle assumes the latter to have been written from "Knottingley near Pontefract," where the letter printed here was written. "Dear Robin" is

feare least our freinds should burne their fingers, as some others did not long since, whose hearts have aked since for it. Howe easy is it to finde arguments for what wee would have; how easy to take offence at things called Levellers, and run into an extremity on the other hand, medling with an accursed thing.[a] Peace is only good when wee receave it out of our father's hand, its dangerous to snatch it, most dangerous to goe against the will of God to attayne it. Warre is good when lead to by o[r] father, most evill when it comes from the lusts that are in our members. Wee waite upon the Lord, who will teach us and leade us whether to doing or suffering.[b] Tell my brother Herne I smyled at his expression concerning my wise freinds opinion, who thinks y[t] the inthroneing

the term by which Cromwell, Ireton, and other intimate friends usually address Hammond. In this letter Cromwell also makes use of the names which he sometimes employed in his correspondence with Vane and one or two others. "Brother Heron" is the younger Vane. "Brother Fountayne" is Cromwell himself. (See Nickolls, *Original Letters and Papers addressed to Oliver Cromwell*, 1743, pp. 78, 84). "Sir Roger" seems to have been one of Cromwell's companions in Scotland, possibly Lambert or Hesilrige. Hesilrige and Cromwell had just been entertained at Edinburgh by the Argyle party (see Whitelock, *Memorials*, ed. 1853, ii., 422, 432). Cromwell defends himself against the charge of granting too favourable terms to the Scots, or as he puts it "turning Presbyterian." The "wise friend" is probably Pierrepont, as Mr. Gardiner suggests. Pierrepont and Vane were both now at Newport, as two of the Commissioners sent by Parliament to negotiate with the King. Both were probably in daily intercourse with Hammond. "It appears from this letter," writes Mr. Gardiner, "that Cromwell had heard that a party amongst the Independents, including Vane, Pierrepont, and Hammond, in their alarm at the thorough-going reforms demanded by the Levellers, were anxious to come to an understanding with the King on the basis of moderate episcopacy and toleration. It was to this state of opinion that he now addressed himself. (*Great Civil War*, iv. 248.)

[a] Compare the letter of Nov. 25. "Dost thou not think this fear of the Levellers (of whom there is no fear) 'that they would destroy nobility,' has caused some to take up corruption, and find it lawful to make this ruining hypocritical agreement? Hath not this biassed even some good men?"

[b] Compare letter II. in Carlyle's collection: "If here I may honour my God, either by doing or suffering, I shall be most glad."

the King wth presbitery brings spirituall slavery, but wth a moderate episcopacy workes a good peace. Both are a hard choice. I trust ther's no necessity of either except, o[r] base unbeliefe and fleshly wisdome make it so; but if I have any logick it will be easier to tirañize haveing that he[a] likes and serves his turn, then what you knowe and all beleeve hee so much dislikes. But as to my brother himselfe, tell him indeede I thinke some of my freinds have advanced too farre, and neede make an hono[ble] retreate, Scotts treaties haveing wrought some perplexities; and hindering matters from going so glyb as otherwise was hoped, especially taking in some doubts that S[r] Roger and brother Fountayne are also turned Presbiterians. Deare Robin, tell brother Herne that wee have the witnesse of o[r] consciences that wee have walked in this thing (whatsoever surmizes are to the contrary) in plainnesse and godly simplicity, according to o[r] weake measure, and wee trust o[r] daily[b] businesse is to approve o[r] consciences to Godward, and not to shift and sharke,[c] w[ch] were exceeding basenesse in us to do, haveing had such favo[r] from the Lord, and such manifestations of his p[r]sence, and I hope the same experience will keepe their[d] hearts and hands from him, against whome God hath so witnessed,[e] though reason should suggest things never so plausible. I pray thee tell my Bro: Herne thus much from mee; and if a mistake concerning our complyance w[th] presbitery perplex an evill businesse (for so I accompt it), and make the wheeles of such a chariott goe heavy, I can be passive and lett it goe, knowing that inocency and integrity looses nothing by a pacient waiting upon the Lord. Our papers are publique; let us be judged by them. Answers[f] do not

[a] "He," *i.e.* the King.

[b] "Day of businesse," Clarke MS.

[c] I should suggest "shirke" instead of "sharke."

[d] "thy heart," Clarke MS.

[e] The King; compare the letter of Nov. 25. "This man against whom the Lord hath witnessed."

[f] "Answers," *i.e.* the answers made by the Scots to Cromwell's declarations. "Cromwell," suggests Mr. Gardiner, perhaps refers to the answer made by the Committee of Estates on Oct 6, in which they speak of "these covenanted kingdoms."

involve us. I professe to thee I desire from my heart, I have prayed for it, I have waited for the day to see union and right understanding between the godley people (Scotts, English, Jewes, Gentiles, Presb^{ns}, Independents, Anabaptists, and all). Our Br^{s} of Scotland (really Presbiterians [a]) were our greatest enemies. God hath iustified us in their sight, caused us to requite good for evil, caused them to acknowledge it publiquely by acts of state, and privately, and the thing is true in the sight of the sunne. It is an high conviction upon them. Was it not fitt to be civell, to professe love, to deale with cleernesse wth them for removeing of preiudice, to aske them what they had against us, and to give them an honest answere? This wee have don, and not [b] more. And heerin is a more glorious worke in our eyes then if wee had gotten the sacking and plunder of Edinb^{r}, the strong Castles into o^{r} hands, and made conquest [c] from Tweed to the Orcades; and wee can say, through God wee have left by the grace of God such a witnesse amongest them, as if it worke not yet [d] there is that conviction upon them that will undoubtedly bear its fruit in due time. Tell my bro: Herne, I beleeve my wise friend would have had a conquest, or if not, things put in a ballance; [e] the first was not very unfeazible, but I thinke not Christian, and I was commanded the contrary by the two houses; as for the later by the providence of God it is perfectly come to passe, not by our wisdome, for I durst not designe it, I durst not admitt of so mixed, so lowe a consideration, wee were lead out (to the praise of o^{r} God be it spoken) to more sincere, more spirituall considerations; but I said before the Lord hath brought it to a ballance; if there be any dangerous disproportion it is that the

[a] "Our brothers of Scotland really presbyterians," *i.e.* not men like the Presbyterian leaders in England professing Presbyterianism for a political purpose.

[b] "and noe more." Clarke MS.

[c] "made a conquest." Clarke M S.

[d] "as if it worke not yet (by reason the poore soules are soe wedded to their governement) yett their is that conviction," etc. Clarke MS.

[e] *i.e.* A mixed government established in which the Argyle and Hamilton parties would counterbalance each other.

honest party (if I may w^th^out offence so call them) in my apprehension are the weaker, and have manifold difficulties to conflict w^th^all, I wish our unworthynesse heere cast not the scale both there, and heere the wrong way. I have but one word more to say. Thy freinds, deare Robin, are in heart and in profession what they were, have not dissembled their principles at all. Are they not a little justified in this, that a lesser p^ty^ of a Parliament hath made it lawfull to declare the greater part a faction, and made[a] the Parliament null, and call a newe one, and to do this by force, and this by the same mouths y^t^ condemned it in others. Thinke of the example and of the consequence, and lett others thinke of it too, if they bee not drenched too deepe in their one[b] reason and opinions. Robin, be honest still. God keepe thee in the midest of snares. Thou has naturally a valiant spirit. Listen to God, and hee shall encrease it upon thee, and make thee valiant for the truth. I am a poore creature that write to thee, the poorest in the worke,[c] but I have hope in God, and desire from my heart to love his people, and if thou hast opportunity and a free heart, lett me heere from thee howe it is wth thee. This bearer is faithfull, you may be very free to communicate wth him; my service to all my freinds, and to my deare brother Herne whome I love in the Lord, I rest.

Thy true & faithfull friend

Herons brother.[d]

(Addressed) For the ho^ble^ Collonell Robert Hammond Governo^r^ of the Isle of Wight.

(Endorsed in another hand) 9^br^ 6^n^ 1648.

A letter from L. G. C.

(Lower down) Cromwell lost (?) letters.

[a] "and made a parliment null and called a new one." Clarke MS.

[b] "if thay bee not drencht too deepe in theere owne reason and opinion." Clarke MS.

[c] "world." Clarke MS.

[d] None of the writing or signature of the letter is in Cromwell's hand.

[*General Council of Officers at St. Albans, Nov.* 16, 1648.][a]

Q[uestion]. Whether this Councill doth approve of the substance and drift of the paper now read to be sent to the parliament and published to the kingdome.

Assented to neme contradicente.

Committee to peruse the paper, and to fitt it for to bee tendred to the parliament.

Com. Gen. Ireton.
Col. Whalley.
Sir Wm Constable.
Col. Scroope.
Col. Ewers.
Lt. Col. Kelsey.
Ad. Gen. Evelyn.
Capt. Cannon.
Capt. Messervey.

Private Instructions for Col. Ewers in reference to the letters & orders herewith sent for the more orderly prosecution of them.[b]

That leaveing the charge of Portsmouth to Lt. Col. Saunders you haste into the island with the letters, and there :

[a] A Council of War, or more properly a meeting of the "General Council of Officers of the Army" took place on Nov. 7, but the Clarke Papers do not contain a record of the votes, though they give a list of officers present. A table of attendances at Councils of War, drawn up from these lists, is given at the end of this volume. Another Council meeting took place on Nov. 16, of which these papers contain no record except the resolutions above. The document referred to is the Remonstrance presented to the House of Commons on Nov. 20. See Gardiner, *Great Civil War*, iv., 236-245.

[b] The date of these Instructions should be Nov. 21. Fairfax's letter to Ewer ("that sealed from the Generall") is the letter dated Nov. 21, in answer to Hammond's letter of Nov. 19. It is printed in *Lords' Journals*, x., 610; *Old Parliamentary History*, xviii., 240, 255. Ireton's letter ("that unsealed from the Commissary Generall") is dated Nov. 22, and is printed in Birch's *Letters to Col. Robert Hammond*, p. 95. The letter from the Council can hardly be the letter of Nov. 25 (or rather warrant) signed by Rushworth in the name of the Council. It must rather be some document like the letter of the 4 officers (Birch, p. 87). Ewer was not to deliver it unless he found Hammond satisfied to act.

1. To deliver to the Governor two of the letters, viz., that sealed from the Generall, that unsealed from the Commissary Generall, but not that from the Councell, unlesse in case as is hereafter expressed.

2 To taste (?) whether upon our Remonstrance, the letters, or otherwise, it please God to satisffye his minde better towards the doeing of the thinges himselfe ; and if soe then lett him knowe by worde of mouth, that hee undertakeinge to doe it himselfe his present comeing to the headquarters is not expected or desired, but rather his staye there ; and in that case for assurance thereof (as alsoe for his better satisfaction to the doeinge of the thinge), give him the letter from the Councell to himselfe.

3. If notwithstanding all this, hee will neather undertake it himselfe nor leave it to you, then keep the letter & proceed as God shall direct & give opportunitye, according to the close of the letter from the Councell to yourselfe, adviseinge therein with Major Rolphe & such other honest officers thereabouts as you finde will be faithfull & secrett.[a]

Att a Generall Councell held in Windsor, Nov. 25, 1648.

That an order be sent in the name of his Excellency & Generall Councell of officers requireinge that the person of the Kinge be secured as formerly in Cairsbrooke Castle, untill upon some resolution to our Remonstrance or otherwise further order shall be given from his Excellency.

To be directed to Col. Hammond or the chief officer commanding in the Isle of Wight.

That the officers above named, or any of them, bee a Committee to consider of such thinges as may bee of concernement for the present affaires, & to make transaction therof.

[a] From a very rough draft.

Commissary Genll.[a]
Lieut.-Genll. Hammond.
Sir William Constable.
Coll. Harrison.
Coll. Whaley.
Coll. Thomlinson.
Coll. Whitchcott.

That an officer of every regiment attend at the headquarters to assist in Councell.

[*A Commission issued by Harry Marten.*]

Henry Marten of Longworth in the County of Berks Esqr.

To Symon Rice, Capt.

Wheras by virtue of that right which I was borne to as an Englishman, and in pursuance of that duty which I owe my said Country, I have resolved to raise and conduct a Regiment of Harquebusiers[?] on horse back on the behalf of the people of England, for the recovery of their fredome, and for common justice against [all] tyranny and oppression whatsoever, theise are therefore to aucthorize and appointe, and I doe herby constitute, you Simon Rice, to be Captain over one troope in my said Regiment of horse consisting of 80 men besides officers, and these to trayne, exercise in armes, and lead, acording to this commission. I doe farther require all officers and souldiers that have or shall putt themselves under your command for this service, to obey such orders as they shall from time to time receive from you, and your self to obey such as you shall receive from me, and from other your superiour officers in the Regiment acording to the discipline of warr. Given under my hand and seale the 25th day of November, 1648.[b]

[a] Names supplied from above.

[b] Mercurius Pragmaticus for Aug. 22-29, 1648, after reading the votes for a personal treaty with the King, says :" The precious Saint Harry, is extream angry

[Robert Saunders to Lord Fairfax.]

May itt please your Excellencie

I sent two letters from the Isle of Wight to give your Excellencie an account of what had bin done in the prosecution of our trust, in the roome of my Collonel,[a] who is (blessed be God) safelie come

that the Houses should presume, contrary to his liking, to proceed so farre as they have done in order to a treaty, for which cause he is resolved to declare against them, in as high terms as ever he did against the King. . . . And therefore he and one Eires are busy in drawing up a manifesto both against King, Lords, and Commons, as confederate to the enslaving of the people; and having already *borrowed a sufficient number of Horse*, on whom he hath set riders, who display their imbellished colours beautified with this misterious motto, 'For the People's Freedom against all tyrants whatsoever,' hee is now imployed about listing of foot; the rusticks of Berkshire resorting to him in great numbers, being mightily taken with [the] novell doctrine, that the supreame power & authority is inherently in the people, & to them doth Harry daily preach in the habit of a Leveller, proposing unto them that they ought not to acknowledge any power above them, or doe homage or yeeld obedience to any, they being a free people subsisting of themselves, & that they ought to pay no tithes, and to confirme them in these opinions, hee hath already forbidden his owne tenants & souldiers, not to yeeld him any manner of reverence, or to be subject unto his commands in ought but what shall concerne them in the warre; & now having begun to act the second part of Jack Cade, hee goes on very prettily, having already distributed the tithes belonging to one of the parsons at Reading amongst the poor of the parish, & also hath divided the spoiles of many prerogative landlords amongst their tenants."

According to Lilburne, Marten also taught the Berkshire jurymen that they were greater men than the judges and ought to sit with their hats on at assizes. *Trial of John Lilburne*, 1649, 4to, p. 123.

Marten's chief assistants in raising these forces were Col. William Eyres and Capt. John Waldron. Their undisciplined soldiers were provided with horses by the simple process of stopping travellers on the highway, or breaking into the stables of the gentlemen of the county (see Gardiner, *Great Civil War*, iv., 268; Tanner MSS., lvii., ff. 197-199; Portland MSS. i., 495; Grey's *Examination of Neal's Puritans*, iii., Appendix, p. 67). On Aug. 21, the House of Commons ordered the forces of the adjacent counties to suppress Marten and his adherents, and sent down Major Fincher to command the local forces for that purpose (*Commons' Journals*, v., 676).

[a] Isaac Ewer, who had succeeded to the command of Hammond's old regiment. Saunders was Lieut.-Col.

to us, and gone over to serve providence in the execution of your commands. I left Captain Joyce behinde privately to agitate businesse with the Governour and other freinds, who is come over this night, that if possible itt may nott bee knowne hee was there, to take off the scandall of an agitating businesse. Hee informes mee, that the Governour doth engage to secure the Kinge.[a] Hee hath passed the businesse of Ormond, and will send a letter, and if that will nott doe hee will proclaime him traitor. The Kinge will nott passe that of Bishoppes. The Commissioners of Parliament will goe on Munday. The Governour is resolved to make proclamation to morrow in the morning, being Sunday, for all Cavaleers that are nott in the list to depart the Island; hee intends to send a copy of the Generalls's lettres to the Parliament, and give them an account of his being sent for by your Excellency. I have drawne in two Companies of foote into Portesmouth Garrison, and have a troope of horse lying att the place appointed uppon any occasions; which is all att present from,

Your Excellencies most humble servant

ROBERT SAUNDERS.

Portesmouth
November 26, 1648.

[*News-letter from Windsor.*]

Windsor, 26 November, 1648.

This day the Generall and Generall Councill of officers mett together about 9 of the clock, and continued together till about 5 in the afternoone, seeking God by prayer to direct them in the great businesse now in hand, that they may bee instruments that justice may bee done uppon those who have caused soe much bloud to bee shed, and that righteousnesse and iudgement may flowe in the land.

[a] See *Lords' Journals*, x., 614, for Hammond's letter of Nov. 28, on the coming of Col. Ewer.

Itt is incredible how wonderfully God appeares in stirring uppe and uniting every man's heart as one man in the prosecution of this businesse, and that there might bee a suddaine settlement made in this Kingedome, and wholesome lawes and modell of Governement may bee speedily agreed uppon, which will bee vigorously prosecuted by the army.

There is a messenger come this night from the Isle of Wight who saith the Treatie broke off there the last night, that the Kinge is secured by Col. Ewers (who deliver'd the Remonstrance and could receive noe answer [a]) hath the charge of him; Col. Hamond is coming uppe to attend the Generall.

This evening about 7 of the clock severall petitions are come from the forces in South Wales, and the regiments of horse in the North, earnestly importuning the Generall to make way for justice against those who have shed soe much innocent bloud in this first and 2[d] warre, desiring the Kinge may bee speedily brought to justice.[b]

[*To Col. Ewer.*]

Sir, Windsor, 27 November, 1648.

Itt has bin formerly intimated to you by word of mouth, that the Kinge being secured in Carisbrooke-Castle, if you founde itt hazardous to keepe him there you should in that case convey him over to Hurst-Castle. Now there appearing to us heere some

[a] The Commons adjourned its consideration to Nov. 27.

[b] A letter to Fairfax from Westminster, dated 27 Nov., after reciting the votes of the Parliament with respect to Hammond on Nov. 27 adds: "These thinges I thought itt my duty to acquaint you with, least the Governor of the Isle of Wight might possibly deale contrary to your Excellency's expectation in a business of soe high concernement, and though letters came this day from Windsor that the King was secured, yett this [letter of Nov. 26] from Col. Hammond, and the orders thereupon, doe make an absolute contradiction. Soe that the honest partie knew not what to thinke of the businesse."

danger in his continuance within the Island, which perhaps is nott soe visible to you there, wee have thought fitt heerby positively to desire you, that for the better securing the person of the Kinge you doe uppon receipt heerof imediately convey him over to Hurst Castle, the best and safest way you can, taking order for a competent Guard out of your Regiment to bee assistant to those in the Castle for the securing of him there. [And] because wee are nott certaine of Col. Eyers his being present att Hurst-Castle, wee therefore desire that you would goe over thither with the person of the Kinge yourself, and take the charge of securing him there untill Col. Eyres himself shall come; for which purpose wee have heerwith sent an order to Col. Eyres his lieutenant, that hee admitt you to command in the Castle untill Col. Eyres returne. Wee suppose that the shippe which now attends you will bee faithfull in this business, butt if before you convey over the Kinge you finde any new shippes come into the roade, which you have nott the like assurance of, wee conceive in that case your best way will bee to take boate att Yarmouth Castle, or else att Freshwater, for your readier passage, and to bee more free from the command of such shippes.

[*To Col. Eyres.*]

Wheras Col. Ewer is appointed to remove the person of the Kinge from the Isle of Wight into Hurst Castle, these are to require you on sight heerof to take the person of the Kinge into your charge, (and to receive such souldiers as Col. Ewers shall bringe alonge with him for that purpose) and to secure him in your Castle untill you shall receive further orders from his Excellency.

[*To the officer in command at Hurst Castle.*]

Wheras Col. Ewers is appointed to remove the person of the Kinge out of the Isle of Wight to Hurst Castle, you are on sight heerof to admitt Col. Ewers with the person of the Kinge, and such guards as hee shall bringe alonge with him into Hurst Castle, and that you observe such orders as you shall receive from the said Col. Ewers, untill such time as Col. Eyres doe returne unto the Castle.[a]

Windsor Castle. Att the Generall Council of Officers. 28th Nov., 1648.

Question. Whether it bee expedient that that Army should bee forthwith drawne uppe to London to quarter in or about the Citty?

Resolved, Nem. Contradicente.

Question. Whether a Declaration shall bee drawne rendering the grounds of the Armie's advance as aforesaid, with relation to the Remonstrance, the thing now in debate, and what shall bee further tendered.

Comm. Generall. Col. Whalley.
Sir Wm. Constable. Col. Hewson.
Col. Harrison.

A committee to drawe uppe that Declaration.[b]

Comm. Generall.
Sir Wm Constable.
Col. Tomlinson.
Col. Barkstead.
Lt. Col. Kelsay.
Capt. Packer.

Or any 4 of them, to bee a Committee to joyne in advice with such as are sent from London, about the preparing of an Agreement, and other thinges of that Nature.

Councell to meete again to-morrow at one of the clocke.[c]

[a] Col. Thomas Ayres, Eyres, or Eyre, was the commander of Hurst Castle. The garrison seems to have been about forty men. Eyres appears to have been absent when the King arrived, and his lieutenant was probably the officer of whose conduct Sir Thomas Herbert so loudly complains (*Memoirs*, ed. 1702, p. 85.) The letter and the two warrants annexed (which last should also be dated Nov. 27), were probably signed by Rushworth in the name of the Council of Officers.

[b] Rushworth vii. 1341.

[c] For officers present see table of attendances.

[*Circular letter sent to the Commanders at Sea.*]

Sir,

The providence of God, together with the sence which hee hath bin pleased to sett uppon our hearts concerninge the condicion of affaires of the Kingdom in relation to the present Treaty, hath led us to prepair and present a Remonstrance to the House of Commons, which wee send herewith to you. Wee have found generall concurance to the same thinge throughout the Army and severall countyes, and wish and hope for the same with you at Sea. It is therefore desired (as the Remonstrance and the thinges contayned herein shall close with what God hath bin pleased to set upon your harts, which wee doubt not of) that you will in a publike way expres to the Generall your and your officers' and seamen's approbation thereof and concurance therein,

By the Appointment of his Excellencie and the Generall Councell of the Armie

Signed

Jo. Rushworth,
Secretary.[a]

28 Nov.,
1648.
Windsor.

[*The General to Lieut. Gen. Cromwell.*]

Sir,

By the Remonstrance which was lately tendered to the House of Commons I beleve your apprehensions are full of the waightines

[a] A similar letter (*mutatis mutandis*) dated 25 Nov. was sent to officers commanding in different parts of England. That directed to Col. Hammond is printed in *Lords' Journals*, x., 614.

of our present affaires, therefore in that particuler I shall not saie any thinge : onlie lett you know that my self with the advice of my Generall Councell of Officers desire, that you would (with all convenient speede possible) come to the Head quarters, whereby I hope our councells and endeavours as formerly j[oining] a mercifull furtherance wilbee giuen to the very great business now in agitation: the importance whereoff I am confident you duely resent.

[T. FAIRFAX.]

Windsor. Nov. 28,
1648.

For Lt. Generall Cromwell.[a]

[*Lieut.-Col. Saunders to Lord Fairfax.*]

My Lord,

In pursuance of your former orders in securing the Kinges person I sent over two companies of foote with Capt. Prettyes[b] troope, pressing boates in the harbour, and stopping those that came from the Isle. Capt. Joyce and some other of our officers are not idle, butt serve providence for the accomplishing all our desired ends.

RO. SAUNDERS.

Portsmouth, 29 November, 1648.

[*Warrant to convey the King to Hurst Castle.*]

You are heerby required forthwith to make your repaire into the Isle of Wight, and to take into your custody the person of the

[a] Cromwell's opinion of the Remonstrance is given in an undated letter to Fairfax, printed in the *English Historical Review* for 1887, p. 149. "Wee have read your Declaration heere," he says, "and see in itt nothinge but what is honest, and becominge Christians and honest men to say and offer." Compare also letter 83 in Carlyle's *Cromwell*.

[b] Henry Pretty, of Ireton's regiment, later a colonel in the army in Ireland.

Kinge, and that you from thence imediately convey him safely to Hurst-Castle; and I doe heerby require Major Rolphe, Captain Boreman, and Captain Hawes, and all officers and souldiers under their command, as neede shall bee, to give you such assistance therin as you shall require of them; and I doe heerby aucthorise you to impress such boates as shall bee necessary for this service; and the Governour of Hurst-Castle is heerby order'd to receive the Kinge into the Castle with such forces as you shall see cause to bringe for the better securing of him there; and in case Col. Eyres the Governour bee absent, the officer who commandeth in his absence is heerby required to obey your orders till the Governour returne. Given &c.[a]

To Lieutenant Col. Cobbett and Capt. Merriman.

[*To Lieut.-Col. Cobbett*]

Sir,

I am commanded by the Generall to desire you to have a speciall care that all civility bee used towards the person of the Kinge in the ordering of that businesse committed to your charge, and that hee have such accomodations whither hee is to remove, as shall bee suitable to the present occasion, that there may bee noe complaint there is any want of conveniencies fitting for him.[b]

[a] This second warrant should apparently be dated Nov. 29. Mr. Gardiner suggests that Ewer had accompanied Hammond to Windsor, and that it consequently became necessary to send new agents. The warrant is from the General Council of Officers. *Great Civil War*, iv., 256.

[b] Probably from John Rushworth.

A list of such horse and foote that are to meet at the Randevouz, 1 Dec., 1648.[a]

Troopes.

12	The Lord Generall Col. Whalley	Horse
5	Commissary Generall	
4	Col. Fleetwood's	
5	Col. Rich's	
2	Lt. Generall's	
1	Col. Harrison	

29 troopes.

2 troopes Col. Okey's Dragoones.

Regiments.

Col. Hewson	Foote.
Col. Pride	
Col. Deane	
Lt. Col. Cooke	
Lt. Col. Ashfeild	

Companies.

3 Col. Inglesby.
5 Col. Barksted.
1 Adjutant Generall.
1 Col. Whitchcott.

Two regiments of horse and 17 troopes.

Two troopes of dragoons. Five regiments and ten companies of foot.

[*Lieut-Col. Saunders to Lord Fairfax.*]

My Lord,

Our God hath done our worke for us, all things are quiet in the

[a] Before the march of the army to London.

Island, the King went without any opposition to Hurst Castle, and is there; your worke now is before you, to putt such a number of confiding men to guard him as therin you may rest, for the old souldiers are rotten. I have sent a party of horse to Capt. Pretty; there will be need of more horse and foote to ly there abouts; the Castle is allsoe much unprovided of victuall. This is all that I can informe your Excellencie, who am, Sir, your humble servant,

Ro: Saunders.[a]

Portesmouth,
December 2,
1648.

[a] *The Moderate* for Nov. 28-Dec. 5 contains the following letter, dated Newport, Dec. 2:

"This morning about six of the clock, five of us came to his Majesties chamber, and desired one of his attendants to aquaint his Majesty with our intentions (according to our orders, to secure his person, which we rather did because he might not be affrighted; which done we secured the town with 40 horse and two companies of foot which we got over last night from Portsmouth, and once in half an hour his Majesty was coached, and soon after secured in Hurst Castle, of which our dear friend and true patriot, Col. Ayers of Wiltshire is governor, whose fidelity can never be poysoned as H. was."

A second letter from the same person, dated Hurst Castle, Dec. 14, adds:

"When the governour of this Castle, Col. Eyres, came down, and came into his presence, his Majesty saluted him with a kind of a jeer, telling him, he hoped he would not take it ill that he came to visit his wife in his absence; but withall that he was sorry to put him up in so narrow a room (meaning, himself and his attendants would take up the greatest part of that little castle, the governour not having one room left for the entertainment of a friend). The governour answered his Majesty, that the place afforded not that accommodation as might be desired, but he should be well satisfied with his present condition, especially now that his Majesty was there in safety (which I believe was more than his Majesty could cordially say himselfe). Upon Sunday last his Majesty was speaking to Lieu.-Col. Cobbet to shew him by what order he was brought to that castle (which till that time he had not seen); the Lieu.-Col. shews him the order, upon the perusall of which he seemed to be well satisfied, after some debate about it, but told us, that as he had no desire to stay long in this place, yet he should be unwilling to be removed hence without the sight of an order beforehand; to which was answered, that necessity was above order; he replyed, that it was true, but necessity was many times pretended, when there was none." *The Moderate*, Dec. 12-19.

[*To Lieut-Col. Cobbett.*]

Westminster, December 5, 1648.

Sir,

I understand you have removed the Kinge to Hurst Castle, and soe manag'd the businesse as itt was carried without incivilitie unto him, or prejudice to others. The Parliament being soe busy att present, there can bee noe orders gotten for monies. That you may nott want for the present occasions, I have assign'd you 100li, which you may dispose with the best husbandry you can for the present occasions of those with you attending that service.[a]

[*A letter from the head-quarters of the Army.*]

Munday, December the 12, 1648.

Sir,

By the last post I acquainted yow in what temper the House of Commons were to comp[ly] with the King, by being ridgedly and passionately bent by voting the King concessions to be a ground of a settlement, which was as much as to say it was satisfactory what he had offered. All good men did soe admire at the weakenes, or rather at the madnes of the Parliament in such a vote, which at Midsommer could not have bin expected; but as it happened about 100 members of the Howse opposed it, who gave incouragement to the Army to thinke of some way to purge the Howse, since they were soe violently bent to a rotten and unworthy peace; to dissolve the Parliament would have bin counted a rash act; to purge it by a force would be thought a bold and unwarrantable attempt; to let both these passe, and to doe nothing, was to continue the same division that was in the Howse, and by consequence the division of the Kingdome, and in conclusion the distruction of it. Upon these considerations, finding the disease being desperate, there could nothing thought upon but a desperate cure; and thereupon the

[a] The letter is unsigned; it is probably from Lord Fairfax to Lieut.-Col. Cobbet.

Army resolved there being noe other way upon the earth left (to my iudgement) to save the Kingdome, but to seaze upon certaine members of the House, who had from time to time obstructed the proceedings in the Howse, and all good motions tending to the welfare of the Kingdome out of faction ——[a] by respect. Hereupon Mr. Prynn, the firebrand of England, Maior Generall Massey, Mr. Gewen, Sir John Clotworthy, and in all about 40 members were seazed upon by the Army going to the Howse; and others desired to forbeare to come thither who were men who were of the same stampe of the same faction. Upon Thursday the Howse sate, and though it was an undoubted breach of theire priviledge to have the Members thus seazed, yet the Members had soe abused the priviledge by the[ir] perpeteutie there, taking advantage thereby, not onely to wronge the subiect, but to vent malice and passion in particular without controwle, as it was frequent with these time serving members; whereuppon the Howse resolved to proceed with the busines of the Armyes Remonstrance and the [settlement of] Kingdome, and to let there members alone till another opportunitie. On Friday the Howse kept a fast, and adiourned till Tuesday; the army being passive all this while, charging the suburbs with provisions, and lying upon bare boords in White Hall, St. Jameses &c., hoping the Citty would not faile to send moneyes for the payeing of the army (considering the Citty was 100,000li. in arreares) and bedds, that soe the souldiers might be accomodated as not to be necessitated to come into London;[b] which the army to avoyde by all meanes possible had patience from Saturday to Friday last, and the Citty of London in all that time not being able (or rather not willing) to advance one 10 dayes pay out of all theire arreares, necessitating the army to resolve to march into the Citty, and there to quarter; which accordingly they did on Friday last, in Paul's, Blacke Fryers, and in parts there abouts. When the Citty see the

[a] A word erased.

[b] Cf. Rushworth, vii., 1349, 1350, 1353.

army was in good earnest, and that theire owne folly, by not advancing that which they owed unto the army had wrought this upon them, then they beganne to vote to raise 10,000li., and to provide bedding for the souldiers, hoping the army would retire out of the Citty; but the army being hitherto deceived with their delitarynes, understood where 27,000li. was in bank at Weavors Hall, went and seazed upon the same,[a] that the Citty might see, that though they could not raise 10,000li. 10 dayes pay for the army, yet the army could tell how to finde a months pay ready in cash. This terrified the malignant merchants and goldsmiths, fearing theire estates should be seazed upon, though there was noe reall cause to suspect them, saide in soe humble a manner that they all professed themselves to be servants to the army. Hereupon the Generall sent some Colonells unto the Citty to assure them never a gold-smith should loose the value of a thimble, or merchant 2d. in his goods, who did not obstinately refuse to pay the just arreares that were behinde from the Citty to the army; and further assured that the 27,000li. that was thus seazed upon should be repaide out of the very arreares that is yet due, out of the Citty arreares to the army, and out of the first moneyes that did come in; and the army having bin there ever since, hath committed noe spoyle more then trouble of quarter, because the Citty are sloe in bringing in of theire debts. Thus you have the true account of this weekes passage. The Lord direct both the Parliament and the army out of these distressed proceedings to bring good unto the Kingdome; and my opinion is this, that you will finde these [members] now sitting in Parliament to goe on more unanimously and more vigorously in the setlement of the peace of the Kingdome, in giving eare unto the subiect, and doeing more capable thinges unto the common wealth in 3 months, then hath bin done by the Parliament for three yeares past.

[a] See Fairfax's letters to the City. Rushworth, vii., 1356, 1358.

[*Thomas Margetts to William Clarke.*]

Deare Billy,

Yesterday wee had a generall meeting of Officers heere and they have resolved upon a declaration, sent to his Excellency by this gentleman Captain Baynes, to which I shall referre you. The Major Generall did expresse himself very sweetly and fully, opposing with aboundance of convincing reason all that gainesaid, so that he gave great incouragement and full satisfaction to all the well affected, and putt much life and strength to the busines, so that he hath clearly taken away all iealous thoughts of non complyance; nay, I can say, I believe no man acts in it with more clearnes and satisfaction in point of conscience, nor can give greater life to the thing; and let no man have any thought against his fidelity and integrity to the publique cause of the kingdome, as I heare he hath been a little too much spoken of in that sence, you may most safely vindicate him against all such.

It is the greate feare of the well affected, that the Army through some temptation or other may fall off, and not act vigorously, (the former defection breeds iealousy) and so they be brought in to further mischeif by being engaged with them. And this is also the enemies hope. If in case this declaration be appointed to be printed I beseech you let it be carefully done, and the presse carefully examined and corrected before it be published; and I beseech you also, when they are done, lett a reasonable proportion of them be sent to mee that am

Thine owne

THO: MARGETTS.

Pont. 13 Dec. 1648.

Present my humble service to Mr. Rushworth, my love to Mr. Hatter, Mr. Wragg and all old Cronies.

This Castle holds out still, the Governor desperate feeds their men with hopes of releif from Scotland; many of them are sick, and many gett away, and [some] came away this day, some yesterday, and some almost every day. Yesterday an officer of theirs standing upon one of their towers had his head shott of by one of our cannon bullets. Wee hope their owne discontents within will shortly put them to extremity. Present my service to Card: Woolsey, tell him by the next post I am for him.[a]

Generall Councell, Dec. 14, 1648.

[List of Names.]

Question debated—

Whether the Magistrate have or ought to have any compulsive and restrictive power in matters of religion.

Adjourned till Saturday at noone to proceede upon the other parte of the Agreement, waiving [?] this first reserve.

The Generall Councell is to meete tomorrow at one in the afternoone in relation to justice.

The Generall Councell is to meete Munday for further proceeding in matter of this dayes debate. Left to the Committee, in relation to the thinges formerly referred concerning the Agreement, to meete tomorrow here or elsewhere in the Cittie to discusse.

Question. Whether to have any reserve to except religious thinges, or only to give power in naturall and civill thinges, and to say nothing of religion?

[a] This letter is one of the few originals amongst the Clarke MSS. On the state of political feeling in the northern army see Rushworth, vii., 1366, 1400. A series of letters from the camp before Pontefract are printed in *The Moderate*. Margetts was secretary to the Council of Officers of the northern army, and probably to Lambert its commander.

Orders for the discussing of this Question.

(1) That those who are of opinion in the affirmative begin (if they will) to lay downe the grounds.

(2) That the discussion be alternate, viz[t]. that when one hath reasoned for the affirmative, the next admitted to speake be such as will speake for the negative, and after one hath spoke for the negative, the next admitted to speake bee for the affirmative.

(3) That if none arguing in the affirmative give grounds for a compulsive power, then none in the negative to speake against any other then the restrictive power.

Col. Rich.	Mr. Taylor.
Col. Deane.	Mr. Collier.
Mr. Wildman.	Capt. Clarke.
Mr. Stapylton.	
Mr. John Goodwin.	

To meete at Col. Titchburne's tomorrow at 4 of the clocke in the afternoone with

Mr. Calamy.	Mr. Marshall.
Mr. Ashe.	Mr. Nye.
Mr. Seaman.	Mr. Russell
Mr. Burges.	Mr. Ayres.
Mr. Cordwell.	Mr. Brinsley.

About the particulars this day debated.[a]

[a] This account of the votes of the General Council of Dec. 14 is from vol. xvi. 4to of the Clarke MSS. The debate which follows is from vol. 67, folio.

General Councill. att Whitehall. 14 *December.* 1648.

Present,

Lo: Generall Fairfax. etc.[a]

The first Reserve as in relation to matters of Religion, read.[b]

The Question,

Whether the Civill Magistrate had a power given him from God?

Col. Tichborne.

How farre the Civill Magistrate had power from God?

[a] For list of names see the table of attendances, given at the end of the volume. Cromwell was absent. *Mercurius Pragmaticus* notes under Dec. 14: "This day Duke Oliver set forth in state towards Windsor, upon an entreaty by letter from Duke Hamilton to come and conferre notes with him, now that design is ripe for execution. It's thought that cunning coward (for as yet we must not call him traytor) hath told tales. . . . ." The same paper adds: "Munday, Decem. 18, came information, that much discourse had passed between Hamilton and Cromwell at Windsor, but in conclusion he protested he was not invited in by his Majesty, nor by any member of Parliament." *Mercurius Pragmaticus*, Dec. 12-19, 1648.

[b] This debate concerns article seven of the original "Agreement" laid before the Council of the Army. It runs thus: "That the power of the people's Representatives extend (without the consent or concurrence of any other person or persons) to the enacting, altering, repealing, and declaring of Laws; to the erecting and abolishing Officers and [?] Courts of Justice and to whatever is not in this Agreement excepted or reserved from them." Eight reservations or exceptions then follow. The first is the one now before the Council. "We do not now empower our Representatives to continue in force, or make any Lawes, Oaths, and Covenants, whereby to compell, by penalties or otherwise, any person to any thing, in or about matters of Faith, Religion, or God's Worship, or to restrain any person from the professing his Faith, or exercise of Religion, according to his conscience, in any house or place (except such as are or shall be set apart for the publique worship,) nevertheless the instruction or directing of the nation in a publique way, for the matters of Faith, Worship, or Discipline (so it be not compulsive or expresse Popery) is referred to their discretion." Lilburne's *Foundations of Freedom*, 4to, 1648; cf. Rushworth, vii., 1358. In the completed Agreement, presented to Parliament on Jan. 20, 1649, there was no reservation concerning religion, but a separate article, the ninth, was devoted to the question of toleration and to religious matters in general. *Old Parliamentary History*, xviii., 533.

Col. Deane.

The law is, that what a man would have done to himself hee may doe to another, and that according to that rule hee did nott undestand the Magistrate to have power.

Mr. Jo. Goodwin.

Offers to consideration, that God hath nott invested any power in a Civill Magistrate in matters of religion; and I thinke if hee had hee might more properly bee called an Ecclesiasticall or Church Officer then a Civill; for denominations are given from those [things] that are most considerable in an office. There is noe difference in that. That the Magistrate hath [not] in any way a concession from God for punishing any man for going alonge with his conscience, I conceive that is nott necessary to bee argued uppon.

That I suppose is [necessary to be argued upon is], whether itt bee proper or conducing to your ends, whether it bee like to be of good resentment of the wisest or generality of the people, that a businesse of this nature should bee of your cognizance, itt being that which hath taken uppe the best witts to determine whether the Magistrate hath power in matter of religion or noe, yett itt being a matter of that profound and deepe disputation as men have made itt, whether it will bee a matter appropriate to the cognizance of you to interpose to determine, and to decide a question which hath bin the great exercise of the learning, and witts, and judgement of the world. And I conceive though there bee reasons uppon reasons of very great weight, commanding why itt should bee inserted—Certainly if soe bee the inserting of itt could carry itt, if itt could obtaine and bee likely to prevaile in the kingdome I thinke itt would blesse the Nation with abundance of peace, and [be] the preventing of many inconveniences, and troubles, and heart burninges that are like to arise. Butt inasmuch as I doe nott apprehend that itt is a matter proper for you to take notice of [or] to intermeddle in, itt being a matter of conscience and matter of religion, whether you will, you must doe itt either then as Magistrates, and then you goe against your owne principles, you doe assume and interpose in matters of religion. If itt bee noe matter of conscience, butt only matter of civill right, itt will fall into those Articles which concerne the civill power of the Magistrate.

Mr. Hewitt.

Every poore man [that] does understand what hee does, and is willing that the commonwealth should flourish, hath as reall an hand heere as the greatest Divine,[a] and all devinity you have had from reading, if you had as many degrees of time since the creation, learning is butt the tradition of men. Hee is properly concern'd and as one of England, and therefore [hath a right] to know whether you give him any power or noe.

Those men that are religious they are those men that has the greatest spiritts and fittest for publique service, and to have religion given under the hand of a Magistrate or two, and all the noble spiritts of the poore to turne them out of the Commonwealth—Therefore iff wee doe honour the Commonwealth of England, itt is best to lett them bee free, that they bee nott banished or injured for matters of Conscience, butt that they may enjoy the Commonwealth.

Mr. Wildman.

I suppose the difference is concerning the Stating of the Question. For what that learned Gentleman was pleas'd to say

[a] "On Saturday the two politic pulpit-drivers of Independency, by name Nye and Goodwin, were at the debate of settling the Kingdom, in the mechanic councell at Whitehall, and one main question was concerning the extent of magistracy, which Nye and Goodwin requested them not to determine before advice had with some learned divines; which saying of theirs turned the debate into a quarrell: for the mechanicks took snuff, told them they thought themselves as divine as any divines in the kingdom, which a brother standing by undertook to prove, and pretended a sudden revelation for the purpose, by which means both Nye and Goodwin were once again made silenced ministers." *Mercurius Pragmaticus*, Dec. 12-19, 1648.

whether itt were proper for this Councill to conceive whether itt were matter of conscience. Through the judgment of God uppon the Nation all aucthority hath bin broken to pieces. Att least itt hath bin our misery that itt hath bin uncertaine whether the supreame aucthority hath bin [here or there], that none have knowne where the aucthority of the Magistrate is, or [how far] his office [extends]. For the remedy of this your Excellency hath thought fitt to propound a new way of setling this Nation, which is a new constitution. Your Excellency thinkes itt that itt can bee noe other way for to governe the people then this way.

And though this Agreement were resolved heere—The Question is now what power the people will agree to give to the Magistrates that they will sett over them to bee their Governours. Now the great misery of our Nation hath bin the Magistrates trust nott being knowne.[a] Now wee being about setling the supreame power I thinke itt is [necessary] clearly to declare what this power is; therefore I thinke the question will bee, [firstly], whether wee shall intrust the Magistrate in matters of religion or nott? [secondly], whether itt bee necessary to express [b] itt or nott?

That then the question must bee thus:

Whether itt bee necessary that after wee have had a Warre for power, to shew what power wee doe give them, and what nott? and I desire that the Question may bee stated: whether itt is

[a] In the "Humble petition of thousands of well affected people inhabiting the City of London," etc., presented on Sept. 11, 1648, this view is clearly set forth. The petitioners address the House of Commons as "the supreme authority of England," and will them so to consider themselves. They are told that they must not admit King or Lords to any share in this supreme authority, "it being impossible for us to believe that it can consist either with the safety or freedom of the nation to be governed by two or three supremes." The petition complains that the Commons have declared that they will not alter the ancient government from King, Lords, and Commons; "not once mentioning, in case of difference, which of them is supreme, but leaving that point, which was the chiefest cause of all our public differences, disturbances, wars, and miseries, as uncertain as ever." *Old Parliamentary History*, xvii., 454.

[b] MS. "exercise," the last line supplies the correction.

necessary clearly to expresse in this Constitution, whether to intrust the Magistrate in matters of religion or nott, whether itt bee necessary to expresse itt or nott?

Col. Hewson.

Noe man hath said that in this Agreement nothing hath bin [granted to the magistrate, save that which hath been] exprest. The maine thinge is nott whether hee[a] should bee intrusted, butt what should bee reserved. I thinke that's sufficient. For to trust them, if they have a power in themselves either to binde or nott to binde, I thinke that will bee a thinge questionable still. For that's doubted by many whether the people can tie uppe themselves to any particular measure of their obedience. Now if soe, if they have nott this power in themselves, then for them to say they reserve itt from others which they have nott themselves——

Col. Rich.

I thinke the greatest cause of the lengthning of the Debate is the mistake of the Question in hand, and I have heard difference in opinion severall [times?] about the Question. As to that the Gentleman that spoke last asserted, I referre itt to your Excellency that whether or noe the [not] empowering the civill Magistrate does nott reserve itt. If wee did not give him this power expresly, implyedlie hee has it not, and therefore to consider whether itt bee a necessary reserve.[b] If itt bee a reserve that concernes the conscience of any of those faithfull freinds that have gone alonge with your Excellency, and this is a reserve that does nott concerne us butt them. . . . . Even for that I referre itt to your Excellency, whether itt ought nott to bee inserted?

Butt as to the equity and reason of the thinge, whether hee hath this from God, or whether hee can have itt, that is soe cleare that

[a] "Hee," *i.e.*, the magistrate.

[b] Order of the two sentences altered.

noe man will argue for itt. That [the question] is, whether the Civill Magistrate hath power to bee exercis'd uppon the outward man for civill thinges. It has bin said wee may intrust the Civill Magistrate with our lives and our estates, butt to intrust the Civill Magistrate with a compulsive power for religious ends does implicitely signify, that wee will submitt to such a power. Now the question is [not] whether wee can impower him over our consciences; it's impossible. Butt this is that which sticks with mee, whether wee ought to countenance the Magistrate, much lesse give him a power over the persons of men, for doing or nott doing religious thinges according to his judgement.

Lt. Col. Lilburne.

To my understanding [in] all that hath bin said to reach this businesse that which hath bin principally aimed att [is] to state the Question. According to [the] Commissary Generall's first stating of itt, [it] is this. That seing there hath bin a great warre about breach of trust (and that unlimited trust), and seing wee are now about to [seek a way to] avoide those miseries that hitherto have hapned, I conceive the substance of the Question will bee this: whether itt bee necessary to represent the trust that is reposed in the Magistrates. That I conceive that is the principall thinge that will reach our end. Whether itt bee requisite to expresse their trust positively in this Agreement, yea or noe?

Com. Gen. Ireton.[a]

I have heard soe many thinges and soe many mistakes that itt makes mee thinke of some other method, and that is to finde out the persons of the severall opinions that are started amongst us, that [they] may apply themselves to answer [each other]. Nott many to speake together of one parte, and that which they have said goe without answer; butt imediatelie as one hath spoken any thinge of one

[a] Ireton, so far as these reports can be trusted, had not yet spoken. I doubt whether the order of the speeches given in the MS. is always correct.

parte that itt may bee answer'd of the other parte. Otherwise wee shall, as farre as my reason goes, perplex ourselves and all that heare us.[a]

My memory is nott able to reach to those many mistakes that I have found in the Debate hitherto, butt I'le speake a worde to the last because itt is very materiall. I perceive by this Gentleman that the foundation of the necessity—the ground of the necessity[b]—[of] the determination of this point now, is fix't uppon this: that wee have had warres and troubles in the Nation, and that hath bin for want of ascertayning the power in which men should have acquies'd in the Nation, and for that men have nott knowne where to acquiesce. If the meaning of this bee, that itt hath bin for want of knowing what power Magistracie hath had, I must needes say that itt hath bin a cleare mistake [to say] that this was the ground of the warres. The grounds have bin these: That wheras itt is well and generally knowne what is the matter of the supreame trust (that is all thinges necessary for the preserving of peace) [it is not so well known] what is the end of civill societie and Commonwealthes. If I did looke att libertie [alone] I would minde noe such thinge [as a Commonwealth]; for then I am most free when I have noebody to minde mee. Nor doe I finde anythinge else that's imediately necessary, nott [as the cause] of making any power amongst men, but[c] the preserving of humane society in peace. Butt withall to looke att such a trust. That you comitt the trust to persons for the preserving of peace that they may use it in such a way as may bee most suitable in civill societie, that are most probable and hopefull for [preserving] libertie, and nott [like] to make us slaves, as itt may bee most hopefull for common and equall right amonge us, as may be most hopefull to provide for the prosperitie and flourishing state of the nation. That the necessary thinge, that which necessarily leads all men into civill agreements or contracts, or to make Commonwealthes, is the necessity of itt for preserving peace. Because otherwise, if

[a] See p. 72. [b] Answering Wildman. [c] MS. "by."

there were noe such thinge, butt every man [were] left to his owne will, mens contrary wills, lusts, and passions would lead every one to the destruction of another, and [everyone] to seeke all the wayes of fencing himself against the jealousies of another.

That which hath occasioned the warre in this Nation, and that which hath occasioned the controversies heretofore is,[a] nott the nott knowing what the limitations are, or of what [nature] the supreame trust is, butt that wee have nott knowne in what persons, or what parties, or what councill the trust hath layne. The Kinge hee hath claim'd itt as his right, as in the case of Shippe Monie, butt the people thought they had another right then. There was a Parliament called, and itt was then cleare and undenied; the Kinge could nott deny itt—that itt was the right of the kingdome that they should nott bee bound and concluded, butt by common consent of their deputies or Representatives in Parliament. Itt [not] being thus farre made cleare where the supreame trust did lie, thus much was cleare, that the kinge could nott doe anythinge alone. Then hee insists uppon itt, that the Parliament could nott doe any thinge without him. This was the difference, because they did assume to doe somethinge without him which they thought necessary for the safetie of the Kingedome. Soe that the ground of the warre was nott difference in what the supreame Magistracie [was, but] whether [it was] in the Kinge alone.[b] Now wee are all that are heere I suppose unanimous, that this bone of contention should bee taken away, that itt should bee determined in what persons or succession of persons the supreame trust doth lie. With us the Question is, what kinde of power wee should committ with those that have the supreame trust. Since itt is cleare in this question itt is nott intended [to determine] whether wee shall committ [to them] a trust of our judgements or consciences, the question is whether wee should give a trust to them for the outward man, and with

[a] The position of several clauses altered.

[b] *i.e.*, a difference not as to the nature of the supreme power but whether the King alone possessed it.

acquiescence butt for peace-sake. That all civill power whatsoever, neither in naturall or civill thinges, is nott [able] to binde men's judgements. The judgement of the Parliament [which] is the supreamest Councill in the World, cannott binde my judgement in any thinge. [Whatever power you give the magistrate], whether you limitt itt to civill thinges or naturall thinges, the effect of that power is that hee hath nott power to conclude your inward, butt your outward man [only]; the effect of all is butt the placing of a power in which wee would acquiesce for peace sake.[a] Take that for granted then. To come to consider whether as to the proceeding to the outward man, and our acquiesce[nce] unto him for peace-sake, itt bee fitt for us to committ a trust to the civill Magistrate for this purpose, concerning spirituall thinges as concerning civill thinges.

Now the ground [of the dispute] is this. There are two pretences of Conscience. There are many men who doe claime a right to the Civill Commonwealth with you, and have nott forfeited that right. They say "Though wee thinke itt bee in your power to determine who shall bee the supreame Magistrate, butt that being determined there is somethinge of Divine Institution that does tell him what is his duty to doe, gives him rules in point of acting betweene man and man, in civill thinges hee ought to have regard to that right. 2[dly] They say, that that same word or witnesse of God left to us, which gives him directions in this case in civill thinges, [which tells him] what is right and what is wronge, and soe must bee the guide of his judgement—that same does tell him, that in some thinges [that concern religion] hee ought to restraine. This is truly the pretence of conscience on one parte.

That which is said against this. First, many men doe nott beleive that there is by the word of God, by the Scripture, any such direction, or power, or duty laid uppon the Magistrate, that hee should exercise any such power in thinges that concerne religion. They differre in that point. Secondly, they say: "Though itt were soe, to your satisfaction that are of that opinion, yett wee

[a] The last three sentences lines are transferred from p. 80.

being nott satisfied that wee ought to thinke soe, itt is nott fitt for us to committ a power to him which God hath nott intrusted him withall." That's the argument. For otherwise itt would follow, that if there bee a pretence of conscience, and some probable grounds and reasons on the one side, that the Magistrate should nott bee bound in matters of religion, butt that hee may exercise this power in this case. When wee are uppon the businesse or uppon agreement itt will bee necessary wee should leave this out. Lett us goe on to make an agreement for our civill rights uppon those thinges wherin wee are agreed, and lett us [not] make such a thinge necessary to the agreement as will inevitably exclude one of us from the agreement, butt lett us make such a distribution of the publique trust in such hands as shall give everyone an equall share, an equall interest and possibility, and lett us submitt ourselves to these future Representatives, and if wee bee nott satisfied in one Representative itt may bee satisfied in the next. This would certainly bee the most reasonable way in all those that have nott admitted this Agreement.

Saving that, [as] itt's alleadged on one hand, "If you putt this into the Agreement you necessarily exclude mee from itt, as my conscience is that the Magistrate should have that power ;" soe sayes the other, "If you have nott this in the Agreement you doe exclude mee from the Agreement for my conscience sake, for my conscience is, that the Magistrate should nott have that power."

Then Sir—For that truly I thinke itt has bin offer'd, to the end wee may come to the neerest possibility that I can see to an agreement—this hath bin offer'd. That you cannot conscientiously intrust the Magistrate with a power which by the rule of God hee ought nott to exercise, butt if you finde itt is alleadg'd to give him a power to all thinges butt those that are reserved, and [if we do] nott reserve this from him then wee give him the power of that. To that itt hath bin offer'd, that in your generall clause concerning the power of the supreame Magistracie of the peoples Representative that wee should [make it] extend to all civill and naturall thinges ;[a] then if nott having right to a power from him if hee will exercise his power without clayming itt from some body else ; if hee have itt in him of God then your Agreement cannott take itt from him ; if hee have itt nott [of God] then itt is nott [given him] in the Agreement.

For that for a setling of the power, there are noe rightfull foundations of this trust [save] either Divine Institution or designation of the person, or else an humane placing of them. Now though itt bee in man (where God doth nott designe) rightfully to elect and designe the persons, yett when the persons are elected and instituted, what is their duty to doe in point of justice, and what is their duty in point of those thinges of religion whereof they are to judge, [those are things] that are nott to bee determined by those that committ the trust to them. Certainly [by] the same reason as wee in only making our choice of the persons and of the time of their continuance, (that are clearly in our power) do[b] leave itt to him according to his judgement to determine and proceede in matters of civill right and civill thinges, [so] wee may uppon the same ground, without further prejudice to the inward[c] man, referre to him a power of determining as to the outward man what hee will allow or suffer in matter of religion.

And thus I have indeavoured as clearly as I can to state the Question and the severall Questions that are in this businesse.

Col. Whalley.

My Lord,

Wee are about preparing an Agreement for the people and truly, my Lord, itt is high time that wee did agree. If we now vary itt is

[a] Cf. Vernon, "The Sword's Abuse Asserted, or a word to the Army; shewing the weakness of carnal weapons in spiritual warfare, the sword an useless tool in temple work; and the bearer thereof an unfit builder. Tendered to the serious consideration of his Excellency the Lord Fairfax and his General Councel, upon occasion of their late debates about the clause concerning religion in the promised Agreement. By John Vernon, sometimes a member of the Army. Imprinted for John Harris, Decemb. 1648."

[b] MS. "to."

[c] MS. "outward."

a ready way to common ruine and destruction. My Lord, I doe perceive in this paper which is prepared for the people to bee by Agreement. There is one Article in itt which hath bin soe much spoken of to the great stumbling of many. Itt causes a great difference amongest us. If soe, wee cannott butt expect that itt will cause a greater in the Kingdome, and soe great as doubtlesse will occasion a new commotion. Since itt is soe apparent to us, I must thinke itt were a very necessary Question to putt, whether this ought nott to bee left out of this paper, yea or noe. For how can wee terme that to bee an Agreement of the people which is neither an Agreement of the major parte of the people, and truly for anythinge I can perceive (I speake out of my owne judgement and conscience) nott [an Agreement of] the major parte of the honest partie of the Kingdome? If the Question were whether the Magistrate should have coercive power over mens Consciences, I thinke itt is a very necessary thinge to putt. Wee have bin necessitated to force[a] the Parliament, and I should bee very unwilling wee should force the people to an Agreement.

Lt. Col. Lilburne.

I agree to that motion of the Commissary Generall, that there might be some of contrary principles or parties chosen out to agree uppon the stating of our Question, that wee may nott spend soe much time in that which wee are to Debate uppon.

Mr. Sprigge.

My Lord,

I should bee loath to taxe any heere with mistakes, though I have nott a better worde to call it by, and itt hath bin used oft already. I conceive there are many mistakes have pass'd in bringing forth the state of the Question. There has bin a mistake I conceive of the true subject that is to bee intituled to this businesse, and a mistake of the capacitie that you are in to act in this businesse, and a mistake of the opportunity that lies before you,

[a] MS. "serve."

and of the fruite and end of your actions. I conceive my Lord, that hee hath not bin intituled to this thinge who ought to be intituled, and that is our Lord Jesus Christ, who is heire of all thinges; and as hee was Gods delight before the world was made, why, soe God did bringe forth all thinges by him in a proportion and conformitie to him, to that image of his delight and content his sonne; and soe retayning this proportion, and acting in this conformitie to him, have all States and Kingdomes stood that have stood, and expect to stand; and declining from this proportion, itt hath bin the ruine of all Governements [that have done so]. Itt is God's designe, I say, to bringe forth the Civill Governement, and all thinges heere belowe in the image and resemblance of thinges above; and when as those thinges that are butt of [a temporary] and representative nature have clash't with that which hath bin their end; and have either sett uppe themselves, or sett uppe thinges that are of this world like themselves, as their end, and soe have made all thinges (I meane the thinges of the other world) to stoope and vaile to these ends, and have measured Religion and the appearances of God according to rules and ends of pollicie, itt hath bin the ruine of all States. I conceive that that is the account that is to bee given of the [cause of the] condition that this Kingdome is brought into att this time.

Now, My Lord, God having thus taken us a pieces, and that righteously, because our Governement did nott stand in God in itts patterne, why hee hath only by his providence now brought forth the Governement of the sword, being that which only wee are capable of, and which wee have brought ourselves into a condition of needing and requiring.[a] Now, My Lord, I conceive that this same goodwill which is in your Excellency and in the Army to promote the spirituall liberties of the Saints as well as the civill liberties of men, cannott butt bee taken well. Itt is that which certainly you shall nott fare the worse for att the hands of God, who will award unto you according to your doinges, and according to

[a] MS. "needinesse & acquiringe."

your intentions. Butt wee must alsoe professe that the Kingedome of Christ does nott stand in [need of help from] any power of man; and that Christ will growe uppe in the world, lett all powers whatsoever combine never soe much against him. Soe that I conceive the Question is nott soe much to bee putt in the interest of Christ and of the truth—I meane in the interest of the neede of Christ of your restraining of the Magistrate,—of your providing against such coercion. Butt if itt should bee, now that the Magistrate is despoyled of all power to oppresse the saints, if you should goe to lay an opportunity before him againe, and offer such a thinge to him, certainly that were to lay a great snare before them,[a] and by thrusting them on to breake their owne neckes the faster. For this I look upon,—that Magistrates and all the powers of the world, unlesse they were in the imediate hand and guidance of God, unlesse hee does superact, they will dash against this stone. Itt is naturall to them nott to retaine themselves in that subordination wherin they are unto God and unto Christ, who are butt to represent [him] in this spheare of theirs in a lower way, and to bee subservient to him. Butt there is an enmitie in all these, there is an enmitie in the powers of the world [against God], and therfore Christ must bee putt downe [by them], as wee have itt att this day. God is in the Kingdome, and hee is growing uppe, and men shall nott bee able to hinder him. Soe that heere's all the question that I conceive can bee made, and all that is concern'd in itt [is this]: whether you will declare your goodwill to Jesus Christ, or noe. For I say, Christ depends nott either uppon this or that, or the truth uppon itt, as if itt should suffer or die, if such a power doe nott appeare for itt. Butt there may bee somethinge else concern'd then [the truth, namely] the flesh of the Saints, which God is tender of; for hee is tender of all of us in our severall administrations and under our severall dispensations; and if soe bee that [the] Saints are nott

[a] "them," *i.e.* the Magistrates, changing abruptly from the singular to the plural.

prepared soe to suffer, or inabled to committ themselves to him in well-doing without such defence as your sword [or] your arme, to restraine and keepe back persecutors—itt may bee God may in mercy putt this into your hearts to accomodate the weakenesse of his people soe. Butt I conceive, My Lord, that this thinge is nott att all essentiall unto your worke; for the power of the sworde and all other power whatsoever being extinct righteously, because itt stood nott and did nott act in God, I conceive that which you have to doe is to waite uppon God, untill hee shall shew you some way, and nott to bee too forward to settle. I perceive by this Agreement of the People there is a going on to settle presently, and [to] make a new constitution, which I thinke wee are nott in such a capacitie to doe. God will bringe forth a New Heaven and a New Earth. In the meane time your worke is to restraine, indeed to restraine the Magistrate from such a power. That the people of God, and that men too, that all men that are, ought to live within such bounds as may bee made manifest to them to bee such bounds that they may nott suffer wronge by might. Certainly if soe bee you shall soe manage your opportunity, I conceive you shall fully answer your end; waiting uppon God untill hee shall [deliver you], who certainly is growing uppe amongst us; and if wee could have butt patience to waite uppon him, wee should see hee would bringe us out of this labyrinth wherin wee are.

Sir Hardresse Waller.

My Lord,

That that I was going about to say was only this: I shall nott take uppon mee to dispute the Question, only tell you I feare I shall goe away with the same opinion I came. That itt was the Question, itt is the Question, and itt will bee the Question to the ending of the world: whether the Magistrate have any power att all [in matters of religion], and what that power is? My Lord, I offer itt to yourselfe and everybody, whether your affaires will admitt of soe much delay as to determine the Question whether or noe. This that is term'd the Agreement of the People, whether you doe alwayes expect to uppehold itt by the power of the sword? Otherwise you must have somethinge suitable to the affections of the people, to correspond with itt. Truly, My Lord, I should bee glad all men might bee satisfied and I thinke, if I know my heart, I could suffer for their satisfaction. Butt since itt is uppon these termes that wee cannott goe together in all thinges, I desire wee may bee soe good natur'd as to goe as farre as wee can, and I hope before that [time for parting] comes God will finde out a way to keepe us together. If the other thinges which are Civill may soe bee termed the Agreement by us, if they may bee gone through withall, and if wee can expresse any thinge to lett the world know wee doe not goe about to give the Magistrate power in that which hee hath noe power, truly, My Lord, this will shew that wee goe nott about to give him more then hee has, if hee have itt att all wee take itt away. Certainly what wee doe heere does nott conclude against right, wee may bee mistaken, if wee give itt nott certainly wee restraine from that usurpation hitherto though I could thinke itt a great-deale of happinesse that every man had as much liberty as I desire I may have nott to bee restrain'd; and since I venture nothing butt a persecution of the flesh, and instead of bringing ease to the Kingedome I should lay itt out, and to that which lies uppon us of destroying Kinges and Parliaments and all that, wee shall destroy a people of our owne, wee shall nott bee thought agreers butt disturbers of the peace. Therfore I shall desire wee may goe on to other thinges and leave this till that time. And truly itt is somethinge to mee that the Spiritt of God has nott thought fitt to determine in this world, as wee are to live uppon such incomes[a] from God, and though itt bee a very pleasing thinge to have God appeare in

[a] incomes, *i.e.* incomings, impressions. Cromwell speaks of "men who know not what it is to pray or believe, and to receive returns from God."

power to us in itt, yett God hath bin as much glorified in the suffering of Saints as in their doing, and therfore I desire wee may goe on to other thinges and nott sticke att this.

Mr. Peter.

May itt please your Lordshippe.

I thinke wee have hardly time enough to spend about those thinges that are very essentially and certainly before us to bee done out of hand.

First of all, wee doe nott know any one's mindes, for I doe nott finde anythinge att all is putt to the Question. For if any one of these three or fower were putt to the Question wee might have noe Question.[a] I know without all controversie there hath bin dispute, and will bee a great while [about this], and I know nott in what Country this will bee first decided.[b] Nott that God and Nature hath left itt soe [doubtful], butt from Diotrephes [c] to this day there hath bin a spiritt of domination. There are two thinges uppon which I will raise the Conclusion. 1. I am mervailous tender that there shall bee nothing done about Religion in England (and I am only tender in England, if I were in another Country I would nott say soe) because the interest of England is Religion.[d] I say itt lookes like the interest of the Kingdome; and I beleive you will finde that [religion is the cause of] those contests that have bin in the Kingdome. And though that Gentleman and others are inabled to know if [it be] soe [better

[a] If any one of these three or four questions propounded were put to the vote we might know the minds of this meeting.

[b] This question of the power of the magistrate with respect to religion.

[c] Peter doubtless refers to Udall's tract: *The state of the Church of England laid open in a conference between Diotrephes a Bysshopp, Tertullus a papiste, Demetrius an usurer, Pandochus an Innkeeper, and Paule a preacher of the worde of God*, published in 1588.

[d] Cf. Cromwell, 4th speech, in which he terms England "the best people in the world. . . . A people that have the highest and clearest profession amongst them of the greatest glory, namely religion."

than I am], I ask why doe wee march with our swordes by our sides? From first to the last wee might have suffer'd under Kinges, or Byshopps, or Parliament or anybody, and wee that [speak] know what itt is to suffer and to bee banish't a thousand miles.[a] You shall know all the disputes all alonge have bin uppon this very point. Itt was the old Question in Pharoah's dayes, Whether the people should worship or no? Yett [though] I thinke in truth, [that] though wee all satt still, yett the worke of God will goe on, I am nott in the minde wee should putt our hands in our pocketts and waite what will come.[b] Wee have bin drawne to this worke, wee have nott bin perswading ourselves. I should spitt him out that would looke for any plantations of his owne from the other side, lett that bee curs't from heaven to minde the thinges of that Kingdome.[c] I only offer these two thoughts. First, God seemes to call for somethinge att our hands about Religion, and that only because wee are Englishmen. The 2[d] thinge is this. That I thinke wee should nott bee too much perplex't about itt; and therfore, if I finde itt move uppon other spiritts that itt is a matter of great intricacie or trouble my thought is this. Doe butt tame that old spiritt of domination amonge Christians, of trampling uppon their Brother, and giving law, and the like. Witnesse the Country next from us that hath all the markes of a flourishing state uppon itt, I meane the Low Countries. Wee are nott soe against or afraid of this toleration, and I am nott soe against on the other side that are to feare some sufferinges. That which I would hinte is, that now wee are come heere to settle somethinge for Magistrates [let us settle something for the Church too]. "If she bee a wall," sayes [Solomon of] the Church, "wee will build a silver palace uppon her, and if shee bee a doore wee will have her of boards of

[a] Peter means to say that he does not agree with Waller's suggestion.

[b] Peter does not ageee with Sprigge's view.

[c] *i.e.* temporal gains.

cedar."[a] For the present case I thinke this, that that last motion made by that noble freind and some others [should be agreed to]. I wish wee would doe as all other Republiques would doe when wee come to such a rubbe as this is, I wish that this thought about this reserve may bee hunge forth in every Markett towne if men will write or speake about itt give itt a time itt may have a month or two that before you goe on with your other worke, and those thinges that can bee agreed to, and the affaires of the Kingdome from such time they may nott have longe debates. And soe you have my thoughts.[b]

Capt. Spencer.

Wee are now about an Agreement of the people, and I perceive one clause in itt is, that if wee have this Agreement wee will acquiesce.[c] I conceive if you leave this [power to the Magistrate] I can never comfortably [acquiesce in it], nor any man breathing, and this surely will bee [a cause of disagreement] if hee[d] bee nott restrain'd in his power.

Mr.[e]

That Gentleman hath mentioned itt 3 or 4 times as if itt might bee taken for granted, that the Magistrate hath power over the outward man [but none over the inward man]. In some case itt may bee done. If hee hath power over my body hee hath power

[a] *Canticles*, viii., 9.

[b] Peter's meaning is clear though the report is hopelessly involved. He recommends that the reserve be adjourned for a month or two, and the outside public invited to give their opinions on it, whilst the council of war continues its discussions on the other parts of the Agreement.

[c] Spencer refers apparently to a passage in the letter prefixed to the Agreement. The Agreement is said to be presented by the Army, "as a testimony whereby all men may be assured what we are willing and ready to acquiesce in."

[d] Hee, *i.e.* the magistrate.

[e] Possibly Wildman or Overton, certainly some layman not a member of the Army. "Tha gentleman" whose argument is refuted is Ireton.

to keepe mee att home when I should goe abroad to serve God. And concerning [yourselves] one worde I would speake. God has pleas'd by your meanes [to give us what liberty we have], which wee looke att as from himself by whome wee have had all the comforts wee enjoy,—I say God hath made you instruments of libertie. In matters of Religion that's preferr'd by us before life. Lett's have that or nothing. Now God hath by your meanes troden uppon that power which should have trodden uppon us. [Let us agree] to prevent any authority from coming uppon us. If you never agree in your Judgements, itts noe matter, [if you] keepe butt authority from beating of us and killing of us, and the like. And wheras that Gentleman spake of this concerning a Representative, concerning what power they should have heerafter, wee have this to say. If you your owneselves cannott helpe us [to freedom] in matters of opinion wee doe nott looke for itt while wee breathe. The Lord hath bin pleas'd to informe you as [well as] any other men. If you cannott agree uppon itt, then I[b] shall conclude for my parte, never to expect freedome whiles I live.

Col. Harrison.

May itt please your Excellency.

I would nott trouble you save that itt may save you trouble. I doe wish that which was offer'd at first might bee entertained to save time. That you would putt the businesse in such a way [as] to have the state of the Question.[a] If itt bee soe longe before you come to the Question, itt will bee longer before you come to a resolution in itt. I offer this: That because this is that which stickes uppon the consciences of men I would nott have itt taken notice of by any that you would soe slight them as nott to doe that now, butt that some of all interests may have the consideration of this, and therin you may have confidence that God will blesse the issue. For what expedient there may bee found in itt that

[a] *i.e.* Have the question stated.

[b] MS. "wee."

may bee left to their consideration, and the blessing of God uppon their indeavours. Whether they should have assistance from some out of London, or those that would bee willing to meete [them from] elsewhere uppon itt, would bee an happy thinge to guide them to the right of itt. That then you would please to goe with the rest of the thinges that I thinke you may more generally concurre in.[a]

Col. Deane.

I should make this motion: whether wee might nott finde some-thinge att this time might satisfie all, and whether in that foregoing clause. . . . "That in all civill thinges," [etc.], wee might nott satisfie all interests?[b]

Col. Harrison.

That will leade you to a consideration of the meritt of the thinge, and will spend much time in debate pro and con, and if itt please God to guide the hearts of some few itt may bee a satis-faction.

Capt. Clarke.

I shall take the boldnesse to offer one worde or two. That Gentleman that spoke last[c] was pleas'd to offer this as an expedient to satisfie all: that if the worde[s] 'civill and naturall' [were inserted, it] might suffice to satisfie all. I suppose [they will] nott [satisfy all], because that all punishments, though for matters

[a] *i.e.* Do not adjourn the consideration of the religious question till we have settled the civil questions, as some propose, but appoint a committee at once to consider the religious question. This proposal was adopted.

[b] Compare the eighth section of the Agreement of the People (as presented Jan. 20, 1649). "That the representatives have and shall be understood to have the supreme trust . . . and the highest and final judgment concerning all *natural or civil things;* but not concerning things spiritual or evangelical."

[c] Refers to Deane.

of religion, are meerly civill for the punishment of the body; and whatsoever the sentence of the Church [may be], if they doe sentence any person, they send him to the secular power. Soe that will bee as himself has spoken. . . . .

Butt I shall adde one worde. This Army by the blessing of God hath done very great thinges for the Nation, and itt's the honour of the Nation that itt hath bin a shelter to honest people that had otherwise bin hammer'd to dust, and as longe as God makes us a shelter to them [it will be an honour to us]. Wee are now closing uppe the day, and I thinke every one heere is willing to see an end of the days, yea yeares [of his life] were itt to see that freedome soe often spoken of, and that common right soe often desired, clearly brought forth to the people. Your Lordshippe and the Army under your command hath taken uppon you to interpose in those times of straightes, to see if you could finde out such a way as might settle the people in formes of common right and freedome. You have remonstrated this to the world; and to that end you have hinted unto a petition of the 11th of September wherin (if your Lordshippe please to looke uppon that itt doth aime att) the thinge principally spoken of [is] that there may nott bee a restriction to the opinions of men for matters of religion, to the[ir] consciences.[a] Wee are conclude[d] men cannott master

[a] "We expected," say the Petitioners to the Parliament, "That you would have exempted matters of religion and God's worship from the compulsive or restrictive power of any authority upon earth, and reserved to the supreme authority an uncompulsive power only of appointing a way for the public, whereby abundance of misery, persecution, and heart-burning would for ever be avoided. . . . That you would not have followed the example of former tyrannous and superstitious parliaments, in making orders, ordinances, or laws, or in appointing punishments concerning opinions or things supernatural, styling some blasphemies, others heresies; whereas you know yourselves easily mistaken, and that divine truths need no human helps to support them: such proceedings having been generally invented to divide the people amongst themselves and to affright men from that liberty of discourse by which corruption and tyranny would be soon discovered." *Old Parliamentary History*, xvii., 456, 458.

passions. I referre this to bee consider'd whether if this bee nott our common right and our common freedome to live under a Civill Magistrate to live by our neighbours, butt as touching religion why should any people bee punished. I thinke, My Lord, that every one heere when hee speakes his Conscience will say plainly [no]. And now whether wee for prudence or policie should protest. Lett us doe that which is right, and trust God with the rest. Noe man or Magistrate on the earth hath power to meddle in these cases. As for meum and tuum, and right betweene man and man hee hath right, butt as betweene God and man hee hath nott. Therfore I desire [that] though all agree that the Magistrate hath noe power to doe soe, and wee have noe power to give him ; yett seing hee hath in all ages usurp't itt ; and in these late yeares, and in this last age[a] almost as in the remembrance of errours and blasphemies had made most of them heere to fall to the ground, and since that is soe wee have great reason to reserve itt soe. Wee might bee willing to reserve itt [hereafter] when wee cannott.

Com̃. Gen. Ireton.

Truly, My Lord, I should nott trouble you agen, butt that I see wee are falne uppon an Argument ; and from the convincing of one another with light and reason wee are falne to an eager catching att that which is our owne opinion, and dictating that which is our apprehension, as if itt were the minde of all, and indeed of God himself; and indeed studying to preconclude one another by consequence, as especially the Gentleman did that spoke last. Hee tells us, that wee are bound by the Remonstrance to doe this thinge that now wee are questioning about whether wee should doe or noe ; and one ground is because in that our Remonstrance wee had referr'd soe to a petition of the 11th of Sep-

[a] May be paraphrased : "Had almost made religion itself to fall to the ground, under pretence of restraining errors and blasphemies."

tember that wee had desired all thinges [in it] to bee granted. Butt if soe itt had bin an ill use of itt; if there had bin generally good thinges in itt, and one thinge prejudiciall, though wee did stand uppon all thinges in itt that were [good] wee were false to our Engagement. When wee had desired the whole wee did nott insist uppon every particle of itt. I desire wee may nott proceede uppon mistakes of this kinde. This conduces only to stifle itt, and I wish wee may nott goe about to sett such thinges uppon men's mindes.[a] I must clearly minde that Gentleman, that all that is said in the Remonstrance concerning the [petition of the] 11th of September is butt this: when wee have prosecuted our desire concerning justice, and our desires to a generall settlement, and amongst the rest a dissolving of this Parliament, [we then desire] that this Parliament would apply themselves for the remainder of the time to such thinges as are of publique consideration, and lay aside particular matters that have interrupted them hitherto, and for the further time they shall sitt nott medling with private matters, butt consider those thinges that are proper [work] for Parliaments, as reformation of laws, and providing better for the well government of the nation, and hearken to what hath bin offer'd to them by persons well-affected for the publique good; and amongst the rest [we mention] that petition of the 11th of September [and we move this as to matters to be taken into consideration, in due time and place, after public justice and the general settlement of the kingdom].[b] Now because wee saw very many and great dreames of good thinges, and therfore have desired they would take itt into consideration with this Agreement and settle-

[a] *i.e.* I wish you would not suggest that the Army has broken its engagements.

[b] The grand army remonstrance of Nov. 20, 1648, to which Ireton refers, supplies the words given here in brackets (*Old Parliamentary History*, xviii., 236). In the text of the speech in Clarke MS. after the word "hitherto" in l. 16. come the following words, which are clearly misplaced, "and for relation to lawes in that kinde and for providing better for the well government of the nation, and wee move this as to advice to matters of justice and of the kingdom."

ment thinges of that nature, and amongst the rest that therfore wee should bee concluded because of that, that wee should nott now have any thinge in this Agreement that shall nott prevaile for that which the petition does [is unreasonable].

Another thinge wee have declar'd [for]: to have a settlement uppon grounds of common right and freedome. Itt is the title of the Agreement.[a] 'Tis true, butt I doe nott altogether remember that itt is in our Declaration. Lett itt bee soe that itt is a common right. Itt is dictated to us by that Gentleman to bee a common right and freedome [that any man] submitting to the Civill Governement of the Nation should have liberty to serve God according to his conscience.[b] This a right, I will agree to that. That is nott the Question amongst us. For if that were the Question, I should bee sure to give my noe to the allowance of any man [to be punished] for his conscience, and if I had a thousand noes I should give itt, and that as loud as any man.

Heere's a[nother] Gentleman[c] that does speake for what is to bee done in this businesse, [as being] a matter that is nott necessary to God and Jesus Christ, butt a thinge wherin wee must shew our good will to him, in preserving his people from sufferinges for that which is his worke, his act. If that were the thinge in Question, I should thinke that wee of this Army above all others should walke most unworthy of the mercies wee have found, if wee should nott indeavour [it].

Butt heere's the case. The Question is now, whether you shall make such a provision for men that are conscientious, [in order] that they may serve God according to their light and conscience, as shall necessarily debarre any kinde of restraint on any thinge that any man will call religion. That's the very Question. Truly, itt is soe, or else you will make noe question. If you could

[a] "An Agreement of the people of England, and the places therewith incorporated for a firm and present peace upon grounds of common right and freedom."

[b] Clarke ?

[c] Sprigge.

bringe itt to a restraint for the Magistrate to punish only men that are members and servants of Jesus Christ, all that are heere would give an aye to itt. Butt to the question: whether admitting that to bee never soe good, and I thinke itt is our great duty and great interest to indeavour [to secure it]—yett whether wee shall make our provision for that in such a way as shall give to all men their latitude, without any power to restraine them, to practice idolatry, [or] to practice atheisme, and any thinge that is against the light of God?

Lieut. Col. Lilburne interrupts.

That is nott the Question; butt [whether] that clause may bee in the Agreement or nott?

Com̃. Ireton.

Whether this bee nott the Question: that[a] [all that] will joyne with you in civill thinges [shall be free from any restraint in spiritual things]? Now I come to tell you of what kinde those thinges are that conscientious men doe thinke the Magistrate ought to restraine. I doe nott thinke any man conscientious [that says] that the Magistrate ought to restraine a man from that which Jesus Christ does teach him; butt men have consciences to say that there are many thinges that men may owne and practice under pretence of religion, that there may, nay there ought to bee the restraint of them in; and that is the ground of our Question. Butt if I have mistaken this, I shall willingly bee mistaken. However I am sure of this in generall: that there is noe exception to the putting of this in this Agreement butt this; that you cannott soe provide for such a reserve as this is for men really conscientious that they shall nott bee persecuted, butt you will

[a] "These things we declare to be essential to our just freedomes, and to a thorough composure of our long and wofull distractions. And therefore we are agreed and resolved to maintain these certain rules of government and all that joyne therein, with our utmost possibilities against all opposition whatsoever." *Foundations of Freedom*, p. 12.

by that debarre the Magistrate of a power that hee ought to have to restraine.

Mr. Sprigge.

There is something offer'd in that which I made bold to speake of. The Question that I conceiv'd to bee canvas'd was: whether your Excellency should improve this opportunity to restraine any power whatsoever from oppressing or vexing any man for the thinges that hee does conscientiously?

Com̃. Ireton.

That's nott the Question.

Mr. Sprigge.

I suppose itt will bee resolved in this, and though the termes may bee different.

Com̃ Ireton.

Doe you make that [clear] that they shall nott punish for any thinge butt that, and wee shall stand to itt.

Mr. Sprigge.

I conceive that there is all alonge a supposition of a provision to bee made to prevent heresies in the world, besides that same which is (as I conceive) the only meanes of suppressing them and eradicating them, and that is the breaking forth of him who is the Truth, the breaking forth of Christ in the mindes and spiritts of men. This is that which does only roote uppe and destroy those heresies, those false conceptions and imaginations; and I conceive that this same is altogether omitted and forgotten in the discourse [of the Commissary General]. For this is the extreamity that wee are reduc't to looke uppon. How shall we avoide, say you, butt that the Kingdome may bee over-runne with such thinges as idolatry and the grossest thinges that are? I conceive that itt is nott proper for Magistracie to bee applyed unto this; and therfore if you doe reserve [from the Magistrate] this power to apply himself this way to the restraint of these, you doe nott reserve [from] him that which is his right, that to which hee beares any proportion, neither doe you withold any meanes that is proper for the suppressing and preventing of these thinges. Itt is a shewing a great diffidence in the spiritt of God, and in Christ, as if he would nott provide for the maintayning his owne truth in the world.

Col. Harrison.

I will only trouble you in a worde. Wee are nott yett resolved uppon a Question. [The Commissary General] and the Gentleman there that spoke last [differ] which ought to bee the Question; though in the issue itt will bee, whether this clause concerning religion ought to bee in [the Agreement]. Yett to the end that you may come to a period [I desire] that you would first take this into consideration: Whether the Magistrate hath any inspection att all in matters of Religion? And when you have concluded that itt will fall under your consideration how much [power] will bee needfull for you uppon any considerations to give to him. Therfore, if you will fall into the Debate of the businesse, I doe humbly offer this to your Excellency as the first Question: Whether the Magistrate hath any power or noe?

Doctor Parker.

I would nott have spoken in this kinde, butt that I have heard divers men speaking, and yett in my owne sence they doe nott come to that which I apprehend concerning the thinge. The Gentleman that spoke last spoke well: that hee would have a Question [stated, whether the Magistrate hath any power or no]. All that I would adde [is, that the question be], whether they have any power to restraine men in their owne consciences acting to civill peace and civill honesty? Whether Jesus Christ under the New Testament hath given any power to the Civill Magistrate to restraine men professing their Consciences before God, while they walke orderly according to civill peace and civill honesty?

Com̃ Ireton.

Itt is good to keepe to the Question which was first drawne, and as it is last (whether Jesus Christ hath given such power) itt is a catching Question. Itt was nott the businesse of Jesus Christ when hee came into the world to erect Kingdomes of the world, and Magistracies, or Monarchies, or to give the rule of them positive or negative. Therfore if you would consider this Question, whether the Magistrate have any thinge to doe in any thinge which men will call Religion (for you must goe soe large), you must nott confine itt [to the enquiry] whether Jesus Christ have under the Gospell given itt, butt you must looke to the whole Scripture. As there is much in the old Testament which hath lost much, yett there are some thinges of perpetuall and naturall right, that the Scripture of the old Testament doth hold forth, wherin itt does beare a cleare witnesse to that light that every man hath left in him by nature, if hee were nott deprav'd by lust. There are some thinges of perpetuall right in the old Testament that the Magistrate had a power in before the coming of Jesus Christ in the flesh. Unlesse you can shew us that those thinges are nott a perpetuall right, nor had nott their perpetuall end, butt had only their temporall end, soe as to determinate by his coming in the flesh, you must give us leave to thinke that the Magistrate ought according to the old institution to follow that right.

Col. Hewson.

I desire your Excellency to consider whether itt tends? If itt bee a Question tending to that, then consider what you doe in putting itt to the Question. Either you resolve that they have a power or nott. I would faine learne if itt bee resolved whether that trust bee infallible, if itt bee liable to a mistake then wee may build a very great foundation.

Lo. Generall.

Now is only to dispute the Question.

Mr. Nye.

My Lord;

[I desire] that your Lordshippe would bee pleased to state the Question. There is one thinge that I have observed, that words of a neere significancie [sometimes lead to confusion], and I conceive these two words doe. Itt is one worde of "matters of religion," and another "matters of conscience." Matters of conscience is larger then "matters[a] of religion." Itt concernes that of the 2d table. Now if itt bee the power of the Civill Magistrate over consciences for a man may make conscience of some thinges. There was a Gentleman cast into Newgate to bee executed for having two wives, and hee had this case of conscience;[b] hee sent for severall Divines, and amongst the rest I had this dispute. All the arguments about persecution for conscience. "Those that were of neerest affinity to sett them farthest off" [etc.].[c] [Say] such matters [of conscience] as concerne the first Table; then you come to distinct termes.

Mr. Walford.[d]

As a servant to your Excellency I desire to speake a worde. There is none concern'd more in libertie then the Lord himself. I know nothing butt that Kinges and Armies and Parliaments might have bin quiett att this day, if they would have lett Israell alone. For men to give away God how well they will answer itt I doe nott know. The Lord is a transcendent thinge. There is a seede gone forth from God . . . and whiles I am in bonds heere you will punish mee, when I shall come to returne to my spiritt. . . . Itt was nott the saints butt God himself. . . . and therfore all that I shall say to this—if you can make by your power a Magistrate a Lord and lett him bee sett uppe assoone as you will. I have noe more to say.

[a] MS. "that of religion."

[b] *i.e.* made this a case of conscience, said he was following his conscience in thus acting.

[c] Specimen of the argument used by the gentleman.

[d] Walford was one of Fairfax's chaplains.

Sir Hardresse Waller.

I should desire the Question if I thought the Question would doe the businesse. I am afraid wee are gotten into the ocean againe. I should desire that might bee minded to save the time. Itt was moved a while since, and that by the way, to putt itt to such a thinge as may bee satisfactorie, for I doe nott thinke that words can satisfie the hearts of men. Butt if your Lordshippe shall take such a course that men of all interests to bee together. Lett the world know you will bring them into their civil quiett. Wee doe nott know butt that they will bee all agreed in this, and when itt is declared to the world, all Gods people may bee free.

Major Barton[a].

An't please your Lordshippe, for ought I perceive there are many presumptions. Many thinke there are great presumptions. I desire there may bee tendernesse had, and that is first, that Justice may bee executed.[b] I feare stating this soe high itt does somethinge putt a demurre uppon that, and uppon what ground I doe nott know. I shall desire, that the meritt of the Remonstrance may bee consider'd, and noe other thinge offer'd that may intermingle, and desire that as itt is of that tender consideration as to bloud or peace. I heare of some thinge that hath bin spoken heere, that there have bin divers invited that as yett doe nott appeare; and [I move] what was by one Gentleman[c] offer'd to your Lordshippe, that the place and time may bee soe determined as to this particular that they may have a further invitation, and soe bee invited that they may come. I shall desire that wee doe nott lay a foundation of distractions.

[a] Of Scroope's regiment of horse.

[b] Apparently refers to the King's trial.

[c] Referring to Harrison's proposal for a Committee.

Col. Titchborne.

I shall desire to move this, that when wee doe putt itt to the Question, first, that you would propose heere what shall bee the Questions in the Debate; and then to referre itt to some persons and some time wherin you may take the concurrence of all persons that doe concurre. And in the meane time that the rest may bee [busied] in the [matters][a] that concerne the whole.

Mr. Overton.[b]

I have observed, that there hath bin much controversie about this point, and severall motions concerning the matters. One thinge offer'd by Col. Hewson and some others, that some of all parties might bee chosen. I humbly conceive the same thinge hath bin already done, for there hath bin fower of severall parties chosen for the drawing uppe of this Agreement,[c] which they have done to try who will agree, and who will nott agree; for itt is a thinge nott of force butt of agreement; and I presume, that there is noe man heere butt is satisfied in his owne judgement what to agree to, and what nott to agree to. I desire itt may passe to the Question, [yea] or noe?

Com̃. Ireton.

I should bee as free as any man to have a catch of his owne Agreement, there was little difference in those that drew this uppe.

All.

Calling for the Question.

C[ommissary-General] I[reton].

My Lord, the Question that men doe call for is nott as to the

[a] MS. "whole."

[b] Richard Overton.

[c] See Preface. The history of the drawing up of the original "Agreement" is given at length by Lilburne.

Agreement—whether that clause may bee fitlie in or noe, or any thinge to that purpose[a]—butt [a question] to bee debated in relation to our judgements.

> The Question was : Whether the Magistrate have any power in matters of Religion, that is, those thinges concerning the first Table ?

Col. Rich.

I shall offer one worde to the Question.

Com̃ Ireton.

> Whether the Magistrate have or ought to have any power in matters of Religion, by which wee understand the thinges concern'd under the First Table ?

Col. Rich.

My Lord, I finde that there is a generall agreement by every person that hath spoken, that itt is nott his desire that the Civill Magistrate should exercise a power to persecute any honest man that walkes according to his conscience in those thinges that are really religious, and nott pretended soe. What is represented in opposition to this is: That wee cannott finde out any way to discriminate this from that[b] exorbitant liberty which those that are nott Religious butt would pretend to bee soe, would take. If you please I should offer my sence to the Question :

> Whether or noe the Civill Magistrate is to exercise any power, restrictive or compulsive, uppon the persons of men in matters of Religion, they walking inoffensive to the Civill peace ?

Com̃. Ireton.

My Lord, I still say, that whoever is eager to catch advantages

[a] Order of clauses altered.

[b] MS. "this."

for his owne opinion that there may be an advantage gained on the other hand, does nott further agreement. That which is propounded I did offer itt, that men under pretence of Religion may breake the peace, [or do] thinges that are civilly evill. Now, My Lord, I suppose that "whether if a man doe walk civilly & inoffensively or noe," is nott att all necessary to bee consider'd in this, which is the first and maine Question that is heere propounded, [viz.] whether in some thinges which [a man [a]] may call Religion, [the magistrate [b]] may have a restrictive power. Whether compulsive or restrictive power you may take itt whether you will. Yett it may still bee the question, if you will have itt putt [c] [after the main question].[d]

Doctor Parker.

One word more I added, that word "civill peace" or "civill honesty."

Com̃. Ireton.

Make itt whatsoever you will according to "civill peace" or "civill honesty;" yett still itt remaines to bee debated [whether the magistrate is to exercise any power in matters of religion].

Major Barton.

My Lord, I doe perceive as I judge, and speake itt with submission, that there are some heere that are too inclinable to follow the course of corrupt Committees formerly, that were forward to putt the Question before there bee satisfaction given.

[a] MS. "hee." [b] MS. "hee."

[c] The order of the clauses given in the MS. has been altered.

[d] Ireton's point is that the question raised by Parker may be considered later after the main question, whether the magistrate has any power at all, has been settled.

Capt. Hodden.

Heere have bin very many disputes what would bee the Question, and if these words bee nott further explain'd in those termes the Question is still, and hath bin, that which I thinke most mens spiritts heere have from the beginning satisfied to bee, [to wit]: Whether you will restraine Magistrates from that tyranny of compelling or enforcing[a] men, and persecuting men for doing those thinges they doe out of conscience, and as to the worshipp of God?

Com. Ireton.

Reades the Question.

Whether [the Magistrate ought to have any power in matters of religion, by which we understand the things concerned under the first Table]?

Col. Harrison.

I desire the word compulsive may bee added, for restrictive will nott bee large enough. If [the words] any power bee nott large enough, [I desire that] then you will take both "compulsive" and "restrictive."

Com̃. Ireton.

My Lord, I perceive itt's every man's opinion, that the Magistrate hath a protective power; and if you will apply matters of Religion to the first Table, itt will bee granted [that he should also have a] compulsive. "Thou shalt have noe other Gods butt mee," "Thou shalt make noe graven image" &c. "Thou shalt nott take the name of the Lord in vaine." And then for the 4th. "Thou shalt nott doe any manner of worke [on the Sabbath day].

Whether the Magistrate have or ought to have any power in matters of Religion?

Mr. Bacon.

I doe apprehend there hath bin much time taken uppe about the

[a] MS. "informing."

restrictive power and [a] the compulsive power; that is concerning the power of the Magistrate in matters appertayning to the Kingedome of Heaven, and the Kingdome of God. They have bin debated, first, whether hee have power; and 2dly what is that power that hee hath; [b] and soe whether the power that hee hath bee either compulsive or restrictive. Now I doe conceive, that any other power [than that] which is purely protective hee hath nott; and I doe give this account. The whole power of the Magistrate is said to bee the power of the sword, an outward power. I doe apprehend [that] really all matters relating to the Kingedome of God are purely and altogether spiritual; and therfore I conceive [that] to allow the Magistrate any other power then that which is purely protective of men to live quietly is to putt a power into the hands of the Magistrate which is nott att all given him by God. I speake somethinge as a man, and I crave leave to speake a word only as a Christian, as touching affaires of this nature, which I doe confesse is a matter to bee acknowledged as the great and wonderfull worke of God. To witt, that there is a time [of] coming forth of captives, according as the Scripture speakes, "I will take off every yoake and remove every heavy burthen from off the people, because of the annointing," [c] that is, because of Christ. Now Sir, give mee leave [to say], this thing is the great matter, and it is the glory of the nation that wee have lived to [see] it, and it is the care of the honourable Councill and all the good people of the Nation, how wee are [to] secure the people of the Nation from the like thraldome they have bin in in times past. I will lay downe only this one position. The ground of all that enmity that hath bin of men one against another, and of the universall enmity that hath bin in all sorts of men against God, I conceive hath bin the state of ignorance, and darkenesse, and pretence of Religion that hath bin amongst us. That nott having the faith itt self which wee have pretended to see wee have rather the forme of godlinesse then the power of itt, and

[a] MS. "to." [b] Order of clauses altered. [c] Isaiah, x., 27.

God hath bin pleased to bringe forth as wee have heard.[a] There are certaine men in the Army that having tasted of the good worde of God and the powers of the world to come, that have bin in the good land, have bin in such a scattered time, wee all having light come, that the land may have her sabaoth in a good sence after 6 or 7 yeares disturbance or trouble now taken away, and therfore the Lord fill the Nation with men of upright spiritts. Whatsoever you doe appoint for the restrayning of men the Magistrate his hands will nott bee bound uppe, butt hee will keepe his power against that Religion that is contrary to himself; and therfore that's to bee prevented att this time as longe as wee goe noe further.

Com̃. Ireton.

A caution that you would use such words as concerne a restrictive power.

Whether the Magistrate have or ought to have any compulsive, or restrictive power in matters of Religion?

1. That those who are of the opinion in the affirmative,[b] begin to lay downe their grounds, and that the discussion bee alternate:

2. That if noe man give grounds for a compulsive power, then those that doe speake against the power of the Magistrate will speake only to the restrictive power.

Mr.——

If there bee noe man heere to speake. . . . . That that, I should offer to consideration is this. When Israell having bin at a losse a longe time had renewed their Covenant with God soe that God accepted them, Hee was pleased to deliver his minde to them (and nott only to them butt to all the sons of men) in those ten words, commonly called, the Ten Commandements. Now as your good Apostle saith, they consist of two Tables, and the commands of the

[a] From this point the speech becomes simply a collection of fragmentary sentences.

[b] MS. adds "or ought to be."

first Table are all negatives. Now God never gave any rules to the sons of men butt hee gave them to bee in force. For my owne parte I apprehend, that they are morall, and soe a rule to all the sons of men as well as to Israell, butt especially to those who are zealous for their God. That there is a compulsive power left to the Magistrates that I cannott alledge ; butt that there is a restrictive [power from the very] nature of the Commandements that I doe hold necessary. Neither did Israell ittself goe about to compell any man, butt were very watchfull and shy whome they did admitt into communion with them, butt wee have observed that they have restrain'd, as itt concernes every Magistrate [to do]. Wee must nott looke att Pagans and Heathens that are revolted from their duties to God, and yett God hath left those impressions uppon the sons of men that you shall nott finde any people butt they worshippe some God. Now the command of God in that kinde is, that they should worshippe noe other God butt him. This is that which I thinke lies uppon all powers, to suffer noe other God to bee worship't butt Jehovah; and soe the 2[d] Commandement does restraine Idolatry. Butt as hee is pure in himself, soe hee will have such a worshipp as himself hath instituted and appointed; hee will nott have the sacred name taken in vaine. Now any that shall breake the 2[d] or 3[d] Commandement comes under the cognizance of the Civill Magistrate. Soe for the 4th, though there bee a Prologue leading to itt, yett itt is restrictive. Soe that though I have nothing to say for compulsive power, yett thus much I have to say, that [the magistrate ought to have a restrictive power]. God deliver'd these thinges to Moses that was a prince in Israell, and itt is a rule to this day, and itt is a rule by the light of Nature [also]; and therfore itt properly concernes the princes of the people, especially those that know [a] God, to restraine corrupt worshippe.

[a] MS. "knew."

Mr. Nye.

I speake to this. That there is noe ground from the nature of the Meeting to conclude every man [as agreeing] that sayes nothing, if your end bee by the suffrage of silence to second your owne judgements, to stampe your owne judgements, butt these have a better foundation then silence, butt least silence should bee soe farre thought of—Truly as the Question is stated I thinke a man may assent to itt, if you will take the words, "those things that are truly religious."[a] If the contests that is betweene us and Byshopps were by way of compulsion they have assum'd soe much as this. That even in that which is truly religious, the worshipp and service of God, they have putt such restrictions[b] as these are: that men shall nott preach though they bee called of God; and soe likewise compulsion, that such a forme of prayer [should be used]. In this sence your Question ought to bee understood, and soe to take the words in your proper speech, and that is religion. For if you say "religion" simply, by itt you understand true religion; and if you speake of any other thinge you will give itt's adjunct "false religion;" and soe a man may easily stand to itt, and yett nott come to what is the drift of the Question: whether a false religion, or such matters as these, are [matters which] the Magistrate hath to doe withall. If itt bee understood in that strict sence, I must stand with you in itt. I doe nott thinke, that the Civill Magistrate hath anythinge to doe determinatively to inforce anythinge that is matters of religion, to inforce the thinge that is that I doe extreamly question. Butt for the other [question], whether the Magistrate have anythinge to doe under any notion or consideration whatsoever, either of setting uppe the false God, which is noe religion indeed, that for my owne parte I must professe that I doe thinke the Magistrate may have somethinge to doe in that. And soe I shall deliver my judgement that noe man shippewreck himself in this thinge.

[a] The last clause has been transferred from a later sentence. Nye proposes to amend Ireton's definition by adding these words.

[b] MS. "reasonings."

Mr. Wildman's Question.

Whether the Magistrate have any restrictive or compulsive power in the time or manner of Gods worshippe, or [as to] faith or opinion concerning him?

Com̃ Gen. Ireton.

Whether the Magistrate have or ought to have any power of restrayning men, by penalties or otherwise, from the profession or practice of any thinge the evill or good whereof relates to God only?

Col. Harrison.

That you will leave [thereby] the judgement to the Civill Magistrate [to decide] whether the doing of such a thinge bee [relating] to God [only] or noe. Whether [when the magistrate punishes] errour or[a] heresie, hee doe nott [profess to] punish them as itt relates to the Neighbour; and whether if soe, wee[b] doe nott leave them to bee punished [by using those words.]?

Com̃. Ireton.

1. I take itt for granted that [the things commanded in] those words which wee call the fower first Commandements they are matters of religion, the fault of[c] non-performance whereof relates to God only, the duty and satisfaction if a man doe observe them relates to God onely. I speake concerning such thinges. As to them I give my ground thus. That as to those thinges the Magistrate hath a power to restraine men, and ought to doe itt. I argue first from the possibility of the thinge. Those are thinges against which there is a testimonie in the light of nature, and consequently, they are thinges that men as men are in some capacity [to judge of], unlesse they are perverted—indeed a man perverted in his owne lusts cannott judge of any thinge even matters of common honesty

[a] MS. "of." [b] MS. "hee." [c] MS. "or."

—2[dly] Those who are subject[s] and nott the judges, they are likewise in [a] capacity to judge of the evill of those thinges even by the light of nature. And in that respect I account itt is proper and nott unsuitable to the judgement of men as men, and of Magistrates as Magistrates, because (if any body will take notes of itt in writing they may [a]) because in such thinges the Magistrate by the light that hee hath as a man may judge, and the subject by that light that hee hath as a man may bee convinc't.

In the next place I goe to grounds of Scripture, and shew that this is the Magistrates duty. And first I will take itt for granted till some body give mee reason to the contrary :

1. That tis the injunction [of the old Testament], and likewise itt hath bin the practice of Magistrates in all the time of the old Testament till the coming of Christ in the flesh, to restraine such thinges. If any doubt itt they shall have proofes : first, that the Magistrates of the Jewes as Magistrates were commanded to restraine such thinges : secondly, that they were commended when they did itt : thirdly, that they were reproved when they did nott. This is cleare through the current of the old Testament

And first because I see the answers to these are obvious, I shall speake to the two cheif [answers], and shew you what is objected. That is first : [that] what the Magistrates of the Jewes might or ought to doe is noe rule to others, for they were to doe itt as ecclesiastical Magistrates, Church matters concerning them ; [that by] the punishment of death or such other punishments, they did butt allude to excommunication, unto the time of the Gospell ; and that you can make noe inference from what they ought to doe as to conclude a perpetuall duty of Magistrates, butt a duty allegorically answer'd in the duty of Ecclesiasticall [officers in ecclesiastical] thinges. This I have have heard to bee one answer ; and to this I shall butt apply one reason to shew the inconveniencie of this answer [to] those grounds that wee give from Scripture, and that is this. Iff

[a] Probably a reference to Clarke's note-taking.

itt doe appeare that those that were the Magistrates amonge the Jewes,—whether they were Ecclesiasticall or Civill Magistrates—that they were to exercise this power, nott only to persons within the Church, butt [to persons] without the Church, professedly noe way within the compasse of the Church, then that objection is taken away. Butt I thinke [it is clear that] they were to extend this power to those that were out of the Church. They were commanded to beate downe the Idolls, and groves, and images of the land whither they went; they were commanded that they should nott suffer the stranger that was within the gate to worke on the Saboath, [and not to] to suffer swearers or idolaters of any kinde. If any man doubt that, itt is an easie matter to produce Scripture for that purpose—Soe that itt is cleare to mee they did [it] consider'd as Magistrates having an aucthority civill or nacturall, not as persons signifying or typifying the power of Ecclesiasticall Officers under the Gospell; and therfore what was a rule of duty to them (unlesse men can shew mee a ground of change) is a rule and duty of Magistrates now.

And that rule or duty to them leades mee to the next evasion: that what was a rule to them under the Law as Magistrates does nott hold under the Gospell. Now to this I answer (and I doe these thinges because I would give men grounds against the next meeting to consider of some thinges); I say that I will acknowledge as to those thinges enjoyn'd the practice whereof was commanded, the neglect whereof was reproved in the Magistrates of the Jewes, whose end was typicall and determinative, to end att the coming of Christ, to all those [I acknowledge] the duty of the Magistrate doth cease. Either as to restriction or compulsion [it] doth cease; because itt relates [not] to the thinges themselves. Butt for those thinges themselves for which they had a perpetuall ground in relacion of the duty to God, a perpetuall rule by the law written in mens hearts, and a [perpetuall] testimonie left in man by nature—and soe consequently for those thinges whereof the ground of duty towards God is nott chang'd—for those thinges I account that what was sin before is sin still, what was sin to practice [before] remaines sin still, what was the duty of a Magistrate to restraine before remaines his duty to restraine still. And thus I have given my grounds why wee ought [not] to binde the hands of tho Magistrate, [so] that they shall nott restraine men from evills, though against God only, that are given as breaches of the first Table only.

Mr. Nye.

I should have made bold to suggest my thoughts this way before. I doe nott professe itt to bee my opinion, butt now I shall doe itt uppon a ground or two.

Under favour I thinke your resolution att first was to propose some objections now, and leave them to consideration.

Mr. Goodwin.

I shall crave leave to speake a few words to what the Commissary Generall hath said.

You were pleased to lay this for your ground. That the Magistrate ought to have a restrictive power in matters of religion, because matters of false worshippe (or att least of idolatry) are matters comprehended within the light of nature, such as may bee perceived by naturall men. I conceive first: That itt is nott whatsoever may bee made out, may bee drawn [a] out by much meditation, or discourse, or inference by the light of nature—you will nott call this matters of the light of Nature; for then every man that is to obey your lawes ought to bee a student, and by contemplations finde those thinges that lie as remote from mens first apprehensions. There are abundance of thinges that may bee made out by the light of nature which are nott lawes or constitutions.[b] All law ought to bee [such] thinges [as may be known] by the light of nature; butt

[a] MS. "driven.'

[b] Order of sentences changed.

such thinges as ought to bee knowne by the light of nature without inquiry, without meditation. Soe [for instance with regard to] thinges as to the being [of God], as to the creation of the world. Itt is an hard thinge for any man to come to frame a notion by such a meditation of such a being as is in God. You must putt in infinitenesse of wisedome &c. Itt will require much of a man's time to frame such a notion which will answer the being of God. For this is nott [to knowe God], to beleive that there is a God, to say there is a being which is more then men, from above that which is of men. Butt to know God is to beleive that there is a true God. "This is life eternall to beleive thee the only true God." [a] That was for that thinge. That though itt bee [possible] by the light of nature to make out [that there is a God, that though] men are capable by the light of nature to conceive that there is a God, yett to conceive this in a right and true manner itt is in the profundities, in the remotest parte, amongst those conclusions which lie farthest off from the presence of men, [even] though itt should bee in the light of nature.

And then againe, [with regard to] what you were pleas'd to observe concerning the Old Testament and the power of the Magistrate, I shall desire to suggest these two thinges by way of answer. My ground is: that there is nott the same reason for the power, and the exercise of the same [b] power [under the] the Gospell [as there was] under the law. My first reason is this. Wee know, that the Magistracie of the old Testament was appointed, instituted, and directed by God himself. The Magistracie under the Gospell is chosen [by men], and they are vested with that power which they have from men. Now God may bee his owne carver. If hee will create and sett uppe Magistrates hee may give them what power hee pleases, and give them charge to exercise such a power as hee shall conferre uppon them. And then further

[a] "This is life eternal that they might know thee the only true God." John xvii., 3.

[b] MS. "samenesse of power."

there is this. There is a peculiar and speciall reason why Magistrates under the law should bee invested with such a power in matters of religion, and that reason being chang'd under the new Testament the consideration will nott hold; itt will nott paralell heere. The reason is this. Wee know the land of Canaan, and indeed all thinges in itt, nott only those that were . . . .[a] poetically, butt the land and Nation and people, was typicall of Churches, and [typical] of the Churches of Christ under the Gospell, of the purity of them and holinesse of them. Canaan is the Kingdome of Heaven as wee all generally know.[b] There was a necessity, that land being a type of perfect holinesse and of the Kingdome of Heaven, that there should bee lawes and ordinances of that nature which should keepe all thinges as pure and free to worshippe as possibly might bee. Otherwise the visage,[c] the lovelinesse of the type, would have bin defac't. Itt would nott have answer'd God's designe in itt. Now unlesse wee shall suppose that the lands and state[s] under the Gospell are typicall alsoe, there is noe reason that wee should thinke to reduce them to those termes[d] [as the land of Canaan was], or by such wayes [as the land of Canaan was]. That is by forcible meanes, by stronge hand, as God did then order and use for the clearing of that land, of that naked piece, which hee intended should bee a type of that whole estate of thinges in his Kingdome and his Church. And that's another thinge. Inasmuch as Magistrates now in [being are under] the Gospell, they are from the first,—and soe consequently to the lowest, for they have all their descent from him—[all instituted by man]. If soe bee wee shall conceive they have power from him, itt should bee part of that power which is putt into him, and vested

[a] Word illegible.

[b] See the argument of Roger Williams in *The Bloudy Tenent of Persecutions*, ed. 1848, p. 272 *et seqq*.

[c] I should be inclined to suggest "virtue" in place of visage, were it not that Goodwin might perhaps have been intending a play upon words.

[d] The MS. continues "for matter of freenesse."

uppon him who made them and sett [them] uppe in the place of Magistrates.[a] For that you were pleas'd to suggest in another parte of your discourse, that there is a certain [inherent] power in Magistracy; [b] for man marks the case and God putts in the jewell, men present and God impowers. I doe nott conceive there is any such thinge in itt, for then there was a necessity that the extent of the Magistraticall power should bee the same throughout the world. Wheras if you looke into the state of all Nations, [you will see] that the power that is putt into the hands of Kinges and princes is moulded and fashioned by the people; and there is scarce any two places in the world where the power[s] of the rulers are the same. Magistrates have soe much power as the people are willing to give them. If [it be] soe now, then if a body of people, as the commonalty of this land, if they have nott a power in themselves to restraine such and such thinges, [as] matters concerning false worshippe, amongst themselves, certaine itt is, that they cannott derive any such power to the Magistrate, butt hee does act itt of himself, and by an assuming unto [himself] that which was never given unto him. There is much more to bee spoken in this point.

Mr. Nye.

The Arguments to abate what the Commissary Generall said are many.

I shall speake butt to one branch, and the last thinge mentioned: that the Magistrate hath noe other power butt what is conveyed to him by the people; for that I thinke is the [great] consideration. For [c] what the Commissary was pleased to say as in relation to the Jewes, wee doe nott beleive that all that was there was typicall, butt much [was] rather morall, judiciall; butt that such a thinge was then in practice as to putt a power in the Magistrate to have somethinge to doe about religion about matters of God. [I]

[a] Cf. *The Bloudy Tenent*, pp. 214, 305, 341.

[b] MS. "magistrates."

[c] MS. "of.'

will take uppe this consideration: that that fundamentall principle of a Commonwealth to act what they are pleas'd to act, does nott in the least lie in the Ministeriall power butt in the Legislative power; and if so itt lie[s] in the people. If soe, then [I would ask], whether itt doe nott lie in the power of the people to consider any thinge that may tend to the publique weale and publique good, and make a law for itt, or give a power [for it]. Whatsoever a company of people gather'd together may judge tending to the publique good, or the Common weale, that they have a liberty [to do], soe longe as itt is nott sinfull. They may putt this into the Ministeriall power to attend itt. Now Sir, suppose this bee laid downe as another principle, [I would ask] whether may nott a company [of people] conclude together and sitt downe in a Commonwealth to doe what may bee done in a lawfull way for the preserving and feeding of the bodie to their good.[a] That the thinges of our God, itt is that which is of publique good and publique concernement, and amonge all other comforts of life I looke uppon this as one, aswell as my house and foode and raiment.[b]

A second consideration may bee this: that there may bee such [and such] sins for which God will take account and make miserable this Commonwealth, those [men] being Christians, or [even] if they have the light of nature [only]. By the light of nature wee are able to say for such thinges God will plague a Nation, and judge a Nation. A companie of men mett together to consult for common good doe pitch uppon such thinges as doe concerne the Commonwealth. They would doe what they can to prevent such sins or provocacions as may [make judgments] come downe uppon their heads. In this case I doe nott goe about to say this, that a Magistrate, as if hee had an edict from heaven, should oppose this [or that]; butt that the people making of them,[c] if itt bee lawfull for

[a] Nye's argument is clearly "If a Commonwealth may provide for feeding the bodies of its members may it not provide also for feeding their souls, etc."

[b] The position of the last sentence has been changed.

[c] "them," *i.e.* laws, or possibly magistrates.

them to make such conclusions or constitutions to avoide such evills, the Magistrate may lawfully exercise that which they may lawfully make; and therfore I say itt was once exercised under the Jewish Commonwealth. Then [if the end of a Commonwealth be to provide] for common good, and if the thinges of God [and blessings] appertayning to them bee a good to bee wish't; if they doe nott [only] tend to that [common good], butt prevent the evill and judgements of God, I know nothing butt in conclusion there may bee some power made uppe in the Magistrate as may tend to itt.

Mr. Wildman.

I suppose the Gentleman that spoke last mistakes the Question. Hee seemes to speake as in relation to the peoples giving that power the Gentleman spoke before, butt to that which hee spoke this may bee answer'd de futuro.[a] That itt is nott lawfull to intrust the Magistrate with such a power. That itt was nott meerly typicall. The Question was, whether itt were morall? If itt were nott morall itt were [not] perpetuall. If itt were morall itt must goe to all Magistrates in the world. That the Magistrate should act to his conscience, destroy and kill all men that would nott come to such a worshippe as hee had. God hath nott given a command to all Magistrates to destroy idolatry, for in consequence itt would destroy the world. To that which the Gentleman said, that the people might conferre such a power uppon the Magistrate in relation to a common good, I answer: that matters of religion or the worshippe of God are nott a thinge trustable, soe that either a restrictive or a compulsive power should make a man to sin. To the 2[d] thinge: that [there might be such a power] nott only in relation to a common good, butt to the prevention of evill; because by the Magistrates preventing such thinges as are contrary to the light of nature—To that I answer itt is nott easily determinable by the light of nature what is sin; and if the Gentleman speake of

[a] The beginning of this speech is hopelessly confused. Wildman attempts to answer both Nye, "the gentleman that spoke last," and Goodwin, "the gentleman that spoke before."

thinges betweene man and man, of thinges that tend to [destroy] humane society, hee is besides the Question; if concerning matters of the worshippe of God, itt is an hard thinge to determine [by the light of nature.] Itt is nott easy by the light of nature to determine there is a God. The Sunne may bee that God. The Moone may bee that God. To frame a right conception or notion of the first being, wherin all other thinges had their being, is nott by the light of nature. Indeed if a man consider there is a will of the Supreame cause, itt is an hard thinge for [him by] the light of nature to conceive how there can bee any sin committed; and therfore the Magistrate cannott easily determine what sins are against the light of nature, and what nott. And to both of those considerations together this may bee said. Supposing both these thinges were thus, yett [to give the Magistrate this power] is butt to putt the Magistrate in a probable condition to doe good, or in a capacity probably to prevent sin. Because the Magistrate must bee conceived to bee as erroneous as the people by whome hee is restrain'd, and more probable to erre then the people that have noe power in their hands.[a] The probability is greater that hee will destroy what is good then prevent what is evill. Soe that to both of them they doe nott putt the Commonwealth into soe much as a probability of any good by such a trust committed to them.

Com. Generall.

I shall desire butt a worde or two. Truly I did indeavour when I began to goe in the way that men might judge whether there was weight in what was said in the reply; and I perceive there was noe other ground laid then what I said, [or] then what Mr. Nye did adde further as a rationall satisfaccion to men why such a thinge might bee intrusted. Butt I suppose the grounds of this are such

[a] *i.e.* "equally fallible and more likely to err." Some word such as "constituted" is required by the sense, in place of "restrained."

as to lay a ground uppon conscience why itt is or should bee the duty of Magistrates in a Commonwealth to use what power they have for the restrayning of such thinges as[a] sins against the first Table, [and] practices forbidden in the first Table; and I would very faine once heare somebody to answer to these grounds that I lay to that. I have heard an answer to one of those grounds: that thinges are subject to men's judgements, ... to the judgement of the Magistrates, and to the conviction of the subject. Butt I have heard none uppon the Scripture ground, and I would heare something of that. 1. That in the state of the Jewes the Magistrate there as a Magistrate,—and as a Magistrate nott of a Church only butt as a Magistrate of a Nation—hee had [the] power and [the] right [to restrain such things]—nay itt was a duty uppon him, hee was injoyn'd to itt, and when hee did itt hee was commended for itt, and when hee neglected itt hee was condemn'd and brought to ruine for itt—and [it was] to bee exercised to others then to those that were members of the Church only.[b] That this therfore which was the rule then, is a rule to a Magistrate as a Magistrate [now], and as the Magistrate of a Kingdome or a Nation. That [which] was then a rule to them that were then [Magistrates] to deserve this commendation if they did itt, and reproof if they did itt nott, is a rule to Magistrates under the Gospell, unlesse in such thinges the evill or good wherof as then was taken away [by the coming of Christ.] If the thinge which hee had a power to restraine [was temporarily or typically evil], then I agree that by the coming of Christ in the flesh itt was taken away. Butt if the thinge were morally and perpetually evill, that which was the ground of the duty [then] will remaine the ground of the duty still, then I conceive the duty as to such thinges remaines the same still. I would I could expresse itt shorter—butt men may take itt shorter,—Butt I would have some answer [these grounds] that is deny that the Magistrates had power to restraine, or [assert that they exercised it not] as Civill Magistrates[b] of a civil

[a] MS. "of."

[b] Position of phrases altered.

society, and [that it] extended only over the Members of an[a] Ecclesiasticall Society; and to shew mee some grounds why if itt were a duty then itt should bee alter'd now, and as subject to men to judge of.

Col. Deane.

The businesse [as] you seeme to state [it] is thus: that in the State of the Jewes there was a Magistrate, and that Magistrate did this and that [to them] that did nott act according to the Jewish religion.

Commissary Ireton.

I will agree [that] all that was in the Jewish religion, the good or evill whereof[b] did tend to typicall institution is nott a rule of our practice.

Col. Deane.

Why should nott the Civill Magistrate in this time punish any man for walking contrary to those rules for which the Jewes were punished?

Com̃. Ireton.

Those thinges which the Magistrates of the Jewes did punish as evill, if they bee of the grounds and evill as they were then——

Col. Deane.

Why will you nott destroy the Turke and the Jewes, and all others as they did the Canaanites?

Doctor Parker.

I would offer this to the consideration of our worthy freinds that are heere.

You say that which was commanded to the Civill Magistrates of the Jewes that is of [moral] right, that is alsoe to bee continued amongst us. I shall offer this objection as to that: that those thinges

[a] MS. "any."

[b] MS. "therof."

that are of morall right as wee conceive, and that they did practice in their religion, were commanded imediately from God; if they were commanded to them imediately from God, without any injunction to bee practized by their successors, and that they should practice the same thinge, then your argument holds good, otherwise nott. My meaning is this. Wee know itt was of morall right, that noe man should kill his owne sonne. Abraham had an injunction to the contrary. God may give out injunctions to his owne will and pleasure, face to face, to any particular person, and to bee obeyed by that particular person, [even if contrary to] those thinges that are of morall right. Itt is of morall right I should preserve my childe, and doe him all the good I can doe. Yett because God did command a contrary thinge itt was practised. Soe on the other side, if God will command thinges to bee done [by particular magistrates], they doe nott conclude all successors of [those] Magistrates that are in the same power.

Mr. Gilbert.

The Doctor sayes, if wee can shew that those commands are now binding uppon Magistrates hee'le grant us the Question as for his parte. Truly I have this to offer. Itt will bee much in compliance with what the Commissary General [said]. There were three lawes amonge the Jewes, the Ceremoniall, Judiciall, and Morall Lawes. I suppose the Judiciall law as to the pains [a] of itt was a fence [b] and guard to the Ceremoniall and Morall law. [In the first place] the law doth aime att obedience to itt, and in the second place a punishment to itt's dissobedience. I conceive the punishment of the Ceremoniall law was nott [a part] of the Morall law itt self, butt [a fence] of the purity of the Jewes.[c] Soe farre as the Judiciall [law] was a fence and out worke to the

[a] MS. "panges."

[b] MS. "sence."

[c] MS. I conceive the punishment of the Ceremoniall law was not of the Morall law itt self the punishment of the Morall law was not of the Morall law itt self, but of the purity of the Jewes.

Ceremoniall law [it] is falne with the Ceremoniall[a] law. Soe farre as itt was a fence and outworke to the Morall law itt stands with the Morall law, and that still bindes uppon men. Soe [that part of] the Judiciall law that was a fence to that, is still the duty of Magistrates.

Mr. Collier.

As farre as I remember the Commissary Generall offer'd two thinges: and the first was, whether that this Judiciall law for the Magistrate to punish thinges which were sin, sin against God, those things in the old Testament mentioned are not commanded by God. And the 2[d], whether they are taken away, and soe have noe relation to the Magistrates under the Gospell. Now to the first, I shall give you the ground why those lawes or commands and that Judiciall law given under the time of the Law hath noe reference to us under the Gospell. I might give you particular grounds, butt one principall ground of that I shall give you is this, as one ground of that which is given already. As itt is Morall itt should have bin given to all states as well as to the Jewes. Butt the ground is this, that the law of the Jewes is nott binding to us under the Gospell. If itt bee I shall then thus inferre, that the Magistrate hath his power from Divine Institution, and soe hath his power from God, and nott from the Agreement of the people, and if soe then they must come to have the same claime from God. If hee have his Commission from God lett him shew itt, soe say I, if hee have his Commission from God wee have nothing to doe to limitt him.[b]

The 2[d] thinge that I would minde you then itt is that wee generally agree in, [and it has been] often minded this day: that the Judiciall law to the Jewes is abrogated to us in the Gospell. I meane in respect of the circumstances of itt, though in respect of the truth of itt there is a Judiciall law to bee executed uppon

[a] MS. "Morall."

[b] Position of clause altered.

the people nott in the way the Jewes did. I shall give you the grounds of itt. One ground is this, that there are some thinges mencioned that was given as commands to Magistrates in the Judiciall law to punish, with which Magistrates in the New Testament have nothing to doe.[a] I shall minde two in particular. The first is that [sin] of Idolatry which was punished with death in the old Testament. Idolaters are to bee putt to death. That under the Gospell the Gospell is soe farre from giving that liberty much lesse power unto a Magistrate to punish an Idolater with death. To mee it is very clear in these words of the Apostle in 1 Corinthians vii.,[b] that if a man or woman had a wife or husband that was an Idolator they were to live with them, and nott to punish them according to the law of the Jewes. The 2[d] thinge I shall minde to you is that of Adultery. Adultery was [under the Law] to bee punished with death. If wee looke to the Judiciall law wee must bee exact as to every particular of itt. Wee shall finde, that this law was done away. The woman that was taken in Adultery was brought to Christ, and they told him that Moses' law was to putt her to death. Christ answers, "Hee that is without sin lett him throwe the first stone att her." Now I looke uppon it to be mysticall. To mee itt was this: that the Gospell would admitt of noe such thinge as this [Judicial Law], butt that there was a New law; and in the Epistles, there was rules given for the excommunication of Adulterers, and [persons guilty of] Incest, and the like, which gives mee ground to judge that the appointing of death under the Old Testament, and the like [penalties to] those which commit such offences doth relate to excommunication.[c]

Col. Hewson.

I am nott satisfied as to the thinge, and therfore I shall nott use

[a] Position of clauses altered.

[b] Position of clause and order of words altered.

[c] In this speech, which is exceptionally confused in the MS., the position of several clauses has been altered.

any argument as from my self; butt having heard some [use an] argument that is nott answer'd I shall desire to hinte itt againe. I shall gather itt uppe in few wordes That which in the Morall law is injoyn'd unto the Jewes is still of perpetuall use amongst us under the Gospell. Butt restriction in the Morall law is enjoyn'd unto the Jewes, as in the 4th. Commandement. Therfore restriction is in perpetuall use now under the Gospell. This I conceive to bee the summe of what you have from the 4th Commandement. To mee itt seemes to bee of some force. There is some thing hinted of that which was typicall, and the like, butt nothing as to this argument from the Morall law.

Com̃. Ireton.

Because this Gentleman doth relate an Argument from mee, I'le tell you how I putt itt.

That which was evill in the time of the Jewes, and remaines as evill now, and hath the same ground of evill now that itt had then, and especially if such a thinge as was evill even before that law [was] given; for such a thinge what was the duty of a Magistrate to restraine then [remains his duty to restrain now], though I cannott say to restraine itt with the same penalty. For the imposing of a penaltie was judiciall, butt the imposing of a restriction was nott judiciall butt perpetuall. This I take for granted: that [what] was evill then and remaines uppon the same ground equally evill now, that if the Jewish Magistrate ought to restraine that even in persons nott under the Ecclesiasticall Jurisdiction, soe ought Christian Magistrates to restraine itt, if they bee Christians, even in those that are nott under the Ecclesiasticall Jurisdiction.

Mr. Goodwin.

Though itt bee supposed and granted, that the same thinges [which] are evill now as they were under the law [are] to bee punished now as they were [then], butt if God hath ordain'd new kinde of punishments [for them] to bee punished with, wee cannott suppose that they are punishable with both punishments. The latter does dissannull the former. If hee that blasphemes is to bee cast out to Satan, that hee may learne nott to blaspheme, itt is impossible that this Commandement of God should bee putt in execution if a blasphemer should bee putt to death.

Com̃. Ireton.

I thinke if wee were now uppon the question of what an Ecclesiasticall Judicature or Church Magistrate should doe, itt would very well bee that that should bee the rule that Mr. Goodwin sayes: that such punishments should bee used by the Ecclesiasticall Officers (and only such) as are warranted by the Gospell, uppon which the outward calling of the Church hath itt's ground; butt itt is concerning a Civill Magistrate, or a Magistrate of a meere civill constitution. I say this, if any man doe butt consider, that in the Gospell there is nothing that is to bee called and taken as of positive institution, butt that [which is expressly so intended]; I will nott desire that itt may bee taken any advantage of. Butt parts of the Gospell[a] are either historicall, expressing what Christ did when hee was in the flesh and how hee was brought to death, as the fower Evangelists, and the Acts of the Apostles. Or else they are exhortatory, written by way of advice to the Churches of the Saints in the severall parts of the world; and they are written to them, [partly] as applyed to what was in generall to bee the condition of all Saints in all ages to the worlds end, and partly [as applyed to] what thinges were the condition of all the saints to whome these Epistles were written. As for the historicall parte of the Gospell—or Propheticall—that's the Revelation—I suppose noe man from the historicall parte will goe to make itt necessary, that in the historicall parte there should bee

[a] MS. "The Gospell the parts of itt."

anythinge of institution of Ecclesiasticall or other Magistrates. In the Epistolary parte, if wee first consider that all the Saints or Churches to whome these Epistles were written were all rather under a condition of persecution under Heathen Magistrates, then having a power of Magistracie in their owne hands, wee have noe reason to thinke that the Epistles written to them should bee intended as to give the rules concerning Magistracie. Butt since there was a rule concerning Magistracie, that is [a rule] by which hee[a] might judge what was evill and what was good—First, Had from the light of nature. 2[dly], Had a more cleare foundation in the Morall law (as they call itt) that gave grounds which way the Magistrate might goe—they[b] doe as well leave the Magistrate [free] in the punishment of those thinges that are in the first Table uppon prudentiall grounds, and nott tying them uppe to the judiciall grounds of the Jewish Commonwealth, butt when there should bee any Christian Magistrates leaving them to those foundations and rules of their proceeding which they had a ground for in nature, leaving that which was good or evill to restraine or nott.[c] I conceive the whole drift of the Gospell hath bin to apply [restraint] in that kind to what thinges are either [un] fitt to bee used amongst men in society as Christians; or else thinges that were the common duty of men nott [merely of] Magistrates [to restrain]; though itt sayes something of that, and if any will say I shall thinke itt to bee very good. Butt this I shall wish to bee consider'd: whether in relation to what is said in the Gospell, if the penaltie does cease then the punishment of itt att all does cease? Then I would faine know, whether by the same ground that Idolatry should [not] bee punished [with death], murther should nott bee punished with death? And [I would fain know] what you can imagine should exempt the Magistrate under the Gospell from punishing Idolaters, should excuse the Magistrate

[a] "Hee," *i.e.* the magistrate.

[b] "They," *i.e.* the Epistles.

[c] *i.e.* leaving the magistrates to decide what was to be restrained or permitted.

under the Gospell, or should deterre him from punishing them with death, or other punishment which under the judiciall law is punishable with death? Whether the same thinge will nott serve to this, that now even for murther, for theft, for all those thinges that are evills against men, which in that law had their particular [punishments] prescribed, whether itt would nott hold as well for this, that now there ought to bee a libertie under the Gospell, itt is a time of mercie, and that wee ought nott to punish those thinges?

Mr. Goodwin.

Those punishments by death of murther and the like, the originall of the equitie and justice was nott to the Jewes only, butt they were by the law of nature. [The old Testament says:] By whome man's bloud is shed. But longe before this [murder was punished by with death].

Coñ. Ireton.

Wee shall desire noe more [than this]. That if the ground of that which made itt sin, and the ground of the punishment does remaine the same now, then the sin is to bee restrain'd as itt was then, and that which was sin then is sin now.

Mr. Nye.

If blasphemy bee punished with two punishments, a sin may bee punished with two punishments; as for example theft. If a man were a Church Member hee might bee excommunicated first, and hang'd afterwards. That was nott a fallacie.

There were 2 places that Mr. Collier had [alleged]. They must nott punish Idolaters then because the Magistrate was soe.[a] Butt for the woman taken in Adultery, this was the reason that Christ did nott judge her, because hee would nott meddle with Magistraticall-matters. All the while Christ lived noe Jewish rite was abolished.

[a] *i. e.* The magistrate was himself an idolater.

Mr. Wildman.

I humbly conceive, that while there is a new saving made whether that such thinges bee null'd by the Gospell, the ground [of your argument is that] which the Commissary Generall sayes.

This is your Argument: that which was sin then, and is now sin, and ought to be punished then, ought to bee punished now. I suppose there is noe consequence att all [in this argument, that] if itt were punished then itt ought to bee punished now. Because itt was [punished then] uppon a judiciall law, which was morall, butt nott naturally morall,[a] and yourself said, that the punishment was nott naturally [moral]. If soe I would desire to know how wee should distinguish which parte of itt was naturally Morall, and what was nott. The Decalogue containes the whole law. If you will extend itt beyond itt I would know where you will terminate itt. Besides, if itt were naturally Morall, you must found it upon nature. If itt had bin given as a thinge naturally morall, and [to a magistrate] as a magistrate, then itt must belonge to every Magistrate that was in the world, and then you must hold that God had ordain'd such a power to bee in every Magistrate. I must confesse, that what was given to them was as Jewish Magistrates, butt nott quatenus Magistrates. Not determining what a Magistrate shall bee you leave us to an uncertainty. Wee finde noe such power att all in any Magistrate.

Mr. Goodwin.

That if this power should have bin destinated in all Magistrates, then every Magistrate in the world had bin bound to have putt all his subjects to death.

Com̃. Ireton.

If I should reply to what was said, and then adjourne the Court, itt would bee thought nott faire; and therfore I shall say nothing

[a] MS. "not morall, but not naturally morall." Wildman's next sentence shows that the first "not" is superfluous. Some repetitions have been omitted, and some corrections from a second version of the speech inserted.

in the world to answer to this, butt leave men to judge whether that which hath bin said bee an answer or noe.

Councell of War held at Whitehall the 15*th of December* 1648.

Resolved:

That the Kinge bee forthwith sent for to bee brought under safe guards, to Windsor Castle, and there to be secur'd in order to the bringing of him speedily to justice.

Lt. Col. Venables.
Lt. Col Goffe.
Major Swallow.
Captain Grove.
Lt. Col. Cooke.
Major Barton.
Major Cambridge.

These are, any three or more of them, to meete at Mr. Hunt his lodging in Whitehall, upon the riseing of this Councell, and thenceforth to meete de die in diem as they shall agree, to consider of the best ways and grounds for the speedy bringing of the King to Justice, and to take advice and assistance therein of any such persons as they shall finde fitt and able to promote this business, and to make some report of their proceedings upon Tuesday next in the afternoone to this Counsell.

The like concerning Duke Hamilton, Lord Goreing, Lord Capell, Lord Loughborow, and withall to consider their cases in respect of Articles given them.

Resolved &c.:

That the Earle of Holland, Sir Lewis Dives, Sir John Owen, Sir Hen: Lingen bee propounded to bee brought to speedy justice.[a]

[a] On Nov. 10 the House of Commons had voted that Holland and Owen and five other chief promoters of the second civil war should be simply banished. *Lords, Journals*, x., 590, 596; *Great Civil War*, iv., 246. But this vote had been rescinded by the Commons on Dec. 13, 1648. *Commons' Journals*, vi., 96. Mr. Gardiner points out that Cromwell was of opinion that these leaders should be tried before the King's trial instead of afterwards. *Great Civil War*, iv., 282.

Resolved &c.:

That Major Boswell, [Mr. Thomas] Holder, Colonel Thomas, Colonel Mouldsworth, Colonel Boynton bee speedily proceeded against as spyes, and the Judge Advocate to prepare a charge against them.

[*Letter to Lt. Col. Cobbett and others.*]

Gentlemem,

In pursuance of these inclosed Resolucions of the Generall Councell of Officers I have sent Colonel Harrison with a convoy of Horse and Draggoons to guard the King from Hurst Castle to Windsor. I desire you therefore upon receipt hereof that you bring away the person of the King to Windsor Castle, at such tyme, and by such way and marches as Colonel Harrisone shall direct, who is to order the Guardes for the convoying and safe guarding of him, but you are (until forther order) still to continue your care about the person of the King for his necessary accomedation and the beter secureing of him from escape.

I remaine [a]

Wesminster December 15th
1648.

For Lt. Col. Cobbett.
Captain Merriman &c.

Generall Councell. Westminster Dec. 16 1648.

Magistrat:

The second Reserve, as to the not impresting of any by sea or land, considered and debated.

[a] Probably signed in the name of Fairfax.

Question. Wether wee shall propound in this Agreement any reserve from the power of the Representative in point of impresting men for the Warre.

Passt in the Affirmative.

Question. Wether there shalbe a Reserve from the Representative to impress for Forraigne Services.

Passt in the Affirmative by all.

[Except Colonel Hewson & Scoutmaster Roe.]

Wee doe not impower them to imprest or constraine any person to serve in forraigne warr, either by sea or land, nor for any military service within the kingdome; save that they may take orders for the forming, trayneing, and exerciseing of the people in a Military way, to be in readiness for resisting of forraigne invasions, suppressing of suddaine insurrections, or for assisting in execution of law; provided, that even in such cases none bee compellable to goe out of the county hee lives in, if hee procure another to serve in his roome.[a]

Resolved &c.:

That this Councell meete againe on Munday next upon the Remainder of the Agreement.

Resolved &c.:

That Dr Pagett, Dr Cox, and Dr Goddard bee added to the

[a] In the Agreement as originally laid before the Council this reservation ran thus: "We do not empower them to impresse or constraine any person to serve in warre, either by sea or land, every man's conscience being to be satisfied in the justnesse of that cause wherein he hazards his life." Lilburne, *Foundations of Freedom*, p. 11; Rushworth, vii., 1360. Compare vol. i., p. 409. In the Agreement as presented to Parliament on Jan. 20 this reserve agrees with the resolution as passed on Dec. 16, with the following clause added: "or for assisting in execution of the laws; and may take order for the employing and conducting of them for those ends; provided etc."

former persons appoynted to goe into London to Colonel Tichburne's house about the first Reserve on Tuesday at 9 of the clock in the morninge.

Major Carter
Captain Hodden } added of the Army.

That at the meeteing of the Councell on Munday they bee remembred of this appointment.

Whitehall Dec. 18 1648. *Generall Councell.*

The Third Reserve allowed and passt thus.

That after the time herein limited for the commencement of the first Representative, none of the people bee at any time questioned for any thinge said or done in reference to the late Warres, or publique differences, otherwise then in execucion or pursuance of the determinacions of the present House of Commons, against such as have adheered to the Kinge, or his interest, against the people: and saving that accomptants for publique moneys received shall remayne accomptable for the same.

4. The 4th Reserve laid aside.

The 5th suspended, as not proper to the place in which it is sett, coming in among the reserves.[a]

[a] The third Reserve was passed as it stood in Lilburne's draft agreement, except that the first sentence ran originally: "That after the dissolution of this present Parliament," etc. See also vol. i., p. 409. The fourth Reserve, now voted to be laid aside, ran thus: "That in any lawes hereafter to be made, no person by vertue of any tenure, grant, charter, patent, degree or birth, shall be privileged from subjection thereto, or being bound thereby as well as others." The bearing of this clause on the position of the House of Lords may be seen by comparing it with the arrangement proposed in 1647. *Clarke Papers*, vol. i., pp. 391, 408. The fifth Reservation was of the same kind: "That all priviledges or exemptions of any persons from the lawes, or from the ordinary course of legal proceedings, by vertue of any tenure, grant, charter, patent, degree or birth, or of any place of residence or refuge, shall be henceforth void and null, and the like not to be made or reserved again. Lilburne, *Foundations of Freedom*, p. 11.

Question. Wether the sixth Reserve shalbe waved or not.

Affirmatives 16.

Negatives 18.

Soe that it was carried in the Negative.

The Councell in relacion to this business of the Agreement meete on Thursday next.

Ordred to bee added to the Committee to goe into London.

Colonel Hewson.

Major Barton.

Colonel Okey.

Memorandum at the meeteing to morrow to consider of some moderate men to meete in London at Colonel Tichburne's.

Whitehall December the 19th 1648.

Tuesday. Day of Humiliation at Wilmott House.

Major Coleman
Captain Spencer
Mr. Cooly } added to those formerly appointed to meete at Colonel Tichburne's.

[*Sir George Booth to the inhabitants of Cheshire.*]

Deare Countreymen,

Most thankfully I acknowledge your respects enhaunct by that your unanimous electing mee, whome yow were pleased to appoynt one of your servants in Parliament, which favour of yours haveinge bin ever in myne eye hath comanded from mee what ever my skill or ability could enable mee unto. This I hope I may modestly and safely say, your business I have intended, without designing aney private advantage of my owne by place of honour or proffitt, and have endevoured soe to smooth and playne my actions, that although in these traduceing tymes 'tis impossible to avoyde, yet may keepe dirt from stickinge on me. I dare not (deare Freinds) soe much weaken my interest in your affections to suppose this declaratory of my selfe necessarie as to you, but shall meane it to those who being strangers to mee and my actions may have just title to it. That which at this time I shall make yours is breifely and exactly to acquaint you, that the 7th of this instant December, comeing as at other tymes, to doe you the best service I could, I was at the stepp which leads to the outward doore of the House of Commons stopp'd by a guarde supposed to bee of the army, who asked mee whether I was a Parliament man, my answer, I was one; then they demaunded my name, I told it them; upon that a long paper was brought out by an officer (as I supposed him) which when they had perused, they told mee I must withdrawe, alledging noe reason at all for it. Knowing it to be both imprudent and vaine to contest with such force I did withdrawe into Westminster hall, where I mett with divers Gentlemen who had received the same usage, with them I joyned in a letter to the Speaker of the House of Commons, telling him what interruptions wee had in the way of our duties, and desireing him to acquaint the House with it, which I may hope hee did. This hold I myselfe obleiged to doe, that soe your undoubted priviledge might be asserted, which is, as part of the free borne people of England, to send your members to act in the Commons House of the Parliament of England without molestation or interruption; though thus farr I had proceeded, yet could not thinke my self to have but very incompleatly discharged my duty, the principle part, as I conceive, being undone, that was acquainting you with it who imployed mee, whose servant I am; haveing faithfully presented you with the whole matter I leave it to you. This consideration I hope in the vacancy of my imployment, will in your thoughts acquitt mee from any share of blame for any inconvenience may fall on you, by free quarter, immoderate impositions or the like, force debarring mee from being there where your commands doe place mee for preventing of such extremities, which to doe my selfe but right I may say I was in a faire way of effectuating, and had made a good progresse in itt when the aforemention'd interrupcions happened, and of this I have very good and plentifull witness. At what time when it shall please the gratious disposer of all things soe to order affaires, that I may with your honour and freedome (for yours it is), I say when thus I may bee permitted to doe you service, I am ready; till that time and alwayes, whether in power or out of power, I have and hope ever shall have an affectionate heart to the reall good of my deare Countrymen the inhabitants of Cheshire, as becomes an Englishman, a Cheshireman, and as you may justly expect from him whome you have obliged. Your faithfull servant as long as life last

G. Booth.

December the 19th, 1648.

Indorsed. For my deare Countreymen the Inhabitants of Cheshire. This is a coppie of a coppie attested under the hands of Peter Drinkewater, John Leigh.

[*Captain Richard Haddock to Mr John Rushworth.*]

Worthy Sir,

I heare inclosed send yow a true copey of the ingagement wee tooke on board the Unickorne before wee sett saille of this last expedition out of the river of Thames, which engagement they did unanimously stand up to mayntayne agaynst the revolted fleete. Sir, the principall motive which induces mee to send itt you is, first, in the way of an acount, that you may thereby see this part of our actions; secondly, that our men for their fidelety to give them further encorigement may see that their names are enrowld in the army; thirdly, to stirre up others when occasion shall bee to act by theire examples. I besech yow have me excuesed for this my troubling you, for the premises aforesayd moved my presompshion, humbly requesting yow to present my service to his excellency, I rest

Sir your servant

From abourd the Unicorne.

R. HADDOCK [a]

Dec. 19 1648.

For the worshipfull Jo. Rushworth, Esq[r], secretary to his Excellencie the Lord Generall, att the Head Quarters nigh London.

Whitehall Dec. 21 1648. *Generall Councell.*

An expedient upon the first Reserve concerning Religion brought in and debated.[b]

Question. Wether the particulars now debated shall bee referred or noe.

Past in the Negative.

All but Officers to goe forth.

Question. Wether the word Morall shalbe in the paper now read or noe.

Affirmatives 17.

Negatives 27.

Soe that it was carried for the word Morall to bee left out.

[a] On Richard Haddock see the Haddock correspondence, printed in vol. viii. of the Camden Miscellany by Mr. Maunde Thompson.

[b] Under Friday, Dec. 22, the *Perfect Diurnal* says : "The General Council of the Army have had many large debates this week upon that reserve in the Representative, in matters of religion ; some Presbyterian ministers have been discoursed withal, and at last an expedient is agreed upon, which will give satisfaction ; much debate also upon the power of the Representative in Civils, as how they might proceed to punish, not being directed by a known law."

Resolved &c.

That the Representatives have, and shalbee understood to have the supreame trust in order to the preservacion and government of the whole ; and that their power extend, without the consent or concurrence of any other person or persons, to the enacting, altering, repealeing, and declareing of lawes, to the enacting and abolishing of the Courts of Justice and publique officers, and to the highest and finall judgment concerning all naturall and civill things, and to whatsoever in such things is not herein excepted and reserved from them as followeth.[a]

Question. Wether under this Generall Article of the power of your Representatives now agreed on, there shalbe any reserve subjoyned concerning Religion.

Affirmatives 12.
Negatives 37.

Soe that it was carried to have noe Reserve.

The Councell adjourned till Saturday.

[*Letter to Col. Harrison.*]

Sir,

Col. Thomlinson is to bee speeded away to Windsor with instructions to himself, Lt. Col. Cobbett, and Captain Merriman, for securing of the Kinge, answerable to the severall Heads you desire resolution in. Soe soone as hee comes you may come away, and

[a] This is practically the eighth clause of the Agreement as presented to Parliament on Jan. 20, 1649, except that the eighth clause, after "natural and civil things," continues "but not concerning things spiritual and evangelicall;" and then enumerates the six reservations, prefacing them thus: "Provided that, even in things natural and civil, these six particulars next following are, and shall be, understood to be excepted and reserved from our Representatives." *Old Parliamentary History*, xviii., 532. In the completed Agreement a separate article, viz. the ninth, was devoted to the question of religion, instead of a simple section amongst the reservations. For the schedule propounded in 1647, see vol. i., p. 407.

your presence heere is both desired and needed. Butt before you come away, wee desire you to appoint 3 or 4 troopes out of your convoy (of the surest men and best officer'd) to remaine about Windsor, to whome you may assigne quarters in the next parts of Middlesex and Surrey, advising with the Governour therin, and to keepe guard by a troope att a time within the Castle, and for that purpose to receive orders from Col. Thomlinson; and wee desire you alsoe out of the cheif of the Kinges servants last allowed (uppon advice with Lt. Col. Cobbett and Capt. Merriman) to appoint about the number of 6 (such as are most to bee confided in, and who may best supply all offices) to stay with and attend the Kinge for such necessary uses, and the rest wee desire you to send away, nott as discharged from the benefitt of their places, butt only as spar'd from extraordinary attendance. This is thought fitt to avoide any numerous concourse which many servants, with their followers and their relations or acquaintance, would draw into the Castle; and for the said reason itt is wish't that such of the servants retain'd as are least sure, and nott of necessity to bee constantly in the Kinges lodginges, may bee lodged in the Towne, or the lower parte of the Castle, wherin the Governour is to bee advised with.

Capt. Mildmay [a] (wee presume) will bee one of those you'le finde to retaine. The Dragoones of your convoy send away to the quarters formerly intended, which (as wee remember) were in Bedfordshire. Wee blesse God by whose providence you are come on soe well with your charge. Wee remaine

Your true freinds to serve you,

OLIVER CROMWELL.

HENRY IRETON.

&c.

Westminster,
Dec. 22, 1648.

To Col. Harrison at Windsor, or by the way
to Farnham thitherward.

Hast.

[a] Anthony Mildmay. See Appendix.

[*Cromwell and Ireton to Col. Whitchcott.*]

Sir,

Capt. Brayfeild of Col. Hewson's Regiment with his owne and two other companies of Foote are ordered to come to you, and to receive orders from you for the better securing of the Castle and the person of the Kinge therin. You may quarter them in the towne and in Eyton [a] (if nott in the Castle). Col : Harrison is alsoe writt unto to appoint 3 or 4 troopes of Horse out of his convoy to remaine neere Windsor, and to quarter in the next parts of Middlesex and Surrey, as you shall advise, and keepe guard by a troope att a time within the Castle, Itt is thought fittest, that the Horse guard or parte of itt bee kept within the upper Castle, and that att least one company of Foote att a time bee uppon guard there, and that the Bridge betwixt the Castles (if you thinke fitt) bee drawne uppe in the night, and kept drawne ordinarily in the day. Alsoe, that noe other prisoners bee lodg'd in that parte of the Castle besides the Kinge, unlesse Duke Hamilton in some close roomes where hee may nott have intercourse with the Kinge, and hee rather to bee in Winchester Castle [b] (where Sir Thomas Payton was), if you can safelie dispose of the other prisoners elsewhere ; butt the Kinge (by all meanes) must bee lodg'd in the upper Castle in some of the safest roomes, and Col. Thomlinson, Lt. Col. Cobbett and Capt. Merriman to have lodginges there, and those Gentlemen of the Army (being about 6 or 7) who are appointed to attend and assist them in the imediate watching about the Kinge to bee alsoe lodged (if itt may bee) in the upper Castle, or att least within the Tower; some of his allowed servants alsoe (that were of imediate attendance about his person) must necessarily bee lodged in the upper Castle, about which Col. Harrison and Lt. Col. Cobbett will advise with you. Col. Thomlinson and with him Lt. Col. Cobbett

[a] Eton.

[b] Winchester Tower ?

and Capt. Merriman are appointed to the charge of the imediate securing of the Kinges person (as you will see by their instructions which they will shew you), and for their assistance and furthrance therin you are desired to appoint such Guards of Foote for the imediate securing of him, and to guard the roomes where hee and they shall lodge, as they shall desire, and that you order those Guards from time to time to observe the orders of Col. Thomlinson, Lt. Col. Cobbett, and Capt. Merriman therin. The Horse alsoe (as to the imediate guarding of the Kinge) are appointed to receive orders from Col. Thomlinson, butt as to the safe-guarding of the Garrison, all (both Horse and Foote) are to bee att your command. Wee thought this distribution better for your ease, and for the leaving you more free to looke to the security of the whole Garrison then to burthen you both with itt, and with the imediate charge of the Kinges person, where you have alsoe soe many prisoners to looke to. Itt is thought convenient that (during the Kinges stay with you) you turne out of the Castle all malignant or Cavalerish inhabitants (except the prisoners), and as many others of loose and idle persons as you can well ridde out, and to stinte the number of prisoners servants to the lowest proportion you well can. You are desired alsoe to restraine any numerous or ordinarie concourse of unnecessary people into that parte of the Castle, of whose affection and faithfulnesse to the publique there is nott good assurance, or who have nott necessary occasions there, and to suffer noe publique preaching in the Chappell, or any like occasion for concourse of people. Tis good the prisoners this while bee strictly kept in, and with-held from intercourse or communication one with another, and that the Guards of the Gates att the upper-Castle have a list of the Kinges allowed servants now retayn'd and their followers, as alsoe of the Officers and Gentlemen of the Army that are to watch the Kinge with their servants, that those Guards may know whome they are ordinarily to lett in, and the Guards att the outer Gate of the lower Castle to have knowledge of the same list, and of all other dwellers and lodgers within the lowest part. The Lord bee with you and blesse you in this great charge. To his good pleasure I committ you and itt.

Your faithfull freind and Servant,
OLIVER CROMWELL.
HENRY IRETON.

Westminster,
Dec. 22, 1648.

For Col. Whitchcott Governour of Windsor Castle [a] hast these.

The 3 Companies of foote now sent have pay for the present, and shall bee duly supplyed; if you can lodge them within the Castle you shall uppon notice have bedding sent for them.

Dec. 23, 1648.

General Council.

December 23.

Instructions for Colonel Thomlinson, Lieutenant Colonel Cobbet, Captain Merriman, and Captain Brayfield, in and for the immediate securing of the King's person from escape.

1. It is to bee understood by you that as to this charge and in the pursuance of those instructions Colonel Thomlinson is to command in chiefe. Lieutenant Colonel Cobbett next, and Captayne Merryman third, and Captain Brayfield last, and in such subordinacion what is herein directed and committed to you is to bee understood.

[a] In October, 1642, Col. John Venn occupied Windsor Castle for the Parliament. In April, 1645, the House of Commons recommended Col. Christopher Whichcote (to use his own spelling of his name) as Venn's successor. Whichcote, who had commanded a brigade under Essex in Cornwall, and had signed the capitulation of Sept. 1, 1644, seems to have been removed from his governorship in 1651. He died about 1655. *Commons' Journals*, iv., 100, 121; Rushworth, v., 706. *Mercurius Politicus*, July 24-31, 1651. Some documents relative to the sojourn of Charles I. at Windsor are printed by Tighe and Davis, *Annals of Windsor*, ii., 228.

2. The Troopes of Horse which shalbe left by Colonel Harrison about Windsor to keepe guard within the Castle, are to receive orders from you or any of you in the subordinacion aforesaid, and the Governor is to order such foote Guards in and about the roomes where the Kinge shalbe kept, for the imediate securing of him, as you shall desire, and the Guards soe appointed are to observe your direccion herein ; but as to the safe guarding of the Garrison all both foote and horse are to bee at the Gouernor's command, and you are to give orders to the horse accordingly (if there bee occasion).

3. Whereas there are some Gentlemen belonging to the Army appointed to bee assistant unto you, and to receive direccions from you in this businese, you are to take orders that two of them with one of your selves (if health permitt) may nightly watch in his chamber or at the doores thereof, and at least one of the three soe watching to bee within the chamber ; and in the day time two of the said Gentlemen, with one of your selves, to bee continually in the roome where hee is, or in view of him, or (when he shalbe private at his devotion, to bee attended at the dore of the roome). But in case of necessary hinderance to any of those Gentlemen in their course you may admitt one of his allowed servants who shalbe willing, or some commission officer of the Horse or foote attending the garrison, to watch in his stead that shalbe soe hindred.

4. You are to suffer noe lettres or writings to pass to or from the Kinge, save what you shall first reade, and soe fitt to pass, and of any writeing which shall be tendered to pass to or from him you are to take a coppie, if you see cause.

5. You are not to admitt any private discourse betwixt him and any other person, save what one of yourselves or one of the aforesaid Gentlemen shall heare.

6. You are to restrayne any numerous or ordinary concourse of people into his presence, or that part of the Castle where hee shall lodge, and to that purpose to desire the Governor's assistance

therein, and his strict care to restrayne the ordinary access of any such people into the Castle, of whose affeccions and faithfulness to the publique there is not good assurance, or who have not necessary occasions there.

7. You are not to permitt the Kinge to walke out of the Castle beyond the Tarras walke.

8. It is referred to your discretion and care to take off and cause to bee forborne all matter of unnecessary state, which might occasion needless charge, take up much roome, or induce recourse of people into his presence.[a]

Whitehall.

Whitehall, December the 23th, 1648.

At a Generall Councell held there, Ordered that Jo[n] Rushworth Esq., his Excellencie's Secretary, signe these Instruccions now agreed uppon, in the name of his Excellency and the Councell, as at other times,

HEN: WHALLEY.
Advocate.

[*Ld. Fairfax to Col. Thomlinson.*]

Sir

You are on sight hereoff to repayre to Windsor Castle, where you are to shew unto Lt. Col. Cobbett, Captain Merriman, and Captain Brayfield this lettre, with the instruccions to your selfe and them heere inclosed concerning the secureing of the King's person, and you are with them to imploy your utmost care and indeavour for the immediate secureing of the King's person from escape, and are

[a] These instructions were all passed unanimously, as Clarke MS., xvi., 61, shows, with the exception of the fifth, which was opposed by Cromwell, and by Cromwell alone. The reason may have been that he thought this particular instruction unnecessarily harsh. Or, on the other hand, he may have considered that it would be an obstacle to the treaty with the King, which, in the hope of saving the life of Charles, Cromwell still continued to advocate. *Great Civil War*, iv., 233-285.

hereby impowered in all things necessary to that end. In pursuance where off the said instruccions here inclosed are to be observed by your selfe and them untill further orders ; I remayne

Your very assured freind

T. Fairfax.

Westminster the
23° December 1648.

For Colonel Thomlinson.[a]

Whitehall Dec. 26 1648. *Generall Councell.*

The Sixth Reserve in the Representative read and debated. Afterwards read thus

(As an expedient.)

That the said Representatives may not exercise the power of

[a] I conclude from this vote and letter that Fairfax, disapproving of the proposal to try the King, had absented himself from the meetings of the Council, in order not to be implicated in the preparations for the King's trial ; but was held nevertheless to be bound by the decisions of the majority of the Council in political matters. From the time when the Council of the Army was first set up, May 1647, the attachment of his signature to the declarations and political manifestos of the army was a mere matter of form. In his "Short Memorial" he says : "From the time that they declared their usurped authority at Triplow Heath, I never gave my free consent to anything they did : but being yet undischarged of my place they set my name in a way of course to all their papers, whether I consented or not." It is certain that Fairfax in writing this, much over-states and ante-dates his opposition to the proceedings of the Army. During 1647 he seems to have been in perfect agreement with the other leaders of the Army. Their differences began in 1648. At some period in the beginning of 1648, probably about April, if the statement of Fairfax himself may be trusted, he prevented a forcible purgation of the Parliament which Cromwell and some others advocated (*Short Memorial*, ed. Maseres, p. 446 ; cf. *Life of Col. Hutchinson*, ii., 149, ed. 1885 ; Rushworth, vii., 1070). In November, 1648, his objections to the acceptance of Ireton's draft Remonstrance led to a last negotiation between the Army leaders and the King (Gardiner, *Great Civil War*, iv., 237). Now, in December, 1648, after giving his support to the Remonstrance, playing the most prominent part in the occupation of London and the interruption of the Newport treaty, he accepted the responsibility of Pride's Purge, but parted company with the Council of Officers on the question of the King's trial.

imediate Judgment in particular questions of right or wronge between one private person and another. Nor may they give imediate judgment upon any man's person or estate for any offence which does not extend imediately to the hurt or damage of the publique, nor for any such offence may they proceede to the takeing away of life or limbe, unless before the fact done it were soe provided against by express law then in force, nor may they inflict or awarde other punishment for such an offence not soe provided against beforehand, save where it is clearely against the generall law of humane society, and where the vindicacion or secureinge of the publique interest does require such Justice.

1. Question. Whether the Sixth Reserve shall pass as it now stands or noe.

Carried in the Negative, Nemine contradicente.

That the Representative may not give Judgment upon any man's person or estate where noe law hath bin before provided, save only in calling to account and punishing publique officers failing in their trust.

2. Question. Whether this clause now read shalbe put to the question as part of the Reserve or noe.[a]

Affirmatives 22.

Negatives 15.

Soe that it was carried in the Affirmative.

Question 3. Whether this clause now read shall pass as part of the Reserve as it is.

Affirmatives 25.

Negatives 13.

Soe that it was carried in the Affirmative as part of the Reserve.

[a] This is the sixth Reserve in the original Agreement, and the fifth in the Agreement as presented on January 20, 1649. The difference is that the sixth Reserve originally began, "That the Representatives intermeddle not with the execution of any law, nor give judgment," &c. Both versions conclude "punishing publique officers *for abusing or* failing in their trust," so that these three words are probably accidentally omitted in the report of the proceedings of December 26, printed above. For the formulas adopted in November, 1647, see vol. i., pp. 407, 408.

C. E. petition of the well affected in Newport Pagnell and parts adjacent.

Directed

To his Excellency the Lord Fairfax, Generall of the Parliament forces &c. and to the officers of your Excellencie's Army now mett in Generall Councell. (Read.)

4. Question. Whether there shall bee any addition made to the 6th reserve or noe.

Affirmatives 12.
Negatives 19.

Soe that it passt for noe addition to that Reserve.

Adjourned till Fryday about 10 of the clock in the morneinge.

The Petitioners call'd in.

Answer returned by Comm. Generall Ireton.

Gentlemen,

Wee have read your petitition, and the Councell have appointed mee to returne you this answer for the present. That they doe very kindlie resent, & thankfullie accept those expressions first in the preamble of the petition of your affections & faithfulnesse in relation to the publique Justice & the liberties of the Kingdome, and for your desire in the prayer of the petition, concerning our prosecution of justice & freedome, they doe heartily close with your desires in itt, & shall indeavour to prosecute the same as God shall direct & inable them in all honest wayes.

And for the last part of your prayer of the petition, for mediating with the Parliament concerning those particulars following, I am to acquaint you, that as the most part of the particulars are such as relate to publique justice & a generall settlement of the liberties of the Kingdome, the Councell hath taken many of them already into consideration, and are in consideration of some other thinges remayning, which soe soone as they have passed the Councell you will see publique, and wee hope to your satisfaction; and the other particulars that you desire mediation in particularly, either concerning the reformation of laws in being, or the making of new, the Councell commanded mee to lett you know that such thinges as those are matters of publique justice & of generall settlement of the liberties of the Kingdome, they shall soe farre as they are proper for their cognizance take them into consideration in their place & time.[a]

General Council att Whitehall 29 *December* 1648.

Elizabeth Poole of Abington first spake, to this effect.[b]

That the businesse was committed to their trust, butt there was a great snare before them.

That God was about to breake the pottesheards of the Earth.

That there should nott bee a sheard left to carry coales now was of finer sort of mettall. I looke uppon all manner of manifestations, formes, and religions which are made uppe in any regard of—

That there might bee a pure life in death—That men might

[a] A large number of petitions both from the army and different counties were presented to Fairfax in December and January, 1648-9. See Rushworth, vii., 1374, 1388, and the Moderate for those months, pp. 200, 210, 211, 214, 223, 224, 231, 233, 239, 251, 263, 285.

[b] A full account of this woman's discourse to the Council is contained in the pamphlet entitled: "A Vision wherein is manifested the disease and cure of the Kingdome, being the summe of what was delivered to the Generall Councell of the Army, Decemb. 29, 1648. Together with a true copy of what was delivered in writing (the fifth of the present January) to the said Generall Councell, of divine pleasure concerning the King in reference to his being brought to triall, what they are therein to do, and what not, both concerning his office and person. By E. Poole, herein a servant to the most High God. London 1648. 4to." In a pamphlet published in 1651 called "A brief narrative of the Mysteries of State carried on by the Spanish faction," etc., she is represented as a "monstrous witch" provided by Cromwell in order to mould the Council to his designs.

bee dead unto all their fairest images, and finde the comlinesse in truth.[a]

After a short speech to this effect, further declaring the presence of God with the Army, and desiring, that they would goe forward and stand uppe for the libertie of the people as itt was their liberty and God had open'd the way to them.

The Commissary Generall said: That for what was said in commendation of the Armie, that they did nott looke for the praise of men; butt for that which shee spoke otherwise, that which shee exprest itt is very good and excellent and worthy consideration.

Woman.[b]

When I had bin many dayes a Mourner for the land with great and sore lamentation, and indeed a sympathizer with your labours, I had a vision sett before mee which was this, for the end of your labours.

There was a Man, a Member of the Army, that some times had bin shewed mee, [expressing] his respect unto his Country, to its liberty and freedome, which hee should gladly bee a sacrifice for. This persone was sett before mee [on the one hand, representing the body of the Army], and a woman which should signifie the weake and imperfect distressed state of the land on the other hand. This woman was full of imperfection, crooked, weake, sickly, imperfect. I [having the gift of faith upon me for her cure] was to appeale to the body of the Army in this man that hee should improve his faithfulnesse to the Kingdome, by his diligence in the

[a] "The great work which lieth upon you is to become dead to every pleasant picture which might present itself for your delight, that you perfectly dying in the will of the Lord, you may find your resurrection in him." *A Vision*, etc.

[b] This account of her vision stands first in Mrs. Poole's pamphlet and was probably delivered before the fragmentary speech on p. 150, but I have preserved the order given in the MS.

cure of this person, by the direction which I should give him for her through the guift of God in mee. There was nothing requir'd att his hand more then the act of diligence ; that hee should before the Lord, act diligently and faithfully to imploy all meanes which I should by the guift of God direct for her cure; and looke how farre short hee fail'd of the meanes, soe farre short hee should bee of her cure; butt soe farre as hee should bee faithfull, soe farre hee should bee for her consolation. Neverthelesse this I was to shew him: that itt was nott the guift of God in mee, nor the act of diligence in him, butt in reference to that spiritt of eternall power which had called mee to beleive and him to act, neither was hee to bee slack in action, nor I to bee staggering in beleiving.[a]

Col. Rich.

I cannott butt give you that impression that is uppon my spiritt in conjunction with that testimonie which God hath manifested heere by an unexpected Providence. What shee hath said being correspondent with what I have made [known] as [manifested] to mee before. The truth is, Itt is true [there are] many thinges in which wee are to take a liberty and use the libertie in reference to the men of the world that wee have to deale withall; butt that principle which is to carry us as in consideration of ourselves before God and the world, [is] after that liberty which the world doeth nott understand. Itt is true wee may use these arguments to satisfie such as understand noe more butt such [things] as the world gives testimonie of;[b] butt if wee have nott another manner of testimonie, such thinges that God hath by his providence given us satisfaction of, I beleive as shee sayes the conclusion of itt will bee butt fleshly [after] having begun in the spiritt. I thinke every man is to search his owne heart, and to see what is within, and nott [to look for deliverance] from himself or from men, or from outward

[a] The words in this speech inserted in brackets are derived from the pamphlet.
[b] The position of this clause has been altered.

meanes; butt from that Kingdome which when itt comes will have noe end. And truly I have had my portion of troubles and thoughts of heart since these thinges have come to their chrysis and to their alteration, and I confesse I can finde nothing that is really and seriously an objection to them butt what does arise from the flesh, which has tempted mee all alonge that might tend to a bearing testimonie against the whole and series of the actions. Certainly these thinges are of God, and 'tis good councill and, 'tis true, that hee that will goe about in a fleshly way to save his life shall loose itt, and hee that will [loose] itt is [in] the way to save [it] . . . them butt they being purified by that fire which is from God and through which all thinges must passe . . . . I doe rejoice to heare what hath bin said, and itt meetes much with what hath bin uppon my heart heertofore and I could nott butt speake what I did to beare witnesse to the same testimonie, and shall rejoice to see itt made out more and more in others.

Woman.

Itt is true that the Lord hath a controversie with the great and mighty of the earth, with the captaines and rulers.[a] Hee will contend for his owne name amongst them, butt beleive itt to your consolations who waite uppon him, that itt is nott with you, or with any butt as the captaines and rulers of the earth; you may bee captaines and rulers uppon the earth and maintaine his controversie, butt if you bee the captaines and rulers of the earth his controversie is against you. Wherfore greater is hee that is with you then they that are against you.

Col. Harrison.

If I doe rightly observe what did fall from you, you said, that

[a] "The Lord hath a controversie with the great and mighty men of the earth, with the Captains and Rulers, and Governors. You may be great and mighty upon the earth, but against the mighty men of the earth is his controversy held: For as you are the potsherd of the earth, he will surely breake you to peeces till there be not a shred left to carry coals on." *A Vision*, etc.

one was represented to you on behalf of the Army, and that through their acting such a thinge was to bee accomplished. Itt was given to you to beleive hee should effect [this by] following somethinge that you[a] ought to suggest unto him. Now that I have to offer unto you is this, whether any thinge was given to you more particularly to expresse then before?

Woman.

Noe, Sir. For itt was represented to mee as the Church, nott that the Church was confined to this, or that, butt as in the body, butt by the guift and faith of the Church shall you bee guided, which spiritt is in you, which shall direct you.[b]

Com̃. Ireton.

For what this woman doth speake of the vision that was sett before her and soe for the judge of spiritts, for ought that I yett see, I see nothing in her butt those [things] that are the fruites of the spiritt of God, and I am therfore apt to thinke soe att the present, being not able to judge the contrary, because mee thinkes itt comes with such a spiritt that does take and hold forth humility and selfe deniall, and that rules very much about the whole that shee hath deliver'd, which makes mee have the better apprehension of itt for the present.[c] Itt is only God that can judge of spiritts of men and women.

I thinke the summe of that which shee offers, that wee ought to doe for God, and you must goe on in the way, and I thinke the exhortation is very seasonable; and therfore I would have you come to the businesse that is before you, and I hope that God will lett that [counsel] goe alonge with you, that wee doe itt nott as men pleasers and men observers, butt as unto the Lord.[d]

[a] MS. "hee."

[b] "She being after demanded, Whether she had any direction to give the Councel? She answerd, No: for the present, for she was in this case presented to herself as the Church which spirit is in you, and shall guide you." *A Vision*, etc.

[c] Cf. vol. i., p. 381.

A petition from Lieut.-Col. Lilburne was read after Mr. Poole's business was finished, and the Council then proceeded to discuss the Agreement.

Whitehall Dec. 29 1648. *Generall Councell.*

The 7th Reserve read, [and] passt as it stands nemine contradicente.[a]

The 8th Reserve read [and] passt in the affirmative, nemine contradicente.

The 8th Article of the Agreement altered, and passed thus:

That the Councell of State (in case of imminent danger or extreame necessity) may in each intervall summon a Representative to bee forthwith chosen and to meete, soe as the Session thereoff continue not aboue fourescore dayes, and soe as it dissolve at least

[a] The seventh Reserve in the original draft of the Agreement was: "That no member of any future Representative be made either Receiver, Treasurer, or other officer during that imployment, saving to be a Member of the Councell of State." In the Agreement as presented on January 20 this was the seventh Article. The eight Reserve in the original draft of the Agreement was: "That no Representative shall in anywise render up, or give, or take away any of the foundations of common right, liberty or safety contained in this Agreement, nor shall levell men's estates, destroy propriety or make all things common." This became in the Agreement as presented on January 20 the sixth reservation of the eighth Article. The following words were also added in the completed Agreement: "And that, in all matters of such public concernment, there shall be a liberty to particular members of said Representative to enter their dissents from the major vote."

The eighth Article of the original Agreement before it was altered, as mentioned above, concluded: "Soe as the sessions thereof continue not above 40 daies, and soe it dissolve two moneths before the appointed time for the meeting of the next Representative." In the Agreement as presented on January 20 the Article, passed as above, is the sixth in order.

The ninth Article of the original Agreement passed as above, became in the completed Agreement the third reservation of the eighth Article. The chief alteration made by the Council from Lilburne's original draft is the insertion of the sentences printed in italics.

The tenth Article now passed by the Council is also the tenth in the Agreement as presented on January 20. In the original draft of the Agreement it ran: "That every officer or leader of any forces in any present or future Army, or garrison that shall resist the orders of the next or any future Representative (except such Representative shall expressly violate this Agreement) shall forthwith after his or their resistance, by vertue of this Agreement, loose the benefit and protection of all the laws of the land, and die without mercy." Lilburne's *Foundations of Freedom*, p. 12.

fifty dayes before the appointed time for the next Bienniall Representative, and upon the fiftieth day soe proceedeing it shall dissolve of course, if not otherwise dissolved sooner.[a]

The 9th Article of the Agreement read and passed (altered thus):

That all securities given by the publique faith of the Nacion shalbee made good by the next and future Representatives, *except to such creditors as have or shall have justly forfeited the same*, and saveing that the next Representative may confirme or make null in part or in whole all gifts of lands, money, or offices, or otherwise, made by the present Parliament to any member or attendant to either House.

The 10th Article read, and thus altered and passed. That whosoever shall, by force of Armes, resist the orders of the next, or any future Representative (except in case where such Representative shall expressly render up, or give, or take away the foundations of common right, libertie, and safty contayned in this Agreement) shall forthwith after his or their such resistance loose the benifitt and protection of all the lawes of the land, and shalbe punishable with death as an enemy and traytor to the Nation. Non contradicente.

The fifth reserve (formerly waved) read.

Question. Whether this shall pass as a reserve or noe.

Resolved in the Negative.

The   of the Agreement read:

Com: Generall Ireton.	Lt. Col. Salmon.
Colonel Harrison.	Major Barton.
Colonel Rich.	Captain Clarke.
Sir Hardress Waller.	Captain Deane.
Colonel Deane.	Captain Hoddon.

These or any six of them to meete at Com: Generall Ireton's Quarters to morrow at 10 of the clock in the morneinge, to con-

[a] *Cf.* vol. i., pp. 364, 365.

sider of a forme of conclusion and subscription to this Agreement as to the officers of the Army. Councell to meete againe on Munday by 10 of the clock in the forenoone.

Some Remarkable Passages out of the Countie of Hereford and Southwales concerning Sir Robert Harley and other Members of the Howse of Comons &c.[a]

In primis Sir Robert Harley and Sir William Lewis and other members of Southwales, &c. did impannel themselves in the name of a Comittee of South Wales, and contrary to all ordinances of Parliament, did order in the said committee that all delinquents in South Wales should not bee sequestred, except Papists in armes and such as defended garrisons in the Kings right, on purpose to make such creatures of theire owne members of Counteyes and shires to sitt in the House of Parliament; and were not at all sequestered till now of late Commissioners were sent down by speciall command from the House of Parliament, and some that were sequestred had their sequestracions taken off on purpose to make members to sitt in Parliament, viz[t] Mr. Lewies in the County of Radnour, and Mr. Rotherway Gwyn who made Majour Robt. Harlow Burges of Radnour, and one Mr. Ansloe[b] a Irishman Knt. of Radnour shire; and soe look on all South Wales, and yow will hardly heare of a man there that serves in the House, but have either bin made by delinquents, or have bin Comissioners of Aray or otherwise assisting the Kinge in party, the Earle of Carbery having a great hand in makeing of them and alsoe your Comittee men and Justices of Peace, this Earle being Generall of all South Wales for the Kinge.

Item, the City of Hereford hath two members that serves in the House for it, one Benjamyne Hoskins always a Comissionour

[a] The paper is given in the MS. at the close of 1648, but from its contents is not improbably of earlier date.

[b] Arthur Annesley.

of array, and one Edm. Weaver a cavalier, both made by delinquents that have bin in armes against the Parliament.

Item, Lemster have two Burges serves for it, Col. Birch and Walter Kerle, lawyer, the first have much enriched him selfe inderectly by the warr, the latter a great Cavalier, and have kept correspoundency with the Enmyes garrisons and by raising moneyes and] provision for them: this Lenpster is within this County of Hereford.

Item, the two Knights of the County are Sir Robert Harlow, one who hath much deserted the godley partey, and did solicite and write to divieres delinquents together with his son and papists for their voyces to make his said son Col. Edw. Harlow, Knight of our County of Hereford, contrary to the freedome of the people.

Item, the said Col. Edw. Harlow, Col. Birch, and one John Hackett a Committee man have bought seaven Lordshipps and woods, 3 parts in 4 less then the worthe of it, of the Bishopps lands within the said County, which much hinders the state in paying the publique debts of the Kingdom.

Item, the said Coll. Edw. Harlow and Major Harlow his brother, with Sir Robt. Harlow their father, would never suffer any Comittee man to bee made within the County of Herford but men of their owne creatures, whereby dyvers summs of money have bin receved by the said Col Harlow and Major Harlow, sons to the said Sir Robt., by order of the said Comittees, themselves being two of them.

Item, the said Robt. Harlow hath by his deputies received great sumes of money out of the Bishopps and Deane and Chapter lands, and how that hath bin disposed of few doe know.

Coll. Burch have enriched himselfe from a man that drove packhorses with Manchester ware, his stock I am perswaded not being 200 li., untill in Bristoll hee married a widdowe which was thought to bee worth 1000 li. more, soe that it is guesed hee was full worth 1200 li.; now sence this warr hee hath purchased in London and Herefordshire

6 or 700 li. per annum, and will purchase more besides his said stock, which was abroad at interest is thought still to remaine. Hee seized on all delinquents estates, almost in the taking of Hereford, raysed what money hee pleased to great summs, gott 2 or 3000 li. by dead pay of his regiment in Kent, and divers others wayes, and I am confident he hath given in a very false account, and I beleive hee hath receved when hee was Govenour of Hereford and comanded in Kent as much moneyes as his pay did amount unto, never the less hee hath 1800 li. charged upon the Excise, and 750 li. outt of Gouldsmithes Hall, besides hee sould the Castle of Hereford which cost him about 130 li., being a garrison, for 600 li. to Sir Robt. Harlow, on purpose that one Coll. More a creature of the said Sir Robert should comand it. Coll. Massey hath much enriched himselfe by the warre, for affter he came from the voyage against the Scottes (when the Scotts first invaded England when the Papists army went against them some eight yeares since) in which expedicion the said Massy was made Capt. of Pyoneeres by Nicholas Davenant, poet Davenant's brother: I say after which voyage hee had not 12d. some time in his pockett to pay for his dinner, the said Nicholas Davenant being now in London at the Feathers in Longe Aker, as is thought now att this present expecting a comand fram Massey. This Massy did raise vast summes of money by his warantes out of our Herefordsheire, Glocestershire Worcestershire & Wiltshire by way of contribucion, and by ceaseing of all delinquents persons and estates, releasing them for money, besides the selling of all the Gentl[emen] and Comanders which was taken at Highnam by Sir William Waller, being 2 or 300 (he receuing for said Kts. as Sir Hen. Lingen, Sir Trever Williams, and others 500 li. apeice, then 300 li. and 200 li. apeice which raised to vast summes of money) the releasing of which caused the garrisones in South Wales to the great prejudice of the well affected in those partes, besides the selling of Mr. Dutton the Knight of Gloucester shire, and others prisoners of note when they were taken, as Sir Richard Ducy, Barronett Tracy and

many others; one tax he ceased Gloucestershire was 17000li. for 3 moneths, besides the said Massey had vast sumes of money from the House of Parliament, and the impost of currants from the Custome House which a Committee of Gloucester received for him, and other great summes hee often received as from the Lord of Essex, besides many prizes that was taken upon the River Severne.

That Sir R. H. hath a thousand pounds in his hands, of one Charles Price a delinquent, and will not deliver it, and hath bought one Mr. Howes his estate, a delinquent which hath been in armes.

Charge against Mr. Thomas Smith.[a]

January 4th, 1648.

The heads of a Charge to a sermon preached by Mr. Tho: Smith at Lancaster parish church, out of the 2d Epistle of Petter, the 2d chap: and the 2d verse.

From which he colected this observation, that every[one] that denies a fundementall doctrin of fayth and after con[futation] . . . . or admonition obstainatly maintaine it.

And now coming to lye downe Antechrist, and what it was like, and heresey to be a pernitious destration.

1. He compared heresey to a canker that did eate the eyes and flesh till at last did consume to the verey bone.

2. He compared it to an overflowing flood that drives away heapes of sand and stones, and indeed nothing is able to withstand it.

3ly. To foxes that devours the little plants or vines of Christ, for as foxes is subtile soe is heriticks.

4ly. To wolves being of a tearing and devouring nature, soe hereticks rent both Church and State.

[a] See p. 187.

5ly. To grinding Marchants that through covteousnesse make marchandiz of poore soules.

6ly. To spaunes of the Divill, or like a spaune of the Divill in a spirituall liknesse which walketh about the City catching soules.

7ly. To doges which are of a snarling nature.

8ly. To Divills or like to Jezabells, the daughters of the Divill being a spirituall bewitching soules.

9ly. To cheaters as in that once famous Citty, which one can sccarsely goe into but they shall have their pocketts pick't, if not their throates cutt, meaneing the Citty of London, where the Parliament and Army resides, haveing their mindes darkened through heresy, denying the Lord that bought them.

I have bin shewing you what they are like, and now I will come to shew you who they are.

(1) Such as leave the truth, and are of this part Independant, and soe to Anabaptize, and then to Antenominisme, and then to meare nothing as they were before.

And that there was such a tolleracion now that every one might follow after his owne lusts, and his owne wayes. I thinke contrary to the lawes of mann, and I am sure contrary to the lawes of God, for if Paul had had might according to his good will, hee would have had them all cutt off that troubled Israell, or the Church of Christ, as Mr. Smith said.

(2) I count those damnable hereticks that would not have their children baptized, or such as would not have a Sabboth or a 7th part of tyme for God's Worship, or that pull downe free Grace and sett up free will, or that preach the law without the Gospell, or the Gospell without the law.

(3) I tearme such damnable hereticks as make seperacion from the ancient Church of England, under what pretence so ever of scandall, untryed without seekeing to bee reformed before the said seperacion, nor ought to leave one Church with lawfull Church ordinance, and to goe to another, both equally scandalous, nor

ought you to depart from that Church, though never soe confusedly disordered, till they bee humbled, and I question whether then or noe; for wee have had two great plagues, namely the sword and pestilence, but now that plague of these heresyes is come which is the worst of all, which destroyes both body and soule.

Soe if heresy bee thus tollerated, then judge whether or noe wee bee not all turning hereticks. But now I will come to lay downe some caution to prevent heresy.

(1) I desyre you not to take up your Religion quickly, nor to change with the tymes, but to learne your principles of catichisme, for now is the tyme comeing that heresy is soe great, that they may come to question you in your principles of Religion.

(2^ly^) Being a people of itching eares which loves to heare noviltyes, and to heare new doctryne, but not allowing old Scripture phrayse to prove it with; therefore I adjure you, as a Minister of Christ, to stand for your old principles, for if you now loose that opportunitty, you never are like to have it againe; for I am not ashamed to confess my selfe one of the scattered tribe of Levy, but I will never turne heretick while I live.

Likewise in his prayer before sermon hee prayed, that if the Kinge were alive that hee might bee restored to his former dignity and honour, and if dead, that his blood may not be layd to the charge of this Kingdome.

And further wee are informed by a very honest man, that the said Tho : Smyth said there would bee noe peace till the Scotts came into the Kingdome to supprese the Independans and Sectaryes armye, and alsoe further said, if they came into England hee would joyne with them, and that the Mallitia of Lancashire was the honestest army in the Kingdome, for they would stand for the Presbyterian Government.

And thus haveing credible informacion that the aforesaid Mr. Smyth have preached this doctryne in divers publique places, and likewise in many private discourses, though often admonished by divers of his owne friends and constant hearers, which wee have bin informed of, Therefore wee humbly conceive him nott fitt or safe to preach to seduce the people, but to remayne in restraynt till hee have cleared himselfe of what is charged against him.

Signed by the Officers of Lancaster Castle.

General Councill 5 *Jan.* 1648 *att Whitehall.*

Elizabeth Poole who came from Abington call'd in.

Eliz. Poole.

Having bin by the pleasure of the Most High made sensible of the many grievances of this land, and of the great trust putt into your hands, I have had some cause indeed of jealousies least you might (through the manifold temptations which will easily besett you) betray your trusts. I know I speake to some amongst you that can judge what I say. I have heard [that] some of you [are busied] uppon that which is called, The Agreement of the People. 'Tis very evident to mee, that the Kingly power is falne into your hands, and you are intrusted with itt that you might bee as the head to the body. Now therfore if you shall take that uppe as an Agreement of the people, I must humbly present this to your thoughts. For itt seemes to mee to bee [intended by the Agreement] that you shall give the power out of your owne hands; whereas God hath intrusted itt with you, and will require itt of you how itt is improved. You are his stewards, and soe stewards of the guift[s] of God in and uppon this Nation. Wherfore I should humbly desire that itt might bee faithfully improved of you; and lett noe jealousies or feares that might suggest themselves to you, or apprehensions in respect of persons whatsoever they are, [prevail] in you to lett goe your trusts. Further another snare on the other hand will meete you: that you beare sway above measure. Butt I am afraid of this alsoe, that you loose your Nobility for feare of what Parliament might say, or people might say, or other judges might say, or such as men have their eyes uppon you. I know itt hath bin the panges (?) of some of you that the Kinge betrayed his trust and the Parliament their's; wherfore this is the great thinge I must present unto you: Betray nott you your trust.[a]

I have yett a[nother] message to declare, which itt's very possible may bee very strangely look't uppon; butt in the law of the Lord I present myself to tender itt, and lett itt finde acceptance as itt is.

(Gives in a paper.)[b]

Col. Deane.

I must desire to aske one question: whether you were commanded by the spiritt of God to deliver itt unto us in this manner?

Woman.

I beleive I had a command from God for itt.

Col. Deane.

To deliver this paper in this forme?

Woman.

To deliver in this paper or otherwise a message.

[a] She being afterwards asked by some of the chief officers; Whether she conceived they were called to deliver up the trust to them committed either to Parliament or people? She answered, No, for this reason it being committed to their care and trust it should certainly be required to their hands, but take them with you as younger brethren who may be helpfull to you. *A Vision*, p. 2.

[b] Against the King's execution.

Col. Deane.

And soe you bringe itt, and present itt to us, as directed by his spiritt in you, and commanded to deliver itt to us?

Woman.

Yea Sir, I doe.

After Debate shee was call'd in againe.

Com. Generall.

The Councill desires to heare [from] you a little further what you say [as] to these 2 thinges. 1. What doe you hold forth to us as the demonstration of the witnesse to us, that this that you have deliver'd to us is from God, and from God given in to you to bee deliver'd to us? The next thinge [is, as to] that particular which you speake of concerning the Kinge: whether you intend itt against his triall or bringing to judgement, or against his execution only? [a]

Woman.

That hee is due to bee judged I beleive, and that you may binde his hands and hold him fast under.[b]

Com Ireton.

What would you hold forth to us as the demonstration or

[a] "Our Counsels run all for the following of Providence by present dispatch, and will not endure any mediations; no, nor hear again of Ireton's proposals, that it were perhaps safer to have the King live prisoner for to dispose him a while to abandon his negative, to part from Church lands, to abjure the Scots, etc." Royalist letter Jan. 8, 1649, Carte, *Original Letters*, i., 202.

Ireton appears to have tried to make use of Mrs. Poole's vision to support the policy he had been urging.

[b] "She was asked, whether she spake against the bringing of him to triall, or against their taking of his life. She answered, Bring him to his triall, that he may be convicted in his conscience, but touch not his person." *A Vision*, p 6.

witnesse that wee should take notice of, that this that you have deliver'd to us to bee read is from God, from him given in to you, and from you to bee deliver'd to us?

Woman.

Sir, I know nott, butt that that is there will beare witnssse for itt self, if itt bee consider'd in the relation that Kinges are sett in for Governement, though I doe nott speake this to favour the tyranny or bloodthirstinesse of any, for I doe looke uppon the Conquest to bee of Divine pleasure, though I doe nott speake this—God is nott the supporter of tyranny or injustice, those are thinges hee desires may bee kept under. [a]

Col. Rich.

I desire to know whether that which is the will of God is nott concordant with naturall reason?—and are refined and purified from itt's heate of which wee know because wee know nothing of itt's fall, but—Whether itt bee the will of God that any thinge in point of Governement should bee inconsistent with the most essentiall being for which itt was ordain'd? Now if then any outward thinge, and [any] state and power and trust [may be forfeited if it is abused], if itt bee nott the will or the minde of God that any man impowred or intrusted for the publique good, for the Governement sake should bee tyrannous to the governed for the welbeing of which hee was sett in the chaire for, then whether for the highest breach of trust there cannott bee such an outward forfeiture of life ittself, as of the trust itt self?

[a] She argues in her message to the Council that they are not to take the King's life. "Vengeance is mine I will repay saith the Lord . . . Stretch not forth the hand against him. For know this, the conquest was not without divine pleasure, whereby kings came to reign, though through lust they tyrannized; which God excuseth not but judgeth; and his judgments are fallen heavy, as you see upon Charles your Lord." P. 5.

Woman.

If these thinges bee mistaken by mee and found out by you, soe God may be glorified I shall bee satisfied.

Lt. Col. Kelsay.

That which was desired to know of the Gentlewoman was, [whether she said] That this message was dictated to her by the spiritt, and by the spiritt presented to this Councill. Now if itt bee this way of demonstration or reason as Col. Rich speakes to [it] will admitt of dispute; butt if itt bee only from God, God doth nott send a messenger butt that there may bee an impression uppon their hearts [that are] to receive itt. Now that which was proposed to Mrs. Poole to know [was], what demonstration or token shee can give that itt is from God; for either itt must bee from extraordinary Revelation from God to you, and from you to us, or else there must bee somethinge of argument and reason to demonstrate itt to us. Now there is nothing of reason in itt, and if itt bee from God the Councill would bee glad to heare what outgoinges there are in that particular ?

Woman.

For the present I have noe more to say then what is said therin.

Mr. Sadler.

I doe desire that I may aske heere 2 questions 1. I thinke you have indeed answer'd to the first already, butt perhaps I doe nott understand you fully, whether itt bee intended [only] to preserve his life, [and] nott att all against his Triall ?

The 2d whether you doe offer this paper or from the Revelation of God ?

Woman.

I saw noe vision, nor noe Angell, nor heard noe voice, butt my spiritt being drawne out about those thinges, I was in itt. Soe farre as it is from God I thinke itt is a revelation.[a]

Col. Whalley.

In case uppon the Kinges Triall that very filthy thinges, murther and all the great crimes that can bee imagined, [shall be proved against him, and] that hee should bee found guilty, then must hee nott die?

Woman.

That Hee will direct you in wisedome, I have presented my thoughts.

Major Barber.

By the favour of this Councill, I would move one question: whether that the spiritt doth give in to her bee, that this Kinge after judgement must [not] die, or that noe Kinge in the world after judgement may die; and if soe, why itt should bee the minde of God that upon judgement and question hee should nott die rather then any other kinge.[b]

Mrs. Poole.

Why surely thus, itt appeares to mee that the Kinge is the highest in subordinat[ion] to God, in respect with the relation over the people His trust he hath betrayed—that I have often bin speaking of, and the charge and care therof is falne uppon you. Butt I speake in relation to the people. A Head once sett off.[c]

[a] This last sentence is attributed by the MS. to Sadler, but is clearly part of Mrs. Poole's answer to his question.

[b] MS. "another kinde."

[c] The sense of her argument, according to the pamphlet, was that the King is to the people as the husband to the wife. The husband is head of the wife (*Ephesians*, v. 23), and therefore apparently may be put under restraint but not cut off. She quotes the case of Nabal.

Col. Rich.

I desire to bee satisfied in one question more. A Triall of the person that may bee is meete and is just, and hee is capable of being judged by men. Now the question is, whether or noe, [in case] hee being nott convinc't that those that were intrusted for the Judiciall power are the proper Judges, and soe when hee [should make] answers pro and con hee stands mute and will nott answer —the question is whether that will hinder the power of judgement?

Mrs. Poole.

I understand itt nott.

Com̃ Cowling.[a]

I have heard mention since I came of two men, Joseph and Moses. The one was a greater provider for the wellbeing of the people, and the other did as much in delivering the people when they were nott well [used]. I desire that as Moses you will nott bee soe full of punctillios as to looke uppon the old Constitution, wherin they have bin uppon us 34 yeares[b] and they could fall uppon noe other forme butt the beastly forme of E[gypt]. [The Jews did] and the

[a] This speech, though given in the MS. at the end of the debate on Mrs. Poole's message, has absolutely no connection with it at all. These debates, as I conclude from a number of signs and other indications in the MSS., were taken down in shorthand on loose sheets of paper at the time, then put up in bundles, and not transcribed or copied into the folio book at present containing them until many years later, probably not till 1662. Under the circumstances it would not be surprising if a speech were sometimes inserted in the wrong place. This speech may very well belong to the debate of Jan. 6, or to that of 13 Jan. Cowell apparently urges the Council not to seek to give up their power to Parliament, as they proposed to do by the Agreement, but to keep the government in their own hands Like the Israelites, he argues, the English people have come out of the house of bondage. Just as the Israelites hankered after the gods of Egypt and set up a golden calf, so the army are making a mistake in too punctiliously adhering to the old Constitution, and striving to set up government by parliaments again.

[b] He perhaps said, "wherein these burdens have been upon us 300 or 400 years."

best they brought forth was a calfe. Now this I should offer to you: Take heede how you sticke unto that Constitution without [leaving] which you are nott able to forme a way by which every man may enjoy his owne.

Whitehall 6 January 1648.

Generall Councill.

Debate concerning the setting a period to this Parliament by the last of Aprill.[a]

Arguments.

Com̃. Generall.

That itt will bee a greater securitie in case the Army should bee forced to remove, when the ill-affected partie may come in againe.

Itt will give much satisfaction to the people, in regard of their expressing their desires nott to sett uppe themselves butt their resolves for a future Representative.

Lieut. Generall.

That itt will bee more honourable and convenient for them to putt a period to themselves.[b]

Commissary Generall.

If the Parliament should vote a day for their dissolution without

[a] The first article of the original Agreement was:

"That to prevent the many inconveniences apparently among from the long continuance of the same persons in authority, this present Parliament be dissolved upon, or before, the last day of April in the year of our Lord 1649." Lilburne, *Foundations of Freedom*, p. 4. In the agreement as presented on Jan. 20, 1649, this article was adopted with merely a couple of verbal alterations; viz. "supreme authority," "end and dissolve." In the third article the first Thursday in May, 1649, was fixed as the date for the election of the new Parliament. In Oct. 1647, the army demanded a dissolution by Sept. 1, 1648. See vol. i., p. 364.

[b] "Them," *i.e.* the Parliament. Cromwell says on 12 Sept. 1654: "I pressed the Parliament, as a member, to period themselves;—once and again, and again, and ten nay twenty times over" (Carlyle, Speech III.). "So willing were we, even very tender and desirous if possible, that these men might quit their places with honour" (Speech I.).

the Agreement, all the indeavours will bee used for Parliaments to come in the old way ; butt if men finde there is noe avoidance of this Parliament butt by this Agreement, there is nothing soe much likely to keepe men's hands off from opposing the Agreement. The people may think if they oppose this Agreement they oppose the ending of this Parliament.[a]

Lieut. Generall.

Then you are afraid they will doe [so]? [b]

Com̃ Generall.

If the generality of people could see the end of this Parliament, [they] would bee for the opposing of any thinge of this kinde ; or would waite for the expiring of that to looke for a succession of new Parliaments in the old way and old forme of a Kinge agen. Nothing of more advantage to this Parliament then to end itt by the Agreement with safetie [to itself], without prejudice to future Parliaments.

Att Whitehall.

Generall Council. 8 *Jan.* 1648.

Mr. Erbury.[c]

Uppon the 3[d] Article, The last Article, That every man beleives his God of all Nations.[d]

[a] This last sentence is added below as a separate speech of Ireton's, but seems clearly to be part of this.

[b] *i.e.* Oppose the Agreement.

[c] A life of William Erbury is given by Wood, *Athenae Oxonienses*, ii., 75, ed. 1721. Wood says he was a chaplain in Essex's army, "and therein he sometimes exercised himself in military concerns, but mostly in those relating to his function, whereby he corrupted the soldiers with strange opinions, Antinomian Doctrines, and other dangerous errors, and by degrees fell to grosser opinions, holding universal redemption, etc., and afterwards became a Seeker, and I know not what."

[d] The debate is evidently on the 3rd clause of the ninth article (concerning religion), which runs thus in the Agreement presented on Jan. 20: "That such as profess faith in God by Jesus Christ, however differing in judgment from the

Com̃ Ireton.

Those that doe nott owne Jesus Christ as a 2[d] person from the Father, yett if you aske them acknowledging the man Jesus Christ as the person through whome God hath revealed himself, whether they have this faith in Jesus Christ?

Debate uppon the last wordes. Soe as they abuse nott this Libertie [to the civil injury of others or actual disturbance of the public peace on their parts.]

Mr. Erbury.

If any man doe offend in relation to the civill injury of others, hee is punishable by the lawes.

Uppon the 4th Article concerning religion. To what purpose will you give that libertie to the Jewes[a] and others to come in unlesse you grant them the exercise of their religion?[b]

doctrine, worship or discipline publickly held forth, as aforesaid, shall not be restrained from, but shall be protected in the profession of their faith and exercise of religion, according to their consciences in any place except such as shall be set apart for the public worship; where we provide not for them, unless they have leave: so as they abuse not this liberty to the civil injury of others or to actual disturbance of the public peace on their parts. Nevertheless it is not intended to be hereby provided, that this liberty shall necessarily extend to popery or prelacy."

[a] "Monday, Decem. 25. Notice was given of what passed in the Councell of Mechanicke at Whitehall on Saturday, where they voted a toleration of all religions whatsoever, not excepting Turkes nor Papists nor Jewes." *Pragmaticus*, Dec. 19-26. On the toleration of the Jews see Carte, *Original Letters*, ii., 233. On Jan. 5, 1649, a petition was presented to Fairfax and the General Council from Johanna Cartwright and her son Ebenezer Cartwright, inhabitants of Amsterdam, for repealing the act of banishment against the Jews, "and that they may be again received and permitted to trade and dwell amongst you in this land, as now they do in the Netherlands." This was printed in 1649 under the title of *The Petition of the Jews*. 4to.

About the same time a negotiation was set on foot between the Catholics and Independents. The Catholics were to support the new government on the promise of a free exercise of their religion in England. See Carte, *Original Letters*, i., 206, 216, 219-222; *Clarendon State Papers*, ii., 544.

[b] *The Perfect Diurnal*, under Jan. 8, says: "The Generall Councell of the Army intended to perfect the Agreement this day, if the sitting of the Commissioners for the trial of the King in the Painted Chamber had not prevented them."

Whitehall, 10 Jan. 1648.

Generall Councill.

Debate concerning the 9th Article, The Magistrates appointing Ministers.[a]

Capt. Butler.[b]

Truth, and light and knowledge has still gone under the name of errours and heresies, and still they have putt these Esau's garments uppon Jacob's back. And in that regard (that for the most parte truth and light go under the name of errour and heresy) wee shall give occasion to our Adversaries to raile against us in every pulpitt; and [they will] make itt their worke nott to discover truth and preach sound doctrine, butt to raile against honest men.

[a] On Jan. 10 and Jan. 11 the discussion is evidently on Article 9, Clause 1, of the Agreement of Jan. 20: "It is intended that the Christian religion be held forth and recommended, as the public profession in this nation, which we desire may by the grace of God be reformed to the greatest purity in doctrine, worship and discipline according to the word of God; the instructing of the people thereunto in a public way, so it be not compulsive; as also the maintaining of able teachers for that end, and for the confutation or discovery of heresy, error, and whatsoever is contrary to sound doctrine is allowed to be provided for by our Representatives; the maintenance of which teachers may be out of a public treasury and we desire not by tithes. Provided, that popery or prelacy be not held forth as the public way or profession in this nation."

The second clause ran: "That to the public profession so held forth, none be compelled by penalties or otherwise; but only may be endeavoured to be won by sound doctrine, and the example of a good conversation." The third clause is quoted on p. 171, note

[b] William Butler of Northamptonshire, afterwards one of Cromwell's major-generals, and throughout his life a great advocate of liberty of conscience. In 1652 he presented to the Committee for the Propagation of the Gospel a paper on behalf of toleration, containing four questions, the second of which illustrates the argument of this speech. "Whether it be not the will or counsel of God that there must be heresies, yea damnable heresies, that such who are approved may be made perfect, and whether it be not the pleasure of God that the judgment and condemnation of such false teachers and heretics be left to Himself?" Masson's *Life of Milton*, iv., 393.

Com̃. Generall.

You agree [to allow them to preach against beliefs], if you doe butt say they must instruct the people as well concerning what is truth as what is false. I would know what latitude you give them to raile [against persons] by this, or that?

A use for satisfaction of conscientious men in those wordes. By our denying [the magistrate] compulsive power or restrictive power to [suppress] errours and heresies, wee doe allow they should bee opposed with spirituall weapons.

Capt. Spencer.

Wee are now about an Agreement, and as if the power were in our owne hands, butt if wee labour for libertie [for ourselves], lett us give itt to others that are as deare to Christ as wee are. Lett them preach what they will, they cannott touch mee only they touch mee in my purse.

Whitehall, 11 Jan. 1648

Generall Councill.[a]

Mr. Erbury.

Question uppon the matter concerning Religion. Whether they doe by that goe about to sett uppe a State Religion?[b]

Men should bee call'd before they can teach publiquely.

[a] *The Perfect Diurnall* gives the following account of this day's proceedings: "Thursday last the Generall Councell of Officers sate at Whitehall. The Agreement of the People as it was fully concluded of was read: and it was referred to some officers to nominate some other trustees for the making the divisions in the severall counties for elections, besides the Lord Grey, Sir John Danvers, etc. Also that two petitions should be drawn up in the name of the Councell to the House; the one for the taking off of Tythes; and the other for the repealing of the statutes for the banishment of the Jews in regard it was not held fit to mention them in the Agreement.

[b] By the first section of Article 9 of the Agreement. The question of the existence of an Established Church was one of the chief causes of division amongst the Independent party. It led to the dissolution of the Little Parliament in 1653, and produced a permanent breach between Cromwell and many persons, officers of the army and Independent ministers, who had hitherto been his strongest supporters. See Masson, *Life of Milton*, iv., 513-518.

Whitehall, 13 Jan. 1648.

Generall Councill.

Mr. Erbury.

Made a longe speech declaring his dissent to the Agreement; setting forth that whilest wee were in a way of putting downe of aucthority wee had the power of God going alonge with us: but as itt was with the Parliament in [imposing] the Covenant, that which they look't for to bee for agreement proved to bee a great disagreement amongst the Nation, soe [with us] this [Agreement would prove] to bee an Hellish thinge, and altogether tending to disagreement; and though hee likes the greatest parte of that Agreement, yett the last [Article] as in relation to religion, is that which will doe much hurt.

Com̃ Ireton.

Answer to itt.[a]

That itt was nott to advance themselves [they offered this Agreement to the nation], butt [as] such a settlement as might bee equally good for all; and when wee did hold this forth without any inforcement uppon any, meerly tendring [it] to them as our utmost essay in this kinde, then itt hath surely itt's proper effect in itt's testimonie to the kingedome of our indeavours in that kinde; and that effect I cannott butt expect from itt, because itt is a duty wee are

[a] The first twenty lines of Ireton's speech substantially anticipate the explanation of the Agreement given to Parliament in the "Humble Petition of the Army," presented with it. *Old Parliamentary History*, xviii., 516-519. That document says:

"To prevent misunderstanding of our intentions therein, we have but this to say: That we are far from such a spirit, as positively to impose our apprehensions upon the judgments of any in the kingdom, that have not forfeited their freedom, and much less upon yourselves. . . . We humbly desire, That whether it shall be fully approved by you and received by the people, as it now stands, or not, it may yet remain upon Record before you, a perpetual witness of our real intentions and utmost endeavours for a sound and equal settlement; and as a testimony whereby all men may be assured what we are willing and ready to acquiesce in; and their jealousies satisfied or mouths stopt, who are apt to think or say, we have no bottom."

led too for avoiding a just offence, and the preventing those evills amongst men that may ensue uppon that offence. Butt indeed if ever wee shall come to use forcible impulsions to binde men uppe in this Agreement; and shall soe sett itt uppe as the necessary thinge without which the kingedome cannott bee, or soe sett itt uppe as that from which wee would promise good thinges to the kingedomes, with a neglect or deniall, or diminution of God, or of his power, then I thinke wee shall incurre (when wee doe come to that end) the same blame as hath bin in the inforcement of the Covenant.

Butt truly, I shall nott trouble your Lordshippe to speake [of] the vast differences both in religious and civill respects that are betweene Covenants of that kinde that that was, and such as this is; I shall say this only in generall: that this businesse of this Agreement is more of the destructive nature to all covenants and to all authorities[a] then itt is of the confirming nature to any. Except itt bee in that last clause of the non-resistencie of the peoples future Representatives by force of Armes.[b] Itt is the[c] contrary to [that, rather] the throwing downe of all destructive power then the erecting of any. Nay, I am confident that itt is nott the hand of men that will take away the power of Monarchy in the earth, butt if ever itt bee destroyed, itt will bee by the breaking forth of the power of God amongst men to make such formes needlesse. Butt the nature of this [Agreement] is, that uppon that ground [that] till God doe soe breake itt there will bee some power exercised, either by a voluntarie dispensation of the power from the people, or by the sword—since in the meane time there will bee some [power], that all the effect of this Agreement is noe more butt as restrictions uppon that power. [We agree as to that power] that itt shall nott bee in the hands of a Kinge; itt shall nott bee in the hands of Kinges or Peeres, or in the hands

[a] MS. "Agreements."

[b] The tenth Article, quoted on p. 156.

[c] MS. "then."

of Commons, butt [in the hands] of such as are chosen [by the people]; and nott in their hands [perpetually], but [only] for soe many monthes as they are chosen; and that there shall bee a new election of another [Representative once in two years]; and for elections, that they shall nott bee in Corporations, butt [in] more equall [divisions]. And for the power [given to the Magistrate], itt gives [him] noe power, butt what the supposition of a Magistracie or a Commonwealth doth imply in itt selfe. The businesse of this Agreement is rather a limiting his power. In time they shall nott sitt soe longe. In the matter they shall nott have power to doe in those thinges that wee reserve from them; and one thinge is a reservation of all other thinges that are in this Agreement which are foundations of libertie. And truly if any man will justly finde fault with this Agreement, as itt is passing from us—to deliver the Nation from oppression, and to settle such a Governement, as there must bee such a Governement—if any man will take any just exception, itt will bee a shewing that wee did nott take away enough of power.[a] The whole Agreement is the taking away of any [undue power], itt is nott a setting uppe of power where there is none, butt itt is a taking off of power, a paring off of those unnecessary advantages which power in this Kingdome formerly had, and is still apt to have, whereby itt may oppresse. Now if itt bee blamable in anythinge; itt is in that itt does nott take away more; and if there were somethinge else wherin power should bee abridg'd, if wee bee unanimous to take away thus farre wee may have patience one towards another till God satisfie us in that alsoe. Under that notion uppon which in my understanding this Agreement doth passe from this Councill, I doe nott understand that itt does come under that sence that Mr. Erbury hath given of itt; and to that purpose itt will bee best to consider the termes

[a] *i.e.* You can argue if you like that we have not sufficiently diminished the power of future governments, but you cannot fairly argue we are setting up new powers.

uppon which wee putt itt forth, and there was a declaration to that purpose to bee drawne to publish to the Kingedome.

Mr. Erbury.

One word, that I might nott bee mistaken [as to] the destruction that I speake of. Itt is nott minded or thought in my heart to destroy any mans person, noe nott to destroy the person of the Kinge, soe his power bee downe. I doe nott looke uppon mens persons or destroying of that power of the Magistrate that is now. The Parliament are a power by whome men may act according to the appearance of God in them. I doe nott looke uppon itt [as a power to be destroyed], neither doe I speake any thinge of that kinde; butt [I speak of] the destroying of those oppressive principalls both in powers and persons, and in courts and lawes. Those [are] thinges that have bin complained of and petitioned [against] by the poore country to the Parliament. The Parliament would never heare them. Many thousand Petitioners have petitioned [first] the Parliament, then the Lord Generall, that they would please to rectifie them; cries against unjust lawes, against tythes, [against] many unrighteous thinges crept uppe amongst us heere, amonge Committees, Receivours of monies. God was with you to take away the oppressions of men, and nott the powers of men,—nott to take away Magistracie, butt to take away those oppressions that lay before you and in your view, to remove them in the power of God.

I conceive the settlement of the Nation is properly to remove those thinges that are [the causes the nation is] unsettled. The thinges that trouble the Nation are these. I doe nott finde they are any wayes unsetled about Governement, butt they are unsetled about those oppressions that lie uppon them. I conceive the removing of these is a setling of them;[a] butt I conceive this [Agreement] will bee a meanes to unsettle them, acting the Nation

[a] "them," *i.e.* the nation.

that should bee settled by the worde of God. Now if God would soe worke and act by his people of this Army as to remove those thinges that unsettle them, they would agree, butt this would unsettle them to see all thinges putt into this frame. For my parte I doe thinke that a dozen or 24 may in a short time doe the kingdome as much good as 400 that sitt in the Parliament in 7 yeares may doe,[a] and therfore that which I would have is to [remove those thinges that] unsettle them.[b]

Commissary Ireton.

I thinke nott that burthens are the causes of unsettlement, or the beginninges of unsettlement, butt [that] the beginninges of unsettlement are the controversies about power, where the power was. Wee finde this, that all the fixing of power to persons hath clearlie tended to the increasing of jealousies amongst men, and soe to unsettlement. Because that men as men are corrupt and will bee soe. Therfore there is probably nothing more like to tend to a settlement then the clearing of power, which formerly hath bin soe much in dispute, and the taking away that controversie of those severall Competitors to the Legislative power of the Kingedome, Kinge, Lords, and Commons. If itt please God to dispose the hearts of the people to [the] Agreement, that in it they[c] may take away [that controversy], and soe taking away power

[a] The order of the clauses has been altered.

[b] Erbury wants to have an immediate removal of the grievances of the nation effected by means of a committee of a few officers and "faithful persons."

Erbury, to use a modern phrase, demanded social reforms, and refused to be satisfied with improvements in the machinery of government. The Agreement had specified 400 as the number of members to sit in future parliaments. The proposal to entrust power to a small body appears again in 1653. Cromwell and his fellow officers urged the Rump "to devolve their trust over to some well-affected men such as had an interest in the nation and were known to be of good affection to the Commonwealth, which we told them was no new thing when this land was under the like hurlyburlies." (Carlyle's *Cromwell*, Speech I.). So too Lambert, after the expulsion of the Rump, "moved that a few persons not exceeding the number of ten or twelve might be trusted with the supreme power."

[c] MS. "to Agreement in itt that they."

from men to oppresse the people, and nott leaving power hereditarie in men is some meanes of settlement. Butt if wee thinke meerly that burthens to the Nation are beginners and are the continuers of unsettlement, or to thinke to take away burthens without somethinge of settlement of another nature that is of clearing of thinges that are in controversie—Wee cannott limitt God to this, or that, or other way; butt certainly if wee take the most probable way according to the light wee have, God gives those thinges [their success]. That if itt please God these thinges should take, and bee received in the Kingdome—Thinges that doe tend to these effects, to the clearing of the controversies that have bin about power and the like, are [things] tending to settlement, and this is a probable way to bringe itt to that. Whether God will bringe itt to passe that or the other way is a secrett in his will, and is further then what is revealed to him, lett him [to whom it has been revealed] speake itt.

Mr. Spencer.

Mr. Erbury speake[s] of taking off burthens. This Agreement doth tend to the power, either the power that is now in the Parliament or the Army, and this Agreement doth leade us to that power to take away that.

Mr. Erbury.

There is as just a power now [in this Army] by which you may act in appearance, as in other following Representatives. This [Army] is call'd now from a just power to remove oppressions. I doe nott speake of Armies and such thinges, butt there are oppressions hidden in and corrupt thinges that may bee removed [by] the power of God if itt appeare in them.[a]

Sir Hardr. Waller.

That all that putt itt off to your hand does a great [dis]service.

[a] Erbury's argument is that the Army is as lawful an authority as any of the Parliaments to be called under the Agreement.

Sure there is att this time a very great dissagreement in the world and in this Kingdome, and if there bee nott neede of an Agreement now, there never was since the sons of men were uppon earth. If all of them [a] bee like't except some particulars, and if they are nott like't the whole must bee left out, I thinke itt will bee hard. Itt hath bin already said itt must bee offer'd to the House before itt comes from them as their act. I am sure there needes somethinge to goe out from you. You promised itt in your Remonstrance. Wee are now gott into the midst of January. Whether every man does nott see that thousands and tenn thousands of men are sencelesse? You have lost two monthes. Itt is nott only necessary that you passe this from you in regard of time, butt that the Agreement—I shall desire itt may bee putt to the Question whether itt shall goe out or noe.

Capt. Joyce.

I desire a worde or two for satisfaction, having bin att a distance for 3 monthes, because itt is desired itt may bee putt to the Question. I begge [to be heard] concerning two thinges which are very much debated in the Agreement: concerning the Magistrates power over men conscientiously fearing God, whether or noe they ought to have any thinge to doe in that thinge: and the other, whether the Magistrate shall have power to punish any man contrary to a law, or without a law.

I have somethinge to speake further: concerning the contending about the power which was the cause of the controversie. I beleive itt is so still, and I am sure itt is the [cause of the] jealousie that is begotten in God's people. God's people they are that have jealousie now att this time over the other. Some say the power is in your Excellencie and the Councill; and some in the Councill when they are there goe to putt itt off to others, namely the men att Westminster, or the Parliament soe called; which for my parte I can

[a] "All of them," *i.e.* all the articles of the Agreement.

hardlie soe call itt. Therfore I must intreate your Excellencie, whome the Lord hath clearlie called unto the greatest worke of righteousnesse that ever was amongst men, that your Excellencie and the Councill goe nott to shifte off that [work] which the Lord hath called you to. For my parte I doe verily believe, that if there were nott a spiritt of feare uppon your Excellency and the Councill, that hee would make you instruments to the people, of the thinges that hee hath sett before you. Itt is that confidence I have, and itt is uppon sufficient ground; because God hath said hee will doe those thinges by his people, when they beleive in him. They by beleif [shall] remove Mountaines, [and do] such thinges as were never yett done by men on earth; and certainly if I mistake nott, the spiritt is now to break forth, soe if itt were nott feare in us, wee should nott bee disputing amonge ourselves. Some are, studying to please men, I shall instance that partie of men called Presbyterians.[a] I dare nott lay itt as a charge, wee doe nott soe much study to feare the Lord our God who is able to satisfie them, and God hath soe farre satisfied some better than wee can Wee hold forth the lives of Christians as being fill'd with the spiritt of Jesus Christ—Soe I say that all that wee now seeme to bee jealous over each other is about power, and truly itt is for want of the power of God that wee are jealous over one another.

[a] "The Lords met this day in Court, and adjourned till to-morrow morning.

"Some of the most rigid Presbyterian Ministers desired (in respect some Officers of the Army had formerly desired a meeting with them, to dispute the Legality of their present proceedings, and having failed the said Officers at that time) that his Excellency would be pleased to give Order for some Officers to give them a meeting this Afternoon, at three of the clock at his Excellencies own house; which granted, they met accordingly, none being admitted to come into the Room, but such as were appointed to dispute the business. Some general Arguments were then insisted on for about two or three hours. The Officers of the Army prest for particulars to be insisted on, to the end they might come to the depth of the Arguments, and a clear satisfaction therein: the Ministers desired another time for that business, which was granted accordingly. The Officers desiring a day weekly to argue particulars with them." *The Moderate*, Jan. 9-16, 1649.

For the other [thing as to which] I have nott received satisfaction (as Mr. Sprigge said once att this Question [a]) iff wee should nott out of goodwill tell the Magistrate plainly that hee had noe power in the thinges of God either compulsive or restrictive. I beleive that God will yett visitt you once more, though I beleive that shall nott keepe itt away, butt lett us bee children unto God, shewing our love unto the Father. I begge that in the name of him I doe nott begge this in my owne name, and in my owne strength. Nott butt that I can trust the Lord. I beleive hee is about to turne some of our swordes into ploughsheares, and to [bid us] sitt still and behold his workes amongst men, and this is the day wherin hee is answering unto that great worke, and that wee should nott soe much indeavour to give away a power that God hath called us unto, or to contend about itt, butt to putt that into your hearts which is in our hearts.

Col. Harrison.

I thinke that it would bee in order to the Gentleman's satisfaction that spoke last, that this [letter] that is in Question before your Excellency bee read; because there are many that have nott read itt since some alterations bee made in itt.

That I doe beleive there are few heere can say that it is in every particular to the satisfaction of their heart, that itt is as they would have itt; butt yett that there are few heere butt can say there is much in one or other kinde [is so]. I thinke that Gentleman that spoke last speakes the minde of others, butt wee finde Jesus Christ himself spoke as men were able to beare. Itt is nott a giving power to men, only while wee are pleading [for] a libertie of conscience there is a libertie [to be] given to other men. This is all the libertie that is given. That if the best Magistrate were that ever were from the worde of God gives the ground of, or the most able men that wee can expect, itt is butt such a libertie given that such a Magistrate can give libertie to one to dispense the

[a] Page 84.

thinges of God. Itt is feared, that wee may nott have such Magistrates because wee have nott had them, nor have them now,[a] nor the men to preach. Now if the Magistrates bee nott such as wee have dispensing the thinges of edification[?] which should bee true. Though I looke uppon itt to bee the truth of God and itt is nott to mee to bee [proved] that the Magistrate should nott have power in these cases, butt since itt is my liberty, itt is my libertie to parte with that which is my right for a weake Brother, and I can beare itt[b] as my owne.

For the Agreement in the whole. I thinke itt hath bin acting uppon the hearts of many of us, that itt is nott an Agreement amongst men that must overcome the hearts of men; itt shall nott bee by might, nor by strength, butt by his spiritt Now this Agreement doth seeme to mee to bee a fruite of that spiritt.[c] That since God hath cast very much uppon your Excellency and those that waited uppon you in the Army, that wee would hold forth these thinges (a setling of that or any thinge which might bee of concerne to others) that wee would nott make use of any opportunity of this kinde—That wee would nott serve them as they have bin served, or as they would serve us, butt that there might bee some conviction that God is in us—For itt is nott a principle of man, when wee have brought downe such men that would have kept us under, to give them a libertie, butt itt is more of God, to putt them into such a condition especially as to thinges of civill concernement

[a] MS. "nott."   [b] "itt," *i.e.* the weaker brother's burden.

[c] Harrison's speech should be read with the address prefixed to the Agreement of the People, which he paraphrases in parts. *Old Parliamentary History*, xviii., 516-9. "We resolved," he says, "that since God had put this power in our hands we would put on record our views of what the terms of the settlement of the nation should be, but that we would not attempt to impose our private views, and 'settle this or that or anything which might be of concernment to others;' nor would we make use of the opportunity to perpetuate our own dominion and keep power in our own hands. On the contrary we resolved to return power as soon as possible into the hands of the people and their representatives in parliament, and content ourselves with merely recommending our scheme of settlement."

that wee neede nott seeke ourselves, that wee will trust God and give them uppe in a common current againe. That hath bin an Argument [of] very much [weight] with many why thinges of this kinde might bee proposed. Though this hath stucke, that the Worde of God doth take notice, that the powers of this world shall bee given into the hands of the Lord and his Saints, that this is the day, Gods owne day, wherin hee is coming forth in glory in the world, and hee doth putt forth himself very much by his people, and hee sayes in that day wherin hee will thresh the Mountaines hee will make use of Jacob as that threshing instrument. Now by this wee seeme to putt power into the hands of the men of the world when God doth wrest itt out of their hands; butt that having bin my owne objection as well as [the objection of] others, itt had this answer in my heart.

1. That when that time shall bee the spiritt of God will bee working to itt, and hee will worke on us soe farre that wee are [to be] made able in wisedome and power to carry through thinges in a way extraordinarie,[a] that the workes[b] of men shall bee answerable to his workes; and finding that there is nott such a spiritt in men, "Itt is only to gett power into our owne hands," "that wee may raigne over them," "itt is to satisfie our lusts," "to answer the lusts within" us,[c] butt rather that itt was in our hearts to hold forth something that may bee suitable to [the minds of] men. That present reproach uppon us doth call uppon us to hold forth somethinge to the Kingdome, and this was all of Argument that did come downe to itt, soe that that objection was answer'd. First to answer that objection, and secondly to take away that reproach. Some that feare God and are against us uppon other grounds. They thinke, that our businesse is to establish ourselves. Now hoping there will appeare much of God in this. That by this wee

[a] The position of this clause has been altered.

[b] MS. "wordes."

[c] These words given in inverted commas represent the opinion of worldlings on the motives which had led the Army to seize power.

doe very much hold forth a libertie to all the people of God, though yett itt may soe fall out that itt may goe hardly with the people of God. I judge itt will doe soe, and that this Agreement will fall short. I thinke that God doth purposely designe itt shall fall short of that end wee looke for, because hee would have us know our peace. Our Agreement shall bee from God, and nott from men; and yett I thinke the hand of God doth call for us to hold forth [something] to this Nation, and to all the world to vindicate that profession that wee have all alonge made to God, [and] that wee should lett them know that wee seeke nott for ourselves butt for men.[a]

[*Orders to the Army during the King's trial.*]

Yow are upon sight hereof, to give strict command to the severall Troopes of your Regiment, in or about London, that the officers doe keepe close to their charges, and the souldyers to their dutyes respectively, and that none of the officers or souldyers doe come to Westminster hall, or any the Courts adioyneing thereto, untill the tryall of the Kinge bee fully finished, save at, and for such time, as they shall by order bee upon duty there, under payne that every officer offending contrary thereunto shall loose his place, and every souldyer soe offending shall bee otherwise severely punished by a Councell of Warre. And every officer in his place is lawfully to see to the observance hereof as hee will answer the neglect at his perill. Given under my hand January the 20th 1648.

To Majour Blackmore or the chiefe officer present with the L[t]. Generalls Regiment.

[a] The *Perfect Diurnal* says, under 13 Jan.: "This day the General Councell of the Army met at Whitehall, with an intention to have subscribed the Agreement, but (some other affairs intervening) it was put off till Monday, against which time a Declaration to be published with the Agreement then read, was ordered to be in readiness." The Declaration was passed on Jan. 15 and the Agreement presented on Jan. 20. Rushworth, vii., 1391, 1392.

The like order to every Regiment of horse or foote now in or about the Towne. And to Capt. Allen or the Cheife officer of Col. Inglesbyes 3 companyes.

With this postscript to the severall Regimentes of horse, (vizt.) Yow are to give strict orders, that the officers of your respective troopes dureing the said tryall, doe cause all the horses belonging to the troopes, while they are in their quarters, to bee saddled all the daie time, and the souldyers to bee in readiness with their pistolls and armes, suddenly to mount if there shalbee occasion, and all to bee in like readinesse in the night tyme alsoe, save such as shalbee come off the guarde but the day before, and that a speciall watch bee keept upon the horses in the respective quarters.

And this postscript to Col. Dean's, Majour Generall Skippon's, Col. Cookes, and the Lord Generall's Regiments of foote, (vizt.):

Notwithstanding any thinge in the late orders for the putting out of new men entertayned since their comeing to London, yow may retayne soe many of them as to make up your Regiment to that establishment, (vizt.) 800 men besides officers, if it were not soe many at your comeing to the Towne.

The Declaration of the Officers belonging to the Garrison of Lancaster Castle &c.

To prevent misunderstanding of, concerning the imprisoning of Tho: Smith Minister upon 2 sermons preached at Lancaster Church, being an eare wittnesse to the same. Feb: the 8th 1648.

To remove the evill thoughts and pernicious opinions that some may have of us, and to give satisfaction to every impartiall spirit, that what we have done to him was not done as to a preacher of the Gospell, but to an incendary of the people to new commocions tending to the disturbance of the peace of the Kingdome, as it may appeare that it was not intended out of malice, or out of any intentions of ours to stopp or silence the mouthes of the publique ministers for preaching the Gospell of Jesus Christ, nor would usurpe that tyranicall authority which they themselves desires to imprison, banish, or brand any in the cheek with the letter B, upon those who out of conscience cannot submitt to the forme of doctrine, to which we reffer you to a catichisme or pamphlett latly sett forth by some of their owne freinds, and presented to the Honorable House of Commons by Mr. Bacon and Mr. Tate, both of them Members of the House. And also we doe declare, that it was soe farr from any intentions or intrest that we had of our owne that we should have been silent, had we not had reall desires of peace towards the Kingdome, and that formerly we have found many Ministers of this County too active in stirring the people both in and since the late warr, and railing against the army which God hath soe often crowned with deliverances, insisting [*i.e.* inciting] people against that army of sectaries as they are called, and now against both Parliament and Army.

And that Mr. Tho: Smith hath some times said that we should have noe peace till the Scotts came to suppresse that army of Sectaries, and being asked what he intended to doe if they came, he replyed that he would ioyne with them ; soe that we could be noe longer silent spectatours of perpeatuall ruine and destruction intended to the peace and setlement of this poore Kingdome, which we have soe long endeavoured with the loss of soe much precious time and blood in hazarding our lives and fortunes for the same, and indeed thinking nothing too deare soe that we might purchase peace, truth, and justice, which we hope God will crowne us at last withall.

But finding the people in this country like tinder ready to receive every sparke of discention sowen or cast amongst them, we conceive it our duty in discharging of that trust comitted or reposed in us, to labour by all possible meanes to suppresse or crush the cockatrice egg least it break forth into a serpent.

And least it should begett a predgedist opinion of any for what wee have done, we doe realy declare, that it was out of our reall and good intentions to the Kingdomes peace and happinesse, and the love that we beare to the truth, and humbly conceives that we were in duty bound to doe no less then what we did.

And had it not happned in such a nick of time, we conceive it had not ben soe dangerous, being done as we conceive mearly in affront to the authoritie which God hath sett up in this Kingdome, and hath made them instruments of, or displayers of the scepter of justice and righteousnesse in our Kingdome, which we have soe much longed and desired after.

And we humbly conceive, that such doctrine or such matter contained in his sermon was neither pertinent nor fitt to be delivered to such people or at such a time, unlesse it were for the elivating or kindling of the fire which formerly was scarsly put forth.

And likewise the said Mr. Smith hath said in his discourse, being asked what he thought of those that he did so much raile against as hereticks, or whether they were deare in the sight of God or noe, to which he replyed he thought noe, for neither Independants nor Anabaptists or Brownists or Seekers are deare in the sight of God; contrary to Paul's opinion against those that did eate herbes and those that did not eate, for he did not say to the eaters of hearbes that they were not precious in the sight of God, and to those who out of conscience could not eate, that they were presious, or likewise in observing of dayes, but if ye eate, eate to the praise and glory of God, and if you observe a day, keep it unto the Lord, and not for debate or strife as many doe. For as Mr. Smith confesseth himselfe that hee had often preached these sermons, though not withstanding he had bin often admonished by honest and godly men, which would gladly doe him what lawfull faviour they could, and is of his parishoners, and they say also that it is noe lesse then what they expected long or this to befall him.

And thus presenting these few lines with the matter contayned in his sermons to be annexed to this, and desires that every unpredgidest or impartiall spiritts to iudge of, and desire not to iudge any thinge till all things be waied in the balance of equitie, and soe knowing and finding truth, you may the better be inabled to stopp the mouth of all gainesayers.

Signed by us the Officers of Lancaster Castle.

THO: RIPPON.
WM. WARNOLL.
JOH: METCALFE.
ROBTE. GOLLIE.
FRAN: ANGLEBY.
GEORGE SMITH.

[*General Council of Officers at Whitehall.* 22 *Feb.*, 1648.]

The first thinge in debate att this Councill was the removing the present burthen of free quarter in many places in this Kingdome, and the prevention of itt for the time to come, uppon which the Generall produced a petition lately presented to him from the officers and souldiers of his Excellencies Regiment of Horse, which was read and approved of by the whole Councill; and it was further agreed, that

Sir Hardresse Waller.	Major Barton.
Comptroller of the Ordnance.	Major Creede.
Col. Hewson.	,, Abbott.
Col. Cooke.	Capt. Packer.
Col. Lilburne.	,, Zanchy.
Col. Goffe.	,, Browne.
Major Coleman.	,, Gladman.

or any three of them, should bee a committee to consider of the particulars of the said petition, and to prepare a draught against the next Councill of such thinges as might bee presented from them to the Parliament, both for the easing the burthens of the

Commonwealth as to free quarter, &c., and for provision of such thinges as are due to the army, the committee to meete to morrow morning in the chamber where the Councill now sitt.

They are alsoe in particular to minde the committee for the army to make uppe the accounts of the army since the 15th of January, 1647.

A printed petition was alsoe now produced, which is dispersed in the severall Regiments of the army; uppon perusal wherof itt was urged by some of the Councill, that divers persons nott of the army did indeavour to seduce and divide the souldiers by such petitions and other wayes; wheruppon after debate itt was agreed [that] Col. Cooke, Col. Goffe, Capt. Browne should goe to Mr. Rushworth, and that by them a proclamation should bee drawne uppe to issue out in his Excellencies name, and by his command to bee read in each regiment att the head of each troope and company; and these following heads are agreed to bee inserted, as:

That there bee noe clandestine contrivances or private meetinges held by any officers or souldiers of the army to the disturbance therof by promoting petitions or otherwise.

The reason to bee given, that some evill, scandalous, and cashiered persons are found out to bee privily working some discontent in the army; to assure them that thinges are now in consideration in relation to the Commonwealth and army, and that the right of petitioning is nott, nor shall bee att all hindred or disturbed; and therfore if any troope or company doe finde themselves any way aggreived they may petition, butt they are to observe these rules:

That every regiment petition distinctly.

That they bee first offer'd to the Captaine of the troope or company, and then to the chief officer in the regiment, and from him to the Generall to bee presented to the Parliament, and in case the officers should refuse them, to present itt to the Generall themselves, &c.

Especiall care to bee had in drawing uppe this proclamation.

And because there is nott in the Articles of Warre any direct or positive power given to punish such persons as breede division in the army, and yett are nott of itt, itt was agreed that Col. Whalley and Col. Hewson should goe to the Lieut. Generall and Commissary Generall to morrow morning, and in the name of the Councill desire them to move the Parliament for some expedient in this case, and that some severe punishment (such as they shall thinke fitt) may bee inflicted uppon any that shall dare to indeavour to breede any discontent in the army, and (if itt bee approved) that they may bee subject and liable to such punishment as a souldier of the army should bee in the like case. And because the first head in the petition from His Excellencies regiment is that all persons may be called to an account for publique monie, itt was agreed on by the Councell, that the two Colonells above-mencioned, and Col. Scrope and Capt. Zanchy, doe to morrow morning alsoe attend the Lieutenant Generall and Commissary Generall, and in the name of this Councill desire them to present to the Parliament an Act which is drawne for taking the accounts of the Commonwealth, and hath bin severall times perused by some eminent Members of Parliament and approved of, and that itt may passe the Parliament as soone as may bee in respect of the great consequence of itt, and the many expectations that are uppon itt, and besides that itt will raise good summes of money hitherto concealed and nott accounted for.[a]

Itt was now alsoe reported to this Councill, that divers souldiers in their march through severall Counties towards Ireland doe much harasse and plunder the Country, soe much that the inhabitants are forced to forsake their dwelling houses, and some almost undone by them. Heeruppon itt was agreed that a speedy order bee issued out in his Excellencies name, to require the officers and souldiers of his army that quarter in or neere such place, to be assisting to the people of the Country

[a] See *Commons' Journals*, vi., 149.

for their relief against the outrages and violence of any souldiers in their march or otherwayes.[a]

Agreed alsoe, That a generall Councill shall bee held uppon Thursday next the 29th instant, and soe every Thursday following, whilest the army is in this Towne, or soe often of the Generall shall thinke fitt.

Whitehall, March 1, 1648. *Att the Committee of Officers for forces & garrisons.*

Nothing done but a consideration of the Petition for the Generall Councell.

[a] A Proclamation by his Excellency the Lord General for the regulating of souldiers in their march to Ireland.

Whereas it is credibly reported, that divers souldiers in their march through several counties towards Ireland have and do still harrass, plunder, and act great violences and insolences in the countrey, to the great injury of the people and dishonour to the army, notwithstanding the power by a former proclamation given to the countrey to suppress and secure them so doing: I do therefore hereby require all officers and souldiers of the army under my command, that do quarter in or near such places, to be ayding aud assisting to the people of the country, for their relief against the outrages and violences of any such souldiers, in their march or otherwise. Provided that it is not intended hereby, that those engaged for the Irish Service be discouraged, disturbed, or interrupted in their march and orderly quartering. Given under my hand and seal in Queen Street this 17 day of March, 1648.

T. FAIRFAX.

The Moderate, March 13-20, 164$\frac{8}{9}$.

[b] In the Clarke MSS. here follows a copy of the petition presented to the general and council of the officers by certain soldiers demanding the re-establishment of the representative council of agitators which had existed in 1647. It is printed in *The Hunting of the Foxes from New-Market and Triploe Heaths to Whitehall by five small Beagles (late of the Armie); or the Grandee-Deceivers unmasked, that you may know them. Directed to all the Free-Commons of England, but in especiall to all that have and are still engaged in the Military Service of the Commonwealth. . . . Printed in a Corner of Freedome right opposite to the Councel of Warre, Anno Domini* 1649. This pamphlet is reprinted in the *Somers Tracts*, ed. Scott, vol. vi., p. 44. The petition is there (p. 54) signed by five soldiers, viz., Robert Ward, Thomas Watson, William Sawyer, Simon Grauut, George Jellis.

Whitehall, 8 *March*, 1648. *Att the Committee of Officers for forces &c.*

The businesse of Duke Hamilton &c. debated.

Three others have their names appended to the Petition as given in the Clarke MSS . viz. Richard Rumball, John Benger, Thomas Harbye. The examinations of Grant, Ward, Watson, and Jellis are printed in the *Hunting of the Foxes*. Richard Rumball, or Rumbald, rose later, obtained a commission in the army. In the summer of 1659 he was lieutenant in Col. Packer's regiment of horse. After the Restoration he became a maltster, and occupied Rye House in Hertfordshire. He took a prominent part in the Rye House Plot, was to have led the attack on the King's person, and was finally executed at Edinburgh in 1685 for his share in Argyle's rebellion. Rumbald had only one eye. "Him, therefore," says Sprat, in his *History of the Rye House Plot*, "as their most daring captain, and by reason of a blemish in one of his eyes, they [the conspirators] were wont in common discourse to call Hannibal." (*A true account and Declaration of the horrid conspiracy to assassinate the late King, Charles II.*, ed. 1696, 8vo, part i., p. 69 ; part ii., p. 53.) On his death see Burnet's *Own Time*, iii., 32, ed. 1833.

The *Perfect Diurnal*, under Thursday, March 1, gives the following account of the proceedings of the Council of Officers : "This day the General Councell of the Army sate in Whitehall where they past a petition to present to the House. . . ."

[The petition was presented March 2 ; the heads are printed by Whitelocke, *Memorials*, iii., and in the *Old Parliamentary History*, xix., 53].

"His Excellency produced at this councell a letter delivered to him that day, subscribed by 8 troopers of severall regiments, the effect of it was to assert the souldiers' right to petition without their officers' consent, expressing much against the Councell of State and High Court of Justice, which was ill resented by the officers, and each officer present being called per poll, declared their disfavouring and disapproving of the said letter, as tending to divide and disunite the Army. And 5 of the 8 troopers ordered to be committed to custody till they were cleared by Court Martiall."

The five soldiers were tried on March 3, 1649 "and after a long debate they were found guilty upon the Fifth Article of War, concerning duties morall, viz. : "That no man shall use reproachfull nor provoking words or act to any, upon paine of imprisonment and further punishment as shall be thought fit to be inflicted upon enemies to discipline and service." And foure of them sentenced to ride the horse, with their faces to the taile, their swords broke over their heads, and to be cashiered the Army. . . . The fifth taken was discharged upon confession of his being misled, and to return to the regiment."—*Perfect Diurnal.*

Major Blackmore.

That the High Court of Justice had taken itt into consideration, and had examined the businesse fully, and that itt was nott proper for the Councill of Warre to consider of itt, and to take notice of itt.

Col. Scrope.

That Civill Warres were nott of the same nature with other warres.

M. Disbrow.

That wee had acted in obedience to the Parliament, and if wee doe act onely as souldiers why doe wee give them into their hands?[a] Our Engagements were to serve the visible power of this Commonwealth, nott to serve our owne wills or our owne judgements to spare any.

When the publique enemy had a publique force in the Kingedome wee were winck't att by the Parliament in the marching by such townes, butt when that was done our worke was to take them. As for Goring and Capell and those, wee were putt uppon itt. Goring and Capell were left to mercy.

Major Blackmore.

That the Parliament had approved of the manner of my Lord Graye's taking of him, and that notwithstanding the Articles with Major Generall Lambert hee should bee tryed.[b]

[a] *i.e.* the hands of the Parliament.

[b] A full account of the trials of Hamilton, Holland, Capel, Norwich, and Sir John Owen is given in a volume amongst the Clarke MSS. (Worcester College MSS., vol 70.) Clarke was one of the witnesses, and probably took down the proceedings himself. Major Blackmore, of Cromwell's regiment, and Captain Spencer, of Harrison's, were amongst the witnesses. The question now discussed in the Army Council was whether the Council should mediate with the Parliament for the lives of all or any of the persons condemned. It was specially urged that the articles given by Lambert to Hamilton involved an assurance of life to Hamilton, and should be made good by the Army.

Capt. Chillendon.

That itt hath bin pleaded this 5 weekes day, and that wee must lett itt alone, and whether itt would nott bee dishonourable to try them?

Sir Hardresse Waller.

'Tis true you went to take delinquents and when you could take them itt was well, butt when you give them conditions [you ought to see that the conditions are observed]. Did Lambert send worde to him that hee had noe power to give him his life? Would any man give uppe 2,000 Horse without some assurance?

Col. Barkestead.

That there could bee noe proceedinges without evidence.

Capt. Pitson.[a]

The Articles are made good. I alsoe broke prison out of Oxford. I went out of the prison, butt did nott breake prison.[b]

Capt Spencer.

That hee was confident hee had Articles. That when the Generall had vile persons in his hands, hee conveyed them to Oxford, and other places out of the power of the Parliament.

Lt. Byfeild.

That hee[c] tooke Capt. Blackwell's Lieutenant, and did freely release him without any ransome, and to shew his cause was nott against Englishmen, butt according to the ends of the Declaration. That if itt had bin declared to him that his life should nott have

[a] Pitson seems to refer to the fact that Hamilton had escaped from prison at Windsor. He was recaptured in a few hours, and it was alleged against him that he had broken his parole to the governor, Col. Whichcote.

[b] Parole?

[c] *i.e.* Duke Hamilton.

bin assured itt had bin more for his advantage [to have fought it out to the death]; hee had nott bin tainted in his bloud and his estate sequestred.

Major White.

That wee did nott mediate before wee knew hee would bee sentenc't to death, butt now wee know itt wee doe mediate for itt.

Lt. Col. Goffe.

The consideration of the providence of God that hath appeared to us for the bringing of us thus farre. These men have all of them past the triall of such as wee have cause to judge are godly and conscientious men. They are satisfied in judgement and conscience that these men ought to die as such as are guilty of that innocent bloud that hath defiled this land.

Capt. Merriman.

That the Articles of Pembroke give them Quarter, leaving them to the mercy of the Parliament. This gives them quarter without any reservation.

Capt. Clarke.

That the faith and honour of the Army was engaged.

Col. Whalley.

That Major Generall Lambert writt, that hee did nott intend hee should bee reserved from the power of the Civill Magistrate. They finde itt cleare that the Generall was nott impowred to give him life against the Civill aucthority.

Col. Barkestead.

That Col. Lilburne had declar'd in Court uppon oath, that they did nott intend to keepe him from the justice of the Parliament.

Hamilton himself said, that hee thought his clothes would serve him as longe as hee lived.

Major Carter.

That hee was sorry in the first steppe to justice they should have soe many blockes in their way.

That God never afforded us an opportunity for us to doe justice till now. The Declarations did manifest [that the war] was against sectaries, which was godly men. That many thousands had bin slaine, wee lost as much precious blould the last summer as in many years[a] before. Lett us looke [to it that] soe much blood bee nott spilt as water uppon the ground. That godly men were their judges; [they were judged] by men meetest to judge them. Since wee shall goe quarrell att all the passages of providence. That I doe nott know a companie of men living that should keepe closer to itt, if wee should nott.

Capt. Baynes.

That hee did wonder they should call this businesse in Question. They have pleaded itt in severall places.

They have pass'd their judgement uppon those Articles. I doe wonder that Col. Hewson (who was one of the Commissioners) should debate itt againe.

Capt. Tomlins.

That which the High Court hath done is either just or unjust. If wee must debate what is just, then lett us goe to Question for all the rest as well as for him.

Capt. Spencer.

The Generall hath written a lettre for two of them.

After the two Questions putt Mr. Peter moved, that the Generall might have a meeting on Sunday next in this roome, to have itt further debated.

[a] MS. "dayes."

[*Lord Fairfax to the Speaker.*]

Right Honorable.

Upon credible informacion [that] William Thompson pretending[a] himselfe a Captain, and to have authorety from mee and the Councell of the army, hath with a party of men, by that pretended power, comitted severall misdemeanours of high nature and dangerous consequence, in breaking open the dores of the dwelling house of one Mr. Littleton att North Okendon in the County of Essex, in the night tyme, fyreing a pistoll, and drawing theire swordes upon the servants and people there, thrust them out of dores, carried them away prisoners, and tooke away some goods; the particulars of all which passages I suppose yow will bee fully acquainted with by Mr. Littleton. For which being apprehended upon examinacion founde to bee noe souldyer, itt was thought fitt not to proceede against him at a Court Marshall, and therefore hee was delivered over to the Civill Magistreate, who as I understand hath bound him with suretyes to answer the same at the next Assizes to be hould[en] for the said County; and hath since his inlargment inveagled divers souldyers of the army who attempted to comitt the like misdemeanours at the same place. My Lord, both I, the Councell, and all others of the army, doe disavow and detest, the giveing of any such authority or power to the said Thompson, or aney other person whomsoever, for acting any thinges of such nature, and theirefore desire that something exemplary may bee done, not onely to deterr others from comitting any thinge of the like nature upon any such pretence, but alsoe for vindicacion of the armye.

[T. FAIRFAX.] [b]

[March 164$\frac{8}{9}$.]

[a] MS. "pretended."

[b] The *Perfect Diurnal*, under March 15, 1649, reporting the proceedings of the Council of the Army which met on that day, says: "Report was made from the Court Marshall by the Judge Advocate concerning the miscarriages of Mr. Thompson

Generall Councill. Whitehall, 23 *March*, 1648.

Itt being for the businesse of Ireland itt was propounded by Col. Whalley, Sir Hardresse Waller, and other officers, that the Lt. Generall would declare himself, whether hee would goe or noe?

The Lieutenant Generall answer'd: That as to will he was uppon the appointment of the Parliament ready to submitt.

That the worke was a greate worke, and would require more of the will and mindes of men to carry itt on, necessary and convenient supplies.

8 Regimentes of Foote and 3000 Horse.

The Councill of State hath by these Gentlemen returned this answer, which in effect was to represent mee Commander in Cheif.[a]

in Essex, and of his putting a man out of possession by a company of disguised persons with false haire and beards, that he was turned over to the Civill Magistrate, and Leiutenant Colonel Lilburne and one Harris offered to be his bayle." William Thompson had been originally a corporal in Col. Whalley's regiment, but was cashiered for his scandalous and disorderly conduct in autumn, 1647, and was for a time imprisoned at Windsor. He then published, possibly with help from John Lilburne, a pamphlet called *England's Freedom Souldiers Rights, or the just declaration, plea, and protestation of William Thompson, a free Commoner of England unjustly imprisoned at Windsor*, 14, Dec., 1647. Allowed to go to London on parole he was found stirring up sedition, and was arrested by Cromwell, and sent back. See *The Kingdom's Weekly Post*, March 2-9, 164$\frac{7}{8}$; and also a pamphlet called *A Vindication of Lieut.-Gen. Cromwell and Comm. Gen. Ireton against a libel signed by one Tompson*, by A. C., dated March 7, 164$\frac{7}{8}$, E 431-16. Other notices of Thompson are contained in *The Discoverer*, 4to, 1649, pt. ii., pp. 7, 19; *England's New Chains*, 1649, p. 8; *The Prisoners Mournful Cry*, 1648; and *The Justice of the Army vindicated*, 1648. Thompson was killed in May, 1649, having headed the rising of the Levellers which was suppressed at Burford. See Whitelocke's *Memorials*, iii., 37.

[a] See *Cal. State Papers Dom.* 1649-50, pp. 39, 41, 49, and *Commons' Journals*, vi., 162, 176.

I told them alsoe my will could nott butt bee subject to those that were over mee, barely consider'd as matter of will; yett inasmuch as this businesse is of soe great importance as itt is, itt was fitt for mee in the first place to consider, how God would incline my heart to itt, how I might by seeking of him receive satisfaccion in my owne spiritt, as to my owne particuler. Nott that I would putt any termes uppon the State in relation to myself, butt that I would bee glad to see a freenesse and a clearnesse in my spiritt to the worke. And a second consideration was, that if their Lordshippes did thinke, that the naming of a Commander in Cheif might bee some satisfaction to persons, to Officers and souldiers to goe, that itt was very fitt for mee to have a little consideration to that in relation to them, that I might nott bee an occasion by any interest of mine to improve that interest to draw men over and nott to bee well satisfied concerning a just and fitting provision for them before they went. And in the last place, the worke being soe weighty, I did thinke that itt would require many thinges. I had had noe serious thoughts of the businesse, and therfore for mee to give an answer, that they might give the Councill an answer, that they had nott only made a Commander in Cheif, and that itt was accepted by him, I did thinke fitt that they should returne back to them [to ask that I might have time to consider of the matter].

That I having taken time till the beginning of next weeke, I hope noe resolution will bee expected from mee before that time. I doe confesse, my Lord, I should desire, that this businesse of Ireland I might nott goe uppon itt out of any personall respects whatsoever ; and I would have personall respects farre from this Army. I doe nott thinke that God hath blest this Army for the sake of any one man, nor has his presence bin with itt uppon any such ground; butt that presence and blessing that God hath afforded this Army, itt hath bin of his owne good pleasure, and to serve his owne turne. That presence and blessing that hee hath afforded us has bin for his owne name sake, because hee would doe amongst the sons of men what seemed good in his eyes for the bringing of his glory and purpose to passe; and uppon this score has this Army undertaken all that itt hath undertaken in the presence of God.

Itt matters nott who is our Commander in Cheif if God bee soe; and if God bee amongst us, and his presence bee with us, itt matters nott who is our Commander in Cheif. Truly I doe beleive that God hath soe principled this Army that there is none amongst us that if God should sett us out any man wee should come to this, to [refuse to] submitt to one another in this for the worke's sake. Therfore I would that I might thinke of this: what is this businesse of Ireland, what are our considerations in relation to England, to Scotland, to freinds heere or there, or enemies any where? And if wee, taking considerations of that kinde and seeking directions from his guidance, answer the best guide that hee shall give to us—And therfore I shall bee bold to offer to you some thoughts of mine, and some considerations which perhaps will best serve to ripen your resolutions as to this undertaking, that soe you may undertake it [a] from the Lord.

You know how itt hath pleased God to beate downe all your enemies under your feete, both in this Kingdome and the Kingdome of Scotland; and you have with simplicitie of heart made this opposition to those enemies uppon those honest and religious grounds that itt is fitt for godly and honest and religious men to propose to themselves; and God hath brought the warre to an issue heere, and given you a greate fruite of that warre, to witt: the execution of exemplary justice uppon the prime leader of all this quarrell into the three Kingedomes, and of divers persons of very great quality who did co-operate with him in the destruction of this Kingdome. Truly, notwithstanding you have brought this worke to this issue, yett itt seemes your worke is nott att an end. You have yett another enemy to incounter with, and freinds to stand by, [and] the interest you have fought for yett further to make

[a] MS. "undertaking."

good; to the end you may bee able to resist those that have bin heertofore your enemies, and are still your enemies, and are more enrag'd, and are not only nott warn'd by those examples and those witnesses that God hath witnessed for you, butt they are[a] removed at a further distance, [and are] joyn'd together in stronge combination to revive the worke heere againe—that is certainly in the Kingdome of Scotland, [and] in the Kingdome of Ireland. In the Kingdome of Scotland, you cannott soe well take notice of what is done, nor of this that there is a very angry hatefull spiritt there against this Army, as an Army of Sectaries, which you see all their papers doe declare their quarrell to bee against. And although God hath used us as instruments for their good, yett hitherto they are nott sensible of itt; butt they are angry that God brought them his mercy att such an hand; and this their anger (though without any quarrelling of ours with them) will returne into their owne bosomes; for God did doe the worke without us, and they that are displeas'd with the instruments, their anger reaches to God and nott to [his instruments.][b] You see they have declared the Prince of Wales their Kinge; and indeavours are both heere and there with that partie to doe what they can to co-operate with them to cause all this worke to returne againe, and to seeke the ruine and destruction of those that God hath ordain'd to bee instrumentall for their good.

And I thinke you are nott ignorant that a great partie heere does co-operate in the worke, and [that] their spiritts are imbitter'd against us, though they might know that if God had nott used this poore Army instrumentally to doe what they have done, they[c] had nott had a being att this time. Butt such is the good pleasure of God as to leave them to the blindnesse of their mindes.

I must needes say I doe more feare—nott that I doe thinke there is a ground to feare itt will bee—but as a poore man that desires to see the worke of God to prosper in our hands, I thinke there is more

[a] Position of words altered.

[b] MS. "him."

[c] they, *i.e.* the English Presbyterians.

cause of danger from dissunion amongst ourselves then by any thinge from our enemies; and I doe nott know anythinge [that is a] greater [danger] then that, and I believe and I may speake with confidence, till wee admire God and give him Glory for what hee has done. For all the rest of the world, Ministers and profane persons, all robbe God of all the Glory, and reckon itt to bee a thinge of chance that has befalne them. Now if wee doe nott depart from God, and disunite by that departure, and fall into dissunion amongst ourselves, I am confident, wee doing our duty and waiting uppon the Lord, wee shall finde hee will bee as a wall of brasse round about us till wee have finished that worke that hee has for us to doe. And yett nott to bee sensible that this [is God's work] is the [cause of the] rage and malice of our enemies. . . .

I wish that they may see their errour (those that are good amongst them), and repent; butt certainly this wrath of theirs shall turne to their hurt, and God will restraine the remainder that itt shall nott hurt us.

In the next place wee are to consider Ireland. All the Papists and the Kinges partie—I cannott say all the Papists, butt the greatest partie of them—are in a very stronge combination against you, and they have made an union with those Apostate forces that were under Insiquene, and the Confederate Catholiques of Ireland, and all that partie are in a very stronge combination against you. The last letters that the Councill of State had from thence doe plainly import, that Preston has 8,000 Foote and 800 Horse, that Taaf has as many, that my Lord Clanrikard has the same proportion, that my Lord Insiquene and my Lord Ormond has a matter of 3,000 Foote and 800 Horse, that these are all agreed and ready in conjunction to roote out the English interest in Ireland, and to sett uppe the Prince of Wales his interest there likewise, and to indeavour as soone as they can to attempt uppon our interest in Leinster and Ulster and Conaught. In all which provinces wee have an interest, butt in Munster [we have] none att all; and though that interest wee have in these three provinces itt is nott soe [in]considerable, [yet][a] if these Confederate forces shall come uppon them, itt is more than probable, without a miracle from heaven, [that][a] our interest will easily bee eradicated out of those parts. And truly, this is really believed: if wee doe nott indeavour to make good our interest there, and that timely, wee shall nott only have (as I said before) our interest rooted out there, butt they will in a very short time bee able to land forces in England, and to putt us to trouble heere. I confesse I have had these thoughts with myself that perhaps may bee carnall and foolish. I had rather bee overrun with a Cavalerish interest [than] of a Scotch interest; I had rather bee overrun with a Scotch interest then an Irish interest; and I thinke of all this is most dangerous. If they shall bee able to carry on their worke they will make this the most miserable people in the earth, for all the world knowes their barbarisme—nott of any religion, almost any of them, butt in a manner as bad as papists—and you see how considerable therin they are att this time. Truly itt is [come] thus farre, that the quarrell is brought to this state, that wee can hardly returne unto that tyranny that formerly wee were under the yoake of, which through the mercy of God hath bin lately broken, butt wee must att the same time bee subject to the Kingdome of Scotland, or the Kingdome of Ireland, for the bringing in of the Kinge. Now itt should awaken all Englishmen, who perhaps are willing enough hee should have come in uppon an accomodation, but [see] now [that] hee must come from Ireland or Scotland. This being soe, I would nott have this Army now soe much [as] to looke att considerations that are personall—whether or noe wee shall goe if such a Commander goe, or such a Commander [do not go], and make that any parte of our measure or foundation—butt lett us goe if God goe. If wee bee still in our calling, prosecuting that cause that hitherto wee have engag'd in, and [if] the opposing those enemies bee a

[a] MS. in each case reads "butt."

parte of that cause (wherein we desire that there may be noe personal respects in it), and if wee bee satisfied in our judgements and consciences that Hee is in itt, that you would lett this bee your motive. And I doe professe itt as before the Lord of Heaven, and as in his presence, I doe nott speake this to you that I would shifte att all from the command, or in any sneaking way or in any politique [way] lead you to an Engagement before I declare my thoughts in the thinge. Whether I goe or stay [is] as God shall incline my heart to. And if you undertake itt uppon these grounds, I am confident there will nott bee soe much dispute amongst us,[a] who shall goe as who shall stay. My meaning is, you will—every honest heart that sees a freedome of their wayes will rather bee whetted on, out of love to God and duty to God, to goe where hee may doe him most service, rather then stay. I say except itt bee that God doe cast [hindrances] in men's wayes by necessity of relations, or laying any law uppon mens hearts, and [other obligations] besides that may otherwise hinder them. I doe nott speake this as thinking butt that hee may bee as honest a man that does desire [to stay as he that desires to go],[b] [but as thinking that] doing service to God, and giving Glory to God will bee the best motive to this worke. Aye, itt will bee much better to have considerations of this kinde then to lay this as the foundation, who shall command in cheif. For my owne parte, though the Councill of State hath putt that uppon mee, yett I have desir'd them to give mee till Tuesday to give in my answer. [I desire you therefore now] to give your resolutions as to the particular Regiments that are to goe, and to state what other demands in that kinde you will make for your going, that may inable those to goe, and to have a subsistence when they goe.

8,000 Foote, 3,000 Horse, and 1,200 Dragoones.

Sir Hardresse Waller.

Made some Objections. That hee thought the worke would nott

[a] MS. those. [b] MS. to goe or stay.

goe forward till itt bee knowne whether the Commander in Cheif named will goe or nott.

Cromwell.

I offer this: That the Army doe move for such provisions as may bee fitt for honest men to aske ; and if you goe uppon that account, I thinke my resolution will bee knowne before yours, and that will bee properly in the nature of thinges; itt will bee best and fittest for you to consider of that first, if there bee a designed parte of the Army to goe as ther will probably.

I hope wee are such a Generation of men, I am sure God soe bindes us about as with a garment—therfore wee are to looke one uppon another as if itt were our owne case, all of us being readie to doe itt ; and therfore I thinke in order to your proceedinges itt will bee better to consider who shall goe, and what is due to him, and to provide for him as to the point of Arreares, and of provision what will serve for honest men to carry on the worke.

And truly this will spend as much time as Tuesday next comes to.[a]

Col. Hewson made a learned speech, and instead of addressing himself to his Excellency [b] said, An't please your Majestie.

Committee of Officers appointed by the General Councill.
Whitehall, 24 *March*, 1648.

After God had bin earnestly sought all the day by fasting and prayer, lettres to the Lieutenant Generall were first read.

[a] "March 23. This day the Councel of the Army met again and named two officers of every regiment of horse and foot of the Army, and divers garrisons of the Kingdom to meet the next morning, to seek God, together with what advice to offer to the General concerning the expedition for Ireland, and to make a report to the Councel Monday next by three of the clock in the afternoon. The Lieutenant General is to give in his answer to the Councel of State on Tuesday next, whether he will go for Ireland or not.—*The Moderate*, March 20-27, 1649.

[b] *i.e.* Fairfax.

Heads of the Lettres to Col. Jones.[a]

Noe Declaration to bee made; itt were to redargute the Parliament.

Col. Whalley.

That these thinges bee offer'd :

1. That their accounts bee stated, Debentures given, and a sufficient security given.

The impowering the Commander in Cheif that goes over soe to capitulate with the Enemy as to conclude a peace; and that noe ill termes bee impos'd uppon him, as either to eradicate the Natives, or to divest them of their estates.

The consideration of those. The names that you would propose in relation to the Army.

To desire Sir Robert Kinge or such other Gentlemen as they shall please to call to them to their assistance in the modelling of the propositions.

To

Sir Hardresse Waller.
Major Generall Mitton.
Col. Coke.
Col. Harrison.
Adj. Stubber.
Col. Reynolds.
Col. Rich.
Lt. Elsyng.

As to the stating of provision, and all those incouragements to make them fitt to goe, the having of Magazines on the English side, the naming of the Navy att whose dispose that shall bee.

8 Regiments of Foote.
6 Regiments of Horse, and
A Regiment of Dragoones.

[a] Here follow extracts from Ormond's letter of March 9, 1648, to Col. Michael Jones, and fragments of Jones's answer of March 19. Both letters having been printed in full these summaries are omitted. For the letters, see Milton's *Prose Works*, ed. Bohn, vol. ii., 170-174.

A great Debate in relation to lotts. Urg'd by Sir Hardresse Waller, that a lott was nott to bee us'd unlesse where the businesse could nott otherwise bee determined.

Col. Cooke offer'd that some might bee appointed as a Committee to consider of some such men.

Itt was urg'd, that [in the case] of Matthias and Barnabas, that there were butt two men, that the Apostles could have chosen one of them two, yett they chose to cast lotts.[a]

[*The Council of State to Lord Fairfax.*]

My Lord,

By the narrative inclosed your Lordshippe will bee informed of what relation hath bin made to this Councill of a disorderly and

[a] March 26 [?] The Councel of the Army sat at Whitehall, and the Committee appointed Saturday last, to propose some particulars for the encouragement of those that shall engage for Ireland made report thereof to the General Councel, upon debate whereof the Councel sate all day and most part of the night. The propositions reported were many.

(1.) That such as shall go shall have three moneth's advance of their pay, and one moneth's advance of their arrear.

(2.) Their accounts to be audited, and security given for them, and to be paid at a certain time, when the Parliament shall appoint.

(3.) That in case they shall be slain in the service, their next kindred or friend may receive the same by will or assignment.

(4.) That shipping may be provided for their transportation, and provisions made ready with expedition.

(5.) That there may be a Court of Admiralty constituted at Dublin, or elsewhere in Ireland, that so the men of war may not be troubled to lose so much time as to their prizes.

These with many other were reported by the said Committee; and if the Councell approve hereof then to be by them transferred to Parliament for their approbation.

The Moderate, March 29-27, 1649.

April 20. This day lots were drawn by the officers of the Army for the service of Ireland; the regiments whose lots did fall to go, were, of horse, Commissary Generall Ireton's, Colonel Scroop's, Colonel Hewson's, and Major General Lambert's: of foot, Colonell Ewer's, Colonel Cook's, Colonel Hewson's, and Colonel Dean's; of Dragoons, Major Abbot's, Capt. Mercer's, Capt. Fulcher's, Capt. Garland's, and Capt. Bolton's troops.

The Moderate, April 17-24, 1649.

tumultuous sort of people assembling themselves together nott farre from Oatlands, att a place called St. George's Hill; and although the pretence of their being there by them avowed may seeme very ridiculous, yett that conflux of people may bee a beginning whence thinges of a greater and more dangerous consequence may grow, to the disturbance of the peace and quiett of the Commonwealth. Wee therfore recommend itt to your Lordshippes care that some force of horse may bee sent to Cobham in Surrey and ther abouts, with order to disperse those people soe mett, and to prevent the like for the future, that a malignant and dissaffected partie may nott under colour of such ridiculous people have any opportunity to randezvouz themselves in order to a greater mischief.

Signed in the name and by order of the Councill of State appointed by aucthority of Parliament.

JOHN BRADSHAW, President.

Derby House, 16 Aprill, 1649.

For the right honorable Thomas Lord Fairfax, Lord Generall.

Information of Henry Sanders of Walton uppon Thames.

Informeth, That on Sunday was sennight last, there was one Everard, once of the army butt was cashiered, who termeth himself a prophett, one Stewer and Colten, and two more, all living att Cobham, came to St. George's Hill in Surrey, and began to digge on that side the Hill next to Campe Close, and sowed the ground with parsenipps, and carretts, and beanes. On Munday following they were there, again, being increased in their number, and on the next day being Tuesday, they fired the Heath, and burn't att least 40 roode of Heath, which is a very great prejudice to the Towne. On Friday last they came againe, betweene 20 and 30, and wrought all day att digging. They did then intend to have two or three ploughes att worke, butt that they had nott furnished themselves with seede corne, which they did on Saturday att Kingston. They invite all to come in and helpe them, and promise them meate, drinke, and clothes. They doe threaten to pull downe and levell all parke pales, and lay open, and intend to plant there very shortly. They give out, they will bee four or five thousand within 10 dayes, and threaten the neighbouring people there, that they will make them all come uppe to the hills and worke, and forwarne them suffering their cattell to come neere the plantation, if they doe they will cutt their legges off. Itt is feared they have some designe in hand.[a]

HENRY SANDERS.

16°. Aprilis, 1649.

[*Captain John Gladman to Lord Fairfax.*]

Sir.[b]

According to your order I martched towards St. Georges Hill and sent foure men before to bring certaine intelligence to mee ; as they went they mett with Mr. Winstanlie and Mr. Everard (which are the cheife men that have persuaded those people to doe what they have done). And when I had enquired of them and of the

[a] The chief pamphlets on the *Diggers* are (1) "*A Watchword to the City of London and the Armie*" by Jerrard Winstanley, 1649. (2) *A letter to the Lord Fairfax and his Council of War . . . delivered to the General and the chief officers on Saturday, June* 9, 1649. Reprinted in the *Harleian Miscellany*, viii., 586, ed. Park. *The true Leveller's Standard*; *or the State of Community opened and presented to the sons of men*, by William Everard, 4to, 1649. On April 20, 1649, Everard and Winstanley had an interview with Fairfax. An account of this interview is given in *Whitelocke's Memorials*, iii., 18, extracted from *The Moderate* or some other newspaper. See also the papers printed on pp. 215-224, *post*.

[b] From Mr. Popham's MSS. This letter is slightly abridged.

officers that lie at Kingston, I saw ther was no need to martch any further. I cannot heare that there hath beene above twentie of them together since they first undertooke the businesse. Mr. Winstanlie and Mr. Everard have ingaged both to be with you this day: I believe you will be glad to bee rid of them againe, espeshially Everard who is no other then a madd man. Sir, I intend to goe with two or three men to St. Georges hill this day, and perswade these people to leave this imployment if I can, and if then I see no more danger then now I doe I shall march back again to London to morrow. . . . . Indeed the business is not worth the writing nor yet taking nottis of: I wonder the Council of State should be so abused with informations. . . . .

Jo. Gladman.

April 19, 1649.
Kingston.

The Committee of Wilts to Sir Henry Mildmay.

Winton, 19 April, 1649.

Sir,

Since your being here wee have had many more complaints come unto us of the ill carriage of Coll. Martins Regiment in this County; among others this day divers honest men of Whitchurch and places adjacent by this inclosed peticon express their deepe sence of the greate oppressions and outrages done upon them very lately by those soldiers; our earnest desire is you would be pleased to comunicate their peticon to his Excellencie, it being in referrence to our late letter written to the Councell of State on the behalfe of this miserable County. Because you were lately upon the place, and therby an eye and eare wittness of the insufferable violences and oppressions this County yett laboureth under, and signed that letter to the Councell of State, wee thinke fitt to intreate your effectuall and speedy care herein ; wherby you will exceedingly oblige the whole County in generall, and in perticular[a]

Your humble servants
Ro. Wallop
Rob. Reynolds
Jo. Hildesley
R. ————
William Wither.

Winton, 19 April, 1649.

Col. Monck to Lord Fairfax.

May itt please Your Excellency,

I am soe deeply obliged to your Lordship for your noble favours, and the good opinion that you have bin pleased to conceive of mee, that I am transported with joy that I have the happines to bee intituled one of your Lordships servants, wherby I may have occasion to manifest my affection. I know itt is the least part of my duty and service to give your Lordship an account of affaires heere. The Scots who were lately under my commaund are now involved into very high distempers amongst themselves, occasioned

[a] This letter, which is accompanied by a petition from the inhabitants of Whitchurch, is from Mr. Popham's MSS. Parliament had voted on 2 Feb., 1649, that the horse under the command of Col. Marten should be made up to a full regiment, but probably in consequence of this and other complaints the vote seems not to have been acted upon. *Commons' Journals*, vi., 129. The officers probably had originally commissions like that of Captain Rice, whose commission from Marten is printed on p. 56. Amongst the Clarke Papers there is a list of officers of this regiment for whom commissions were desired, Feb. 1, 1649, viz.: Capt.-Lieut. William Yate, of Marten's own troop ; Capt. William Ware (commander of the troop lately Rice's) ; Capt. Richard Pechell, of the Wilts troop ; Capt. Greenwood, of Derbyshire ; Capt. Dolphin, of Nottingham ; and Arthur Evelyn, for his own troop. The regiment was evidently intended to be made up from what were termed the "loose troops" raised in different counties, and not forming part of any regiment, and Evelyn was probably to be its major.

by their desencion from this service. Sir George Monro is advanced into their quarters, and is sate downe before Colrane with 4 regiments of Irish foote, and 300 horse of Ormond's party, the Lord of Ardes holding complyance with him, butt all the rest of the regiments and troopes of the Scotts forces are marched to oppose Monroe. Sir Robert Steuart hath ben very active since his arivall comaunding the leaguer before Derry, but I receaved intelligence this day that the Scotts have drawen off their siege before Derry, butt uppon what occasion I canot informe you, only I conceive ther is some agreement concluded betweene Sir Cha: Coote and them.[a] I understand that the supply intended to bee transmitted hither are ready for transportacion. I hope there is some horse ready amongst them, which is much wanted here. Coll. Jones is drawen into the feild, and I am ioyned with him; wee lye in the way to stoppe Ormond from advancinge towards Dublin. Inchiqueene is ioyned with him, which makes him too stronge in horse for us, the daily distractions that happen in the North prevents the well affected party there from joyninge with us, or sending horse to aid us, soe that I hope your Lordship will send a supply of horse heare speedily to enable us to cope with them, and then I doubt not but your Lordship will receive a good account of our endeavours, which shall bee wholy imployed to advaunce the service for the interest of England. I desire that your Lordship will honor mee with your comaunds which I will faithfully observe to the utmost power,

My Lord, Your Excellencies
most faithfull and most humble servant
GEORGE MONCK.[b]

For his Excellency Lord Fairfax,
Lord Generall of all the forces in the Kingdome
of England.

[a] An agreement was concluded between Coote and O'Neill, 22 May, 1649.

[b] This letter is not dated, but it is inserted amongst news-letters dated June, 1649, and was probably written either early in June or towards the end of May.

To his Excellency the Lord Fairfax and the Counsell of Warre the Brotherly Request of those that are called Diggers sheweth

That whereas wee have begun to digg upon the Commons for a livelihood, and have declared to your Excellency and the whole world our reasons, which are four. First, from the righteous law of Creation that gives the earth freely to one as well as to another without respect of persons. Secondly, by vertue of yours and our victory over the King, whereby the enslaved people of England have recovered themselves from under the Norman Conquest; though wee doe not as yet enjoy the benefitt of our victories, nor cannott soe long as the use of the Common land is held from the younger bretheren by the Lords of Mannours, that as yet sitte in the Norman chaire, and upholde that tyranny as if the kingly power were in force still; and a third reason that moved us to digg was the perswasion of our hartes that the Parliament and Army would make good their bargaine with us; for you promised that if wee would adventure person and purse to recover England from under that Norman oppression you would make us a free people, and you have obtained the victory by your owne and our assistance, and there is nothing wanting from you to us but makeing good your bargaine to us, for by the law of reason and contract wee have bought our freedom of the Parliament and Army, who have the power of the sword in your hands, by our blood, taxes, and free quarter. And wee are perswaded of your faithfullness to us for two reasons. First, your promises, which as you are Gospell professours wee expect you will make good, and soe give us our freedome, which wee have dearely paid for, and you have received our moneys the fruits of our labours. Secondly, your Covenant to God, unto whome first wee kept fasting dayes, and praied him to help and deliver this oppressed Nation, and then after any victory over our oppressour Charles you apointed daies of thanks-giving unto God. Now in the third place, God expects from you and the Parliament to performe your Covenant in deede and worke as well as in words, and let the oppressed goe free unto whom you promised freedome; and though you have fought for it, yet wee have paid for it, and soe have purchased that same freedome with you, that is that wee may live in the earth without poverty; for (fourthly) wee digg upon the Common to make the earth a common treasury, because our necessity for food and rayment require it.

Now Sirs, divers repulses wee have had from some of the Lords of Mannours and their servants, with whome wee are patient and loveing, not doubting but at last they will grant liberty quietly to live by them; and though your tenderness have moved us to bee requesting your protection against them, yet wee have forborne, and rather waited upon God with patience till hee quell their unruely spirits, and of prosecuting Sauls to make them righteous Pauls; and in regard likewise the souldiers did not molest us, for that you tould us when some of us were before you, that you had given command to your souldiers not to meddle with us, but resolved to leave us to the Gentlemen of the Cuntry and to the law of the Land to deale with us; which wee were satisfied with, and for this halfe year past your souldiers have not meddled with us.

But now Sirs, this last weeke upon the 28th of November, there came a party of souldiers commanded by a cornet, and some of them of your owne Regiment, and by their threatneing words forced 3 labouring men to helpe them to pull downe our 2 houses, and carried away the wood in a cart to a Gentleman's house who hath bin a Cavaleer all our tyme of warrs, and cast 2 or 3 old people out who lived in those houses to lye in the open feild this cold weather, (an action more becomeing the Turks to deale with Christians then for one Christian to deale with another); but if you inquire into the business you will finde that the Gentlemen that sett the souldyers on are enemyes to you, for some of the cheife had hands in the

Kentish riseing against the Parliament, and wee know, and you will finde it true if you trust them so farr, that [they] love you but from the teeth outward.

Therefore our request to you is this, that you would call your souldiers to accompt for attempting to abuse us without your commission, that the Cuntry may know that you had noe hand in such an unrighteous and cruell act. Likewise wee desire that you would continue your former kindnesse and promise to give commission to your souldiers not to meddle with us without your order, and wee shalbee very thankfull to you and remayne

Yours and England true borne sonnes and frends.

JOHN HEYMAN
AN: WRENN
HEN: BARTON
JO[N] COULTON
ROBERT COSLER
JOHN PALMER
JACOB HEARD

in the behalfe of others called the Diggers.

To my Lord Generall and his Councell of Warr.

Sir,

I understand that Mr. Parson Platt with some other Gentlemen, have made report to you, and the Councell of State, that wee that are called Diggers are a riotous people, and that wee will not bee ruled by the Justices, and that wee hold a mans house by violence from him, and that wee have 4 guns in it, to secure ourselves, and that wee are drunkards, and Cavaleers waiteing an opportunity to helpe to bringe in the Prince, and such like.

Truely Sir, these are all untrue reports, and as false as those which Haman of old raised against sincere harted Mordecay to incense Kinge Ahasuerus against him. The conversacion of the diggers is not such as they report, wee are peaceable men, and walke in the light of righteousness to the utmost of our power. Our enemies have sent divers tymes to beate us, and to pull downe our houses, yet wee never gave them bad language, nor resisted againe, but tooke all their abuses patiently, waiteing upon God till hee make their harts quiett, that wee may live in peace by them; but truely the same things which they falsely report of us, wee and all the people round about us, can and would prove to their faces, if yow should call us face to face, some of them were alwayes Cavaleers, and had a hand in the Kentish riseing, and were cheife promoters of the offensive Surry petition; but wee doe not speake this to ripp up old quarrells, neither doe I desire to mencion their names, least yow should thinke wee were enemies; for truely it is our desire to conquer them with love, though they much abuse us that have alwayes bin your freinds, as the enemy themselves, if they were face to face, can say not otherwise.

Now Sir, the end of our digging and ploughing upon the common land is this, that wee and all the impoverisht poore in the land may gett a comfortable livelyhood by our righteous labours thereupon; which wee conceive wee have a true right unto, (I speake in the name of all the poore commoners) by vertue of the conquest over the King, for while hee was in power hee was the successour of[a] William the Conquerour, and held the land as a conquerour from us, and all Lords of Mannours held tytle to the common lands from him; but seeing the common people of England by ioynt consent[b] of person and purse, have caste out Charles our Norman oppressour, wee have by this victory recovered ourselves from under his Norman yoake, and the land now is to returne into the ioynt hands of those who have conquered, that is the commonours, and the land is to bee held noe longer from the use of them by the hand of anye whose those[c] will uphold the Norman and kingly power still; and if soe, then wee that are

[a] MS. "over." [b] MS. Possibly "consert" or "concert". [c] *Sic.*

impoverished by sticking to the Parliament and you, shall loose the benefitt of all our taxes, free quarter, and blood, and remayne slaves still to the kingly power in the hands of Lords of Mannours, which wee have cast out of the hands of Charles.

Therefore wee poore oppressed Commoners claime freedome in the common land, by virtue of the Parliaments promises and ingagement, and of the armies actinge ; for wee did beleive and rely thereupon, being as wee conceive it a firme bargaine betweene you and us ; for you and the Parliament in effect said to us, 'Give us your taxes, free quarter, excise, and adventure your lives with us to cast out the oppressour Charles, and wee will make yow a free people', therefore by the law of contract as wee expected was firmly made and confirmed on our part by performance, wee claime this freedom to enioy the common land for our livelihood, for wee have bought it by our bloud and money.

Secondly, wee claime this freedome by equality in the conquest over the Kinge, for the Parliament told us what they did they did it for the safety and peace of the whole nation, the army told us they fought not for themselves, but for the safety and peace of the whole Nation, and yow and wee ioyned our forces togeather to procure our freedome, and have obteyned it ; therefore if there bee a spoyle of the common land to be gathered, as there is, it is to bee equally devided betweene yow that went to warr, and wee that stay'd at home and paid you, that is, as the Gentry have their inclosure free to themselves, soe wee the poore impoverisht commoners claime freedome in the common land by vertue of this conquest over the Kinge, which is gotten by our ioynt consent.

Thirdly, wee know that England cannott bee a free Commonwealth, unless all the poore commoners have a free use and benefitt of the land ; for if this freedome bee not granted, wee that are the poore commoners are in a worse case then we were in the King's dayes, for then wee had some estate about us, though wee were under oppression, but now our estates are spent to purchase freedome, and wee are under oppression still of Lords of Mannours tyranny; therefore [unless] wee that are poore commoners have some part of the land to live upon freely, as well as the Gentry it cannott bee a common wealth, neither can the kingly power bee removed soe longe as this kingly power in the hands of Lords of Mannours rules over us.

Now Sir, if you and the Counsell will quiettly grant us this freedome, which is our owne right, and sett us free from the kingly power of Lords of Mannours, that violently now as in the Kings dayes holde the commons from us, (as if wee had obteyned noe conquest at all over the kingly power), then the poore that ly under the great burden of poverty, and are alwayes complayning for want, and their miseries increased because they see noe meanes of releife found out, and therefore cry out continually to you and the Parliament for releife and to make good your promises, wilbe quietted.

Wee desire noe more of yow then freedome to worke, and to enioy the benefitt of our labours—for here is wast land enough and to spare to supply all our wants—but if yow deny this freedome, then in righteousness wee must raise collections for the poore out of the estates, and a mass of money will not supply their wants; because many are in want that are ashamed to take collection money, and therefore they are desperate, and will rather robb and steale, and disturb the land, and others that are ashamed to beg would doe any worke for to live, as it is the case of many of our diggers that have bin good housekeepers; but if this freedome were granted to improve the common lands then there would bee a supply to answer every ones inquire, and the murmurings of the people against yow and the Parliament would cease, and within a few yeares wee should have noe beggers nor idle persons in the land.

Secondly, hereby England would bee enriched with all commodity with in it selfe which they each would afford; and truely this is a stayne to Christian religion in England, that wee have soe much land ly wast, and soe many starve for want; and further, if this freedome bee granted, the whole land wilbee united in love and strength, that if a forraigne enemy like an army of ratts and mice come to take our inheritance from us, wee shall all rise as one man to defend it.

Then lastly, if yow will grant the poore comoners this quiett freedome to improve the common land for our livelyhood, wee shall reioyce in yow and the army in protecting our worke, and wee and our worke wilbee ready to secure that, and wee hope there will not bee any kingly power over us, to rule at will and wee to bee slaves, as the power has bin, but that you will rule in love as Moses and Joshua did the Children of Israell before any kingly power came in, and that the Parliament wilbee as the Elders of Israell, chosen freely by the people to advise for and assist both yow and us.

And thus in the name of the rest of these called Diggers and Commonours through the land, I have in short declared our mynde and cause to you in the light of righteousness, which will prove all these reports made against us to bee false and distructive to the uniteing of England into peace.

Per me Gerrard Winstanley for my selfe and in the behalfe of my fellow Commoners.

December the 8th,
1649.

[*The Diggers Song.*]

You noble Diggers all, stand up now, stand up now,
You noble Diggers all, stand up now,
The wast land to maintain, seeing Cavaliers by name
Your digging does disdaine, and persons all defame
Stand up now, stand up now.[a]

[a] From vol. xviii. of the Clarke MSS., in Worcester College Library; undated, but, from the accompanying papers and internal evidence, clearly written in 1649.

Your houses they pull down, stand up now, stand up now,
  Your houses they pull down, stand up now.
Your houses they pull down to fright poor men in town,
But the gentry must come down, and the poor shall wear the crown.
          Stand up now, Diggers all.

With spades and hoes and plowes, stand up now, stand up now,
  With spades and hoes and plowes stand up now,
Your freedom to uphold, seeing Cavaliers are bold
To kill you if they could, and rights from you to hold.
          Stand up now, Diggers all.

Theire self-will is theire law, stand up now, stand up now,
  Theire self-will is theire law, stand up now.
Since tyranny came in they count it now no sin
To make a gaole a gin, to sterve poor men therein.
          Stand up now, stand up now.

The gentrye are all round, stand up now, stand up now,
  The gentrye are all round, stand up now.
The gentrye are all round, on each side they are found,
Theire wisdom's so profound, to cheat us of our ground.
          Stand up now, stand up now.

The lawyers they conjoyne, stand up now, stand up now,
  The lawyers they conjoyne, stand up now,
To arrest you they advise, such fury they devise,
The devill in them lies and hath blinded both their eyes.
          Stand up now, stand up now.

The clergy they come in, stand up now, stand up now,
  The clergy they come in, stand up now.
The clergy they come in, and say it is a sin
That we should now begin, our freedom for to win.
          Stand up now, Diggers all.[a]

[a] Three of the Diggers, Henry Bickerstaffe, Thomas Star, and Jerrard Winstanley, were brought before the Court at Kingston for trespass in digging

The tithe they yet will have, stand up now, stand up now,
The tithes they yet will have, stand up now.
The tithes they yet will have, and lawyers their fees crave,
And this they say is brave, to make the poor their slave.
Stand up now, Diggers all.

'Gainst lawyers and gainst Priests, stand up now, stand up now,
Gainst lawyers and gainst priests stand up now.
For tyrants they are both even flatt against their oath,
To grant us they are loath, free meat, and drink, and cloth
Stand up now, Diggers all.

The club is all their law, stand up now, stand up now,
The club is all their law, stand up now.
The club is all their law to keep men in awe,
But they no vision saw to maintain such a law.
Stand up now, Diggers all.

The Cavaleers are foes, stand up now, stand up now,
The Cavaleers are foes, stand up now;
The Cavaleers are foes, themselves they do disclose
By verses not in prose to please the singing boyes
Stand up now, Diggers all.

upon St. George's Hill, and infringing the rights of Mr. Drake, the Lord of the Manor. Winstanley was sentenced to pay for fine and law costs £11 9s. 1d.; Bickerstaff was imprisoned for three days, and Winstanley's four cows were seized. "They took away," he complains, "the cowes which were my livelyhood, and beat them with their clubs, that the cowes heads and sides did swell, which grieved tender hearts to see: and yet these cowes never were upon George Hill, nor never digged upon that ground, and yet the poore beasts must suffer because they gave milk to feed me." He adds that the "parish priest, and the Surrey ministers, and sorry ones too they are, that have set up a lecture at Cobham for a little time, to preach down the Diggers, have bid the people neither to buy nor sell with us, but to be at us imprison us or banish us."—*Watchword to the City of London.*

To conquer them by love, come in now, come in now,
 To conquer them by love, come in now;
To conquer them by love, as itt does you behove,
For hee is King above, noe power is like to love.
 Glory heere Diggers all.[a]

[*Charles Fleetwood and others to Colonel John Downes.*[b]]

Sir,

Wee doe understand, that Capt. Deane is to be imployed by the Commissioners appointed by the Parliament for Ireland, and therfore doe recommend to your thoughts for that place Mr. Clarke, who hath long served the Army, and who hath bin longe acquainted with most businesse that hath pass'd betweene your Comittee and this Army, whose diligence and readinesse in that way and faithfulnesse to the publique service wee have had good experience of, and wee doubt nott but many of your selves alsoe;

[a] These verses are probably by Winstanley, who inserts similar compositions now and then in his pamphlets. To his *Law of Freedom in a Platform* he prefixes the following lines:

"In thee O England is the Law arising up to shine,
 If thou receive and practise it, the crown it wil be thine,
If thou reject and stil remain a froward son to be,
 Another land wil it receive, and take the crown from thee."

And on the title-page of his *Watchword to the City of London* he writes:

"When these clay bodies are in grave, and children stand in place,
This shewes we stood for truth and peace and freedom in our daies;
And true born sons we shall appear of England that's our mother
No Priests nor Lawyers wiles t' embrace, their slavery wee'l discover."

[b] This letter and Kympton Hilliard's letter on the next page are from Mr. Popham's MSS.

your kindenesse to him heerin will bee a very good obligacon unto

Your humble servants

CHARLES FLEETWOOD.
EDW. WHALLEY.
MATT. THOMLINSON.
GEORGE MONCKE.
R. OVERTON.
WILL. GOFFE.
HEN. WHALLEY.
C. FAIRFAX.
E. GROSVENOR.
WILLIAM DANIELL.

Edinburgh
19° octobbris
1650.

For our honoured freind Col. John
Downes, in the chaire of the
Committee for the Army.

[*Kimpton Hilliard to Mr. William Clarke*].

Deare Brother,

Although I have beene in towne about this sennight, yet I protest I have not had the leisure of writing to you ; the Governor commanded the Major (who hartily desires to be remembered to you) and my selfe hither about perfecting our muster rowles, which have soe imployed mee that it was a burthen is now become facile through much use of it. I showed Major Harding your letter which I received yesterday, wherein you promise to send his commission as captain by the next, for which hee thanks you, and wee have one request more to you, for John Beere, storekeeper and master gunner in Waymouth. I shall take care to gett your money for them. I am from my hart sorry for Mr. Moss, his wife is rann like a woman distracted, poore hart, she is a miserable wretch, and will not admit any thing that's comfortable to be receaved by her. Men having not higher aymes then themselves, and those too high when they end in earth, bringe desolation. I could wish that wee may yeild ourselves to bee conquered by the spirit of love and humility that will teach us moderation in all our actions, especially in those things that concerne our selves, when nature and flesh onely will bee boundlesse and imoderate; they are blessed that live upon the good testimony of Jesus Christ, waiteing or daily attending how they shall bee guided rather then to seeke to guide our selves. When wee thrust ourselves forth into the world with thoughts wee can never bee satisfied enough with it; if we did but thinke they that trust in it shall perish with it, surely it would make us not to love [?] our owne ruine; every nature desires mixture with its great element, even soe wee with the world, as if wee had not a portion, nor did not desire to partake of the never failing condition of glory; 'tis very comfortable to live humbly prudently, and moderately, and still to waite for a more perfect manifestation, that soe wee may bee acted through all fleshly darke dispensations into the true light that whosoever walkes in it their foote will not stumble. It is noe small joy to us here to heare that you and honest Mr. Hatter (to whom I pray kindly remember mee) escapt a danger soe neare; I hope it wilbee a warneing to you hereafter; you see 'tis ill trusting such cruell men whose desires are after the blood of the righteous, and Kaine like, because their formall sacrifice can not be accepted, know not how to vent that rage which dominates in them, but by killing innocent and harmlesse Abell, but certainly their fall is nigh, their rage and cruelties are soe great.

For newes I shall not undertake to trouble you with, but leave it to my brother Mabbott; onely thus much, being by chance upon the water not knowing it to bee the Lord Mayor's day, I met his Lordshipp and all in companies in severall barges attending him to Westminster, and on the head of every barge new colors with the commonwealth armes, which now they begin to both see and taste. I profess wee are soe tender of you and the Commonwealth in our parts that a little dogg dare as well pluck a lyon by the jaw as any man in the least to speake in the derogation of you, soe loved are you in any of our spirits that if you are wounded wee are wounded, if you are healed wee partake of it; this sympathye in affection must dwell in the hart of the upright, 'tis a companion to them, and they must delight in it. I am loath to trouble thee in this important affaire in which the Lord Almighty guide you, but mythinks I could ever lett forth my soule to thee ; thy deare wife was in such an extasie of joy to heare of your escaping that danger that Capt. Pitson[a] perisht in shee fell into an extreame passion; shee hopes when it shall please God to send thee home to her againe to prevaile with thee to stay with her. I have noe more but my truest love which shalbee at thy commaund while I am

KYMPTON HILLIARD.

Ax Yard, the 29 October, 1650.

[Addressed] :

For my deare brother Mr. Willm. Clarke
at the head Quarters in Scotland.

[*William Clarke to the Commissioners of the Great Seale.*]

To the right honourable the Lords Commissioners of the Great Seale of England.

The humble peticion of Wm. Clarke one of his Excellency the Lord Generall Cromwell's secretaries now in service with his Excellency in Scotland,

Sheweth,

That your petitioner having purchas'd from the State part of S. John's Wood parcell of the late King's land, one Mr. John

[a] Taken prisoner by the Scots, Whitelock, iii., 255.

Collins unjustly claimes some part of that he hath purchased and paid for, and his conveyance sealed and inrolled, and for the same hath proferred a long bill in the Court against your peticioner and James Staresmore, Henry Curtis, and others, freinds and agents of your peticioner's.

That the entrest and title is solely in your petitioner and the other defendants noe wayes at all concerned herin. And your petitioner being so spetiall employed in Scotland with his Excellency in the service of the State, as wilbe made appeare by oath, humbly desires that according to the votes of Parliament, all proceeding in the said suite may be stayed untill your petitioner can attend the same, for that if it should proceed now in your peticioner's absence, the same might be much to his prejudice, none being able to make good his title and intrest to the premises in question.

And your Petitioner shall pray &c.

WM. CLARKE.

2°Junij 651

[*Kimpton Hilliard to William Clarke.*][a]

Deare Brother,

Colonel Heanes regiment with six companies of Sir Hardress Waller's regiment of foote, two troopes of horse, (vizt.) Capt. West's and Capt. Margerum's,[b] being shippt at Weymouth, on Fryday

[a] This letter is from Mr. Popham's MSS. In *Mercurius Politicus*, Oct. 30-Nov. 6, 1651, p. 1175, is a relation of the taking of Jersey, which is also printed in *Several Proceedings in Parliament* for the same date, p. 1698. Heane's letter, dated 27 Oct., and Blake's letter, dated 26 Oct., are also to be found in the latter newspaper, p. 1700. Heane's correspondence with Philip Carteret about the surrender of Montorgueil Castle is printed in *Several Proceedings*, p. 1734, and *Mercurius Politicus*, p. 1213. See also *Mercurius Politicus*, 1307, 1318, 2156, 2551. Hilliard's letter seems to have been used in compiling the official relation, but contains many additional details.

[b] "Margery." *Mercurius Politicus.*

the 17th instant at 4 in the afternoone we hoysed sayle, and bended our course towards Guernsey there to take in 200 men more, who were to join with us in the reduceing of Jersey Island; but we had not sayled above 5 leagues before the winde rose soe high that our open boats could not live upon the seas, that we were forct to returne again; the 19th in the morneing we agayne set sail, and though the winde was yet high by 12 at night wee cast anchor under Sarke Island near Guernsey; the 20th in the morning we launcht forth and steered directly for Jersey, and about 12 at noone came to an anchor in St. Wons Bay, where we lay all that day, not being able to hoyst our smale boats out of the ships to order our businesse, the winde being soe very high; the 21th wee steered round the shoare and came before St. Brelades Bay, where we droppt anchor; the day before the Eagle Frigate running nere the shoare to fyre upon the enemy received a shott which peirct through her side, and dropped in her howld, but did noe further harm. After we had anchored before St. Brelades Bay we descried several bodies upon the shore, and receaved from them divers shott from a lyne on which they had planted several guns from one end of the Bay to the other. All this while the winde continued soe high that wee were put to a stand, and could not tell what to doe, wee seeing apparent ruin to us all if the winde ceased not. About six at night wee considered that though the weather was not seasonable, and 16 sayle of our fleet left at Guernsey, our horse provisions was quite spent, soe that they must bee lost if wee either lay still or returned; and wee being willing to do the worke wee were sent about resolved to throw ourselves upon the Lord, and to morrow to endeavour to doe it; and it so pleased the Lord that within an hour after we had a calme sea and quiet weather, which gave us opportunity to fitt ourselves with such necessaries as our businesse required. The 22nd about three in the morning we held a Councell on board the Admirall, where wee resolved to improve the Lord's goodnesse to us in that seasonable weather which yet continued, and that morning to goe on; to which purpose there wee craved a blessing on our undertaking. About 5 that morning wee began to boate our men, and came round the shoare in them to St. Wons Bay, leaveing our shipps to keepe them in alarum at St. Brelades Bay; before our boates could get ashoare the tyde was spent, and wee forct in much danger, without bread or beere, to lie there till the next tyde, and about 11 at night for expedition sake wee cutt our cables and run ashoare, our boates after they were on ground drawing 3, 4, 5, 6, and some 7 feet water, but those that were in those that drew most gott over [to] the rest and run ashore, most middle and some neck high, so willing were they either to live or die together. This day while wee lay in our open boats the Elizabeth friggott came, and rid as nere the shoare as shee could, and let fly at their colours uppon the shore, and killed one horse and 2 men of theirs. We were noe sooner landed but the enemy entertayned us with a desperate charge, they being a body of horse, which our foot withstood as stoutly (our horse not being yet landed), and after halfe an houres dispute (their horse being upp to the muzles of our musquets) the Lord was pleased to give us the victory, and made the enemy fly before us; after which wee drew ourselves into a posture fitt to receive them upon the sands, where wee continued about an houre, and finding noe enemy to assault us (onely some great shott from the hills) we thus marcht a mile in to the Island, in which time we seized 7 or 8 guns they had planted uppon that shoare. After we had marcht about a mile there wee continued till about 5 the next morneing (being the 23rd October, the same day on which the bataile of Edgehill was), when wee marcht round the shoare towards St. Brelades Bay, and drew uppon a hill before wee came to it, whither our parties aboard brought divers prisoners and colours. Here wee endeavoured to gett in provision for our hungry and tyred soldiers, but before wee could gett any (still keeping ourselves in a fighting posture) wee marcht down to Brelade Bay, where wee found about 12 guns but their men fledd; after which we drew upp upon a hill on the other side this Bay in sight of Elizabeth Castle, under which hill was a fort which had in it 2 demi culverins, which they forsook. Upon this hill wee received several great shot from a strong fort of theirs called St. Albans Tower. Here wee understood that the enemy were all fled into their 2 strong Castles, (vizt.) Mount Orguill Castle which they call the Old Castle, and Elizabeth Castle which they call the New Castle; and my Colonel being unwilling to loose time (notwithstanding his souldiers former hardshipps) marched that night to their chief towne called St. Hilarys, with his owne regiment and Capt. Wests troope of horse onely, to keepe the enemy into the New Castle, which is within muskett and halfe shott of this towne upon an Island in the sea. While wee were on our march hither the Colonel sent in a summons to St. Albans Tower (which likewise stands upon an Island on the other side of the Harbour), and gave them two houres time to send him an answer, in which time they surrendered it, upon terms to remove from thence to Elizabeth Castle, which that night they did by water. In it wee had 14 guns and a convenient place under which our shipping may ly in despite of their Castle. Our quarters being this night taken upp in St. Hilarys towne, whereby the New Castle was blockt upp. The 24th the Colonel sent Sir George Cartaret a summons, to which he returned but a scurrilous answer. This day the Colonel ordered his own regiment with Capt. Wests troope of horse to martch to their Old Castle, and Major Ebzery with his 6 companies and the 3 companies from Guernsey with Capt. Margerum's troope to possess our quarters; and that night about 9 o'clock wee drew upp on a coney warren before Mount Orguill Castle, after which wee were disposod to keepe guards within muskett shott of the Castle, and the 25th the Colonel sent the Governor thereof (Sir George Carteret's brother) a summons. His answer was that hee had noe power to surrender that place. It is of it selfe very strong, were it not for a hill close by which commands it, from whence our mortar peeces (when wee have them hither) will I hope force him to deliver it. Thus hath the Lord given into your hands this brave Island with the loss of not above

3 or 4 men, and about 24 wounded, of which one is since dead. The enemy carried a cart load of dead in their New Castle, of which one was Colonel Bovill as I am informed. The enemy at our landing are reported to be about 3000, but their numbers 2 daies before were reported to bee twice as many more. Since which the Old Castle called Mount Orguill Castle is surrendered. The conditions were to martch away with their swords, which they did, only the Governor had with him 2 horses and the liberty of carrying away some of his goodes. The Islanders are to live peaceably at home, and have protection, and not bee troubled for any thing done during the late warr; the strangers to have passes to go into their own countries. Truely I cannot but wonder to see how the Lord doth strike these people with feare and terror that they should soe suddenly deliver upp such a strong hold. It is seated very high upon a round rock, and many vauts in it cut out of the firme rock, that in my judgment 'tis neither stormable or to bee injured by mortar pieces. This is the Castle in which Mr. Prynn was prisoner. Wee had in it nere 50 guns great and smale, 5 or 6 whereof are brass, one of which is demi cannon. The New Castle is indeed a most invincible place, but the Lord Almighty is able to overcome them. This day we here from St. Malloes in France, that upon notice given them of our fleete comeing this way, they turned all the English out of the towne, and planted 50 guns more about the towne than there was before, fearing wee would attempt them. This day I received one from you, I am glad you are well, my true love to you and my dear sister. I am well blessed bee the Lord, onely a litle louzie. I am

thyne while

KYMPTON HILLIARD.

Jersey Island, this 30° Octobr, 1651.

For my deare brother Mr. William Clarke at the Head Quarters in Scotland these.

[*Extracts from News-letters*].

Nov. 15, 1651.

All this weeke hath bin spent in debate of the New Representative. The Judges sitting upon the benches, members of Parliament, were called in to give their vote in this greate businesse. Yesterday (after a long speech made by his Excellency to set a time for the sitting of this Parliament) these large debates came to a question, vizt. that it's a convenient time [to declare a certain time] for the continuance of this Parliament beyond which it shall not sit, and this question being put the house was divided and carried in the affirmative by two voyces. Tuesday next is appointed to nominate the time.

Nov. 16.

Yesterday the Parliament came to a conclusion, after 6 dayes debate, to name the time, and on Tuesday they resolved when this Parliament shall end ; a dreadfull vote to some who have large accounts or unworthy actions to ans[wer], for the Committees in the country begin to look about them. The House was devided at the putting of this question 49 noes 51 yeas, my Lord Generall and Lord Chief Justice St. John tellers for the yeas, Mr. Bond and Mr. Morley for the noes, and 2 latter being against it. I beleive things will draw to some conclusion and speedy settlement.

[*The trial of Mr. John Erbury.*]

Checquer Chamber, 8th Febr. (52).

Committee of Plundred Ministers.

Mr. Millington, Chayreman.

Present.

Maj. Gen: Skippon, Mr. Cawley, Coll: Rich, & divers others Mr. Phelps Clark. Neere the Barr on the Right hand Capt. Chillenden & witnesses against Erbery.

[a] "Yeares" MS.

Spectators.

Coll: Cobbett, myself, & about 4 or 500 more, 2 or 3 files Musqteers & 2 Officers.

All other Motions layd aside & checkt.

Prisoner call'd.

Then Phelps reade how farr they proceeded last time.

Capt[n] Chillenden.

I heard Mr. Erbery say, That these saints are much against the sinnes of Adultery outwardly, but comitt them wholly inwardly; also a poore Ranter hes but one night in a moneth with a whore, but these saints this wel-favor'd harlott can lye with twenty betweene this and Westminster.

Maj. Gen. Skippon.

I think hee said Christ was a Beast.

Erbery.

Right Reverend, give mee leave to speake a word for my self.

Mr. Millington.

Stay you a while. Capt. Chillenden declare what hee said concerning Christ being a Beast.

C: Chillenden.

Mr. Phelps hath it already. Butt hee declared all the Prophettes were Beasts, soe hee came to Christ, & that hee would confound all formes etc.

Mr. Erbery.

I hope the Lord in you is judge this day.

Chillenden.

Hee said. Don't wee see a morall man hee continues in his morality still, but your Church Members & holy men continue in sin, & the Ranters were the holyest in the nacion but their knowledge came to nothing, & that Christ was a Beast, the apostles & prophetts were Beasts & knew nothing, the Saints or Church Members knew nothing, nor hee knew nothing. God in us knew all, but wee nothing, 65 Isaiah 20 etc. 'There shalbe noe more an infant of daies' etc. That hee knew God was coming to destroy the knowledge of all the Saints as they call themselves.

Mr. Millington.

Mr. Gray what can you say. But why appear'd you not att first sumons?

Grey.

I onely received the last sumons. It was not out of feare, favour, or affeccon.

1. Mr. Erbery called the bread of the Lords Supper uncleane bread, & hee said because it was the bread of mourners, & will yee sitt downe att the Table of whores; yee cannot discerne the Lords body lyes in Babilon.

2. Concerning Baptisme, 9 Proverbs, 17, 'Stolen waters are sweete.' The waters of Babilon are stolen, they are wordes of the whore. 18 Rev. 22, "And the voice of Harpers musick, etc. Yee shall have Baptisme noe more, Lords Supper noe more, preaching noe more.

3. 30 Isaiah. By removing there into Corners is ment pulpitt preachers, such yee shall have noe more; every object shall teach you, your food & rayement shall teach you.

4. That prayer was a work of God, & when the Spiritt of Christ came in the flesh it did consume, 66 Isa. Christ as a worme will consume, corode, & destroy the flesh, faith etc.

5. When Christ was neerest dissolucion of his flesh then the Spiritt of prayer forsook him, hee prayed onely these few words, 'Father lett this Cupp pass,' etc. I tell you this came from the darkness of his Spiritt.

2d. Article. Mr. Phelps reads:

'That hee blasphemously preached downe the Godhead of Christ.'

Mr. Gray.

That Christ would consume our faith. I wonder what evill men see in the Turkish Alcheron. When Christ comes into your flesh, hee will make you in love with all Religions, yea Papists & all. Hee dyed the just for the unjust is mistaken, for Christ in the Spiritt will destroy your flesh that hee may bring you to God.

Luke saith hee was Crucified in the 9th houre, & John who was onely present att his death the 6th.

That Christ dyed not for pardon of sin, or [to] satisfy the Father, but [to] declare the Father's love.

Those Churches call'd Anabaptists etc. & State governments, all those formes, saith hee, God will destroy.

Mr. Millington.

What can you say Mr. Pemberton?

Mr. Pemberton.

I was att Somersett House & heard Mr. Erbury on the 8th Revelacon 1st, uppon opening the 7th seale, 'and there was silence in heaven for ye space of half an howre.' Hee said Christ was going out of all formes. 12 Rev: 1st, concerning the woeman clothed with the Sun & the Moone under her feete, [those] were the Ordinances which shold now cease. 18 Rev: [22nd], when the noise of the Harpers shalbe noe more, which was the comon preaching & singing wee now have. This noise was hee said the musick of Babilon, & further as hee said, as God was going out of all these formes soe that there was a more glorious manifestacon of God coming out this day, viz[t]. a 3[d] dispensacon never knowne to the Saints of old, diffring from the law & gospell Order. What saies God, remember not former things, I will doe a new thing saith God, soe are wee, as hee was perfectly one with God soe are wee. When Christ came to suffrings the Spiritt of prayer dyed in him, shewing the feebleness & confusion of his Spiritt hereby. It pleased the Lord to bruise him, his understanding was confounded, hee was afraid & knew not what hee said. Hee tooke Peter & James with him because hee was afraid to goe alone; that the darkness then was the confusion of his understanding.

And the Vaile of the Temple was rent fro topp to bottome, hee was onely amased, for what was the Vaile but our pure flesh, our guifts, our graces, our performances. This is the flesh of Christ, all of them shalbe torne from highest attainements to lowest performances.

Mr. Millington.

What have you to say Mr. Erbery?

Mr. Erbery.

I humbly thank this Honorable Committee for having liberty once more to speak heere before you. It is thus, I told you the first time the power of the Lord uppon my Spiritt. I came to London to preach onely the New Jerusalem. I confess most what the last evidence said is true; but because I am charg'd by Capt: Chillington [with saying] that Christ is a Beast, & that the Saints & all men knew nothing, I knew nothing. But had I nów withheld my coming Capt. Chillington had slided his necke out of the collar; and for mee to say that hee was worse than a Beast, I onely said hee was worse then a goose.[a]

[a] "Hee," *i.e.* Chillenden.

Mr. Millington then checkt him.

Erbery.

True I said the Churches were a welfavor'd harlott, Ezek. 30. I told the old prelatick Churches they were an old rotten whore, but these a fayre whore, but the Presbytereans call the Independent Churches whore, & the Independent call them whore againe, & I say they are all whores together. Isa. 47, that whore said, I am a Queene, but the Scripture saith shee is a whore, her knowledge hath deceived her. I speake as in the presence of God, I meane nothing against the Saints, but [against] Apostates; nay it hath been preacht publiquely in Blackfryers, if men would have good places they must goe into the Independent Churches.

11 Job. 12. Vaine man would bee wise, though born as an Asses Colt. 49 Psal.: 12,[a] man being in honor abideth not, but becomes as a Beast that perisheth, & wisest men have proved the greatest fooles.

Moses a Minister of the law, some say his face shined, but the originall renders it horned, beastlike.

As Christ to the theife on the Cross—This day shalt thou bee with mee in Paradice. God onely is wise, & that any man account himself soe Ile say hee is as the wild Asses Colt. Every man is a Beast. The prophett speaking of Christ, 30 Pro: saith, 'I am more brutish then any man.' Christ is the Glory of the Father. The word wisedome & power of God in the Father. Christ was in God from Eternity, but became man. The words in Hebrew, Adam signifies weakness or dust of the Earth, 2[d] Ish: man also but signifies heat. 31 Jer: A woman shall compass a man. All that appeared to Christ was in the power of the Father.

Baptisme & Lords Supper, as in the Anabaptists & Independent Churches, were not Gospell Ordinances. Baptisme of the Spiritt was by power from on high, but the apostles could not goe forth till it came, though comaunded.

[a] MS. 46 Gal. Several errors in the refs. to chapter and verse have been corrected.

They delude their hearers with this word teach & baptize etc. But they mince & cutt the word in halfs.

As breaking of bread among the Churches is uncleane to them it is the bread of mourners.

There was in Gospell times noe breaking of bread but by a spirituall breaking; there was formerly but one body, one bread, one Church, one Baptisme, but heere all is in a confusion; therefore Christs body is in Babilon, & one clashing against another, & now I waite when the spiritt will appeare to make us all one & convince us of our being yet in Babilon.

Mr. Millington.

Must wee have candles or withdraw?

Some said noe candles, but deferr it till next Tewsday.

Mr. Millington.

Then lett the Company withdraw.

C. Chillenden (aloud).

He said that Christ in flesh was a Beast, & that I was worse than Balaams ass, for that spoke truth, but I a lye; consider it.

Mr. Millington.

Wee'le withdraw, [and] heare noe more now. [a]

[*Oliver Cromwell to Lieut.-Col. Wilks.*]

Sir,

I received your lettre, and as to the parte which concernes the colleccion for Marlebrough [b] I shall speake with Major Haines [c] thereaboute, by whom I expect to know what Colonell Read hath

[a] From Mr. Popham's MSS. [b] See Preface. [c] Or "Baynes."

done thereuppon. The other parte of your letter[a] is full of very loving and kind expressions of the heartinesse of your affection to me, and of your tendernes and sensiblenes of the burden of my condicion; and truly it was to me very seasonable, because if I mistake not, my exercise of [that] litle faith and patience I haue was neuer greater; and were it not that I know whom I haue beleeued the comforts of all my friends would not support me, noe not one day. I can say this further to you, that if I looked for anything of helpe from men, or yet of kindnes, it would be from such as feare the Lord, for whom I haue been ready to lay downe my life, and I hope still am, but I haue not a few wounds from them; nor are they indeed, in this sad dispensation they are under (being diuided in opinion and too much in affection ready to fall fowle uppon one another, whilest the enemy to be sure unite to purpose to their common destruction), in a capacity to receiue much good or to minister good one to another, through want of communion in loue; soe that whosoever labours to walk with an euen foote between the severall interests of the people of God for healeing and accomodating theire differences is sure to have reproaches and anger from some of all soarts. And truly[b] this is much of my portion at the present, soe unwilling are men to bee healed and attoned; and although it be thus with mee, yet the Lord will not let it bee alwayes soe. If I have innocency and integrity the Lord hath mercy and truth, and will owne it. If in these things I have made my selfe my ayme, and designed to bring affaires to this issue for my selfe, the Lord is ingaged to disowne mee; but if the worke bee the Lord's, and that they are his purposes which hee hath purposed in his owne wisdome, he will make his owne councils stand; and therefore let men take heed least they bee found feighters against him, especially his owne people. I heare things are very troublesome through the discontent of some amongst you, who will quickly bee made manifest by theire fruites. And I am perswaded the

[a] "Of your letter" omitted.

[b] "Surely."

Lord will not suffer his people alwayes to bee deceived by such pretenders and pretences to Righteousnesse and Justice, and care not how unjustly and unrightiously they walke, not to bring forth Righteousnesse and Justice, as[a] they pretend, but most abominable unrighteousnesse, wickednesse, impiety, and confusion upon all the world God hath wrought in the midst of us. I doe veryly suspect most guilty herein, because I finde men acting here vppon the same principles who have conceived to themselves alsoe greate hopes from the devisions and discontents amongst you, who have had such expectacions from some notable designe to bee acted in Scotland from some considerable person there, that they have formed theire worke here of like wickednesse and confusion to bee contemporary here; and truly it is thus they are exciting all discontented humours and persons to stir, and to goe into Armes, haueing framed their declaraccions wherin they have a singular compliance with the malignant partie, as theire declaracions will manifest, wherin they gratifie them beyond what euer was done for them, by which the cavalier partie is soe encouraged that they doe accompt this spirit, principle, and motions of these men, as the likelyest way to bring them into their former interest that ever yet they had, and of this we have a very full discouery. Besides we find that divers are very highly acting that interest, and are preparinge great quantities of armes to that purpose, of which through the goodnes of God we haue made a full discouery, and the busines is become soe naked and open, that indeed if all the people of God had one hearte and spirit, yet it would be all litle enough to man's[b] iudgment to preserue the interest of the people of God. We have apprehended divers persons of quality who haue comissions from Charles Stuart and are possest of many armes to carry on their work, and in the discouery herof the Lord hath appeered very gratious to us. The Lord stablish, strengthen, and keepe your minds entire,

[a] "and as."

[b] "Many."

and make his people of one heart, and giue them one lip ; and I pray you shew your fidelitie in standing by and sticking to your honest Generall Geo. Monck, who is a simple hearted man, and as you have opportunity [a] exhort all to doe the same ; [b] and let the honest officers be as diligent to make peace and keepe it there as wicked men who are the instruments of Satan are busie to bring in confusion. I commit you to the Lord and rest,

Your louing friend,
OLIVER P.[c]

[*Secretary Thurloe to General Monk.*]

Sir,

I suppose you will heare from other hands of the imprisonment of Major-General Harrison, Mr. John Carew, Mr. Courtney, and Colonel Rich. I will trouble you with the particular reasons and grounds therof, and that truly not knowing how they may be represented by others. About 10 dayes since they with some others came to his Highnesse, (after that Mr. Rogers with very many of his people had been with him concerneing the imprisonment of himselfe and Mr. Feake), and demanded of him that the prisoners of the Lord might be set at liberty. Whereunto his Highnesse answeared them, that if they were the prisoners of the Lord they should soone be set at liberty, but that hee was sure there was noe body in England in prison for the Lord or the gospell sake. And these two persons were soe far from being in bonds uppon any such account, that they were in prison as evill doers, as for railing,

[a] "At your own opportunitie." [b] "soe."

[c] There are two copies of this letter in the Clarke MSS. One is headed "Letter to Lieut.-Col. Wilkes." The variations in the two texts, when of any importance, are given in the notes. From its position amongst the other letters it should be dated between 14 and 18 January, 165$\frac{4}{5}$.

reviling, telling untruthes, stirring up the people to armes, &c., which he said he had already made appeere to Mr. Rogers himselfe, and could alsoe satisfie them when there was time for it; and to that end he told them, hee should desire to speake with them at some more convenient time (it being then too late), when he should deale very plainly with them, and would be content to be soe dealt with by them, and to heare what they had to say against the way that he was now in. And soe they went away. About two daies after his Highnesse sent to them that he would speake with them the next day at 9 of the clocke. Harrison and Courtney promised to come, but after it seemes they repented, for they came not. My Lord thinking there might be some mistake in the message, sent a second time, haveing appointed some Christians to be present, who might heare the discourse. But Major-General Harrison then said, that if he had been required to come he should have been more free, but was not free to come uppon a desire; the rest had all notice but all refused to come. Then his Highnes summoned them by a warrant in writeing, required them to appeare before him or the Councell uppon a certaine day to answer such things as shalbee objected against them concerning the peace of the Nation. When they were served with the warrant Harrison said hee would come, but did not, nor any of the reste. Upon this contempt, and because of the certaine information that my Lord had of theire endeavour to stir upp the people against the Government, and to seduce some persons from theire trust (and that of the greatest moment) which they held under the State, hee sent for them in safe custody, and they were brought hether upon Friday in the afternoone. And because things might bee carryed on in a Christian manner his Highnesse had present, when they were called in before him and the Councell severall sober Christians and Ministers, as Mr. Carryll, Mr. Brooks, Mr. Cradock, Mr. Recorder, and others, some whereof were the Irish officers, and at the desire of Major Generall Harrison and the others, there were alsoe called in Mr. Sympson, Mr. Bankes, Mr. Pendarvis &c. That which was first asked them was, why they had in contempt of authoritie refused to come uppon the summons which had bin sent; whereunto, after they had desired to know whether there was any thing against them but theire contempt, they plainely answered, that they could not come, because in that act they should acknowledg the Governement, which they could not doe, it being a Governement set up against the will of God, and in oposition to the Kingdome of Christe, and was antechristian and Babilonish, and they did expect that God would power out his wrath uppon it, and those that did adheere to it, and they did not come, least some of the dropps of wrath should fall uppon them, and therein they obeyed the Scripture, which calls to the daughter of Syon to come out of Babylon. Mr. Carew added that My Lord Protector, when the little Parliament was dissolved, tooke the Crowne off from the heade of Christ, and put it upon his owne. It would be too large to tell all particulars; some of the principalls they layd downe are these. That the present authority is not any authority, nor to bee obeyed, and consequently armes may bee taken upp against it. That the Magistrate which is carnall hath no right, nor can have; and the greate objection which they made againste this Goverment was because it had a Parliament in it, whereby power is derived from the people, whereas all power belongs to Christ. And it beeing demaunded of them, whether they would engage to live peaceably and not disturbe the peace of the Nation, the[y] refused to doe it; and it being pressed uppon them to doe it, because of the protection they had, they denyed they received any protection from the present Governement, and that they owed theire protection onely to God, and they should expect the same quiet protection from God if the whole army were disbanded to morrow. This was the sume of what they saide, and indeed it seemed strange to all that heard them. Mr. Cradock professed hee would not for any thing he had bin absent, saying hee could not have beleved that theire principles were such as they did discover, and soe said every body else. After the company was with drawne the Councill did offer to them, that if they would retire into theire owne Counties, and promise not to come forth without leave, it would bee all that would bee expected, vizt. Major-Generall Harrison into Stafford-shire, John Carew and Courtney into Cornewell, and Rich into Kent; but they utterly refused it. And thereupon they are ordered to stand comitted, which I assure yow is done of pitty to them, and some other people who are led by them, as well as for the sake of the Nation, that they may not putt things into blood and confusion, and bee made use of by the Caveliere and vile leavelling party to destroy and utterly roote out all that are good and godly in the land. Before they were committed, his Highnes tould them that they were not onely comitted for the contempt, but because they had acted against the Governement and the peace of the Nation, and particularly tould every one of them what hee had against them: Major-General Harrison, that hee had not onely countenanced those who declaymed publicquely against the Governement, but had perswaded some of the lawfullnesse of takeing up armes against it; John Carew, that he had not onely done what Major-General Harison had, but endeavoured to seduce some greate officers from theire trust; that Colonel Rich endevoured to hinder the raiseing of the tax, and Courtney had bin in Norfolk and there perswaded the Churches to take armes, and in the West hee declaired his opposicion, and saide that at London hee should finde both hands and hearts enow to overthrow this Government. To this they made noe answer at all. Thus you have had a very long account of this businesse, which I was willing to doe to prevent misinterpretacions. And it is certaine theire party will endeavour to doe it, as they do heare, and labour to perswade that all Christians are concerned in this imprisonment, when the contrary is true to one of the saints of this nation, [who] doe disowne them, and their courses, and take these things to bee the effect of wrath and envy, and judg them to bee under a greate temptacion.

Many, very many of the Churches of Christ, as well those under baptisme as others in Scotland and England, have acknowledged the

Governement in writeing under theire hands since the disolution of the Parliament. I know it is a trouble to my Lord Protectour to have any one who is a sainte in truith to bee greeved or unsatisfied with him; but he is comforted that what hee doth in these cases, hee doth it for God's and the Saints' sake, and opposes therein that spirritt which is of the world, which God in his Providence all all along hath borne witnesse against, vizt. that spiritt which would impose upon the consciences of others, and breake all in peeces who will not bear[a] downe to theire apprehencions. The Presbyterians[b] speakes as well of the Kingdome of Christe as these men, and many of them as holy, and I am sure much more knowing even in spirituall things.

J. T.[c]

[a] MS. "beere."

[b] MS. "Presbyterrars."

[c] Two fragmentary letters from Thurloe's collection of MSS. in the Bodleian, printed at the end of the Preface, further elucidate the opposition of the Fifth-Monarchy men to the Protectorate.

APPENDIX.

APPENDIX A.

TWO LETTERS FROM CLARKE PAPERS IN THE POSSESSION OF MR. LEYBOURNE POPHAM.

Capt. Lieut. Ingram to Sir Thomas Fairfax.

May it please your Excellency,

It having pleased God lately to send some of his messengers to your Excellency and others in your army to intimate to your Excellency and them that he was departed from your Excellency and the army,[a] since which tyme God hath I beleeve in some measure possest your Excellency and some of them with the truth thereof, as appeares by his inclining your hearts and theirs to seeke him, when providentially I was there and heard him constraine Lt. generall Cromwell to make some ingenuous acknowledgements to that purpose. I heard also the same God speaking in your Excellency (to which the testimony within you at that tyme will testify) presently after Mr. Knight had done speaking, your expressions tending to set forth your Excellencies delight in waiting upon God in that way (as it is indeed the only way, the wisest and best way), and therefore your Excellency desired some others to continue that duty, which Mr. Allen was constrained to doe, and that sweetly and spiritually; before which day and since having heard many complaine of those messages sent to your Excellency and others, tending to declare God's

[a] Cf. Rushworth, vii., 940, 953.

departure from your Excellency and them, but not what he would have you to doe; since which tyme it hath pleased the Father to incline my heart to wayte upon him for a word of wisedome to declare to your Excellency and them (as an answer in parte to your petition then breathed up to him, that soe you might be directed what God would have you doe that he might againe delight to be with you): which having receaved I was constrained (though with much weakenesse) to declare yesterday (according to that little measure of light given to me, out of the abundance of my love to your Excellency and them) at the Councill of Warre, for which I was (though a member of that Councill) commanded to withdraw, and a charge immediately drawne up against me, sentenced, and confined; whereof I thought it my duty to give your Excellency an account, being made willing to give in my reasons in writing why I spake it, my answear to the charge exhibited against me, as allso to that Quere then propounded to me, vidt.: Whether I would submitt to the justice of the Generall Court Marshall, and unto the whole discipline and government of the Army (according to lawes and ordinances of warre made for this Army) at the tyme appointed by your Excellency and that Court. In the mean tyme I thought fitt to declare to your Excellency (having receaved a commission from your Excellency), as parte of my answear to the aforesaid Quere, vidt.: That so long as your Excellency shall act according to your first principles (manifested in your Excellencies commission given to me), and according to the publique declarations of the whole souldiery at Triplowe Heath for Justice, Justice, (which was my particular answeare to the Commissioners before your Excellency), and according to the solemne ingagement of the Army to which your Excellency hath given your assent, soe long I shall manifest my willingnesse to yeeld obedience to your Excellency by my future actions and my present subscribing my selfe

A faithfull servant to your
Excellency
JOHN INGRAM.

December 21
1647.

Endorsed: Capt. Lt. Ingram.

Thomas Margetts to William Clarke.

My dearest friend,

I was very short in my last, but I hope I gave you a satisfactory reason, now I shall a little enlarge, being somewhat reconciled, and give a few thoughts in answeare to yours by last post. The relation of Mr. Saltmarsh (which I had more fully by Col. Overton) is very remarkable, and certainly he saw an evill in the imprisoning and punishing of men for acting not according to other mens lights, or contrary to the wisdome, reason, and policy of flesh and blood; and though I am a little unsatisfyed with the keeping on his hatt etc. yet I beleive his appearance in that manner may justly give a checque to all violent proceedings and prosecution against honest men though in some things of other judgment. As I know flesh and bloud is the ground of all difference and contention, as well among the saints as others, so I see flesh and bloud also in their late action, both in the prosecutor and prosecuted; yet I beleive the sufferer shall see more glory then the other because he is nearest humility, the mortification of flesh, and the spirit of meekenes, which if that were predominant then how would the saints agree and trample downe the other powers of the world and flesh! I feare the glory of the flesh in the great saints wilbe a great gaul (and a great while yet) to the little; and though I think the time of Levelling is not come, yet the time will come that all the enemies of Christ (and I think all flesh and bloud wilbe found in that number) shalbe made his footestoole. And nothing satisfies mee so much concerning Mr. Saltmarsh as that I know he was a man of a meeke and humble spirit, and I am apt to think it was not pride made him keepe on his hatt, but I conceive to shew how baseley he esteemed even the greatest glory of flesh in that transportation and extasy of spirit, and doth hint on something of prophesy that the despised prosecuted spirit of Christ shall triumph over and not be subject to the glory of the world and flesh, and his dying in this condition gives mee to draw this conclusion, that as the glory of God appeares flesh decayes, the more of glory, the lesse of flesh, and the one (as in him) shall overcome and destroy the other. Mr. Pownell [?] I perceive had some sight and sence with him, but the bright morning star hath not appeared so glorious on him as yet.

Concerning your prisoners being high spirited and pragmaticall, I know not who they are, nor of what spirit, but conceive they are those that are called Levellers; and if they are of the good spirit no wonder they are high, for that cannot be suppress in a prison, and he that is acted by that cannot be idle; if of the other I pitty their pride, and like not their activity; their new plea I think will not hold water, and for Thompson's conclusion to his Excellency I think it did proceed from an evill spirit such as I would have discouraged and destroyed.

I perceive the heads of the Army are now imployed cheifly about getting security and satisfaction to the souldiery in point of arreares and disbanding supernumeraries. Arreares are good when they can be gott, but I think disbanding is not seasonable; it may doe good in one way in easing the Countries burthen, but more hurt another in giving occasion to great enemies to plott and act (according to their principles of ignorance and malice) the destruction of freedom and justice. Thers more need of union then the other, and surely could the comon enemy divide he would rule. I am more for strict discepline to prevent oppressions and complaints then disbanding, as affaires stand; and, as I said once before, had wee guided our reynes right wee needed not have feared so sudden a dismounting for another to take the saddle that perhaps may gal'd the horse worse. I received yours yesterday by Mr. Cadwell, for which great paynes I am truly thankfull, and very glad to heare of the great harmony in the Officers at the Castle the late fast. I observe the harmony sprung from humility and yeilding of high spirits; love and agreement must needs followe meekenes and humility. I am glad Col. Rainb[orowe's] former services and late humility have gayned so good an aspect. I received one of the Scotch declarations and cursorily read it over, and shall give thee my present apprehensions. In the generall I think they have proudly and pragmatically medled with what they had nothing to doe; and though they pretend something of joynt interest, yet it is no older then the Treaties, and I think there is nothing there to bind this kingdome to doe nothing without them; though I feare they were a little too hard for us, and gott ground and advantage upon us by those Treaties. The late vote of the house of Commons hath given them a notable nipp, and they felt it, for you see they winch in the latter end of their declaration. I doe not discomend their policy (though I doe their honesty) in endeavoring to gett a joint interest, no otherwise then I would discomend a beggar from endeavoring to become a Lord, or one that lives upon long cale to gett roste meate, and I beleive they would very gladly fight for it, if they thought they should overcome, but I think this large expression of their anger (though they are very cuning in their anger) will make us a little more to eye them.

In particular—

I value not their reasons for a personall Treaty. And though there be not so much cause to fear the King's power now, as when hee had an Army, yet the kingdome is as farre from settlement, and as free from disturbance as ever, but they would faine have him there to make the other step into Scotland, that they might gett the other £200,000. They are very angry Religion is not made the first proposition to the King, and say wee ought to builde the house of God before our owne. The house of God is like to be well built by such masons and carpenters as they are; they surely will never measure with a straight line and rule, nor lay the stones with faire colours, and the foundation with saphires etc. Uniformity, discipline, rooting out sects, blasphemy, heresy, destroying all but their owne opinions way and practice is their language; is this the language of the Lamb or the Beast? What a stirre doe they keepe about the Covenante, as if all were lost unles the black tribe be kept up, and how cuningly doe they prosecute the advantage they gott upon this kingdome in its lowe estate? Oh what an eyesore is that Army to their interest and designes, whome they are so angry at, and would so faine have disbanded. You see what names they give; if they can once prevayle to take away your power, have at your coates. Not a bitt of toleration or favour ile warrant you. Doe you see how they jeare the Parliament, saying they tolerate all sects and heresies, and after all protestations &c. give no more then a toleration to the Presbyterian Government, their great Diana. How mightily doe they plead for the King (cuning Karles) for their owne ends more then love. And what have they to doe with the militia of England or London, they must be judge what it is fitt for us, or what wee must doe, or what have they to doe with titles of honor, Court of Wards &c. At last their desires are so unreasonable that I think they are not fitt to be taken notice of, and I think the Parliament of England need not feare their snappish laying of violation of the Treaty upon their score. I might be very long, and if I thought none would goe about to onfute this booke I would doe it my self, for I think it is a very good and easy work.

The Parliament and Army are now thinking to ease the Kingdome of burthens, as free quarter, supernumeraries &c. there is a close cuning Army or Assembly that march alwaies in black in this Kingdome, which I think may goe under Supernumeraries, I hope they wilbe disbanded too with the rest; I wounder no party hath sett upon them to route them. I think their Arreares will not be much, for their 4s. hath been duly paid them, besides their severall fatt benefices.

I find by the declaration of Parliament you last sent concerning taking off of free quarter &c. a very bad consequence in my judgment. No man must goe into any house except Tavernes &c. without the consent of the owner. Now no man will willingly enterteyne a souldier, so that necessarily the Army must alwaies lye in Innes, Tavernes &c. The souldiers will not be able to live upon Inne and Taverne rates, and my thinkes of all houses in the Kingdome they should be kept out of those, or els wee shall have nothing but a drunken Army, and laid open to all disorders and mischeifs. If the Army must have constant pay and discharge quarters, they might have the liberty to quarter in private houses. I think this is the ready way either quite to destroy, or at least to bring dishonor and disorder upon the Army.

I received the Lawes and Ordinances and also the £4 13s. 4d. of Mr. Cadwell, and perceive I have but £14 of the other money, but did conceive there had been 3 moneths paid since I came away. However if Generall Lambert desire it, I pray make it up £20 for him, and trust mee till you receive more for mee. I perceive Sir William Constable hath Generall Lamberts Regiment given him; though he is willing to submitt to it yet he hath now no regiment, nor any other place of benefitt, for hee hath received none since hee came into theis parts. Wee have little stirring heere. Some late orders of the Counsell of Warre, are made concerning quartering and regulating the Army heere, and I have sent some by Mr. Cadwell; I could have sent the one last weeke, but thought it not worth the sending. The Commissioners left heere in the Generall's absence are Colonel Bethell, Colonel Bright, Colonel Thornton, Lieutenant-Colonel Goodrick and Major Rookeby, likewise Colonel Lilburne and Colonel Overton are named though not present. Three make a quorum.

Tis time to end, I am
Thine owne
T. M.

York, 29th December, 1647.

Commend my service to Mr. Wragg and bid him take heed of falling into the fire. Cap. Wisdome is now going towards you, he is yet destitute of a place. I pray be his assistant while he stays there as much as you can. Forget mee not to Mr. Hatter and all the rest of my friends.

Endorsed : Mr. Margetts. Dec. 29, 1647.

APPENDIX B.

An account of the Origin of the Agreement of the People and the Negotiations of the Officers of the Army with the Representatives of the Levellers, extracted from John Lilburne's Pamphlet, "The Legal Fundamental Liberties."

The Legal Fundamental Liberties of the People of England.

Although Oliver had his hands full with Poyer, Goring, Holland, Hamilton, and Langdale the last year; but especially with the general odium that was then in both houses against him, upon the notable impeachment of his Major Huntingdon, August 2, 1648, and I then by my absolute freedom was a little up, and could have at my pleasure been revenged of him, if I had so pleased either by divisions in his army, which was easily then in my power; or by joyning in impeaching him with Major Huntingdon; which I had matter enough to do, and was earnestly solicited to do it again and again, and might have had money enough to boot in my then low and exhausted condition to have done it, yet I scorned it, and rather applied my hand to help him up againe, as not loving a Scotch Interest (then likely to swallow us up) as is very well and fully known to his present darling, Mr. Cornelius Holland, and also to Colonel Ludlow, and Mr. Thomas Challoner, with other Members that I could name; and which was demonstrated to himself by a Letter I sent him by Mr. Edw. Sexby, whom on purpose I procured to go down to him; the true copy whereof thus followeth:

Sir,

What my Comrade hath written by our trusty bearer, might be sufficient for us both; but to demonstrate unto you that I am no staggerer from my first principles that I engaged my life upon, nor from you, if you are what you ought to be, and what you are now strongly reported to be; although, if I prosecuted or desired revenge for an hard and almost starving imprisonment, I could have had of late the choice of twenty opportunities to have paid you to the purpose; but I scorn it, especially when you are low, and this assure yourself, that if ever my hand be upon you, it shall be when you are in your full glory, if then you shall decline from the righteous ways of Truth and Justice: which, if you will fixedly and impartially prosecute, I am

Yours, to the last drop of my heart bloud,
(for all your late severe hand towards me),

JOHN LILBURN.

From Westminster this 3 of August 1648, being the second day of my Freedom.

Which Letter etc. as I have been told by the Bearer, was not a little welcome to him.

But his dealings with me now manifest that Proverb to be very true, viz., Save a thief from the Gallows, and for your requitall he will be the first shall hang you. But to this I shall say no more but what the Spirit of Truth saith in Prov. 17, 13. That he that rewards evil for good, evil shall not depart from his house.

And being at liberty, not liking in the least the several juglings I observed in divers great ones in reference to the personal Treaty, and that there was nothing worth praising or liking thought of or presented by the Parliament in reference to the People's Liberties or Freedoms (especially considering their late large expences and hazards for the procurement of the settlement of them) I was compelled in conscience to have a hand in that most excellent of Petitions of the 11 of September, 1648, which (I am sure) was no small piece of service to Cromwel and his great Associates; though his Church-men now my chiefest Adversaries, durst not joyn with it, nor own it for very fear. And having been in the North about my own business, where I saw Crumwel, and made as diligent scrutinies into things about him, as I could, which I then to myself judged, savoured more of intended self-exalting, then anything really and heartily (of what before I had strongly heard of him) to the through-advancement of those things that were worthy to be accounted indeed the Liberties and Freedoms of the Nation.

And being come to London, my self, and some other of my friends, by two messengers, viz., Mr. Hunt, one of Cromwels creatures, and another sent a message down to him to Pomfret, to be delivered to himself, and to debate it with him, and bring his express answer back again speedily : the effect of which message was,

That to our knowledg God hath caused him to understand the principles of a just Government, under which the glory of God may shine forth by an equall distribution unto all men.

That the obtaining of this was the sole intended end of the Wars : and that the War cannot be justified upon any other account, then the defence of the people's right unto that just Government, and their freedom under it.

His answer to which message by Mr. Hunt was principally directed by the Independents; some of whom appointed a meeting at the Nags-head Tavern by Blackwell Hall at Mrs. Wilson's, and invited Mr. Wildman and myself, etc., thither, whether we went accordingly, and where we met with Colonel Tichburn, Col. John White, Dr. Parker, Mr. Taylor, John Price, and divers others (where we had a large debate of things, and where the just ends of the War were exactly laid open by Mr. Wildman, as ever I heard in my life). But towards the conclusion, they plainly told us, the chief things first to be done by the Army, was first to cut off the King's Head, &c., and force and thoroughly purge, if not dissolve, the Parliament. All of which we were all against, and pressed to know the bottom of their center, and in what they would absolutely rest for a Future Settlement; and I plainly told them in those words, or to this effect.

Its true, I look upon the king as an evil man in his actions, and divers of his party as bad, but the Army had cozened us the last year, and fallen from all their promises and Declarations, and therefore could not rationally any more be trusted by us without good cautions and security: In which regard, although we should judge the king as arrant a tyrant as they supposed him, or could imagine him to be, and the Parliament as bad as they could make them ; yet their being no other ballancing power in the kingdom against the Army, but the king and the Parliament, it was our interest to keep up one Tyrant to balance another, till we certainly know what that Tyrant that pretended fairest would give us as our Freedoms; that so we might have something to rest upon, and not suffer the Army (so much as in us lay) to devolve all the government of the Kingdom into their wills and swords (which were two things we nor no rationall man could like) and leave no persons nor power to be a counter-balance against them. And if we should do this, our slavery for future (I told them) might probably be greater then ever it was in the Kings time; and so our last error would be greater then our first, and therefore I pressed very hard for an Agreement amongst the People first, for a new Parliament, etc., utterly disclaiming the thoughts of the other till this was done. And this (I told them) was not onely my opinion, but I believe to be the unanimous opinion of all my friends with whom I most constantly conversed.

At which the Gentlemen Independents were some of them most desperately cholerick: but my opinion being backed with the speeches of some others of my friends, we came calmly to chuse out four and four of a side to debate and conclude of some heads towards the accomplishment of an Agreement of the People: and (as I remember) their four were, Colonel Titchburn, Col. White, Dr. Parker, and Jo. Price: and our four were Mr. William Walwyn, Lieut. Col. Wetton, Mr. John Wildman, and myself. But John Price sent some of the company to tell us (after we were parted, and some of us drinking a cup of wine below) he would not make one, if Mr. Walwyn was one, for he had a prejudice against him. Unto which I replied, Mr. Walwyn had more honesty and integrity in his little finger then John Price had in all his body; and therefore no meeting for me, seeing John Price was so base, unless Mr. Walwyn was one, though we had but two of a side: but the business being much debated and expostulated, Mr. Walwyn and John Price both (for peace sake) were at present laid aside: and according to appointment (as I remember) all the other six met the fifteenth of Novemb. 1648, being Wednesday, at the fore-mentioned Nags-head; and there, after some debate, unanimously agreed in those words, viz.: That in our conceptions, the only way of Settlement is:

I. That some persons be chosen by the Army to represent the whole body: And that the well-affected in every County (if it may be) chuse some persons to represent them: And those to meet at the Head-Quarters.

II. That those persons ought not to exercise any Legislative power. but onely to draw up the foundations of a just Government, and to propound them to the well-affected people in every County to be agreed to: Which Agreement ought to be above Law; and therefore the bounds, limits, and extent of the peoples Legislative Deputies in Parliament, contained in the Agreement, to be drawn up in a formall contract, to be mutually signed by the well-affected people and their said Deputies upon the dayes of their Election respectively.

III. To prevent present confusion, the Parliament (if it be possible) may not be by force immediately dissolved; but that the day of its dissolution be inserted in that Agreement, by virtue whereof it shall be dissolved.

IV. That this way of settlement, (if it may be) should be mentioned in the Armies first Remonstrance.

V. That the matter of the Petition of September 11, 1648, be the matter to be setled.

Which agreement of ours (as I remember) was immediately sent away to the Head-Quarters at St. Albans by Mr. Hiland of Southwark, where (as it was afterwards told us) it was very well accepted and approved of by the great ones there; whose high and mighty Declaration of the 16 Nov. 1648, (drawn by Ireton at Windsor, when he pretended to lay down his Commission) against the King coming to our view, we made divers objections against many passages in it: but especially at divers lashes that tacitely at the beginning of it hinted at us, which we told some of their friends could not be put in with a spirit of peace towards us, or intention of good to the Nation, in those good things we desired and propounded for it: But it was with many fair expressions salved up by them, upon which we judged it requisite for some of us to go to Windsor, to speak with Mr. Ireton the Stear-man himself; and accordingly (as I remember) Lieut.-Colonel Wetton, Mr. Petty, Mr. Wildman, and myself met there, and having drawn up our thoughts in writing, we communicated them to Col. Tychburn, Col. White, Mr. Moyer, and divers others of the Independent Party, who went with us to the Governors house, where we met with Mr. Peters, the grand Journey— or Hackney-man of the Army; And after we had acquainted him with our mindes, we delivered him a copy of our Paper, containing distinctly the Heads of what we desired, and intreated him to deliver them to Commissary Ireton, with whom we desired to discourse about them; who sent us word, at such an hour he would come to our Inn at the Garter, to speak with us about them; and accordingly he did, accompanied with a whole train of Officers; and a large and sharp discourse we had; our principall difference lying at his desire in the too strict restraining Liberty of Conscience, and in keeping a power in the Parliament to punish where no visible Law is transgressed; the unreasonableness of which was much spoken against by divers of the principall Officers with him, but especially by Col. Harrison, who was then extreme fair and gilded: And so little satisfaction had we at that meeting, from Ireton (the Armie's Alpha and Omega) that we despaired of any good from them, and were in a manner resolved to come away in haste to London, and acquaint our friends with our conceptions, and so improve our interests forcibly, as much as we could, to opose their intended designes. But Colonel Harrison coming to us again at ten a clock, according to our desire, we had a private and large discourse with him, and fully and effectually acquainted him with the most desperate mischievousness of their attempting to do these things, without giving some good security to the Nation for the future settlement of their Liberties and Freedoms, especially in frequent, free, and successive Representatives, according to their many Promises, Oathes, Covenants and Declarations; or else as soon as they had performed their intentions to destroy the King (which we fully understood they were absolutely resolved to do, yea, as they told us, though they did it by Martiall Law), and also totally to root up the Parliament, and invite so many Members to come to them as would joyn with them, to manage businesses, till a new and equall Representative could by an Agreement be setled; which the chiefest of them protested before God was the ultimate and chiefest of their designes and desires. I say, we pressed hard for security, before they attempted those things in the least, lest when they were done we should be solely left to their wills and swords; by which, we told them, they might rule over us arbitrarily, without declared Laws, as a conquered people, and so deal with us as the poor slavish peasants in France are dealt with, who enjoy nothing that they can call their own. And besides we plainly told him, we would not trust their bare words in generall onely, for they had broke their promise once already, both with us and the Kingdom; and he that would break once, would make no conscience of breaking twice, if it served for his ends, and therefore they must come to some absolute particular compact with us, or else, some of us told him, we would post away to London, and stir up our interest against them, yea and spend our bloods to oppose them. To which he replyed to this effect, It was true in what we said; for he must ingenuously confess, they had once broken with us and the Kingdom, and therefore acknowledged it was dangerous trusting them upon generals again: But, saith he, we cannot stay so long from going to London with the Army as to perfect an Agreement, and without our speedy going we are unavoidably destroyed: For (saith he) we fully understand that the Treaty betwixt the King and Parliament is almost concluded upon; at the conclusion of which, we shall be commanded by King and Parliament to disband, the which if we do, we are unavoidably destroyed for what we have done already: and if we do not disband, they will by Act of Parliament proclaim us Traytors, and declare us to be the only hinderers of setling peace in the Nation; and then (saith he) we shall never be able to fight with both the interest of King and Parliament: So that you will be destroyed as well as we: for we certainly understand that Major Generall Brown, etc. are under hand preparing an Army against us. And therefore I profess, I confess, I know not well what to say to your reasons, they are so strong; but our necessities are so great, that we must speedily go, or perish; and to go without giving you some content, is hazardable too.

Well Sir, (said we) we have as much cause to distrust the Parliament men, as we have to distrust you; for we know what and how many large promises they have made to the Kingdom, and how little they have performed; and we also know what a temptation Honor, Power, and profit are even to those spirits that were pretty ingenuous and honest before; and when you have done your work, and got, as you pretend, fourty or fifty of the honest members of the House to you; alas, (said we) it will be a mockpower ; yet they may finde such sweetness and delight in their pretended power, that they may fly to your swords for their protection, and bid us go shake our ears for our Agreement, and go look for it where we can catch it. And therefore we will trust generals no more to your fourty or fifty Members of Parliament, then to you : for it's possible, if we leave the Agreement to their framing, they may frame us such a one as will do us no good, but rather make us slaves by our own consents, if signed by us : and therefore we pressed him that we might agree upon a finall and absolute Judge of the matter and method of the Agreement, that so we might not spend months and years in dispute about it. And therefore we would propound this unto him, That if their honest friends in the Parliament, as they called them, would chuse four from amongst themselves, and the Army four from amongst themselves, and the Independents four from amongst themselves, ; we that were nick-named Levellers would choose four from among ourselves ; and these sixteen should draw up the Agreement finally, without any more appeal to any other ; and we for our parts, so far as all our interest in England extended, would be willing to acquiesce in, and submit to the determinations of these sixteen or the major part of them. And we would be willing the Presbyterian party should be invited, and desired to chuse four more to be of equal authority with the other sixteen ; provided, they did it by the first day we should appoint to meet upon.

Which proposition he approved of extraordinary well, and said, It was as just, as rational, and as equitable, as possibly could be ; and said, He doubted not but all Interests would center in it, and he ingaged to acquaint them with it ; and so we parted, very glad that we were likely to come to some fixed agreement for the future enjoyment of our dear-bought and hard-purchased Freedoms.

And the next morning we went to the Gentlemen Independents, that lay the next door to us, who were almost ready to horse for London, and we acquainted them with it, who liked it very well ; and with whom we fixed a night for several distinct meetings in London, to chuse our respective Trustees for this work, and also appointed a day to meet at Windsor again about it, and from them we went to Master Cornelius

Holland, who then was the chief stickler for those they called honest men in the House of Commons; and as I remember we met Colonel Harrison, Master Holland, and Captain Smith, a Member, and his son in law, in the street, and Master Holland seemed exceedingly to rejoyce at the Proposition, Colonel Harrison having told him of it before, which we repeated over again distinctly to him, that so in conclusion we might not be gulled through pretence of mistakes or misunderstanding, which we were continually afraid we should meet with; so we went all together to Commissary General Ireton's Chamber, to have his concurrence, which of all sides was taken for the concurrence of the whole Army, or at least for the powerful and governing part of it; he being in a maner both their eyes and ears. So when we came to his Chamber in the Castle, he was in bed with his wife, but sent us out word by Colonel Harrison, as he averred to us, That he did absolutely and heartily agree to the foresaid Proposition, which to avoid mistakes was again repeated; so we seemed joyful men of all sides, and appointed a day speedily to meet at Windsor about it, Master Holland again and again engaging for four Parliament men, and Colonel Harrison with Commissary Ireton for four of the Army, as we Londoners had done for each of our Tribe; and so to Horse we went, and I overtook upon the Road the whole gang of Independents, with whom I discoursed again, and acquainted them all fully with the absoluteness of our Agreement, which they acquainted their friends with in London, who chose Colonel Tichburn, Colonel John White, Master Daniel Taylor, and Master Price the Scrivener; And for our party, there was by unanimous consent of the Agents from our friends in and about London at a very large meeting chosen Master William Walwyn, Master Maximilian Petty, Master John Wildman, and myself; and for the honest men of the Parliament as they were called, they had severall meetings at the Bell in Kings-Street, and at Somerset house, where, as I was informed, they chose Col. Hen. Martin, Col. Alexander Rigby, Master Thomas Chalenor, and Master Scot, with one or two more, to supply the places of those of them that should be absent at any time about their occasions; so when we came to Windsor, the Army men had chosen Commissary-General Ireton, Sir William Constable, and, as I remember, Colonel Tomlinson, Colonel Baxter, Lieutenant Colonel Kelsey, and Captain

Packer, some two of the which last four should always make up the number ; so we had a meeting in their Council-Chamber at the Castle, where we were all of all sides present, but only the Parliament men, for whom only Col. Martin appeared, and after a large discourse about the foundations of our Agreement, we departed to our lodging, where Colonel Martin and we four nick-named Levellers lockt ourselves up, and went in good earnest to the consideration of our Agreement, but much was not done in it then, because of their haste to London, to force and break up the Parliament (which journey at all was very much opposed by Mr. Walwyn, and many reasons he gave against their march to London at all), the absolute dissolution of which, their friends in the House would no wayes admit of, although Ireton, Harrison, etc., commonly stiled it then a Parliament that had forfeited its trust, a mock-parliament, and that if they did not totally dissolve it but purge it, it would be but a mock-parliament, and a mock-power however; for where have we, say they, either Law, Warrant or Commission to purge it, or can anything justifie us in the doing it, but the height of necessity to save the Kingdom from a new war, that they, with the conjunction with the King will presently vote and declare for, and to procure a new and free Representative, and so successive and frequent free Representatives? which this present Parliament will never suffer (and without which the freedomes of the Nation are lost and gone, and the doing of which can only justifie before God and man our present and former extraordinary actings with and against legal authority) and so all our fighting will be fruitlesse ; and this was their open and common discourse with more of the like nature ; and to those that objected against their total dissolving or breaking the House (and the illegality of their intended and declared trying of the King, which also was opposed by us, till a new and unquestionable Representative was sitting) as I am able sufficiently, by plurality of witnesses, to prove and justifie, yea when they were come to London, Ireton, etc., and some Members of the House (in a Chamber near the long Gallery in White-hall) had a large conference, where and to whom he stifly maintained the same to their faces, calling this purged Parliament a mock power and a mock-parliament, which Members, I believe, if there were a necessity of it, I could produce to justifie it; for I am sure one of them told me the substance of all the discourse immediately after it happened; so that if it be treason to call this a pretended parliament, a mock-power, a mock-parliament, yea, and to say in plain English, that it is no Parliament at all, then they themselves are the prime, the chief and original traytors; and if this be true, as true it is; then there is neither legal Judges, nor Justices of Peace in England; and if so; then all those that are executed at Tiburn, etc. by their sentences of condemnation given against them are meerly murthered, and the Judges or Justices that condemned them are liable in time to be hanged (and that justly) therefore, for acting without a just and legal commission either from true Regall, or true Parliamentary power; see for this purpose, the notable arguments in the 13, 14, but especially 15 page of the second edition of my late Picture of the Council of State. But to return to our acting to compleat the Agreement, all parties chosen of all sides constantly met at Whitehall after the Army came to Town, saving the Parliament men failed only Master Martin was most commonly there, and a long and tedious tug we had with Commissary Generell Ireton only, yea sometimes whole nights together, principally about Liberty of Conscience, and the Parliaments punishing where no law provides, and very angry and Lordly in his debates many times was he; but to some kinde of an expedient in the first, for peace sake we condescended in to please him, and so came amongst the major part of the 16 commissioners, according to our original agreement, to an absolute and final conclusion; and thinking all had been done, as to any more debate upon it, and that it should without any more ado be promoted for subscriptions, first at the Council of War, and so in the Regiments, and so all over the Nation. But alas, poor fools, we were meerly cheated and cozened (it being the principal unhappiness to some of us (as to the flesh) to have our eyes wide open to see things, long before most honest men come to have their eyes open; and this is that which turns to our smart and reproach, and that which we Commissioners feared at the first (viz. That no tye, promises, or engagements were strong enough to hold the grand Juglers, and Leaders of the Army) was now made clearly manifest, for when it came to the Council there came the General, Cromwel, and the whole gang of

Creature-Colonels, and other Officers, and spent many dayes in taking it all in pieces, and there Ireton himself shewed himself an absolute king, if not an Emperor, against whose will no man must dispute, and then shittlecock Roe their Scout, Okey, and Major Barton (where Sir Hardress Waller sate President) began in their open Council to quarrel with us, by giving some of us base and unworthy language, which procured them from me a sharp retortment of their own basenesse and unworthinesse into their teeth, and a Challenge from myself into the field besides seeing they were like to fight with us in the room, in their own Garrison, which when Sir Hardress in my ear reproved me for it, I justified it, and gave it him again for suffering us to be so affronted. And within a little time after I took my leave of them for a pack of dissembling, juggling Knaves, amongst whom in consultation ever thereafter I should scorn to come (as I told some of them) for there was neither faith, truth, nor common honesty amongst them: and so away I went to those that chose and trusted me, and gave publikely and effectually (at a set meeting appointed on purpose) to diverse of them an exact account how they had dealt with us, and cozened and deceived us; and so absolutely discharged myself for medling or making any more with so perfidious a generation of men as the great ones of the Army were, but especially the cunningest of Machiavilians, Commissary Henry Ireton; and having an exact copy of what the greatest part of the foresaid sixteen had agreed upon, I only mended a clause in the first Reserve about Religion, to the sense of us all but Ireton, and put an epistle to it, of the fifteenth of December, 1648, and printed it of my own accord, and the next day it came abroad; about which Master Price the Scrivener and myself had a good sharp bout at Colonel Titchburn his house, within two or three days after, where I avowed the publishing of it, and also putting my Epistle to it of my own head and accord. And after that I came no more amongst them, but with other of my friends, prepared a complaint against their dealing with us, and a kinde of Protest against their proceedings; which with my own hand I presented to the Generals own hands at the Mews, the twenty-eight of December, 1648, being accompanied with Major Robert Cobbet, Mr. Thomas Prince, Mr. George Middlemore, Mr. Robert Davies, Mr.

Richard Overton, Mr. Edward Tench. Mr. Daniel Linton, Mr. William Bottom, Mr. John Harris, Mr. Thomas Dafferne, Mr. Tho. Goddard, Mr. Samuel Blaiklock, Mr. Andrew Dednam, Mr. John Walters, and Mr. Richard Pechel; and which was immediately printed by Ja. & Jo. Moxon, for William Larnar, at the sign of the Black-moore near Bishops gate; within two or three days of the delivery of which, I went towards my journey to Newcastle; and about five weeks after my arrivall in those parts I heard that the Generall and his Councel had presented their Agreement to your House: which, when I read the title page of it, I found it to be upon the 20 of Jan. 1648, which is compleat 35 dayes after my publishing of that which is called ours.

APPENDIX C.

A letter from Captain Anthony Mildmay, one of the attendants on the King, to his brother, Sir Henry Mildmay.

My worthy good Brother,

I am resolved to continue here one month more, to see what that time will produce, but longer I will not stay upon the terms I am now, my danger being very great and certain, and my reward uncertain: for you may very well conceive that the malignant party will be stil practising against me, to make me suspected by the Parliament and their Army, hoping to remove me by that means: all other ways they practised in vain. Many things are omitted in the last declaration which I hope you wil mention in the next. Some little time before the first expedition against the Scots, Ship-money and other taxes coming in slow, it was resolved by the King (at a juncto) that a regiment of horse should be presently raised, the pretence for a guard for the Kings person; but there was no need of that, there being a Band of Pensioners, and the Yeomen of the Gard. The old Countesse of Devonshire paid £2,000 to Marquess Hamilton, which he was to have as a gift when this Lord Wilmot was established Commander in Chief of this regiment. If M. Haughton, an Attourney living in S. James, and one Mrs. Barrow, that lives in Cheneys in Buckinghamshire, Sir Edward Wortley, and Franc Wortley be examined, they will satisfie the Parliament that this horse guard was to be imployed absolutely to force the King's will upon the people. Sir, this day our worthy Governour and the King had some disputes in my hearing and others. In short, the King had very many bitter expressions against your proceedings and said, That any King that should do such abominable things as you did, deserv'd to have his Crown pull'd off his head. I was astonish'd to hear him say so: for formerly his opinion was, that no King could deserve to be deposed: that he was accomptable to none but God: Who then should pul off his Crown? He said, That the passing the Act to make Strafford a traitor lay heavie upon his conscience: That it was the greatest sin that ever he committed: that he was forced to do it, and if he had power, he would say as much against all the Acts he had passed this Parliament. In some of his Declarations from Oxford he expresseth with what freedome hee passed all the Acts that hee passed this Parliament, and if they were to passe, he would passe them; and now you hear he professsed the contrary in the hearing of divers of us. He is the most perfidious man that ever lived; and if ever he gets power, he will make no more difficulty to hang you then I will do to eat my dinner this cold day. Our charge is great and dangerous, our attendance insupportable, did not God enable us. You know what discouragements I have, when strangers are placed before me, and, although they be honest men, yet they have not performed the service to the Parliament that I have. I was servant to King James in an honourable condition, and to this King ever since he was crowned; and your self and all that knew me must affirm, that I was ever a great opposer of tyranny and Popery. Eighteen yeers since I was sworn Gent. of the Privie-Chamber, and so continued; and now I am lesse, and must so continue, or come away. I desire your advice, without which I will do nothing.

Your Brother and Servant,

A. Mildmay.[a]

Carisbrook,
29 Feb., 1647.

[a] Printed in Mercurius Veridicus, 27 April-8 May, 1648. How this letter came into the possession of the editor of a royalist newspaper does not appear, but it bears internal marks of genuineness. It is interesting as revealing the manner in which the King was watched by the agents of the Parliament

APPENDIX D.

APPEN

LIST OF OFFICERS ATTENDING AT COUNCILS

	Nov. 7.	Nov. 16.	Nov. 25.	Nov. 28.	Dec. 14.	Dec. 15.
Abbott, Major . .					+	+
Allen, Capt. . . .					+	+
Arnold, Capt. . .						
Ashfield, Lieut.-Col.						
Audley, Major . .		+				
Axtell, Lieut.-Col. .	+	+				
Babington, Capt. .						
Baker, Capt. . . .					+	
Barber, Cornet . .					+	
Barkstead, Col. . .			+	+	+	+
Barrow, Capt. . .						
Barton, Major . .					+	+
Bayley, Capt. . .						
Baynes, Capt. . .						
Beale, Capt. . . .			+	+		
Bethell, Major . .		+				
Billers, Capt. . .			+			
Blackmore, Major .						+
Blackwell, Capt. . .		+	+		+	+
Bowen, Lieut.-Col. .						
Bowen, Capt. . . .						
Bradford, Capt. . .						+
Brayfield, Capt. . .		+				
Bridge, Capt. . .						
Browne, Capt. . .	+					

DIX D.

and Committees, Nov., 1648—March, 1649.

Dec. 16.	Dec. 18.	Dec. 21.	Dec. 23.	Dec. 26.	Dec. 29.	Feb. 22.
					+	+
+		+				
					+	
+	+	+		+	+	
		+				
+		+		+	+	
	+	+				
+		+		+		
	+			+	+	+
		+				
		+			+	
					+	
				+	+	
		+				+
	+	+			+	
		+				
	+	+				
				+		
	+				+	

	Nov. 7.	Nov. 16.	Nov. 25.	Nov. 28.	Dec 14.	Dec. 15.
Browne, Major . .		+				
Burgess, Capt. . .			+	+		
Bury, Adjt.-Gen. .						+
Butler, Capt. . . .				+		
Cadwell, Capt. . .						
Cambridge, Major .						+
Cannon, Capt. . .		+			+	
Carter, Major . . .	+		+		+	
Carter, Lieut. . . .			+	+		
Chamberlaine, Lieut.						
Chandler, Lieut.-Col.						
Chillenden, Lieut. .	+	+	+		+	
Clarke, Capt. M G.S.					+	
Clarke, Capt. S.H.W.					+	
Cobbett, Major . .						
Cobbett, Lieut.-Col.			+			
Coleman, Major . .				+		
Constable, Col. Sir W.		+	+	+		+
Cooke, Col. . . .		+				
Cooke, Lieut.-Col. .	+	+	+		+	+
Creede, Major . .						+
Cromwell, Lieut. Gen.						+
Cromwell, Capt. . .						+
Dancer, Capt. . .				+		
Davis, Capt. . . .		+				
Dawes, Capt.-Lieut.			+			
Day, Lieut. . . .						
Deane, Col. . . .					+	+
Deane, Capt. . .			+	+		
Dennison, Capt. . .						
Disbrowe, Col. . .		?				

Dec. 16.	Dec. 18.	Dec. 21.	Dec. 23.	Dec. 26.	Dec. 29.	Feb. 22.
						+
+	+	+		+	+	
	+	+				
+	+	+		+	+	
				+		
					+	
		+		+		
				+		
	+	+				
	+	+		+		+
	+	+			+	
	+	+		+	+	
	+	+			+	
					+	+
+	+			+		+
		+				
		+				+
+	+					
						+
					+	
+				+		
	+				+	
	+			+		
+		+			+	
+	+	+		+	+	
		+		+		

	Nov. 7.	Nov. 16.	Nov. 25.	Nov. 28.	Dec. 14.	Dec. 15.
Disher, Capt. . . .						
Disney, Capt. . .				+		
Dorney, Capt. . .						
Ellis, Lieut. . . .				+		
Ely, Capt. . . .		+				
Empson, Lieut. . .		+				
Evanson, Capt. . .					+	+
Evelyn, Adjt.-Gen. .	+	+	+			
Ewer, Col. . . .		+				
Fairfax, Gen. . .	+	+	+	+	+	
Freeman, Capt. . .					+	
Gladman, Capt. . .	+					+
Goffe, Lieut.-Col. .	+				+	+
Goddard, Capt. . .						
Grimes, Capt. . .	+	+				
Groome, Capt. . .						+
Grosvenor, Qr. Mr. Gen.						
Grove, Capt. . . .		+	+			+
Hacker, Col. . . .						+
Hammond, Lieut.-Gen.			+	+	+	
Harding, Capt. . .						
Harrison, Col. . .		+	+	+	+	+
Hawes, Capt. . .		+				
Heane, Capt. . .		+				
Hewson, Col. . . .	+	+	+	+	+	+
Heydon, Lieut. . .			+			
Hodden, Capt. . .					+	
Husbands, Major .					+	+
Ingoldsby, Col. . .		+				
Ireton, Comm. Gen.	+	+	+	+	+	+

Dec. 16.	Dec. 18.	Dec. 21.	Dec. 23.	Dec. 26.	Dec. 29.	Feb. 22.
	+					
				+		
						+
					+	
						+
+						+
				+		+
	+					+
						+
		+				
		+		+		
+	+	+				+
	+					+
	+					
				+	+	
						+
+	+			+	+	+
+		+		+	+	
	+	+				
+	+	+		+	+	

	Nov. 7.	Nov. 16.	Nov. 25.	Nov. 28.	Dec. 14.	Dec. 15.
Jenkins, Capt. . .						
Jennings, Lieut . .		+				
Joyce, Capt. . . .	+				+	+
Jubbes, Lieut. . .						
Judge Advocate, the	+	+				
Kelsey, Lieut.-Col. .	+	+	+	+		+
Kerbey, Capt. . .						
Lagoe, Major . .				+		
Lawrance, Capt. . .						
Lilburne, Col. . .						
Lloyd, Capt. . . .						
Lydcote, Col. . . .					+	
Malin, Cornet . .						
Mason, Lieut.-Col. .						
Mercer, Capt. . .					+	
Merest, Capt. . . .						
Messervy, Capt. . .	+	+	+		+	+
Moore, Capt. . .						
Morgan, Capt. . .		+				
Mosse, Capt. . . .						
Neale, Capt. . . .		+				
Newman, Lieut. . .		+				
Okey, Col.						+
Packer, Capt. . . .				+		
Parsons, Capt. . .				+		
Peck, Capt. . . .						
Peverell, Capt. . .						
Phillips, Cornet . .						
Pitson, Capt. . . .						
Porter, Cornet . .						
Pretty, Capt. . . .		+	+		+	
Pride, Col. . . .		+		+		

Dec. 16.	Dec. 18.	Dec. 21.	Dec. 23.	Dec. 26.	Dec. 29.	Feb. 22.
					+	
	+					
				+		
+						
					+	
						+
						+
					+	
+						+
	+					
		+		+		
						+
+	+	+		+	+	
					+	
						+
						+
	+	+		+	+	+
						+
		+		+	+	
					+	
					+	+
	+					
					+	
	+				+	

	Nov. 7.	Nov. 16.	Nov. 25.	Nov. 28.	Dec. 14.	Dec. 15.
Rainborowe, Major .						+
Rawlins, Capt. . .		+				
Reade, Lieut.-Col. .						+
Reynolds, Capt. . .						
Rich, Col.		+			+	+
Rippon, Capt.. . .						
Robinson, Capt. . .		+	+	+		
Rogers, Capt. . . .		+				
Rosse, Capt. . . .			+			
Rowe, Sct.-Mr.-Gen.			+			+
Sabberton, Lieut. .		+				
Salmon, Lieut.-Col. .					+	+
Saunders, Col. . .					+	+
Savage, Cornet . .		+				
Sedascue, Major . .						
Scotten, Capt. . .					+	+
Scroope, Col. . . .	+				+	+
Sherer, Lieut. . .						+
Skippon, Maj.-Gen.[a]						
Smith, Capt. . . .		+				
Southwell, Lieut. .						
Sparrow, Capt. . .						
Spencer, Capt. . .				+	+	+
Spooner, Capt. . .						
Stanlie, Lieut. . .						+
Stiles, Capt. . . .		+	+			
Strange, Cornet . .						
Stubber, Adjt.-Gen. .	+			+		+
Swallow, Major . .					+	+
Symonds, Capt. . .						
Tichborne, Col. . .					+	

[a] Absent throughout.

Dec. 16.	Dec. 18.	Dec. 21.	Dec. 23.	Dec. 26.	Dec. 29.	Feb. 22.
					+	
+	+	+		+		
	+			+	+	
+		+		+	+	
					+	
	+					
+	+	+		+	+	
+	+	+		+	+	
		+		+		+
				+		+
						+
+		+		+	+	+
+		+			+	+
						+
					+	
	+	+				
				+		
				+		
+				+	+	
	+			+	+	
	+					

	Nov. 7.	Nov. 16.	Nov. 25.	Nov. 28.	Dec. 14.	Dec. 15.
Tomlins, Capt.-Compt.	+	+	+	+	+	+
Tomlinson, Col. . .		+	+		+	+
Tracy, Cornet. . .						
Twisleton, Col. . .						
Venables, Lieut-Col.						+
Wagstaffe, Capt. . .						+
Waller, Col. Sir H. .					+	+
Wallis, Cornet . .						
Walton, Col. . . .						+
Ware, Capt. . . .						
Warren, Qrtr.-Mstr.						
Watson, Capt. . .						
Weekes, Major . .						
Whalley, Col. . .	+	+	+	+	+	+
Whichcote, Col. . .		+	+	+		
White, Major . . .						
White, Col. . . .					+	
Whitie, Capt. . .						
Wilkes, Major . .					+	
Wilkinson, Lieut. .						
Wilton, Col. . . .					+	
Winthrop, Capt. . .						
Wolfe, Capt. . . .					+	
Woolsey, Cardinal .		+				
Zanchey, Capt. . .	+	+	+	+		+

Dec. 16.	Dec. 18.	Dec. 21.	Dec. 23.	Dec. 26.	Dec. 29.	Feb. 22.
	+					
+	+	+				
						+
					+	+
+		+		+		
+	+					
+	+	+		+	+	+
					+	
	+					
		+				
						+
	+					
+	+	+		+		
					+	+
					+	+
					+	+
	+	+		+	+	
		+				+
				+		+
+		+		+	+	+

NOTES ON THE TABLE.

There is no list of attendances for December 23, and that of November 7 is imperfect. The handwriting of some of the lists is very bad, and it is difficult to be sure of the correct reading of all the names. Other persons than officers were occasionally present. On November 16 two chaplains, Mr. Floyd and Mr. Knight, were present. Knight was again present on December 14, when a number of representatives of the Levellers and Presbyterian and Independent clergy also attended, viz. : John Goodwin, Hugh Peter, Brooke, Seaman, Denne, Sprigge, Nye, Bacon, Gilbert, Parker, Collier, Walford, Estwick, Hewitt, Russell, Wollaston, John Wildman, Lieut.-Col. John Lilburne, and Lieut.-Col. Wilton. John Wildman and William Walwyn were present on December 18.

The following notes on individuals will explain the list. Capt.-Lieut. Babington is styled captain on December 21. Capt. Baker in the list of December 14 should possibly be Barker or Barber. Lieut.-Col. Bowen's name is given in the list of November 16, but noted as absent. Adjutant-Gen. Bury is probably Captain James Berry. The two Clarkes are distinguished as of Major-Gen. Skippon's regiment and of Sir Hardress Waller's. A Captain Clarke is mentioned as present on December 15 and December 16, without any note to show which is meant. Captain Cromwell was probably Henry Cromwell, captain in Harrison's regiment of horse. The name of Major Davers or Danvers appears in the list of December 14. Adjt.-Gen. Evelyn is styled major in the list of December 29. Ensign Fairbanke appears in the list of December 21, and Captain Helsum [?]. Col. Lilburne is Robert Lilburne. Lieut. Lloyd is mentioned on February 22, and Ensign Lucas as present on November 16. Captain Merest, whose name is difficult to read, is probably the Captain Richard Merest who was Adjt.-Gen. in 1652. Captain Moore, December 29, should possibly be read Mosse. Two lieut.-cols. named Reede, or Rede, are named as present on December 18. The lists of December 18 and December 29 mention Captain Reynolds, that of December 26 Colonel Reynolds. Major Wilkes is styled Lieut.-Col. Wilkes on February 22. Cardinal Woolsey is a joke of Clarke's. A letter dated February 15, 1651, says : "This day Mr. Wolsey, assistant to the Quartermaster-General, died." This is probably the person referred to.—*Letters from Roundhead Officers*, p. 10. Bannatyne Club, 1856.

INDEX.